Anglo-Saxon Somerset

Anglo-Saxon Somerset

Michael Costen

Oxbow Books
Oxford and Oakville

Published by
Oxbow Books, Oxford, UK

© Michael Costen 2011

ISBN 978-1-84217-988-8

This book is available direct from

Oxbow Books, Oxford, UK
(Phone: 01865-241249; Fax: 01865-794449)

and

The David Brown Book Company
PO Box 511, Oakville, CT 06779, USA
(Phone: 860-945-9329; Fax: 860-945-9468)

or from our website
www.oxbowbooks.com

A CIP record is available for this book from the British Library

Library of Congress Cataloging-in-Publication Data

Costen, M. D.
Anglo-Saxon Somerset / Michael Costen.
      p. cm.
   Includes bibliographical references and index.
ISBN 978-1-84217-988-8
1. Somerset (England)--History. 2. Anglo-Saxons--England--Somerset. I. Title.

DA670.S5C747 2011
942.3'8015--dc22

2011004960

Front cover: Weare, Chedder. Photo: author.
Back cover: Glastonbury Tor. Photo: author.

Printed by
Information Press, Eynsham, Oxfordshire

Contents

Acknowledgements and Thanks   vii

Introduction   1

1.   Post-Imperial Politics: defence and offence   12

2.   Settlement and Soldiers   32

3.   Settlements and Estates   51

4.   Eorl and Ceorl, Theow and Freo   74

5.   Ancient Agriculture   95

6.   Tenth Century Agriculture   119

7.   Early Trade   139

8.   Trade and Town   159

9.   Old Religion   177

10.   The Church Reformed   202

11.   Conclusions   225

Abbreviations, Manuscript Sources and Bibliography   237

Index   253

Acknowledgements and Thanks

Figures 5.3, 5.5, 5.6, 6.1, 6.11 and 7.8 make use of material from the first and second editions of the six inch Ordnance Survey maps and The Survey's kind permission is acknowledged. Figures 2.6 and 3.2 are reproduced by kind permission of the Somerset County Museum, Taunton. The aerial photographs are all the copyright of Professor M. Aston and are reproduced here with his permission. The cover photo is by Angela Costen.

My thanks are due to:

Professor Mick Aston for allowing me to make use of his work in progress on a gazetteer of Somerset Radio-Carbon dates 400–800 AD and for the use of a number of his aerial photographs. Dr Nick Corcos for help and advice. Dr John Davey, for advice on South Cadbury and permission to publish figures from his doctoral thesis. Jodie Dubber for allowing me to use material from her unpublished MA dissertation. Julie Dunne for the use of material from her unpublished BSc dissertation on Shapwick. Jane Evans of the Weston-s-Mare Museum. Joyce Jefferson and the East Somerset Study Group. Dr John Knight for permission to refer to material from his unpublished PhD thesis. Sarah McClean for material from the HER of North Somerset Unitary Authority and Bath and North-East Somerset Unitary Authority. Mr Steven Minnitt, Director, Taunton Museum for permission to photograph the Queen Camel Sword and Beads from Buckland Dinham. Pippa Osborne, for use of unpublished material on Chewton Mendip from her undergraduate dissertation. Dr Naomi Payne, Archaeological section of the Planning Department, Somerset County Council, for help and advice about the Portable Antiquities Scheme and for the supply of information about coin finds. Clare Randall and the South Somerset Archaeological Research Committee. Bob Smisson for permission to refer to material in his unpublished undergraduate dissertation and for introducing me to Gatcombe and to its importance. Dr Richard Tabor for advice about South Cadbury.

Last and most importantly, I owe a great debt of gratitude to Mrs Susan Grice of the Department of Archaeology and Anthropology, Bristol University for drawing (and redrawing) most of the figures.

Introduction

Another book about Somerset needs to be justified on a more than local level if it is to have relevance for the study of the most difficult period in our history – from the end of Roman administration up to the coming of the Normans. Can we say anything which helps us to understand this long era if we look only at a single shire? (We are of course dealing with the ancient Somerset, existing before the manufacture of 'Avon' and its subsequent, not always noted, disappearance.) If integration into the emerging kingdom of Wessex took place in the later seventh century, then there are about 250 years of history to study before that time. We cannot understand later Somerset without some attempt to understand post-Roman Somerset. It may well have had some existence as a province or a kingdom during this period and it is quite clear that it was part of an integrated and organised society. In addition Somerset has a history as a shire which reaches back well before 1066. The authors of the Anglo-Saxon Chronicle specifically mention the men of Somerset in 848 when they fought against a Danish raiding army at the mouth of the river Parrett (ASC 'A', 848). Asser, writing towards the end of the ninth century, referred to '*Summurtunensis paga*', the district belonging to Somerton (Keynes and Lapidge 1983, 84). Since it is clear that there were local Ӕaldormen in Somerset by that date, the likelihood is that the boundaries of their jurisdiction were well defined by the middle of the ninth century, if not before. Probably few people thought in purely geographical terms, but rather of men who owed some kind of duty or allegiance; but as we shall see in the course of this study, there is every reason to believe that some of the boundaries of late Anglo-Saxon Somerset had been defined very early indeed, probably before the seventh century. Although Somerset was never an Anglo-Saxon kingdom, its long history outside Wessex and then its subsequent integration into the Old English kingdom served to give it a character and identity of its own, which makes it a worthwhile study.

This book is an attempt at writing a history for a shire which has very few written records before the Domesday Book. It is therefore a history of a society seen largely through the archaeological record, through its place-names and charters and through its landscapes. It is shaped in part by the writer's belief that the stories of societies are largely the record of the relationships among the powerful and their attempts to control and exploit their environment, physically and socially, to meet their needs. It would be good to think that the mass of the peasantry pursued lives which were little affected by the doings of the great, but realistically that was not the case in Britain. What the powerful perceived as their interests profoundly influenced the direction of English society. The picture is therefore one of a society which was dynamic and which experienced many changes as its rulers struggled for control among themselves and did their best to retain their positions against external forces. Some of those forces were aggressive and it would be wrong, for instance, to treat the attacks of the Northmen which afflicted most of western Europe in the eighth, ninth and tenth centuries as anything but serious. They were clearly the most important of all outside pressures.

It is too often assumed that economic expansion

Figure 1. Somerset and the surrounding Wessex shires.

and population growth are external factors to which societies react. Population growth in particular is often treated as a *deus ex machina*, something which occurs as a natural process and is beyond control, a force of nature which shapes society. A thesis of this book is that both are the result of the actions of the powerful in society; that kings and aristocracy shaped both the economy and the population to meet their own needs, which included maintaining their position and power against the threat posed by the Northmen.

The expansion of the power of the kings of Wessex and then of the kings of the English was part of the evolutionary pressure upon English society, which saw a remarkable development of its economy and bureaucracy, especially in the tenth and the eleventh centuries.

The native Old Welsh were already Christian by the sixth century and the English followed them by adopting the religion of post-Roman Europe early in the seventh century. Christianity provided an ideological cement which helped to bind together a violent society, while providing it with norms of thought and behaviour which moved it back towards the main stream of European life. Here again, the adoption of Christianity by the powerful, chiefly at first the petty kings, enabled them to use the new religion as one of the tools with which to shape their society to meet their need for control of resources, both intellectual, physical and political.

The early fifth century

Early in the fifth century the formal Imperial administration of Britain collapsed. In 407 the army in Britain, which was the guarantor of administrative continuity, elevated one of its leaders to the purple as Constantine III (Orosius, VII, 40, 4). Anxious to overturn the outcome of the barbarian invasion of Gaul which had taken place on 31st December 406, he and the army left Britain, never to return. This was a sudden end to colonial rule, leaving behind several centuries of acculturation: a social system which had absorbed much of the Roman urban and rural styles of life, at least for the aristocracy; an urban life based upon trade and local government administration; a system of local government which was common to much of the rest of western Europe; a religion which linked it to the rest of the Empire; and above all an economy which was heavily dependent upon the Imperial government.

There is little evidence to suggest that provincial magistrates in Britain or members of the Imperial government realised that this was a defining moment. There is some evidence that later historians and chroniclers thought that practical political contact with Britain ceased around about 410, although contacts with the south-east were maintained by the continental Church for some decades after this date (Wood, I. 1984, 1–25). Procopius remarked 'however, the Romans never succeeded in recovering Britain, but it remained from that time under tyrants' (Dewing 1916, bkIII, ii, 38). As we shall see, there is every reason to believe that less formal contacts never ceased in the west.

Although it seems unlikely that any one at the time realised what was happening, a gradual loss of administrative and military contact was inevitable once the army was gone. The practical effects of this rupture were two. The first was that the army was no longer a consumer of goods and services. As the most expensive part of the late Roman state, consuming a very large proportion of its annual revenues, the army's expenditure was a major part of the economic cycle. It has been suggested that supplies, mostly grain, which had previously been sent from the west of Britain to the Rhineland in the fourth century had helped to stimulate the economy of southern Britain (Salway 1981, 359–60; Walters 2001, 130). It may be that the relatively settled nature of British society in the late fourth century meant that an export trade continued until the departure of the army disrupted it. This alone would have been enough to trigger a decline in the economy.

Secondly, the disappearance of soldiers and officials who were paid in precious metal meant that the normal import of coin ceased. We do not know how much contemporaries understood about the loss of their coinage. They may have believed at first that this would be only a temporary difficulty and only slowly realised, as they adapted, that life had changed for ever. For us, dealing with a period which has left almost nothing in the way of written records, durable coins provide important evidence from which inferences can be drawn.

For everyday purposes only the coin in circulation continued to be available. One result was an increase in the number of hoards of coin buried. Such hoards are of course not specific to the early fifth century. In a world without banks people frequently buried their money simply to protect it from thieves; the number of burials may well be related to the quantity of coin in circulation and be part of normal everyday life, but there is an increased number from the later fourth century/early fifth century, many of which contain coins up to the reign of Honorius (reigned 393–423), with a terminus of c. 405, though some coins of the usurper Constantine III (407–11) also occur, though not in Somerset, taking us up to c. 411 (Kent 1979, 21–2). The hoards are widely distributed through the county (Fig. 2). Those deposited after c. 383 (25 in all) are grouped into three areas.

The first comprises the region north of the river Axe. Here there is a scatter running down the Chew Valley, a small number along the Avon valley, a couple near the coast, one of which was discovered in the

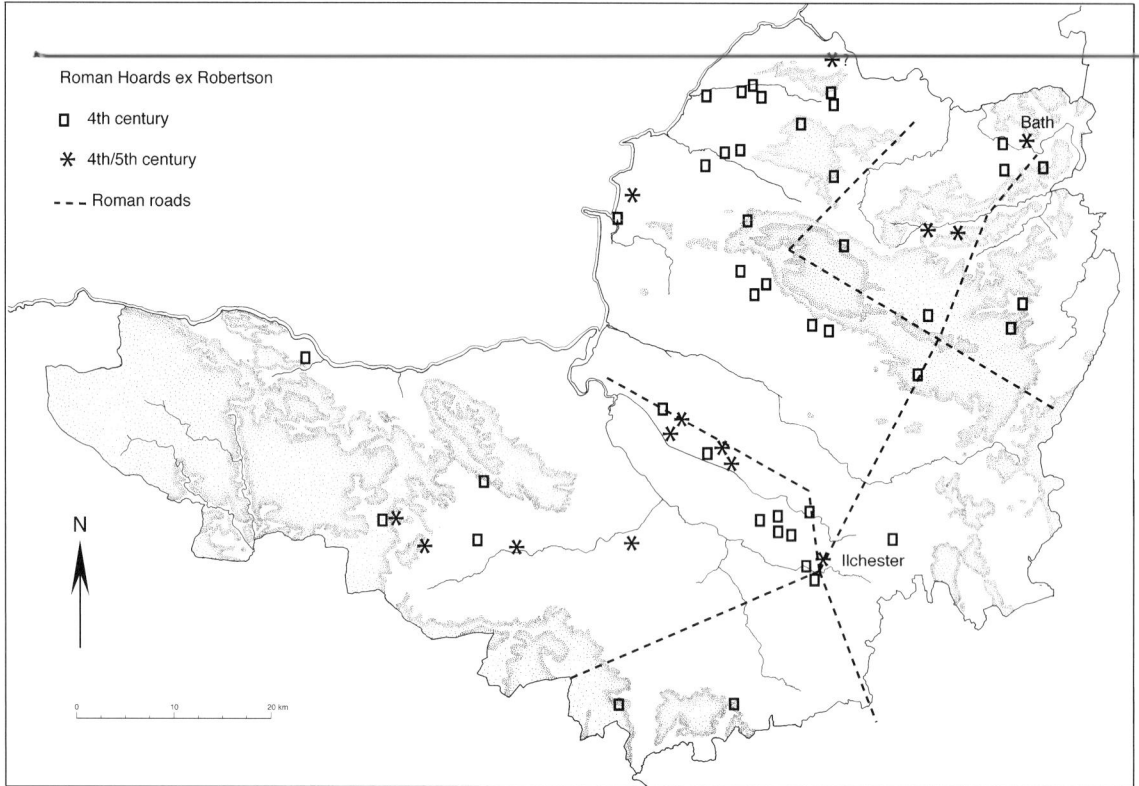

Figure 2. Hoards of the fourth and fifth centuries.

Worle hill-fort, and two along the south side of the Mendips at Cheddar and Wookey. There are no signs of hoards of this period from the area between Bath and Frome, which had several large villas. The next area covers the low ground of the central Somerset region, running from Ilchester along the Polden ridge towards the mouth of the river Parrett. Here Shapwick and Chilton Polden both provided examples of multiple hoards. Finally an area stretching from the southern marshes, at North Curry, along the river Tone to the edge of Exmoor provides another area of concentration. The distribution of hoards where the terminus coincides with the end of coinage, in the early fifth century, is contained within these three areas, suggesting that they are a subset of the whole movement to deposit coin and not an extraordinary response. Perhaps people in these areas felt particularly threatened, but there are later indications, discussed

elsewhere, that the pattern may reflect real post-Roman economic activity. It is also noteworthy that many of the sites of these deposits emerge as important estates in the later Anglo-Saxon period. Clearly commercial activity and organised economic life which needed coins continued in the early fifth century in these most densely occupied areas. Except for the hoard at Ilchester these are rural discoveries, so the countryside was still using money in the first quarter of the century.

There are actually about 118 hoards of coins known from the historic county, of which not all can be dated (Robertson 2000). Of the datable hoards only three are of the first century, another three of the second, 37 are from the third century and 57 from the fourth century. Of the 57 remaining hoards, 14 had coins of Arcadius (383–408) or Honorius (393–423) as their last dated component and could therefore have been deposited at some point in the early fifth century.

Some of these hoards are quite small: the hoard found on Shapwick Turf Moor in 1868 contained only 14 coins (HER10005), but the find made in 1821 at Holway, near Taunton was described as containing 'a great number of silver coins' (HER44244). The hoard found at Frances Plantation near Priddy in 1887 contained nearly 1500 silver coins (HER24236). The widely varying sizes of the deposits suggest that they were made by people of all classes except the very poorest. They were sometimes deposited close to a building as at Charlton Mackrell, where the hoard was close to a Roman building and to a number of burials (HER53689). At Shapwick Heath four separate hoards were found all buried within about 15 m of one another (HER10723). Here the deposits were out on a peat moor, though the existence of so many deposits close to one another suggests that it was a well marked site of significance in the early fifth century.

We cannot know what was buried and recovered by its owners, or sometimes by thieves who stole it, or how many hoards were discovered in post-Roman and medieval times (the crock of gold at the end of the rainbow has a basis in fact) or await discovery still. What we do have is probably only a small sample of the coin buried. The fourth century Somerset examples were deposited over a period which ranged from the mid-380s up to c. 410 but we cannot be certain how long after 410 money continued to be used in commercial transactions. Clipped coin may well point to its continued use in markets where its value was rising and no more could be found. Archer, in his survey of coin hoards, suggests that clipping begins with those hoards which were deposited after AD 400 (Archer 1979, 29–64). Dr Esmonde Cleary thinks that most of these late hoards were accumulated early in the fifth century (Esmonde Cleary 1989, 139). When discussing finds of Roman coins, both stray losses and hoards in Wiltshire, Dr T. S. N. Moorhead suggested that coin may have circulated as late as the 420s (Moorhead 2001, 96). In the hoard found at Burtle (HER10940), the coins were all clipped, suggesting that they had been in circulation for a long time and that they had been clipped as their value rose. We can imagine that once the steady supply of

coin from the mints on the continent broke down, existing coin in circulation increased in value as coins were lost or were traded abroad. It seems clear that hoards with a large number of clipped coins were deposited late, probably well after 407–11 (Burnett, A. 1984, 163–85). Recently Abdy has suggested that the clipping of coins was carried out by the *civitas* authorities who taxed their populations and re-issued the clipped coins to the point where they were no longer acceptable, at which point their use ceased (Abdy 2006, 76–95). If that is true, then some sort of market activity must have continued for some years after AD 410 and he suggests that the whole process had ceased by about AD 470. This would suggest that some of the Somerset hoards could have been deposited well after the date of their last coins. His analysis of the Patching (Sussex) Hoard shows that coins minted on the continent in the fifth century were present in Britain in the mid-century, though whether they had been circulated for trade is not at all clear. A diametrically opposed point of view is taken by Reece, who considers that the idea of coin use as tokens after the very early fifth century is a fantasy (Reece, 2002, 63–4). Such diametrically opposing views cannot be reconciled without further data, but it would not be surprising if coin use continued in different places to different dates as society became more localised and circulation more restricted.

Gradually the coin became so valuable that people first reduced its value by clipping and then became reluctant to spend it and buried it instead. An alternative view might be that increasing disorder and political uncertainty induced people to hide their money. It is illuminating to consider Heinrich Härke's analysis of the breakdown of the old Soviet empire in the late years of the twentieth century. 'US dollars are Russia's second currency and the preferred currency for savings; and because Russians do not trust Russian banks, such savings are kept at home, creating a horizon of post-Soviet hoards exclusively in US dollars' (Harke 2007, 65–6).

This discussion assumes that the motive for the deposition of so many hoards was economic. People were hiding their wealth until better times arrived. There is some evidence which might point to coin being deposited for other ritual reasons. Dr James Gerrard has suggested that a group of ten silver coins from the Baths at Bath, dating from the later fourth century and showing some signs of clipping and thus possibly in use into the early fifth century, were deposited together as a ritual group. They are the only coins from this late period found among a vast deposit of over 12,000 coins excavated from the spring. The same writer also suggests that some other hoards may also have been deposited for non-economic reasons and cites the hoards from Shapwick Heath as likely to be in this category (Gerrard 2005b, 271–3). However, it seems likely that ritual reasons for deposition can only have been relevant in a minority of cases.

Two facts stand out from the mass of data about the hoards. The first is that Somerset has a very high concentration of hoards, although they are attested across a belt of territory which runs from Norfolk to Devon. The second is that the deposition of hoards was not a once only event, it was a process which had always occurred and which continued until coin ceased to be available to be buried. But there was a distinct rise in burial frequency from c. 380 onwards, showing that people of all classes were burying their money throughout a roughly 30 year period at least, and perhaps more if those hoards which end c. 410 were deposited after the coin had been in use for some time. Additionally, there was almost certainly a rise in the proportion of currency in circulation being deposited during the 30 years. If as suggested above by the modern Russian example, putting one's money under the bed or in the ground is a common and rational response to turmoil in society, we should recognise that the death of Roman Britain was a long slow process and that 404 or 410 are significant dates, especially for us, but in fact only markers in a drawn out process of decline and separation.

We have to ask next what happened to all the money that was never buried. Coins of the late-Roman period are found continually, although not in quantity. N. S. Ryan remarked that 'The apparent failure of the system of coin supply and the resulting limited distribution of post-388 issues would suggest that, outside the towns, coin use did not survive beyond about 400. This however, is only to be expected from the overall picture of declining rural money use throughout the second half of the century' (Ryan 1988). It has also been suggested that the practice of clipping brought about the collapse of the

coinage because the coin was no longer worth its face value and without the support of the silver coinage bronze could not circulate. Thus, it is suggested, coins would cease to circulate by c. 409 – an abrupt end to the monetary system (Burnett 1984, 163–85). The few coins found have to be set against a background of their declining availability and a case has been made for coin clipping in the years immediately after 404. Remarkably few casual losses recorded in Somerset are from the end of the fourth century, though doubtless there are more to be found. A coin of Arcadius and Honorius, found at Wiveliscombe, is clipped, suggesting that it was in use in a period of coin shortage. A single coin, a *siliqua* of Arcadius, found at Bradley Hill, had also been clipped[1] as had an example from Curry Rivel (SOM-29ADC2). As we have seen above, coin in hoards can also show traces of clipping and, as has been suggested above, there are grounds for believing that coin did continue to circulate in the first 20 years or so of the fifth century. The fact of clipping, along with continued circulation, would suggest that commercial life of some kind continued with lack of coinage becoming a problem. Clearly burial removed a proportion of the finite supply from circulation, increasing the value of that which remained in use. If local trade, facilitated through money, continued in the early fifth century we might expect that its general level would have declined, sharply at first as the impact of the migration of the army to Gaul affected producers, and then more slowly as the purchasing power of the well to do fell off following the loss of central government spending. In the modern world a loss of spending power caused by a drop in demand would lead to a deflation and money would become cheaper. However, in a world where money was no longer being produced, the currency could appreciate if money disappeared faster than the economy declined. People might bury coin to keep it safe hoping that its value would rise even more. An alternative explanation might be that elite purchasers continued to buy imported goods and that as the country's bullion was drained off coin became scarcer and more valuable. Clipped coin might reflect their real silver value, rather than their nominal currency value. In these circumstances we might expect wealthy people to consider melting down their plate for coining as was normal in the Middle Ages

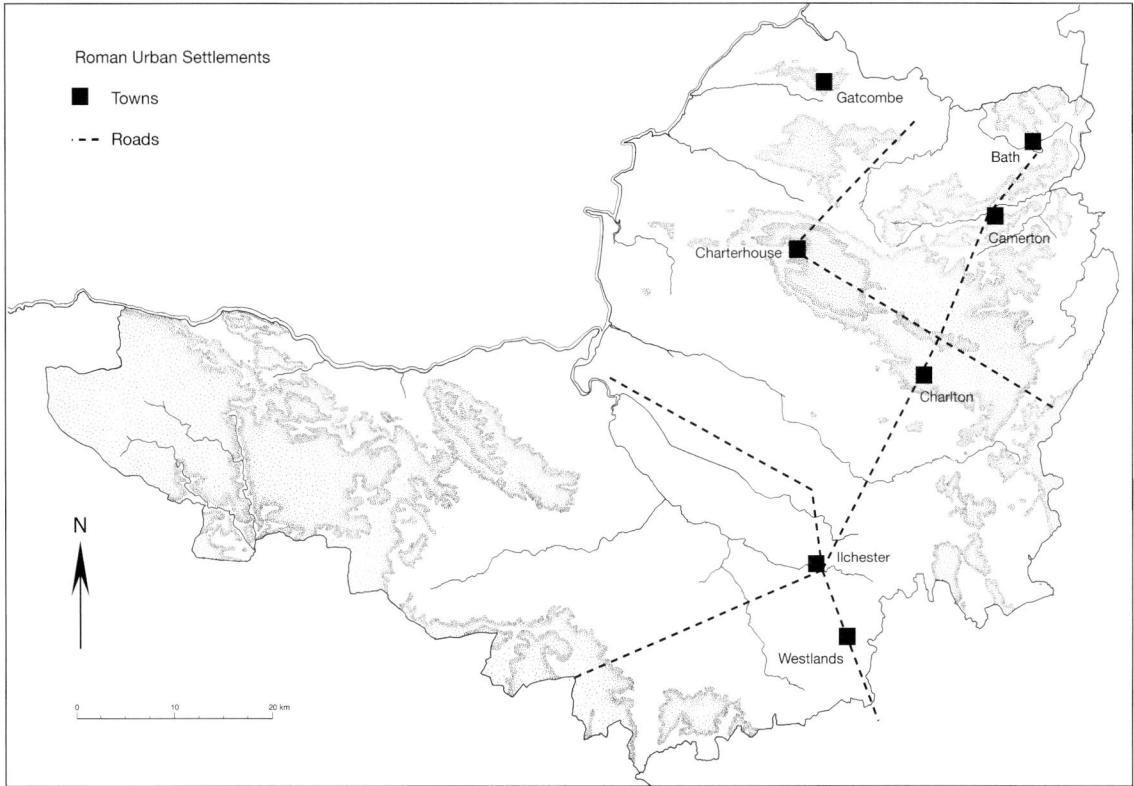

Figure 3. Late fourth century urban settlements.

and in early modern times. This did not happen, either because there were cultural impediments to the idea of a local mint for precious metals, or because economic and political circumstances prevented it. Given that Honorius had encouraged *provinciales* to take up arms in their own defence (Wood, I. 1984,5), one might have expected local rulers to think in terms of minting their own currency, especially when we consider the traditional power of coins as symbols of political authority and legitimacy. Again, this did not happen. People in authority may have hoped for restoration of normality at first. Minting was an Imperial prerogative, so there were probably strongly inhibiting taboos associated with such an idea and by the time it was apparent that that a return to normality would never happen the need for coin had declined so that minting was no longer worthwhile.

One thing is clear, we have not found evidence of extensive jewellery or ornament in the area. Wealth in the form of plate and jewellery was not buried in quantity. It may be that the elite who owned such precious objects had gradually disposed of it as they became poorer. The long drawn out nature of the crisis which destroyed late Roman society would have encouraged such a reaction. Alternatively, as members of the rural elite left for Armorica during the first half of the fifth century they took their treasure with them.

The towns

The failure of the towns of Britain in the immediate post-Roman world is normally seen as part of the collapse of the monetised economy and of the European-wide system of government in the later Roman Empire (Fig. 3). The Empire at large has been described as a 'proto-industrial economy' or an 'industrialising economy' (Dark 1996, 1–21). Britain certainly supported a pottery industry which produced large quantities of goods from manufacturing centres which were widely distributed, and it also supported a major iron-smelting industry. Somerset had a salt-boiling industry, which was rural and which must have produced for a market, and there were probably many other locally based craft workshops which produced every-day items of metal-ware, leather, wood and pottery, all of which were to some extent dependent upon a monetized and integrated economy. Like the rest of the British provinces it was not highly developed compared with the inner core of the Empire, around the Mediterranean, but was essentially an agricultural economy which produced some mass-produced goods for mostly regional consumption. In practice the towns of the late fourth century were already in decline before money vanished. In a society which was becoming increasingly a command economy, the towns could not continue as major manufacturing and trade centres. The demands of the imperial government for men and materials to maintain the administration and the army were too great for the economy to sustain. Although they continued as centres of government administration and as market centres, municipal life had weakened, with baths, theatres and other public buildings no longer used. Urban populations had declined sharply and many towns had areas which were no longer built over (Faulkner 2000, 121–30).

Somerset was not well provided with towns in the Roman period, but *Aquae Sulis* (Bath) to the north was certainly very important, both as a cult centre and as a market and administrative centre on the Fosse Way, where it crossed the Wiltshire Avon. Of all the towns locally it has the best claim to late survival of some kind of urban life. Professor Barry Cunliffe, writing in 1995, thought that the town continued to show signs of urban life in the post-Roman period which may have continued right through until its re-emergence as a major centre in the tenth century (Cunliffe 1995, 119). Dr Davenport goes much further and suggests that there is a parallel between Bath in the fifth and sixth centuries and the situation in many of the towns of Gaul in the late Antique period, where the much reduced towns continued as urban communities, though often very small indeed (Davenport 2002,

22–4). Recent work on deposits from underneath the debris in the precinct of the temple suggests that the area ceased to be used for any pagan religious purpose in the mid-to-late fifth century and suggests that this may have been a deliberate demolition by Christians (Gerrard 2007, 159–61). In Gaul the most common cause for the continued existence of the town was as a religious centre, normally as the seat of a bishop. This was how places such as Le Mans, Tours, Poitiers, Lyons, Clermont, Toulouse, Arles, Nimes, Narbonne and many others survived, with the bishop as the continuing authority and probably, with his household, the major consumers of goods and services. Of course Bath was not Tours – it was much smaller and crucially it was embedded in an economy which had lost its coinage, unlike the cities of Gaul and other parts of the old Roman Empire. Nevertheless it seems possible that a centre of activity and perhaps authority, possibly based upon the seat of a bishop, continued to exist to the north of Somerset and may have exercised some influence for a distance round about. However, the occupation of the area which is now Gloucestershire and of Bath and its immediate hinterland was an early success for the emerging Anglo-Saxons. Any connection Bath may have had with the area to the south was ended with the appearance of the Hwicce in the later sixth century. The area around the town which later became the hundred of Bath is likely to have been the land which lay in the territory of the Hwicce until the early tenth century (Thorn 2005, 9–27).

Much further south lay '*Lendiniae*', Ilchester. Here there is much less evidence for any kind of urban survival in the post-Roman period. There are suggestions that the urban life of the town finished in the early fifth century and that any continuing use was at a very low non-urban level. As is evident from the map (Fig. 2) above, coins of the early fifth century do appear in a hoard from Ilchester (Robertson 2000, no.1508). Someone in Ilchester was still conserving coin in the first quarter of the fifth century. Excavation suggests that buildings were dismantled after dereliction, immediately raising the question as to why this should happen and when. However excavation also produced sherds of a sandy grey-ware jar which has been likened to fifth or sixth century imported 'E' wares and a few sherds of fifth and sixth century 'A' or 'B' Mediterranean wares have also been reported (Leach *et al.* 1982, 12). There may have been some continuing activity at or near Ilchester, to which we shall return later.

There were three other small towns in Somerset which have been identified and excavated, all on the Fosse Way. Camerton was excavated between 1926 and 1956 (Wedlake 1958). There were indications that the settlement continued as a town into the fifth century and also of commercial activity, including a small hoard of minims of the early fifth century (Wedlake 1958, 96).

The settlement at Charlton near Shepton Mallet is a much more recent discovery (Leach and Evans 2001). This was a thriving small roadside settlement which was active right through the fourth century and into the fifth. However the outstanding feature of this site was the discovery of burials which seem to indicate continued use in the fifth century and the possibility that activity on the site continued into the sixth at least (Leach and Evans 2001, 95–6). The excavators remark that 'By the end of the seventh century all occupation by the living or burial of the dead had probably ceased' (Leach and Evans 2001, 97). Elsewhere Peter Leach remarks 'there is clear evidence here for continuing occupation well past the conventional end of Roman Britain, even though we might by then no longer call this place a town' (Leach and Evans 2001, 144).

At Westlands in Yeovil excavation of the site took place in 1927–8 (Radford 1928, 122–43). The excavator proposed a date of c. AD 370 as a terminus for the site, but recent commentators have pointed out that the coin evidence points to a later date than this and that the there is evidence of reuse of part of a building (HER54751).

There may also have been a small town, or at least a heavily defended and well populated settlement at Gatcombe, in the modern parish of Long Ashton. This site was known in the nineteenth century from the works on the railway, but not investigated systematically until the period 1967–76, when Keith Branigan led a series of excavations. His cautious verdict was that it was probably a very grand villa which had been destroyed by the railway works and from which extensive workshops relating to a production site had survived (Branigan 1977). Recent

investigation reveals that the area was surrounded by walls some 15 ft thick, which may have started as earthen banks, perhaps in the third century AD, and were then reinforced with stone facings in the fourth century, as happened at Caerwent (Smisson 2009). Nineteenth-century accounts suggest that coins of the later fourth century and even of Arcadius were found on site and Branigan's work revealed buildings which were being repeatedly refurbished late in the fourth century. There is every likelihood that Gatcombe continued to be occupied well into the early fifth century at least. Major questions still remain concerning the precise functioning of this place which will only be answered by further archaeological investigation. If it was a town it looks to have been rather isolated; there are no known 'Roman' roads nearby. Why was it so heavily fortified? What was its function? How was it related to the surrounding countryside? And was its ending related to the commissioning of the hill-fort at Cadbury-Congresbury to the south, towards the end of the sixth century?

Taken overall, the evidence of coin hoards, finds of lost coins and the decay of urban settlements would seem to point to a collapse of organised town life in the region at the end of the fourth century or in the early years of the fifth. However there are signs that all may not have been quite as bleak as first suggested. Some sort of community seems to have survived in Bath and there is strong evidence that settlement and activity continued at both Camerton and Charlton into the post-Roman period. Something organised clearly continued at Gatcombe, though what this was is unclear. Evidence from Ilchester is less strong, but even here too there are hints of activity. If we were to adopt the position that Bath was the seat of a post-Roman bishop the continuation of some activity in the other towns might not be so implausible. All except Gatcombe are linked to Bath by the Fosse Way and one might suggest continuing communication along the road and possibly some trade movement as long as Bath remained free from the control of the barbarian rulers of the east. If any reliance can be placed upon the early entries of the Anglo-Saxon Chronicle this arrangement might have persisted until 577 or thereabouts, when Bath was said to have fallen to Cuthwine and Ceawlin (ASC 'A', 577). However, if this really happened, we need to be clear that the type and extent of activity in these centres would not have qualified as 'urban' by the standards of the first or second centuries AD. What was left was impoverished and debased, probably supporting only a handful of people who were little different from their neighbours in the nearby countryside.

The Countryside

The picture presented by rural settlement is even more difficult to evaluate. Writing in 1976, Keith Branigan was confident that many villas in the south-west, including Somerset, had been attacked in the mid-fourth century, though he also agreed that many showed signs of re-building or occupation after AD 367 (Branigan 1976). In fact it is surprisingly difficult to say much about the villas at the end of the fourth century, since so many are hardly recorded and few have been excavated under modern conditions. Of 67 recorded in modern Somerset, 24 have sufficient evidence for us to be confident that they were occupied in the fourth century. At Ilchester Mead there seems clear evidence that the building was in use in the fifth century (HER53104). But we have to consider what we mean by that. Were they occupied as they were built, for a gentry and aristocracy who relied upon a plentiful supply of cheap labour to enable them to maintain a large house and a great *familia*? Or did they see their standard of living decline, leaving a relatively impoverished owner, living beyond his means in a house which deteriorated for lack of maintenance? At Ilchester a fourth century extension to the villa had ovens built into a major room and in the early fifth century part of a veranda wall was demolished to allow a new structure to be built. This certainly suggests a degree of 'downsizing', if nothing else. Elsewhere, coins suggest some villas continued to be occupied into the early fifth century. This was certainly true of the villa at Newton St Loe, where a coin of Honorius has been found, but more general evidence is lacking (MBN1661).

Generally the evidence suggests that the decline of the economy which had allowed these great houses to flourish through much of the fourth century meant that by the end of the century they were all falling into decay and that most were abandoned or were

inhabited on a much reduced scale in the early fifth century. Their decline is an index of the decline and fall of a particular group of wealthy people, who may have retained some pre-eminence and power among their neighbours, but for whom the standard of living had been drastically reduced. Thereafter their houses became ruins and sources of re-useable material.

Few rural settlements of a lower social standing have been extensively excavated, but where they have significant information has emerged. On Lansdown, near Bath, a rural settlement with signs of industrial activity has produced a coin of Arcadius (MBN2008). At Catsgore a substantial group of farmsteads was constructed in the early second century and rebuilt over the centuries. In the fourth century a considerable number of new stone buildings were erected, replacing earlier timber structures. At least one of these buildings remained in use until at least the early fifth century (Leech 1982, 7). The same excavator also examined the settlement at Bradley Hill, near Somerton (Leech 1982, 177–252). A number of the buildings here were occupied into the early fifth century. Building 1 was abandoned in the first half of the fifth century. Building 3 was abandoned after 402 and deliberately demolished at a later unknown date. These two examples are well known and are part of widespread and dense settlement across the south-east Somerset area. Both show that activity continued at these settlements into the fifth century. A recent scholar, using the cemetery at Bradley Hill, has suggested that activity may have continued here into the sixth century (Gerrard 2005a, 1–9). These were large sites, groupings of farmsteads, probably the dwellings of peasants originally dependent upon a villa. How representative they were of the wider landscape is impossible to say. Other sites have not produced precise information about the ending of settlement. At Wearne Roger Leech was unable to do more than note that there was pottery of the third and fourth centuries on site (Leech 1976, 45–50). The difficulty has been that of recognising and dating pottery from the early fifth century. Dr James Gerrard has boldly suggested that it may be possible to extend the date range of Roman Black Burnished wares, made in south-east Dorset, into the fifth century (Gerrard 2004, 65–76). If his argument is valid then it does indeed suggest that trade of some kind persisted into the fifth century. However, even this evidence disappears as the century goes on and we are left with the sites themselves and 'invisible people'.

The evidence of decline suggests very strongly that the population itself was falling. By the end of the fifth century there were probably far fewer people in Somerset than at the beginning. Loss of urban populations is matched by the abandonment of many rural settlements also. A recent commentator has suggested that the population of Britain may have halved during the fifth century, but he started from a suggested figure of somewhere between two and four million at the end of the fourth century (Härke 2002, 150). Peter Fowler prefers a higher starting figure and thinks the early fourth century population must have been at least four to five million, though his use of the date AD 300 for the high point implies that he thinks there was a fall during the fourth century. He is in no doubt that there was a severe fall during the fifth century and perhaps beyond (Fowler 2002, 16–18).

The hiatus which follows, where it is obvious that a society of some kind continued to exist, but left little if anything recognisable to us, continued for perhaps twenty-five to fifty years. The colonial withdrawal can be seen as an ongoing process, spread over the second half of the fourth century and culminating in the military withdrawals of the early fifth century and the accompanying collapse of the currency. This economic catastrophe was in itself enough to cause a fall in population, but the onset of the plague in the mid-century must have added to the general decline. There followed a post-colonial world in which Old Welsh society began to construct a new political settlement. E. A. Thompson argued as long ago as 1950 that there was a social revolution which caused the land-owners to appeal to Honorius (Thompson 1956, 163–7). For Neil Faulkner, a theoretical Marxist model for this period would demonstrate that 'Popular ('bagaudic') resistance to tax-collectors and landlords, supported by Christian radicals, challenge(d) ruling class control over land, labour and the social surplus' (Faulkner 2004, 5–12). There is little evidence to support this interpretation and also little to refute it, and it is from this point of collapse and obscurity that we must begin to suggest the outline of a new society. If we accept that the Somerset region continued to be dominated by an Old Welsh, not Roman, culture until the mid-seventh century we need to construct a model for the political and social structure of that society.

Note
1. Information from Mr S. Minnitt, Taunton Museum accession no. is 76.AA.93/118.

1

Post-Imperial Politics:
defence and offence

The Old Welsh societies of western Britain were in a fundamentally different position from their Anglo-Saxon neighbours. They were post-Roman, but they were not merely a pale remnant of the world they were cut off from. The Celtic language, which had continued to be spoken as the local vernacular, eventually became the language spoken by everyone, but there is also evidence that a Latin Romance had begun to develop in the fifth and sixth centuries and may have been spoken by the elite and often understood and spoken at a functional level by many others (Woolf 2003, 271–3). Contact with the Latin speaking world was not lost. It is clear that the language of the Church remained Latin and that some literate contact with continental Europe continued, if only through the Church, which became a binding force in Celtic society in Britain as it became elsewhere in western Europe. Gildas was able to write literary Latin for an educated audience, so that material decay did not necessarily mean a collapse of culture or indeed of education. Nevertheless as far as we can tell the vernacular became the language of the rulers as well as of the ordinary people by the later sixth and early seventh centuries and it is likely that the existence of Germanic speakers close by helped to engender a feeling of community among the Celtic speakers (Woolf 2003, 376). Their polities were the result of the decay and collapse of late-Roman society and had been born from the need for local responses to the loss of contact with the Imperial administration, the final collapse of the proto-industrial economy and then the need for self defence against the effects of the new and aggressive Anglo-Saxon settlers appearing to

the east and the north. These new societies were not, however, based upon loss and decay, although they were a product of disruption. There is no evidence that the first problems they faced were caused by organised kingdoms in the east. The Anglo-Saxon Chronicle, with its stories of early leaders from whom later kings were descended, carving out new kingdoms for themselves, has a very shaky foundation. Had the post-Romans of the west of Britain been faced with a unifying and charismatic Anglo-Saxon leader, such as for instance Clovis among the Franks, it is likely that the whole of lowland Britain would have succumbed very quickly, but the emergence of well organised Anglo-Saxon polities took a long time. As it was, the post-Roman kingdoms of the west resisted political domination by the new eastern groups for a period of about 250 years. In view of this timescale we must consider them a reasonable success, but there is nothing to suggest that they were prepared to try to win back control over eastern Britain. Their stance was defensive.

Geography

In order to construct a political environment for post-Roman Somerset we need to build a likely physical environment. We cannot assume that the later boundaries of the shire were in evidence in AD 400 or 450. Professor Dark has suggested that there may have been as many as nine post-Roman kingdoms in the west of Britain in the fifth century. One of those kingdoms is 'Dumnonia' in south-west England (Dark 1994, 111). Such a kingdom would have embraced Devon, Cornwall, Somerset and Dorset, or some area which approximates to those counties. It would have made a very large kingdom, when compared to others in western Britain, so it would be quite surprising if it were not actually broken into a few smaller units.

The best preserved Roman roads are those which run north-east to south-west or north to south, the most famous of which is the Fosse Way (Figs 1.1 and 1.2. It is followed by modern roads, mostly 'A' roads from south-eastern Somerset northwards as far as Bath (Margery 1955, 113–6). Only in just a few places, on the steeper parts of the Mendips for instance, does the Fosse Way disappear (HER55101). Much of the road from Ilchester to Dunball is also still in use, but the road along the Mendips, (Margery's 45b) is only partly followed by modern roads and seems to have been lost where it crossed the eastern part of the Mendips to the east of Shepton Mallet. However, the road from Charterhouse north to the Avon (Margery 540) survived for a while in part, as is evidenced by the extant Stratford Lane in Compton Martin parish, and fields in Chew Magna parish (tithe no. 1075). The road which ran from Ilchester to Dorchester has never gone out of use. Just outside Ilchester seven phases of the road to Dorchester together with the remains of a Roman bridge were discovered. The lowest three were Roman and culminated in a substantial paved surface. Evidence was recovered of a timber bridge associated with the first two roads and a stone bridge with the third. These were followed by medieval and post-medieval surfaces and two tarmac surfaces (HER55359). Continuity of use is therefore certain for both these roads, suggesting strongly that communications southwards remained important throughout the area in the post-Roman period and beyond.

These roads were, of course, well made metalled highways, meant for the use of the imperial and provincial administration and clearly maintained until the end of that administration. The Fosse Way was certainly well known in the early Middle Ages. The name occurs as *fosse streat* in the Anglo-Saxon charter for Clifton, near Bath (S777 of 970), as *foss* in the charter for Radstock (S854 of 984), and *fosse* at Pilton (S247 of 705 – actually tenth century). Although some of the charter bounds from which

these examples are taken may not be of the dates they bear, but rather post-Conquest, they are still evidence of the antiquity of the name (Watts 2004, entry 'The Fosse Way'). Their survival until today, in the case of the Fosse Way with an ancient name, points to continued use throughout the post-Roman period. On the other hand, the comparative difficulty of tracing the Fosse Way into Devon suggests that continuity of communication towards Exeter was not so strongly maintained and that contact was probably by sea through the Bristol Channel.

The disappearance of the east-west road from Charterhouse towards Old Sarum strongly suggests that there was a real dislocation of communications in that direction which lasted long enough for the road to fall into disuse and to be forgotten. It runs through an area in which it is likely that boundaries were ill-defined until the tenth or eleventh centuries and so was not used as a boundary marker either. It may be that the disappearance of the lead-mining and smelting industry caused the roads to become disused, but it may also be the result of loss of regular trading and political contacts with the east. Further south in Dorset a somewhat similar pattern of loss emerges. Although the road from Dorchester towards Exeter mainly survives as metalled lanes, the road eastward from Dorchester towards old Sarum via Badbury Rings has fallen almost entirely into disuse, although it survives as a conspicuous landscape feature for much of its length (Margery 1955, vol. 1, 95–6, 99–101). It seems likely that the loss of this eastward contact is a result of the political situation in the fifth century, while the survival of the westward road along the Poldens in Somerset and the westward road from Dorchester towards Exeter point to continued contacts by sea in the Bristol Channel and by land from Dorchester, westward along the coast.

The eastern boundary is more problematical. In Somerset it might follow much the same course as today, using the wooded ridge of Selwood Forest as a boundary in what is now south-east Somerset. It has been suggested that the wood defined the boundaries between Roman cantons (Eagles 2001, 214). Its continuance as a boundary is also marked by its use as the point of division for the western diocese formed in 705 for St Aldhelm (ASC 'A' 709). So well recognised was it that it gave its name to the

Figure 1.1. The Fosse Way, looking south-westwards from Lopen towards Dinnington.

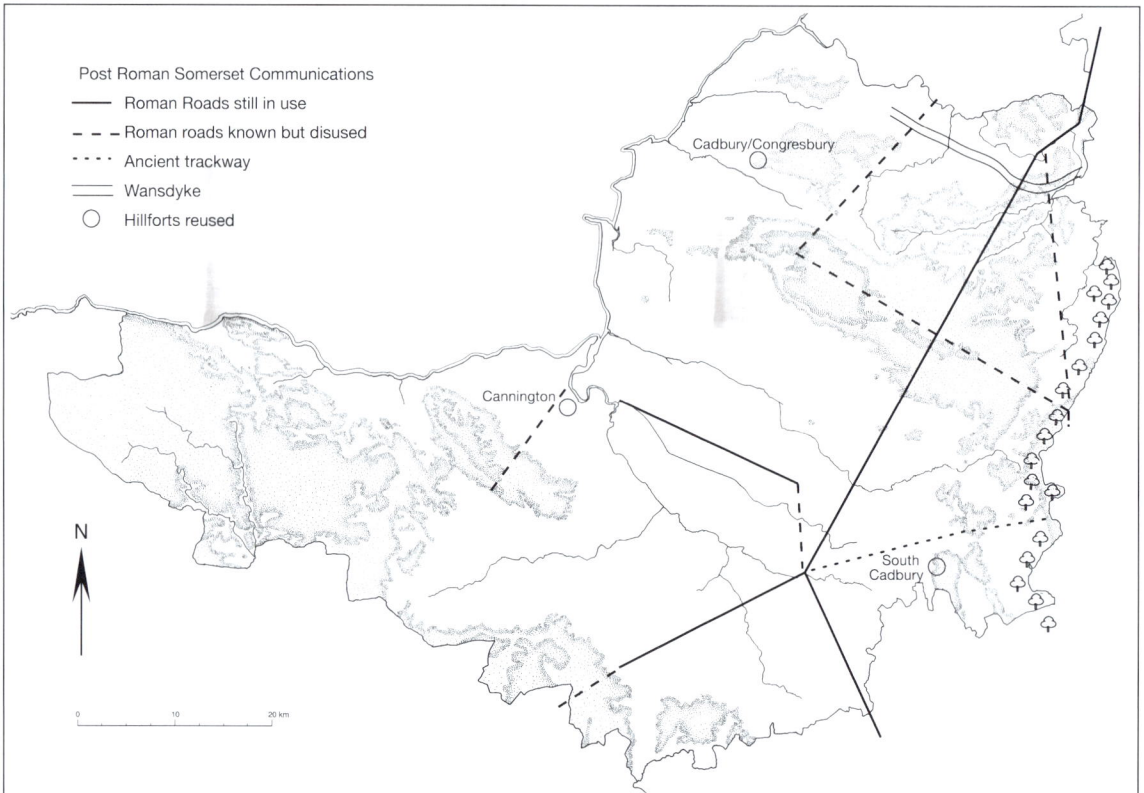

Figure 1.2. Road communications in post-Roman Somerset.

diocese itself which was often called 'Selwoodshire' according to Æthelweard, writing in the tenth century (Campbell 1962, 21). This boundary may well have extended down to what is now the northern part of Dorset, since the woodland extended well south of Penselwood in the middle ages. The northern edge may have included Bath and followed the Avon initially, but this turned out to be a very vulnerable line. However, there is no evidence that what is now western and north-western Wiltshire was part of an organised barbarian polity in the early fifth century. The road from Bath towards Old Sarum was another casualty of the post-Roman period, but may not have disappeared immediately. Just over the border at Bradford on Avon there is some evidence which suggests a well organised post-Roman Christian presence at a possible monastery based in a villa. The discovery of a suggested baptistery inserted into a major room in the villa certainly makes this a possibility (Corney 2003). In addition the retention of a number of Brittonic names in north-western Wiltshire suggests a continued use of the Old Welsh language there (Coates 2000, 95–6). It may for a time have been part of an area ruled from Old Sarum if from anywhere, or possibly continued as a region of British influence through the first half of the fifth century and probably later. A military boundary in north-east Somerset may not therefore have been needed initially. In north-eastern Dorset Bokerley Dyke may have marked the edge of Durnovarian territory, though the existence of a well developed Christian community in Wareham in the post-Roman period suggests that Durnovarian influence may have stretched as far as Poole Harbour to the east (Radford 1975). The retention of the road system, the continued existence of a small population in the town, the importance and longevity of the monastic community there and the relative decline of Ilchester suggests that Dorchester may have remained the main urban centre for this eastern part of the post-Roman region in the first half of the fifth century (Sparey-Green 2004, 103). Bath to the north was on the northern side of the Avon and although connected with the rest of the south-west by the Fosse Way, was probably more closely connected with the region around Cirencester than with Ilchester or Dorchester.

In the late Roman state the provinces of Britannia were divided into *civitates*, each of which consisted of a municipal centre and surrounding *vici* and countryside. The *civitas* was in turn divided into *pagi*. Unfortunately we have no information about the division of the late Roman countryside of south-west Britain. It may be that Ilchester was a *civitas* capital or merely an important *vicus* and head of a *pagus* with Dorchester as its *civitas* capital. The later boundary between Somerset and Dorset lies about half-way between Ilchester and Dorchester, while the boundary between Somerset and Devon is about half-way between Ilchester and Exeter. It is tempting to speculate that this reflects a continuing recognition of late-Roman administrative practices, but this seems unlikely and it is more probable that they are the result of later Anglo-Saxon administrative developments. In any case, the collapse of Roman administration may have over-ridden any such local boundaries.

Politics

Along with this new political geography there was a new social structure driving political activity. The fourth and fifth centuries saw a large-scale immigration into Armorica from southern Britain (Giot, Bernier and Fleuriot 1982). At first this movement may have been stimulated by the drafting of British recruited troops into the region. They may have been followed by civilians (Galliou and Jones 1991, 133). By the mid-fifth century there seems to have been a migration of members of the elite political and social classes who came as organised settlers, retaining their social structures, probably with their household dependants, slaves and servants and even with their own bishops. Knight suggests that the villa owners were fleeing the more militant and proselytizing, radical Christianity espoused by St Martin and his followers (Knight 1981, 60). While this is, of course, a possibility, it seems unlikely that such a group would have been powerful enough to cause a mass migration. Furthermore it would have been a migration into an area closer to the influences of the radical tendency. It is more probable that the villa owners were leaving because of economic hardship, caused by the growing dislocation of the British economy. They moved into an area where the

Roman 'proto-industrial' economy still functioned; they were following their colonial masters. Perhaps they took their treasure with them into exile, leaving little to be buried and re-discovered.

In such situations it would be odd if a whole class, along with their dependants, had fled. If that were the case, then there would have been a serious dislocation of landowning, together with other serious social changes. Some at least of the magistrates and other rural landowners must have remained. When Constantius wrote about the visit of St Germanus to Britain in c. AD 429, he described the saint as meeting notables who held office of some sort, possibly urban (Knight 1981, 56). In Devon and in South Wales, though not in Somerset, contact between the émigrés in Armorica continued as evidenced by the spread of the fashion for funeral monuments bearing the '*hic jacet*' inscription, which were probably inspired by examples in the Vendée and the Bordelais (Knight 1981, 57). Even though many members of the elite had left, some must have remained behind, since there was continuation of contact between the two parts of western Celtic society. Certainly organised political life continued and it seems possible that other systems connected with the towns survived. An education system seems to have survived in some sort, since it produced at least one bishop in Gaul who was of British extraction – Faustus of Riez who was noted for his classical training (Lapidge 1984, 32). St Patrick, if his account of his early life is true, lived the life of a young nobleman before his capture and again must have received his education in the early fifth century, but certainly after the collapse of Roman administration though probably not in the west-country (Thomas 1979, 87). There is some evidence that the religious polemicist, Gildas, although undoubtedly a monastic, had been educated through a system which was still intended to provide lawyers and administrators for the Roman administrative system (Lapidge 1984; Winterbottom 1978, 28, 1, 2). He was writing towards the middle of the sixth century, so that he must have received his education at the beginning of the century, probably privately. If the observations about the education available are true, then a fairly sophisticated society existed into the early sixth century, even if it has left few physical traces.

Both Procopius and Gildas explicitly stated that Britain was governed by tyrants, which was almost certainly a recognition that the men who ruled no longer relied upon Roman administrative forms to bolster their legitimacy. It does not necessarily mean that their rule was violent or unpopular. Procopius clearly used the term to describe any unofficially elevated leader (Dewing 1914–18, vii. 40.4). He and Gildas were writing long after the collapse and their perspective signalled the emergence of a new form of government.

Gildas mentions five kings in his own time, whom he accused of tyranny because they did not follow the accepted rules of the civilised governor. They plundered and terrorized, waged civil wars and failed to administer justice impartially. One of these was Constantine, the king of Dumnonia. 'This unspeakable sin is not unknown to Constantine, tyrant whelp of the filthy lioness of Dumnonia' (Winterbottom 1978, 29). This is clearly a reference to Constantine's mother as a powerful person and part of a governing group, perhaps a queen. Gildas accused Constantine of the murder of 'two royal youths'. The foulness of this deed was accentuated by its commission in a church. Whether we should believe the gory details is unclear, but this story, along with Gildas's earlier description of the tyrants as surrounded by their military companions, 'bloody, proud and murderous men' clearly shows that what had emerged in Dumnonia was a polity ruled by a warrior king and his military retinue (Winterbottom 1978, 28, 1, 2). The murder of 'royal youths' is typical of a dynastic struggle, where the most powerful and ruthless member of a ruling family disposes of younger relatives who may one day offer a challenge to his power, perhaps by claiming a legitimate right to rule, or because they are the heirs of a ruler killed by the tyrant. Such patterns were to become commonplace in Britain among the Anglo-Saxon kings and in Gaul among the Merovingian and the Carolingian dynasties. As the history of the Merovingian and Carolingian kings shows, there is nothing inherently improbable in the existence of a society where militarised rulers, surrounded by their warriors, were unrestrained in their actions but literate commentators, moving in such societies, recorded events and often played a part in them, as Gregory of Tours demonstrated in his History of the Franks (Thorpe 1974).

When local military rulers emerged it was normally because of the failure of recognised and inherited institutions to provide adequate protection against internal or external enemies. It has usually been assumed that the coming of barbarian invaders, whether Picts and Scots or Anglo-Saxons, would be the catalyst, but this does not have to be the case. The loss of an army which could act as an internal police force and the reduction in the number of powerful noblemen in the towns and countryside might have been enough to stimulate the rise of opportunists among the remaining members of the elite, who would then take over ruling functions on their own terms and provide for their own security by recruiting their own military forces. This would have been facilitated by the structure of late Roman society, in which members of the aristocracy were surrounded by their clients and their servants and slaves, and expected to have links with other similar groups. As central authority weakened, the competition between *familiae* would have intensified and British society would have become increasingly dangerous. The *familia* was a potentially large body, which could easily be militarised. The fruitless appeal to the *magister militum*, Aetius, in AD 446, may have been the point at which the tyrants' power was confirmed, since there was now no hope of help from conventional Roman forces (Winterbottom 1978, 20, 1). According to the Gallic Chronicle, it was only just before this date, in 441, that the Anglo-Saxons had arrived in Britain and for them this was an age of expansion and aggression, for the Old Welsh a time of defence and resistance. It is against such a background that the hill-fort society of Somerset in the later fifth and the sixth century must be viewed.

Hill-fort sites and the fifth–sixth century aristocracy

The excavators of the hill-forts of Cadbury-Congresbury and of South Cadbury were both adamant and definitive in characterizing the two sites as the settlements of an elite group (Rahtz *et al.* 1992; Alcock *et al.* 1995). Both sites were old Bronze Age/Iron Age hill-forts which had been re-used in the post-Roman

period. In the case of the site at South Cadbury there is extensive evidence of Iron Age use which ended with the violent storming and destruction of the settlement in the 70s of the current era (Alcock 1972, 170–1; Alcock *et al.* 1995, 99) and then use in the later Roman period with a temple site (Alcock *et al.* 1995, 173). Both sites have produced ample evidence of reuse as hilltop settlements in the period c. 475–550, though Cadbury-Congresbury has some evidence suggesting that it was in use until the late sixth or even the early seventh century. Both have also produced evidence of contact with the Byzantine eastern Mediterranean through the assemblages of pottery, type Bi amphorae from the Peloponnese, Bii from Cilicia and Antioch, Biv jars from Sardis, and Phocean Red-Slipped Ware plates for the smart table services. Cadbury-Congresbury, however, has produced a wider range and greater quantity of the pottery than South Cadbury, as well as glass-ware. Glassware at Cannington came from graves and was similar to glass recovered from Cadbury-Congresbury and from Dinas Powys and may be related to the hill-fort there (Rahtz, Hirst and Wright 2000, 308). There are also some indications of re-use of Ham Hill (Burrow 1981, 269), and there is evidence of finds of exotic pottery from Glastonbury Tor, suggesting that it too was an important site even in the sixth century. The presence of large quantities of animal bones and five ferrules from the base of spears suggests that it should be viewed as a secular site, not the seat of an early religious community (Rahtz 1971). However, more recently Philip Rahtz has come to the view that the site was probably an early Christian site (Rahtz 1993, 59–60). Cannington has also produced Bii amphorae sherds and African red slipware (Rahtz, Hirst and Wright 2000, 295). The hill-fort at Worlebury, near Weston-super-Mare, produced a 'Saxon' spear-head of the fifth-sixth century (Burrow 1981, 282). Athelney and Beckery have also produced some evidence of 'prestige' occupation at this period (Campbell 2007, 118). There may have been other hill-forts which were also re-occupied, but there has been insufficient exploration or evidence to be certain. The strongest candidate is Cadbury-Tickenham. There has been very little investigation of the site since an excavation by H. St G. Gray, whose work was published in 1913, and some unpublished survey

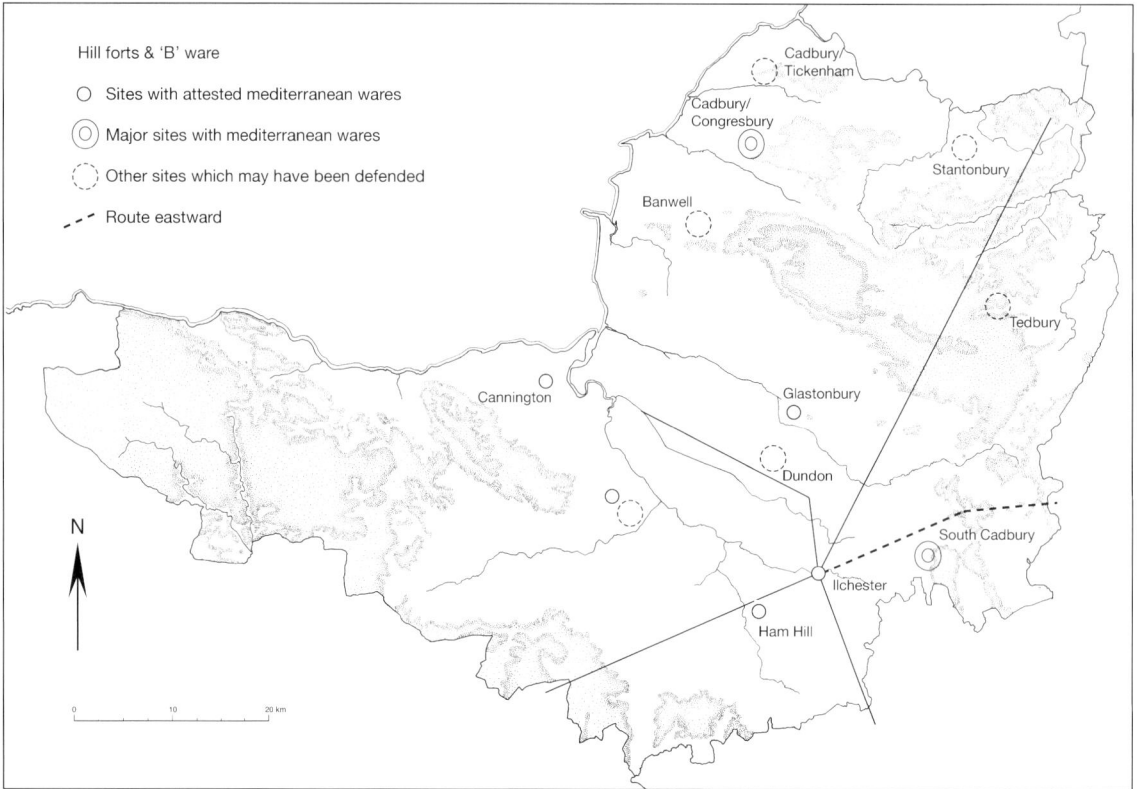

Figure 1.3. Hill-forts and the distribution of 'B' ware.

work (V. Russett, pers. comm.). It is one of three hill-forts in Somerset which have the same 'Cadbury' name. There is a further example in Devon (Gover, Mawer and Stenton 1931–2). There is also a 'Cadbury Farm' in Hampshire and 'Cadbury' in Shropshire (Watts 2004), so that the name is well evidenced and means 'the hill-fort of Cada' (an Anglo-Saxon male personal name). Since the personal name rarely occurs elsewhere it is likely that this is a reference to a mythological personage and may be connected to sites which were used in the post-Roman period. In view of the nature of the evidence at Cadbury-Congresbury and South Cadbury, Cadbury-Tickenham must be a candidate for re-occupation, especially as the Roman 'town' of Gatcombe is so close by.

Rightly, much has been made of the discovery of this material at the two major sites. They are not of course unique in the South West. Dinas Powys in

South Wales was at least as important as Cadbury-Congresbury and must be taken into consideration when assessing the meaning of the Somerset sites (Alcock 1987, 20–66), as must Tintagel (Thomas 1982, 17–34), St Michael's Mount in Cornwall and High Peak in Devon (Turner 2004, 25–32). However exotic material from the Byzantine world is not found only at these major sites. The discovery of eastern Mediterranean pottery at 'beach-markets' at Bantham and Mothecombe in Devon and at sites such as Tregurthy and Gwithian in Cornwall makes it clear that contacts with the East were not confined only to these great hill-forts but were quite widespread, at least in Devon and Cornwall, and there are several dozen sites in western Britain where this material occurs (Campbell 1996, 83–96). B-ware has also been found at Carhampton, on the north Somerset coast, where it was associated with a metal-working site (Campbell 2007, 118). It may be that contacts and the pottery were more widespread than we know and that a more complete picture will emerge from continuing research. The metal-working may be connected with a post-Roman monastic site (HER 33449).

Analysis of the pottery assemblages shows that they were imported directly from the eastern Mediterranean and from the North African coast, not carried along as part of commercial ventures which moved aggregate cargoes along the shores of western Europe (Fulford 1989, 1–6). Anthea Harris has suggested that these contacts were essentially diplomatic in origin, for it is difficult to imagine what commercial gain could come from a long and hazardous voyage from the eastern Mediterranean to western Britain, a part of the western Empire which had always been on the edge of the world (Harris 2003, 147). An alternative would be that the imports represent the results of a trade in tin originating in Devon and much in demand in the Byzantine world (Wooding 1996, 82). The ruler who controlled the tin through the demand for tribute and perhaps through organising and controlling the trade itself would be in an extremely powerful position. A purely diplomatic initiative would also have been concentrated upon the high status site of a ruler and potential client, rather than scattered through relatively minor sites. Trade in itself, however, does not need to be seen as purely commercial and divorced from government policy and interests, as modern experience shows. Towards the end of the fifth century and during the first half of the sixth century diplomatic trade contact between the Byzantine world and south-western Britain may have involved the supply to high-ranking groups of quantities of vessels containing wines and oils as well as fine wares for dining. In addition, the pottery is practically all that survives from these contacts and the imported goods probably included perishable items such as textiles, primarily silk, but also perhaps books and people. It is possible that precious metals and other manufactured items also arrived. Such contacts, with gifts of valuables and coin, were widespread across western Europe in the fifth and sixth centuries and may be related to the more general diplomatic efforts of the Byzantine emperors in the later fifth and early sixth centuries. More recent analysis of

materials from sites in western Britain has shown that there were two components to the seaborne contacts, goods which arrived directly from the eastern Aegean and items which came from other continental sources (Campbell 1996, fig. 2). Although the driving force behind one assemblage may have been primarily connected with royal policy and monopoly and the another more commercial and carried on at a lower level, the two were not mutually exclusive and both may have been stimulated by the appearance of local rulers who were recognisable to diplomats and merchants and who offered the chance of valuable contacts with a part of the Europe formerly within the Roman world and still linked to it by the ties of religious belief.

It is apparent that Somerset was not at the forefront of these contacts when we compare the distribution of pottery in the county with Devon and Cornwall. In particular the size of the site at Tintagel and the signs of the scale of its connections to the eastern Mediterranean world make it clear that it was the pre-eminent high status site in the south-west, perhaps the seat of a king (Barrowman, Batey and Morris 2007). This was probably the site from which the high status material was re-exported to the Somerset hill-forts as part of the initiative which maintained the authority of the ruler at Tintagel. In Somerset it may be that the major contact was always directly with Cadbury-Congresbury. Certainly this site has more imported material than South Cadbury, though we should not ignore the differences in the areas excavated at the two sites. The difference in the quantity of material may simply be the result of Cadbury-Congresbury's proximity to the Severn Estuary, while supply of luxury material to South Cadbury might be more difficult given that goods would have had to be brought up river some distance. The fortifications at Cadbury-Congresbury were certainly substantial (Rahtz *et al.* 1992, 231), but are not as powerful as those at South Cadbury. At Cadbury-Congresbury the excavators thought that display was a major factor in the use of the site (Rahtz *et al.* 1992, 231). The same may be true of South Cadbury, but the strength of the defences suggests either that the occupants were more concerned about possible attack than their confrères at Cadbury-Congresbury, or that they needed more in the way of defences to impress their neighbours.

There the fifth century rampart was 4–5 m thick and was faced with stone laced with timber. About 1100 m of walling were erected and there was also a substantial timber gatehouse (Alcock *et al.* 1995, 22). The excavator estimated that the timber uprights used (approx. 200 mm square posts) amounted to some 3000 m of wood. This was a massive construction and must have taken a considerable time to build (Fig. 1.4). Forced labour on the site may have been a way of reinforcing the subjugation of a reluctant population as well as a response to fears of attack from the east and might mark political weakness. A recent commentator has concluded that South Cadbury was a central place for much of Somerset and regards Cadbury-Congresbury as its import-export centre (Campbell 2007, 118–9). However at Cadbury-Congresbury the relatively weaker defences would suggest that the occupants were surer of their political position, perhaps because they had diplomatic relations with their neighbours across the channel at Dinas Powys and because of the prestige attached to relations with the distant eastern Empire.

The choice of South Cadbury as a fortified site was clearly made with strategic objectives in mind (see Fig. 1.3). The Fosse Way carrying communications from the midlands to Exeter runs only a few kilometres away to the east and the hilltop replaces the urban site at Ilchester, which is at a nodal position, with access to water transport and control of the road to Dorchester and the south coast, as well as local roads (Alcock 1988, 34). The line of the modern A303, immediately to the north of South Cadbury, probably follows a major route-way from the east, while the hill-fort itself guards the forest of Selwood, which was a major barrier between Wiltshire and Somerset in the early Middle Ages. The commander of the fort must have had a considerable force of men at his disposal, perhaps mounted, to patrol the area, but it is worth noting that we have no trace of the arms and armour which they would have used.

At South Cadbury a coin of Honorius, found in the make-up of the fifth century rampart, suggests that the site was in some sort of use at the beginning of the fifth century and there are indications that wine was being imported and drunk on the hill-top before the refurbishment of the ramparts. This serves to remind us that the commencement of the pottery does not necessarily mark the commencement of re-use of the hill-forts (Alcock *et al.* 1995, 114). It is probable that the movement to such sites pre-dates the growth of contacts with the eastern Mediterranean and that the social changes which led to their re-use itself facilitated the contacts.

Being on the coast, or having easy access to it and thus to external relations, may well have helped the occupiers of Congresbury-Cadbury to become dominant in the region. Control of access to high-status goods is an enduring feature of hierarchical societies in Late Antiquity and in the early Middle Ages. Access to these goods and control of their distribution was both a sign of dominance and a method of control over followers. The Somerset sites can be seen as subordinate to Tintagel, which may have relied upon the export of tin, gathered as tribute or tax, as the method of obtaining the high status goods, some of which were then redirected to the aristocratic groups at the hill-fort sites.

While it is necessary to acknowledge the problem caused by varying degrees of knowledge about the sites, a possible hierarchy of hill-forts and defended sites at the end of the fifth century and during the first half of the sixth century may have existed. Politically, South Cadbury would probably rank second in the hierarchy, after Cadbury-Congresbury with Glastonbury Tor, Ham Hill and Cannington hill-fort as less important sites, perhaps third rank. The nearest port-site for South Cadbury would have been Ilchester, where the river was navigable for small boats or barges, but it would have been much less convenient as a shipment centre than Cadbury-Congresbury. Finally we should not overlook the possibility that there are other sites, not distinguished yet by discoveries of eastern Mediterranean pottery, which could have formed part of the pattern of high status sites. One such might be at Portishead/Portbury, just south of the Avon and on the Bristol Channel, where a cemetery, similar to those found elsewhere, including Henley Hill very close to Cadbury-Congresbury, suggests a large and well organised community (Watts and Leach 1996). Similar cemeteries at Banwell, which has a hill-fort which has never been investigated (Eagles 1994, 20), and at Wembdon (Langdon 1986; Croft and Woods 1987; Croft 1988; Hollinrake and Hollinrake 1989;

Woods 1990), show the existence of other large and well organised communities, which would fit into the pattern.

The western Wansdyke, which runs intermittently from Maes Knoll in the west to the head of Horsecombe in the east (Fox and Fox 1960), is an earthwork which can most easily be attributed to this period (Dark 2000, 146–7). The Foxes thought that it was probably mostly of the early seventh century on the basis of its name, Wansdyke, from the Old English *wodnesdic*, which is how the name appears in later Anglo-Saxon charter bounds (S777). However, the name may well simply reflect the historical ignorance of the later Anglo-Saxon speakers in the area. It was quite normal to attribute a large and mysterious earthwork to a supernatural being and Woden did not cease to exist simply because the Anglo-Saxons had become Christians. The Foxes thought that the most easterly portion of the dyke, from the top of Horsecombe, across the Fosse Way and to the top of the drop down into Englishcombe, pre-dated the rest of the construction and was intended to block the route of the Fosse and the hilltop across which it runs. It is a noticeably straight and well engineered section of the ditch. Since the blocking of the Fosse Way shows that it was in use at the time, the dyke might represent a boundary between a Dubonnic polity to the south and a state based on *Aquae Sulis*, and date from some point in the fifth century. Its construction shows that it faces northwards and so belonged to the polity to the south. The later extension of the dyke westward may have followed when the Bath-Cirencester region passed into English hands, perhaps in AD 577 (ASC 'A'). As the Foxes also pointed out, the dyke utilises two hill-forts, Stantonbury and Maes Knoll, but neither of them seem to have a military role. There are no entrances into the forts made to accommodate people moving along the line, suggesting that its primary purpose was not military. There are gaps in the boundary which have been attributed to woodland (Fox and Fox 1960, 37–8), but it is also possible that sections were never built because the dyke was never finished. An alternative explanation might follow that proposed by Peter Fowler for Wansdyke in Wiltshire, that it was constructed to meet a short-lived emergency in the late fifth century by the inhabitants of southern

Wiltshire, an emergency which was ended by the battle of *Mons Badonicus* (Fowler 2001, 196). The earlier section of the dyke would therefore represent the power of the polity with its local power centre at Congresbury, with its most powerful military site at South Cadbury, guarding the central lowlands of Somerset from the routes from Wiltshire, through southern Selwood. The more westerly section may merely represent a brief military and political development, but would nevertheless demonstrate that the local society was well organised and under significant political control.

A more recent and much more radical appraisal of the evidence relates the dyke to the origins of the Wessex polity at the beginning of the seventh century (Reynolds and Langlands 2006, 13–44). This view, like Peter Fowler's, sees the dyke as a single construction and argues for the reality of an extension westward as far as Portbury. They see the use of Woden's name as part of the process of identity creation, in which the mythical founder of the Wessex dynasty and 'father' of the men of Wessex was associated with a construction project which marked out their territory from that of their Mercian neighbours to the north.

Since the post-Roman people of Somerset were the resident population when the Anglo-Saxons began to affect them it might be expected that their stance was entirely defensive, but that does not mean that it was peaceful. Gildas tells us that post-Roman society was riven with internecine struggles. It would be normal in such circumstances for small polities to be prepared to ally themselves with groups of outsiders, as the Anglo-Saxons were, if it conferred an immediate advantage. Contacts of this nature would lead to some cultural exchanges, even if political differences remained strong. What was important for the continuance of the post-Roman culture of Somerset was that the people of Wiltshire cannot be regarded as uniformly 'Anglo-Saxon' in the fifth and early sixth centuries. Although one needs to be cautious about the historicity of Gildas's work, he must be correct in describing the battle of Mount Badon, since he dates it by his own birth (Winterbottom 1978, 26, 1). This battle probably took place somewhere in northern Wiltshire and as we have seen, it has been suggested that the eastern Wansdyke was built as a counter to a threat to the post-Roman population of central

Figure 1.4. South Cadbury Castle, from the south.

and southern Wiltshire from the Thames valley area in the late fifth century. The failure to complete the dyke is put down to the battle of Mount Badon and the subsequent setback to aggressive expansion by the emerging 'Anglo-Saxon' polities (Fowler 2001, 196).

The spread of Anglo-Saxon culture across Wiltshire is marked by the cemeteries which display their burial practices (Eagles 2001, fig. 11.1), but it does not follow that Wiltshire in the sixth century contained an aggressive and expansionary group of Anglo-Saxon warriors and there is no evidence to suggest that the groups who later formed the kingdom of Wessex had yet come together. Bruce Eagles has suggested that the mid-sixth century entries of the Anglo-Saxon Chronicle may indicate warfare between Anglo-Saxons in northern Wiltshire and the Thames Valley and others in southern Wiltshire (Eagles 2001, 205). This is possible, but the Anglo-Saxon Chronicle is not a source to be relied upon for detail of this nature. It seems likely that the southern part of Wiltshire, at least in the west, was not a powerful unified polity in the mid-sixth century. This was not a period when graves with grave goods suggest that an elite ruler existed or that an intense struggle for power was in progress. The analysis of cemeteries which contained graves with weapons and graves without weapons

shows a clear division in terms of stature between those buried with weapons and those without. This has been interpreted as an ethnic division, with people of both ethnic groups buried in the same burial plots; Anglo-Saxons together with members of a local post-Roman population. They are seen as groups where the 'Anglo-Saxon' element formed the elite while the 'post-Roman Celtic survivors' were part of a subordinate group (Härke 1990, 42). Whether or not the ethnic interpretation holds true, the observation that weapon burials relate to family status, not to warrior status, is important, since it suggests that weapon burials do not reflect a warlike and aggressive society. Furthermore, burials of this type peak towards the mid-sixth century and decline steadily thereafter. The peak of weapon burials, it is suggested, coincides with a period of comparative peace, in the aftermath of the battle of Mount Badon (Härke 1990, 31–2). This was essentially a society of peasant-cultivators.

After the middle of the sixth century the contacts with the eastern Roman Empire withered and the supplies of exotic material began to dry up. The result was the collapse of the polity of Dumnonia whose king could no longer exercise control as his wealth vanished with the collapse of the export of tin (Green 2007). This in turn was followed by the retreat of the local elites, who lost much prestige, but probably exercised a freer local authority with the loss of their distant ruler at Tintagel. The decay of sites such as South Cadbury could, therefore, be the result of a loss of wealth and authority. However, there is no reason to see the people of Wiltshire as expansionary, since there is little evidence that they had yet developed a large military aristocracy which lived by plunder. The military stance of post-Roman society in Somerset was accordingly reactive and defensive when viewed in the context of the Anglo-Saxon *adventus*. They were well organised enough to control the labour resources and the materials necessary to re-fortify hill-forts and to begin to build linear earthworks. This is not surprising, given that some of the elite must have emerged from among local officials of the late Roman local government system. Gildas suggests that the post-Romans were also able to combine on a large enough scale to inflict a crushing defeat on the Anglo-Saxons, perhaps enough to destroy their leadership locally and cause them to withdraw to consolidate their gains in the east, or to fight among themselves. The rulers of Somerset were perhaps able to scale back their military activities and devote their resources elsewhere. Like their contemporaries further east, they were primarily part of a peasant farmer based society, with little incentive for military activity. It was not until the incorporation of Wiltshire into the emergent kingdom of Wessex that Somerset faced a renewed military threat and this must be due to the appearance of leaders who built kingdoms by military expansion and the cultivation of war-bands from whom came the warrior aristocracy of Wessex. They were aided in their expansion into Somerset by the contraction of Old Welsh society with the loss of connection with the now collapsed Tintagel, which might at an earlier date have supplied military aid. The Anglo-Saxons moved into the area of least resistance.

Prior to this development there are signs that Anglo-Saxon influence and perhaps even settlement had already begun to appear in the areas close to the borders with Wiltshire. The major evidence comes from the extensive cemetery at Camerton which was excavated between 1926 and 1932 by the Very Reverend Prior Ethelbert Horne (Horne 1929; 1934). The cemetery was discovered through quarrying and an unknown number of burials were destroyed before

investigation. One hundred and nine graves in all were excavated, yielding evidence of 114 individuals. The excavator considered this to be an Anglo-Saxon cemetery on the basis of the goods found in the graves (Horne 1933, 42–46). All the graves were orientated east-west and so the excavator thought they must be Christian burials. This last point clearly seems sustainable, but the question of whether these were 'Anglo-Saxon' is more difficult to answer.

It would be worthwhile to consider this judgement in the light of more recent work on the subject of burials with grave goods. The work of Heinrich Härke is particularly interesting in this context (Härke 1990). He has constructed a large database of graves of 'Anglo-Saxon' type which cover the period from the mid-fifth century up to the seventh century, drawn from excavations of cemeteries across southern Britain. During this period grave goods were a regular feature of burials and he notes the frequency of various types of weapons in graves. The most commonly found item is the spear, nearly 84% of weapons, followed by the shield, 45% and the sword nearly 11%. The seax, axe and arrow make up the remainder, just under 6.5% (Härke 1990, 26, table 1). In comparison, the cemetery at Camerton produced no swords, shields, seaxes, axes or arrows. There were two spears among 29 male burials (Appendix 1). One 'iron dagger' (Horne 1929, 64, grave 8), may have been a seax. Härke also suggests that in his sample there is a clear anatomical difference between males buried with weapons and those without. This is a systematic height difference of 2 to 5 cm and he suggests that the taller males with weapon burials represent a socially superior group who were heads of households and were of Germanic stock (Härke 1990, 40), while the shorter group represent the native Celtic stock, who were present in a subordinate position in the household, a position marked by the absence of weapons in their graves. This is a very clear and attractive proposition, which would place roughly half the males in his sample within the Germanic and thus colloquially 'Anglo-Saxon' stock.

At Camerton there can be little doubt that the assemblages found in the graves are very similar to many found in 'Anglo-Saxon' burials. This is particularly true for female burials. There are four female burials from a total of 13 with beads and similar female attributes. The number of children with beads is slightly greater, five out of a total of 34 children. There were seven children with knives, suggesting they were little boys. Adult males with knives totalled about 8% of the 114 bodies recognised and males without knives 9.8%. (Appendix 1) Accompanied and unaccompanied burials were therefore split almost evenly. However there is no statistically valid distinction in average heights between those with knives and those without (Appendix 2). The inhabitants of these graves could not be distinguished ethnically by their height. Camerton contrasts quite sharply with the cemetery at Cannington (Rahtz *et al.* 2000). Although there are burials with knives and some beads (Rahtz *et al.* 2000, 311–2, 324–39) they are nothing like as plentiful as at Camerton. This is especially the case for the beads; at Cannington only seven beads were retrieved, while at Camerton beads were found in ten of the graves. There would seem to be real differences in the way in which disposal of the dead was regarded between the two areas.

There are two possibilities arising from these differences. The first is that the burials at Camerton represent a smaller community than at Cannington. Again, if they were a Christian group it might be that this was a native community which was adopting burial customs more akin to those used by their near neighbours in Wiltshire, but without the weapon burials found further east. It has certainly been seen as a late-to-sub-Roman cemetery and placed in the same group as Cannington, Henley Wood and Exeter (Morris 1983, 25) and definitely regarded as sub-Roman by Philip Rahtz, who places it as one of a group of cemeteries related to a town or villa (Rahtz 1977, 54). Fowler and Rahtz make the point that the finds with the burials suggest the cemetery was in use over a fairly long time span and also suggest it might be the cemetery for the inhabitants of the nearby Camerton post-Roman settlement (Rahtz and Fowler 1972, 200–1).

The alternative explanation is that this was indeed an Anglo-Saxon burial ground, in which case it might date only from the seventh to eighth centuries, since the regular east-west grave orientation would suggest a strong Christian influence. It seems unlikely that the cemetery would have begun in the pagan period, unless the burials destroyed by quarrying were of a much earlier period. Further weight is given to this possibility by the discovery of escutcheons from hanging bowls. It has been suggested that these bowls are mainly from seventh century graves (Geake 1997, 85–6). This would point to a substantial community, if the burials cover a relatively short time-span, and this raises difficult questions about the location of settlement and its relationship to the burial site. On balance it seems most likely that this was the cemetery of a local 'Old Welsh' population, perhaps from a quite large district, rather than from a small community, who were influenced to some degree by their near neighbours. They were not 'Anglo-Saxons', but we do not know how they described themselves.

The post-Roman period saw the appearance of an aristocracy which based its claim to rule on its ability to preserve the post-Roman society of the region. It did this by re-organising government defensively, setting up strong points in re-used hill-forts, which it was able to re-fortify using local labour. It became a military aristocracy, probably with a king or kings. The continued use of the Roman roads from Bath and down to Dorchester suggest that movement and contact between society in what is now Somerset and Dorset, particularly the Dorchester area, continued throughout the fifth and sixth centuries. This would fit well with Ken Dark's view that there may have been a 'Dubonnic' area which embraced much of eastern Somerset and much of Dorset (Dark 1994, 124–5). In the north the early construction of part of Wansdyke may represent control over passage down the Fosse Way from areas to the north and east, where the English were beginning to become dominant, perhaps in the second half of the fifth century, and the later part of the dyke may have been begun in response to a later emergency, perhaps in concert with the inhabitants of southern Wiltshire. Despite the size and power of the fort at South Cadbury it is likely that political power in Somerset lay nearer to the coast and that Cadbury-Congresbury was the most important local site. The aristocracy bolstered their claim to rule through their contacts with the Empire, mediated through the major centre at Tintagel, for a while enjoying relations with the Eastern Empire and distributing to favoured followers products of Mediterranean civilisation, otherwise long unobtainable. In the later sixth century and in the early seventh century the claim to military competence was never seriously put to the test, since their neighbours in west and south-west Wiltshire were relatively under-organised. However, the rise of an Anglo-Saxon polity based upon predatory warfare and led by warrior princes and their land-hungry kinsmen sealed the fate of this post-Roman society.

The Anglo-Saxons

English literacy began with the coming of the missionaries, but no-one documented the history of the English in the early seventh century and by the time Bede began to write in the early eighth century he had little information about Wessex. The Anglo-Saxon Chronicle is a ninth century document, and as Barbara Yorke has observed, tells us 'how some of the West Saxons of the ninth century saw, or wished to see, the origins of their kingdom' (Yorke 1989, 84). Patrick Sims-Williams in writing about Bede and the Anglo-Saxon Chronicle shows that the early material is very unreliable so that the Anglo-Saxon Chronicle's account of the taking of Somerset by the West Saxons should be treated with some care (Sims-Williams 1983, 33–5). It has recently been suggested, on etymological grounds, that the Anglo-Saxons fought a battle against the Welsh at Brean Down in 614 (Breeze 2004, 234). 'In this year Cynegils and Cwichelm fought at Beandun and slew two thousand and sixty-five Welsh' (ASC, 'A', 614). The number slain seems highly improbable. From what we know of early medieval armies a force of 2000 would have been extremely large and that many dead extraordinary. Armies were probably numbered in a few hundreds rather than thousands. A battle at such a site might be possible as the result of a raid into Welsh territory in search of plunder, but not strategically important, and in any case the internal politics of the West Saxons at this time were confused and inward looking, so that systematic aggression is unlikely. The greatest danger to the men of Wessex came from the north and the Anglo-Saxon Chronicle for 628 says that Cynegils and Cwichelm (his son) fought against Penda at Cirencester and 'they came to an agreement', strongly suggesting that Cynegils was defeated and submitted to Penda (ASC, 'A' 628). There were probably many

raids into Somerset by war-bands seeking plunder, but no real attempt at conquest. The revisionist view of the nature of Wansdyke may be relevant here. Although it would be hard to ascribe it to the earlier part of the seventh century, since the Anglo-Saxons do not seem to have controlled the region before the mid-century, it might be part of a later political boundary. In Somerset the clinching topographical arguments in favour of a seventh century, rather than a fifth/sixth century date, lie in the fact that the later Anglo-Saxon estates and the post-Conquest parishes of northern Somerset do not use it as a boundary. The estates around Stantonbury hill-fort – Corston, Priston, Marksbury – have boundaries which were probably set by the tenth century and are probably much older and which mention the dyke, but which do not use it as parts of their boundary. It certainly looks as if the dyke was built across already demarcated estates, with no regard to their existence (Costen 1983, 25–35). The place-name 'Marksbury' itself, meaning 'the boundary fort', suggests that the purpose of the dyke was well understood by local inhabitants. Such a construction need not be older than the mid-seventh century and would represent the response to an emergency. Once the Mercian kings had come to dominate in the second quarter of the eighth century it would have become obsolete in any case. The alternative, of course is that the dyke is in fact sixth century and crosses estates already laid out by that time.

But we have to ask, who were the West Saxons the men of Somerset were being forced to join? Writing in 2000, John Moreland argued strongly for an approach to the problem of the appearance of Englishness which takes into account new views about the nature of the barbarian-Roman interaction as it has been explored on the continent of western Europe and which sees the English take-over of British society as based largely upon a revised understanding of ethnicity among the native population. An 'Anglo-Saxon' society is seen as emerging from the redistribution of power and the reconstruction of local societies in the sixth century. Medieval peoples expressed their sense of community through a belief in a common ancestry, 'blood communities', but in reality they came to believe in this common ancestry because they acted together. They were a political and perhaps a linguistic group. While this revisionist view of Englishness is attractive and a welcome antidote to the view of English identity as something brought into Britain by cohesive groups of warrior-settlers, and also provides for simpler and clearer ways of understanding the material evidence of graves in the fifth and sixth centuries, it does seem almost to avoid acknowledging that there were actually incomers from continental Europe in the fifth century and that they settled here permanently (Moreland 2000, 23–51). The evidence of the spread both of new ways of burying the dead, which pointedly ignored the growing traditions of Christian belief exemplified in plain east-west burial, and the growth of Old English as the dominant language indicate the development of a powerful new culture which did not have all its roots in Celtic-Roman tradition.[1]

The debate about the numbers of incomers, who, whatever their backgrounds, do seem to have shared the Old English language, has proved inconclusive as yet. A persuasive group has suggested that the total number of incomers was quite small, with Higham (1992) estimating as few as 25,000. This would indeed have been a small elite, but Härke has suggested a figure of 100,000 to 200,000, which given the likely fall in the indigenous population after c. 450 would represent a very large group of incomers (Härke 2002, 150). A recent study of 'Y' chromosome samples taken across England, North Wales, Norway and Friesland suggests a very large mass migration of males from Friesland, affecting the Midlands and East Anglia (Weale *et al.* 2002). If the interpretation of the data is correct this would have been an event which overwhelmed the native population of the Midlands. However more recent studies have begun to undermine this conclusion. A study by C. Capelli *et al.* (2003), has shown that continental genetic input from Denmark/Schleswig-Holstein into the population of Great Britain was strongest in the central Midlands, but that even here there was a continuing indigenous component. The level of continental introgression was lower in southern England which they describe as having a 'limited continental input' and that the genetic make-up of the population 'appears to be predominantly indigenous' (Capelli *et al.* 2003, 982). A further study has suggested that the Anglo-Saxon incomers

achieved dominance by early reproductive isolation and by differential social status. Thus the incomers would tend to marry within their groups and to exploit their relative economic and social advantage to achieve a higher reproductive success rate than their native contemporaries (Thomas, Stumpf and Härke 2006, 2651). This is certainly consistent with the current view that medieval families were usually structured so that the elite males fathered the most children while low status men had fewer children. Breeding success was not spread evenly throughout the population. In a world where the political and cultural leaders were incomers we might expect them to dominate the early breeding patterns in the fifth and sixth centuries, until cultural differences were eliminated. Taken together this suggests that the Anglo-Saxons of Wiltshire, and indeed further east in Wessex, were predominantly Old Welsh genetically, with a strong admixture of continental genes, and that they had been absorbed into the new dominant culture.

The Anglo-Saxon Chronicle is a major source for the political events of the period, and this remains true until the Norman Conquest. The chronicle was composed towards the end of the ninth century and was part of the programme by which the kings of Wessex, starting with Alfred, set out to strengthen their monarchy in Wessex and expand it throughout the rest of Britain. The early part of the Chronicle, therefore, was not a contemporaneous record of events but a reconstruction, based on early annals and calendars (Swanton 2000, xviii–xix). As with any work of history its compilers had an agenda, in this case clearly linked closely to the fortunes of the West Saxon kings and their aristocracy. It may be therefore that the narrative of events, as related in the Chronicle especially for the seventh and eighth centuries, has more coherence than the material passed down to the chroniclers. Recent judgements on the *Annales Regum Francorum* suggest that the construction of such records was an activity of the highest sophistication and should be judged accordingly (McKitterick 1997, 116). All historians try to bring order and coherence to their material and thereby 'interpret' the past. The writers of the Anglo-Saxon Chronicle were no different as they tried to explain the present by recourse to the past of their people.

By the time the 'Anglo-Saxons' entered Somerset in the mid-seventh century it is almost certainly the case that they had been brought together to form the kingdom of Wessex only very recently. It has been suggested that the origins of the kingdom of Wessex lay in the period 660 to 690, actually after their likely arrival in Somerset. In c. 660 the seat of the bishop of the West Saxons was moved from Dorchester-on-Thames to Winchester, by division of the diocese at the instigation of the West Saxon king Cenwalh (Bede, 114). According to the Anglo-Saxon Chronicle the minster at Winchester had been founded some years earlier in 648 (ASC, 'A' 648). Whether or not this is true, it does suggest that the Winchester area was seen as important in the early history of Wessex and the conquest of the Isle of Wight and the Meon valley in 686 has also been seen as marking an important moment in the early history of the West Saxons (Yorke 1989, 92). Cenwealh and Cædwalla were major leaders, establishing an aggressive personal over-lordship, involved in the politics of the emerging Anglo-Saxon kingdoms and subsuming smaller groups of people into their polity. Despite the baptism of their predecessor Cynegils c. 635 (Bede, 112–3), Cædwalla was not baptised until his pilgrimage to Rome after his abdication in 688 (Bede, 232). The presence of under-kings, perhaps leaders of subsumed groups, is important. When Cenwealh died in 672 his widow, Seaxburh, was reported to have ruled for a year (ASC, 'A', 672). Bede thought that Cenwealh's under-kings had taken over from her at her death and ruled for ten years. In this confused period Æscwine ruled for a period and was then succeeded by Centwine, who may have been able to suppress the under-kings (Yorke 1995, 82).

This is an extremely interesting statement, since it hints at the possible earlier formation of the 'Wessex' area. The 'under-kings' who probably emerged as ealdormen in the later seventh and early eighth centuries may well have been the leaders of much smaller and less hierarchical regions which had been subsumed by the new Wessex, but who were only too ready to try to reassert their power or independence at an opportune moment. These under-kings would fit well with ideas expressed by Alex Woolf about the nature of the formation of early Anglo-Saxon polities, where the purpose of early leaders is to reconcile differences and reduce conflict (Woolf 2000, 91–109). Cædwalla, however, was able to subdue and remove them (Bede, 182). On the other hand Aldhelm who was Centwine's son claimed that he ruled successfully (quoted in Stenton 1947, p. 67 fn. 3). It may be that Centwine succeeded by utilising his under-kings and that Cædwalla simply took advantage of the achievements of his predecessor.

Rule by one man or one family was by no means established, therefore, and the narrative of the Chronicle probably conceals a much more fluid political situation than its writers wished to project. It has been suggested that the very confused dating of the kings of the seventh century points to deep ambivalence on the part of the later chroniclers about the rulers of this period. It is by no means certain that the list of father-son relationships has any connection with the truth, which was probably much messier (Kirby 1991, 50–3). At the time of the attack upon Somerset the rule of one undisputed king was therefore not yet the norm. Cenwealh's assault may well have been intended to enlarge his own power against that of potential rivals and provide those who would follow him with territory, plunder and status. Taking Somerset was therefore part of the process by which the new identity of the Anglo-Saxons of Wessex was created. It was by acknowledging and following this new royal house that the men of Wiltshire and then of Somerset, became Anglo-Saxons. Ine's Laws, promulgated between 688 and 694, contain well-known evidence of the position of the Welsh inside Wessex. In what is essentially a political statement the wergilds of Welshmen of varying statuses were laid down. A Welshman with 5 hides of land had a wergild of 600 shillings and a Welshman with a single hide 120 shillings (Whitelock 1955, 367), but a penally enslaved Welshman could be flogged as the result of an oath taken on behalf of 12 hides of land, while an enslaved Englishman would only be flogged for his crime with an oath taken on behalf of 34 hides of land (Whitelock 1955, 370). The first sign of acculturation into the group must have been the adoption of the English language, which was probably regarded as a sign of 'Anglo-Saxon-ness'. It was probably already widely spoken as the language of the dominant group in Wiltshire well before the kingdom itself emerged and the acceptance of English and of the authority

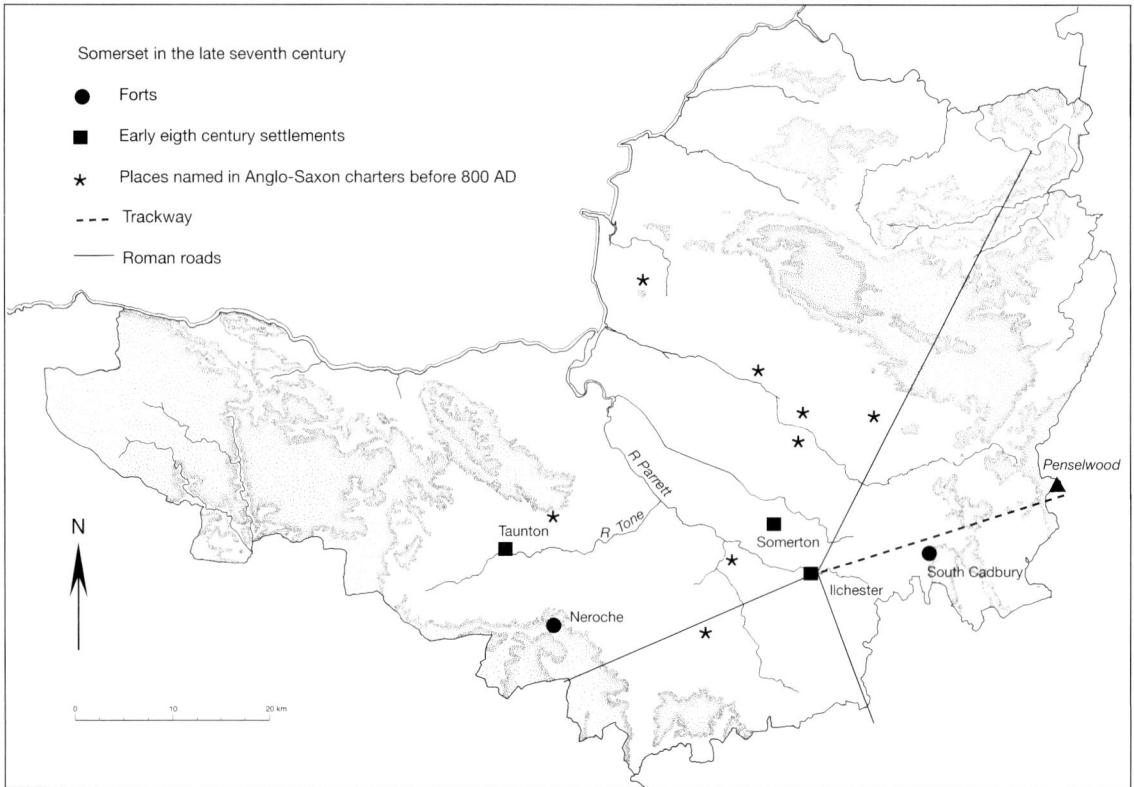

Figure 1.5. Somerset in the late seventh century.

of the new kings must have been made somewhat easier for remaining Welsh speakers as the new kings became Christians, though it is unlikely that all their Anglo-Saxon followers were in the mid-seventh century. The adoption of the new religion by the English accompanied their new status as part of the kingdom of Wessex. It may also be the case that the very aggressive phase through which the Anglo-Saxon societies of the early seventh century passed was itself part of the process of 'Anglo-Saxonisation'. A common response to a call to arms helped to promote a sense of a common identity.

The Winchester Manuscript of the Anglo-Saxon Chronicle for 658, says that 'Here Cenwalh fought at *peonnum* against the Welsh and drove them in flight as far as the Parrett' (ASC, 'A' 658).[2] Almost all commentators have taken this to be a reference to Penselwood, on the border between Somerset and Wiltshire. The Peterborough manuscript of

the Anglo-Saxon Chronicle also has a reference to Penselwood, as *peonnan*, in 1016, and this time referenced as near Gillingham and thus certainly Penselwood. Both references are to an English dative plural form of the Old Welsh word *penn,* 'a hill-top' (Smith 1970, pt. II, 61). It looks very likely, therefore, that Penselwood is meant in both instances. This entry in the Chronicle at least seems to be accurate. A battle close to Penselwood somewhere near the modern main road, would have taken place on the border between Wiltshire and Somerset as they now are, and at a natural point of entry to the county, with the high ground of the Penselwood ridge to the north and lower marshy land further to the south. In the later fifth and early sixth centuries this gap was policed by South Cadbury castle, but by the mid-seventh century the hill-fort had been abandoned and the major objective, the site of Ilchester, with its control of the major roads and the river basin, would have

Figure 1.6. The Queen Camel sword.

been open to attack. Once the roads were gained it would be quite easy to push a defeated army back to the river Parrett, a natural dividing line. In the central south of the shire it is possible that a fortification was built on the ridge in Neroche forest. It has recently been suggested that the earthwork which was utilised by the Normans as the basis for the Castle of Neroche dates from the Anglo-Saxon period (Prior 2006, 105). If so it would have controlled a route which ran from north-west Dorset towards Taunton and from there westward to the sea (Fig. 1.5).

Of course, none of this may have happened. Such a decisive conquest might be wishful thinking written by an Anglo-Saxon historian two centuries later, building bricks without straw, but the only physical evidence, currently known, for the presence of the Anglo-Saxons in seventh century Somerset comes from Queen Camel, 8 km to the east of Ilchester. Here nine burials were discovered in 1931, one of which included a sword of the seventh century. This has been described as a Germanic style sword of a 'household warrior' (J. Naylor, pers. comm.) and might suggest the burial of a man who had been granted an estate in newly captured territory (Fig. 1.6). Fanciful speculation might make the remaining burials those of local peasantry from his newly acquired land.

Both Taunton and Somerton are mentioned in the Anglo-Saxon Chronicle in the early eighth century, Taunton as being destroyed by the queen in 722 after it had been built by Ine (ASC, A, 722). The involvement of these two places in military operations suggest very strongly that they were in some way fortified. By Ine's time it was normal for the residence of a nobleman to be described as a '*burh*', a fortified place, so it is likely that the king's own estate centres were normally fortified in some way. Somerton would clearly replace Ilchester and South Cadbury as a site to

control the Fosse Way and the route from Dorchester to Glastonbury and Wells. Taunton guards the crossing of the Tone and gives access to the valley along the southern side of the Quantocks, to reach sites along the Somerset coast, particularly Watchet, the likely site of a port or trading place. Two other sites may also be of interest. At Milborne Port there was an earlier site called Kingsbury, alongside which the later town was built, and Kingsbury Episcopi (Lib. Alb. 1065) shows that a king had a *burh* there also at some point. It has been suggested that Kingsbury was originally a part of South Petherton (Aston 2007, 70). If so, then Kingsbury may have been set up as a strong point on the river Parrett, guarding access to South Petherton and thence to the Fosse Way. There are a number of other important early sites which were later strongly associated with the Anglo-Saxon kings, but it is not possible to be certain that they were under direct royal control in the later seventh and early eighth centuries. Cannington, Cheddar, Crewkerne and Carhampton are first mentioned as royal property in King Alfred's Will written between 873 and 888 (S1507) but they may originally have been founded for or as minster centres and only later come under direct royal control. This is also likely to have been true for Bruton, Frome and Williton, each of which was royal property in 1086 (DB), and also for other sites given to the early bishopric at Sherborne, such as Wells and Chew, and later transferred to the new bishop at Wells (Blair 2005, 325–7).

The conquest of Somerset was driven by the king's need to provide his warriors with land as a reward for their services. The warriors were keen to join ventures of plunder and conquest, for it was in this way that they proved themselves as worthy of gifts of land from their lord and thus gained the chance to take a wife and have a family. It is likely that the later sixth and seventh centuries were the very period during which the aristocratic warrior ethic was becoming most firmly established and the rapid expansion of the number of available estates was of particular importance to them. That expansion continued into Devon in the later part of the seventh century, but thereafter the space for expansion of the new kingdom became very limited. At this point the 'frontier' era was over and the kings and their aristocracy settled down to a long period of consolidation, during which Somerset emerged in a recognisable form.

Notes

1. See B. Ward-Perkins, (2000) Why Did the Anglo-Saxons Not Become More British? in *English Historical Review*, 115, No. 462, 513–33)
2. Alex Woolf has an interesting suggestion, that Geraint fil Erbin, king of Dumnonia was killed as a result of this attack at *Llongborth*, Langport on the Parrett. See Woolf 2003, p. 376 fn. 149. The problem of course is the identification of the two names. There is no direct evidence to link the two and the earliest English references to Langport are all tenth century (see Watts *et al.* 2004).

Appendix 1

Grave goods at Camerton

Children with grave goods	12	10.7%
Children without grave goods	22	19.64%
Adult with grave goods	16	14.28%
Adult without grave goods	17	15.1%
Female with grave goods	4	3.57%
Female without grave goods	9	8.03%
Male with grave goods	11	9.82%
Male without grave goods	21	18.75%
Total burials	**112**	
	(excluding foetus)	

Total males	32
Total females	13
Total adults undetermined	33
Total children	34
Total	**112**

Adult + adult males with knives	19
Children with beads	6
Children with knives	6
Adults and female adults with beads	4

Appendix 2

Femur lengths in inches as recorded by Horne 1929 for 29 males with and without grave goods

Femur length in inches	Goods
16.5	none
17.25	none
16.25	none
16.12	none
17.0	goods
16.7	goods
18.5	none
17.0	none
15.7	none
17.1	goods
16.5	none
20.3	none
17.9	none
19.4	goods
18.4	goods
17.5	none
18.8	goods
18.8	none
17.9	none
17.9	none
16.8	none
18.8	none
17.7	none
18.5	goods
18.1	none
19.6	none
18.2	goods
19.0	goods
16.7	goods

Comment

Type	Mean	SD	Num
Without	17.64	1.22	19
With	17.98	1.01	10

Gives us: t = 0.7595, d.f. = 27

From tables:

$t(P=0.25, d.f.=27) = 0.683685$
$t(P=0.10, d.f.=27) = 1.313703$

This means that if the total populations of men buried with and without weapons are the same, we can expect a difference, of this size and number of individuals, somewhere between one fourth and one tenth of the occasions when we sample them. The standard limit for accepting something as significant is one twentieth. Thus it appears that there is no difference between the samples.

(I am grateful to Dr N. P. Costen of the Department of Mathematics and Computing, Manchester Metropolitan University, for this comment.)

Settlement and Soldiers

The charters written by the early kings of Wessex may offer the best direct evidence we have for Anglo-Saxon dominance of the area in the later seventh century. However, the problems of authenticity presented by the Anglo-Saxon charters, especially those of an early date, are formidable. It is extremely difficult to disentangle muddle from forgery and faulty transmission from deliberate deception. The charter S1249[1] for lands at 'Lantocal' and at 'Ferrameare', possibly Leigh in Street and Meare may represent an early grant by a bishop, Hæddi, to the *monasterium* at Glastonbury. Dr Heather Edwards thought that the charter is probably authentic (Edwards 1988, 19), while Dr Lesley Abrams is more sceptical (Abrams 1996, 153–4). This charter is dated to about 680. The charter S237 which was a grant by King Centwine to Abbot Hæmgils, of land at Creechbarrow, just outside Taunton, and land near the Quantocks, later identified as West Monkton, near Taunton, is dated to 682. Both Edwards and Abrams regard this as a charter with much genuine material in it. The charter for lands at Brent, S238, is dated to 688–726 and claims to be a confirmation by King Ine of an earlier grant by Baldred. Baldred was the grantor of the charter S236 of c. 680 and so his original grant may have been made at about the same time. The grants all concern Glastonbury Abbey, but Muchelney Abbey was also receiving lands at much the same time. A grant of 693 by King Ine (S240) is probably substantially genuine (Edwards 1988, 198–201). This was for land somewhere in south-eastern Somerset, near the Fosse Way. The Anglo-Saxon kings certainly controlled central and south-eastern Somerset and the Creechbarrow charter shows that they had reached the Taunton area, on the western side of the Tone, by the early 680s. From that position there was little to stop an advance along the valley to the south of the Quantocks until they reached the Bristol Channel and mastered the coastal strip.

In central Somerset control of the Ilchester area gave ready access to the Fosse Way which would have carried the Anglo-Saxons up on to Mendip. From there the northern coastal region and the Chew Valley would have been accessible by moving westward, along the top of the hills. Charters are much less helpful here. A lost charter by Ine to Abbot Berwald was for land '*ad pedem de Munedup*'. Although the charter was likely to have been genuine (Edwards 1988, 68) its position is completely unidentifiable (Abrams 1996, 172–3), but it demonstrates that political control over the Mendips had been secured by the end of the seventh century.

Taken together these charters strongly suggest that political control of central Somerset had been achieved by the early 680s and that the kings of Wessex were reinforcing their authority by making grants to new-founded or re-founded monasteries. This control should not be seen as simply an exercise in administration of newly conquered peoples. By an alliance with the church the king must have hoped to consolidate his personal power in the kingdom as well as the shire. Centwine, who granted land near Creechbarrow, may have been an under-king (Kirby 1991, 53) and Ine was far from well established in 688–9, probably being still associated with his father (Kirby 1991, 122). Ine, however, was able to control his expanding kingdom more successfully than any of his predecessors, extending his influence across Sussex and Surrey and pursuing war against the Welsh into Devon, so that by 710 he had pushed King Geraint of Dumnonia back to the Tamar (ASC, 'A' 710).

Ine's laws make clear that the relationship between his new Welsh subjects and his English followers was something which needed regulating. The sheer number of them, and the continuance of their 'welshness' is evident from the systematic way in which their wergilds are laid down. Their status was recognised, but was one of a subject population, normally ranked as worth half the wergild of their new English neighbours (Whitelock 1955, 364–72). The laws as they have survived are not a single codified exposition of a static position, but rather the accretion of years of judgements (Wormald 1999, 103–6). As such they are a political statement about the amalgamation of the two groups into the new Wessex.

Ine's period of undisputed rule was probably quite short, however, since in 721 he killed the *aetheling* Cynewulf, suggesting dissension inside the ruling family, and the Anglo-Saxon Chronicle records a pattern of external warfare and internal division. For most of the seventh and eighth centuries the Mercians were the dominant force among the Anglo-Saxons and when the kings of Wessex fought outside Wessex it was usually against the Mercians, but they also fought the English of Sussex and of Kent. In 725 Ine killed Ealdberht, who was in exile among the South Saxons. He had been implicated in the 721–2 episode and had fled into exile in 722 (ASC, 'A' 721–5). The existence of other nearby small kingdoms made it easy for failed revolutionaries to go into exile while waiting for more favourable circumstances and helped to promote further cause for war.

This pattern continued for much of the eighth century and father to son succession never occurred until 839. Kingship could not in any real sense be regarded as hereditary. The centres of authority in Wessex were therefore situated much further east in Wessex, in eastern Wiltshire and in Hampshire. Winchester was the seat of the eastern bishop and the trading centre at 'Hamwih' was close by. In 757 Cynewulf seized power and used the ealdormen and probably other members of the aristocracy to depose King Sigeberht (ASC, 'A', 757). Sigeberht

was 'allowed' to retain Hampshire as a sub-kingdom, but lost that too when he murdered an ealdorman who still followed him. It is probable that Sigeberht managed to retain control of Winchester and Hamwih and that at first Cynewulf was simply not powerful enough to seize Hampshire. Cynewulf was himself killed by Sigeberht's brother, Cyneheard, some twenty-nine years later (ASC 'A', 757). Other entries in the Anglo-Saxon Chronicle show the eighth century kings fighting the Mercians and also the Welsh, presumably on the frontier on the far west. By the late eighth century there is no doubt that the kings of Wessex were subject to Offa, the Mercian king. Beorhtric was probably not related to his predecessor and Ecgberht, the grandfather of King Alfred, spent some time in exile at the Frankish court. In 789 Beorhtric of Wessex married Offa's daughter and it was not until the Battle of Ellendun (AD 825) at which the West Saxons defeated the Mercians that Ecgberht achieved a dominant position among the English (Story 2003, 216–7). The division of the now much expanded diocese of the West Saxons, with its base at Winchester, into two territorial dioceses, one with its seat at Sherborne, marks the start of a new period in the history of the region.

Early administration probably rested on the under-kings who had more or less complete control over the land. Cuthred, the relative of King Cenwealh, who was granted 3000 hides at Ashdown in 648 (ASC 'A', 648), seems to have been just such a ruler and the Baldred who is styled '*Baldredus rex*' in S236 of c. 681 may well have been a similar local under-king in Somerset. The same man seems to have sold an estate in Wiltshire to abbot Aldhelm between c. 676 and c. 686 (S1170). He may have exercised authority in Wiltshire as well as Somerset. By the eighth century under-kings had been replaced by ealdormen, and we know the king had a group of councillors (ASC, 'A' 757). Cynewulf in 774 referred to the '*patriciis et principibus,*', 'important and chief men' who consented to a grant he made to Sherborne and the bishop there, and the charter signatories appear elsewhere as his '*praefecti*', the ealdormen, as witnesses of a charter (S263 and O'Donovan 1988, 4–5), showing that a group of great noblemen who were also royal office holders had been created and the early shires of Wessex had probably been defined as the territories for which these men were responsible. Somerset would therefore have been recognisable as a shire from the mid-eighth century at the latest.

A boundary between Somerset and Dorset existed from an early date, since there are two settlements with names which relate to boundaries. Rimpton, to the east of Yeovil is in Somerset. The name, *rima tun,* is the 'boundary tun'. It is not on the historic boundary with Dorset, but has the parish of Trent between it and the ancient bound. It may not refer to the boundary of the shire, but perhaps to the boundary of an extended territory around Cadbury. However, on the southern side of the river Yeo and south of Yeovil, the settlement of Ryme, in Dorset, again OE *rima*, a 'boundary or edge', lies on the county boundary with Somerset, here marked by a stream. Such impersonal topographical names are usually regarded as early, which in the case of Anglo-Saxon names in the south-west cannot be before c. 650, but are likely to have been formed by the earlier eighth century (Gelling 1978, 126). It may be that the boundary was defined soon after the English coup and was negotiated to define the territories of the *reguli* or ealdormen of the two shires. To the north, as we have seen, the boundary was defined by the territory of the Hwicce and this boundary was perpetuated when the Hwicce were absorbed into Mercia.

The king's direct interest in the Somerset landscape need not have been great in the early years of rule. Those places which can be most directly tied to the king are in central Somerset. There was nowhere west of Taunton, or north of the Mendips, where the king held a power centre, suggesting that he relied heavily on the churches in existence or being founded at important sites in the west and the north to maintain his influence. We probably misunderstand the nature of the king's approach to property to see these *vills* in terms of either royal or church lands. The early kings may have regarded church settlements as their own, staying at them and depleting their resources as needed by their followers, as well as using their dependants as needed. It suited the king to maintain the dominance of the Church as the occupier of lands if he was rarely in the area. The ealdormen would probably have been able to use the resources of royal property in order to carry out their duties and there was always a danger that the king's property would be subsumed within the lands of the ealdorman, which he probably held as a support for his position, as he strove to build a patrimony of his own. It would have been much harder for the ealdorman to appropriate church property, especially the lands immediately around the minster itself.

The ealdorman's task was to administer the courts of the shire and collect the tribute owed to the king from his estates, but his most important duty was to raise and control the soldiers needed by the king in his incessant wars. Unfortunately we have little firm idea of the size of the army which could be raised from the shire or of that commanded by these early Wessex kings. Historians of an earlier age were convinced that early Anglo-Saxon society was one of free Anglo-Saxon peasants who were also warriors, fighting for their chiefs as needed. It is a thesis of this book that Anglo-Saxon society was founded upon inequality and that 'freedom' was a rare commodity and an anachronistic idea in the world of the warrior. Writing about the seventh century ceorl, Professor Abels suggests, very reasonably, that the ceorl who followed the king into battle followed because he was commended directly to the king himself, the corollary being that other ceorls, not commended to the king, might not have to follow him. Commendation did not of course mean unfreedom. This conclusion is the result of a careful dissection of the nature of military obligation in middle Anglo-Saxon England. The king might expect to be followed into battle by his own military household and by members of his nobility, surrounded in turn by their followers. That nobility, at least in the seventh century, might not all automatically follow the king, since not all might necessarily be commended to him (Abels 1988, 22). We need to be careful not to give the impression that there exists a consensus on the question of the composition of armies of this period, or indeed that the reality was as neat and tidy as suggested above. Timothy Reuter has pointed out that there are still conflicting views about the nature of military service in this period and that they differ wildly (Reuter 1997, 32–7). However the picture drawn is one where although the king might command the loyalty of most men in his kingdom there might be some – powerful men – who had never personally submitted to the king and who might be lord over, as it were, islands

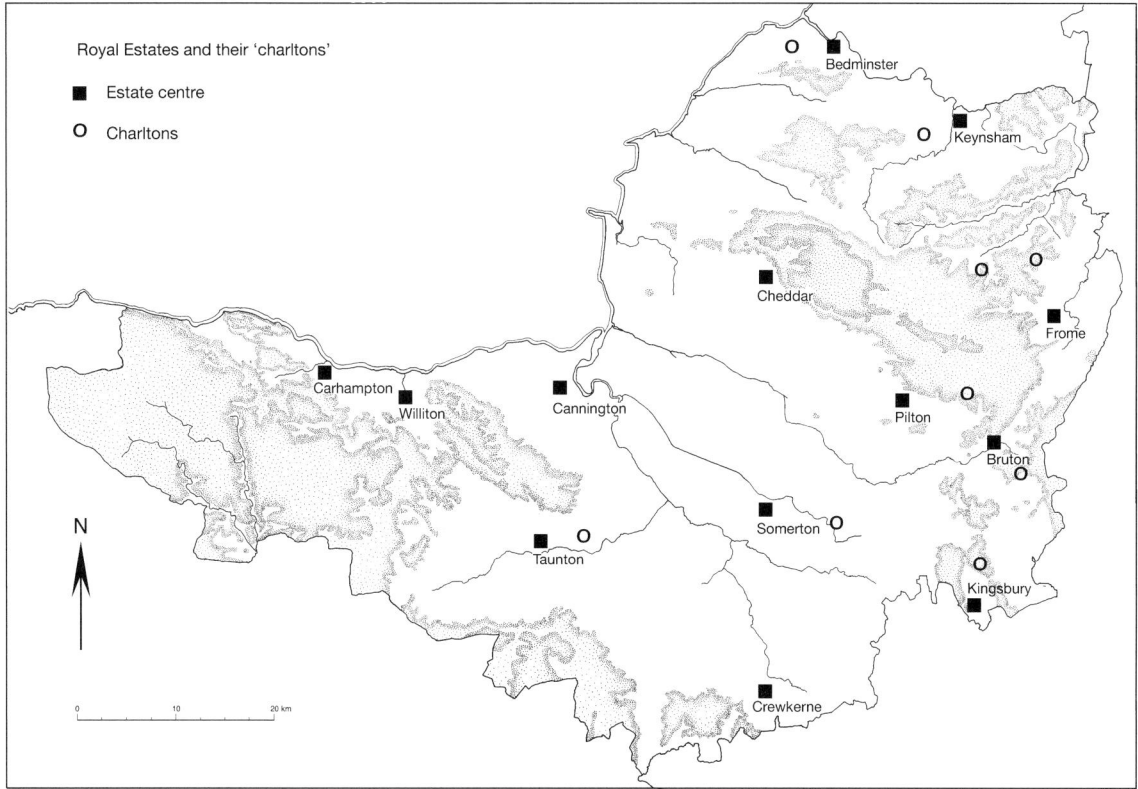

Figure 2.1. Royal estates and their associated 'charltons'.

within the kingdom where the king's authority could be much less than complete. The power of the king would be reflected by the ability to reduce such islands to an absolute minimum and thus command the biggest possible army.

In Somerset the king could command peasant soldiers or supporters from a number of settlements. The place-name 'Charlton' means the *tun* of the *ceorls*' (Ekwall 1960). The ceorl was simply a peasant farmer and writing as long ago as 1964 Professor Finberg pointed out that by the time of King Alfred they were not to be regarded as 'free', that is able to leave and go where they would, although they were certainly not slaves (Finberg 1964, 146–7). The loss of 'freedom' by ceorls was probably connected to the social changes which accompanied the rise of the warrior aristocracy. Control of the peasants was a natural part of the change since the warriors depended upon them for

their material support. For the ceorl the compensation for the loss of status was probably his control of the land he farmed. Warrior lords might come and go, but the ceorl and his family remained on the land. The best explanation of these place-names is that they were settlements of free peasant farmers who were directly responsible to the royal central place for the payment of tribute and who were the king's direct dependants and therefore his followers. There are nine 'Charltons' in Somerset, most of which were clearly dependent upon a nearby royal centre (Fig. 2.1).

The position taken by Professor Abels is that the warrior aristocracy of Anglo-Saxon England, at least in the sixth and seventh centuries, had no permanent family land holdings of their own. They did not have the luxury of permanent customary tenure available to the ceorl. Instead, as young men they needed to establish their right to a grant of land from the king by their military service (Abels 1988, 29–34). As members of the aristocracy they had no alloidal land, but depended upon the king's favour for their support. As a result they could not marry and produce legitimate heirs until they had proved themselves as loyal followers and as warriors. The idea of land or rights over land as a gift for service was long-lived. The poem *Deor,* perhaps from the late ninth century, certainly conveys that feeling, perhaps with some deliberate archaism.

> For a while I was Heoding's bard, a dear lord. My name was Deor. I had a worthwhile office for many years, a loyal lord, till now Heorrenda, a song-skilled man, has the land-right which the noble protector previously gave me (Muir 1994, 284–5).[2]

Hornblotton, 'the hornblower's tun', looks as if it was just such a grant for a service and we might envisage a patchwork of lands, some held by right and others held from the king as loan-land which is likely to have been especially common in Somerset since it was conquered territory.

However, others consider that prior to the conversion, noble families did have lands which could be passed on to heirs (Reynolds 1992, 215). A nobility with no permanent land would seem unlikely. Ine's Laws state that a *gesith-born* man (that is nobly born) who owns land will pay a fine of 120 shillings and forfeit his land if he neglects military service (Whitelock 1955, 370). Clearly Ine expected noble men to have land of their own. Bede makes it clear that this was indeed the case in northern society, about which he knew most, and it seems unlikely that the society of Wessex differed radically in this matter. However it may be that conquests made it possible for the king to expand the area of loan-land under his control, increasing his hold over younger members of the nobility. One consequence of this was the need for the king to provide plenty of opportunity for war and this need drove much of the aggressive politics of the seventh and eighth centuries. The other side of the coin was that if young men remained in the king's war-band until they received a grant of land, they might be quite mature before that happened, especially if there was little in the way of warfare. The warrior class might expand only slowly as their reproductive success was checked by lack of opportunity and the numbers of men available to the king may therefore

have been limited, unless the king could expand the land available for distribution. Expansion of the noble class therefore would go hand in hand with the king's success in conquering new territory, much of which he could retain to distribute as loan-land, especially around the edges of the large new estates he had acquired.

It is normally not possible to determine where such loan-land might be, but Faulkland in Hemington parish (Fig. 2.2) may be an example of just such an estate. The name is *folc land*, that is 'folk land' (Ekwall 1960). The consensus of an earlier age would have seen this name as proof of the existence of a primitive 'free' peasantry, for in all probability this is a very early English name in Somerset and it has been pointed out that by the ninth century folk land was rapidly disappearing (John 1966, 74). It was seen by Professor Stenton as land which paid tribute to the king, in contrast to land held by warriors (Stenton 1947, 306–8). Actual references to 'folk land' in documents are very few and far between (Reynolds 1992, 215) and the Somerset place-name is unique (Watts 2004). It now seems likely that the 'folk' were not a free peasantry, but instead were the noble warriors, who may well have regarded themselves as the only 'true' folk, the real Anglo-Saxons. Such a stance would be quite natural if they saw themselves as the product of a couple of centuries of carefully nurtured ethnic exclusivity, even if genetically that were not true. So Faulkland stands in contrast to its near neighbour Buckland (OE *boc land,* land held by charter), although it is not necessarily the case that the two names are contemporary. Faulkland was probably loan-land, granted to a warrior in reward for his service, and was part of the great estate centred at Frome (Abels 1988, 214, n. 67).

The political story of Somerset between the time of Ine and the fall of Harold is one of gradual expansion of the class of aristocratic warrior land-owners. Increasing military demands in the ninth and tenth centuries, caused by the attacks of the Northmen, impelled the kings to increase their political and social control over society in order to extract from it greater and greater resources, chiefly at first as soldiers, but also in other material resources, weapons, horses, ships. The aristocracy for their part exacted a price for this. The king could only expand his warrior corps

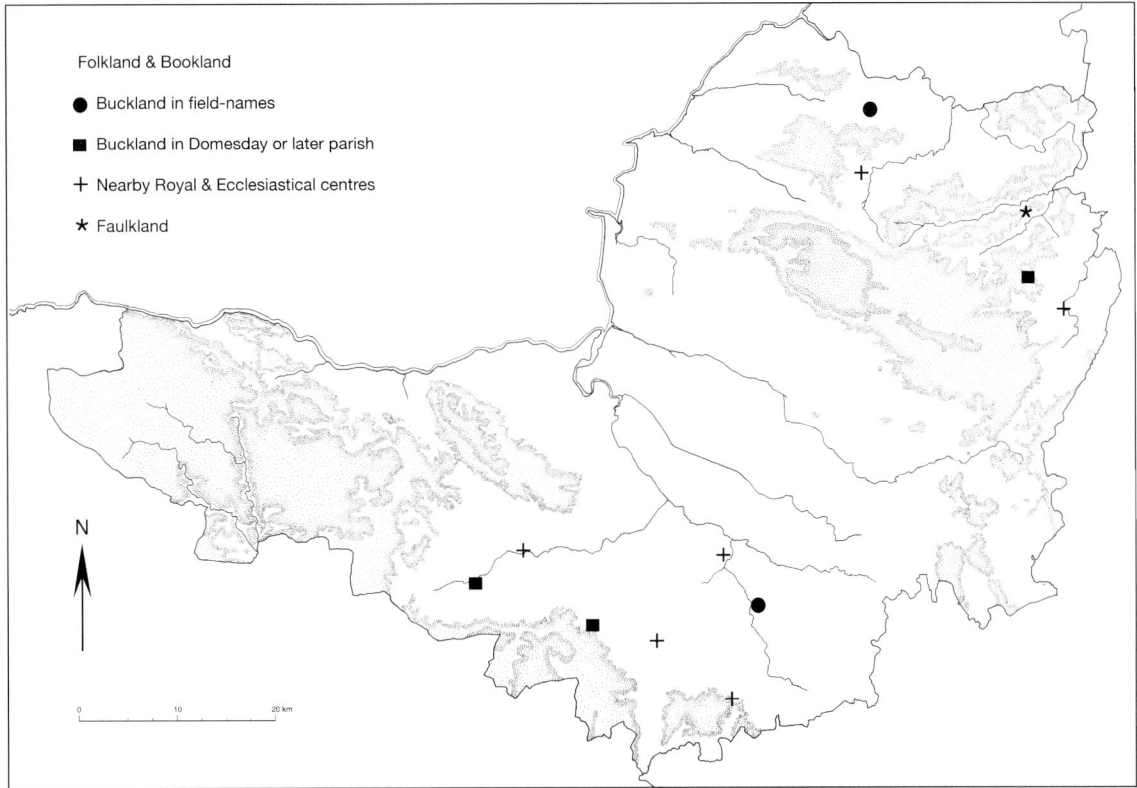

Figure 2.2. 'Folkland' and 'bookland'.

by alienating land. As we have seen, at first loan-land meant alienating the land only on a temporary basis, but in the eighth and ninth centuries this land had to be granted on a more permanent basis and bookland became established, enabling the aristocracy to break the close link between warfare and land, although this did not mean that they ceased to be warriors. Bookland was land held by a written charter or '*boc*'. The most important feature of bookland seems to have been the right of alienation of the property, although clearly the right to leave the land to heirs was also immensely important (Reynolds 1992, 216). In a famous passage Bede complained about the practice in Northumbria whereby noble families purchased land by charter from kings which was ostensibly intended for the foundation of a monastery. In fact the property was then used for secular purposes, allowing its owners to establish hereditary rights over

it by reason of the *in perpetuum* nature of the grant (Bede, 170). Bede was writing in 734, but recognition of the practice of emancipating property by grant of a charter does not seem to have become accepted until later in the century. The first known example is a grant by Offa of Mercia to a follower of land at Salmondsbury in 779 (S114). In Somerset the earliest example is of land 'on the north bank of the river Parrett'. King Beorhtric granted ten '*cassati*' of land to Wigferth, his '*prefectus*' in 794 (S267). Wigferth, who was almost certainly an ealdorman, was given the right to give the land as he chose or to leave it to any heir he liked. The charter has survived because the land eventually came to the Abbey of Athelney, and with it came its charter.

This grant to Wigferth was an early example of 'bookland' in Somerset. Tenure by 'book' was to become the normal way for members of the Old

English warrior class to hold their land and possession of bookland became a sign of aristocratic rank. By the time of the Norman Conquest this had become a type of alloidal tenure which gave its owner almost complete freedom of disposition of his property. In Somerset there are at least three certain examples of 'Buckland' place-names, the form the word '*bocland*' normally takes in modern place-names: Buckland Dinham, West Buckland and Buckland St Mary. There is also an example of a field-name 'buckland' in Martock (t. 1639) which may be a reference to a lost site and another in Stanton Drew. There is a charter for Buckland (S555), in which King Eadred granted Buckland Dinham to his kinsman, the Ealdorman Ælfhere. In 1066 the estate belonged to Dunn (DB 47, 19) and paid tax for 12 hides, although the tenth century grant had been for an estate of 20 hides. It seems that the estate never belonged to Glastonbury Abbey, despite appearing in its chartulary (Watkin 1956, 610). The chartulary mistakenly groups the charter with other documents relating to Buckland Newton in Dorset, suggesting that Glastonbury Abbey had merely acted as a repository for the document. West Buckland formed a part of the group of estates exchanged by King Edward the Elder with Asser the bishop of Sherborne between 899 and 909 (S380). It was a 5 hide estate and was included inside Wellington in 1066. Buckland St Mary first appears in the Domesday Book as two small estates amounting to 2½ hides together. The three estates are therefore quite various in size, suggesting that there was no particular policy in the disposal of land by the king. Buckland Dinham may be connected with an early royal centre at Frome and West Buckland with the royal centre at Taunton (ASC 'A', 722). All three estates may well be early examples of the use of the name. As bookland became common the name would no longer be applied. It has also been suggested that the use of the name may indicate an estate which had been especially created, perhaps by being carved out from a larger unit (Rumble 1987, 221).

During the later eighth century and the ninth century bookland was to become a normal part of the policy of kings, available to grant to members of the aristocracy either to secure their loyalty or for cash. In 801 Egbert made a grant of the estate of Butleigh to his thegn Eadgils. The grant allowed Eadgils to leave the land to whom he pleased, but imposed the duties of following the king in war, working on fortifications and bridge-works, the three common burdens applied to all bookland granted to laymen (S270a). According to the *De Antiquitate* Eadgils subsequently gave the land to Glastonbury Abbey, the reason the contents of the charter have survived (Scott 1981, 110, 142). Eadgils probably made the grant on his death-bed but had enjoyed the income from the property during his life-time.

The problem of the Danes

In the first half of the eighth century warfare between the kings of Wessex and their neighbours continued but the need to encourage and placate the aristocracy was undoubtedly also driven by the ongoing attacks of the Northmen. Sporadic attacks had occurred on the north-east coast of England in the late eighth century. Alcuin wrote to King Ethelred of Northumbria in 793:

> We and our fathers have now lived in this fair land for nearly three-hundred and fifty years, and never before has such an atrocity been seen in Britain as we have now suffered at the hands of the pagan people. Such a voyage was not thought possible. The church of St Cuthbert is spattered with the blood of the priests of God, stripped of all its furnishings, exposed to the plundering of pagans – a place more sacred than any in Britain (Allott 1974, 18).

Attacks by people from the Scandinavian region occurred throughout all of western Europe in the ninth century. The first recorded attack upon Frankia took place in 799. Thereafter the attacks were increasingly frequent, until as in England, in the middle of the century, the raiders ceased returning home each winter, preferring to make a fortified camp in the area they had chosen to pillage (Graham-Campbell 1994, 143). The Anglo-Saxon Chronicle records that for the first time three ships arrived from Hordaland (in Norway) and that the crews of the ships killed the king's reeve who had ordered them to go to the king's *burh* (ASC 'A', 789 and 'E' 789). Æthelweard's Chronicle adds the additional information that the Northmen landed at Portland, that the king's *burh* was Dorchester and that the reeve assumed they were merchants (Campbell

1962, 26–7). Alcuin was astonished that a seaborne attack had occurred; the reeve was not surprised by the arrival of 'merchants' by sea.

There is ample evidence to show that sailing ships from the continent, Anglo-Saxon, Frankish, Frisian and Danish were commonplace around the shores of Britain in the seventh and eighth centuries (Haywood 1999, 93–110). The arrival of seaborne merchants would not, therefore be so surprising. The shock was that now these were raiders and over the course of the ninth century the danger they presented became considerable as the size of the raiding forces increased and the scope of their attacks widened. Richard Hodges has warned about the danger of seeing the Vikings as *dei ex machina* of change in the ninth century (Hodges 2006, 157–62). Instead it may be that the decline in effectiveness of the Carolingian monarchy, as Louis the Pious and his sons quarrelled, took the cork out of the bottle and allowed the Vikings to expand into Christian Europe. It may also be that a group which had been prospering as intermediaries on trading routes between the East and the Carolingian West was affected by the fall off of that trade and turned to aggression as a means of replacing its lost wealth.

Other historians have more recently re-evaluated the role played by the 'Northmen' – mostly Danes, in Western Europe in the ninth century. The picture which emerges is much more nuanced than has previously been usual (Nelson 2003). The depiction of the attacks was in part intended to help reinforce a sense of unity among the aristocracy of Wessex in a time of immense change, but there can be little doubt that they were real enough and did constitute a genuine danger. As the events in East Anglia showed, there were plenty of Danes willing to start a new life as settlers in Britain and their leaders were anxious to establish themselves as leaders in English society.

After the initial shock the first thirty years of the ninth century were quiet enough in Wessex as the Danes turned their attention to Ireland. However, in 836, 35 (or 25) ship-loads of Vikings attacked Carhampton. King Egbert fought the Vikings, but the Chronicle entry shows that the Danes won the battle (ASC 'A', 836). King Æthelwulf similarly fought the Danes at Carhampton in 843 and also lost (ASC 'A', 843). The Chronicle states that there were again 35 ships, which suggests that there was some confusion between the two accounts, but it seems likely that the Danish forces were relatively small on both occasions. Since neither king was killed in the two encounters which they lost we can assume that the forces on both sides were about evenly matched, or that the kings were somewhat outnumbered, but not to such an extent that they were overwhelmed. If the 35 ships were all large warships then a force of over 2000 men could have been carried.

The newly constructed Danish longship, the *Sea Stallion*, launched in 2006, a replica of the '*skuldelev 2*', is a 30 metre vessel (Vinner 2002, 36–7) (Fig. 2.3). This copy of a ship which was built near Dublin c. 1040 represents what must have been the battleship of the day, a craft constructed for rich and powerful men, and would have carried at least 60 men, since she needed that number to row her. She may well have carried over 100, bearing in mind that she would have been fit for a king, or at least a self-confident jarl, and that he and his chief warriors would have been passengers, not oarsmen (Swanton 1999, 12). However, such vessels must have been very expensive to build and to maintain and it seems unlikely that the fleets of adventurers, however aristocratic, could have contained many of these thorough-bred machines. It seems more likely that many of the vessels used must have been smaller and more like the cargo ships of the tenth and eleventh centuries. Of the 20 ships described as dating between 900 and 1100 which have been excavated from the Baltic regions only two, '*skuldelev 2*' mentioned above, and the Hedeby warship were as much as 30 m long, pointing to the relative rarity of such monsters (Crumlin-Pedersen 1997, 184–94). Some were like the '*Helge Ask*' a modern reconstruction of '*skuldelev 5*', a warship of about 17.5 m, capable of carrying a crew of approximately 30 men. Most were between ten and 20 m long and were cargo or merchant ships of some kind. '*Skuldelev 3*', a 14 m cargo carrying vessel would have been typical. Carrying about 5 tons of cargo, she needed a crew of five to eight men and would have needed six men to row her (Fig. 2.4). She may well be representative of northern European shipping at this period (Crumlin-Pedersen 1972). Writing in 1972, Ole Crumlin-Pedersen clearly felt that the Danish fleets of the late tenth century consisted mostly of the large ships mentioned above. In part at least his argument is supported by the evidence of the '*leding*', the Danish national defence system, which was based upon the collective construction and maintenance of ships of this type. On the other hand he also suggests that the 60 footer, with twelve pairs of oars and carrying perhaps 40 men was typical (Crumlin-Pedersen 1972, 182–207). In any case, the fleets provided by the *leding* were a century or more later than the attacks on Britain and it is difficult to argue backwards.

Whatever the size of the ships, such a fleet was an enormous investment. The '*skuldelev 3*' cargo ship replica took 20,000 man hours to build using tenth century techniques and tools (Vinner 2002, 27). In the tenth century this might have represented the labour of 16 or 17 men working 60 hour weeks for 20 weeks. Despite a probably unreconstructed attitude to workers' rights it seems unlikely that even Danish warrior chieftains would have been able to get more than an average of 60 hours work a week from valuable craftsmen, when they were engaged upon long term projects. Furthermore the difficulties of supply, especially of timber which was not plentiful in tenth century Denmark, would have slowed the process as well. It would surely have been impossible to build a complete fleet of 200–250 ships (a typical fleet of the later part of the ninth century), over a single season, since it would have been impossible to assemble a large enough group of shipwrights or to collect the supplies needed in such a short time. Indeed, if the ships lasted about 20 years on average, then a fleet of 200 would lose about ten ships each sailing season, which would need to be replaced each year. This would represent the work of about 160 men every year and most of those men would need to have been ship-wrights. The sails were woven of wool and required an enormous quantity of material and hundreds of hours of labour by skilled women to complete. Such a fleet represented an investment in labour and materials built up over many years and would have needed careful conservation. For the Viking adventurers a very high return on the investment in warfare would have been needed to maintain such a fleet, since the ship-wrights, blacksmiths, timber cutters, the women who made the sails, all needed to be supported. In turn, their demand for food, clothing and perhaps modest luxuries such as personal ornaments, knives, combs and so on, would have stimulated other crafts and stimulated agriculture. It might not be too fanciful to see the growth of such a large body of shipping as the foundation of later volume trading across the North Sea region. One can at least see that the need for trade and the desire for plunder were two aspects which had been characteristic of Danish society for a long time and both drove the introduction of the sailing – as opposed to the rowed – ship. Certainly the technology was fully matured by the end of the millennium and had probably been developed by about AD 800 (Crumlin-Pedersen 1981, 271–86). It was a high value and high risk investment option. This must have fuelled aggression as well as, at the same time, making war easier over a much wider area (Sawyer 1971, 85).

Although John Haywood accepts the idea that an army from a fleet of this size would have been 'potentially well over 1000 men' (Haywood 1999, 171), I conclude that the 35 ships were mostly manned by an average of about 30 men each, which would give a raiding party of about 1000–1100 men. The argument for this number as a typical size for a raiding party is reinforced by estimates of the size of Viking armies in Northumbria (Sawyer 1971, ch. 6) and by estimates of the size of contemporary Viking raiding forces in Ireland (Clarke 1999, 39–40). The king must have raised a force of about the same size and it is possible that this would be the men of the shire, augmented by the king's own household troops. An army of about 1000 men would be a respectable number to be raised from the shire and the account of the raid of 843 suggests that an army of about the same size was raised on that occasion also. In 840 the Ealdorman Æthelhelm fought 35 shiploads of Danes at Southampton and won, suggesting that he must have had a force of about 1000 men, presumably the shire levies (ASC 'A', 840), while in 845 Ealdorman Eanwulf and the men of Somerset, together with the bishop Ealhstan of Sherborne and Osric, Ealdorman of Dorset with the Dorset men fought and defeated a Danish force at the mouth of the river Parrett (ASC 'A' 845).

As long as the size of the Danish raiding parties remained at about 1000–1100 men it was possible,

Figure 2.3. A 30 metre long Viking longship under construction at Roskilde, July 2004. The shipwrights are using the same construction techniques on this replica as were used on 'skuldelev 2', the wreck of a longship, built in Dublin in 1042 and excavated close to Roskilde. Clearly visible are the marks of the adze where the plank has been trimmed ready for the addition of the top strake, part of which is visible in the background (author's photograph).

Figure 2.4. Here a much smaller Viking ship, capable of carrying a crew of about 15 men, is seen under sail off Roskilde, in very fresh conditions (author's photograph).

though not inevitable, that the shire levies would be able to defeat them, although no doubt the raiders did much damage before a counter-attack could be launched. However, in 851 the raiders began to over-winter in England and the size of the attacking army rose enormously. Some 350 ships arrived in the Thames. In 866 the Great Army, a force which had spent some years ravaging the Carolingian Empire, arrived with the intention of settling rather than merely raiding and extorting. This was a highly organised force, which had spent years away from its Scandinavian homelands. It almost certainly consisted of warriors with women, children and followers, including slaves and craftsmen. Even with an average of 30 people per ship the total numbers involved must have neared 10,000. If half were non-combatants, wives, concubines, children, slaves, craftsmen – then the army itself might have numbered about 5000–6000 warriors.

The Irish, Frankish and English chroniclers, writing independently of one another in the ninth century, tend to suggest that a typical Great Army arrived in a fleet of 200 to 250 ships (Brooks 1979, 2–11). Such fleets were still being used at the end of the tenth century, so that the change in the size of raiding armies in the second half of the ninth century marked the beginning of a new era in English warfare. Until the Norman Conquest it seems that armies were of about this size, 5000–6000 warriors. The challenge faced by the kings of Wessex was to manage their political and social system in such a way as to make it realistic to be able to raise an army of that size from year to year as needed. What must have seemed like an emergency in the mid-ninth century became a normal way of life by the early tenth century. A subsidiary consideration was provision for the raising of large sums of money with which to buy off the Danes when military means failed. As early as 865 the men of Kent were attempting to buy peace with the Danes (ASC 'A' 865), although with little success. The extraction of loot in the form of silver was a major part of the modus operandi of the Danes and was used with great success in Gaul. It became a regular feature of their operations in England also.

In order to maintain a body of fighting men of a suitable standard the king may well have needed to grant away more land to warriors in return for their loyalty. Place-names which are of the type 'personal-name + *ing* + *tun*', ('the estate of a person named x'), may represent land granted in this way; estates which took their names from the first permanent tenant. Groups of these names exist around major royal and ecclesiastical centres and may be evidence of this practice. Close to Frome, a major ecclesiastical site and an estate centre which was in royal hands in 1066 (DB 1.8), were Lullington, Hemington, Hardington, Egford, Babington, Tytherington, Beckington, Woolverton (Fig. 2.5). Six of these eight places appear in *Domesday Book* as manors, of varying hidages. Hemington was the largest at 21 hides and Egford the smallest at 1 hide. All except Lullington were in the hands of laymen in 1066. At Lullington King Harold was the owner, suggesting that he had obtained the land at some point before his rise to the throne, since the manor had not stayed with other royal lands (DB 5.51). Another group lay around Ilminster; Barrington, Chillington, Dillington, Dinnington, Puckington and Whitelackington. There is Domesday information for only three of these manors and only Whitelackington was of any size – 10 hides (DB 22.3). In 1066 Ilminster belonged to Muchelney Abbey, but despite its early charter of AD 705 it is very likely that the abbey did not gain control of Ilminster until the tenth century. The charter (S249) is probably a concoction of that period (Edwards 1988, 204–6). It is therefore likely that Ilminster was an independent collegiate church until that time. Cannington was a royal estate in the time of King Alfred in the later ninth century (Keynes and Lapidge 1983, 175). Here there is only Fiddington, a 4 hide estate held by Alfward in 1066 (DB 22.8). Much further west lies Bossington, a detached portion of Porlock parish.

It is likely that Frome and Ilminster and possibly Cannington were the sites of religious communities which controlled major territories which were employed by the king as sources of rewards for his followers at a time when the Viking raiders needed a response. Further lands taken from the church may also have been used to endow followers by the kings of the later ninth and the early tenth centuries. There are suggestions from the charters in monastic chartularies that many of the lands given to them in the second half of the tenth century were being

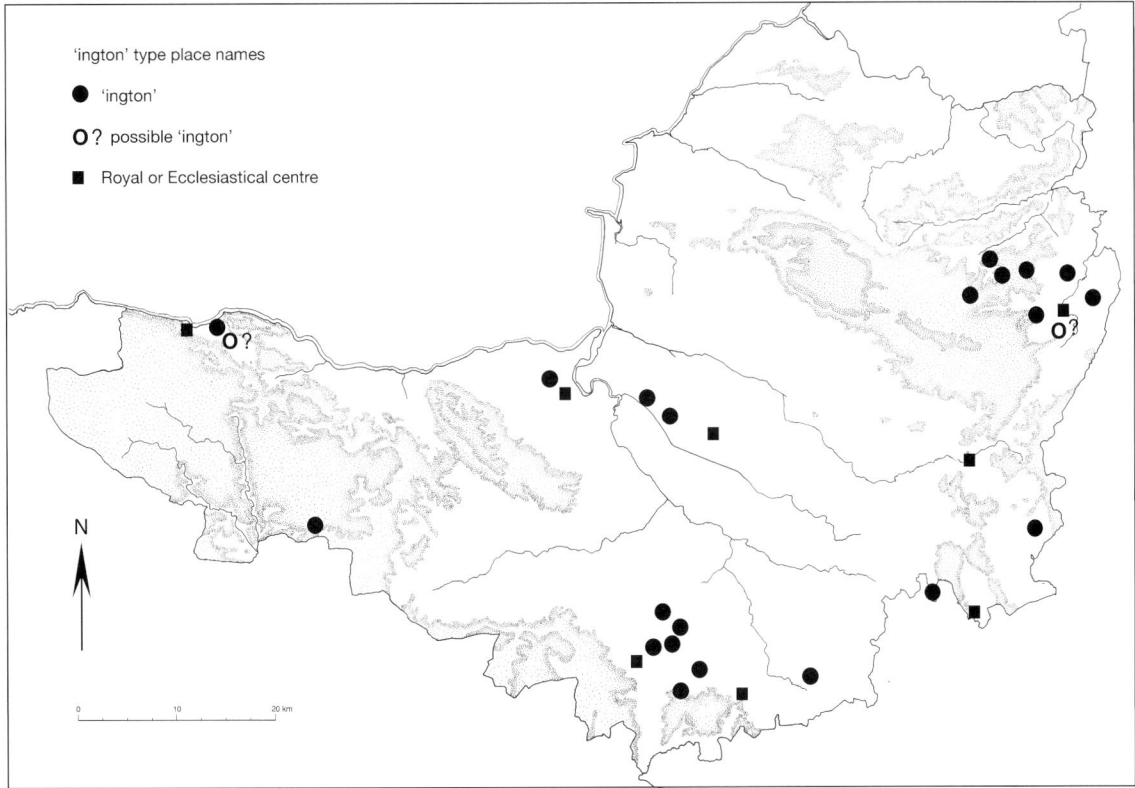

Figure 2.5. 'Ingtun' place-names.

returned after their loss. Professor Fleming has argued on the basis of an analysis of charter grants and exchanges that the Wessex kings, particularly Alfred and Edward the Elder, used church lands for their own strategic purposes on a large scale and she cites several examples from Somerset (Fleming 1985). Some of her examples are difficult to sustain. Creech St Michael near Taunton, which was granted by King Alfred to one of his thegns in 882 (S345), may not be the same estate as that granted much earlier in 682 to abbot Hæmgils of Glastonbury (S235) (Abrams 1996, 100, n. 144). In 901 Edward the Elder made an exchange with the *familia* at Malmesbury, giving them Hankerton in Wiltshire for Farmborough in Somerset (S363). This was an exchange sought by the community, since nearby Hankerton was a far more convenient possession for them than the quite distant Farmborough. Nor does the exchange by Winchester

Old Minster, of Banwell, Compton (Bishop), and Crowcombe for privileges for its minster dependency at Taunton necessarily mean that the bishop's arm was twisted (S372). The estate of the minster at Taunton was enormous and a grant of privileges may have been worth the loss of several other estates. In 1086 the bishop's estate at Taunton paid tax on 54 hides and had a further 20 hides of untaxed land. The bishop also had extensive financial and judicial rights, including jurisdiction over cases of housebreaking and theft and the right to collect Hundred pence, Peter's Pence and Church taxes, as well as holding courts and commanding the military service of the men within the estate (DB 2.1–2). For his part the king gained holdings close to his estate centres at Cheddar and Wedmore amongst other lands.

On the other hand, it is possible that Berrow, which was part of the great Brent estate in the

Figure 2.6. Aller looking westward. The church is just visible in the foreground of the settlement. To the west is Aller Moor.

seventh century (S238), had been taken away. It was apparently granted to a thegn, Wulfmær, by King Edgar in 973 (S793) and may have found its way to Glastonbury as a grant from the family of the thegn when he died. Many other ecclesiastical properties may have passed into royal hands or been granted to laymen by ninth and tenth century kings, but the statements by monasteries in charters of the later part of the tenth century, that the lands granted to them were restitutions of unjust seizures, may not always be true. Both South Stoke, near Bath and Weston, also near Bath, were said to have been restored to St Peter's in Bath (S661 of 956 and S694 of 961). Both charters are spurious, probably compiled long after their supposed dates (Keynes 1994, 176–7, 182). It is the later reformed Benedictine monasteries from which we have the records where lands are supposed to have been restored after loss, Glastonbury, Bath, Muchelney, but it is likely that the greatest losses were suffered by the monastic establishments which were never restored and which have left nothing in the way of written memorials.

When King Alfred defeated the Danes at Edington in Wiltshire, near their winter camp at Chippenham, he was supported by the men of Somerset, Wiltshire and the western part of Hampshire (ASC 'A' 878). His army was probably depleted as the result of Danish raiding, but nevertheless could have numbered as many as 2000 men. The Danish army was not annihilated, since it was able to retreat to the fort, but Alfred was able to attack the fort, seizing the

supplies and the defenders. 'He destroyed the Vikings with great slaughter, and pursued those who fled as far as the stronghold, hacking them down; he seized everything which he found outside the stronghold – men (whom he killed immediately), horses and cattle – and boldly made camp in front of the gates of the Viking stronghold with his army' (Keynes and Lapidge 1983, 84–5). Hunger made the Vikings submit and they found it politic to treat with the king, offering him hostages and submitting to baptism, deep inside English territory at Aller (Fig. 2.6). For the rest of his reign Alfred pursued policies intended to provide a systematic defence system for his lands as well as providing him with an army and rudimentary navy (Abels 1998, 194–207).

The *burhs*

The principle that bookland carried a public obligation to go on military service, to carry out bridge-works and to build strongholds was well established in Wessex by King Alfred's time (Brooks 1971). The charter of Beorhtric of 794 for land on the river Parret is the first extant Somerset grant which imposed this burden (S267). However, Alfred was responsible for the construction of a series of defended sites, forts, around Wessex which presented the Vikings with formidable obstacles provided they were garrisoned. The larger picture, examining the system across the whole of Wessex, has been admirably studied in Hill and Rumble (1996) in their survey of the Burghal Hidage. In Somerset these forts were sited at Bath, Axbridge, Langport, Watchet and Lyng (Fig. 2.7). With five forts Somerset was well endowed with defences. At this point we should note that Professor Brooks thinks that the forts had existed since at least the mid-ninth century, before Alfred's time as king (Brooks 1996, 129). This idea seems difficult to sustain. Famously Alfred built a refuge at Athelney in 879 (Keynes and Lapidge 1983, 84), which he would not have needed to do had Lyng, the fortress immediately across the Yeo, been available to him (Fig. 2.8). Lyng may have been built when Athelney was converted into a monastic site, or used to provide a fortified bridge crossing of the river Yeo. The fort at Watchet is close to Carhampton, the site of two battles against the Vikings (see above) and it seems unlikely

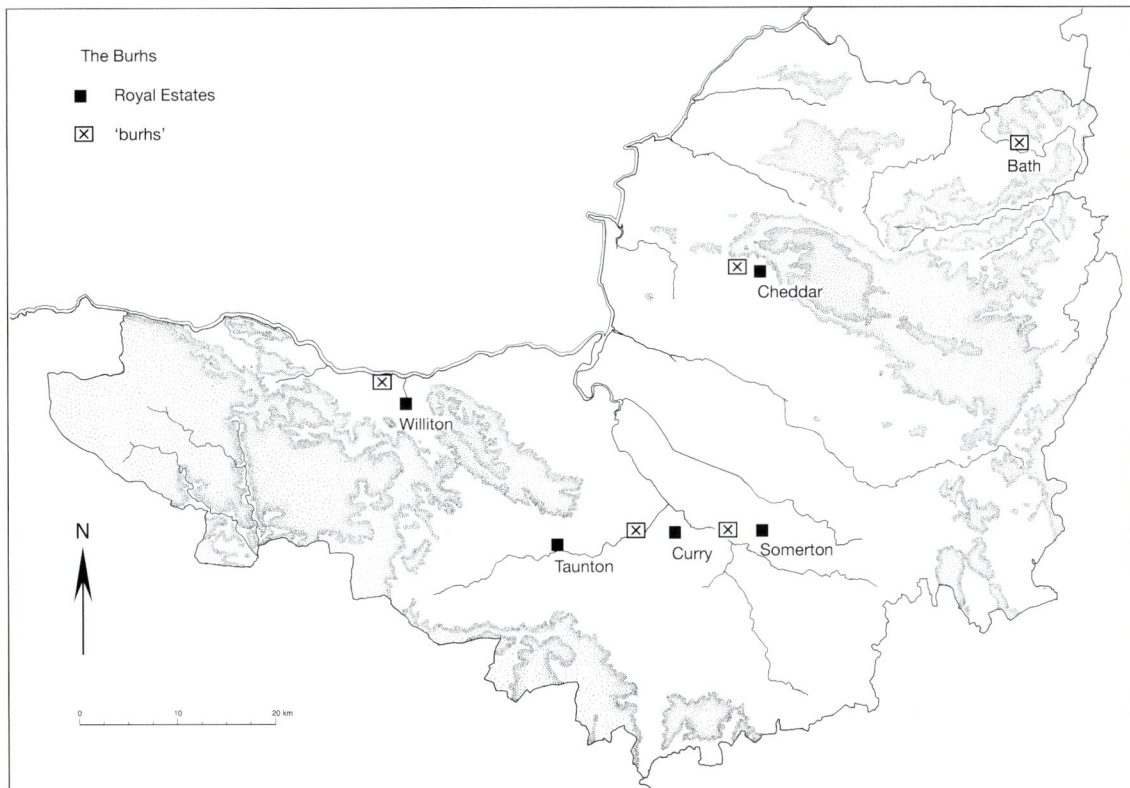

Figure 2.7. The 'burhs' of the later ninth and early tenth centuries.

that it would not have been utilised had it existed.
It is not mentioned in the Anglo-Saxon Chronicle.
Jeremy Haslam has persuasively argued that the forts
were built as part of a carefully planned system of
defence for Wessex, with the peripheral forts – in our
case Bath and Watchet – acting as first line control
of access to Wessex (Haslam 206). It seems simpler
to assume that the forts of the Burghal Hidage were
constructed during Alfred's reign and that they are
part of a systematic approach to defence of the whole
of Wessex and not built on an ad hoc basis.

Figure 2.8. The burh *at Lyng and King Alfred's fort at Athelney.
The* burh *lies under the houses of the village of East Lyng in
the foreground. The river Tone, now visible on the right of the
picture then flowed from right to left through the gap between
Lyng and King Alfred's fort which was situated on the lower
of the two pale coloured fields in the mid-distance. The top-
most of these two fields is the site of King Alfred's monastery of
Athelney (photograph Michael Aston).*

Prior to Alfred's time fortifications were probably royal houses which had palisades or earthworks around them, rather than very large constructions which could withstand an assault by a Viking army. Kingsbury Regis at Milborne Port and Kingsbury Episcopi near South Petherton might have been sites fortified in this way, but no positive evidence yet exists (Draper 2008, 240–53). It is likely that the system of labour which contributed a man per hide towards the construction of each fortification was an extension of an already existing practice. Work on fortifications was a part of the common burden imposed on all bookland and some sort of systematisation almost certainly existed and was adapted. Much later when great estate owners came to build parks, which relied on bank and ditch with palings to fence them, each villein tenant was expected to provide a specific amount of labour, enough to fence four perches around the park at Pilton, on Glastonbury Abbey manors every year, for construction and maintenance (Egerton 3321). In 1327 his work was valued at a penny per perch, but there is no way of projecting such a value back to the year 900. We probably need to envisage the construction of the *burhs* as proceeding in much the same way as the building of a park, with peasant labour contributing so many perches of rampart from each hide until the work was complete, even if the ratio of hides to rampart length cannot always be reconciled. On that basis the construction of the earthworks for each site need not have been too onerous a burden for the surrounding district, while maintenance would have been a relatively straightforward affair. The major problem would have been enforcing the construction of something which was not of obvious benefit to landowner or tenant, unless they lived within sight of it.

The siting of Alfred's forts was clearly intended to protect important royal estates, as well as being part of an overall defence system. Thus Axbridge guarded Cheddar, principally by blocking or controlling the approach via the river Axe. This river was certainly tidal for some miles inland and had a greater flow than today, since the Brue also discharged to the sea through it (Williams, M. 1970, 64). The proposed site for the fort at Axbridge is slightly to the south of the current town centre and seems to look south towards the Axe (Batt 1975, 22–5). It may be that it

commanded a bridge over the river, impeding access to Cheddar. Certainly the name means the 'bridge or causeway on the Axe' (Watts 2004 and Dodgson 1996, 112–3). Cheddar provided access onto the Mendips, with the potential for easy travel to Wells, with its important minster and its estate and beyond that to the Frome estate, again a minster site. The same concern appears at Lyng. Here the fort lay across the river Yeo from the fort and later monastery site of Athelney, and very close to the point where the Yeo joined the Parrett. The confluence of the Tone and the Parrett lay just to the north. A causeway and bridge joined the two sites (Aston 1984, 183–4). Here the forts and bridge may have served to block the river and provided protection for royal estates at Curry and Taunton. Langport was also placed on a river, at the point where the Yeo passes through a gap in higher ground. In this case the fort on the Yeo protected the royal centre at Somerton from advances up the river. It also controlled access by water to Ilchester and from there to the Fosse Way, with its potential for rapid movement north-east or south-west.

The two remaining forts, at Watchet and at Bath, were on the edges of the shire. Bath provided a site on the boundary between Mercia and Wessex, which had only recently been appropriated by Alfred. Coins were minted in Edward the Elder's name from the mint at Bath as early as c. 900, suggesting that the town was fortified by that date (Lyon 2001, 69). Its importance lay in its control of the Fosse Way and of the Avon valley, impeding travel from Wessex into the Midlands and also controlling routes running from Gloucestershire towards western Wiltshire. At Watchet, within the royal estate of Williton, the fort occupied an old hill-fort on the coast (Aston 1984, 192). It not only overlooked the landing place and trading site at Watchet; it also commanded a route towards Taunton and central Somerset, and a prospect along the Somerset coast towards Carhampton, a royal site attacked by the Vikings on at least two occasions.

All five of the forts are placed to command movement through the shire, with a special emphasis on attack from the sea and up rivers, but also to control the major north–south communication from Mercia towards central Somerset and Devon. Quite apart from the overall plan for the defence of

Wessex, of which these five forts formed only one small part, the local threat was well established. At Downend there is some evidence for the earthworks of a typical Viking camp. Predating the Norman castle at Downend, two earthworks together make a 'D' shaped enclosure, utilising a now extinct stretch of the river Parrett as the remaining side of the defence (Prior 2007, 85–6).

But forts are of no use if they are not maintained and defended and it was by constructing a permanent system of building, maintenance and defence that Alfred and his son Edward the Elder showed their administrative abilities and their political acumen. What was important was the arrangement used to support the forts which made use of a pre-existing system of apportioning liability for renders and tribute, which had been used from the first entry of the Anglo-Saxons into Somerset, the hidage system. This measure, based upon the notional size of the estate needed to support a family, was extended to cover the liability for support of the forts and for performance of military service. The Burghal Hidage, composed early in the tenth century, preserves a list of the forts in Wessex and the west Midlands and gives information concerning the way in which forts were supported from the surrounding countryside (Hill and Rumble 1996, 1). Each fort was allocated a certain number of hides of land, related to its size, expressed in terms of the length of its wall. 'For the establishment of a wall of one acre's breadth, and for its "defence", 16 hides are required. If each hide is represented by one man, then each pole (of wall) can be furnished with four men' (Rumble 1996, 34). However, it is not possible or productive to make the hidage needed for the Somerset forts fit the later hidage of the shire as it existed in 1086 at Domesday (Hill 1996, 92–7). The Burghal Hidage gives Watchet 513 hides, Axbridge 400 hides, Lyng 100 hides, Langport 600 hides and Bath 1000 hides, a total of 2613 hides (Hill 1996, 84). The total hidage of Somerset in 1086 was 2993 (Darby 1986, 336). After a century and a half of change it seems unlikely that there would be a very close agreement, but nevertheless the figures are close enough to establish the reality of the system. The size of the support for each fort may well correlate with the length of walling, but we should perhaps avoid trying to make the fit too

exact (Hill 1996, 94). There is no trace in Somerset of the duodecimal system of hidation apparent in the midland counties, where the process of hidation took place as Edward the Elder gained control of the region (Campbell 2000, 2–5). Athelstan demanded that the boroughs should all be repaired by a fortnight after the Rogation days, suggesting that ongoing maintenance was a problem (Whitelock 1955, 384).

The system clearly worked by the time of Edward the Elder, when the Vikings were busy in the Bristol Channel and Severn estuary. In 914, after Edward had driven a Viking sea-borne army out of Gloucestershire, he stationed men all along the Somerset and Devon coasts to forestall a landing and when one was attempted near Watchet and then at Porlock the attackers were driven off (ASC 'A', 914). Both the fort at Watchet and the system for raising men seem to have been successful. The coast was not troubled again until the reign of Æthelred when there was a renewal of invasion and destruction. A seaborne raid in 998 did much damage at Watchet (ASC 'E', 998) and in 1001 the Danish army landed at Exeter defeating the combined forces of Devon and Somerset at Pinhoe (ASC 'E', 1001). In 1013 Swein and Cnut ravaged the district and camped at Bath with their army. The ealdorman Æthelmær of Devon and all the western thegns submitted to Swein and gave him hostages (ASC 'E' 1013) but in 1015 the shire was attacked again. Finally, during the disturbances of Edward the Confessor's reign, Earl Harold, in rebellion, landed at Porlock in 1052 (ASC 'E', 1052) and a force was raised to oppose him. The Abingdon Chronicle ('C') says he killed 30 good thegns of Somerset and Devon after the landing.

Soldiers

Of course this view of the tenth and early eleventh centuries is myopic, since it takes no account of the extensive military operations throughout the Midlands and the north of England during Edward the Elder's reign and those of his successors, particularly Athelstan, nor of the wider political implications of the extension of the power of the kings of Wessex across the greater part of England, but it is evident that the need for warriors was ongoing and important throughout the tenth and the eleventh centuries. A bigger kingdom necessarily demanded bigger military forces. Of immediate concern is the question of how many soldiers Somerset could supply, bearing in mind that, at least in the time of Edward the Elder and perhaps during Athelstan's time, the *burhs* needed to be defended as well as a field army raised. Without a garrison the *burhs* were of no value. They needed to be defended by competent soldiers, though there are plenty of examples of later medieval towns being fortified and defended successfully by their citizens, women included. It is hardly credible to suggest that the Burghal Hidage figures actually tell us how big the garrisons were, despite the suggestion that each hide owed a man to its *burh*. This would mean a literal application of the figure of '27,070 men' as garrison in Wessex (Brooks 1996, 128). Professor Brooks remarks that 'the 27,070 men whom the Burghal Hidage commits to the construction and defence of the forts must have represented a very high proportion (probably as many as one in five or six) of the adult male population of the West Saxon kingdom of King Alfred or Edward the Elder'. Given the relatively small population of the day, this is clearly absurd, as Professor Brooks points out. It seems hardly credible that so many able-bodied men could be found or if found, spared from their agricultural duties. It may well be that this is a reference to the overall obligations of construction and repair, rather than garrison duties. However, the defences without manpower were nothing and each fortification must have needed at the least a few hundreds of men, if it were threatened or under attack. Thirty-three such defences, even with an average of 100 men only, would need 3300 to man them. Professor Brooks suggests skeleton garrisons, but such garrisons need not be seen as in some way inferior. Later castles often ran with garrisons of a dozen men or so and it was only in times of grave emergency that they would be strengthened with more soldiers. Somerset's five forts might have needed a total garrison of about 500 men, which does not seem an impossible number to raise, but may well have been smaller.

By the end of the Anglo-Saxon period the Domesday Book provides a way of estimating the men available for military service. Aethelstan demanded that each landowner should provide two well mounted men for each plough he owned

(Whitelock 1955, 384). However, there is the famous example from the Berkshire Domesday, where 'If the king sent out an army anywhere only one thegn went from each 5 hides, and for his sustenance or pay 4s for two months was given him from each hide' (Williams and Martin 2002, Berks DB fo. 56). Each man would need to have his arms and his horse, ready to go, but might expect to serve his turn in the king's army only occasionally, perhaps at every fifth callout. His pay of one pound for the two months was a substantial sum and an indication that the warrior himself was a man with the training and the weaponry to be an effective soldier. This suggests that the training and perhaps the status of the soldier had risen between the time of Athelstan and the time of King Harold.

A theoretical maximum call-out for Somerset would be 598 thegns on the basis of 2993 hides in the assessment of the shire (Darby 1986, 336). Such a crude mechanical estimate is very risky and no medieval king ever achieved complete efficiency in his administration; nevertheless there is material in Domesday Book which suggests that this number might be quite easily reached. Wulfstan (Archbishop of York 1002–23), in the *Geþyncðo* assumed that in his ideal world the thegn had an estate of 5 hides – indeed that was how you judged his status as a thegn (Whitelock 1955, 431–5).

> And if a ceorl prospered so that he had fully 5 hides of his own land (agenes landes), church and kitchen, bell house and burh-geat, seat and special office in the king's hall, then he was thenceforward entitled to the rank of thegn.

In the minds of some contemporaries at least he was therefore primarily defined as a landed proprietor, a man with bookland and a direct relationship to the king. The Archbishop was probably describing a real group of people at the beginning of the eleventh century and there were certainly some men in the Domesday Somerset who fitted his description. There were 77 estates of exactly 5 hides and 52 of them were held by individuals who were laymen and probably therefore 'thegns'. But there was nothing exceptional about an estate of 5 hides. Out of 895 separate holdings in 1066 they amount to 8.6% of all estates. One hide holdings were much more common; 129 of them amount to 14.4% of all estates. Although nearly all the large estates were held by the church or by the king and his family there were many laymen with estates larger than 5 hides and with holdings spread across the shire. One such was Edmer Ator who held Cranmore in 1066 (DB 8.32). He also had estates at East Chinnock and at Odcombe, at Aldwick and Mudford and at Dinnington and Camerton (from Glastonbury), as well as extensive lands in Devon and Dorset and elsewhere which were not held from Glastonbury (DB 19. 44, 19. 47. 37. 5, 37. 12. and DB 15.12–13, 15.14–30). Presumably these men were summoned to the army with a following of soldiers drawn from their estates. Those with only one estate of 5 hides went themselves and were not typical of men from Somerset. Although it is likely that most of these men owned their lands as bookland, it is clear that in many cases they held land which had been deliberately broken up into holdings of this size, probably as a way of endowing warriors. For example, if we rebuild East and West Harptree, (*harper's tree or gallows*?) which the names suggest were probably one estate at an early date, we find a 20 hide estate. In the Domesday Book East and West Harptree are not distinguished from one another; both are simply *Herpetreu* (DB 5.60, 19.37, 5.60, 24.31). By 1086 the two settlements were in different hundreds, strongly suggesting that the division into East and West had taken place much earlier in the tenth century or even the ninth. East Harptree was in the Winterstoke Hundred, while West Harptree was in the Chewton Mendip Hundred, although physically separated from Chewton Mendip by East Harptree. Between them the two Harptrees contained four units in 1086 and each entry in Domesday Book was for a 5 hide estate, so that there were two estates in each settlement. It looks as if a large estate was first divided into two 10 hide units. This probably took place before open-field agriculture was well established. Much later the two estates were each sub-divided, although the agricultural system and the village developments were not affected.

Among the owners and holders of estates in 1066 there were many who were either not named, or whose names were recorded in the Exeter Domesday and were omitted from the final Exchequer version. The most likely reason for this omission was their low social status. Where the occupiers were not named they were almost always described as 'thegns'. There

were some 295 of them in Somerset. Many were on Church estates and they were clearly in a subordinate position, since very frequently we are told that they could not leave the land. That is they could not seek a new lord and retain their estates. The land on which they lived is often described in Domesday Book as 'thegn land'. They were lease-holders, probably for lives. Forty-eight of these thegns are to be found on Glastonbury abbey estates. It is clear also that the average holding of each of these men was very small, if we assume that they each held only the one estate. (It seems likely that if a man had held several estates and thus a substantial acreage, he would have been named). Thus on the Glastonbury estates in Somerset they amounted to an average of about 1½ hides a head, far from the 5 hides suggested as the correct minimum holding. Glastonbury with 240 hides of taxable land in Somerset had exactly the correct number of thegns to fill its quota, but they were endowed with much less than 5 hides each. It seems likely that these men were soldiers, or the descendants of soldiers who had been settled on small estates by the abbey as a way of meeting its military obligations to the Old English Kings as well as to perform other services (Abels, 1988). Many others were living on their own lands, but their estates were very small as units of taxation. Three thegns held the now lost estate of Dodisham and paid tax for 3½ virgates and 5 acres of land (DB 21, 20). There were over 180 small estates of less than a hide, recognised by the Domesday commissioners as independent in some way. Many were as small as a single virgate, sometimes smaller. Many of these men living on their own lands may have clubbed together with their neighbours to meet the 5-hide obligation or have performed service for their much richer neighbours who owed more than personal service on their extensive estates, but there is reason to believe, as we shall see later, that many of these small estates were very much under-taxed and may have returned their owners a better living than the bare tax record would suggest.

The theoretical 600 soldiers were probably quite easily raised, since it seems that they could live off not much over a hide each. Whether more were actually supplied to the king's army is unknown, but it is clear that land-owners could if needed, raise or hire more military retainers than were required by the king and a force of about 1000 men would not be impossible. The call-up of soldiers and the supervision to make sure the call was answered needed a considerable bureaucracy and the hundred system, which had developed as a method of providing regional courts and as the basis upon which taxes were collected, probably served for that purpose as well. The system may well have worked without much outside instruction, since the siege of the new Montacute Castle in 1068 needed to be broken by the Bishop of Coutance (Page 1911), suggesting that the attack was well organised. It does not sound like an attack by local peasants, but more likely involved thegns from Somerset and Dorset, fighting within the structure of the shire levies, with which they were familiar.

Anglo-Saxon Somerset was moulded by its warrior aristocracy. It became English by force in the late seventh century and the structure of its secular society was driven by the needs of the warrior aristocracy and of their kings. Although these were early medieval kings they were able to use the fact that their conquest of Somerset had coincided quite closely with the emergence of kingship to impose a tight grip upon society. The highly personalised nature of their kingship was reinforced by the ideology of the new Christian religion which encouraged the written formulation of law. The absorption of so many Welsh people gave the kings an important opportunity to exercise law-making and establish the legitimacy of the activity. The conquest of Wessex more than doubled the area of land available to the early kings and careful control over its disposition helped to strengthen the king's grip on his aristocracy. By judicious grants of estates he could increase the number of warriors available to him, and by keeping a monopoly of the grants, at first by use of loanland, later by the use of bookland, could tie warriors to himself.

The system was tested to extremes in the later eighth and early ninth centuries and provided the Wessex kings with a large enough following to withstand their Viking enemies. The reform and expansion of the system for providing warriors and for defence of the shire worked well for almost a century, but could not withstand the power of the battle-hardened and professional armies of Swein and Cnut, nor the impact of the superior technology and the good fortune of the Norman host.

Charltons in Somerset
Charlton Adam/Mackerell ST53565/28673
Charlton Farm in Failand ST494/737
Charlton Farm in Hemington ST76016/53949
Charlton Farm in Kilmersdon ST68520/52199
Charlton Horethorne ST66545/23123
Charlton in Creech St Michael ST29235/26743
Charlton in Shepton Mallet ST63150/43174
Charlton Musgrove ST73001/31799
Charlton, Queen ST63405/67059

Notes
1. All references to Anglo-Saxon charters are to the numbering used in Sawyer 1968
2. My translation of the last part of the poem.

3

Settlements and Estates

Most commentators are agreed that the fifth century saw a considerable fall in population all across post-Roman Britain. Such a fall was probably inevitable once the stimulus of commercial farming was removed, but there are good grounds for believing that it was exacerbated by the plague which swept across the Roman Empire in the years immediately after 541 (Little 2007, 4–13). It is clear that it reached Britain and since this was undoubtedly an outbreak of bubonic plague, the mortality would have been very high, perhaps reaching as much as a third to a half of the population. It is likely that the plague returned on a number of occasions during the sixth century and the pandemic continued through the seventh century and into the eighth (Maddicott 1997). Recurring outbreaks, which are a feature of the disease, were noted in continental Europe. Although we can put no figures on the size of the population by c. 600, it is likely that it had fallen to a fraction of the fourth century levels and that it remained stagnant through the seventh century. Our investigation of settlements after the mid-fifth century must be influenced by this knowledge. It should be no surprise therefore that so many of the low status rural settlements which have been excavated should show signs of abandonment or impoverishment in this period. It is likely that there were simply not enough people to maintain them all.

Unfortunately the best evidence for settlements of the living in the fifth, sixth and seventh centuries seems to be through the dead (Fig. 3.1). We have already seen the cemeteries of this period as adjuncts of the revived hill-fort system, but it may be that they offer more information about the wider settlement patterns of the period also. Somerset is surprisingly well provided with 'Dark Age' cemeteries and therefore some information concerning actual settlements. Current archaeological work continues to provide more and more firm evidence from excavation and the associated dating, normally through radio-carbon sampling.[1] Current examples are Bishops Lydeard, Bradley Hill, Brean Cliff, Buckland Dinham, Camerton, Cannington, Henley Hill, Lamyatt Beacon, Portishead, Portbury, Charlton near Shepton Mallet, South Cadbury, Wembdon, West Harptree, and Wint Hill (Banwell). As far as we can tell there are no enclosures around them, fitting well with the view that these early cemeteries were open. We are not dealing with circular or sub-circular graveyards (Petts 2002, 27–9). However, there is little uniformity as between cemeteries making it worthwhile to look at each one in some detail to extract what information we can about the settlements to which each pertained. To begin with we need to recognise that the currently known cemeteries must be only a selection of the total number within the county. There may be many awaiting discovery, probably associated with hill-forts which have not yet been explored.

The Bishops Lydeard cemetery was located at Stoneage Barton in 2000. The site is close to the boundary between the parishes of Bishops Lydeard and Cothelstone. Five burials were discovered, one of which was of a child. The graves at this site were surrounded by square ditches, which formed a demarcation area for each burial. The excavators compared the site with other similar sites and

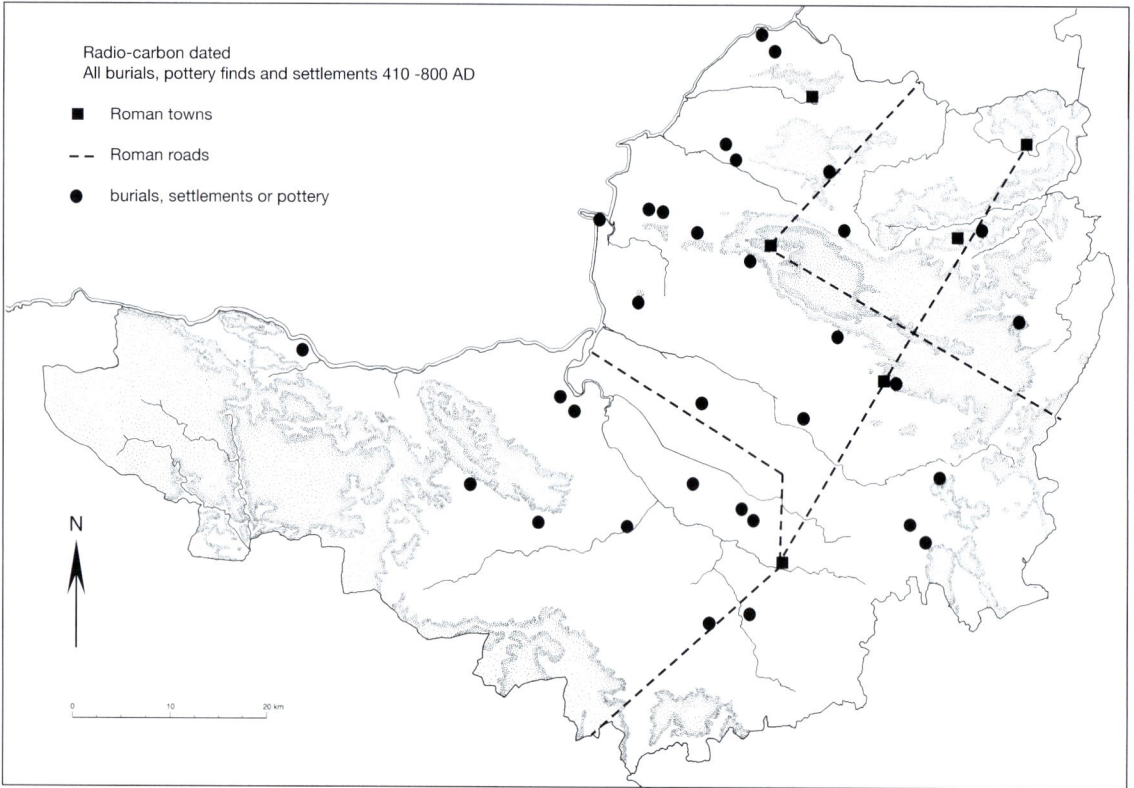

Figure 3.1. Settlement evidence, AD 400–800.

Figure 3.2. Beads from a grave at Buckland Dinham.

concluded that the burials were probably those of high status individuals (Webster and Brunning 2005). The excavators do not know how extensive the cemetery may have been originally.

Bradley Hill, near Somerton, was the site of 46 east–west burials in three groups and closely associated with a small farmstead complex (Leech 1981). James Gerrard has argued that the site may have continued in use into the sixth century and the same is true for the settlement nearby at Catsgore (Gerrard 2005a).

At Brean Cliff eight burials of the post-Roman period were excavated (Levitan 1990, 74–80). All were east-west burials without grave goods, though an earlier discovery was reported as including a knife. A radio-carbon date of AD 650 ±80 years places the burials firmly in the post-Roman period (HER10131). Since they were discovered eroding from the soft cliff face, it seems likely that the graves recovered were only a part of a larger cemetery and the excavator speculated about the possibility of settlement in the area, but would not commit himself to a conclusion (Bell 1990, 82–3). Peter Fowler has suggested that a field system located on top of Brean Down could be of this period (Fowler 1975, 130). In addition there are many examples of fish-traps on the beach at Brean and it is difficult to imagine that none of them were in use in the post-Roman period (HER 12574 and others). It would be unlikely that the cultivators would live too far from their fields and the rest of the estate, probably defined by the boundaries of the present parish, was marsh-land which would have been given over to seasonal cattle grazing. In the north Somerset Levels there is clear evidence that the landscape became flooded in the late-Roman/post-Roman period. It is not clear how long the flooding lasted, but it covered large areas of the low-lying ground (Rippon 2006, 80). It was probably the result of a tidal surge caused by a storm over-topping neglected embankments. It is likely that something similar occurred at Brean, making the marsh land almost useless for long periods. This can never have been a large community, perhaps only a few families, probably living along the foot of the Down in a hamlet.

Close by on Brean Down, just above the Brean community, stood a late Roman rural temple and close to the temple a second building which has been interpreted as a possible late/post-Roman church. There is a possibility that this was a small religious group, living at a post-Roman church on the hill-top. If so they may have represented a small, self-contained, celibate group, leading a monastic existence.

At Buckland Dinham a small cemetery, discovered while quarrying, produced evidence of four or five burials and an additional burial was excavated by the Reverend Horne and Arthur Bulleid. They found a female skeleton buried with silver earrings and several beads of quartz, glass and shell (Horne 1926, 77–8) (Fig. 3.2). The assumption was that this was an 'Anglo-Saxon', probably sixth century burial, but in view of the similarity with the burials at nearby Camerton it might be better to regard this as another cemetery attached to a small post-Roman settlement. We do not know how large it was, but the area of the hill-top where it is situated suggests that it was not extensive. The site of the settlement is unknown, though Romano-British pottery has been observed on Murty Hill, about 1.5 km away (Stokes 1995, 175).

We have already seen that at the Camerton cemetery 109 graves were excavated (see above Chapter 1). Dating evidence spanned the period from the fourth century to the seventh (Rahtz 1977, 61). It seems unlikely that the cemetery was complete as excavated, but nevertheless it may not have been very much larger than explored. A cemetery of that size, spread over such a long period, would again suggest a small community.

At Cannington, on the other hand, the excavator has made it clear that he thinks the cemetery was very extensive, with up to 2000 burials being likely (Rahtz, Hirst and Wright 2000, 59). This is thus by far the largest cemetery in the county, and suggests a continuing population of a minimum of about 200 persons. As the excavators suggest, these may not all have lived in a single settlement (*ibid.*, 420–1). This was a carefully organised cemetery with the graves aligned into family groupings (*ibid.*, 129), and evidence of a grave of superior importance, perhaps developed as a shrine and with a path leading to it (*ibid.*, 51–7), an indication of some kind of authoritative direction. Further more, it was in use for a long period, certainly up to the mid-seventh century and perhaps into the early eighth.

At Henley Hill the cemetery was in use for a much shorter time than that at Cannington. The number of burials excavated was about 75 and the central period of use of the cemetery was the fifth to sixth centuries, connecting it with the hill-fort nearby. Disuse of the cemetery probably corresponded closely with abandonment of the fort. (Watts and Leach 1996, 51, 69). The relatively small number of burials at such an important site and its disuse when the fort was abandoned shows that this was a cemetery of the elite. There must have been another cemetery somewhere else for the rest of the community.

A small cemetery of at least sixteen burials was excavated on the hill-top at Lamyatt Beacon, very close to the late Romano-British temple and a small building, not connected with the temple. Of the 16 burials nearly all were females and were described as being of above average height and showing few signs of hard labour. Carbon dating produced dates ranging from AD 559 to 782 (Leech 1986, 259–328).

Portishead produced a cemetery of 43 burials which have been classified as post-Roman fourth to seventh century (Pretty 1969, 51). The relatively small number of burials may be due to failure to find further parts of the cemetery or suggest that this was a small community. Not far away at Portbury, close to the church, another Romano-British period cemetery was found during construction of the school (Ponsford 1979, 7–8). Here, unlike at Cannington, the burials were not at a centrally placed cemetery, showing that local groups had more autonomy.

The site at Shepton Mallet has already been mentioned above. Here the burials 'need not have ceased before the sixth century and perhaps even later', although the settlement itself appears to have been abandoned before the burials ceased (Leach and Evans 2001, 95).

At South Cadbury a small group of burials were excavated over a considerable period of time. Four burials were found in 1966 (Taylor 1967) and were considered to be Anglo-Saxon on account of the grave goods, including a spear head and part of a shield-boss. In 2001 further excavation revealed two more burials, both with evidence for grave goods. Examination of the teeth revealed that both individuals were born and lived locally and extends the possible period for the cemetery from the seventh century, back into the sixth (Davey 2005, 169–186). We do not know the full extent of this cemetery but the excavator thought that it was connected with a community at or near South Cadbury Castle.

At West Harptree in the early nineteenth century the Reverend Skinner reported that quarrymen had found more than 100 burials, mostly with heads to the west, though some were aligned north-south. A few had weapons and other grave goods. Rahtz and Watts certainly thought that this may have been a cemetery similar to Cannington (1989, 338).

At Wembdon at least 20 burials were located with indications of a larger cemetery. The carbon dates obtained (HER12470) suggest that the cemetery was still in use in the early Anglo-Saxon period (Langdon, 1986).

At Wint Hill in Banwell there was a cemetery which produced 27 burials. Here a Roman building on a hillside had been demolished and burials put through the building. There was evidence from the presence of medieval pottery, including glazed ridge tiles, that the site had continued in use for a long period. The excavators regarded the burials as 'post-Roman', but they may well have covered a long period, into the high Middle Ages (Hunt 1964, 35–9). There is evidence of extensive buildings of the Roman period, showing that there was a large community. It seems unlikely that the settlement continued to function in the fifth, sixth and seventh centuries, but the site clearly remained very important. It may have been used as a burial ground for small groups from the surrounding area and an element of continuity is possible. It has been suggested that there was a chapel on the site – and the medieval green glazed ridge tile would support that possibility (Hunt 1964, 35). The fields where the excavation took place are called 'chapel leaze', (t. 1472 of 1838) and 'chapelyard', (t. 1477 of 1838). However, the ascription of the chapel to St Romanus is erroneous, as that chapel was located in Winscombe (Hunt, W. 1885, 92).

Of all the cemeteries discussed Cannington is pre-eminent. It is by far the largest site investigated – 542 individuals were excavated – and probably once contained more burials than anywhere else – up to a maximum of 2000! The nearest rival is Camerton with 109 graves. Unfortunately we cannot make close comparisons relating to the extent of the cemeteries, simply because it is not possible to know how large they were at the point when they ceased to be used. There are traces of settlement on the hillside below the hill-fort at Cannington (Rahtz, Hirst and Wright 2000, 11), but it seems possible that the site served as a cemetery for many other small settlements scattered about the Cannington area. This might suggest that some central authority or presence encouraged surrounding communities to bring their dead to the site and that the practice was a manifestation of wider authority with religious significance.

Apart from Cannington, none of the cemeteries so far discovered or reported seem to be very large, suggesting that there is little evidence for large settlements in the fifth or sixth centuries. Most of the population, even high status groups, lived in small communities as the burials at Stoneage Barton suggest. The burials at Shepton Mallet seem to have continued beyond the end of occupation of the site, suggesting that a traditional cemetery continued to be used while the settlement had moved away and it may be the case that elsewhere some traditional burial sites continued to be used while settlements moved.

The cemeteries fall into a number of overlapping groupings, each of which is significant and may illuminate the larger settlement pattern. Hill-forts are clearly important in the history of the region in the later fifth and early sixth centuries, but the cemeteries are only tenuously connected with them. Cannington with its 625 burials is the biggest site, but may have been primarily a religious centre for scattered communities. The cemetery on Henley Hill, close to Cadbury-Congresbury hill-fort, was clearly associated with it, but it may represent an elite group, rather than people living in settlements in the area. The small cemetery near South Cadbury at Hincknoll Slait is only tenuously connected with the hill-fort and may be the result of settlement nearer at hand at Sigwells just to the south. There is a much stronger association when we look at 'coastal' cemeteries. Brean, Cannington, Henley Hill and Portishead are all of this type. These correlate well with sites which have a connection with religious communities, Henley Hill, Wint Hill, Brean, and Lamyatt and perhaps Cannington also. Sites which

were important in the post-Roman period as centres of political power and were close to the sea and thus in contact with the continental late-Roman world are well represented. The cemeteries point to some concentrations of population and power along the coast, and the connection with religious communities is strong.

There was a subsidiary focus in the east with Camerton and Charlton near Shepton on the Fosse Way and Lamyatt Beacon close enough to the Fosse to be grouped with these two. Sites such as Buckland Dinham, Bradley Hill and Wembdon may be the closest we can get to minor settlements scattered across the landscape.

Turning to recognised settlement sites, at Shapwick the Sladwick site is not associated with a cemetery and shows some evidence of re-use of a Roman period building at a quite rudimentary level which is attributed to the mid-fifth to early seventh century period (Gerrard and Aston 2007, 384–8). This is therefore an example of a site which came into existence in the post-Roman period and was deserted before the mid-seventh century. The hearths found at East Lambrook, which returned radio-carbon dates for the sixth to seventh centuries, probably represent the remains of dwellings of this period. They were within a Neolithic causewayed enclosure which may still have been recognisable at that period (HER 28391). Doubtless there are many more similar, probably quite low-status sites of this type to be found across Somerset.

Clearly some continuity of settlement did take place and there is a possibility that some of the small hamlets and farmsteads which certainly appear in the Domesday Book all over the county, despite the tenth and eleventh century moves towards nucleated settlement, preserve some measure of continuity. Tantalising glimpses of what may have been occasionally occur. The hamlet of Woolston, near South Cadbury was in two parts in 1066: one of 3 hides and 1½ virgates and the other of a single hide (DB 19, 55, 36, 7). The larger unit seems to survive today as the hamlets of Woolston, Lower Woolston and Woolston Manor Farm, all in Yarlington. The smaller unit, clearly taken from the larger estate, probably in the tenth or eleventh century, has been absorbed into Yarlington (Dubber 2006). Test pitting and gradiometry at the site showed that Bronze Age, Romano-British and medieval settlement were all present, often overlying one-another and reusing features such as ditches. In one test pit a single sherd of fifth/sixth century imported ware, similar to the material from South Cadbury hill-fort, was discovered (R. Tabor, pers. comm.). It would be idle to build too much on this one piece of pottery, but it does point to the need for more careful excavation on similar sites to assess whether this was a stray find or a hint of further more systematic evidence to come. However Dr Tabor believes there is enough evidence from the excavation to suggest continuous occupation of the site (Tabor 2008, 95) Apart from this one rather dubious case it is not yet possible to link the post-Roman period directly with the seventh century Anglo-Saxon landscape, though there must have been many hamlets and farmsteads present in the mid-seventh century which still have a presence today. The real difficulty may prove to be the discovery and elucidation of the pattern of settlement in the post-Roman period itself. Dr Gerrard has made a vigorous case for settlement at the Bradley Hill site into the sixth century and if this be accepted, then the same is probably true for other post-Roman sites of a similar nature, but this is not settlement which survived into the Anglo-Saxon period. The most promising example is at Marchey Farm in Wookey parish. The site which takes its name from a chapel there dedicated to St Martin produced Romano-British, Anglo-Saxon, medieval and modern pottery from ditch cleaning and some Romano-British pottery from under the floor of the farmhouse (Ellis 1978, 107–8). The survival factor here was probably the isolated nature of the tiny settlement, in the marshes of the Levels in the Axe valley, and the very real possibility that it was the site of a very early church. What is not at all obvious, in general, however, is how we make the jump from the sixth century to the seventh and the eighth. Since there is no pottery recognisable between the fifth or perhaps the sixth century and the end of the ninth and beginning of the tenth century it would be possible to argue that the site was abandoned and reoccupied. Even the documentary evidence for the antiquity of the name and perhaps the site is shaky (Abrams 1996, 165).

This is the point at which to introduce the problem of 'wics'. This is a place-name element which is not uncommon in the Somerset landscape. Its meaning has been exhaustively examined, with Smith (1970) needing six and a half pages to categorise it. Dr Margaret Gelling first studied a special case of 'wics' when she wrote about *wichams*, showing that they were closely related to the Roman settlement pattern (Gelling 1967) and re-visited the subject ten years later (Gelling 1977). More recently another scholar, Richard Coates, has produced an elegant and insightful examination of the element (Coates 1999). His conclusions are complex, but he shows that there is running through the many uses of the word a sense of 'dependency'. Other scholars have seen it as describing dependencies such as outlying dairy farms (Hooke 1998, 134). However, Simon Draper, writing about Wiltshire, has tried to establish that *wic,* either as a simplex or in compound forms, can have a relationship to the Roman landscape (Draper 2002, 37–44). Writing in 1992 I suggested that there was a statistical relationship between *wic* sites, and villa sites. I contrasted an examination of 61 *wic* sites in Somerset, of which 45 can be identified, with a large number of 'tun' sites, also from the county (Fig. 3.3).

> The mean distance between villa sites and *wics* is 3.46 kilometres and the mean distance between a large (134) sample of *tun* settlements (place names ending in OE 'tun') is 5.73 kilometres. The difference between the two means was 2.245 kilometres and the standard error of difference was 0.68. There is a less than 1 per cent probability that this difference is random (Costen 1992, 66).

To say that the difference is not random is not to say that there is necessarily a causal link between *wic* sites and Roman villa sites. It might be that there was a very strong tendency to place dependent settlement sites in the same areas as lost Roman villa sites, or that *wics* are concentrated in the same parts of Somerset as the villas. However, it may be that *wics* are survivals from a pattern of settlement from which the villas were absent as a result of their collapse in the late fourth/early fifth centuries. The implication is that they were recognised by the newcomers in the mid-seventh century as part of the existing landscape and that the sense of dependency which the element clearly has, was an appropriate term for settlements which were those of the now subject population. They may also

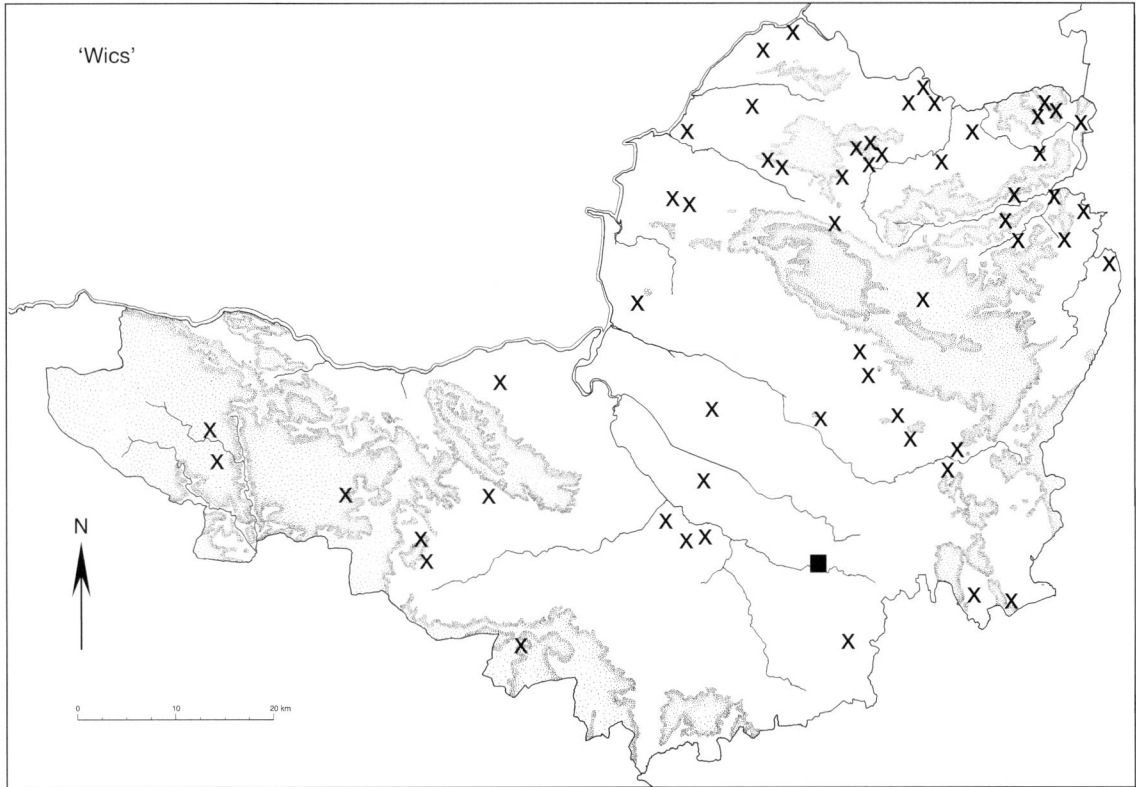

Figure 3.3. Distribution of 'wics' *in Somerset.*

have been regarded as dependent in a new and much more hierarchical landscape introduced by the Anglo-Saxons. Such a post-Roman pattern does not demand that the *wics* be all of Roman origin, but rather that they were part of the post-Roman landscape, so that some may have had Roman or even earlier origins while others may have arisen in the post-Roman period as a result of the continuance of a particular pattern of settlement. Their survival is likely to have been the result of continuing agricultural relevance. The way to finally settle the question will be a detailed archaeological examination of a number of sites, both at deserted sites, as at Sladwick in Shapwick (above) and at farms and hamlets still active.

Some further evidence about the nature of settlements in the late post-Roman period might also be provided by two places which have Old Welsh names. Tarnock in 1066 consisted of two 1 hide

holdings, each with land for 2½ ploughs. In 1086 one holding was farmed directly by its tenant and the other had only one villager and two smallholders (DB 24, 12–13). Tarnock, in Biddisham parish, is low-lying and marshy and must have been primarily a cattle raising settlement. Winterhead was a similar 1 hide unit in 1066. It belonged to Glastonbury Abbey and was tenanted. Here too the land for ploughs (probably an estimate of its arable capacity) was two. It had no demesne and seems to have been entirely cultivated by the peasants who lived there – two villagers, two smallholders and two slaves. This estate had access to the Mendip hills nearby and was probably mostly concerned with cattle and sheep raising (DB 5, 12). There are probably many other small settlements of this type where continuity is no longer recognisable because their names have become anglicised.

Simon Draper has also suggested that there

might be a connection between settlements containing the element *wealh*, 'a Welshman', and the Roman landscape. He examined 'waltons', the *tun* of the Welshman or men (Draper 2002, 37–44). Unfortunately all the Waltons in Somerset are either from the OE *weall*, 'a wall' or *weald*, a 'woodland'. This is certainly the case for Walton near Glastonbury, Walton-in-Gordano, and Walton near Kilmersdon (Ekwall 1960) and probably applies also to a lost Walton in Drayton. However, the three '*walcots*' (the cot of the Welshman or men) are more promising. The Walcot now in Bath, but originally just outside the northern gate, is a good candidate as are the lost *walcot(t)s* in Banwell (t. 439–40 and 1443) and in West Harptree (t. 209). At Banwell the 'w*alcott*' is inside the large estate with extensive Roman settlement and at West Harptree the '*walcot*' is close to the very large post-Roman cemetery. The place-name is of course English, but it described a minor settlement, a 'cot', which may well have been owned or tenanted by a Welsh speaker, perhaps in the seventh century. Such a settlement would certainly be a candidate for continuity from the post-Roman period.

Finally there is the evidence from Church Field at Shapwick. Here a timber building has been dated as being constructed in the period 540–760 (95% probability) and continuing in existence to 810–980 (95% probability) (Gerrard and Aston 2007, 418–420). This building may have been constructed just before the point at which Anglo-Saxon rule began and have continued in use until the later ninth or early tenth centuries. Its survival as archaeology is probably due to the abandonment of the whole church site in the early fourteenth century and it may be that other similar buildings lie under modern villages. It is not possible to say if this was connected with the church here, but it was almost certainly a dwelling site. If it was, as appears, an isolated building, rather than part of a larger settlement, it may represent part of a landscape of isolated farmsteads and hamlets.

The conclusion, then, is that the late post-Roman landscape was not tightly organised. Some major post-Roman sites, such as Banwell or Cannington, may have retained a large degree of organisation in the countryside round about, but over much of the county the landscape was much more loosely tied together in a mosaic of small settlements. The

implication, as we have already seen, is that by the early seventh century, society itself was rather loosely structured, with a lack of any real central authority and no rigid hierarchy. That is not to suggest that there were no nobles, warriors, peasants or slaves; merely that groupings were small and connections local and probably not particularly systematic and that social ties were not rigid. In addition, if the pandemic of plague and the reversion to a subsistence economy combined to keep the population quite small, we might expect settlements to be small and for many in existence in the later fourth century to fail or to shrink. New settlement would have been influenced by changes in agricultural practice as well as new social structures, such as those caused by ecclesiastical development. It is noticeable that what evidence there is for these centuries often occurs at or near places which were important centres in the Anglo-Saxon period, so that some element of continuity is implied. However, simple lack of physical evidence makes further analysis simply speculation.

The Anglo-Saxons

The problem which confronts us in trying to determine the pattern of landholding and the form that the holdings took in the mid-to-late seventh century and through into the early eighth is how to explain the transition from the Old Welsh to the Old English. One way of dealing with this problem has been to posit the existence of large regions of authority which passed into Anglo-Saxon hands to be resurrected as 'multiple estates' and this has certainly been an approach used in the past. The issues of transition and early Anglo-Saxon administration are not, however, necessarily linked. I think we can see evidence of very large areas of lordship and control, some of which may have roots in a post-Roman organisation of the landscape, but others may be better understood as re-organisation as the result of a much more authoritarian and hierarchical social structure introduced by the kings of Wessex and their followers.

In the mid-seventh century and beyond, under the authority of the kings of Wessex, Cannington became a royal ecclesiastical estate (Fig. 3.4). In a later chapter it will be argued more fully that these great estates, of which Cannington is only one example, should not be regarded as either 'royal' or 'ecclesiastical', but as a mixture of the two – estates with a major religious community at their centre which was under the patronage and control of the king and was used by him as a local political centre of control and as an economic resource when he was in the area. It is likely that as the churches lost influence in the face of the emergency and danger caused by the Viking attacks of the ninth century, the military priorities of the kings and their followers placed the control of these estates more fully in the king's hands.

This was certainly true in the time of King Alfred when Cannington was mentioned in his will (Keynes and Lapdige 1983, 175) and was still royal land in 1066 (DB 1.6). Burials at the Cannington post-Roman cemetery ceased during the seventh century, which strongly suggests that the change of political and religious authority with the coming of

the Anglo-Saxon kings was marked by a transfer of the overlordship of the area to the kings themselves and the transfer of religious activity to the new site, close to the present village and centred at the present church site. The church at Cannington, dedicated to the Blessed Virgin, replaced the cult centre at the old cemetery and became the seat of authority. Possession of land is normally a sign of the importance of a church and St Mary's at Cannington had lands, though the full extent is unknown, at the time of the Domesday survey when Erchenger the priest held 2½ virgates in the lands of Cannington church (DB 16,6). The settlement itself, with the church, lies within 2 km of the hill-fort and its associated post-Roman graveyard. The choice of the site for both the church and the royal centre is not a coincidence. The kings of Wessex were making an 'ideological statement' when they formed their new centre (Turner 2006, 113).

Early forms of the place-name 'Cannington' show

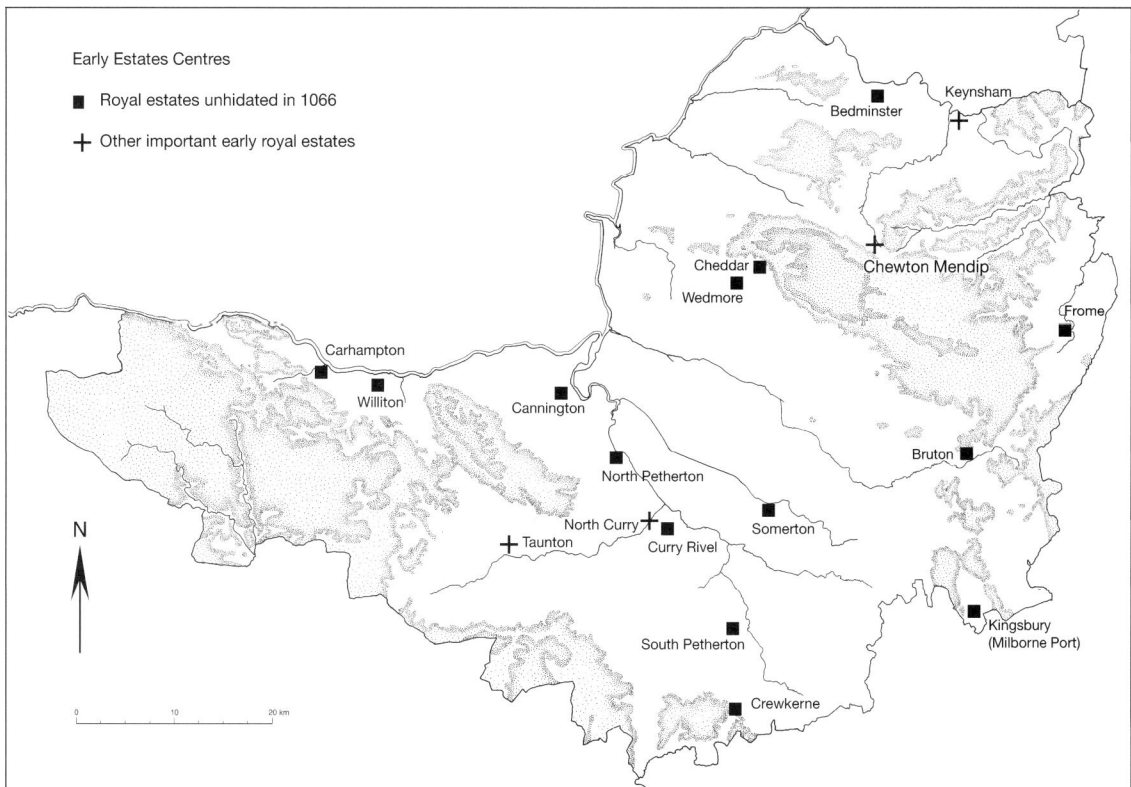

Figure 3.4. Early Anglo-Saxon estate centres.

that it is derived from the form *cantuctun*, meaning 'Quantock tun' (S1507, King Alfred's Will, AD 873–888). 'Cantuc' is in turn a word from an Old Welsh source and may have the meaning 'an edge, or a border'. This would certainly be an appropriate way of describing the Quantock Hills, which do cut off the Cannington area from the countryside to the south, while the Parrett does the same to the north. Cannington is one of a group of early names given by the Anglo-Saxons to their new settlement centres in Somerset, all of which use the names of rivers or other features to locate them (see below). The estate centre at Cannington is therefore to be regarded as a successor to some earlier centre, rather than an actual continuation, a new beginning under a new regime.

At the time of the Domesday Book Cannington was linked with Williton and Carhampton to produce a combined estate of 100 ploughlands (DB 1.6). This was a highly artificial grouping which leaves no way of knowing how large Cannington was, but it might be possible to tentatively reconstruct the early estate around Cannington, using the Domesday Book as a starting point. In 1066 the Cannington hundred contained about 50 hides (DB). This hidage was divided between 48 different holdings, most of which were very small and often represent the sub-division of already tiny units. The place-names often suggest that the holdings were small and the result of clearance activity. Rexworthy contains a *wyrth* element, normally associated with small settlements or individual farmsteads. It was only taxed as a 1 virgate (a ¼ hide) unit (DB 21.11). Beere, probably Old English *bær,* 'woodland pasture', was also an estate of 1 virgate (DB 16.8). The largest estates were Stogursey with 4½ hides, Stockland with 4¼ hides and Fiddington with 4 hides (DB 27.1, 25.1, 22.8). There were eight estates of 1 hide only and eleven of 1 virgate only. Some estates had been split. Combwich had been divided into two 1½ hide estates and Chilton Trivett into two half hide estates (DB 17.2, 32.1 and 21.10, 46.12). Stockland was divided into three parts which had originally totalled 8¾ hides (DB 21.26, 25.1, 31.1). The divisions were probably the result of the need to provide land for followers and clearly took place well after the settlements themselves had formed and received their names, but other

settlements, such as Swang, earlier *suindune*, 'pig hill', or Gothelney, earlier *godelege*, 'Goda's wood', were small settlements, often not more than individual farmsteads. Cannington had also lost small parts of the estate, a half hide unit and 2½ virgates (DB 16.3 and 46.9). The remaining part of Cannington itself was only a small core of what was once a much bigger jurisdiction.

The ancient, though post-Conquest, parish boundaries show that Cannington itself was not a self-contained unit. There were five holdings belonging to Cannington inside Otterhampton. Stockland Bristol had five plots inside Otterhampton. Charlynch included a large detached portion containing the Domesday estates of Currypool and Swang cut off by Spaxton. Spaxton in turn included a large area between Fiddington and Stogursey. A further complication was that Nether Stowey, in Williton and Freemanors Hundred, held two enclaves inside Spaxton (Fig. 3.5). The most likely explanation of these detached portions is that they represent assets awarded to estates as they were released from inside the main estate, or new land reclaimed from marshland which was not allocated to any of the dependent settlements of Cannington, but retained as part of the central estate.

The hundred also includes a number of '*stoc*' names. These are Stogursey, Stockland and Edstock. A '*stoc*' could be either a religious site, or a dependent settlement (Smith 1970, II, 153–4). Stogursey, post-Conquest, was the site of a priory founded between 1100 and 1107 by William de Falaise and his wife Geva (Dunning 1992, 142). It is noticeable that priories were founded at many sites which were collegiate churches prior to the Conquest and so it is possible that Stogursey was one such. It was certainly important enough to have a dependent chapel at Lilstock (Dunning 1992, 154). Stogursey could be either a religious site of pre-Conquest origin or a secular site, but in either case a dependency of Cannington. Stockland was a substantial estate, but may have been a dependency in its turn of Stogursey, while Edstock was a small estate with a personal name attached to it, 'Icca's stoc'.

There are also a number of place-names of the form '*personal-name + tun*'. As we shall see in more detail later, this type of name is associated with late,

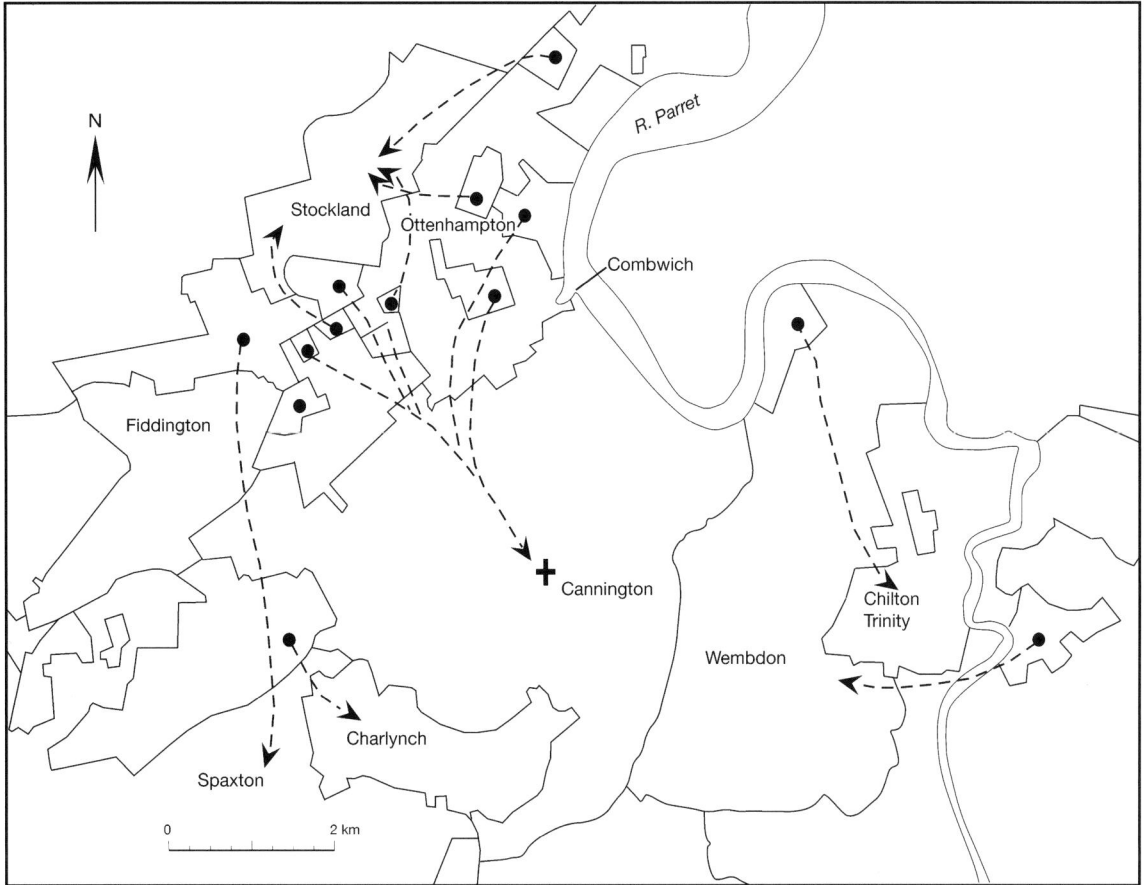

Figure 3.5. A simplified plan of Cannington and the surrounding settlements.

probably later ninth and tenth century estates. In some cases these may have been newly formed, in others existing estates were permanently alienated and took the name of their new owner. Woolston, Stringston and Spaxton are certainly of this type. Fiddington is a place name of the type '*personal-name + ing + tun*' and may have been an early alienation. Spaxton is certainly late, since the personal name, 'Spakr' is Norse and so likely to post-date the influx of Danish noble-men under King Cnut at the beginning of the eleventh century.

It seems possible therefore that the early estate core contained at least the lands in the Cannington hundred, since so many of them are linked to Cannington, either through physical inter-

relationships or through place-name patterns. In its earliest phases the estate may have consisted of no more than the central area around Cannington church with outlying tributary 'stocs' and individual farmsteads, many of which survive to the present day. The 'tun' settlements represent 'infill' growth of population and settlement in the later Anglo-Saxon period, so that the estate assumed its Domesday appearance quite late.

Other similar regions may have existed around the coast. Banwell too was the centre of a great estate and in this case, although we do not as yet have evidence of a hill-fort with high status dark-age imports, there was a substantial Roman building close to the present church site, and we have seen that there was a post-Roman cemetery and substantial Roman buildings at Winthill, about a kilometre from the present village. Banwell was a very large Domesday estate and it probably included Weston-super-Mare, which lies just to the west, but has no separate existence in 1086 and hence no Domesday Book entry (DB 6.9). 'West', 'north', 'south' and 'east' *tuns* were usually dependent settlements, named from their geographical relationship to their central place. Christon, Puxton, St Georges, called *Puttingthrop* in the Middle Ages, Churchill (DB 6.9 and see note p. 354) and Sandford, now part of Winscombe, were all included within Banwell at an early date (Aston and Costen 2008, 139–58). There may also have been a connection with Kewstoke, to the north-west. There was intercommoning between Kewstoke and Banwell in the Middle Ages as evidenced by the ancient parish boundaries (Kain and Oliver 2001). In addition, the Domesday Book records that Banwell had woodland of more than six square miles. It is hard to imagine where this lay, although it did not need to be in one block alone. It may have included woodland in Churchill and Christon as well as in Banwell itself.

Kewstoke is one of a group of -*stoc* place-names in the Mendip region. Eilart Ekwall studied the place-name element in great detail (1936, 11–43). He demonstrated that the element has a very varied and flexible history. It could mean 'monastery' or 'cell', 'city' or 'town'. Another meaning might be 'a meeting place' and finally, a 'dependent settlement', possibly an 'outlying cattle-farm'. He also suggested that the name was in use at an early date, since it occurs in documents of the eighth century. Dr John Blair has suggested that many of the -*stow*,[2] -*ciric* and -*burh* place-names reflect a dependent site, and that they may often be monastic dependencies such as hermitages (2005, 216–7). Professor Pearce also suggested that some -*stoc* names might sometimes have been used to replace a 'lost British name of an establishment in existence in the sixth century' (Pearce 1978, 74). It may be that some of the -*stoc* names in the region denoted a similar status, or were dependent religious sites. The place-name Kewstoke, with the meaning 'St Kew's (holy) place', might suggest a hermitage of the Old Welsh period. There have been suggestions that the church stands close to a well-site which may have had religious or ritual uses, which would further strengthen this possibility, and a sub-oval enclosure around the church site may also point to the possibility of a *llan* or early cemetery site (Calder 2002, 10). Banwell would have been a religious site with the settlements round about controlled by its *monasterium*.

Just to the north of Banwell lies Congresbury. We have already seen how important it was in the post-Roman period and it would be odd indeed if it were not at the centre of a large territory. A model proposed by Professor Aston (personal comment) would have a church site develop on the hill-fort after the site ceased to be used as a military or aristocratic high status site – that might have been in the later part of the sixth century or early seventh century. It would be at this time that the connection with Cyngar was established, but the place-name itself is an English coining and so likely to be about or just after the mid-seventh century, which is when the English arrived here, although the first reference to the name is by Asser in the later ninth century (Keynes and Lapidge, 1983, 97). The land surrounding the hill-fort may comprise its *regio*, part of which we see as Congresbury Parish, perhaps with the addition of Wick St Lawrence, which was not recorded in Domesday Book and which was a chapelry of Congresbury in the Middle Ages (Hobhouse 1887, vol. 1, 251), and possibly with Yatton and its dependencies also. The hill-fort is situated on the boundary between Yatton and Congresbury, as if it had been used as an important boundary marker, while the temple on Henley Hill, surely connected with the hill-fort, lies in Yatton. In 1086 Congresbury and Wick formed the lands originally belonging to the *monasterium*. Political manoeuvring by Earl Harold Godwinson had removed the lands from church control, but Congresbury and Wick remained the remnant of the estate which it once controlled (Oakes and Costen 2003). It seems to offer an example of an estate whose origins lie in the post-Roman period, the core of which may have survived because of its continuation as the lands of a long-lived and conservative church. Yatton, probably detached at a very early date, remained an important place with 20 hides at Domesday in the possession of the bishop of Wells (DB 6.14). In 1086, Wemberham was described as a pasture, belonged to Yatton, but had previously been a part of Congresbury, despite lying on the northern side of the river Yeo, reinforcing the possibility that there had been strong links between the two places (DB 6.14). In 1066 Yatton was held by John the Dane, possibly on a lease, and it may be that it was left to the bishop after Harold's seizure of Congresbury.

Other places with a claim to be central to a region in the post-Roman period would include Portbury and Carhampton. In the case of Portbury the place-name may be important. As with nearby Portishead the first element is the Old English *port*, a 'port', from the Latin '*portus*' (Gelling 1977). The use of the word would indicate recognisable commercial activity when the Anglo-Saxons arrived, or in the period before their take-over, when the geography of the region was probably well known. Stephen Rippon has suggested that it lay at the centre of a *regio* which embraced Portishead, Clapton-in-Gordano, Easton-in-Gordano, Walton-in-Gordano, Weston-in-Gordano, Abbots Leigh, Wraxall, Nailsea, Flax Bourton, Backwell, Tickenham and Clevedon (Rippon 2006, 127–30).

At Carhampton the signs of a monastic community may also suggest that there was a substantial estate there supporting the church. In 1066 Carhampton was included with Cannington and Williton for administrative purposes in a unit which was unhidated but assessed at 100 ploughlands (DB 1.6). There are indications that the earlier Carhampton had strong links with other, more minor estates. Oare (DB 30.2) and Allerford (DB 32.4) were both 1 hide estates in 1066 and each owed a customary due of 12 sheep to Carhampton. Rodhuish, to the south, was a large detached portion of the parish, but was a separate Domesday estate which was assessed at 1 virgate only (DB 35.15). It later had a chapel attached to St John's Church in Carhampton. In addition there were two small detached portions of Carhampton parish, Knowle and Totterdown, inside Dunster (D/D/Rt/M/277). A part of Rodhuish Common lies in Withycombe parish, and this may be a sign of the lateness of defined boundaries in this unenclosed landscape. Carhampton at an early date probably consisted of the estate centre on the low ground at the coast, surrounded by satellite settlements in favourable valleys on the moor to the south and the

west. It may well have included other settlements beyond those now identifiable as a part of the *regio*.

These regions may be distinctive because they were strung along the coast, where the wealth and possibly the political power had accumulated in the post-Roman period. It is impossible to do more than speculate about the extent of the territory controlled from these places. It is possible that other great regions existed in the interior, but there is even less evidence to support what must be, by any standard, a flimsy case.

Analysis of the development of early landscapes which relies upon ideas of 'multiple estates', that is important centres with wide lands around them, which then are broken up into smaller units, has recently lost ground (Hadley 1996; Lewis *et al.* 1997). I do not intend to argue for the existence of large multiple estates in Somerset, but I do want to stress the real possibility of the existence of large areas of jurisdiction which were organised around the needs of a powerful central authority, whether secular or ecclesiastical, although later I shall put forward the view that we would do best not to draw too sharp a distinction between the two. The idea that such large jurisdictions might be 'planned' in some sense is clearly possible. Charlotte Fabech, writing about Scandinavian settlements, alludes to the Icelandic Sagas and describes an expedition to Iceland to settle. The hero builds a farm on a high point and calls it Borg (meaning 'a hill') and settles his foremost follower opposite, on the other side of the fiord. Six other followers are granted farmsteads around the lord. He also creates five 'production units' each of which is devoted to a different speciality, stock rearing, fishing, hunting and iron-work (Fabech 1999, 42). We are thus presented with an idealised view emanating from the Scandinavian world of how a great man's estate should be organised. It is laid out to display status, but it also is founded upon the exploitation of resources which will support the particular needs of the aristocratic group. It depicts an ideal situation without pre-existing landscapes and the competing power structures actually in place. It is a literary conceit but it illustrates the mentality behind the real great estates of the seventh and eighth centuries. It does not seem possible, except in the cases outlined above, to see a large degree of continuity at a high level between the major settlements of the

Anglo-Saxon period and the post-Roman world. Thus it is not possible to regard the Cannington estate as a direct descendant of a post-Roman estate. What is possible, however, is to argue that it is not a co-incidence that in at least two cases, Cannington and Carhampton, and possibly at others, the centre of the estate was based close to sites of significance in the post-Roman polity. It would be most useful to think of the minor settlements as carrying the largest element of continuity between the post-Roman and the Anglo-Saxon landscapes. It was probably the peasantry who felt the impact of the Anglo-Saxon conquest least.

Royal centres

We may find surer ground if we look at the important centres of Anglo-Saxon royal power in the later seventh century, without trying to link them too closely with the pre-seventh century. Among the estates named in the Domesday Book as belonging to the king was a group which had never been hidated – rated for tribute. Some of them had appeared in King Alfred's Will; Cannington, Carhampton, and Wedmore and Cheddar (these two were almost certainly regarded as parts of one estate) (Keynes and Lapidge 1983, 175–7). In 1066 the king also had unhidated land at Cannington, Williton, Bruton, Frome, Crewkerne, South Petherton, North Petherton, Somerton, Curry (Rivel), Bedminster and Milborne Port (DB 1.1–10.20). The lack of hidation strongly suggests that these lands had been possessions of the kings of Wessex since the seventh century and represented land which had never been alienated to noblemen as loan-land, probably because of their ecclesiastical connections. However we need to be careful not to assume that because these lands were taken and held by the kings or their representatives at an early date, that this means that they were already integrated estates. That may be to transfer back onto the post-Roman landscape a large scale organisation which it did not have, but which was appropriate to the more highly structured English society. The apparent centralisation at Cannington, signalled by the large cemetery, may relate to the religious landscape, rather than the secular.

Some of the king's estates have names which

suggest a pattern; they are names which consist of a simple topographical element with the addition of '*tun*', meaning farmstead, settlement. These were 'royal settlements' or 'vills', they were estates which on one interpretation, the king used himself and from which he might draw supplies and revenue and in some cases where he might have a residence (Sawyer 1983, 273–299). Certainly the king had a documented association with some of them – Somerton (ASC 'A', 733) and Taunton for example (ASC 'A', 722). The topographical element is often a river name. Thus Bruton is the '*tun*' on the Brue; Williton the '*tun*' on the Willett; North and South Petherton are both on the Parrett; Chewton is the '*tun*' on the Chew, this was a royal manor in 1066, but had been hidated (DB 1.29). This pattern is continued by estates which were not royal in 1066. The best known is Taunton – the '*tun*' on the Tone. The Anglo-Saxon Chronicle attributes the founding of this estate to King Ine (ASC 'A' 722). The two Pethertons, North and South were large unhidated royal estates (DB 1.3–4). Ilton, on the river Isle, was a possession of Athelney Abbey in 1066 (DB 10.1) and was an 8 hide estate. Athelney was King Alfred's foundation, so it is probable that he gave them the land from his own resources in the later ninth century. Camerton, the '*tun*' on the river Camelar, was a substantial estate of 10 hides, but it had come to the Glastonbury abbey as an exchange with the Count of Mortain for Tintinhull after 1066 (DB 8.31). In 1066 it had belonged to Eadmer Ator, an important thegn with extensive holdings in Somerset. Wrington, on the river Wring, was a 20 hide estate belonging to Glastonbury Abbey in 1066 (DB 8.27). It may have come to Glastonbury via the Ealdorman Æthelstan when he entered the monastery as a monk, but it was certainly in the possession of his family in 904 when King Edward the Elder is said to have re-issued their charter for Wrington because the previous charter had been destroyed by fire (Abrams 1996, 254–256).

Another group contains other topographical elements. Cannington has already been discussed, but not far away was Kilton, Old English, possibly *cylfa*, 'a knob shaped hill' + *tun* (Ekwall 1960 and Watts *et al.* 2004). King Alfred left Kilton to his eldest son, Edward (Keynes and Lapidge 1983, 175), but by 1066 it had been granted away and was held as two manors which together paid tax of 10½ hides (DB 25.30). Carhampton, another unhidated estate, means the *tun* at *carrum,* 'the rocks' (Ekwall 1960 and Watts *et al.* 2004).

Names which consist of a river name *alone* form an important group of estates, all of which are likely to have started as major royal assets. Doulting, Curry, Frome and Chew Magna are of this type. Doulting seems to have been the early name of the great estate at Pilton, though Dr Lesley Abrams has shown that there is probably confusion and deception involved in its charter (1996, 112–14). The name presented may apply either to Doulting or to Pilton, but it consists of the early name for the river Sheppey, *Duluting*. We are on firmer ground with Frome, which was an unhidated royal estate in 1066 (DB 1.8) as was Curry (Rivel) (DB 1.5). Chew was a large estate of 30 hides (DB 6.13) which belonged to the Bishop at Wells, but had probably belonged earlier to the bishop of Sherborne (see below, Chapter 10). The grant had clearly come from the kings of Wessex at an early date, probably in the early eighth century and again is a simple river name, although its current name 'Chew Magna' is clearly intended to distinguish it from its neighbour, Chewton.

Finally there is a group of miscellaneous names, Crewkerne 'the barn on the hillside', Somerton, 'the *tun* used as a transhumance centre', or possibly 'the *tun* used as a summer residence'. Both these places were unhidated royal ancient demesne and both were large estates (DB 1.1 and 20). Cheddar has a name of very obscure origin, while Milborne Port is a late name, related to the tenth century *burh*, but the earlier name for the estate seems to have been Kingsbury, 'the king's fortified residence'.

Only two of the royal or possibly royal estates have personal names as an element; Bedminster, 'the monasterium of Bedæ', and Keynsham, which is *Cægin's hamm*, 'the enclosure belonging to *Cægin*'. All the others have names which are impersonal in their construction. This would seem to point to their deliberate foundation as royal centres in the seventh century. In some cases it is possible to suggest that they were founded inside an ancient post-Roman estate but on a new site. Bruton would certainly seem to be an example of this procedure. There are strong arguments for seeing this foundation and

others of a similar nature as centres dominated by early *monasteria* (Blair 2005). This view of these 'central places' will be discussed later, but for the present purpose it is enough to note this possibility. It does not preclude their use as royal centres also. Bruton lies close to the hill-top late Roman temple and the post-Roman cemetery site at Lamyatt Beacon and it is clear that an ancient road, which runs from south-west to north-east, crossing the eastern flank of Lamyatt Beacon and continuing towards Frome, was diverted to serve the new site. The size of primitive Bruton is difficult to determine, but must have included Brewham, 'the enclosure on the Brue', as well as Ditcheat. In 1066 Ditcheat was Glastonbury Abbey property (DB 8.30) and this 30 hide estate included the later estates of Lamyatt (within which the Beacon stands), and Hornblotton. This last place was 'the *tun* of the horn-blower'. It may be that this was an estate granted to the man who led the king's hunts in the Selwood forest, which covered much of Brewham and extended from Frome in the north as far as Gillingham in Dorset in the south. Ditcheat was granted by King Æthelwulf to his *princeps*, Eanwulf in 842 (S292). A lost charter of 855 X 860 may record the grant of Hornblotton to the same man by king Æthelbald (S1699). As with all Glastonbury lands, nothing is ever straightforward. The grant of 30 hides included the settlement at Lottisham, on the western side of the Fosse Way. In the Middle Ages Lottisham was never a parish, but always part of the parish of Ditcheat. In the charter S292 both Ditcheat and Lottisham have boundary clauses (Figs 3.6 and 3.7). That for Ditcheat is solvable (Costen 1988, 46–7) and shows that Ditcheat included Alhampton. (The clause for Lottisham, however, has not yet been elucidated). Domesday Ditcheat is a much more complicated affair. The *Liber Terrarum* records a grant of Lamyatt by King Eadwig to Cynric (S1756). There is no indication of how it may have come to Glastonbury, but it was presumably a gift along with its now lost charter. These estates were included inside the Domesday Ditcheat, which was still said to contain 30 hides. Cutting the Gordian knot might involve the surmise that Glastonbury simply placed these extra estates inside Ditcheat and thereby reduced its tax burden. Such duplicity does not affect the idea that the estates thus covered came from the king's stock

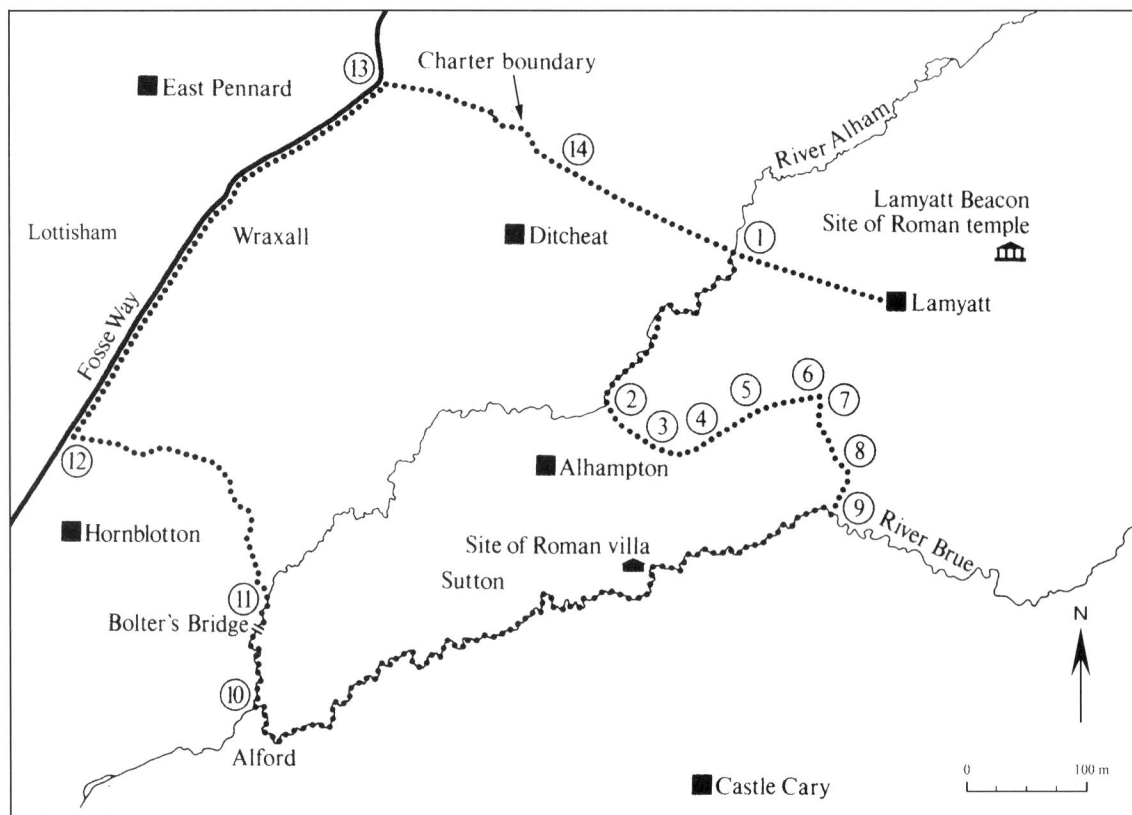

Figure 3.6. Ditcheat and its charter. The numbers indicate points on the boundary identified from the charter.

of land surrounding his royal vill at Bruton. A more conservative view would see the surviving medieval parish of Bruton, which embraced the chapelries of Wyke Champflower and Pitcombe, as the early estate.

To argue for a large estate with significant assets is not to deny the existence of many smaller units within the estate and neither does it follow that the Anglo-Saxon estate replicates the patterns of settlement and organisation which existed prior to the mid-seventh century. It may be that an important site – important perhaps because of the status of its previous Old Welsh owner; important because as befitted a '*potens*' the estate was large and productive; important because it represented a site of traditional high status in the local landscape, linked perhaps to a temple and then a Christian site of significance – was a natural place for the new ruler to appropriate. He may then have enlarged his estate by gathering control over other smaller settlements round about, reordering and redirecting them to fit the hierarchical structure of the newly emerged Anglo-Saxon kingdom of Wessex.

Other vills may also have been included in the royal estate, but identifying them is more difficult. Names which indicate an activity, rather than ownership, may be part of this extended estate system. Shepton Montague, south of Bruton, has a name which simply means 'sheep tun'. This may indicate that it was a settlement which specialised in sheep production for the royal centre, or perhaps that it paid tribute in sheep. Added to Shepton Montague after 1066 was Stoney Stoke (DB 19.57). As noted with the Cannington example the name indicates it was a dependent unit, probably of Bruton. 'Charltons' have already been mentioned above and there is an

Figure 3.7. Bolter's Bridge. This medieval 'packhorse' bridge is at the spot where the Anglo-Saxon charter speaks of 'Bola's tree', which probably means 'Bola's gallows' and refers to a gallows belonging to this man. It stood beside a road or path where passers-by would see the bodies of malefactors hanging.

example not far from Bruton – Charlton Musgrove, a 5 hide estate in 1066 (DB 33.1). If Brewham was included in the Bruton estate in the seventh century, then it is likely that Witham (later Witham Friary) should also be included, since it was described as within Brewham before 1066 (DB 21.90). The settlements of Brewham, Pitcombe, Redlynch and Wyke Champflower were all chapelries of Bruton in the later Middle Ages. Pitcombe was a separate 5 hide manor in 1066, but the entry shows that it had a strong connection with Bruton, since it controlled eleven burgesses in the borough of Bruton (DB 36.1). Its chapel was dedicated to St Leonard, suggesting that it was a post-Norman foundation, since St Leonard, often associated with hunting and the forest environment, though much more the patron of prisoners, did not really become popular

in England until after the First Crusade (Farmer 1987, 264). Redlynch and Wyke Champflower do not appear in the Domesday Book and so are almost certainly included inside Bruton.

This tentative reconstruction involves a large area, but its borders are impossible to define. This is true for other groupings also. Dr Corcos has argued that Chew Magna, in the north of the county, stands out as another possible large estate which was dismembered. Together with its neighbour Chewton Mendip it makes a fairly coherent unit (Corcos 2002, 50–8). Chew Magna was a large manor of 30 hides, with land for 50 ploughs in 1086 (DB 6.3). It had probably been an endowment of the church at Wells from its foundation in AD 909 and a property of Sherborne before that (O'Donovan 1988, xxxvi–xlvii). It is of course named after the river on which it stands. This name has not been satisfactorily explained. Within the manor, and almost certainly a part of the pre-Domesday settlement, lay Stoke, now Chew Stoke, already broken up into smaller dependent units by 1066 (DB 3.3–4, 47, 16). This dependency may also have been the site of a subsidiary religious settlement. The whole estate probably came to Aldhelm, bishop at Sherborne, from the West Saxon kings at the foundation of his diocese 'West of the Wood' in c. AD 705. Chew Stoke is the site of the famous Pagans Hill Temple, parts of which were visible above ground into the modern era and which must have stood as substantial ruins in the sixth and seventh centuries. Here there is evidence of activity into the fifth century. Chew Stoke was also the site of a Roman villa. It has produced evidence of contact with the Anglo-Saxon world in the blue glass jars which have been dated to the early seventh century, before the Anglo-Saxon take-over of the area (Wooding, 1996, 87–8). The large post-Roman cemetery at West Harptree may also be connected with this estate. Chewton Mendip stands out as a royal estate with a church endowed with land in 1086 (DB 1.29) which became the mother church for a group of nearby parishes; Emborough, Ston Easton, Farrington Gurney and Paulton, as well as chapels at Hallatrow and Easton Minor. It is possible that here the royal tun was founded as a substitute centre to replace the site at Chew which had been granted to the church.

Centrally placed in the shire is Somerton. As noted earlier it was mentioned in the Anglo-Saxon Chronicle as having been captured by King Æthelbald of Mercia (ASC 'A', 733). It was the first of the royal lands to be enumerated in Domesday Book and was clearly regarded as a major administrative centre (DB 1.1). Somerset is the 'shire of the dwellers around Somerton'. It was a large agricultural settlement with land for 50 ploughs and it included the *burh* of Langport. The manor of Kingsdon, to the south-east of Somerton, is not included in the Domesday survey and probably lay in Somerton at this time. On the western side, the estate at Huish Episcopi was claimed by the bishop of Wells and his lands were set out in the charter S1042 of 1065. This document, which cannot be reconciled with the property detailed in the Domesday Book, has been accepted as a post-Conquest forgery. Simon Keynes has suggested that it

should be seen as part of the campaign by Bishop Giso to recover the lands which he believed the Church of St Andrew at Wells should rightly hold (Keynes 1997, 203–71). Huish was almost certainly part of the estate of Somerton therefore. Also on the western side of Somerton was the Glastonbury estate of High Ham. The monastery claimed to have received the land from King Edgar (S791 of 973), though it is by no means certain that the charter is genuine (Abrams 1996, 134–5). However, the estate probably did come from the royal fisc at some point. To the south the estate of Long Sutton had been given to the abbey of Athelney by King Alfred. The charter which is extant (S343) is unacceptable as it stands, but may be based on a genuine charter of the 870s (Keynes 1994b, 1134). In the Domesday Book Long Sutton clearly belonged to Athelney Abbey (DB 10.2 and 6). It is plausible that this was originally part of the Somerton estate and was granted away by King Alfred. Thus the whole of the 'island' of Somerton would seem to be the royal estate. Connected to it on the south-east is the estate of Charlton Mackrell/Adam, two estates which appear in Domesday Book, Charlton Mackrell being of 3 hides (DB 22.19) and Charlton Adam of 5 hides (19.43). Their lands were so intertwined that it is clear they were once a single unit, which was divided before the Norman Conquest. This 8 hide unit may fill a 'charlton' role for Somerton as suggested above at Frome and at Bruton. The Charlton estate brings the boundary of a 'Greater' Somerton up to the Fosse Way on the east, giving the whole unit clear boundaries with the marshes and rivers to north and south. On its boundary to the south lay Ilchester, an important junction on the old Roman road system and the site of the church of the estate at Northover, which was Somerton's mother church.

A rather different royal estate is revealed further south at 'Curry'. There were three estates called 'Curry' in 1066, North Curry, a royal estate of 20 hides including Stoke St Gregory, which was not otherwise surveyed (DB 1.19), Curry Rivel, a royal estate of ancient demesne (1.5), and Curry Mallet, two small 3½ hide estates in the hands of thegns in 1066 (DB 21.1–2). The two major estates stand on either side of a marsh which is now divided between the two. The place-name is a river name (Ekwall 1960) and is well attested in the tenth century (S455,

Places owing dues to Curry Rivel in 1066 (DB)
(those with interests in Curry Moor underlined)

Figure 3.8. Domesday Manors owing renders to Curry Rivel.

AD 934 X 9 and S352, AD 879). Domesday Book shows that a number of settlements in the area had close ties with one or both of the royal estates. There was a group which was connected to Curry Rivel by renders, of sheep and lambs or payments – Ashill (DB 19.18) 30 pence; Hatch Beauchamp (DB 19.29) a sheep and a lamb from one of the hides; Bradon (DB 19.17, 19.23, 19.25), four sheep and four lambs, Donyatt (DB 19.24), five sheep and five lambs; Bickenhall (DB 19.27) five sheep and five lambs (see Fig. 3.8). Another group was connected to Curry Rivel by including within its territory land which had belonged to Curry Rivel in 1066 – Capland contained half a hide which had been 'in' Curry Rivel (DB 47.5) and Swell had a virgate inside Curry Rivel (DB 19.15). Also connected with Curry Rivel was Drayton, an estate of the Abbey of Muchelney (DB 9.6), which had a detached portion of woodland inside Curry Rivel (Drayton tithe map). Earnshill (DB 21.71, 46.20) was an ecclesiastical dependency

of Curry Rivel in the later Middle Ages, suggesting an early close relationship.

A different group of estates had detached portions which lay in the marsh dividing North Curry and Curry Rivel. The largest portion of the marsh belonged to North Curry and Curry Mallet. Fivehead, Swell, Beercrocombe, Broadway and Buckland St Mary also had interests. The detached parcels each represent rights in the marsh, either for grazing or for reeds, osiers or peat (Fig. 3.9). Hatch Beauchamp had a detached parcel as well as owing a sheep and a lamb. Together these connections suggest that the Curry Rivel estate was once the centre of a much larger agglomeration which may have included Drayton before it was passed to the abbey of Muchelney.

Each of these royal or ecclesiastical centres was probably exploited as large demesnes, mostly worked by slaves and by families who were bound to the estate. Surrounding the central place was an array of minor settlements of varying sizes and ages, owing

Interests in Curry Moor as revealed by
detached parts of parishes

Figure 3.9. Domesday Manors with an interest in Curry Moor.

rents and services, but inhabited by a variety of people, ranging from members of the aristocracy, dependent upon the king, to peasant farmers of Welsh or English extraction.

Other important royal centres also existed at Chewton, Kingsbury Episcopi, Crewkerne, North and South Petherton, Williton and Kingsbury Regis (Milborne Port), but there was still room left for other land-holders. Some of them were important ecclesiastical institutions, but there was probably some room left early on for other lords to hold land as well as to receive it as loanland from the king. The growth of these great royal estates was part of the process by which the kings of Wessex gained a decisive superiority over their burgeoning aristocracy. Kings began to alienate land to laymen at an early date and the example of Beorhtric's grant of land at Wigferth (S267 of AD 794) and that by Egbert to Eadgils (S270a of AD 801) of land at Butleigh are probably lucky survivals of transactions revealed to

us when the land eventually ended up in the hands of a monastery which preserved the charter.

Somerset is very unusual in that a late ninth/early tenth century hall complex excavated at Cheddar can be regarded as a palace or hall site belonging to the kings of Wessex (Rahtz 1979). Cheddar was named in King Alfred's will when it was bequeathed to his son Edward (Keynes and Lapidge 1983, 173–8) and in 1066 it was still a royal manor and had never been hidated, suggesting it had been in royal hands for a long time. It was a regular stopping place for the kings of the tenth century (Hill 1981, 156–7, 160). It is likely that the site was chosen for meetings precisely because there were facilities for a large assembly of the king's followers. There were of course any number of other sites belonging to the king in Somerset in the tenth century: Somerton, Milborne Port, Crewkerne, Curry Rivel, Cannington, Williton. None have evidence of a palace or hall like Cheddar, despite the Eadred 'wearing his crown', a formal ceremony which would have been attended by a host of noblemen, at Somerton in 949 (Hill 1981, 158). The Cheddar site was very large but similar sites do not seem to exist on other estates. It seems likely that the kings of Wessex rarely visited these places in the tenth century, though they may have done so in the eighth and ninth. Cheddar palace must be evidence for the growing size of the royal court at the end of the ninth century as the Wessex kings became more important and their rule spread. Although the kings of the eighth and ninth centuries may have had halls on their estates it is also possible that they relied upon the minsters at these places for hospitality. As long as this practice continued the kings marked themselves off from other landowners through their close association with centres of spiritual power. They were, as lords, qualitatively different from other men. The king's retreat to a palace marked the beginning of a different relationship with his church, but also provided a new social and political focus. Other royal estates became increasingly removed from the king as an individual and became much more centres for the production of supplies or, increasingly, cash to meet the needs of the court. They were much more like the estates of other great landowners and like them were under pressure also, to provide for a burgeoning class of military retainers.

Planned settlements

By the tenth century it is clear that the proliferation of smaller estates, often formed by the sub-division of larger existing units, was becoming commonplace. Examples of such settlement creation include the Chinnocks, East, West and Middle, East and West Lydford, North and South Barrow, East and West Harptree (already mentioned above), Charlton Adam and Charlton Mackrell and the settlements on the Polden estate of Glastonbury Abbey, Shapwick, Catcott, Edington, Chilton Polden, Cossington and Woolavington (Costen 1991, 39–55). At the Lydfords, East Lydford belonged to Glastonbury Abbey in 1066 and was thegnland (DB 8.4). West Lydford was held by Brictric who was probably an outright owner (DB 4.21). It is clear from the arrangement of lands within the two manors that they had once been one unit (Costen 1991, 46–48).

Lydford as a single unit may have been part of the grant of 744 (S1410). It was probably the abbey which made the division of the estate into two parts in the tenth century. The great hill-fort of Cadbury Castle gave its name to both North and South Cadbury. By 1066 North Cadbury was the larger and more important settlement. It was a 12 hide estate held by Alfwold (DB 36.5). South Cadbury was also held by Alfwold (surnamed 'The Bald') in 1066 (DB 36.7) but was only a 3 virgate (¾ of a hide) estate. Another 2 hides and 1 virgate, un-named, had been added to it after 1066 and a hide at Woolston and 2 hides at Clapton had also been added to make a respectable estate. There is no indication of how South Cadbury came to be detached from North Cadbury, but it may have been intended as land for a retainer.

A much grander newly planted settlement was developed at Charlton Horethorne, just north of Milborne Port of which it was a subsidiary. The present village was planted in the midst of the ancient Iron-age and Roman landscape of dispersed settlement. A north/south alignment, which was an intrusion within the existing alignment of boundaries, marked the development of a double row settlement. Similar settlements at Abbotsbury, Stalbridge and Sturminster Newton in Dorset have been dated to the late Anglo-Saxon period, suggesting a likely date for the Charlton Horethorne village (Davey 2010)

Puxton near to Banwell was included in the Domesday description of that manor (DB 6.9). It was an ecclesiastical dependency of Banwell and probably included within the estate as it appears in the charter (Aston and Costen 2008). The name 'Puxton' is the 'tun of Puca', a typical formation of the tenth century. It is likely that Puxton represents a reclamation settlement in the marshes of the North Somerset coast. It seems to have begun as a small unit using an infield/outfield system of agriculture (Rippon 1997, 172–3). It was probably only one of several settlements of this kind on the marshes in this period and must owe its beginnings to the needs of the Bishop, the lord of Banwell, either for more income, or to provide for secular followers.

The creation of these settlements, complete with villages and open-field systems, was a response to the pressures upon the aristocracy, monastic institutions and the thegnage, both to produce means of support for warriors and to increase money incomes. Many of these estates seem to have been bookland properties, but we have no clear evidence of how so much land came to be bookland. Nor do we know how frequently the many small landowners had a charter which proved their status. Clearly some men had charters which have sometimes survived when the land in question was donated to a monastery. The history of Rimpton illustrates the way in which quite important men of the tenth century dealt in land. In 938 King Æthelstan granted Rimpton to Æthelred (S441). There is no indication of whether the land was actually purchased or whether it was a grant for services. Then in 956 King Eadred granted Rimpton to Brihtric Grim (S571). Maybe the land had returned to the crown and then been re-granted, but when Brihtric made his will (S1512, 964 X 80), he left Rimpton to Winchester Old Minster and he mentioned the two charters in his will, suggesting that he had received the first charter (S441) as part of a purchase. It was a proof of title. Brihtric also mentioned in his will that he had bought and added a hide of land to Rimpton.

Unfortunately the Domesday Book for Somerset does not tell us about the status of secular estates in 1066. We do not know whether the holders named were tenants of some greater lord or whether they were outright, alloidal owners. However, if we look outside the south-western circuit of the Domesday Book, it is possible to see a pattern which might also be applicable to the shire. Hampshire is in the south of England and was part of Wessex, but it was surveyed in a different circuit from Somerset, and so the questions asked by the Domesday surveyors and answered by landowners were probably worded a little differently. The Hampshire survey does indicate the lord of each manorial tenant (Munby 1982). A random sample of a hundred manors not held from the Church shows that 85 of them were held directly from the King. The manors were not chosen because of the high social standing of their owners. On the contrary many were very small and belonged to men of low social status. Forty-two of those who held from the king had manors described as 'allods'. That is to say, these men were people who had commended themselves to the king but the land they held was

their own and not his. They owned it as bookland which they could sell or bequeath as they pleased. If the Hampshire pattern was common across Wessex, the majority of the small secular estates of Somerset were alloidal.

This spread of ownership by bookright probably reached well down the social scale, but we do not know if it always involved a written charter. Grants made by laymen other than the king have survived, though they are relatively rare, so it may be that by the mid-tenth century most lay landowners had some documentary proof of possession. Ownership of land, as well as lordship, was therefore commonplace and this may well explain why the tenth century sees the appearance of places with names formed quite simply by the addition of '*tun*' to a personal name. Thus Alstone was *Alsistone* in 1086 (DB 24.33) and is formed from the personal name *Aelfsige + tun*. Fifteen names of this type occur in the Domesday Book for Somerset, (see Appendix) although there are probably more which are not recorded and some were still being formed after 1066. Pardlestone (DB 21.47) was held by Perlo in 1066 and the name is formed from his name. The name was only recently coined in 1066. Shearston (DB 21.8) was held by Sired in 1086, so that the name had been formed after 1066 but before 1086 and Dodington was still *stawe* in the Domesday Book (DB 4.12), but was held in 1086 by Doda. Regardless of when they were formed these estates were all small, averaging $2\frac{1}{5}$ hides each, though their sizes ranged from 6 hides at Lovington to a virgate at Stringston. Names of this type do not occur anywhere in England before the beginning of the tenth century, so that they are a record of a change in social structure and land-owning patterns taking place in the tenth century. It does not mean, of course, that only those places with names of this type were owned as allods, merely that personal ownership was becoming commonplace well down the social scale. If the appearance of so many small, independent estates was caused by the need of the kings and of greater lords for followers, the new status of so many of these estates was the price they paid for their followers. They extracted security of tenure and with it the right to move to any lord they chose in return for their political and military support.

Conclusion

The pattern of settlements outlined above depended upon the dominance of the king and his followers in its earliest form. The conquest of Somerset gave the king enormous wealth in the form of tribute from his estates and control of resources which could be delegated to the Church and to his warrior followers. It was in this way that the status of the nobility was promoted and preserved, for no king could or can exist without an aristocracy of some kind upon which he rested as he delegated authority and to which he looked for support, political and military, to hold the polity together and to repel aggressors from outside the kingdom. The redistribution and the re-ordering of lands mirrors the increasing complexity of that aristocratic class as challenges, political and military, pressed upon it. However, even after four centuries the imprint of that first conquest is clear in the survival of the dominant position of the king as landowner and in the structure of estate ownership so clearly shown in the Domesday Book.

Notes

1. I am indebted to Professor M Aston for his generosity in sharing with me his database of radio-carbon dated burials and settlements for the period 400–800 . Some of that material has been used in Figure 3.1.
2. Stow and stoc are very closely related words: see Smith 1970, vol. 2, 153–4 and 158–61.

Appendix

Personal names + *tun* in Somerset Domesday Book

The name of each settlement is followed by its Domesday Book reference, the name of the 1066 holder, the form of the name in Domesday Book and then the meaning of each name

Allerton	DB 24.11	5 hides	Wulfnoth	Alwarditone	= Ælwearde	+ *tun*
Alston Sutton	DB 24.14	4½ hides	2 thegns	Alnodestone	= Ælnoth	+ *tun*
Alstone	DB 24.33	1 hide	Alfwold	Alsistone	= Ælfsige	+ *tun*
Houndstone	DB 19.81	1 hide	3 thegns	Hundestone	= Hundes	+ *tun*
Lovington	DB 37.8		3 thegns	Lovintone	= Lufa	+ *tun*
Lufton	DB 19.82	1 hide	Alwin	Lochetone	Luca	= *tun*
Runnington	DB 25.45	2 hides	2 thegns	Runetone	= Runa	+ *tun*
Spaxton	DB 35.5	2½ hides	Alfwy	Spachestone	= Spakr	+ *tun* (ON)
Stringston +Stringston	DB 21.34 35.4	¼ hides 1 hide	Siward Alfwy	Strengestone Strengestone	= Strenge	+ *tun*
Tetton	DB 18.1		Ednoth	Tedintone	Tedda	+ *tun*
Torweston	DB 25.37	1½hides	Leofsi	Turvestone	= Tovi	+ *tun*
Woolston (ST0939)	DB 25.32	½ hides	Brictmer	Ulvretone	= Wulf	+ *tun*
Woolston (ST2344)	DB 21.18	½ hides	Ulf	Ulwardestone	= Wulfweard	+ *tun*
Woolston (ST6427)	DB 19.55 36.7	3¼ hides + 1 hide	3 thegns Alnoth	Ultone =	Wulf	+ *tun*

4

Eorl and Ceorl, Theow and Freo

We have no direct access to the structure of the post-Roman society of Somerset. We know that the early post-Roman period was characterised by the appearance of kings or tyrants and it is obvious from the existence of the refortified hill-forts and the discoveries of imported pottery that an aristocracy of some kind emerged in the fifth century, but all we have to tell us about the Welsh comes from the Laws of Ine. They may already be describing a group with a very changed structure by the early years of the eighth century and one which had in any case been cut off at the top by the displacement of its rulers. Ine's Laws show that there were Welshmen with 5 hide estates as well as lesser amounts of land, suggesting that there were still men of quite high social status, but we know nothing about their relationships with other men above and below them in economic terms before the Anglo-Saxon coming (Whitelock 1955, 367). We need therefore to turn to Anglo-Saxon society in Somerset, conscious that it had absorbed the local Old Welsh population which was almost certainly a substantial majority of the population in the mid-seventh century.

The slaves

A society in which slavery is a central institution is inevitably one which has quite marked and often rigid divisions. It is difficult to avoid thinking in terms of the Marxist 'class' and indeed this seems to have been a 'mode of production', but contemporaries would have seen it in terms of rank or degree, high or low, above all slave or free. The laws of the Wessex kings are permeated by such thinking. They set out a society with rigid boundaries, but we know from other medieval writing that what was described was often a construct, an abstracted and idealized view of something which was actually a much less formal social structure. Nevertheless the rigid forms evident in Ine's Laws and still apparent in King Alfred's time must have had an impact on how men viewed their position in society, if only because the laws provided the framework through which practical matters, such as wergild, were calculated.

Of all the forms of lordship in society nothing can be more complete than the lordship exercised over a slave. This is a particular and special form of lordship in that the lord owns the person of the slave and in Anglo-Saxon society could do much to the slave that he or she could not do to a free man. The slave's subjection was complete. The slave had no rights or expectation of reciprocal support from his master. However, a slave in early medieval society was not merely an economic object to be exploited; he or she was also a sign of the status of the owner and a living re-assurance to all those who were not slaves about their relative worth and standing (Wyatt 2001, 341). Slavery was an institution of long-standing in the early medieval world, an inheritance, as so much else, from late Roman society. It pervaded the barbarian societies which surrounded the Empire. Gildas wrote of the Britons as being enslaved by their Anglo-Saxon conquerors, but perhaps we should not place too much emphasis upon Gildas the polemicist (Winterbottom 1978, 27). St Patrick was captured and enslaved in Ireland, but tells us nothing about the slaves in Britain among the British themselves. It seems inconceivable that this social institution had not persisted among the post-Romans of the south-west in the fifth and sixth centuries, simply because it continued to exist in every other European society, 'civilised' and barbarian alike. Recent work has shown how powerful an influence the trade in slaves was in the whole of the post-Roman world, from Britain to Persia and Egypt (McCormick 2001; 2002). Throughout the whole of our period we should bear in mind that slaves were extremely valuable, not only for their everyday use in the local economy, but also as a potential source of money in return for their sale and export.

During the post-Roman period and throughout the later period also, enslavement of those defeated in battle seems to have been normal (Pelteret 1985, 121) and it is likely that the expansion of Wessex led to some enslavement of the local post-Roman population. This is certainly borne out by the semantic development of the word '*wealh*'. Initially this meant 'a foreigner', but soon came to mean 'a Welsh man' (Pelteret 1985, 319–22). In Wessex it also had the meaning of 'slave', again pointing to one of the most important sources of slaves at the period when Wessex itself was being formed. However, we have little documentary or material evidence to support such a view, and our first real information comes in the laws of the early Wessex kings. It was certainly possible for slaves of Anglo-Saxon origin, probably acquired as the result of war, to be available in the seventh and eighth centuries. Between 709 and 731 Brihtwold the Archbishop of Canterbury wrote to Bishop Forthhere of Sherborne, seeking to buy back a girl from his region who was owned by Beorhwold, the abbot of Glastonbury. He offered 300 shillings in ransom for her, the appropriate wergild for a woman of very high rank (Whitelock 1955, 731).

Ine's Laws, as we have already seen, are a compilation from the end of the seventh century (Whitelock 1955, 364–72). Very early in the laws we come to a ruling that the slave who works on Sunday at his master's behest will gain his freedom. The slave who works without his master's knowledge is to be whipped, or pay a fine to avoid the punishment. Immediately it becomes clear that slaves in Wessex had a more complicated existence than we might

expect.[1] He might work without his master's knowledge. For whom? Presumably not his master. Then perhaps for some-one else, or more likely on his own behalf. He may avoid a lashing by paying a fine. He must have money which is his own, or some-one else is to pay his fine for him. As a slave, in theory, he cannot have money which is not his master's, but Wessex slaves would certainly seem to have been able to earn money privately. Law 23.3 discusses the wergilds of a Welsh gafol-payer and of his son. It then remarks that a slave is to be paid for with 60 shillings or in some cases, unspecified, 50 shillings. This may of course simply be his commercial value, but it may on the other hand be a wergild of some kind. Sixty shillings was also the wergild of a landless Welshman (law 32). The impression that the slave had a standing in law is reinforced by law 74 which lays down that if a Welsh slave kills an Englishman he can be redeemed from the kin of the dead man with a payment of 60 shillings. If his master refuses to pay the 60 shillings he loses control of the slave, who may then be redeemed by his free kin. If he has none then he would be handed over to the relatives of the dead man. The remark about the free kin of the slave shows that the slaves position was a complicated one. He was not a member of a 'caste' with no close ties outside the slave class. A 'free' kin group might also encompass the unfree.

A common practice from an early time was for the very poorest to sell themselves or more often, their children, into slavery in order to survive. The practice was certainly well established by the later seventh century since authorisation of the practice by the Church occurs in Theodore's Penitential (Haddan and Stubbs 1869–78, III, 202). The Penitential allowed a family to sell a child under seven years old without the child's consent. A child of seven or above needed to consent and a child of 14 could sell himself. This extreme practice was probably the result of general insecurity during times of warfare. Those without a protector of some kind were often reckoned as 'poor' and slavery may have offered such people security and protection.

Several laws discuss the treatment of men, both English and Welsh, who have been penally enslaved, showing that it was a common practice, even in the later seventh century. Those who suffered this fate were people unable to pay the penalties laid down for crimes such as acts of violence. The fact that there are several clauses discussing slaves suggests that they were a substantial part of the population. However, more knowledge about the existence of slaves does not come until the tenth century, when surviving wills begin to mention them. When Ealdorman Ælfheah left lands which included Batcombe in Somerset he requested that all the penally enslaved men on the estates he had bequeathed should be freed (S1485). The will of Wynflæd (S1539) contains much detail about lands and goods. She ordered the release of several slaves by name, including Gerburg, Miscin, Hi….., Burhulf's daughter, Ælfsige and his wife and elder daughter and Ceolstan's wife, all of whom seem to have lived at Chinnock. She also freed Pifus and Eadwyn and …..'s wife at Charlton Horethorne and she freed the penally enslaved men on her estates. Another group of slaves, from Chinnock, including one called Ceolstan, she bequeathed to her son Eadwold and another named group to her daughter Eadgifu. There were clearly two distinct groups of people. On the one hand the penally enslaved, who were possibly single men, did not warrant names and were simply set free, their sentences commuted by her death. We do not know what they had done to be enslaved, but it may have involved offences against Wynflæd or her household, or they may have been enslaved as the result of her rights of justice. The other slaves were clearly long-term dependants, part of a group of families with long histories of slavery.

There are of course many records, usually inserted in Gospels, of slaves being freed and by the middle of the tenth century slaves were certainly buying themselves out of slavery, together with their families, and establishing their continuing freedom.

> Here is made plain in this Christ's Book.[2] Leofenoth, Ægelnoð's son at Corston has bought out himself and his offspring before Ælfsige the abbot and all the convent at Bath, with five 'ora' and 12 sheep as witnessed by Kascill the port-reeve and all the townspeople at Bath. May Christ make blind he who ever alters this. (Hunt 1893, 33)

Although they could be bought and sold, slaves were therefore not entirely without means. This was a feature of slavery common to the institution across northern Europe. In Francia north of the Loire in the eighth and ninth centuries slaves had been granted land by their lords and given the right to pass this land on to their heirs (Verhulst 1991, 196). In England also, by the middle of the tenth century their status went beyond being mere chattels. They could own property and by Æthelstan's time the law recognised that the slave might own cattle and be a buyer and seller (Pelteret 1985, 85). We should not be unduly influenced by the views of Roman lawyers. They may have seen the slave as a speaking 'object', but it is clear that the status of the slave of the early medieval world was much more complex. There is no doubt, though, that their status was a degrading one which men wished to be free of.

It is undoubtedly the case that male slaves were used primarily as agricultural labour and this link becomes clear when we look at the evidence of the Domesday Book, which is the first point at which we have information about numbers and distribution. John Moore has shown that the male slave of the Domesday Book was normally a householder with wife and children (Moore 1989, 217–9). As heads of household, 2120 are recorded for Somerset, which would probably give a population of about 9500 to 10,000 people altogether, including wives and children, a substantial labour force, some 16.3% of the total recorded population, although we should be wary of spurious accuracy (Darby 1986, 338). Slaves are normally accounted for in Domesday Book within the demesne entries and John Moore has pointed to the connection between plough-teams and slaves (Moore 1989, 209), showing that they were normally the demesne ploughmen. It is possible to show that the number of slaves in relation to the area of cultivated land was very similar across the whole of Wessex. If we look at the figures for slaves per hide there is a considerable diversity across Wessex (the Domesday shires of Hampshire, Wiltshire, Dorset, Devon and Somerset). Devon, with 2.9 slaves per hide, has the highest ratio, while Somerset comes next with 0.72 slaves per hide (see Table 4.1). The trend seems to be for slavery to become more important as we move westward.

However, if we use *ploughlands* as the basis of our enquiry the picture becomes much more homogeneous. Slavery is actually at its most intense in Hampshire and becomes less prevalent as we go

Table 4.1. Relationship of slaves to hides and ploughlands in 1086

	Slaves	Hides	Ploughlands	Slaves per Hide	Slaves per Ploughland
Devon	3318	1142	7934	2.9	0.41
Dorset	1244	2357	2287	0.52	0.54
Hants	1765	2785	2932	0.63	0.60
Somerset	2120	2933	4815	0.72	0.44
Wilts	1588	4032	3475	0.39	0.45

(All figures taken from Darby 1977)

westward, although overall the numbers of people involved are not huge. This of course looks only at heads of slave households, but even if we include families at 4.5 persons per household the numbers available are only 1.98 persons per ploughland in Somerset. These figures strongly suggest that there was a correlation between the amount of ploughland being cultivated and the amount of slave labour being used and that this held true across Wessex. The figures also add weight to the view that hides are not always a useful way of estimating the agricultural value of estates in 1086. This has implication for our ideas about agriculture and will be considered again elsewhere.

What we cannot be sure of is that the slave population expanded to keep pace with a general population growth in the tenth and eleventh centuries. There are clues which may suggest that it did not. The laws of Æthelberht of Kent in the early seventh century refer to the existence of 'grinding slaves', women who were employed in grinding corn (Attenborough 2000, Æthelberht 11). They were evidently important enough or common enough to warrant a law preventing their use as sexual objects. However, water-mills were common features of the manors of the Domesday Book. In Somerset about 35% of all manors had at least one mill. This might suggest that the expansion of female slave numbers had not kept pace with the growth in the number of aristocratic households or the expansion of corn-growing and that water-mills formed a cost-effective alternative.

Rosamund Faith has discussed the widespread employment of slaves as estate workers of all kinds, showing that they were often skilled at specialist agricultural tasks, such as dairying or animal husbandry, and were probably found on small farms as well as in great households, even if they are not recorded as such in Domesday Book (Faith 1997, 62–70). In the centuries prior to c. 900 slaves may have formed the chief cultivators on the estates of the king, the aristocracy and the church.

Chewton Mendip is a large estate on the northern side of the Mendips, which is first mentioned in King Alfred's Will of c. 872–88 (Keynes and Lapidge 1983, 175). In the Domesday Book it was described as a 29 hide estate with land for 40 ploughs (DB 1.29). The manor church held a further half hide. It may be possible to see in Chewton some trace of an earlier estate which was worked by slave labour. The early modern boundaries of the parish preserve considerable information concerning the likely early history of the place. The contorted boundary between Chewton and Emborough to the east, Ston Easton to the north-east and Litton to the north-west suggests that the arable land of the four manors already stretched across the whole area and joined one another at the point when the boundary was first laid out. This is likely to have been before 1086 as Emborough appears as a manor of 3 hides in Domesday Book (DB 5.61). It was, however, part of the ecclesiastical parish of Chewton, suggesting that it had once been part of Chewton. Ston Easton was also an ecclesiastical dependency of Chewton and consisted of three units of 4½ hides (DB 5.59), 1 hide (DB 42.3) and 1¼ hides (DB 46.25). Litton belonged to the canons of Wells Minster and was a 8½ hide estate (DB 6.17).

East and West Harptree, adjoining Chewton on the west, had probably started as a dependency of Chewton Mendip. As we have seen in Chapter three the primitive 'Harptree' had been divided at an early date and then perhaps in the tenth century both East and West Harptree were divided again.

In addition, at Domesday the two settlements were in different hundreds, strongly suggesting that the physical division into East and West had taken place much earlier. East Harptree was in the Winterstoke Hundred, while West Harptree was in the Chewton Mendip Hundred, although physically separated from Chewton Mendip by East Harptree. We might reasonably infer that Harptree was divided into two settlements at some unknown early date, almost certainly before hundreds began to be formed in the early tenth century. However, *Harptree* had probably started as a dependency of Chewton Mendip, since Chewton Mendip had a detached area of woodland in Compton Martin Parish, to the west of Harptree.

The core estate, still existing in 1086 and now extant as Chewton parish, is probably therefore the core of a much larger estate. That core may well have been worked by slaves grouped at an estate centre, perhaps close to the existing church site. The modern landscape and earlier maps (MAP/DD/WG\MAP2) show a curvilinear boundary marked as a lane, running across the northern open field, and a similar curved road to the south, close to the foot of the Mendip slope (Fig. 4.1). This boundary between hill-land and lowland is marked by a series of farmsteads, each with access to hill-grazing. It may be that central Chewton was a primarily arable estate, worked by slaves and marked by long curving boundaries which divided the inland from the rest of the estate. The extension for open field beyond the northern curved boundary would represent expansion of open-field cultivation in the later Anglo-Saxon period.

Even in 1086 there were still 20 slaves and 2 freedmen on the estate and the demesne was of 18 hides. The 9 ploughlands of the demesne therefore had 2.4 slaves (freedmen included) each; more than twice the average for the shire. By 1086 the community had grown to include eighteen *villani* and 25 bordars and the church estate of a half hide had 2 slaves, 2 villeins, 8 bordars and 8 cottars. The addition of so many peasant farmers would explain the extension of the arable until it intermingled with neighbouring settlements.

Similarly large numbers of slaves can also be found on large estates of the church. At Taunton, a very large estate of 100 ploughlands, the Bishop of Winchester had 20 ploughlands which were untaxed (DB 2.1). He had 70 slaves, 16 freedmen and 17 pigmen. These last may well have been recently freed and were certainly dependants. It is not at all clear how long the Bishop of Winchester had held Taunton, but it was certainly in his possession in 904 when it was described as a *monasterium* (S373). Again a church centre may well have worked extensive arable lands with the aid of a large slave labour force which formed the nucleus of their operations and to which the large numbers of peasant farmers – 80 villeins and 82 bordars – provided an important supplement.

While it is probable that slavery had always existed inside early Anglo-Saxon society, it is also likely that the institution received impetus from the profound changes which took place in the early seventh century. Prior to the appearance of the early kings there were probably few very large estates. The process of early state formation was accompanied by the formalisation of control of large numbers of men and the land they worked by the new warrior aristocracy led by the early kings. In a world where land was plentiful manpower was the scarce resource and it made sense to tie as much labour as possible to the new estates, since tribute paid by the ceorls and by lesser warriors would not provide sufficient surplus to support the pretensions of the new leaders. Slavery made good economic sense as well as being morally unobjectionable.

Parallel with the rise of the kings, their admission into the circle of Christian rulers in western Europe demanded that the new church should be provided with lavish grants of land. This too needed labour to provide the surpluses the new clergy needed and again a large demesne staffed by slave labour was the only way to provide substantial returns. Slavery was therefore changed from what was probably an important domestic arrangement in both post-Roman and Anglo-Saxon society into a large scale institution aimed at increasing surpluses for the burgeoning warrior and clerical groups. Large scale slavery, as opposed to domestic slavery inside the household, may therefore have been a social and economic consequence of the growth of lordship at the highest levels among the king and his aristocratic warrior followers. In Somerset as in other parts of Wessex the persistence of the extensive cores on so many large ecclesiastical and royal estates probably helped perpetuate large scale slavery as long as labour was relatively scarce. By the time of the Domesday

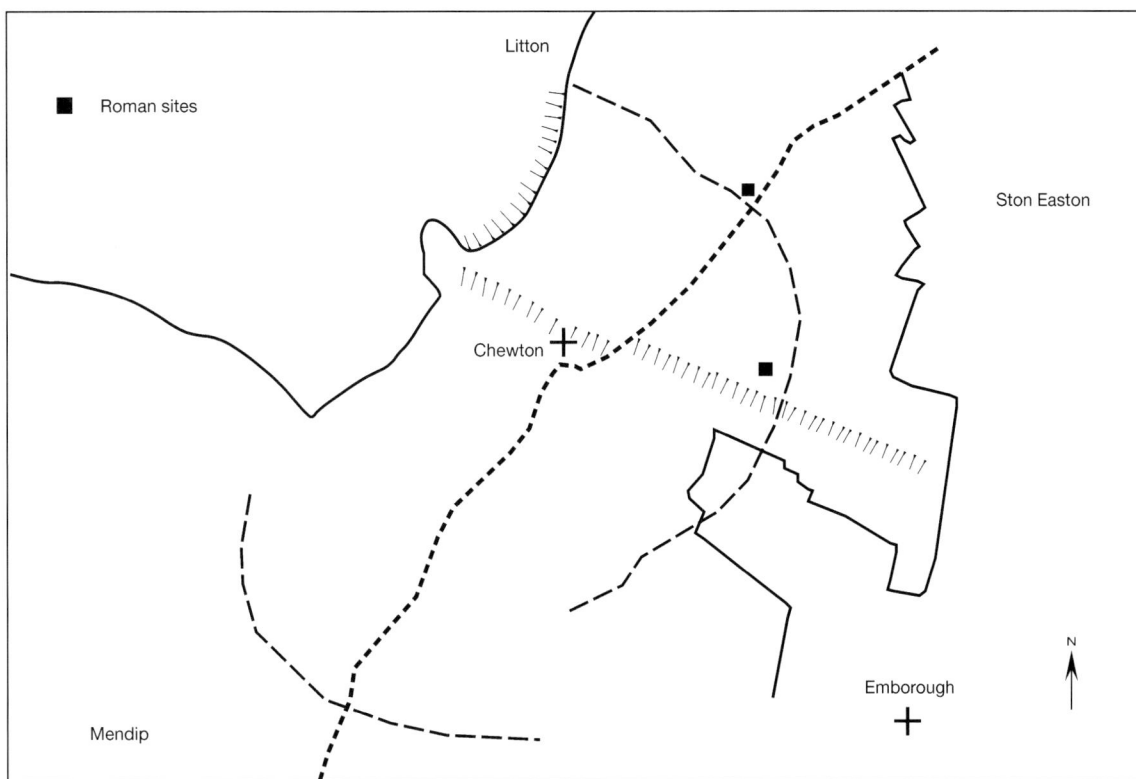

Figure 4.1. Chewton Mendip; The curving roads may represent the remains of the bounds of the inland of the estate, with the road from Wells to Bath running across the estate and passing close to the centre.

Book slavery was still a flourishing institution and it was only in the next century as the population grew still further that it made economic sense to free the slaves and place them on the bottom rung of the semi-free peasantry. *Pace* Professor Dyer, it seems to me likely that the decline of slavery was the result of the growth of population facilitated by the agricultural revolution and the consequent surplus of labour which appeared during the twelfth century (Dyer 1996, 174–93).

Great ecclesiastical and royal estates were the most obvious employers of slave labour, but the practice spread far more widely. Chilton Trinity was an estate which paid tax on only 1 virgate and had one ploughland in 1086 (DB 46.12). It was not therefore more than about 200 acres in extent. Ansger who held it clearly had a demesne of some sort there since he had a few cattle. The population consisted of a villein and a slave. Probably the slave worked Ansger's demesne land and the villein farmed the rest. Ansger also held Shovel which paid tax on a virgate and had land for half a plough (DB 46.14). No population is recorded, but clearly some-one farmed it. It was probably worked by a slave and his family. How many villeins themselves owned slaves is impossible to say, but Rosamund Faith has advanced the view that slave owning spread far down Anglo-Saxon society and slave labour must have been of real economic value for the peasant farmer in the later Anglo-Saxon period (Faith 1997, 66–7). Certainly King Alfred assumed that ceorls would own slaves when he laid down the compensation to be paid to the ceorl if his female slave was raped (Whitelock 1955, 377). The real slave population of Somerset may have been considerably larger than the Domesday Book suggests.

The half free

Rosamund Faith writing about 'cottars' suggests that they and the 'bordars' of the Domesday Book were virtually indistinguishable (Faith 1997, 70–5). As a group they were originally workers on the lord's demesne lands, the 'inland'. As such their status was not much above that of slaves. Since their farmsteads were probably too small to support them they supplemented their livelihoods by labouring on the lord's lands. The 'cotlands' of Porlock were small plots of land behind the village used by slaves and bordars for growing their own crops (Everett 1968, 60). Similar 'Coteland' existed at Englishcombe, near Bath (T\PH\dcl/10–11). 'Cot' is an old English place-name element which is clearly related to the cottars of the Domesday Book. It means a dwelling of low status. Smith (1970) thought that the rarity of the name in charter material as compared with the later frequency of the name implied that it was a late formation as a name. This is not necessarily the case. 'Cot' names may not appear in charters simply because they represent settlements which were too lowly to be the regular subject of grants. Ten places with the place-name element occur in the Somerset Domesday Book. They are not large estates, but nevertheless they are not all very small. Pitcote (DB 5.43 and 46.22) was divided into two units which totalled 5 hides. Carlingcott (DB 19.60) was a 3½ hide estate and Ashcott 3 hides (DB 8.11 and 8.14). It may be that these estates began as very small units, a cottage and a few acres, and were then transformed by the addition of extra lands to make a modest estate which could be granted to a follower whose status was well above that of the original cottager. The name in itself implies that the early holders were of the low status, and occasionally a complete early 'cot' estate can be distinguished. Draycott near Cheddar is an excellent example. Here a tiny square plot of land, now almost completely built upon by the village of Draycott, is distinguishable from the surrounding parish of Rodney Stoke, because it remained within the parish of Cheddar, to which it was attached during the Middle Ages (DB 47.15) (Fig. 4.2). It appears to have been carved from Rodney Stoke, perhaps at a period when Rodney Stoke was a part of the Cheddar estate.

In the Domesday Book it was recorded as paying tax on a virgate only. It was held by 'Godwin the Englishman', whose mother had held the land in 1066. He was recorded as one of the king's thegns in 1086. It is likely that he inherited the land from his mother who perhaps held it as the widow of a thegn established at Draycott and responsible to the king through Cheddar. Draycott is a fairly common minor place-name and Smith (1970) suggests that the name is related to Old English 'dræg' meaning something dragged, or a track suitable for a sled. The Draycott near Cheddar might be a dwelling or a group of dwellings for men who worked in the woods on the slopes above Cheddar and who dragged the timber down the steep hillside using horses. The deep runnels left by this practice are still visible today in Cheddar Wood (V. Russett, pers. comm.). If so Draycott was clearly later elevated in status by being granted to a thegn, however minor he may have been. By 1086 Godwin had two oxen to work his half ploughland. There were no other people recorded on his estate, although he would have needed some labour.

In a similar way, Allercott is recognisable as a detached portion of Timberscombe parish (Fig. 4.3). It was an independent manor in 1086, but paid tax on only a half virgate (DB 25.23). It was reckoned to have two ploughlands, though Durand the holder in 1086 had only one plough. There were also two villeins and two bordars there. It looks as if Allercott began as a small farmstead in a fold of Exmoor, which was worked by low status dependents of a larger estate. Although Allercott was later attached for ecclesiastical purposes to Timberscombe it is possible that it had originally been an outlier of another estate centre. Eventually it became a holding of slightly higher status held by Leofwin who was probably its alloidal owner in 1066.

Gilcott (DB 21.64), now lost, was also very small, only half a hide, and Holnicote (DB 16.13, 21.65) was also only just over half a hide. Other 'cotts' were larger. Carlingcott was a 3½ hide estate and both Foxcote and Pitcot were 5 hides. The positioning of these estates may explain why there was so much difference in size. Most of the small estates were tiny islands of cultivation on Exmoor and in the Brendon Hills. They probably functioned as outliers of larger

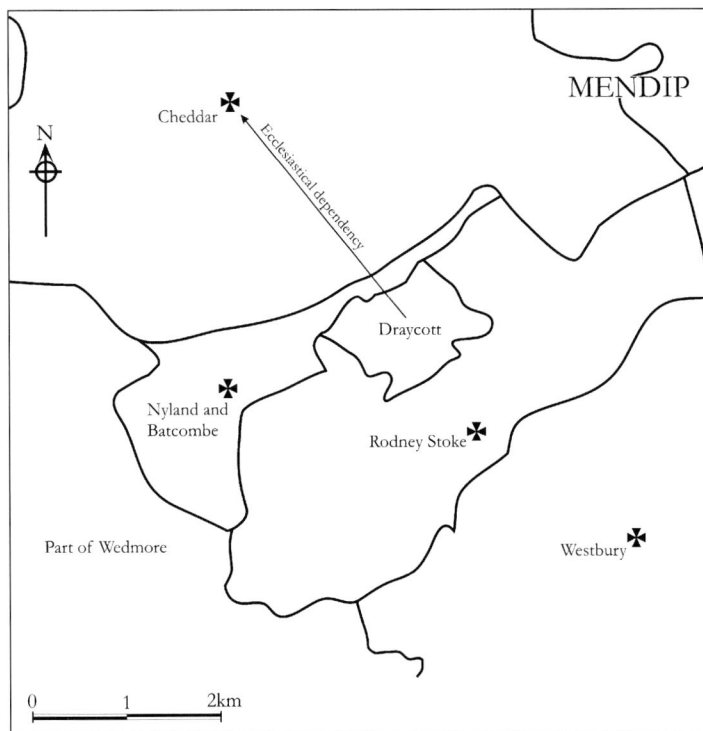

Figure 4.2. Draycott and Cheddar.

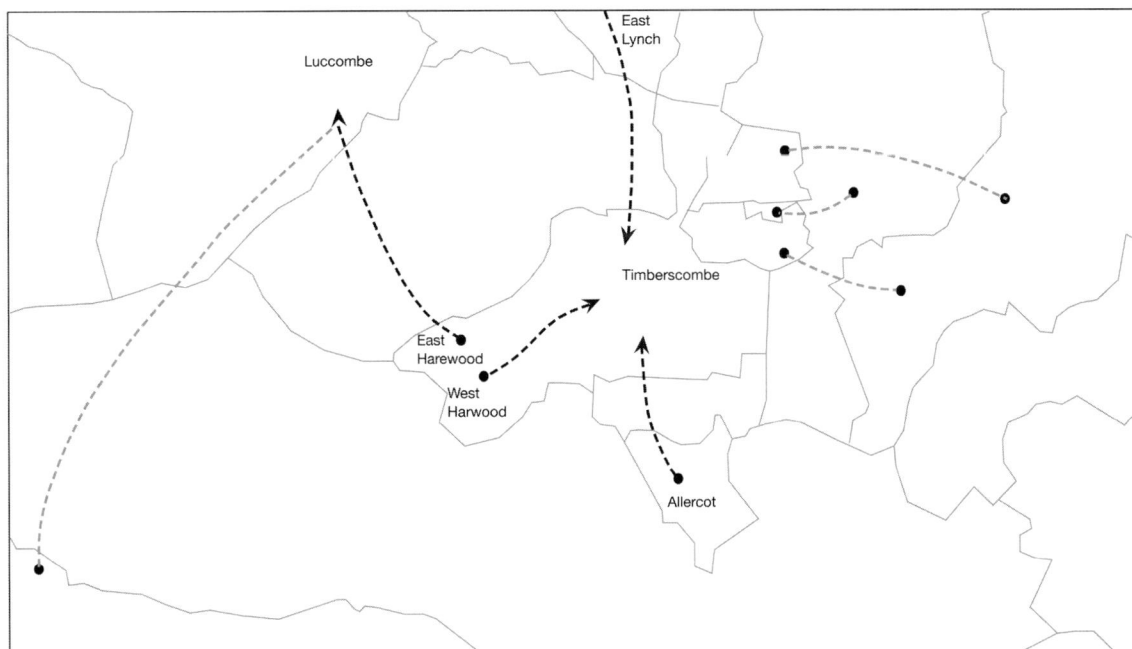

Figure 4.3. Allercot and Timberscombe.

centres which were sited closer to the sea, on lower ground. There are other 'cotts' in the same region which have no record in Domesday, but which may well be ancient settlements also. Although small, they may also have had access to extensive grazing on the hills around. The rest of the 'cotts' lie on the lower ground north and east of the river Tone. It may be that they were originally areas of land allocated to the bordars of an estate. At later dates when open-field agriculture had absorbed the ceorls into the communal system the bordars were placed alongside them in the open fields and their former settlements, perhaps augmented to make respectable holdings, were granted, leased or even sold to thegns for their support. The great Shapwick estate belonging to Glastonbury (DB 8.5) contained within it Catcott, a 5 hide unit in 1086, which was one of a number of sub-estates held by groups of thegns who were abbey dependants. Ashcott, a 5 hide estate (DB 8.1, 14), on the same Polden ridge was connected with Walton nearby. It contained within it another settlement, Buscott. It is possible that the 'cott' was merely the nucleus of an estate which was put together long after the 'cott' came into existence and that the name alone connected it with its distant past.

There are many 'cott' names inside modern parishes which show that such settlements were quite common. Knightcott in Banwell was a functioning holding in 1598 (D\P\ban) and there was also a 'Walcott'. Dulcote which exists as a modern village, but never attained parochial status, was a small unit inside the great Episcopal manor of Wells.

If the surmise about the status of 'cotts' is correct their occasional appearance as small but independent estates in the eleventh century marks a change in the position of their erstwhile *famuli*. Originally part of the demesne labour force, settled on a site where they might partly support themselves, they were now no longer closely bound to the demesne of their lords' estates, but were integrated with the other farmers on the tenanted land, while their 'cott' was turned over to a new sort of dependant, the thegn. Their remote successors were probably the peasants who appear in the surveys of Glastonbury manors holding tiny farms. In 1327 John le Irrische held a messuage and a ferdel of land at Shapwick in the open-fields. His labour services were extensive, much more than a

quarter of the services of the virgators (BM Egerton 3321). He was one of 19 such men; in 1086 there had been 16 bordars.

The most conspicuous peasants in the Domesday survey are the '*villani*' or 'villagers'. Both the Domesday term and the modern expression are used to describe the 'standard' Somerset peasant farmer of the eleventh century. On the classic manor he held a virgate of arable land in return for his labour services and rents. He was probably the *gebur* of the will of Wynflæld who granted to Shaftesbury Abbey '*þara gebura þe on þam gafollande sittað*, 'the peasants who live on the gafol land'. These men were unfree to the extent that they could not leave the estate, although they were not slaves, who, as we have seen, were a quite distinct group in her will. They paid '*gafol*', a rent, although they almost certainly also did labour services as well (S359 of AD 900). The 'Rectitudines', possibly written for the estates of Bath Abbey in the tenth century, show the *geburs* bearing heavy labour services and rents in return for their lands (Harvey 1993). The gebur's land was a grant from the land-lord and was stocked with oxen, sheep and sown land, as well as tools for working the land and utensils for his house. Although the writer made it clear that the burdens varied from one estate to another as a result of local custom, the gebur's work normally involved two or three days' labour a week, depending on the season, including ploughing and sowing the lord's land with his own seed. He paid a cash rent of 10 pence and dues of barley, hens and sheep, as well as taking his turn at guarding the lord's sheep in the fold, feeding the lord's dogs and giving bread to the estate swineherd. When the gebur died his belongings reverted to the lord. The 'bowermead' (t. 829 *etc.*) at Pilton, a Glastonbury estate, may preserve the name of an area where such men had their meadow and 'bower grove' (t. 109) in Flax Bourton may be where the geburs cut wood. Bourton in Compton Bishop parish (ST412553) is the 'tun of the *geburs*', and so may be a site where a group of them farmed.

Freemen; the ceorls

Most of the *villani* of Somerset Domesday were probably men in this semi-free situation, but many of their predecessors had been ceorls and as such men of some standing in their communities, freemen. Ine's Laws contrast them with the nobly born gesith, but the ceorl could clearly be a man of some substance or have access to wealth. If he needed to pay a wergild in connection with a homicide he might offer slaves, swords and mail-coats as part of the reparation (Whitelock 1955, 370). It has already been suggested that the 'Charlton' estates were places farmed by men of such a status and who owed their services directly to the king, with no lord at their settlement. It may have been similar ceorls who held the '*hwysces*' which still survive in Somerset as Huish or Hewish.

This place-name was in active use before the Norman Conquest and does not seem to have been in use in the later eleventh or twelfth centuries (Kurath and Kuhn 1956). It has an etymological connection with the word *hid*, 'a hide of land', through a common root in *higan*, 'a family' (Smith 1970). It is considered to mean 'the land for the support of a family' (Bosworth and Toller 1882). A survey of such places in Somerset made in 1992 examined 20 '*hywisces*' (Costen 1992b, 65–84). Further searches have produced more examples in Bruton, Churchill, Compton Pauncefoot, Crewkerne, East Harptree, Hornblotton, Ilton, Kilmersdon, Luccombe, Puxton, Tintinhull, Thornfalcon, Stoke-sub-Hamdon and Wells Without parish – a further 14, all from field-name material. It looks as if such settlements were quite common. In some cases it is possible to reconstruct *hywisces* and it becomes clear that the area of the *hywisc* varied according to the nature of the landscape in which it was situated. Thus on the high ground of Exmoor Rodhuish has an area of 586 ha., while at Rimpton, on low land near Yeovil, the *hywisc* had an area of 80.9 ha. (Costen 1992b, 65, 67) (Fig. 4.4).

It is clear that the size of the *hywisc* depended very much on the quality of the land, as might be expected if it was intended to support a family. Although these farms were substantial it seems unlikely that they could have been intended to support the young warrior of the seventh and eighth centuries. The inference must be that they were the farmstead of ceorls and that the ceorl represents the typical Wessex 'family' whose holding formed the basis of the hidage system and ultimately in the later tenth century, the unit of collection for the geld.

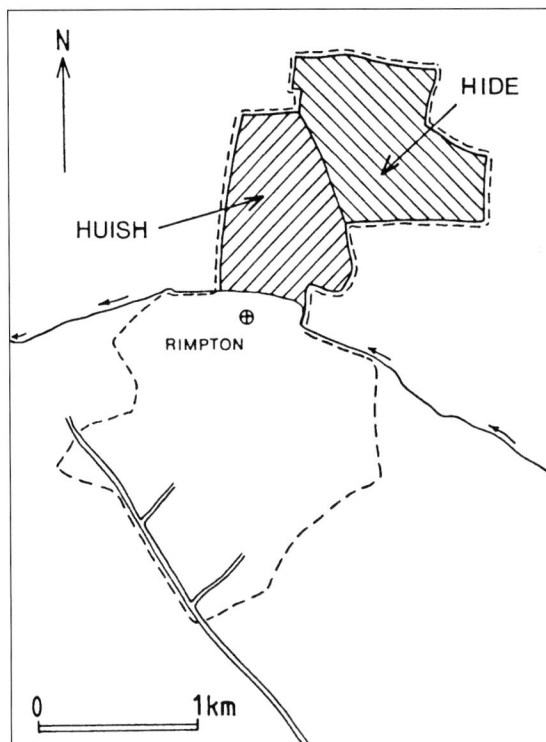

Figure 4.4. The 'hywisc' at Rimpton.

By the time the Anglo-Saxon ceorls came to Somerset they had been part of the developing English society for at least 200 years and it is very unlikely that they still retained the same social status as in their early days in Britain. It has been suggested that the hide or *hywisc* upon which the ceorl lived had its roots in the Roman *centuria* of 200 *iugera*, an area which would come to 124.7 acres and would thus approximate to the conventional 120 acres of the hide (Barnwell 1996, 53–61). Thus the unit may have had its origins inside the Roman Imperial system of land apportionment and taxation and have been present in Britain when the Anglo-Saxons arrived. This is an attractive idea, but until we can definitely tie some of the known *hywisces* to a pre-Anglo-Saxon estate such a case would be difficult to prove. It may also be the case that the early settlers arrived with a culture already influenced by the administrative arrangements of the continental Roman Empire and imported the system as appropriate for the ordinary warriors of the

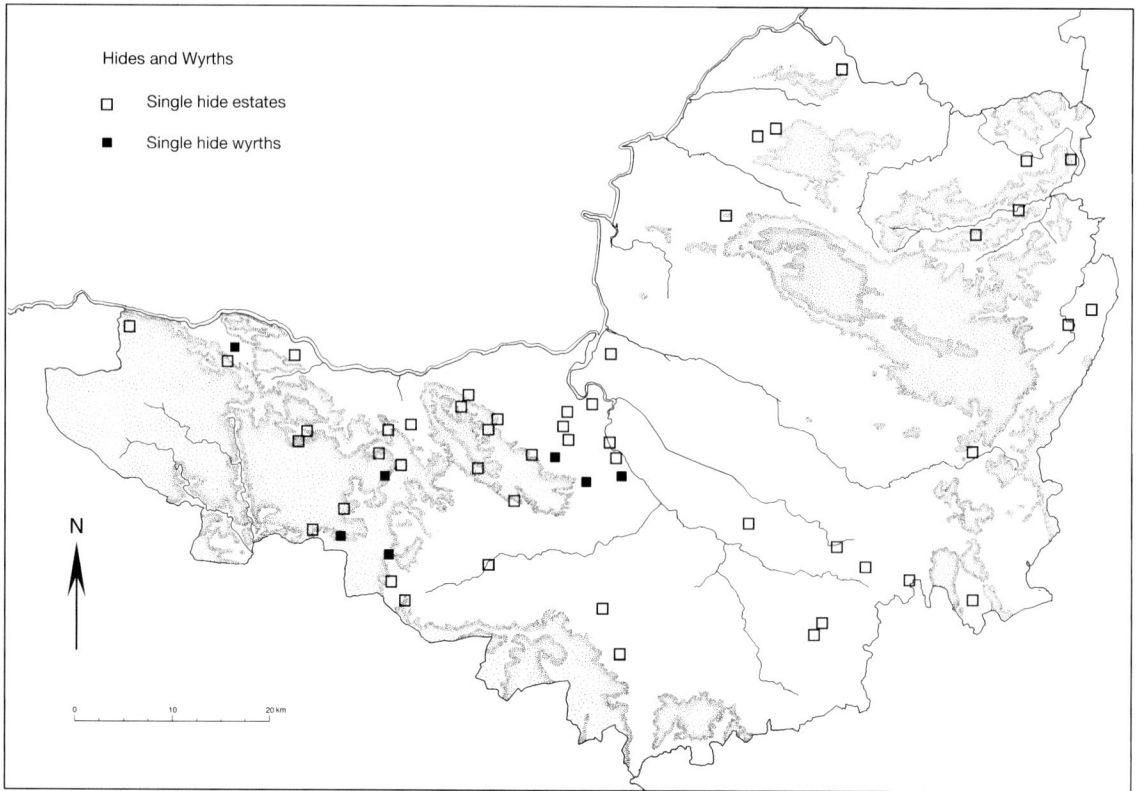

Figure 4.5. Hides and wyrths.

earliest days – the *ceorls*, in a society where money no longer functioned and pay in cash was impossible.

If the 1 hide farm was the normal support of the early ceorl family it is likely that there were many more than the 34 examples already quoted. They would not necessarily preserve the *hywisc* name, since that was a description of their purpose and status, and it is possible that many of the small estates of Domesday Book originated as such farms. There are 57 estates in the Somerset Domesday survey which are of exactly 1 hide and are not sub-divisions of larger units. Of particular interest are the estates in that group with 'worth' names, Chubworthy, Elworthy, Huntworth, Lexworthy, Manworthy and Selworthy. The element *wyrth – wyrthig* means 'an enclosure' (Smith 1970, 273–7) and by extension came to mean an enclosed dwelling or farm. Ine's Laws say that 'a ceorl's wyrth (homestead) must be fenced

winter and summer' suggesting that such holdings were well known in the eighth century (Whitelock 1955, 368). Some of these names may preserve the name of the farmer – Chubworthy, 'Cib's worth', (DB *cibewrde*). Elworthy, 'Elli's worth' and Lexworthy, 'Lecc's worth'. Huntworth may contain either a personal name Hunta or Old English 'huntere', a hunter, while Selworthy is Old English '*sele*', sallow plant. Manworthy was '*æt monawyrþige*' in AD 963 (S709), 'at the men's worth'. Perhaps it was exploited by a group of peasants. Elworthy is the only 'worth' settlement of 1 hide which is now a parish. As a parish it also contains the manor of Willet which was a half hide estate in 1086 (DB 25–34). The two manors were both held by Dodman in 1086 (DB 25, 33.34) which probably explains why they ultimately became a single parish. The ecclesiastical parish contained 1490 acres, of which Elworthy farm amounted to

202 acres at the time of the tithe award. Chubworthy was still a farm at the time of the tithe award and contained 190 acres, neither of them too far from the notional 120 acres of the hide.

Other Domesday *wyrths* did not amount to exactly a hide of land. '*Lodenwrde*', now Edingworth in East Brent was a 2 hide estate (DB 8.34). Almsworthy '*Edmundesworde*' in 1086 (DB 21.56) was rated at only a virgate. It is now represented by Almsworthy Farm in Exford, which was of 49 acres at the time of the tithe award.

The boundary clauses of Anglo-Saxon charters contain two references to *wyrths*. At Charlcombe, near Bath, the bounds of the charter of c. 1066 (CCC 111) have '*Andlang brokes to dealla wyrde dic*', 'along the brook to the ditch at the shared worth', suggesting that the worth was farmed by several people. The Anglo-Saxon charter for Ditcheat and Lottisham (S292 of 842) contains '*on scheobanwergthe*', 'at Sceobba's worth'. This boundary is probably tenth century or later, rather than ninth century and the site of the worth is not identifiable. Neither is it possible to identify the '*wirte*' somewhere on the southern side in the bounds of Ditcheat (also S292 of 842). At Ashwick there were '*þreon worðigan*', 'three worths', perhaps three permanent enclosures (S1149). Berrow had a '*bischapes werthe*' in the charter (S793), which is no longer identifiable. The charter for Compton Bishop, of 1066 (Lib. Alb. Vol. 2 fo. 246 v) has a reference to '*gemera land uf bufen melc weg and eall seo wyrð on sundran*'. This separate *wyrth* was probably above the north-western side of Cheddar Gorge and may be of one of the many small farms whose remains lie along the southern escarpment of the Mendips.

A number of *wyrth* settlements have risen to the status of parishes. Badgworth, Bishopsworth, Chelwood (Celeworde in 1086 (DB 17.5)) Clatworthy, Closworth, Cudworth, Elworthy, but generally they were small in 1086 and remained small settlements and parishes thereafter.

Other worth/worthy names include a personal name element and they often survive as modern farms and hamlets inside bigger parishes. The best example is at Exford, where almost all the settlement of the parish consists of a group of farms each with a personal name attached to the *wyrth*. Almsworthy has already been mentioned above. In addition there

were Buckworthy (69 acres), Lower Pitsworthy (55 acres), Higher Pitsworthy (51 acres). The bulk of the *wyrths* with personal name elements are concentrated in the west of the county, on the higher ground (Fig. 4.5). This may be because tiny estates of this type were destroyed by the advance of new methods of farming and the creation of new estates in the tenth and eleventh centuries, but it may also be the case that the broken highlands and the edges of uplands such as the Brendons and the Mendips provided the semi-independent ceorls with opportunity to acquire or create their own small estates. This was land which did not suit the large royal, aristocratic and ecclesiastical holdings of the seventh and eighth centuries. The margins provided the opportunity for relative independence. Relationships between lord and man were therefore to some extent influenced by the landscape in which they lived. A world of small estates and isolated farmsteads meant that men could not be so tightly bound as on the great arable estates of the flatlands. If ties were looser relative status may not have been so easy to distinguish in the hills. Unfortunately we do not know if these holdings, or some of them, were already in existence in the early seventh century. It seems unlikely that they were all carved out new at the beginning of the Anglo-Saxon period. More likely some at least of these places were occupied long before the coming of the kings of Wessex and their followers, 'eorl and ceorl'. By King Alfred's time such '*ceorlisc*' men were almost certainly commended either to the king or to some other great man. Their freedom was relative by King Alfred's time and the numbers of ceorls may never have been very great. They were probably heavily outnumbered by the much more unfree geburs and bordars of the great estates (Finberg 1964, 146–7).

Some other units can be recognised from their morphology. Dr John Davey has documented seven of these small estates in the South Cadbury area. Each of them is a 1 hide unit. Some have curving boundaries and it is suggested that these were formed in open land landscapes, others have much more regular boundaries and must have been formed inside already established units or pre-existing field systems (see Fig. 4.6). Similar small estates may have existed inside Chewton Mendip, where settlements were formed on the edge of the large central farmlands

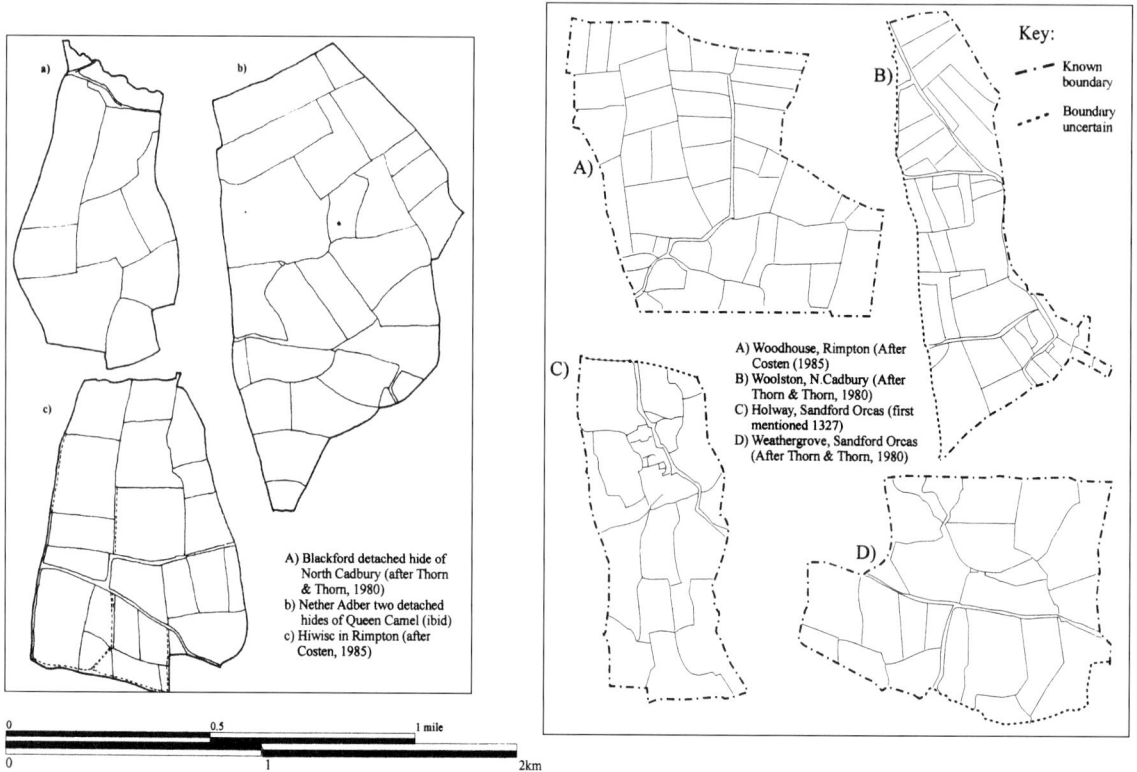

A) Blackford detached hide of North Cadbury (after Thorn & Thorn, 1980)
b) Nether Adber two detached hides of Queen Camel (ibid)
c) Hiwisc in Rimpton (after Costen, 1985)

Key:
— · — Known boundary
— · · — Boundary uncertain

A) Woodhouse, Rimpton (After Costen (1985)
B) Woolston, N.Cadbury (After Thorn & Thorn, 1980)
C) Holway, Sandford Orcas (first mentioned 1327)
D) Weathergrove, Sandford Orcas (After Thorn & Thorn, 1980)

Figure 4.6. Single hide units in south-east Somerset (after John Davey, 2005).

of the royal demesne, possibly when it passed from ecclesiastical to royal hands.

We need to be careful to recognise that simply because a Domesday holding was very small, it was not necessarily very ancient. Clearly some small units had arisen by division of a developed settlement. Often they still shared a name, distinguished by 'East' or 'West', 'North' or 'South' This is likely to have been a recent development as lands were divided by lords or by inheritance or marriage gift. Others may be the result of a division to settle a thegn with land at a quite late period, probably in the tenth century. At Blackford, near South Cadbury, there were two Domesday holdings. The smaller (DB 36.8) was of 1 hide only, the larger (DB 8.9) was a 4 hide estate belonging to Glastonbury Abbey, but held by a thegn. The origins of the Glastonbury estate are obscure (Abrams 1996, 59–62), but there is some evidence

to suggest that this was a 5 hide estate from which a 1 hide unit had been taken. It looks as if here too the common-fields were already functioning when the estate was divided. Late field-name evidence shows common-field spread across the whole of the later parish. However, the village in the later nineteenth century still had two farms called East Hall Farm and West Hall Farm (1st ed. 6" OS map). One of these farmsteads, West Hall, is described as being of eleventh century and later construction, which must make it the oldest farmhouse in Somerset (English Heritage loE 263351). It would be a reasonable conjecture to suggest that these two buildings are related to the manorial centres of the two Domesday estates. Both are in the village, though at either end of the settlement, suggesting that the settlement, probably with its church, was already in place at the time of the division.

By the time of the Domesday Book it is clear that the men who held these small settlements, *wyrths* or *hywisces* or simply very small units, were not the 'ceorls' of Ine's day. They seem to have been independent landholders, presumably holding their estate by bookright, which would imply that they were minor members of the warrior aristocracy, the beginnings of a gentry. Some may indeed have been the descendants of ceorls who had prospered, others of minor members of the aristocracy. The ceorl was effectively buried by major changes in the structure of late Anglo-Saxon society which had probably reduced most of his class to the status of dependent *geburs* during the ninth and tenth centuries or seen some rise by prospering as farmers or through attachment to a great man to become thegns. The *Gepyncðo* says rather wistfully that 'if a ceorl prospered, that he possessed fully 5 hides of land of his own, a bell and a burh-gate, a seat and a special office in the king's hall, then was he henceforth entitled to the rights of a thegn' (Whitelock 1955, 433). The *Norðleoda laga*, said of a ceorl that 'even if he prospers so that he possesses a helmet and coat of mail and a gold-plated sword, if he have not the land, he is a ceorl all the same' (Whitelock 1955, 433). The connection between land and the thegn's status was thus made most effectively. The status of the thegn no longer depended upon his connection to the king or other great man but was becoming a property qualification. Clearly times were changing if the writers needed to dwell upon the rules of the past. However much it may have irked tidy minded clerics like Wulfstan it is unlikely that the boundary between the ceorls and their descendants and the minor thegns was very easy to distinguish.

Freemen; the gesiths and thegns

Originally the word 'thegn' meant 'a servant', but as with its much later successor the knight – from the Old English '*cniht*', a 'youth or serving boy', it came to have a much more distinguished meaning and by the end of the Anglo-Saxon period was used to describe someone who bore arms and normally was a landowner or landholder with lordship over others (Clark Hall 1960). The earlier Anglo-Saxon warrior and nobleman was normally referred to as *gesith*,

'nobly born'. It was of course normal that such men should be warriors and it was from this group that the major land-owners were drawn.

Eanwulf was ealdorman of Somerset in the mid-ninth century and led the shire forces to victory against the Vikings in a battle somewhere at the mouth of the river Parrett (ASC (A) 845 (848)). Land at Ditcheat (S292), and probably at Binegar (S1701) and Hornblotton (S1699) is recorded as granted to him. Evidently his family maintained their connection with Somerset, since it is likely that the lands at Ditcheat and Hornblotton were passed to Glastonbury Abbey in the tenth century. We do not know if his family lands reached outside Somerset or what else he held, but usually the lands of such great families were widely spread across a region. Æthelfrith, *dux* (a term often used to describe an ealdorman), was holding land at Risborough in Buckinghamshire in 903 (S367) and at Wrington in 904 (S371), where the charter was said to replace one lost in a fire. Later tenth century wills show that such families held many estates and it would seem difficult to imagine that lordship could mean much in personal terms for such people. When the ealdorman Ælfheah made his will between 968 and 971 he mentioned 21 places spread across Wessex, including Batcombe in Somerset (S1485). His wife Ælswyth was also a landowner in her own right. Charters for Corston (S593), Winscombe (S1726) and Nyland (S1761) were all issued to her alone. The survival of the charters or references to their existence is due to the subsequent grant of the land to monasteries. Many grants made directly to women were probably made in order to facilitate a pious gift. Ælswith become a nun after her husband's death. Both she and her husband were buried at Glastonbury, the privilege of the great benefactor (Foot 2000, 182–3). These great people probably spent much time at court or going from one estate to another. For most of their people they must have been quite distant figures, who lived surrounded by their own court, made up of thegns and priests from their own estates. However wills in which slaves were freed, such as the will of Wynflæd, (S1539) quoted above, show enormous attention to detail. Such wills were normally written when the testator was already gravely ill and seem to show a personal knowledge of individuals which is unlikely

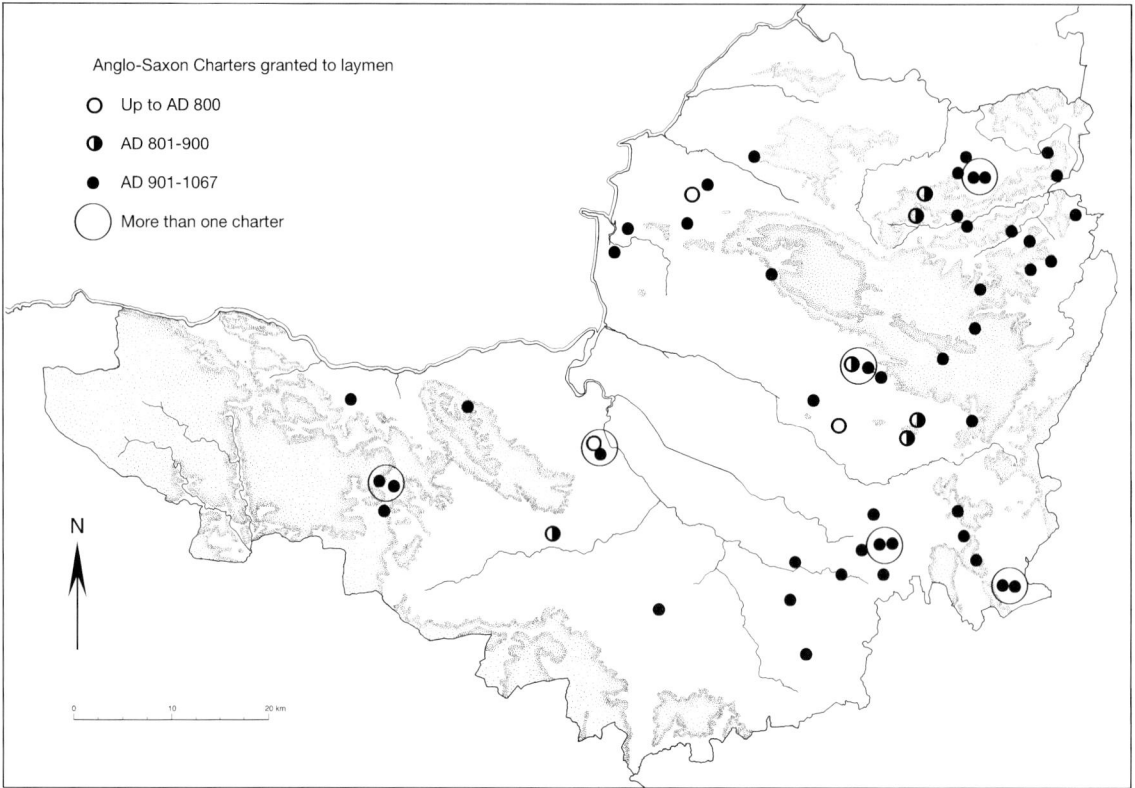

Figure 4.7 Anglo-Saxon charters in Somerset granted to laymen.

to have come only from the clerks who attended such people.

Other members of the nobility had their lands less widely spread. Wulfwaru, who died between 984 and 1016, held land at Freshford, Claverton, Compton, Butcombe, Leigh, Holton and Winford, though land holding in one shire alone seems to have been relatively unusual for the people important enough to make a will.

As well as the very great people, close to the king and often related to him, there were many other people who had roles at court, probably as administrators and councillors. These men were often described as 'King's Thegns' in the tenth century. Many of them were substantially wealthy and there are many surviving charter grants of land to these men. How many of these grants were gifts which rewarded service or were intended to tie the recipient to the giver, and how many were sales for cash is impossible to know. However, it is noticeable that some estates seem to have been granted to lay people on a number of occasions, suggesting that they were not outright grants despite the existence of a charter. Æthelræd, who was described as 'minister', received a grant of land at Henstridge from King Athelstan (S1712 of 924 X 39). He also received a grant of Rimpton in 938 (S441). In 956 Rimpton was again granted, this time by King Eadred and this time to Brihtric Grim (S571). Both charters were acquired by Winchester Old Minster when Brihtric left Rimpton to the minster. His will (S1512 964 X 80) mentions both charters which went with the property. It may be that Brihtric actually bought the land from Æthelræd or his family and that the grant of a new charter was simply Brihtric fortifying his position as the new owner by obtaining a new charter.

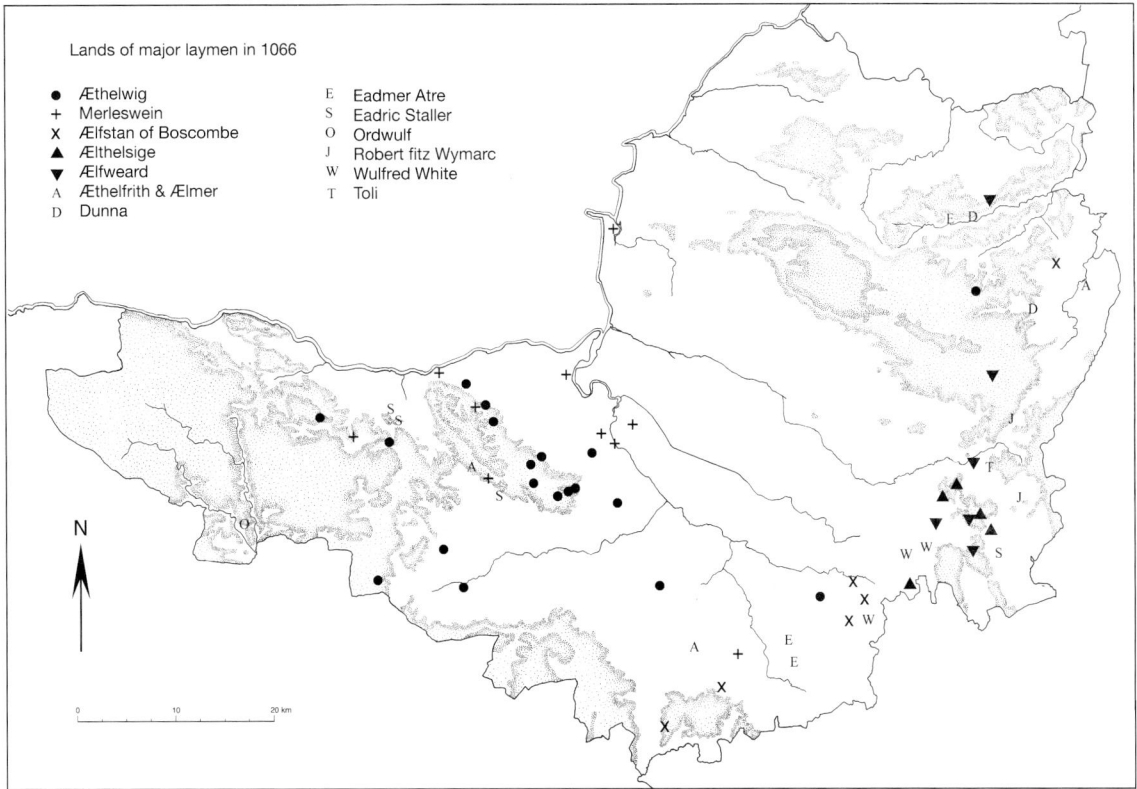

Figure 4.8 Distribution of the lands of major lay landowners in 1066.

There are 49 surviving charters or records of charters of the tenth century which record grants to laymen and women in Somerset (Fig. 4.7). These have survived because they all passed into the possession of a monastery or church or were deposited in a church for safe-keeping and were recorded. Many other grants must have existed but have disappeared without trace because they were concerned solely with the lands of lay men and women. There was a lively market in land by the end of the tenth century, probably driven in part by the rising quantity of silver in circulation. It is not until the mid-eleventh century, with the making of the Domesday Book, that we can get some idea of the scale of landowning by the upper levels of the thegnly class. P. A. Clarke's painstaking study of the lands of the earls and of the thegns with more than £40 worth of land shows clearly that land ownership among the richer thegns was widely spread

across the shires (Clarke 1994). Ælfstan of Boscombe had estates at Whatley in Winsham, Hinton St George, Yeovilton, Laverton, Yeovil and Chilton Cantelo. He also held one estate in Hampshire, one in Berkshire, 15 estates in Wiltshire, of which three were leases, five in Dorset, six in Hertfordshire four in Gloucestershire and six in Bedfordshire (Clarke 1994, 229–231). He was typical of the 16 men who were worth more than £40 a year, holding land in Somerset. His estate in Hampshire was at Silchester and the Domesday Book states that he held it from King Edward '*in alodium*' (Munby 1982, 32, 4). He was thus the outright owner of the land, with an obligation to the king himself. It is probable that his land in Somerset was owned in the same way. Direct ownership of land implied a commendation directly to the king himself or to some other great man – one of the earls. Whether such an arrangement can be projected back to the time of King Alfred seems unlikely, but the personal commendation may well have preceded the granting of booklands to laymen in such numbers. As we have seen above in Chapter 2, the imposition of military service upon all bookland in the ninth century made such a commendatory relationship almost impossible to avoid.

In Somerset the lands of this group of well to do men were concentrated in a broad belt of territory running along the border with Dorset (see Fig. 4.8). Another smaller concentration lay along the foot of the Quantocks and scattered across the high ground of the Brendons. In the south-east the land was generally good for agriculture and many of the estates were small. In the west, the land had lower agricultural value, but was often exploited as small isolated farmsteads in a largely unenclosed area of upland pasture and wood-pasture. There was thus a sharp division between the lands held by the king and the church in the centre of the county, which were mostly large estates, and the smaller ones held by laymen. A conjecture would be that these were areas where estates had always been small and as a result were suitable for grants, which were not too big, and also for sales for cash. Once the land had been alienated there would be a tendency for these estates to remain lay estates as people bought, sold and inherited them perpetuating the pattern.

For these landowners, men with a direct relationship with the king and in some cases administrative responsibilities at his court, personal relationships with lesser landowners and even their own tenants must have been difficult to maintain. We do not know where such people were ordinarily resident and it seems unlikely that we should envisage a hall at every manor. As in later times, they may already have maintained one or two rural residences, dividing their time between them and spending time away on their official duties, following the court. They could not easily develop a 'county aristocracy' when their lands were so widely dispersed and when purchase, inheritance and marriage redistributed estates so freely. Such a group did not appear until well after the Norman Conquest when the nature of land-holding changed. A settled relationship with the landscape was probably more likely among the minor landowners who held no more than a single estate.

Lesser Men

Manworthy, near Milverton, was granted by King Edgar to the thegn Ælfric in 963 (S709). It was a small 1 hide estate the charter for which begins '*Ðis is þare anre hyde land boc æt monawyrþige þe eadgar cyng gebocade ælfrice his þegene on ece yrfe*'. 'This is the land-book of the 1 hide at Manworthy which King Edgar registered in favour of his thegn Ælfric for his personal use'. The estate was still held by a layman, Ulf, in 1066 (DB 25.44). We do not know if Ulf was a descendant of Ælfric, but a copy of the charter for the estate is preserved in the records of Wells Cathedral (Liber Albus II fo. 289). It was probably deposited there for safe keeping, for there is no record of the Bishop holding the land.

Saeward and Aldeva held Horsington in 1066 (DB 28.1). They '*quo volebant ire poterant*'; 'could go where the would'. They owned the land and were free to give their allegiance where they pleased. Horsington was divided unequally between them. They were probably related and the division may be the result of inheritance. Aldeva held 10 hides and 3 virgates while Saeward had only 1 virgate. However, they held the land jointly, suggesting it was a single settlement in which they each held their share. Lordship would therefore be divided, with each commanding their own tenants. They must have co-operated to allow a single settlement to function, so that even at this level lordship was depersonalised and nearly equated with land-lordship, but a landlordship which included control over slaves, cottars, bordars and villeins, all of whom were unable to leave the estate without their lord's permission. An 11 hide estate was of course a substantial holding. In contrast the two brothers, Ælfric and Wulfa, who held Clapton, had 3 hides jointly and ran the estate between them (DB 19.68). We see these people in the Domesday Book as they appeared in 1086. Unfortunately we know very little about their predecessors. We can envisage some of them coming from among the ceorls and others being the younger children of more important land-owners. Some were probably placed on their estates as military followers of important families, particularly in the tenth century, but we do not know how such people might become holders of bookland. As we saw above (Chapter 3), East Lydford belonged to Glastonbury Abbey in 1066 and was thegnland (DB 8.4). West Lydford was held by Brictric who was probably an outright owner (DB 4.21). It is clear from the arrangement of lands within the two manors that they had once been one unit (Costen 1991, 46–8). Lydford as a single unit may have been part of the grant of 744 (S1410). It was probably the abbey which made the division of the estate into two parts in the tenth century. Perhaps Brictric or a predecessor actually purchased the estate from Glastonbury, but it is unlikely that the abbey would sell land. His ancestors may have taken a long lease, normally for three lives, and managed to convert it into bookland. We can see how Manworthy came into the hands of a layman and how this very small holding came to have a 'book', but we cannot be certain of how Brictric's ancestors came to own West Lydford or how countless other minor land-owners first obtained their estates and then proved their title.

Some men of military rank clearly did not own their own estates but leased the land upon which they lived. Such leases are often noticed when the land failed to return to its monastic owner after the three lives of the lease had run their course, but we can see an example of how an agreement might work through a lease drawn up by Bath Abbey before 1086, but after the Norman Conquest. In it the abbey leased the estate at Charlecombe to William Hosatus who held it in 1086 (DB 7.8). The monastery 'let the land to him and ten oxen and 60 sheep and 100 sown acres, for life. He is to pay each year two pounds to the minster for rent and to do the king military service and pay the geld'. Failure to keep to the bargain would result in forfeiture and 'be he cursed by Christ, St Mary and St Peter that the minster is abused' (Hunt 1893, 37–8).

What distinguished such men from their *ceorlisc* neighbour was their obligation to perform military service and the duty of paying a heriot when they died. This was incumbent upon them as owners of bookland and of course this was what made them so vulnerable after the defeat at Hastings in 1066. Otherwise they may have looked very like their neighbours. The sharpest distinction was probably between these minor landowners and the thegns retained chiefly on monastic estates to fulfil the military obligations of their ecclesiastical masters.

They were real soldiers but as we shall see often much poorer than their bookland fellows.

By the mid-eleventh century such people were completely overshadowed by the rise of the great earls. In Somerset the House of Godwin was represented by Earl Harold and his family held over £180 of land. He ravaged and plundered in western Somerset in 1052, killing local thegns who opposed him (ASC 'E', 1052). Opposition would not have been expected if he had had many commended men in the region and neither would he have killed so many local warriors. When he and his father appeared along the coast of south-east England just a little later 'they enticed to them all the local people along the sea-coast and also up inland' (ASC 'C', 1052). In contrast with Somerset this suggests local commendation and support in Sussex and Kent. The only places he held in West Somerset were Dulverton and Old Cleeve. At Dulverton an estate held by thirteen thegns had been added into the manor after 1066 (DB 1.12). It may be that this group were actually commended men of Harold. There is no mention of dependent thegns at Old Cleeve (DB 1.3). However, further north-east at Winsford, Tosti had three thegns (DB 1.17) and Harold had another three at Congresbury (DB 1.21). At Banwell Harold had six commended men, some with considerable estates (DB 6.8) and he may have had a thegn at North Curry (DB 1.19). Other estates held by the House of Godwin do not seem to have had thegnland and Earl Harold's influence in the region was not, perhaps, very great, despite the size of the estates he held.

The king

There can be no doubt that the greater the land-holding the greater the influence exercised and the king was by far the largest single landholder in the shire. We have already seen how the king was able to gain influence by rewarding men and women with lands and probably also by having a near monopoly of the granting of charters when land changed hands between nobility, thus authenticating their holding as book-right land and overseeing the transactions. In King Alfred's time personal lordship meant that he was able to raise a troop of warriors from the shire, even when his power and influence were at the nadir. In

878 when he had withdrawn to Athelney he was able to command the support of the men from 'that part of Somerset-men nearest to it' (ASC 'A' 878). Asser talks of 'the thegns of Somerset' (Keynes and Lapidge 1983, 84). It looks as if the king could command all the warriors within the area he controlled, regardless of whether they were settled on their own lands, the king's or those of the church. It is unlikely that this would have included land south of Bath, which would have been vulnerable to Viking attack from north-east Wiltshire and from south-east Gloucestershire, but it may have included all the land south of the Mendips. The Vikings certainly did not control Ilchester, which would have made Alfred's move through Selwood and up towards Chippenham impossible. Control of Ilchester would have given Alfred access to men from the estates around Bruton as well as those from the royal lands spread through south-eastern Somerset, around South Petherton and Crewkerne. Later in his reign when he was well established, he certainly had paid warrior retainers at his court, including pagan Danes (Nelson 1983, 17), and it is likely that this was a feature of the households of other noblemen.

Alfred's success in 878 was in part due to his personal lordship which was effective as long as the men he commanded were not too widely spread or too numerous. When the ninth century command structure of an ealdorman and the shire forces failed, as they did in early 878, a more old-fashioned method of leadership was invoked, personal lordship on the battlefield, and it succeeded. However the consequence of the struggle was a reorganisation of lordship, especially as it applied to war, through Alfred's famous system for providing for a permanent field army and in the longer term, by encouraging the growth of the warrior class. A further consequence was the formalisation of the king's control of justice through the organisation of the hundredal system with its courts. They provided the setting for laws which made 'lordship' a legal obligation for all adult males , something which applied to all free men, not just the warriors.

The Hundred Ordinance of the mid-tenth century shows that the court was probably not yet fully settled as an institution. The very first clause enjoins that the court should be held every four weeks. Much of the rest of the ordinance concerns how the hundred should deal with thefts, particularly relating to cattle, including procedures for passing policing duties from one hundred to another (Whitelock 1955, 391–2). This may be a locally produced document laying down protocols for the benefit of local officials (Wormald 2001, 378–9). There is nothing to suggest that the hundreds themselves were particularly old and they may have sprung from the need to apportion and control work on the Alfredian forts and to systematise the raising of soldiers. They seem to be very much part of the institutionalisation of justice, a process which probably began with King Alfred. King Ine assumed that men would have lords (Whitelock 1955, 368), but also expected that their kin would be responsible for them. Tenth century kings clearly saw lordship as the method which provided the community with the means to bring wrong-doers before the courts and used their law-making powers to make every man responsible to a lord.

The Hundreds, within which justice was administered and where the system of sureties was controlled, may well have started as a reasonably regular division of the shire into manageable units. Dr Thorn's dissection of the hundred of Bath shows how an early hundred may have been formed, with 100 hides of land, but by the time of Domesday Book, when some details of the system first becomes discernible it had become chaotic (Thorn 2005, 9–27). Dr Thorn's 'Exon List II' was probably an index list for the hundredal returns upon which the Exon Domesday was based (DB, p. 370–20). This lists 58 names, some of which were single manors. The actual composition of each hundred is not clear, since the hundred names were not associated with the manorial entries in the Domesday Book. However, it is likely that many of the hundreds were formed by grouping estates around a royal or ecclesiastical centre. The later hundred of Whitley embraced two Domesday Hundreds of Ringwoldesway and Loxley. The land within them belonged entirely to the Abbey of Glastonbury. The two hundreds consisted of estates strung along the Polden Hills, except for the estates at Sowy and High Ham. Sowy, along with the other estates along the Poldens, had belonged to the abbey from a very early date. There is no evidence to suggest that High Ham belonged to the abbey before the mid-tenth century (S791 and see Abrams 1996,

134–5). Possibly Ham would have been attached to the royal estate centre at Somerton prior to its gift to Glastonbury and may have moved from the Somerton hundred to Loxley hundred at that time. It is likely that many estates were moved between hundreds and sometimes detached altogether to suit new and powerful owners. Hundreds controlled by powerful lords, such as the abbot of Glastonbury, would have seen public justice mediated through his officials, but hundreds with a royal centre would have been administered by royal officials. All the hundred courts administered justice according to the common law and those laws laid down by the kings in their doom-books.

Meeting places for the courts were often in the open countryside and may have been designed to provide a neutral site for meetings which must often have been tense affairs in a society where weapons were commonly carried, violence frequent, and punishments often savage. The Bempstone hundred met on the top of a slope on the Isle of Wedmore, at a point quite close to a road and with a wide view across the moorland towards the sea. The hundred meeting point itself was a stone marker, the '*bemereres*' stone – the trumpeter's stone. Such meeting places may well be older than the formal hundred court system and relate to traditional sites for local meetings.

The hundred system and the shire court which probably met to consider business relating to property disputes and to promulgate the king's business to his thegns provided the tenth century kings with a formal method of government of the shire, but the way in which the king's power was most directly felt was through his rights as a major land-owner. It is necessary to use the Domesday ploughland assessment, since so much of the king's land had never been rated for taxation. The king's own lands in 1066 amounted to 653 ploughlands, including the queen's property. This was about 13.5% of the 4815 ploughlands in the shire (Darby 1986). The next greatest landholder was the abbey of Glastonbury with 508.5 ploughlands – 10.5% of the ploughlands. Between them the monasteries and bishops held 1162 ploughlands. The king had an economic advantage, in that his estates were nearly all very large. They averaged just over 36 ploughlands each, while those of Glastonbury averaged just over 13.5 each and

the estates of other churches were similarly smaller than the king's. Insofar as the king could expect to command the support of the Church he controlled 1815 ploughlands, over 37% of the land in Somerset, along with all its military resources.

Of course the Church in Somerset had been nothing like as well endowed as this at the death of King Alfred. As we have seen, throughout the ninth and tenth centuries the kings of Wessex were alienating land to their followers. Some of this land of course returned to the king, but much was permanently alienated. Here the mid-tenth century monastic revival was of enormous importance, since some of the land granted to lay supporters found its way into the hands of the church as pious gifts from laymen. Ditcheat was initially granted by King Athelwulf to the Ealdorman Eanwulf (S292 of AD 842). The estate was probably willed to Glastonbury by a descendant after its revival. As a result the land became attached to an institution which was to hold it until the dissolution of the monasteries in the sixteenth century. The land was effectively 'sterilised'; removed from the process of re-distribution through marriage, sale and gift in wills which was ongoing inside aristocratic families. In addition land granted by the king himself directly to monasteries and to bishops was similarly permanently removed from the aristocratic land-circuit. The king thus built up an enormous reservoir of patronage which he could expect to call upon to support his position in the shire, through influence over individuals exercised by abbots and bishops and if necessary through military power.

The clerics who helped kings to draw up the laws with which they asserted their role as arbiters and guarantors of order in society probably helped to systematise its structure. In providing conceptual tools with which to understand the way in which men related to one another, they introduced a powerful means by which ranks and degrees could be defined and each man and woman's place marked out. The laws came at an important moment, when the kingdom of Wessex was coming into existence. The new definitions of each man's place in the world were closely intertwined with the expansion of Wessex, especially in its drive westward and were a counterpart to the physical conquests of the seventh century.

Conclusion

It is evident that the attempt to define a society by a description of the different sorts of men within it cannot be more than a snapshot of a particular moment. Presumably King Alfred preserved Ine's Laws because he felt that they were relevant to his own day, but it is clear that by the time of the Norman Conquest real changes had taken place. The law was becoming less interested in the status of those who offended and more concerned about the ways in which justice might be administered. Justice had become less personal and was much more formal. The king was mostly anxious that men should be answerable to the courts through the sureties provided by the people who lived around them, rather than by their kin. The lines between the noble and the non-noble had become blurred as the kings sought to increase their military followings and provide a defensive system which was no longer concerned with plunder and expansion but sought to protect the integrity of the kingdom. For the king, lordship meant a military tie to men he hardly knew, and to the landowners in Somerset it was expressed through land-ownership and the patronage which might be exercised through it.

A common theme which unites the men of the seventh century with those of the eleventh was their concern about the ownership of land. Both *gesith* and *ceorlisc* men were defined in terms of the land they held and it was the ownership of land which determined status in the eleventh century, though not in such formal terms as in the seventh. That relationship to the land was often expressed through the kind of landed holdings they lived upon and sometimes fossilised in the place-names of the countryside. At the bottom of society men were marked by their failure to own land outright and their increasing subjection to those who did. The line between the slave and the unfree peasant had become increasingly blurred and their relationship to the land one of subjection rather than control. They changed hands with the land – theirs was not a personal relationship with a lord. To a large degree they were the victims of changes in agricultural practice driven once more by the needs of the king and his aristocracy for increasing control of the resources of the countryside to meet the demands of a much enlarged kingdom and expanded military capability. To put it crudely, they needed both to increase total output and to expand their share of the surpluses.

Notes

1   The apparent directness of the Ine's Laws is complicated by the possibility that they were in fact compiled over a period of years, and may contain additions by later rulers. See P. Wormald, *The Making of English Law: King Alfred to the Twelfth Century, Vol. 1. Legislation and its Limits*. Oxford, (Blackwell, 1999), 103–5.

2. Ælfsige was dead by 1087, so this entry, originally in a copy of the Gospels, must have been written before the time of Domesday.

5

Ancient Agriculture

The post-Roman condition

If, as suggested above in Chapter 3, the first half of the fifth century saw the collapse of the towns and the market system, the reduction of the population by plague, as well as social disruption, it is clear that agricultural practice must also have changed. Much later a similar upheaval associated with the Black Death in the mid- to late fourteenth century was marked by an unsuccessful attempt by the ruling elite to maintain the old social patterns and agricultural regimes, followed by an adjustment in social structure and relationships during which extensive arable cultivation gave way to sheep and cattle rearing. However the fourteenth and fifteenth century agricultural revolution took place in an environment where towns and markets continued to function. The fifth century experience was more traumatic. It might be assumed that the agricultural reaction would be dramatic also.

We actually know little about the agricultural practice of the post-Roman period. As a result it may be helpful to propose a theoretical model and then to test it against what evidence there is.

The post-Roman agricultural regime needed to provide for a population which was divided between a small elite of rulers and their associated warriors on the one hand and the mass of the rural peasantry on the other. The surviving craftsmen were probably closely associated with the ruling warrior elite and shared in their economy to which they contributed. For part of the period the rulers and their followers lived in or close to re-used hill-forts and when those were abandoned they probably transferred to rural centres

nearby. They needed to exploit the labours of the peasantry to provide themselves with adequate food supplies, plenty of high protein foods, such as meat, fish and dairy products as well as grain, a substantial part of which could be converted into alcoholic drink. They would also have needed adequate foodstuff for their horses, which were probably used for prestige transport as well as being symbols of status. They would also have needed plentiful supplies of raw materials such as wool and flax for conversion into cloth for their clothing, as well as hides, the leather from which was used extensively in many different household items as well as things such as horse harness. There was also a need for worked timber for use in construction. They may also have needed to command an agricultural surplus which could be used to trade for items otherwise unobtainable, such as metal for weapons and tools or other specialised manufactured items. Of course the system could not be static. Over a period of two and a half centuries the size of the population may have changed and the numbers demanding support may have changed also.

There were two ways in which these surpluses might be obtained. One was to continue to exploit estates directly, where possible using bond labour. As we have seen earlier there is every reason to conclude that slavery continued to be an important institution in post-Roman Britain and this could be one method used to work such estates. In a society where people were relatively scarce every effort would be made to maintain the slave population, unless they were used as a resource to be exchanged for goods. The other method was to simply demand a share of the peasant cultivators' surplus as tribute, effectively rent, but otherwise allow them to cultivate as they wished. The two methods are not mutually exclusive and we might expect to find them running side by side as complementary strategies.

Theory would also suggest that with a fall in population and the cessation of food supply to towns, the extent of cultivation would decline and there would be a move away from arable farming towards less labour intensive methods, particularly towards cattle and sheep rearing in open areas and cattle and pig rearing in wooded regions. The question is: do we have any evidence to confirm or refute this model?

So far there is little detailed evidence to suggest that woodland regeneration was extensive across the shire. The most detailed studies using pollen analysis have been conducted around Exmoor and unfortunately mostly in Devon. Evidence from the Somerset part of Exmoor at Hoar Moor in Exford Parish suggests that these high lands were exploited by a system of shifting arable cultivation and animal husbandry and that this pattern persisted from c. 1600 BC until c. AD 500 (Francis and Slater 1990, 19). Woodland does not seem to have been advancing, and the general farming pattern persisted through into the post-Roman period. A similar study at Codsend Moor in Cutcombe again suggested that arable farming continued during the whole millennium somewhere nearby, though grazing decreased in the later half of the period (Francis and Slater 1992, 27). At the Chains on Exmoor there is some evidence for the retreat of farming and some return of woodland (Dark, P. 2000, 143).

These studies are inevitably on high ground and very localised. Studies made in Devon around the edge of Exmoor on valley sites show that there was little change in the region between the fourth and sixth centuries. This was a pastoral landscape which showed no sign of woodland regeneration. There is little sign of abandonment of settlement or of the traditional field systems (Rippon, Fyte and Brown 2006, 49). If that result can be extrapolated to similar areas of Somerset around the northern and southern edges of Exmoor and the Brendon Hills, a picture of a farming society which chiefly relied upon livestock rearing and management and which was mainly static for the two and a half centuries after the end of Roman

administration would seem plausible. Small pastoral communities would have farmed in their traditional manner, exploiting the moorlands as areas for the grazing of cattle and sheep, cultivating some grain crops in sheltered areas, but not advancing settlement. Such a region, not much affected by the commercial world of the late Roman Empire, lacking both towns and a villa economy, would have suffered less of a shock than places nearer 'civilization' when the fifth century collapse occurred and so would have had little reason to change practice. It might also be possible to extend this view to suggest that since there was little in the way of 'romanisation' west of the Parrett and few signs that the area was much affected by the rise of the hill-fort culture of central and northern Somerset, this whole area may have continued to function in much the old way.

As around Exmoor, so in other parts of Somerset woodland advance was not general, but this does not mean that there was no change in the proportion of land given over to woods. Some additional woodland cover might well be expected with a population fall and less intensive use of the countryside, even if agriculture continued. An advance of woodland does not imply cessation of cultivation, but its contraction. Work by John Knight on woodland in north Somerset has shown that the earthworks of abandoned Romano-British field systems underlie a number of sites. In a sample of 50 ancient woods no less than nine were shown to have earthworks. They are likely, therefore, to be examples of woodland regeneration in the post-Roman period. Examples are widely scattered across the whole region north of the Mendips, suggesting that the regeneration was not an isolated or exceptional event (Knight 2003, 45–7). If we were to extrapolate this finding across the county east of the Parrett, we might expect to find quite frequent evidence of woodland advance, particularly where the topography is broken and hilly.

The levels behind the coast, to the north of the Parrett estuary, were mostly salt-marsh, used for salt production. By the mid-fourth century the industry was already in decline and at Burnham and Huntspill after this time the levels were sealed by alluvium at least 0.5 m deep. North of that area, around Brent Knoll, there is ample evidence of Romano-British settlement which was also buried under sediment

(Fowler 1970). To the north of the Mendips the Levels were farmed and after the Roman period went into a slow decline which saw the gradual disappearance of cultivation. The sea level rise which caused this may have been quite slow and the ingress of tides may have been the result of the gradual degradation of sea defences over a considerable period. The accumulation of silt was much smaller here and there are signs that flooding was mostly by fresh water (Rippon *et al.* 2000, 95–6). This probably made it impossible to maintain settlements on the lowest land. Of course, periods of flooding would have made the land much less productive, but the marshes would still have been very valuable as fishing and fowling grounds and would have provided seasonal grazing for people living around the edges of the lowest land.

Parts of the inland levels had also been well cultivated and around Ilchester, on the edge of the low ground, there is evidence that Roman-period fields were abandoned. Land which had been used to grow cereals, with drainage, hedges and ditches, had been buried under about 0.30 m of silt, which was probably deposited by seasonal flooding from the rivers. On top of this silt post-Conquest medieval ceramics mark the re-appearance of cultivation (Leach 1987, 121). We might expect that land which needed extensive maintenance to keep it under arable cultivation would be the first to be abandoned, but cessation of ploughing does not mean cessation of use and it was probably grazed.

It is noteworthy that there are three dedications to St Bridget in lowland areas of Somerset (Fig. 5.1). The churches at Brean and at Chelvey are both dedicated to her. The saint is associated with cattle rearing and the place-name 'Chelvey', although it is Old English rather than Old Welsh, means the 'calf wic'. Bridget is of course an Irish saint whose cult was widely established outside Ireland under the influence of Irish evangelisation on the continent and her cult was well established in Wales also (Farmer 1987, 62). Near Cannington there were fields called 'Saint Brides meadow' in 1607 (SRO, DD\BRbn10), there was a field called 'brides' at Stowell (t. 199–200) and a 'brides field' at Timberscombe (t. 247). 'Bride' or 'Bridie' were common diminutives for Bridget and close to the St Bridget's chapel on Beckery, near Glastonbury, there are still fields called 'bridies'. The

cult in Somerset may well have developed before the coming of the Anglo-Saxons, and if so would suggest that cattle-rearing was important to the area in the post-Roman period. There are other important traces of her cult locally which may also preserve traces of devotion to a saint who might protect cattle. The chapel on Beckery Island, near Glastonbury and an abbey possession, which was certainly there in the eighth century, was dedicated to her (Rahtz and Hirst 1974). It was a site with strong associations with the Irish pilgrims who passed through on the journeys between the European mainland and Ireland and this may explain the cult. However it stood on the edge of the Levels, on the margin of an enormous tract of moorland grazing, which might also have fostered the cult. Both Glastonbury Abbey and Muchelney Abbey were surrounded by marshes. This was especially the case at Muchelney, where the abbey and its earliest possessions were on quite small islands in the moors. At both monasteries St Bridget figured in their Kalendars as she later did at Wells. In the case of Glastonbury her cult was celebrated by c. 970 at the latest (Wormald 1988, 45) and at Muchelney she also appears in the medieval breviary in the later thirteenth century (Schofield 1927).

The east of the shire has a much gentler landscape and was always much more heavily populated. In addition it was the area closest to the threat from the east and it had the hill-fort of South Cadbury as its elite centre. One might expect the agriculture of the area to reflect different needs, with a larger non-agricultural group demanding support. Some idea of the strategies employed by agriculturalists in this lowland area has been provided by the work of John Davey. He has identified three very extensive field systems: the first of which (his system 'B') covers a wide area of countryside in the south-east of Somerset, running from the Blackmore Vale in Dorset westward as far as Rimpton and Sherborne; another system ('A') adjoining which runs northwards through North and South Barrow; a third system ('C') which covers Maperton and Yarlington (Fig. 5.2). In the first system he shows that the field alignments throughout the Horethorne Hundred run with their long axes east-north-east to west-south-west, respecting the western slopes of the Blackmore Vale. The fields, about five times as long as they are wide, are typical of the later

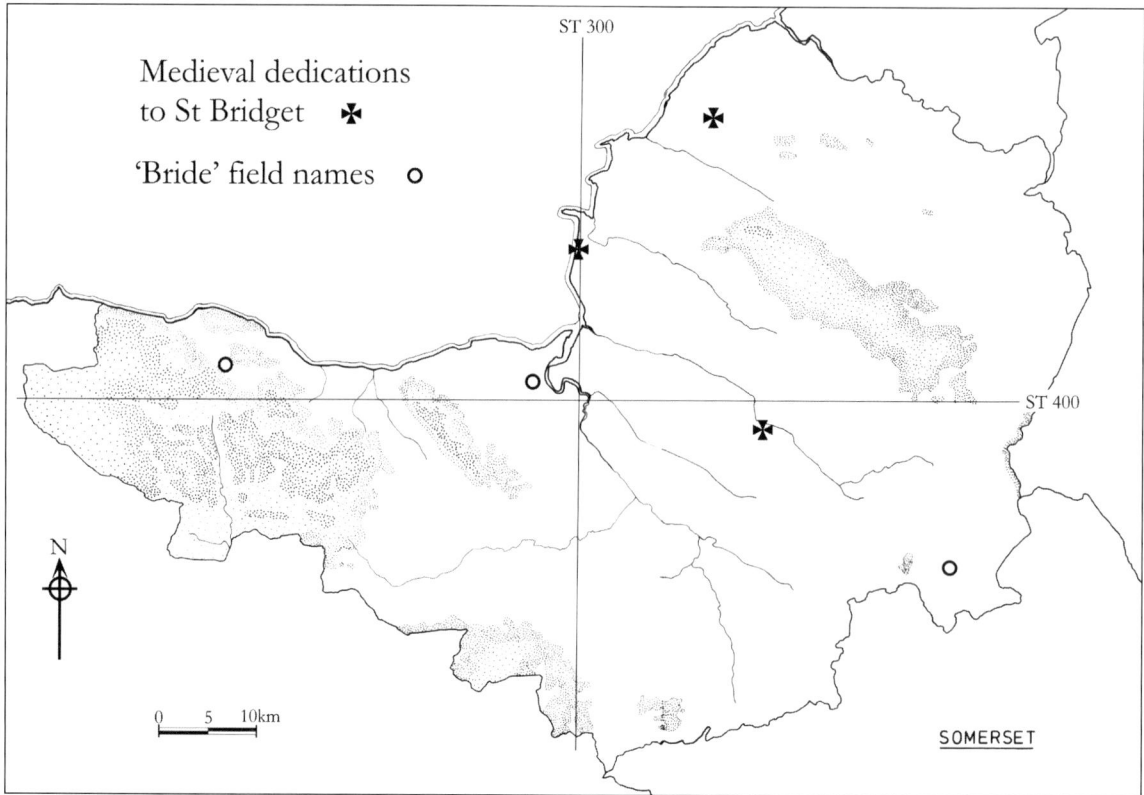

Figure 5.1. Bridget and Bridie.

Roman period. He suggests that the estate around Sherborne in Dorset was carved out of this rectangular landscape and that it must therefore be younger. This would indicate a Roman or pre-Roman origin for the system. His system 'A' is the earliest. These fields in turn may be related to late-prehistoric droves running perpendicular to the major river valleys (Davey 2005, 66–72). Earlier work had already identified parts of this system, showing that it probably extended westward (Rawlings 1992, 37–8)

The clear implication of the survival of this landscape is that it has been continuously cultivated since the Roman period at least and the deposition of silt across the previous arable fields at Ilchester suggests that the catchment area of the Yeo within this landscape was subject to some degree of continuing arable exploitation. The later tenth and eleventh century open-field systems are superimposed upon the old system without obliterating it and the

boundaries of Anglo-Saxon and later estates respect it. Much of the land in this area is relatively flat and fertile and in the Middle Ages supported numerous arable estates. It does not follow, however, that the land was always used in the same way. Arable need not have dominated in the fifth and sixth centuries as it did in the mid-eleventh century. At Castle Farm, South Cadbury, the excavation of a ditch close to a Romano-British settlement showed that the fifth century ditch fill consisted mostly of sheep bones (Davey 2005, 79). It may be that much of the region saw a rise in animal husbandry, utilising the existing field pattern, but there is little evidence to suggest widespread abandonment of land and certainly not of re-growth of woodland (Davey 2005, 50). The increased importance of animal husbandry does not preclude the continuance of arable cultivation, but suggests that it became less important. It may be that an early period of demand for supplies from the

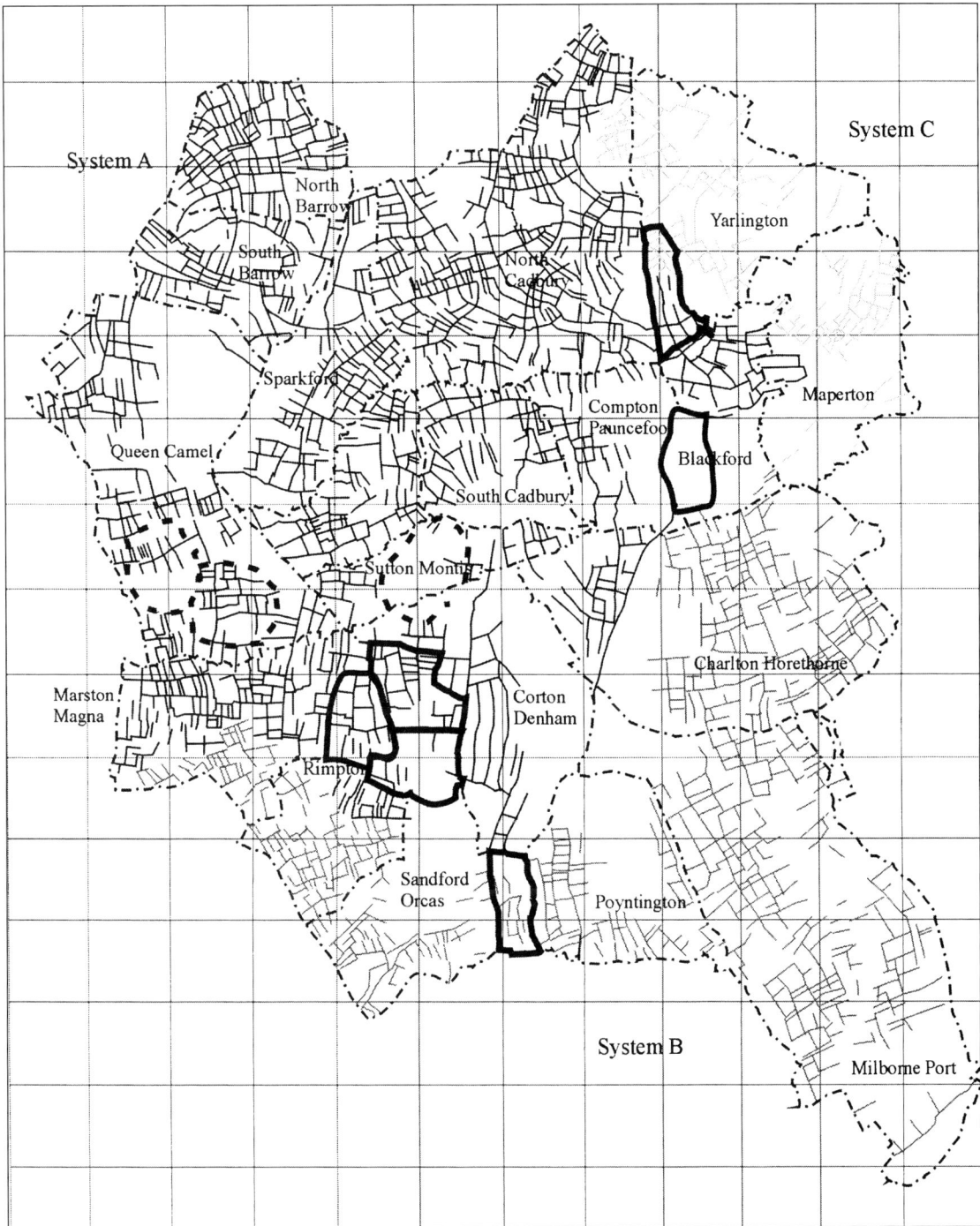

Figure 5.2. Post-Roman field systems around South Cadbury (after John Davey 2005).

South Cadbury hill-fort helped to keep this whole region active and that the pattern of fields persisted over such a wide area because of demand or control from the elite centre at the hill-fort.

There is also some evidence to suggest continuity of agricultural practice at Bleadon. Here there are clear signs that the later medieval open-field system has been superimposed upon earlier field patterns. 'The boundaries of the early fields appear to run into the medieval strip fields, which themselves have been fossilized by later enclosure' (Iles and Stacey 1984, 55–6). It could of course be the case that the later open-fields were simply laid out over the earlier field boundaries because there was nowhere else for them to go, in an area squashed between the steep hill to the north and the wet levels to the south, but it seems unlikely that there was no cultivation or use of the earlier Romano-British fields on arable land. Work by Peter Fowler drew together much information about the survival of pre-Anglo-Saxon field systems in northern Somerset, demonstrating their existence in many areas where cultivation did not resume in the medieval period, but there is little evidence linking them with later cultivation (Fowler 1978, 29–47). In the Roman period the whole of the Chew Valley had been well settled and the existence of large estates in the Anglo-Saxon period suggests that continuity of occupation was widespread. Evidence of much post-Roman agricultural activity probably lies buried under later medieval fields.

The Chew valley contains the estate of Chew Magna. This was a large manor of 30 hides, with land for 50 ploughs in 1086 (DB 6.3). Chew Magna had probably been an endowment of the church at Wells from its foundation in 909 and a property of Sherborne before that (O'Donovan 1988, xxxvii–xlvii). It is of course named after the river on which it stands. This name has not been satisfactorily explained. Within the manor, and almost certainly a part of the pre-Domesday settlement, lay Stoke, now Chew Stoke, already broken up into smaller dependent units by 1066 (DB 37.3–4, 47.16). As mentioned in an earlier chapter, the estate had important Roman antecedents. Chew Stoke is the site of the famous Pagans Hill Temple, parts of which were visible above ground into the modern period. Here there is evidence of activity into the fifth century

and beyond. It has been suggested that the temple kept its roof into the thirteenth century (Rahtz and Watts 1989, 330, 333). Chew Stoke was also the site of a Roman villa. It has also produced evidence of contact with the Anglo-Saxon world in the blue glass jars and these have been dated to the early seventh century, before the Anglo-Saxon take over of the area (Wooding 1996, 87–8). This strongly suggests that settlement in the area was of high status and that it was organised with a degree of sophistication. This in turn implies a substantial population needing agricultural resources for support. It seems very likely that this area continued to be worked agriculturally. It certainly did not revert to uncultivated land.

There is then, some evidence to suggest that the agricultural system continued to function much as before, though some of those areas which were used for arable on a large scale seem to have retreated to grass. Many marshland areas also ceased to be intensively utilised and instead became grazing grounds, while those areas which had always been pastoral continued in much the old way, particularly in the west.

Farming early Anglo-Saxon estates

The agricultural needs of the early medieval world were of course conditioned by the structure of society. Post-Roman Somerset was dominated by a very few power-centres and it is likely that there was a relatively loose structure to society with a fairly 'flat' hierarchy, especially after the collapse of the central authority at Tintagel. This might favour an unstressed pastoral economy which relied chiefly on tribute to support the economically inactive. In contrast the much more hierarchically self-conscious Anglo-Saxon militarised society favoured the growth of quite large households surrounding the newly emerged kings and probably around the ealdormen also. Parallel with the growth of royal and aristocratic entourages went the reorganisation of monastic communities which also had the potential for major growth. As a result the kings, princes and abbots needed to organise their agricultural support to meet the needs of large and growing groups of economically non-productive followers, whether they were warriors or monks. As we have seen, the necessary manpower in a society where labour was relatively scarce was to hand in the institution of slavery and its associated states of dependence and semi-slavery. The prominence of slavery in Ine's Laws is evidence of the importance of the institution in the economy of Anglo-Saxon Wessex and penal slavery was an expression of this economic imperative. The great estate was necessary but only possible because of the strict social organisation behind it. It was the economic and social expression of the inexorable pressure of a warrior society built around loyalty to the new royal institution.

Writing about the *villae* of Merovingian Gaul, Adriaan Verhulst has drawn attention to the way in which the arable demesne was cultivated by slaves or bond men attached to the estate centre. The arable, though important, did not occupy more than 20 to 40% of the estate and peasant tenants performed very little in the way of labour services (Verhulst 1992, 1 145–7). He points out that these estates in north-western Gaul were not simply successors to the Roman *fundi*, but normally had their estate centres built well away from the old Roman sites. It would be too simplistic to imagine that the estates of seventh century Wessex were modelled upon or sought to emulate those of the continental world, but it is the case that the kings of Wessex and their aristocracy and especially the church were faced with much the same challenges when organising their economic base, a challenge which was for them relatively new and had developed only as the kings accrued power and prestige through recruitment of a large armed following. For the first time they were faced with the need to support a large number of people who were mostly gathered together in one place for long periods.

Ine's Laws contain a surprising statement about food renders; 'As a food rent from 10 hides: 10 vats of honey, 300 loaves, 12 ambers of Welsh ale, 30 of clear ale, 2 full grown cows, or 10 wethers, 10 geese, 20 hens, 10 cheeses, an amber full of butter, 5 salmon, 20 pounds of fodder and 100 eels' (Whitelock 1955, 371). Of course we do not know if this was actually a law of Ine himself and therefore of the late seventh or very early eighth century or whether it dates from a little later in the eighth century, but in any case it shows a remarkably clear view of the output to be expected from an estate. This may have been a measure of what was expected on the king's lands, or

perhaps an attempt to enforce a uniform render on estates loaned out to his aristocratic followers. What it does demonstrate is the wide range of foodstuffs expected to be available from what was clearly a mixed farming environment, with access to rivers large enough to carry salmon. This, together with the reference to Welsh ale, makes it likely that this ruling was promulgated for estates in the west of Wessex. It also reveals the expectations and frame of reference within which the great estates functioned. It would be difficult to describe something so comprehensive as merely 'subsistence'.

It has already been proposed that the typical royal and ecclesiastical estates of seventh and eighth centuries consisted of a core area, surrounded by dependent smaller settlements, sometimes with specialist functions. This core area seems to have had arable agriculture at its heart and a topography which is common to several of them is still discernible. Often the estate lay on an area of extensive arable land, the scale of which is often apparent from the Domesday record. In some cases the estate centre, typically marked by the site of the church, lay towards the edge of the arable area. The great estate of Somerton is a good example. The church and the likely settlement centre stood on a bluff overlooking a valley to the north-east, on the edge of the Somerton 'island'. The area was one which had been heavily settled in the Roman period (Fig. 5.3) and the fairly level ground to the west and south of the present village was the site of the later open-fields, with a strong north/ south pattern. The cultivation and pattern extended westward as far as the manor of Pitney which was a 1 hide estate in 1086 (DB 1.34). The nature of its boundary suggests it was taken out of Somerton after cultivation extended that far. To the south-west was the manor of Long Sutton, which was probably granted to Athelney Abbey in the ninth century by King Alfred (Keynes 1994b, 1134). The indented nature of the parish boundary again suggests that there was already ploughland here when the boundary was drawn, though the nature of the surviving charter boundary clause makes it difficult to be certain (S343, 852 for 878) (Fig. 5.3).

At Curry Rivel also, the church again lay to the north-east corner of a large arable area which was later cut by the boundaries of dependent settlements, and

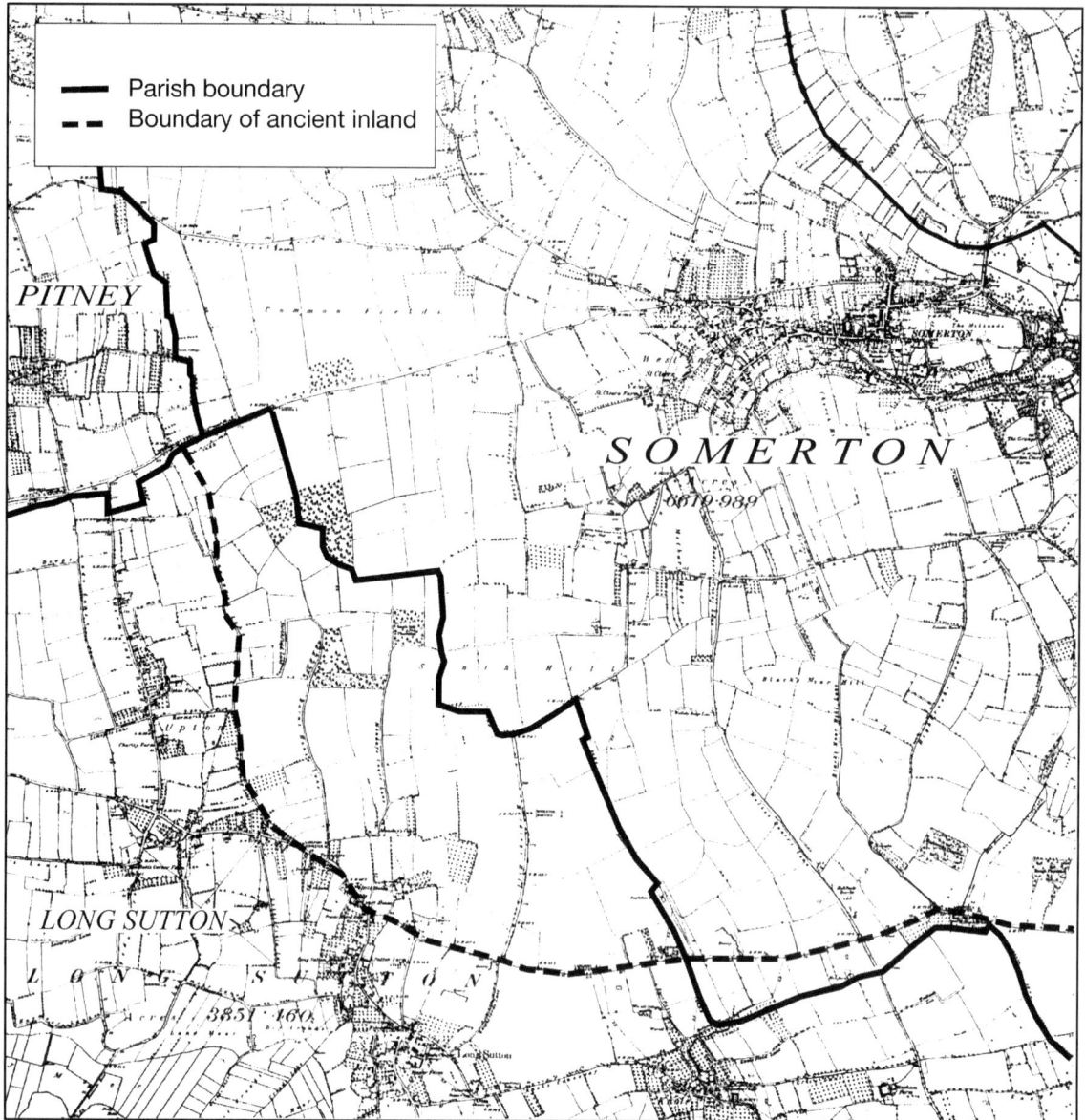

Figure 5.3. Somerton and its possible inland.

its boundary with Drayton to the east, an estate which passed to Muchelney Abbey at some date in the Anglo-Saxon period, also betrays a division made when cultivation had already reached the area (Fig. 5.4).

Similar patterns are discernible at Keynsham, Frome and North Petherton and at Milborne Port, which was still 'Kingsbury' at this point. At other places – Crewkerne, South Petherton, Chewton Mendip – the manorial centre is more centrally placed. The example at Chewton Mendip has already been explored and may preserve a fossilised boundary of just such an estate before expansion. In each case

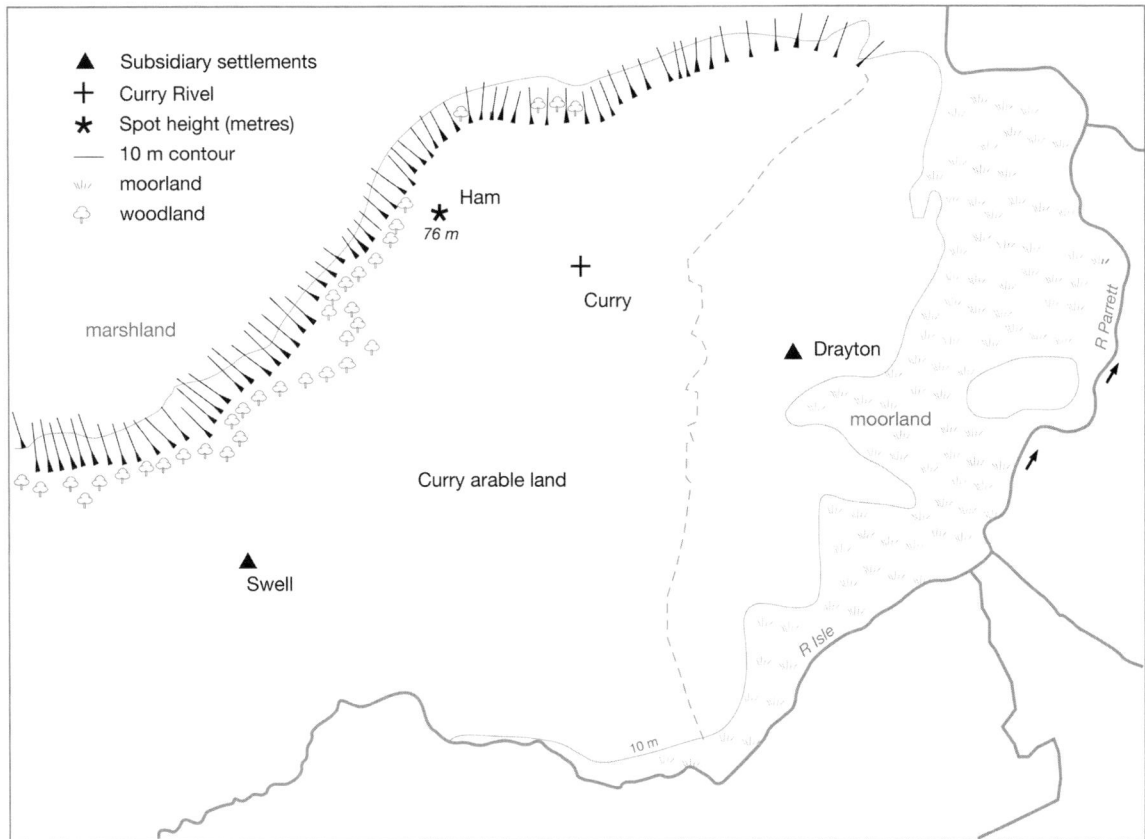

Figure 5.4. The early Curry Rivel estate.

an area of fairly flat and easily cultivated land is surrounded by dependent settlements, some of which were recognised as independent manors by 1086, some of which remained within the parent estate. At North Petherton, for example, Thurloxton was fairly obviously a detachment from the ancient estate, but other sites, such as Huntworth and Hadworthy, outlying settlements, never broke free.

South Petherton still exhibits an extraordinary plan. The centre of the settlement, with its important church, stands on a low bluff overlooking a stream. Surrounding it were the open-fields, which were arranged in an enormous circular pattern. The outline of this circle is still very marked on modern maps, on early Ordnance Survey maps (OS 6" 1st ed.), and on the tithe map (D\D/Rt/M/291). In contrast the probably later manor of Over Stratton, described as

a subsidiary of South Petherton in Domesday Book (DB 1.4) on the south eastern side of the Fosse Way, has a rectilinear plan as do its fields around it. Compton Durville, another manor within South Petherton Parish, lies immediately to the west of the circular fields, as if it was planted on open ground, outside the central estate fields, and also has a mainly rectilinear field plan (Fig. 5.5).

That this pattern is not unique to Somerset is evident from the work of Keen (1984) on Sherborne and Dorchester. Both places exhibit a large scale pattern of boundaries suggesting an extensive field system, surrounding the central settlement, in the case of Sherborne the monastic site and at Dorchester the important royal manor. As we have seen, this Sherborne estate intrudes upon the earlier large-scale pattern of Roman and post-Roman fields and must

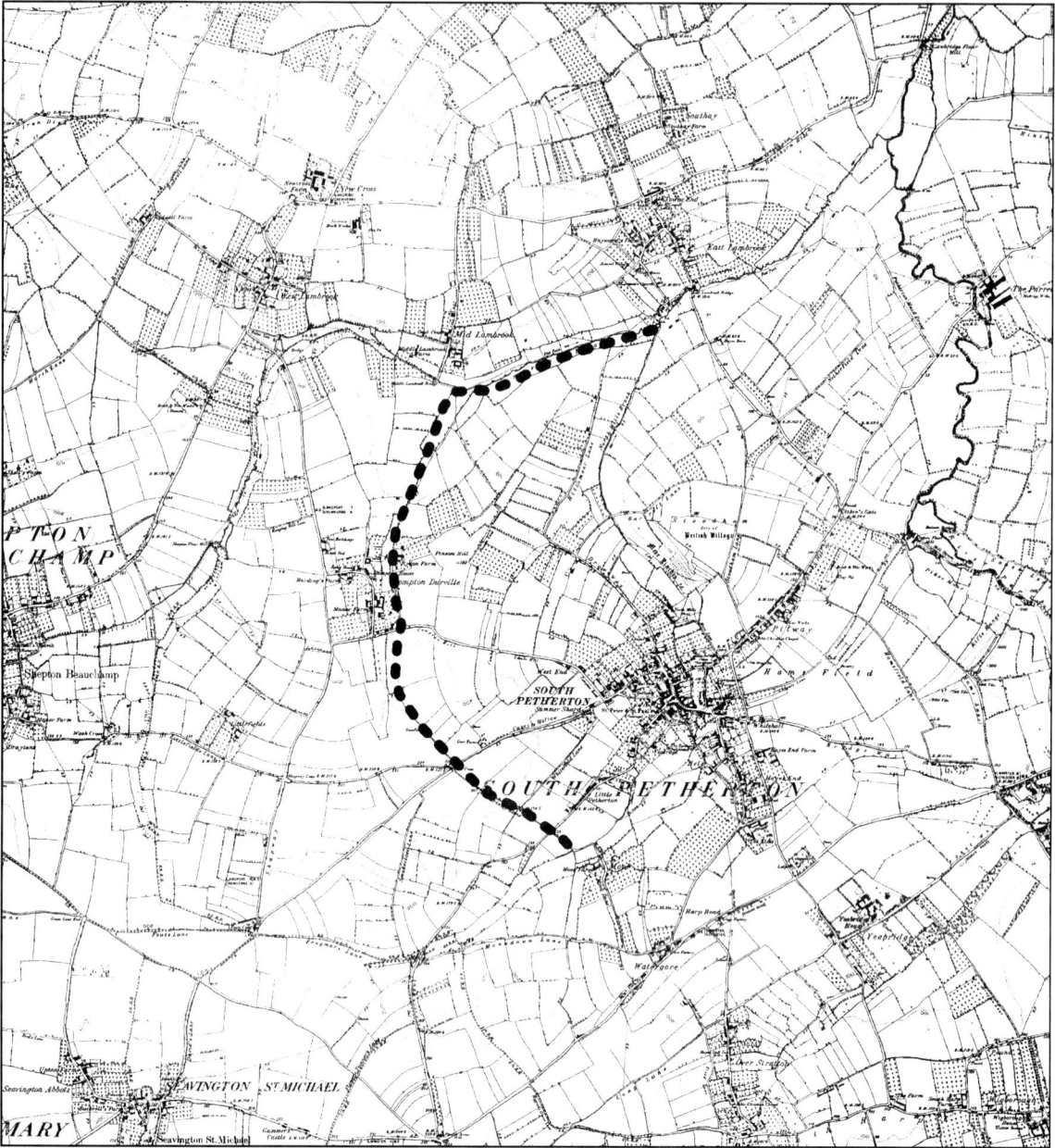

Figure 5.5. South Petherton showing the boundary of its early arable inlands.

therefore post-date them. It adds weight to the idea that there was a characteristic structure to important royal and ecclesiastical settlements and that this was something which emerged in the early Anglo-Saxon period – probably the later seventh or early eighth

centuries. I am not suggesting that these early central estates had common-field systems working in the later seventh or eighth centuries. A common-field system would imply that there were tenants integrated into the system which was run on a fairly rigid basis, with two great fields, alternately cropped and fallowed. What existed instead was an open-field system, where the land was cultivated as arable on a permanent basis, but not in a communal way. Susan Oosthuizen has made the distinction between open-field and common-field crystal clear in her important paper on the origins of common-fields (2007).

West of the Parrett the topography made it more difficult to farm in this extensive manner, but Taunton was clearly an estate of this type, although probably founded for strategic control of the crossing of the Tone and of the valley running west of the Quantocks to the sea. Williton, at the seaward end of this valley, did have considerable areas of good level agricultural land and Williton itself would have been founded to work that ground, inland of the post-Roman landing place and religious site at Watchet, while Cannington also commanded extensive land suitable for arable.

Such large areas of arable would have consisted of the lord's land and the small tenements of his unfree dependents. They must have been devoted to grain crops and can only have been worked by dependents. We have little idea to what extent free peasants were required to provide services within such a system as well as giving tribute renders. In Gaul the demesne was worked chiefly by slaves with the addition of labour services from the holders of peasant tenements (Verhulst 1992). Whether peasant proprietors, the ceorls, already owed some labour services as rent at this early date we do not know, but it seems likely that Ine's laws already show such services developing. 'If anyone covenants for a yardland or more at a fixed rent, and plough it, if the lord wishes to increase for him the [rent of the] land by demanding service as well as rent, he need not accept it, if he does not give him a dwelling; and he is to forfeit the crops' (Whitelock 1955, 371). As Rosamund Faith has pointed out, the crucial point here is that accepting a dwelling from the lord meant accepting perpetual control by the lord (Faith 1997, 76). It is likely that as necessity drove peasants to accept the house they found themselves performing labour services as well as paying rents in kind. In this way the estate could build a group of dependants who worked their own yardlands, probably outside the area dominated by the lord's lands, but who were available to add their labour to the lord's demesne as need arose.

If this analysis of estate sites in Somerset is valid it would suggest that early important centres, whether royal or ecclesiastical, would have been marked by extensive arable on good quality, flat lands, laid out close to a centre which was not necessarily in the middle of the cultivated area, but often sited in a dominant position. Exactly how the lands were worked is not clear. There may already have been a rotation system of some sort in operation, but it may not have been organised in a formal 'two-field' system. In such large systems there would have been room for a kind of shifting cultivation inside the lord's land, with a return to particular plots taking place at quite long intervals. The area reserved for cultivation may have been large, but the actual land under plough in any one season may only have been a fraction of the land available. Physically the lord's estate might consist of his own lands grouped on the best land and fairly easily accessible from his court, while the tenants lived, some close to his court and owed services, others scattered on other parts of the estate in their own houses. The tenants' land would lie around the periphery of the lord's holdings and beyond that would be the pastures, meadows, woods and in some cases major dependent settlements, later to appear as independent manors. The ceorls who had their own dwellings and were superior to those who lived in a house provided by the lord probably worked small farmsteads, separate from the lord's arable, since Ine's Laws tells us that 'A ceorl's homestead must be fenced winter and summer. If it is not fenced and his neighbour's cattle get in through his own gap, he has no right to anything from that cattle; he is to drive it out and suffer the damage' (Whitelock 1955, 368). The homestead or wyrth must have contained his arable crops, which could be damaged by straying beasts. His animals, along with those of his neighbours, would have fed on the common pastures. Similar problems arose over meadow land (Whitelock 1955, 368). The Laws envisage a common meadow belonging to the ceorls which was divided into lots, which would be fenced around against cattle by common effort – each man would have fenced a section. If someone failed to fence and the cattle damaged everyone's hay then those who had suffered would be compensated by the offender. The promulgation of the laws suggests that the problems of unfenced arable and meadow were something which was growing or had only recently arisen. Perhaps the ceorl with his small fenced arable, common meadow and animals on the pastures was becoming a common part of the landscape of large estates. Such a common pasture formed a boundary point in the charter of 909 for Bishops Lydeard and is named as *fasingafeld*, 'the open land of Fasa's men' (S380). If the Laws suggest a meadow used by the peasants and there was pasture used by a lord's men, then there were probably similar areas used exclusively by the lord and his slaves and other bond-men. The *swan mere* 'peasants' boundary' in the Anglo-Saxon bounds of Long Sutton is a similar reference and the *swan mead* at Wellow (t. 1097–8) may also be a meadow reserved for these peasants.

For the ceorl or minor aristocrat on a smaller estate it is possible that they practised some form of shifting agriculture, with an infield which was more or less permanently cultivated and a larger area on which crops were grown on a portion only and cultivation was shifted around from year to year. The middle field at Tatworth near Chard might preserve some remnant of such a system (Fig. 5.6). What later became a large area of open-field may have started as two large enclosures, surrounded by common waste (Down and Carter 1990, 117). This may have been the outfield area. The manorial centre, the 'wyrth', lies in an area of irregular, curving enclosures, surrounded by lanes.

At Badgworth near Axbridge, the manorial centre, now the site of the village, exists as a large rectangular area, bounded by modern lanes. It amounts to about 6.75 hectares or 16.6 acres. It lies at the foot of a low hill, just on the edge of the moors. The 10 m contour runs through the square from north to south. This may have been the central 'wyrth' and to the south the outfield may have lain in part of the later rectangular open-field of Badgworth. In 1066 it was regarded as two manors, probably each of 1 hide, held by two thegns, though this looks to have been a late division (DB 24.10). Stephen Rippon has also identified a number of settlements in the Levels as beginning with an area of infield. In addition to the settlement at Puxton he suggests a number of sites in East and West Huntspill, East Brent and Lympsham as well as other sites in the northern Levels. All the places are distinguished by an irregular oval central area, with

tracks leading into it (Lane and Coles 2002, 60–1). On average these 'infields' are of about 13 hectares. The outfield here would have consisted of grazing in the moors rather than extensive outfields.

Smaller farmsteads occupied by ceorls would mostly have been subsumed inside later field systems as cultivation expanded in the late Anglo-Saxon period. However there may be traces of some of these settlements surviving as deserted sites. At Chewton Mendip a group of fields on the outskirts of the parish have the names 'sacerfield'. This may mean land belonging to priests (OE *sacerdland*, land allotted to priests, Clark Hall 1960). These fields are associated with a number of large oval areas, now enclosed by banks and lanes in a hilly area on the edge of the Mendips. Chewton Mendip Church held half a hide of land at Domesday and these farmsteads may have started as land allocated for the support of the church and its priests (DB 1.29).

Fisheries

Arable cultivation was of course only one part of the exploitation of the landscape. Ine's 'rent' makes it clear that the rivers were regarded as important sources of food. For Anglo-Saxon society fishing was an important activity which provided a useful source of calories for relatively little effort and little capital outlay as long as it did not involve the use of boats. There is little to suggest that fishing at sea, or even by boat, was a normal activity prior to the tenth century. It is likely that river fishing and fishing from the seashore were the major methods used. Fishing in rivers was probably an activity which supplemented the incomes of people who otherwise were cultivators. The material evidence consists of the extensive remains of fish-traps along the Somerset coast, particularly in the west, and the survival of a number of 'weir' names indicative of the existence of fluvial fish-traps. Evidence from radio-carbon dating of fish-trap posts surviving around Bridgwater Bay show that fishing for sea-fish by this method was well established in the Anglo-Saxon period with dates ranging between the early eighth century and the Conquest. Ten different samples provide robust evidence, but there are no dates suggesting that the practice existed before the mid-seventh century. For

Figure 5.6. The suggested 'wyrth' at Tatworth.

the moment it looks as if fish-traps first appeared after the arrival of the Anglo-Saxons in the area (Straker 2008, 187). It may be that the arrival of the English, with the development of great estates as the result of the more hierarchical society they introduced, placed greater demands than hitherto on traditional fishing, pushing people to exploit the more difficult environment on the coast.

The parish name 'Weare' is derived from the Old English '*wer*', '*wær*', a dam or weir (Smith 1970, 255). The estate lies on the south bank of the river Axe, which was then tidal. A fish-weir built there would

have trapped sea-fish as they moved with the tide. The word is also incorporated in the place-names Dunwear (on the lower Parrett) and Warleigh (on the Avon to the east of Bath). All these names probably indicate fishing stations which were in operation in the eighth century and the Butleigh charter of 801 (S270a) also contains a reference to '*Bregedeswer*', 'Breged's fish trap'. Sometimes the fish-trap alone could be sufficiently valuable to be granted. In 708 Bealdhun granted Froda, the abbot of Muchelney, a fish-trap at Swynwere on the Parrett (S1174). There are now lost records of grants of fisheries to

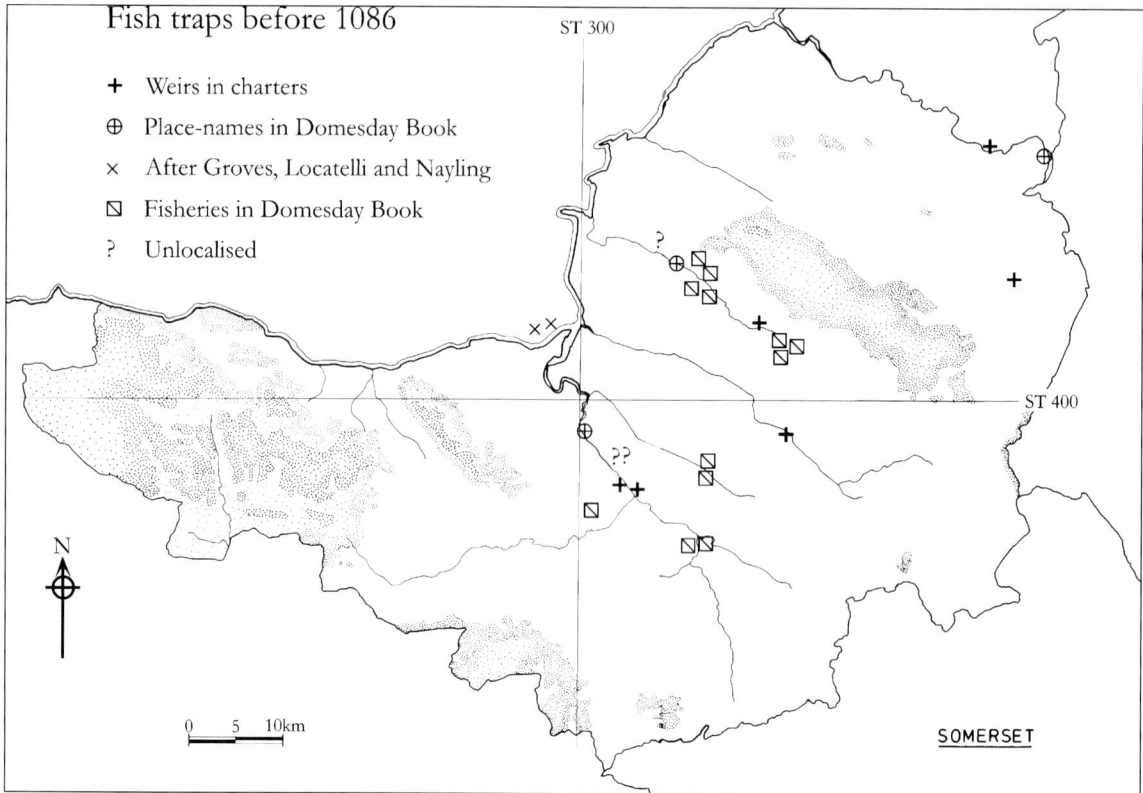

Figure 5.7. Fishtraps in the Anglo-Saxon period.

Glastonbury Abbey in the eighth century. King Baldred is supposed to have granted a fishery on the Parrett to Glastonbury (S1665, 676–685). King Ine may have given Glastonbury a fishery and half a hide of land at a place called *Escford* (Scott 1981, 114 and 142) and the grant was repeated by King Edmund (S1723, 939–46). Finberg thought it might be on the river Axe (Finberg 1964b, 113). Glastonbury did not own the place by 1086.

As might be expected, most references appear in later documents and are mostly of the tenth and eleventh centuries (Fig. 5.7). However, the spread of dates, starting early in the eighth century, shows that fisheries were important sources of food and income at all times. Royal grants are evidence that they were regarded as lucrative and perhaps prestigious possessions and point to the king exercising control over the rivers as sources of wealth and as highways,

since the weirs would have often impeded river traffic. Fish-traps were mostly situated on the major rivers of the central levels, many in positions where the trap could take advantage of the tides to bring in sea fish and to enable fish to be caught in the current of the ebb and flood. Most also seem to be connected with major estates held by the king or by the monasteries. The traps on Stert Flats, for instance, are probably connected with the Cannington estate. Weare lies on the northern side of the Wedmore island and was probably attached to Wedmore which was a royal possession. There were probably many other fisheries, on the rivers of north Somerset, for example, which are unrecorded. On the Axe at Tarnock there was a 'ffysshing at Black Lake' in 1536 (T/PH/Vch 38). We have no idea how old this weir was, but it was probably one of many standing along the tidal rivers.

Most of the surviving fish traps named in charters,

like the example in the Butleigh charter, combine the element with a personal name. This is true for *Brihtwoldes were*, on the Avon, near Bath, (S508, 946), *Tunsing Were*, at Panborough (S626 of 956), and *Hengest were* at Lyng, (S432 of 937). Dunwear incorporates the personal-name *Dunn* (Ekwall, 1960). It looks as if the operation of a fish-trap was something rented out, at an early date, to an individual, perhaps a man with the special skill required to work it, rather than being something controlled directly from the lord's estate centre. The named individual would have paid a rent from the catch for his right to fish in this way. There may well have been many other fish-traps which were controlled more directly. Those which we know of are fortuitously mentioned in charters. Probably quite arduous obligations were imposed by the lord who controlled access to the river banks. At Tidenham in Gloucestershire, alongside the river Severn, the numerous fish-traps were burdened with obligations to supply the lord with certain types of fish caught and to allow the lord access to the catch on very advantageous terms (S1555). Similar schemes probably existed in many other places but at Muchelney the two fish-traps are simply recorded as paying a render together of 6000 eels each year to the abbey (DB 9.1). As that was the rent the total catch must have far exceeded that number and since they could not be eaten all at once they must have been preserved, either by smoking or by salting. Either method suggests a lively trade, but how large the trade was in the seventh or eighth century, or if it existed at all at that time we cannot tell. In the later medieval period there is ample evidence that the monasteries and the king, with interests in the Levels all exploited fisheries. In 1180–1 Henry II had a fishery called *Morcock Eswere* at North Curry which yielded 5000 eels a year and another called Stathewere, at Stathe which paid 1000 eels (Bates 1899, Athelney 129) and in 1170–83 Gilbert de Helleworthy owned fisheries at Estwere, Merewere and Ianswine, all on the river Tone, as well as rights in Hengestwere (Bates 1899, Athelney 134).

The earliest fish-traps may have been in existence before the coming of the Anglo-Saxons, but it seems more likely that they were connected with the growth of the large estates with their need for large and varied supplies. This may have spurred the construction of the fish-traps which were large and needed considerable quantities of timber as well as much labour. They were probably a capital investment which would mostly be made by an estate or individual with considerable resources.

Exploiting the woods

Although Somerset is not now a heavily wooded county, woodland is widely dispersed, despite the large area occupied by the Levels, which are generally quite open. As a generalisation it would be fair to say that the woodland lay chiefly in the hills and valleys of north-east Somerset and on the great sweep of higher land to the east and south east and across the south towards Exmoor and the Brendons, where the tops of the moors were open, but the sides and the valleys well wooded. To the north the woodland occupied the high ground of the Failand ridge and the flanks of the Mendips.

The two largest areas of woodland were the Selwood, on the eastern boundary and Neroche, on the border with Devon. Selwood was described by Bishop Asser as *Coit Maur*, 'the great wood', in his life of King Alfred (Keynes and Lapidge 1983, 84). 'Neroche' means 'the nearer hunting place'. That these two woods stood on borders may not be chance. Although the land on which they stood was not of great agricultural value, their existence as large tracts of wood, used in the case of Neroche as common woodland for several settlements, may owe something to their value as buffer zones between polities. For Selwood this would be for post-Roman Somerset and the English dominated Wiltshire of the sixth and seventh centuries. Neroche, though, would have served as a barrier zone with part of Dumnonia, another Old Welsh polity.

The lower ground of the centre of the county was considerably less well wooded, but not bare. Woodland was a major amenity for any medieval community and in 1086 about 70% of manors had some woodland, although by that date only about 11% of the county was wooded (Rackham 1980). Only Huntingdonshire had a higher percentage of settlements with woodland (76%). It is impossible to know how much change there was during the post-Roman and Anglo-Saxon periods in the total

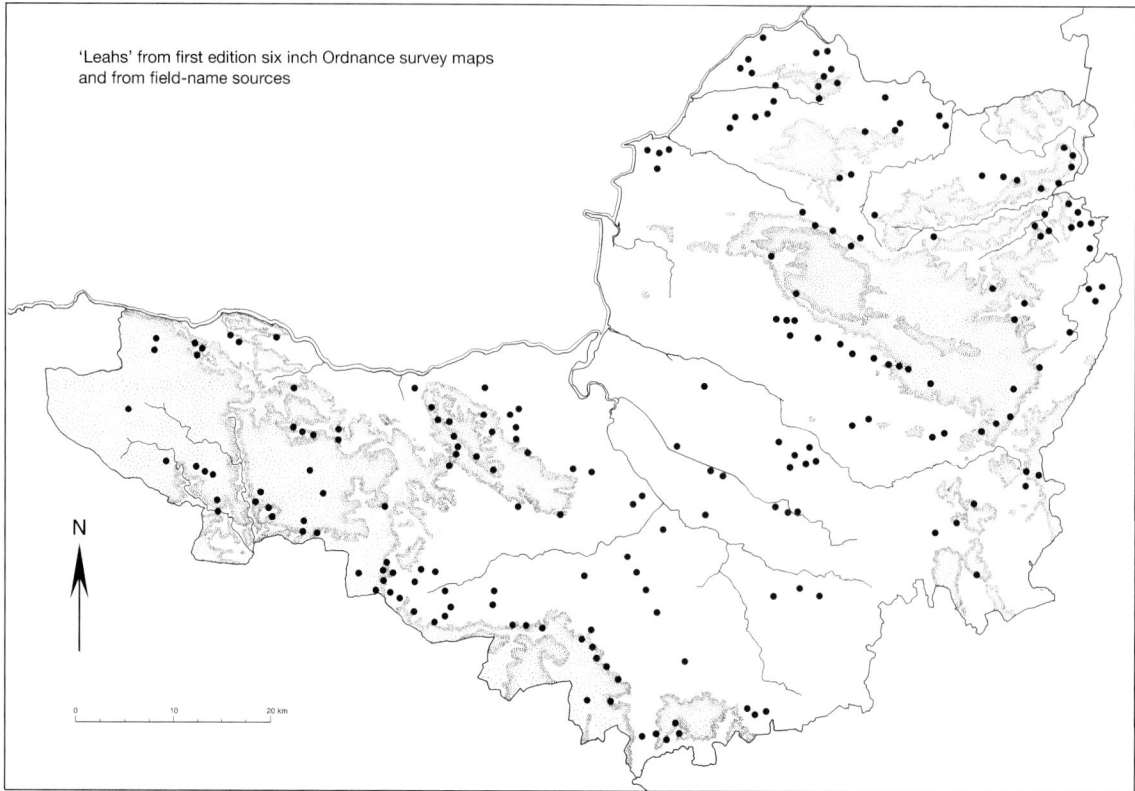

'Leahs' from first edition six inch Ordnance survey maps and from field-name sources

N

0   10   20 km

Figure 5.8. 'leahs' as indicators of managed woodland.

woodland cover. The consensus is that that the region did not revert extensively to woodland in the post-Roman period, though sporadic advance is always possible (Rippon *et al.* 2000, 107), and as we have seen there is some evidence that perhaps about 10% of Somerset woodlands east of the Parrett show some sign of advance. By 1086 the median size of woodland for all Somerset settlements was about 35 acres. The area in a manor could be very small. Near Bath one of the two holdings at Tadwick (DB 45.8) had one acre of woodland. The manor paid tax for half a hide and had land for a single plough. At the other end of the scale Staple Fitzpaine (DB 19.26) had about 240 acres of woodland, while Bathford had about 1440 acres (DB 7.6). It is clear that from the start woodland was a resource which the Anglo-Saxons exploited to great advantage and it is probable that it was most important as wood-pasture, land which was treed,

but had enough open ground to provide grazing for cattle and sheep. The very common element 'leah' was normally used to describe such woodland and names containing the element are widely distributed (Fig. 5.8).

In 1086 there were 18 manors which had 'leah' names, so that as a major settlement name it is rare, especially when we consider the ubiquity of the element in field-names and minor place-names (Fig. 5.9). Of the 18 Domesday manors, only nine became parishes, since the rest were too small to support a church of their own, while West Bradley does not appear in Domesday Book but did become a parish. The element was in use in Somerset quite early since Butleigh as '*bodecanleighe*' appears in a charter of 801 (S270a). Apart from Butleigh only Farleigh Hungerford is recorded before 1086, in the charter S867 of 987. Settlements rarely developed from

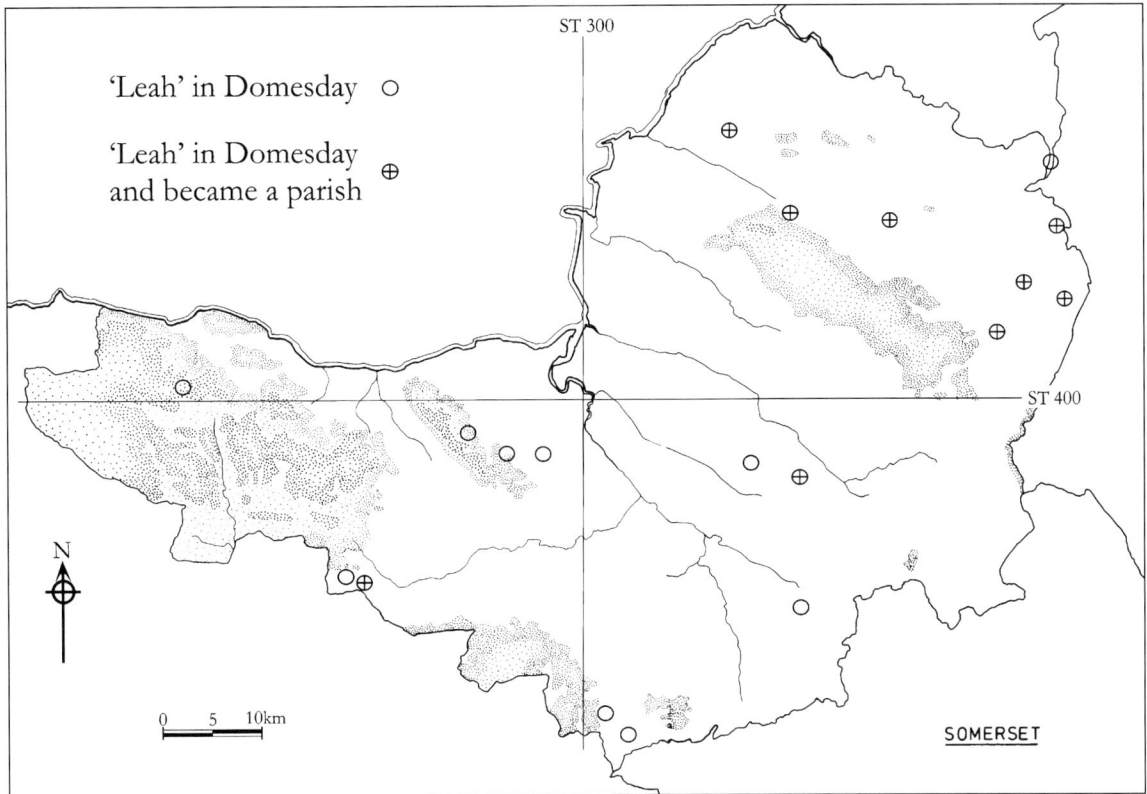

Figure 5.9. 'leah' settlements in Domesday Book.

wood-pastures, but wood-pastures were enormously important as resources.

These areas of woodland grazing were often quite close to the boundaries of the estates and a study of the boundaries of Anglo-Saxon charters and later data provides considerable evidence to flesh out the rather bald Domesday account. Bathford was not inside Somerset in the seventh century, but came into the shire when Bath was transferred, perhaps during King Alfred's time. It is a parish strung along a steep hillside beside the river Avon. The boundary of the Anglo-Saxon charter reads;

Ðis synd þa land gemæra to Forda. Ærest of afene andlang stræt on þane annestan. of þam stane on beonnan lehe. Of beonnan lehe innan wæfer. Andlang wæfer on wibyrhtleage. Of wibyrhtleage on hnæf leage. Of hnæf leage on cunuca leage. Of cunuca leage ut on afene.

These are the bounds of the land at Ford. First from

the Avon along the Roman Road to the single stone. From the stone to Beonna's wood-pasture. From Beonna's wood-pasture to the (river) Weaver. Along the Weaver to Wibyrht's wood-pasture. From Wibyrht's wood-pasture to the wood-pasture on the promontory. From the wood-pasture on the promontory to the hill-wood-pasture. From the hill-wood-pasture out to the river Avon.

There are good reasons for thinking that this boundary clause, which is attached to a tenth century charter (S643 of 957) is actually somewhat later than the tenth century. It may have been compiled in the early twelfth century but provides information about the early estate boundary, complete with woodland names; '*beonnan lehe*', *wibyrhleage, hnæf leage and cunuca leage*. Later documentation supplies the names of yet more 'leahs'. These include *hagelega* 1180–1220 (Kemp and Shorrocks 1974, 118), *bradleye*, 1270

(Hunt 1893) and *rokeleya*, 1180–1220 (Kemp and Shorrocks 1974, 120). Warleigh was the name of a manor which lay inside the later Bathford parish, but was a separate 1 hide manor in 1086 (DB 45.9). Its name shows that the settlement was carved out of a woodland.

It is interesting to notice that all the 1440 acres of woodland in Bathford was described as *silvae minutae* 'underwood' in 1086 (DB). This was almost certainly coppice and would not have been suitable for wood-pasture. It looks as if the Bath Abbey, the owner of Bathford by the tenth century, had converted the wood-pasture to provide firing for the monastery hearths. By the twelfth century there is evidence that many of the old 'leahs' had been brought under the plough, but there was probably a time, early in its Anglo-Saxon history, when this was a mostly woodland pasture estate.

East and West Pennard belonged to Glastonbury Abbey and both have Anglo-Saxon charters with bounds (S236 for West Pennard and S563 for East Pennard). Despite the very obscure early history of the relationship between the two places, the charter bounds do provide evidence which dates from the tenth century (Abrams 1996, 195–8). At West Pennard there were *tatanlegh* and *obanlegh*, all in the bounds of the tenth century charter. Tatanlegh appears as *tadelege* in c. 1307 (BL Add mss 22934), as *tadley* in c. 1527 (BL Egerton 3034) and can be identified today as modern fields, *tadley* (D\D/Rt/A/310, t. 781, 759, 762, 782, 783). *Woolley* appears only in the tithe award, but can reasonably be assumed to belong to the pre-Conquest period. East Pennard had *ferley* in 1261 (Longleat 10682) and also *stodleage* in 955 in the charter. There was also a *bradley* in 1265 (Longleat 10683). The *bradley* names lie on the parish and estate boundary with West Bradley and may provide a clue about the origins of that settlement. It may still have been a part of East Pennard for administrative purposes in 1086 and have been originally a large area of wood-pasture used by the inhabitants of East Pennard.

In a block of 32 parishes on the eastern side of the county (see Appendix), *leah* names in charters and in field names are distributed rather unevenly. The areas of Domesday woodland vary quite widely and *leah* names do not always occur where woodlands were extensive. West Lydford had no less than 1100 acres of wood in the estate of 1900 acres, but no *leah* names. It seems that the woods of West Lydford were not used as wood-pasture. On the other hand the Glastonbury Estates of East and West Pennard and Pilton, which included the later parishes of West Bradley, Shepton Mallet, Pylle, North Wootton and Croscombe, a total of 14453 acres, had 42 *leah* names. It looks as if these estates were widely used for grazing cattle, sheep and pigs.

As soon as we can recognise woodlands in place-names and in documentation they seem to be attached to particular estates, but in the case of Neroche it may be that there was a more general right to the use of the woodland spread across a wide area. The reference in the early charter S240 of 693 to *silva q(ui) dicit(ur) stretmerch*, may be to part of Neroche. Detached portions of Barrington, between Ashill and Bickenhall, of Whitelackington inside Broadway, of Donyatt also inside Broadway, of Ilton south of Ashill and of Curland inside Staple Fitzpaine represent land granted in return for loss of woodland and grazing rights inside Neroche Forest. Rights to grazing in the forest also existed for tenants of Curry Rivel (DD\CTV/210 of 1566). It looks as if inhabitants of many of the settlements in south Somerset had access to Neroche for grazing and for woodcutting and this may be a remnant of much wider rights to use of the woodland at an early date.

Ine's Laws suggest that by the early eighth century there was already pressure on woodland. 'If anyone burns down a tree in the wood, and it is disclosed who did it, he is to pay full fine: he is to pay 60 shillings, for fire is a thief' (Whitelock 1955, 369). One guesses that a tree might be burnt down in an attempt to assart for cultivation. Similarly the penalty for cutting down a tree 'under which 30 swine could stand' may have been an attempt to control assarting of wood-pastures. The very fact of such laws points to a problem as seen by the king and his advisers.

Flocks and pastures

The keeping of animals, particularly sheep, has been a recurring theme in European agriculture for centuries. Commercial sheep-rearing on a huge scale was certainly practised in the late Roman Empire. In the Rhone Delta, near Arles, the Crau, which is an area of thin, stony, dry soil, supported as many as 100,000 sheep (Badan, Brun and Congès 1995, 263–310). Until recently 'the shepherds abiding in the fields, keeping watch over their flocks by night' were still a living reality in many parts of western Europe and they were certainly part of the Roman world. For the Anglo-Saxons Somerset presented an opportunity to expand a part of agriculture which was already important in Wessex. Wiltshire, after all, embraced Salisbury Plain, the largest area of open grazing land in southern England. Somerset did not offer anything quite so large, but the Mendips were still a worthwhile prize. The open ground on top of the Mendips, treeless since the bronze age, was an area available for grazing which stretched from Uphill on the coast of the Severn Estuary as far as the Fosse Way in the east, a distance of about 35 km, but was rarely more than 5 km wide. To the east of the Fosse Way the land becomes more broken and was often wooded. In Devon the open grazing of Dartmoor was common to practically the whole shire (Fox 2006, 79). Perhaps this was the case for the Mendips in the seventh century, but early in the Anglo-Saxon period it is obvious that the whole of the Mendips was ringed by important estates, more often than not controlled by the kings of Wessex or by the Church and this continued to be true up to the Norman Conquest. Late Anglo-Saxon charter boundaries, for example those for Bleadon (S606 of 956) and Banwell and Compton Bishop (Lib. Alb II, fo. 246, 1068), show that boundaries of estates already ran up onto the top of the Mendips, suggesting that the area had been carved up by king and church. However, there is evidence to show that the Mendips were used for transhumance by the estates controlling the lands, with sheep brought up onto the hills from the townlands in the summer to graze and returning in the autumn. The work of Bob Smisson has shown that there was a drove which ran from Bleadon in the west onto the highest parts of the hills around Priddy and he has suggested that a system somewhat like that of the 'Great Flock of Lansdown', near Bath was in existence (see Chapter 6) (Smisson 2004).

West of the Parrett the tops of the Quantocks, the Brendons and Exmoor all offered pasture for sheep and cattle. Despite the important royal estates along the coast there is little to indicate that there was systematic control of the hills by the great. The Quantocks had areas of common grazing available into the later sixteenth century (Dunning 1985 16), but Domesday Book also shows that pasture was already allocated to each manor. Similarly, manors such as Brompton Ralph and Clatworthy had common pasture on Brendon into the sixteenth century (Dunning 1985, 22 and 31), but also had their own grazing in 1086 (DB). In the seventh and eighth centuries boundaries adjoining the Brendons and Exmoor may not yet have been definitely established and the existence of so many isolated small settlements, the *wyrths* and *cotts* for example, points to large areas of open ground, not yet appropriated to any one estate. It may well be that the lack of major royal and ecclesiastical estates meant that there was less pressure upon resources and a slower development of intensive sheep farming.

The other type of pasture was that provided by the marshlands. As we have seen above it is likely that the lowland moors were chiefly used for cattle grazing, though sheep could also be kept on marshes. The huge area of the Levels occupies the whole of the centre of the shire and was the subject of numerous attempts at drainage from the later Anglo-Saxon period right down to the twentieth century. In modern times, high water spring tides can be over 4 m higher than the low points in the Brue valley. At all times during from the post-Roman period up to the Norman Conquest the Levels were subject to inundation, particularly in the winter when heavy run-off from the surrounding higher ground met high tides flooding up the rivers. In summer time, when the run-off was much less and storms which could drive the tides higher were less common, the moors could provide large areas of grazing. The number of animals which could be kept was not dependent so much upon the area of moorland available as on the number of cattle which could be stocked on higher ground over the winter. When we consider that the cattle would compete with sheep brought down from high ground, for winter grazing and for stored fodder, we can see that numbers could be quite severely limited.

Generally in the post-Conquest period the central moors were open to all the tenants and freeholders of the manors which bordered them. Manorial boundaries did not normally include land out on the Levels. At Shapwick in the first half of the fourteenth century the perambulation of the bounds used the edge of the moor to the north of Shapwick as its boundary (Egerton 3321 of 1327). It seems unlikely that this was not the case in the Anglo-Saxon period and most pre-Conquest estates lying close to the moors may have used the edge of the moors as their bound, but then used the moors in common for unrestricted grazing. During the post-Conquest period there were many disputes concerning commoning rights[1] and it is clear that the great monasteries and the bishop at Wells along with the crown had become the effective owners of the moorland, but this seems to have been a post-Conquest development. Glastonbury's gradual extension of the area 'Twelve Hides' was an attempt to expand jurisdiction and immunities but it also had the effect of extending control over the moors. Appropriation of the moors by the monasteries was driven by rising populations and land hunger, which raised the price of grazing and the wealth of the institutions, but in the pre-Conquest period the pressures were probably much less. Somerton is generally held to derive its name from Old English *sumortun*, the 'tun used only in summer' (Ekwall 1960), though this seems unlikely in view of the importance and early origins of the place. The name must refer in some way to the summer-time use of the moors around the Somerton high ground. It may carry the meaning 'the tun which controls the summer grazing'. The large area of land available on the Somerton plateau would have made it possible to keep large numbers of animals there over winter and to have used the moors extensively as a result.

Scattered across the Levels are a series of isolated higher spots, often only a couple of metres above the surrounding marshes. These 'islands' are often distinguished by the '*ieg*', Old English 'island', in their names. These vary in size from large blocks such as the '*Sowy*', now Middlezoy, Westonzoyland and Othery, a 12 hide estate belonging to Glastonbury Abbey, to tiny areas such as Panborough, also a possession of Glastonbury Abbey and entered as having only 6 acres of arable land and a vineyard in 1086 (DB 8.1). Although those islands mentioned in the Domesday Survey all had arable, their situation in the moors meant that they were well placed to take advantage

of the grazing and fishing available around them. Some of the islands are mentioned in charters at a very early date. Muchelney Abbey was situated on one of these islands and also held Thorney and Midelney nearby as part of the core estate. Its name means 'the great (*micel*) island'. Many others also belonged to the early monasteries. Athelney, the 'nobleman's or prince's island' was also used for the foundation of a monastery. Even Glastonbury itself stood on a very large promontory pushing out into the marshes, almost like an island. There were, of course, good spiritual reasons why monasteries should be sited in the midst of marshes, but one should not imagine that they were therefore disadvantaged at their foundation. The marshes offered physical security, but also ready communications by water and above all, access to extensive grazing and fisheries (Fig. 5.10).

Confirmation of the value of the Levels to the Anglo-Saxons comes from a distribution of royal and ecclesiastical estates. Many of the larger estates had ready access to the moors, with 23% of royal and 44% of ecclesiastical lands bordering moorland (Fig. 5.11). This was, of course, the position in 1086 and the preceding century had seen a dramatic rise in the land available to the Church; the acquisition of new estates scattered across the shire probably affected the final position quite markedly. In the case of the king, his holdings were much affected by the dispersal of lands as gifts and the acquisition of estates by confiscation and inheritance. In the case of the monasteries, the lands in the central lowlands were mostly acquired in the eighth century and those on higher ground were tenth century endowments.

Conclusions

Inevitably any study of the agricultural regime of a region with so little written information and scattered archaeological data is bound to be heavy on generalisations and sparing with detail. This is especially the case when considering the earliest post-Roman period, but there is one theme which emerges. This is the enduring power of the elite to bend the system to meet their needs. The hazy outlines of the post-Roman world around South Cadbury certainly point that way. The survival of a landscape in which the ancient field-patterns were

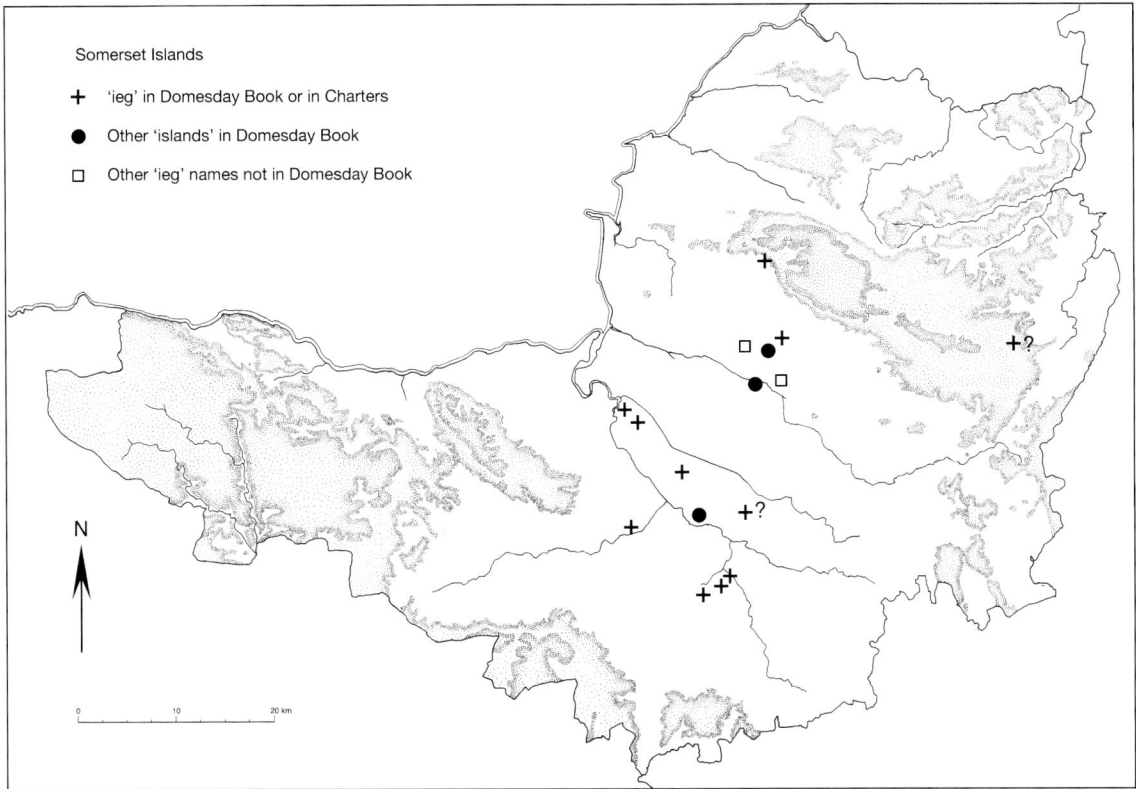

Figure 5.10. 'Islands' in the marshes.

so strong that they have influenced later medieval layouts suggests that a widespread authority kept it in production. The power of an elite is much more evident once the kings of Wessex and their followers took over. The potentially important arable centres on the great royal estates could only have been productive if they were carefully supervised and exploited by highly controlled labour – slaves. A large entourage of economically inactive warrior followers inevitably demanded either plunder and rapine or a carefully exploited landscape. The demands of the rapidly expanding ecclesiastical groups, organised in much the same way as a king's household, also needed major supplies of foodstuffs. The importance of Glastonbury Abbey's core estates as food producers will be explored in a later chapter, but the monastery's exploitation of the isle of Avalon was not unlike the royal farming at Somerton or South Petherton.

Arable farming notoriously controls its workers and is often marked by their depressed status. The woods offer a different perspective on getting a living from the land. The wooded landscapes of Somerset are so often in hilly, broken areas and they provided the opportunity for many small settlements and farmsteads, the *wyrths* and the *cotts* of Exmoor and the Brendons for example. Living chiefly by grazing their animals as well as cultivating some arable, the peasant farmers and lesser members of the warrior group were much more independent than the peasants who lived on or close to the great estates. They probably gave tribute rather than being constrained to provide renders or pay rent. Yet even here, as early as the beginning of the eighth century as we have seen, the king was legislating over problems associated with woodland use and perhaps clearance. The great pastime of aristocracy and of kings was the chase and

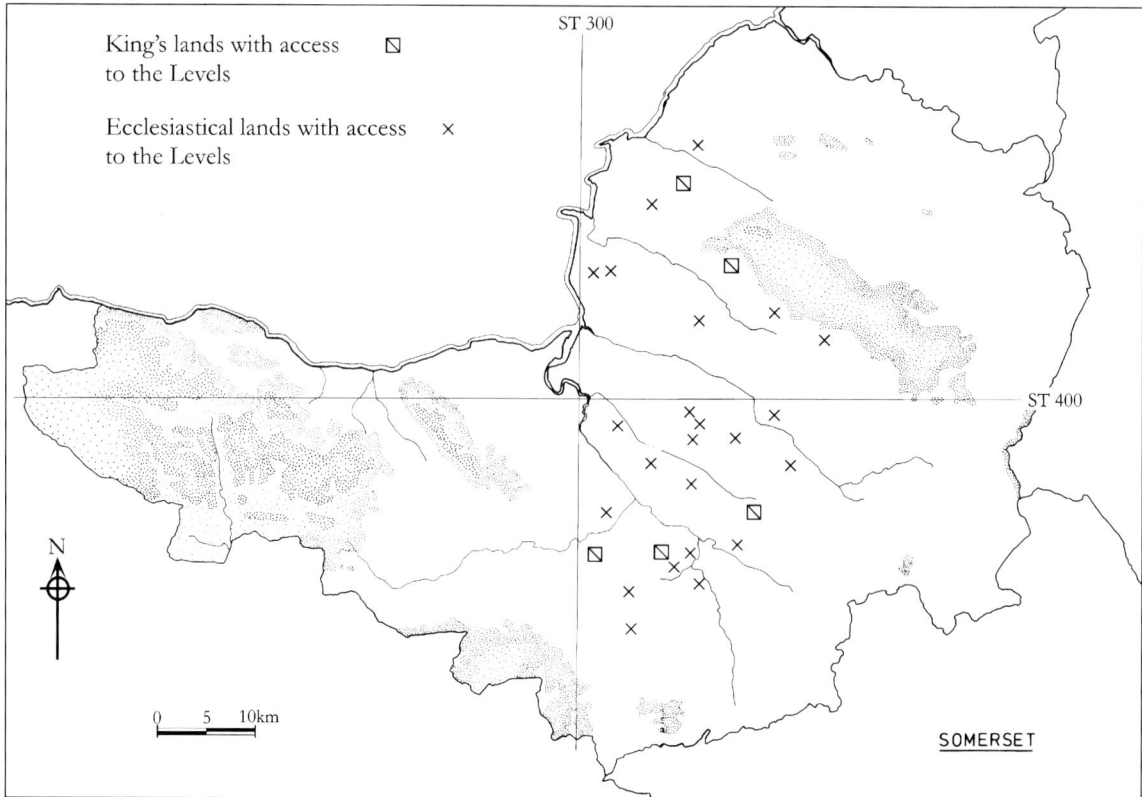

Figure 5.11. Access to the Levels for royal and ecclesiastical estates.

an intensification of the hunt was probably also one of the consequences of the growth of the king's court and entourage. Ekwall thought that Neroche got its name from a connection with hunting dogs, Old English '*raecc*' (Ekwall 1960, see entry for 'Neroche'). At the beginning of the tenth century the monastic establishment at Taunton was required to provide support for eight of the king's hunting dogs and their handler for one night and his hawker for nine nights (S373 of 903). This was evidently a long standing duty and was probably replicated on all the other great estates which were or had been royal. The need for a greater agricultural output was to drive a major change in the way the landscape was used and in the process many of the smaller independent farm units were to be swallowed up, along with their proprietors.

Control for purposes of exploitation was also important where pasture lands offered major returns.

'Sheep' elements in place names are not uncommon in Somerset, giving us Shepton Beauchamp, Shepton Montague and Shepton Mallet as well as Shipham and Shapwick. The Mendip Hills provided the most important of the sheep ranges and the estates lying around the hills could all benefit from the activity. If sheep farming was important at this early stage, in the eighth and ninth centuries we are driven to the conclusion that there was something more than subsistence farming occurring here. What happened to the wool, which is likely to have been the most enduring and transportable crop? It will be suggested later that it may have been a substantial item of trade, even at this early date. Elsewhere in Somerset, particularly in the far west, around the Brendons and Exmoor, the exploitation of sheep and cattle was not so intense. Centres of royal and ecclesiastical power were further away and such very large areas were not so easy to control. Neither were outlets for products so easy to access.

The presence of the powerful, at least in the early Anglo-Saxon period, is also manifest in the Levels. The use of extensive arable land was often complemented by the widespread grazing for cattle and also for sheep available in the summer. The Levels were part of the central river system of the shire and they provided comparatively easy transport and facilities for harvesting, preserving and moving fish. Control of the fisheries put the king or the Church and aristocracy in command of a major food source, available all year round, especially in the spring time, a notoriously difficult time of the year for food supplies.

Whether it was exploitation of arable, the pasturing of sheep or the grazing of cattle, the impetus given to agricultural production by the influx of this group of conquerors was of the greatest importance. Most elite groups who conquer a new land expect to become wealthier and more powerful as the result of their success. I do not think the Anglo-Saxons of the new Wessex were any different in that respect from the Normans of 1066 or the Europeans in Central and North America in early modern times. The addition of new layers of rulers to the rural Old Welsh society of the seventh century gave fresh impetus to the agriculture of Somerset, pushing it to exploit the landscape more intensively than before. The influx of an enlarged class of noble followers who needed land upon which to settle and who received estates as a reward for their service must also have stimulated agricultural production. Their demands were probably greater than those of the aristocracy they displaced.

The scale of the estates outlined above and the potential for production seems too great to be aimed solely at subsistence, even a rather grand subsistence for aristocracy and warriors. The system would have been capable of producing agricultural surpluses which could be sold or exchanged, providing cash for the elite with which they could purchase the high status goods they needed in order to confirm their positions. As we shall see later there are real signs of trading activity in Somerset, particularly in the eighth and early ninth centuries, and behind the transactions must lie production of some kind.

Nor did the needs of the kings and their followers diminish with time. Anglo-Saxon society in the eight and ninth century was riven with internal quarrels which led to bloody fighting and kept the warriors employed. The advent of the Northmen merely intensified the pressure, as well as introducing another group who hoped to exploit the countryside through pillage.

Note
1. See Williams 1970, 32–8 for a discussion of the rights of commoning and the bitter disputes between Glastonbury and Wells in the high Middle Ages.

Appendix

The parishes used for survey of leah names.

Pilton, North Wootton, Croscombe, Shepton Mallet, Doulting, East Cranmore, West Cranmore, Cloford, Witham Friary, East Pennard, West Pennard, Butleigh, Barton St David, Kingweston, Keinton Mandeville, East Lydford, West Lydford, Alford, Castle Cary, West Bradley, Hornblotton, Ditcheat, Ansford, Bruton, Brewham, Penselwood, Charlton Musgrove, Shepton Montague, Yarlington, North Cadbury, North Barrow, South Barrow, Babcary, Charlton Mackrell, Charlton Adam, Milton Podimore, West Camel, Bratton Seymour, Wincanton, Stoke Trister, Cucklington, Baltonsborough, Compton Pauncefoot, Maperton, Holton, Wanstrow, Batcombe, Upton Noble, Milton Clevedon, Evercreech, Lamyatt.

6

Tenth Century Agriculture

Agricultural change in the tenth and eleventh centuries was driven by two major related forces. The first of these was the expansion of the warrior class caused by the king's political and military demands which encompassed first the expansion of the kingdom of Wessex into the kingdom of the English and then the drive to protect the new kingdom against the external attacks of the Danes. Secondly, the growth of a larger aristocratic elite together with a rapidly expanding reformed monasticism demanded that greater surpluses be produced. England was still a profoundly rural society and there is nothing to suggest that manufactured goods could have formed more than a tiny part of the total growth in output in the south-west. Agricultural expansion necessarily had to provide the basis for an increase of wealth.

The normal way to understand population growth in medieval history has been to see it as a sort of 'deus ex machina', a natural phenomenon, which occurs as the result of human fertility and which drives economic change, particularly economic expansion and the increase of wealth in society. I want to argue that this is not necessarily the case and that we should see the growth of medieval populations as the result of the economic and social structure of society. That in turn was moulded by the decisions made by rulers and people in positions of power at all levels within Anglo-Saxon and medieval England. English society was not simply the passive recipient of a growth in population of Malthusian nature, but rather the active promoter of that growth, albeit unconsciously, through the decisions and actions of those with power and authority. Changing agricultural practice, particularly the introduction and spread of the common-field system, was what provided the means by which agricultural output could expand and which made it possible for the population to grow. A more intensive agriculture needed more hands to cultivate the land, providing an incentive to the landlord to encourage that growth, chiefly through increasing the number of tenements available in the common-fields.

The common-fields

The introduction of the plough was of prime importance to the agricultural economy, probably the most important single innovation of the high Middle Ages, since it multiplied the productivity of the farmer, by allowing him to cultivate far more ground more efficiently and more quickly than before. Peter Fowler suggests that the plough, as distinct from the ard, which was a scratch plough, was gradually introduced in the tenth and eleventh centuries (Fowler 2002, 182–204). Its ability to cut long furrows, turning the sod completely over, was a technological advance which drove the development of the full common-field system. The plough encouraged the cultivation of long furlongs. Once set in the ground it was an advantage to be able to break the ground without stopping or turning, which was time consuming and cumbersome. Breaking and turning the ground made cultivation much more effective but it was an energy intensive activity and as a consequence a large plough-team was needed to provide the necessary power to make this possible (Hill 2000, 12). The long strips of ploughland this produced could only be efficiently laid out if they were grouped in blocks. Looked at from one point of view, the introduction of the plough and the common-fields was a single technological development. The plough was therefore the reason for the growth of the common-fields and quite incidentally the common-fields were the drivers behind the appearance of nucleated village settlements. There were of course other aspects of the particular form of the common-fields, not least the need to provide for grazing animals, which was a powerful reason for the grouping of the furlongs into great fields. If it were intended that the animals of the estate should all graze the fallow field, particularly that the lord's animals should do this, then the land in fallow or crop needed to be grouped to make the process practical and economic where a great many animals were involved. This was especially true for sheep. There was, too, the element of fairness in the allocation of strips, though the tenth century concept of fairness was probably far removed from ours, and also the economic importance of being able to fence the fields against animals breaking in or out. However, all these needs were consequent upon the requirements of the plough with its team as a machine.

David Hall has remarked that the furrows at Raunds in Northamptonshire overlie older Anglo-Saxon settlements and that they cannot be earlier than the ninth century (Hall 1995, 130), while Della Hooke has shown that references to intermixed acres frequently occur in Anglo-Saxon charter bounds in the tenth century (Hooke 1981, 58). In Wiltshire the charter S719 of 963 has *singulis jugeribus mixtum in communi rure huc illacque dispersis*, 'single acres mixed in the common-lands scattered here and there'. This would fit well with Peter Fowler's ascription of the plough to the tenth century. No doubt the spread of the new plough and the appearance of the strips grouped into the great fields was a slow business, with estates still using the older methods of infield/outfield and stirring the ground with an ard running side-by-side in the same district with those using the new system and it is entirely possible that in Somerset the plough and the ard were to be found in use simultaneously within a few miles of one another for long periods of the tenth and eleventh centuries. Just

like the early modern movement towards enclosure and re-development in severalty, such a movement would be quite slow and would appear among early adopters all over the country and be taken up by the generality of landowners quite slowly. It could of course, only be implemented where the topography made it feasible, but perhaps even more where the economic and social climate was right.

The use of the plough made it possible to develop the common-fields of Somerset in the tenth and eleventh centuries, but also dictated social change. The new machine needed more oxen than the ordinary peasant farmer could maintain and co-operation with his neighbours was therefore essential if he was to benefit from the development. There is, however, nothing to suggest that pooling of resources and co-operation of this kind would have come easily to the late Anglo-Saxon peasantry. It is much more likely that the changes were driven by the landlords and by their interests. Laying out the fields and if necessary bringing the peasantry together in an enlarged manorially centred settlement was a preliminary to a system which placed new burdens upon the ceorl. In the Laws of Edward men were forbidden to leave their lord without his permission and Æthelstan's Laws demanded that the relatives of a lordless man should find him a lord. These injunctions were designed to reduce crime by providing guarantors who would produce a wanted man or answer for him in court, but the practical effect was to limit freedom of movement for the ceorl. He became bound to the lands of a particular lord (Whitelock 1955, 416). Such control facilitated the extension of labour services which would have increased to enable the lord to plough a larger area of demesne than ever before, using the peasants' labour to supplement the labour of his slaves, cottars and bordars. It is likely that the ploughs they used were at first supplied by the lord and the ability to plough co-operatively by pooling their oxen was a by-product of the need to supply the lord with teams for demesne ploughing. The lord may also have needed to increase the supply of oxen for the peasants' use, thereby binding them closer to him and depressing their status, which was still further depressed as they were drawn together into new settlements, often carefully planned to replace the hitherto scattered tenements. The effect of the new system was therefore to increase dependency. By the middle of the eleventh century in Somerset the normal peasant farmer held a customary tenement of a virgate, a quarter of a hide. In practice he had about 30 acres of arable, divided between the two great fields, and also had access to pasture, meadow and woodland.

The enlargement of the lord's demesne enabled him to extract more wealth from his tenants than hitherto, through their labour as well as encouraging the expansion of numbers of families, who thus provided extra workers on the demesne. This could be done by adding acres and furlongs onto the newly established fields, so that younger sons of peasant households could start a villein tenancy of their own, rather than staying unmarried in the paternal or fraternal household.

The first question to ask about the growth of the common-field system is how widespread it was in Somerset by the eleventh century. Some years ago I looked at evidence for the practice in Wessex by analysis of the terms employed in charter boundary clauses in Anglo-Saxon charters. I suggested then that the paucity of references to acres, headlands and furrows in Somerset (all terms normally used in describing common-field ploughland) betrayed estates where arable cultivation had not reached the borders, in contrast to evidence from Wiltshire which showed far more examples of ploughland reaching the boundaries (Costen 1994, 100). It may be, therefore, that Somerset was not as intensively cultivated as parts of Wiltshire were in the tenth century, but topography may also have played a part, with Wiltshire estates in river valleys, constrained by the plain above them and the river flood-plains below them to plough outward to their boundaries.

That examples of common-field systems did exist in the late Anglo-Saxon period is clear from study of the early maps, which preserve the evidence of compromises and expedients adopted at an early date to accommodate tenurial changes inside existing settlements which already had working field systems. Such a case is clear at Stocklinch, near Ilminster. There were two Stocklinches, Magdalen and Ottersey, which existed as two estates before the Norman Conquest and survived into the nineteenth century as two parishes. In 1066 and in 1086 Stocklinch Ottersey

was a manor of 3 hides (DB 47.14). Stocklinch Magdalen was a manor of 2 hides (DB 25.48). The tithe maps show the outline of an estate which had clearly started as a single 5 hide unit, from which two parcels had been carved. Stocklinch Magdalen was formed by taking a block of land, which may have been the lord's land of the new estate as the core (tithe map D\D\Rt\A\462, for Stocklinch Magdalen). To this were added other strips in the common-fields and blocks of meadow (Fig. 6.1). The rest of the land belonged to Stocklinch Ottersey, which was therefore the residue of what had once been a 5 hide estate (tithe map D\D\Rt\A\129, for Stocklinch Ottersey). Two distinct settlements also existed, with Stocklinch Ottersey a planned and now deserted settlement (HER 54574). Despite the two settlements and their two churches, the two tithe maps and even the late nineteenth century six inch Ordnance Survey maps show the remnants of the single common-field system quite clearly, indicating that the fields were laid out before the manors were divided one from another. Since both existed in 1066 the common-fields must pre-date the Conquest.

At Overstowey in the later twelfth century the old castle was described as standing on land which was clearly common-field: *in orientali parte culture ad eandem ecclesiam pertinentis in cuius parte occidentali sedet castellarium* – 'in the eastern part of the furlong belonging to the said church on the western part of which stands the castle' (Ross 1959, 275). Thus the castle stood upon land which had been part of a furlong. Since the castle was constructed before 1086 it is very likely that it was built over a pre-existing common field (Prior 2006, 71).

Another clear example is provided by the three settlements of West Chinnock, Middle Chinnock and East Chinnock. Chinnock was mentioned in the will of Wynflæd c. 950 (S1539), though it is not clear if she owned the whole of Chinnock, or only a part of it. By the time of the Norman Conquest it had certainly been divided into three estates (DB 19.44, 19.48, 19.49). Edmer Ator, an important landholder, with lands in Dorset and Devon also, held a 7 hide estate at East Chinnock and the other two estates were each held by un-named thegns as 3 and 4 hide estates respectively. The original 14 hide estate had first been divided into two 7 hide units,

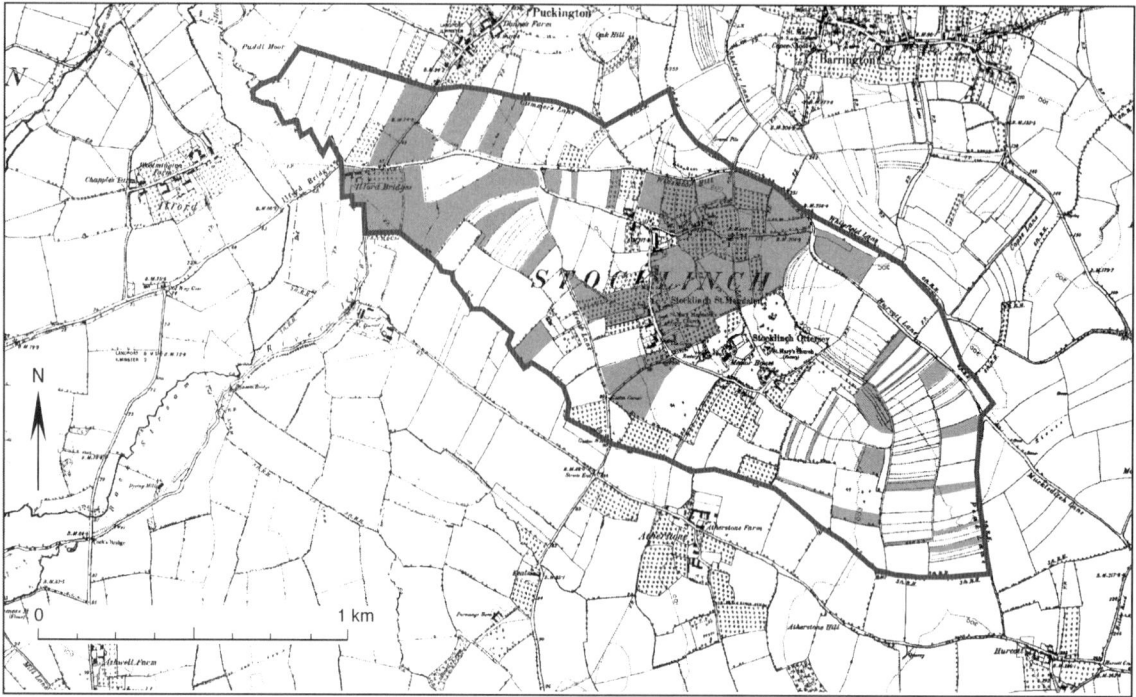

Figure 6.1 The Stocklinches; Stocklinch Magdalen comprises the areas shown in grey. The rest of the estate, within the marked boundary, was Stocklinch Ottersey.

one of which had then been further sub-divided. The settlement at West Chinnock lies so close to the boundary with Middle Chinnock as to suggest that it was already there when the division of lands took place. This might explain why the East Field of West Chinnock lay to the east of Middle Chinnock so that farmers from West Chinnock needed to pass through Middle Chinnock in order to get to half their land (Fig. 6.2). Middle Chinnock must be an insertion and it is difficult to envisage a situation where groups of peasants would voluntarily devise such a system. The common fields of West Chinnock must have been laid out first at the time that a division was made and then re-worked when the sub-division which created Middle Chinnock took place, certainly before the Conquest (Costen 1991, 44–5). It is probable that the two thegns who held the smaller estates were commended men of Edmer Ator, since all three estates were granted to the Count of Mortain as were Edmers's other Somerset holdings at Odcombe and

Camerton. It may be that Edmer had actually carried through the re-organisation in order to provide for his thegns.

I have made a similar argument for the origin of the villages and the common-fields at the settlements along the Poldens at Shapwick, Ashcott, Catcott, Woolavington and Cossington. Pairs of settlements with east/west or north/south names, such as East and West Lydford and the Charltons, Mackrell and Adam also provide useful ways into the problem of estate and village formation (Costen 1991). In the case of the Charltons the entangled nature of the two parishes suggests that, like the Stocklinches, a single common-field settlement had been sub-divided (Fig. 6.3). This was accompanied by the creation of two settlements, each with its own parish church. By 1066 Charlton Adam was a 5 hide estate, held by three thegns and Charlton Mackrell was a 3 hide estate held by Alfward (DB 19.43, 22.19).

East and West Lydford and North and South

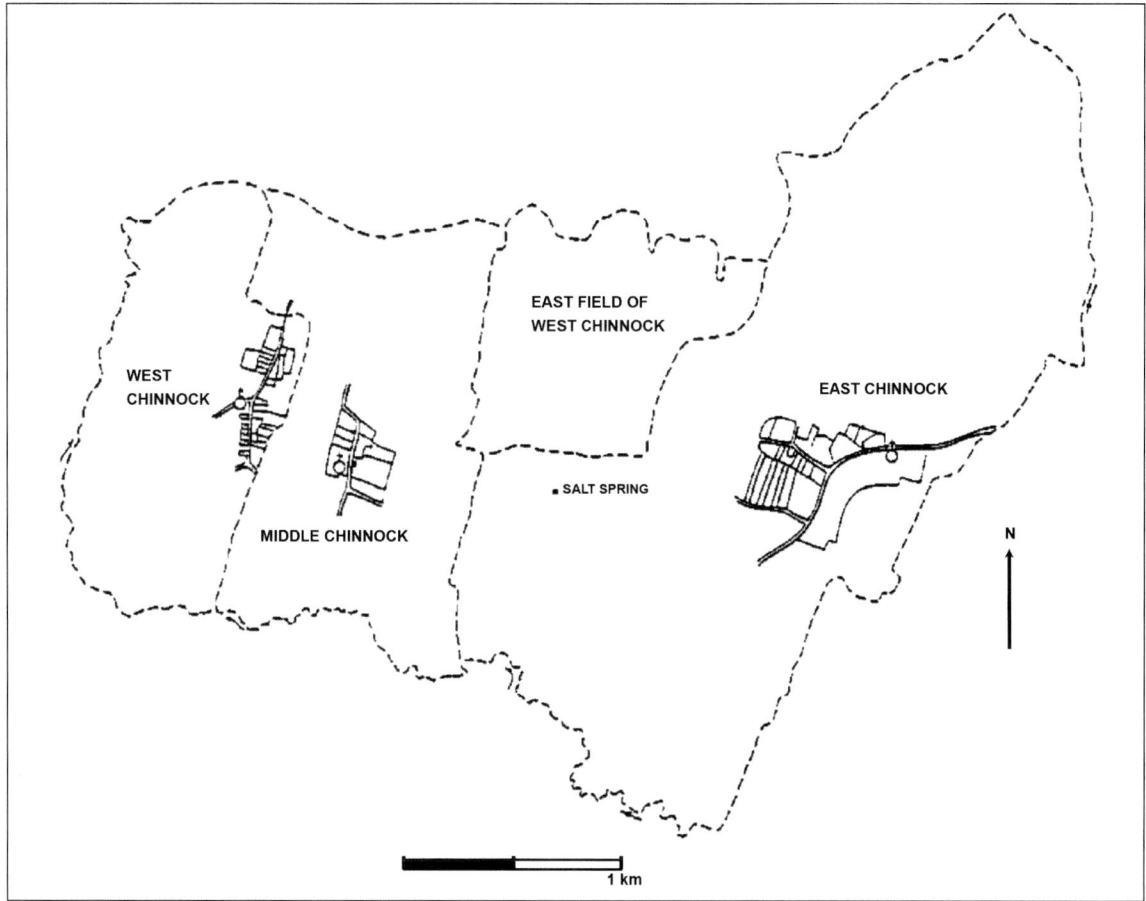

Figure 6.2. The Chinnocks.

Barrow, on the other hand, look as if they were separated before their fields were laid out. The Lydfords had separate village centres and separate field systems, but betrayed their origin as a single estate unit with East Lydford's woodland lying cut off on the western side of the Fosse Way and to the north of West Lydford (Fig. 6.4). East Lydford was a 4 hide estate held by Alfward from Glastonbury Abbey in 1066 (DB 8.4) and West Lydford was owned by Brihtric and was 9 hides in extent. North and South Barrow show a simple outline for the original estate, cut across the middle by a later boundary. Mossmoor on the west side and Blackmoor on the east side are areas which are shared between the two settlements (Fig. 6.5). We might extend the same argument to

the example of East and West Harptree mentioned above in Chapter 3.

Christopher Thornton has shown that at Rimpton a pattern of dispersed peasant farmsteads was replaced with a nucleated settlement and a common-field system during the Anglo-Saxon period, although this was not linked to the formation of a new estate (Thornton 1988). The appearance of a fully functioning common-field system, therefore, can be linked in some of these cases to a process of settlement formation.

In an attempt to throw further light on the problem, Figure 6.6 plots information about common-field agriculture in 82 settlements mentioned in Domesday Book. It uses field-name data collected by the author

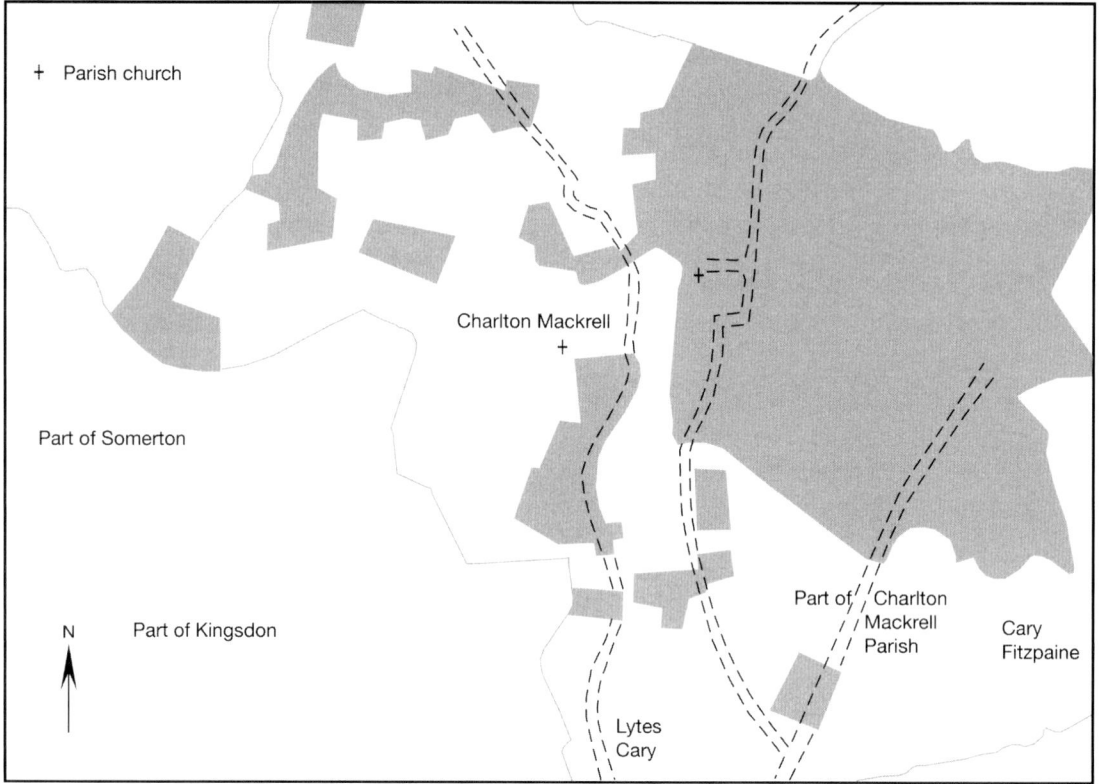

Figure 6.3. Charlton Adam and Charlton Mackrell. Charlton Adam consists of the shaded areas (simplified).

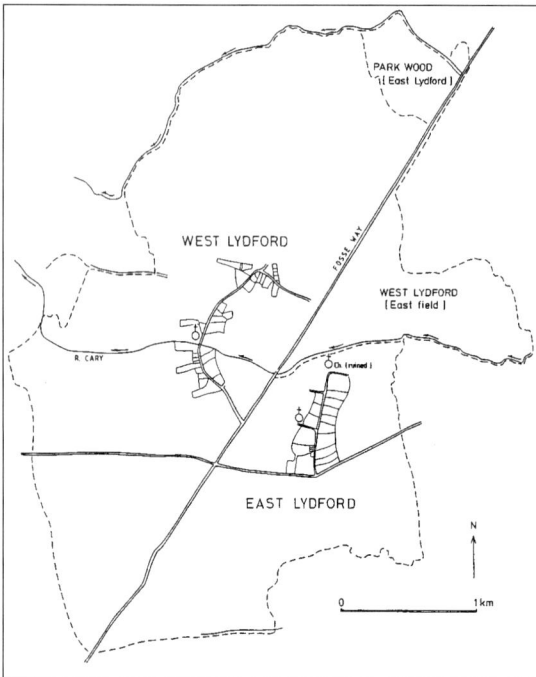

Figure 6.4. East and West Lydford, redrawn from the tithe maps.

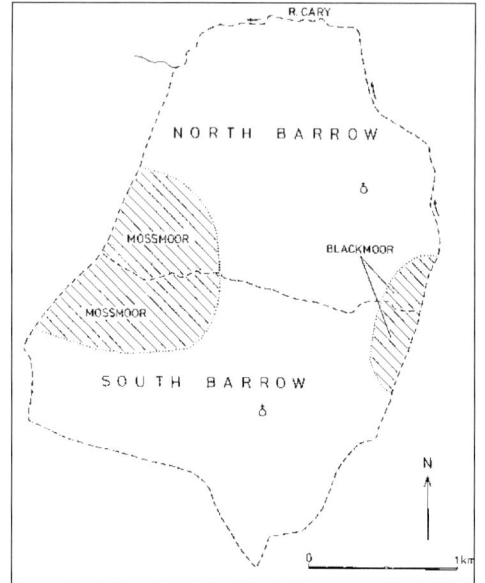

Figure 6.5. North and South Barrow, redrawn from tithe maps.

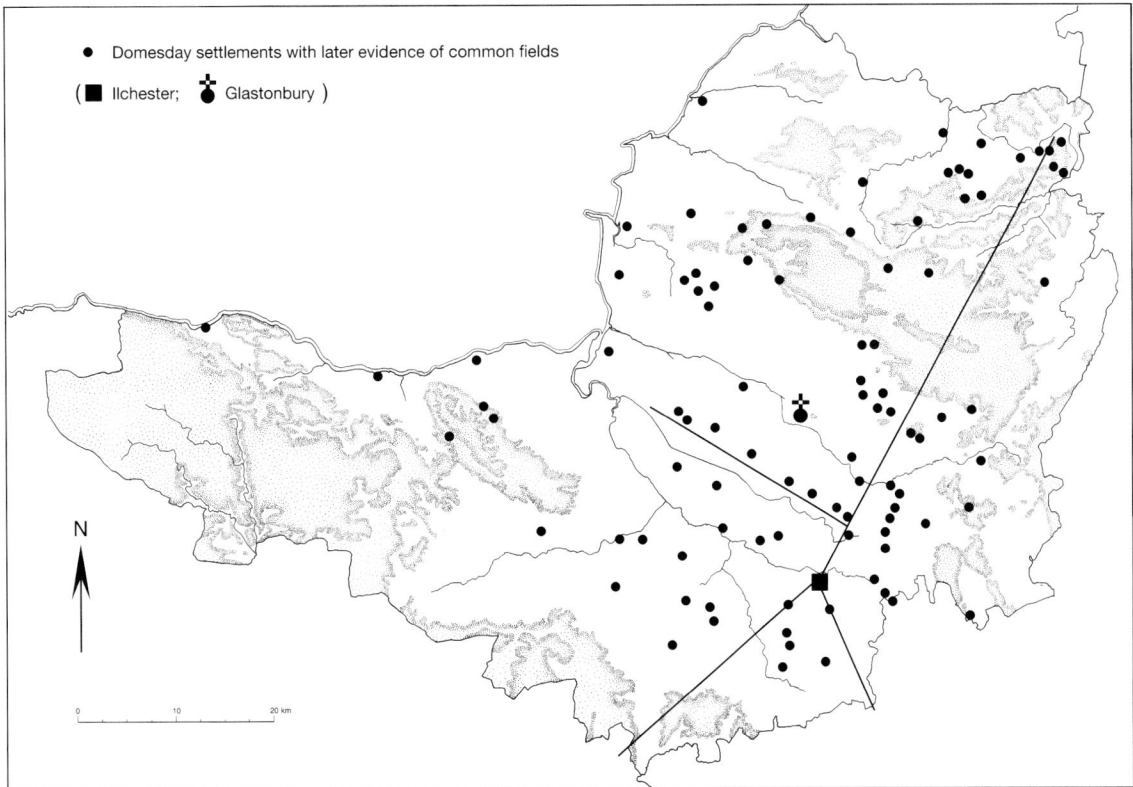

Figure 6.6. Domesday settlements with later evidence of common fields.

and looks at the survival of common-field names and expressions such as 'north/south field' or 'east/west field', 'campo orientalis', or 'australis' or 'in the common field'. The material was collected over many years and includes field-names from a scatter of parishes from all across the county, and consists of a corpus of over 100,000 names. Information in the far west of the county is probably under-represented. As might be expected it shows the bulk of the common-field on the lower ground and in the centre and east. The area around and to the north of Ilchester has a great many points, and this is partly due to the relatively small size of the manors here, but also reflects a real density of common-field agriculture. Lack of evidence on the author's part does not mean that a particular manor had no common fields. Mary Whitfield's study of south-east Somerset shows evidence of later medieval common-field systems in almost every parish (Whitfield 1981, 17–29). Unless

the examples which have been demonstrated are particularly unusual it seems likely that common-field agriculture was the norm, at least in Somerset east of the Tone and Parrett, by 1066.

Wooded areas and the Brendons and Exmoor have very little in the way of common-fields, though we should also note that many of the manors immediately west and north-west of Taunton may have had fields which disappeared in the fourteenth and fifteenth centuries and which have left few traces in later field-names. The map does not show that there was no arable west of the Tone, but rather that it was not organised in the classic common-field pattern. The settlements detailed above as examples of early common-field systems are all within the eastern area and it seems possible to assume that estates in this area first adopted common-fields and that it is probable that they were widespread by the eleventh century.

One of the problems with such sketchy information

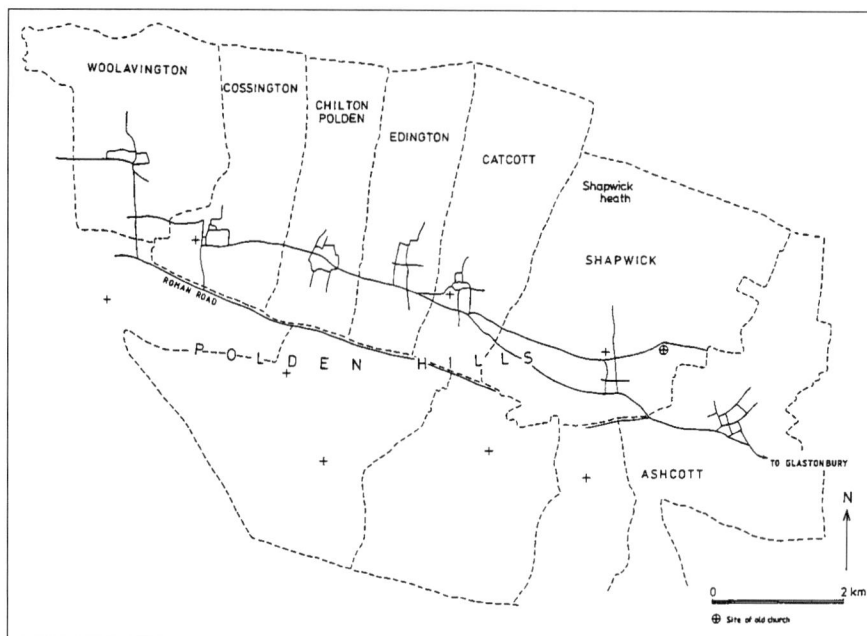

Figure 6.7. The Polden estate and its sub-units.

is that we do not have a relative chronology for the introduction and spread of the system and we do not know who introduced it. An obvious candidate would be the reformed monasteries, in particular Glastonbury Abbey, since it was the first in Somerset to undergo reconstitution and reform and was the institution with the largest landholding also. Glastonbury acquired most of its lands in the second half of the tenth century, and the sheer scale of its endowments provided it with considerable resources which would certainly have been needed to reorganise estates and provide the working capital needed to fund new plough-teams. The Shapwick estate was in the hands of the abbey from the early eighth century onward (S253 of 729). This initial grant was of a block of land which covered all the western part of the Polden Hills. The Domesday survey shows that Shapwick in 1086 included the present villages of Sutton Mallet, Edington, Chilton Polden, Catcott and Woolavington (Fig. 6.7). They were already separate units, but were included under the Shapwick entry (DB 8.5). Cossington, which was clearly part of the original estates and was still a Glastonbury holding in 1066 (DB 8.7) was a separate manor.

At some time a division of the primitive Polden estate into these units had taken place. Nicholas Corcos argued that Shapwick was part of a multiple estate which had been broken up, possibly in the tenth century (Corcos 1983, 47–54). The church of Shapwick stood in the east field, isolated from the village, until it was demolished and the present building in the village centre was newly constructed in October 1331 (Holmes 1896, 73). The church is therefore related to an older landscape which existed before the common-fields and the settlement were laid out (Fig. 6.8). Had the re-planning taken place before the church was constructed it would have been placed inside the settlement it served. Other settlements in the same Shapwick group had chapels rather than parish churches and these stood in the settlements, showing that they were contemporary with or later than their villages. The same is true for Cossington (outside the Shapwick group by 1066) and for Woolavington, which both had parish churches. The early church at Shapwick, therefore, may well predate the tenth century re-arrangement of the estate.

The regular layouts of each of the villages and their surrounding fields all look as if they were part of a

Figure 6.8. Site of Shapwick old church. The outline of the church foundations are clearly visible in the centre of the picture. The churchyard boundary shows as a dark line and lighter marks reveal other structures which once stood in the church precinct. Open-field furlongs called 'Old Church' ran across the site in the later Middle Ages (photo M. Aston).

concerted plan and Nicholas Corcos suggested that the planning might date from the re-foundation of the Abbey and be linked to St Dunstan. While this might well be the case it is more likely that it was a development of the years of expansion at the abbey in the second half of the tenth century. The small establishment of clerks which Dunstan reformed would have needed much less support than the growing community of monks he replaced them with and the re-planning of estates may be the result of that expansion of numbers. Even more pressing for the community was the need to support a large number of warriors. This must have been an imposition upon the new community and was related to the extent of the estates granted to it by the king and his followers.

In 1066 there were 48 thegns on Glastonbury estates in Somerset alone. No less than 14 of them had held the Shapwick estates jointly (Shapwick itself excluded) in 1066 (DB 8.5). This strongly suggests a re-planning in the second half of the tenth century and it also shows that there existed a person or group of persons with knowledge of the value of the new plough and the system of agriculture it demanded and the power and resources to push through a radical change. If the monks of the abbey were the people who introduced the plough and common-fields the movement cannot have begun before the mid-tenth century. It is noticeable that Glastonbury's estates in central Somerset were largely common-field communities in the post-Conquest period. Sally

Harvey, writing about demesne agriculture in the later eleventh century, has shown that Glastonbury ran a very intensive demesne agricultural system by 1086, with almost as many plough-teams on the lord's land as the peasantry owned (Harvey 1983, 58). It may be that this is the result of a consistent policy of extensive arable exploitation on their estates in the tenth and eleventh centuries.

However, another possibility is that the introduction of the common-fields went hand in hand with the creation of new settlements by the king and great aristocracy as they sought to provide land for their warrior followers. As we saw above, the 5 hide estate at Stocklinch was a secular estate and typical of the common-field holdings of the pre-Conquest period. It could still be divided between two owners before 1066. Similarly, at the Chinnocks the two small estates, West and Middle Chinnock, were of 4 and 3 hides respectively and probably needed to be constructed as common-field units to make them productive enough to support their new warrior lords. This is probably also true for many of the 'personal-name + tun' settlements which appear in the tenth century. Secular estates were generally much smaller than those of the king or the church and in many cases may have needed the new technology to make them viable as support for a warrior.

Hides, ploughs and ploughlands

Anglo-Saxon estates in Wessex were measured in hides, a measure of the tax-paying liability of the land. It was not a measure of area, though of course there was a general connection between area and capacity to pay. In its origins the hide as a measure was very ancient. It appears in the earliest charters and in Ine's Laws and is connected with tribute renders (Brooks 1996, 132). Officials thought in terms of the 'family' unit for tribute purposes and used that as a scale to measure the capacity of an estate as compared with its neighbours. This provided a fairly objective yardstick which could be recognised by all and seen as fair. As we have seen earlier, some small estates, often called 'hiwisces' in Somerset, retained that primitive connection to the hide as a measure of land capable of supporting a 'family', but where it was used to describe larger

estates there was clearly an element of formalism about it. Although early Anglo-Saxon charters always measure their grants in hides there is little correlation between the figures in early grants and the hidage of the estates named in the Domesday Book. We cannot say that estates retained their hidages over the course of many centuries and it is dangerous to assume that comparison between the hidages given in Anglo-Saxon charters and the hidages given in Domesday Book proves stability, even for the tenth and eleventh centuries. For example, Bishops Lydeard was named as a 12 hide estate in the charter S380 of 899–909. In Domesday Book it had 9.75 hides. At Rimpton the charter S411 of 938 was a grant of 5 hides. It is not surprising therefore to find that the Domesday hidage of Rimpton was also 5 hides. However, Brihtric Grim's Will, by which he bequeathed Rimpton to the Old Minster at Winchester between 970 and 984, states that he left the land, the charters and an extra hide of land which he had purchased and added to the estate (S1512). On that basis Rimpton should have been a 6 hide holding in 1086. It is likely that divisions and sales and purchases gave an opportunity for tax liabilities to be altered sometimes to avoid or reduce payment. However, it is likely that estates which did not change their boundaries retained their rating over long periods. If this is truly the case, then the record in the Domesday Book provides a measure of the relative value of estates at an early period. Other assessments may then be seen as more up-to-date measures and thus provide a method of measuring change.

John Moore long ago showed that the ploughland of the Domesday Book was a real measurement of areas of arable land and that the actual size of a ploughland varied according to the quality of the land (Moore 1964, 125–6). The Domesday description *terra est x carrucae*, 'there is land for x ploughs', he suggests was an estimate of the total arable land which could be cultivated, while the number of recorded plough-teams measures the actual cultivation. Nicholas Higham's later analysis re-inforces the idea that ploughlands are a real areal measurement of available arable in 1086 (Higham 1990).

A test of how intensively land was cultivated by 1086 can be made by comparing the number of ploughlands recorded with the number of teams available to work them. The total of the teams includes both demesne and tenant ploughs. The royal estates amounted to 807 ploughlands and had 578 plough teams working on them (DB 1.1–25). This means that there were 71% of the teams needed for a full complement. By this measure nearly 30% of the land available to plough could not be cultivated in any one year. On Queen Edith's lands which were enumerated separately, there were 223.5 ploughlands and 163 ploughs (DB 26–31). Thus there were 72.93% of the necessary teams. For comparison Glastonbury Abbey had 548 ploughlands and 396 ploughs which meant 72.26% of the necessary teams (DB 8.1–41). For all practical purposes the regime in place on both royal and ecclesiastical estates was the same. If the same exercise is pursued with the estates of laymen a rather different picture emerges. In thirty-six estates chosen at random (and thus including estates in the far west, where the crown and the church had few lands), there were 175.5 ploughlands and 144.5 plough teams. The ratio was 82.33%. There were on average more plough-teams available to work the secular estates than the great estates of king and church. We might expect the king or the church to be able to provide the capital to maintain plough-teams on a much larger scale than the resources of a random collection of laymen, some great and some anonymous, would allow. It may be, however, that the great estates provided so much income that church and king did not need to work their assets so hard. The lay-men, conversely, were usually living on much smaller units and may have needed to work them harder in order to extract their desired income. All this is of course based upon an assumption that arable was the measure of value upon which tax-paying ability was based. In fact the pastoral side of the economy was almost certainly as important and this should be borne in mind when considering the relative lack of arable in the west of the shire. The lower rates of arable exploitation on the royal and ecclesiastical lands may be the result of a greater attention to pastoral farming, made possible by the sheer size of the estates and their greater access to other resources, such as pastures and moors, while on small estates with little pasture it became imperative to exploit the arable as fully as possible.

Nick Higham thinks that there was a tendency for the survey to show an equality between the number of plough-teams and the number of ploughlands on the large estates and that this was due to a strategy for estimating the number of ploughlands available by a count of the plough-teams. He also thinks that elsewhere manorial lords were anxious to get ploughlands and plough-teams to correspond to avoid the possibility that fresh tax demands might be made on the basis that the estate was under-utilised (Higham 1990, 39–40). This seems to me to place too heavy a burden of interpretation upon the evidence to imagine the landowners of the later eleventh century seeing the discrepancies between the two as fiscally dangerous. This is too much like a twentieth century economic interpretation to apply to the eleventh. The real danger for the landowner was surely the risk that the discrepancy between the available ploughlands and the geld rating in hides would be noticed, suggesting that the estate was under taxed. If a new tax was contemplated (and avoided by King William's timely decease), it is likely that the number of plough-teams would have been ignored in favour of a tax on estimated possible output, based on ploughlands, since using actual teams would lead to a fluctuating tax yield and massive avoidance. In any case, in Somerset it is clear that the greatest 'underutilisation' comes on royal and ecclesiastical estates where lords were least concerned about taxation. Clearly ploughlands were not estimated on the basis of plough-teams, but were generally truthful answers to the commissioners' question about potential.

All this leaves open a further question. How often did plough-teams and ploughlands coincide and what interpretation can we place upon the event? On Glastonbury Abbey's estates, five out of 36 properties (15.3%) had as many plough-teams as ploughlands and just two estates had a small surplus of teams. On royal properties 19.4% had equal numbers of teams and ploughlands and one estate had a surplus team. The sample of secular estates shows a closer correspondence, with 32.7% of the sample having equal teams and ploughlands and 10.8% surplus teams. Secular estates were more heavily cultivated than royal or ecclesiastical estates. Having extra plough-teams was not necessarily a disadvantage. It provided an opportunity for more rapid and thorough

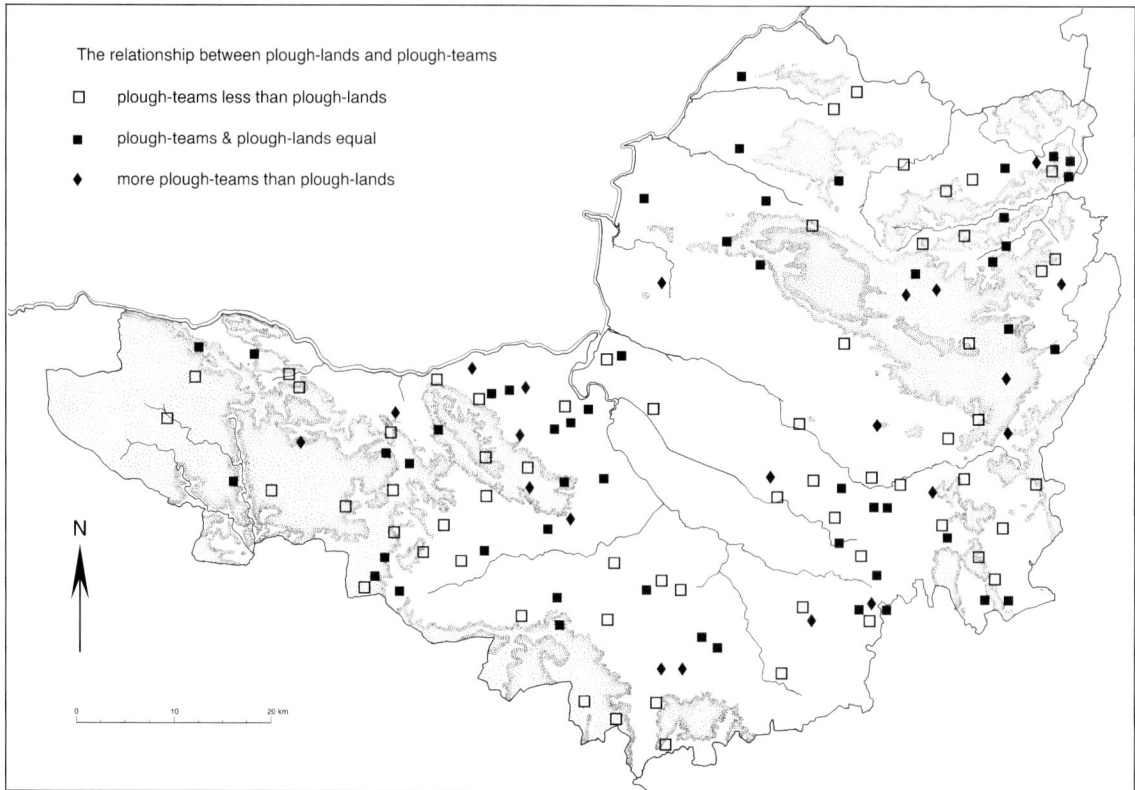

Figure 6.9. Plough teams and ploughlands.

cultivation of the arable, giving greater security and the possibility of increased yields. An illustration of this trend is provided by the two Stocklinches already mentioned. In 1066 Stocklinch Magdalen was held by Edith (DB 25.48). She was succeeded by a Norman tenant by 1086, but at Stocklinch Ottersey the manor was held in 1086 by Alfward and his brothers and they had succeeded their father (DB 47.14). The value of the manors had remained constant during the period 1066–1086 so that the situation in 1086 was probably very similar to that which pertained in 1066. The Domesday Book shows that Stocklinch Magdalen was a 2 hide estate, with 2 ploughlands and 2 plough-teams, both of which belonged to the demesne. Stocklinch Ottersey was a 3 hide estate, but had only 2 ploughlands and had 2 demesne ploughs. The tenants on this estate also had a half plough. Almost all the land was lord's land. The tenants at

Stocklinch Magdalen held 1 virgate and 1 furlong and the men of Ottersey had 1 virgate only. Of the whole 5 hides only 2 virgates and 1 furlong were available to the tenants, who must have worked on the lord's land for wages in order to get a living, since there were few other resources available. Between them the two manors had only 4 acres of coppice, 8 acres of pasture and 23 acres of meadow. All the rest of the land must have been arable. Here were two estates which were almost entirely cultivated intensively by their owners and were overwhelmingly devoted to arable farming, using the labour of their tenants, nearly all of whom were of servile status.

As can be seen from Figure 6.9 the scattering of estates with more, less or equal numbers of plough-teams to ploughlands is random.[1] They are intermingled across the shire. It was the smaller usually secularly owned estates which were most

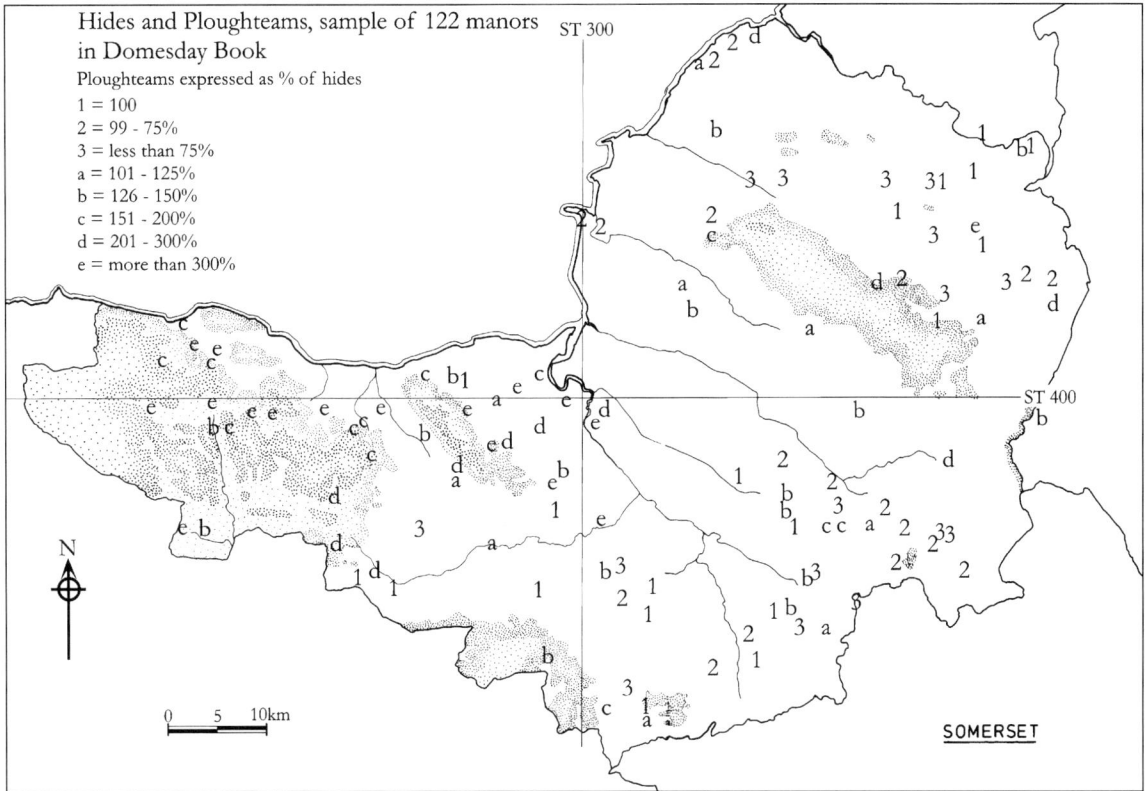

Figure 6.10. Plough teams expressed as a percentage of Domesday hidage.

intensively cultivated and the real division is between the larger, often ecclesiastical or royal estates and the smaller estates available to the lay nobility. A much more significant pattern emerges if we ask what the relationship is between the hidage and the number of plough-teams recorded for each manor. Again a random (though different) sample of 122 manors has been distributed (Fig. 6.10). Here the relationship of teams to hidage is expressed as a percentage. Those manors where the hidage and teams match are marked '1' and falling percentages, where teams are fewer than hides, '2, 3'. Manors where teams exceed hidage are marked with alphabetical letters 'a–e'. Quite clearly there is a marked geographical division, with high percentage manors being much more common west and north of the Parrett–Tone line.

The best explanation of this phenomenon is that the disparity, where teams are far in excess of hidage,

is a crude measure of agricultural expansion over the course of the tenth and eleventh centuries. If the initial hidage was assessed on the basis of the arable in use, perhaps in the early tenth century when the assessment for the support of the *burhs* was made, but the plough-teams in use by 1086 reflect the area of arable in use by that date, then the disparity between the two is a measure of the growth of arable during a century and a half. That expansion had been greatest in the west of the county, but had affected the whole to some extent. The remarkable correspondence of slaves with ploughlands (see Chapter 4) strengthens the case, since it shows a consistency across the south-western counties which the hidage figures obscure. In terms of output ploughlands are contemporary and realistic; hidages are not.

It seems unlikely that the expansion could be solely down to new, foreign entrepreneurial proprietors coming in after the Conquest. The scale of the changes is too large to have taken place in so short a time. This is not to suggest that hidage was calculated on the basis of the number of ploughs or part-ploughs found on a manor, but rather that a manor being first rated, for example at a half hide, would be small, with a low population and necessarily not much in the way of arable. Part of the expansion of activity on the manor would involve some expansion of arable, even if the main activity was pastoral, simply in order to help feed the inhabitants. The commissioners noted the potential of many of these manors when they recorded the potential ploughlands, even if the number of teams had not yet caught up with that target.

The demesne

As Rosamund Faith has made clear, the terms 'inland' and 'demesne' are not synonymous (Faith 1997, 48–55). I have reserved the term 'inland' for lands which were outside the taxation system and which in Somerset seem always to have been ecclesiastical lands, apart from the great royal estates which were 'ancient demesne' which had never been assessed because they belonged to the royal house. The term 'demesne' I use to describe the 'home farm' of the estate, the land set aside to be administered and cultivated directly by the lord, rather than let to his tenants.

The existence of slaves and other servile dwellers on Anglo-Saxon estates suggests that a cultivated demesne was a longstanding feature of land management. As we have seen, there is a clear relationship between the numbers of slaves and the amount of available arable in Wessex. That measure used available ploughlands rather than ploughs actually in use, but the more rational measure it provides is a good reflection of the density of the slave population, the cultivators of the lord's land. Estates where slavery was an important feature would have been especially favoured in the move towards common-field agriculture. They had a labour force immediately available which could be put to use. Taunton with its 70 slaves and 16 freedmen in 1086 could easily work the 20 ploughlands with the 13 teams (DB 2.1). Probably many of these men worked at other manorial jobs besides arable agriculture. One effect of the move towards common-field cultivation

was an increase in the labour available to work the demesne. The output of arable is closely linked to the intensity with which it can be worked. More labour meant more attention could be paid to activities such as weed control, and systematic manuring also became possible. Most surveys of labour services from the twelfth and thirteenth centuries show weeding as an obligation, particularly for the lower status tenants. It was probably first imposed during the move to common-fields. Furthermore, the increasing number of tenants meant that there were more animals feeding on pastures and wastes and the manure could be turned to advantage, with the practice of penning animals, particularly sheep, on the fallow. In later medieval practice the lord's land was the first area to be treated in this way and it seems probable that the practice developed along with the new methods of cultivation.

Generally, in 1086, the lords were themselves cultivating a major proportion of their estates as arable. At Kingsbury, for example, the bishop and the tenants had 6 hides each, the rest of the land being a subsidiary holding (DB 6.5) and at Ilminster Muchelney Abbey had 9 hides 1 virgate and the tenants 10½ hides (DB 9.3). However, at Batcombe the Abbey of Glastonbury had 9 hides 3 virgates while the tenants had only half a hide (DB 8.24). Almost all the 20 hide estates in Somerset were owned by the king or by churches and it might be that there were special circumstances at such places, but a similar examination of 10 hide estates, nearly all of which were in lay hands, shows similar proportions. Although at Crewkerne the lord's land amounted to 2 hides and the tenants to 4 hides 2 virgates, on many others the lord held the lion's share of the land. At Blagdon the lord held 7 hides and 2 virgates and the tenants 1½ hides, and at Laverton the lord's land was 6 hides 3 virgates and the tenants' land 3 hides 1 virgate. It may be that the 20 years after the Norman Conquest had seen a radical increase in the areas farmed directly, but it is more likely that increases had been modest. Laverton, for example, had seen its value increase from £7 to £8 per annum over the period (DB 26.4). On the estates of the bishop of Wells only two holdings had increased in value between 1066 and 1086, two had decreased in value and the remaining eleven were unchanged. The estates

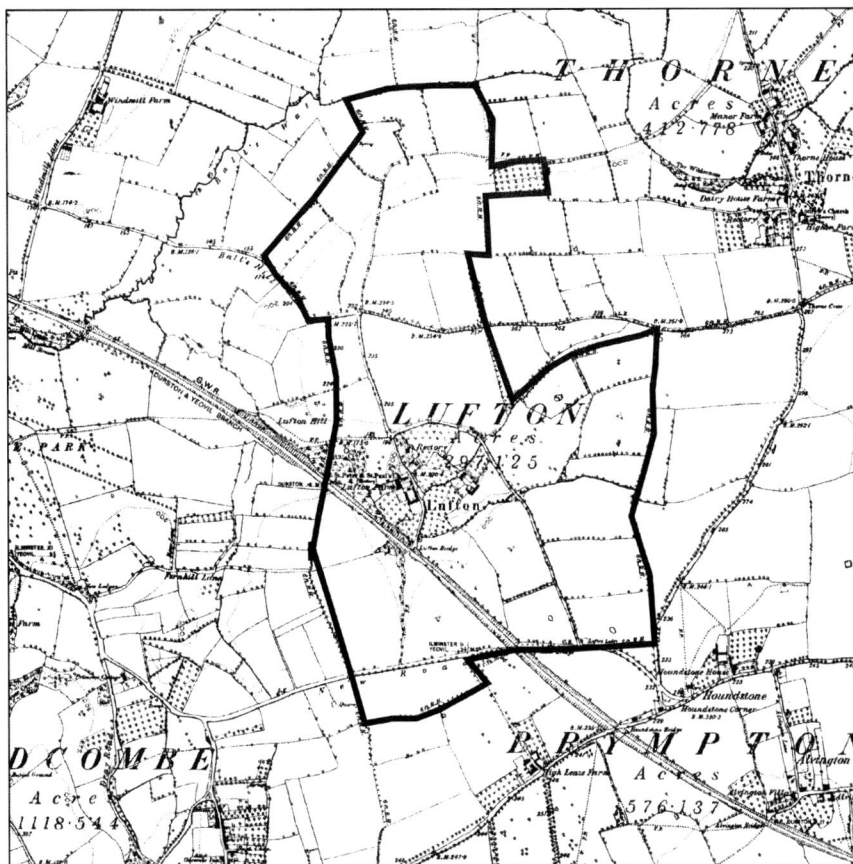

Figure 6.11. The Domesday manor of Lufton still visible as a parish.

granted to secular magnates probably changed more. The count of Mortain had 86 manors in Somerset. Most of them were sub-infeudated to his followers by 1086, so most of the income was going to them, rather than to the count. 40% had increased in value; 24% had seen a fall and 36% were unchanged. The scale of the changes in money values was positive but not dramatic, as the aggregate rise in values amounted to £21 3s over the 86 manors – about 1.26 s per hide. This suggests that the scale and intensity of demesne farming had not changed markedly over the 20 years after the Conquest and that the Domesday Book actually provides a reasonably accurate picture of demesne farming in 1066.

The smaller estates had the largest proportion of their land devoted to the demesne. Some of the

smallest jurisdictions cannot have looked much like a classic manor, since nearly all their area was devoted to the home farm. White Ox Mead paid geld for 1 hide (DB 21.89). It had land for two ploughs and those were both on the demesne. There was a slave and otherwise the population consisted of six bordars who held 1½ virgates between them. They had no ploughs and so must have been dependent upon the lord for their cultivation, as well as working on his land for part of their support. Most of the estate was lord's land. Eckweek, next door, seems to have had a single common-field system, which may have predated the division into two manors, evident in the Domesday Book (Kidd and Young, ND). Lufton, near Yeovil, was a 1 hide estate held by Ansger in 1066 (DB 19.82), and was still visible as a tiny parish of approximately 300 acres, at the time of the tithe award (Fig. 6.11). The tithe map certainly suggests that two fields had existed and that it once had a common-field system, but the only plough-team belonged to the demesne and the only inhabitants were two slaves and three bordars. It may be that the estate was farmed on a two-field rotation, with the land divided into furlongs, but the bordars' acres must have been very thinly scattered amongst the lord's. The technical demands of the new machine would thus be met, but labour input from tenants would have been negligible.

There were, of course, also estates with no demesne. At 'Petherham', an estate near Cannington, there were four bordars with one plough-team working the whole estate of one ploughland (DB 21.21). Before the Conquest the landowner had been a Godwin. In 1086 it belonged to Roger of Courseulles. It may be that the bordars simply paid a cash rent to Roger and had paid Godwin similarly. If so it is a reminder that small estates are not always easy to fit into a regular pattern and that our ideas of how the countryside was organised are profoundly constrained by the format which the Domesday commissioners imposed upon the survey. Individual low status farms did still exist in the mid-eleventh century. At Eckweek there were two separate 'manors'. The smaller consisted of a single ploughland and paid tax on a virgate. The population consisted of a single villein and a slave. The farm was owned by Alstan of Boscombe in 1066 (DB 19.61). An excavation at Eckweek, near Bath, 1988–9, revealed a single farmstead of the late Anglo-Saxon period, along with its accompanying farm buildings. This may be Alstan of Boscombe's farmstead, since there is a demesne only at the other manor. The other 'manor' at Eckweek was really no larger, being a single ploughland but paying tax for 1½ virgates and 8 acres. Here the whole of the land was in a demesne farm with a single bordar resident (DB 24.32).

To a large extent we see what the commissioners wanted their contemporaries to see – a neatly organised landscape. They in their turn were deeply influenced by the bureaucratic impositions of the Anglo-Saxon administration, with its emphasis upon tax-raising which necessarily placed great weight upon regularity and systematic ordering.

Animals

The cultivation of arable was only one part of the life of the common-field estate. The agglomeration of the lands of the tenants with those of the lord made possible the efficient use of the animals of the estate as a method of manuring the land. The single great fallow field provided an area upon which the animals of the community might all graze together, supporting them and fertilising the ground. If the manor also had substantial areas of pasture and waste the communal herds and flocks brought back their load of dung and deposited it on the fields at night. There is evidence from other parts of western Britain that pasture and meadow land was regarded as for common use at earlier periods. Della Hooke has pointed to the charter for Ardington (S691 of 961) where there is the explicit statement that 'the nine hides lie both in common and allocated land, pasture in common, meadow in common and arable in common' (Hooke 1989, 21). It is possible that one aspect of the new agricultural regime was that lords took a greater interest in the common wastes and pastures than previously. Although later medieval customary tenant farmers normally had rights in the common pastures, these rights were paid for through their services and cash rents. It may well be that it was at this point in the later ninth and in the tenth centuries that the lord first began to appreciate the real value of his manorial pastures and woods and to see that they could increase his income and so extended his control over what had formerly been regarded as simply a common resource. The intensification of crop production also implied a rise in the number of animals being kept and control of grazing probably became valuable. The new fields needed oxen in considerable numbers to plough them and herds of cows would have been needed to produce the necessary bull calves. If the manor could not rear them for itself then a sufficient surplus would be needed to enable the purchase of oxen from outside. The classic ox team is of eight animals, but it may have varied according to the stiffness of the ground being worked. There were 316 teams on the lands of the Count of Mortain and his tenants (DB 19). Four oxen to a team would mean 1264 animals in the plough-teams and eight oxen teams 2528. Obviously such mechanical

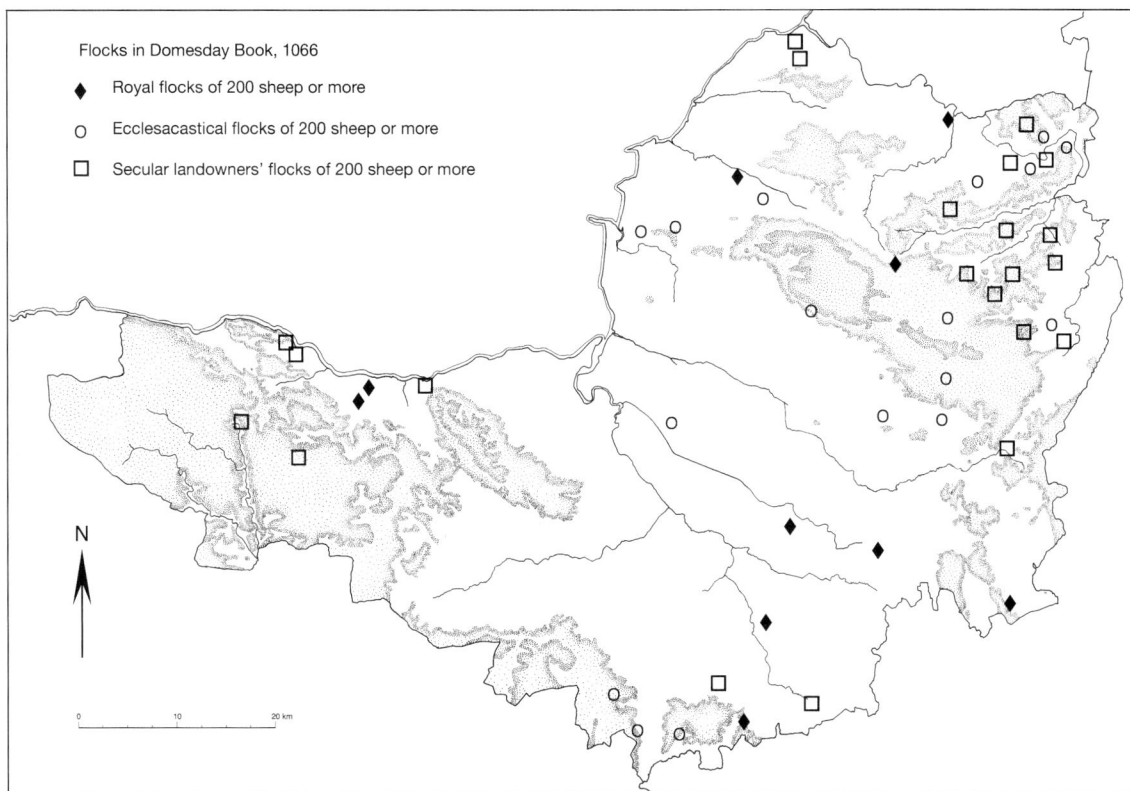

Figure 6.12. Domesday flocks of 200 sheep or more.

calculations are bound to be far from the truth, but they serve to suggest the very large numbers of oxen needed by the common-field system and behind them a large and constant breeding programme and a lively market in animals. The cows which were needed for the breeding programme would have also produced milk which could be turned into cheese, as well as providing valuable leather, but that would have been subsidiary to the need to provide the oxen. There is some evidence to support this conjecture from work on animal bones which has shown that as the Anglo-Saxon period progressed cattle were kept to a greater and greater age. Thus where in an earlier period most cattle were slaughtered when they were quite young, optimising meat output, by the end of the Anglo-Saxon period they were being kept much longer, to optimise their output as beasts for traction and burden (Sykes 2006, 56–7).

Much more important in numerical terms were sheep. The Domesday Book for Somerset records over 40,000 demesne sheep. It is likely that the number is somewhat inaccurate. Some manors with recorded pastures have no demesne sheep, which is unlikely. Returns often give the numbers of sheep in round numbers, 40, 50, 100, 200 sheep. Clearly these were estimates of approximate numbers. However, other numbers are very specific, showing that some returns were very detailed, so the numbers in the Domesday survey may convey a realistic estimate. Most estates stocked some sheep and the total numbers must have far exceeded 40,000 with the addition of tenant flocks – perhaps as many as 80,000.

The great royal and ecclesiastical manors around the slopes of the Mendips all ran sheep in great numbers. In fact the crown and church between them controlled nearly all the access to the upland grazing, dominating the plateau from Bleadon in the west to Frome in the east. This is certainly not an accident. As we shall see in a later chapter, the Abbey of Glastonbury pursued the acquisition of lands in and around the Mendips in the mid and late tenth century. The desire to increase access to extensive grazing may well have prompted expansion in that direction.

The geographical pattern of sheep-raising shows that although the greatest flocks were to be found on ecclesiastical and royal estates, chiefly around the Mendips, the greatest concentration of large flocks (over 200 animals) was in the eastern Mendips, east of the Fosse Way and to the north of Frome (Fig. 6.12). Many of these flocks were on secular estates, suggesting that secular landowners were also deeply concerned with the wool trade. Most of the estates with large flocks were taking advantage of the extensive areas of open grazing in the more broken and wooded eastern Mendips, but some estates, such as those at Hinton Charterhouse and Norton St Philip, were on land which also had a great deal of arable. The sheer numbers of sheep kept and the clearly well-developed nature of the industry suggest that all landlords were interested in a substantial business which provided a cash crop as well as fitting into the mixed farming regime which gave the common-field system its stable character. Here was the embryonic production process which was to drive future manufacturing and hence trade in woollen cloth.

Fisheries

In the previous chapter we considered river and shore-line fishing and it is clear that this source of food was heavily exploited throughout the Anglo-Saxon period. In Ælfric's Colloquy his fisherman describes fishing by boat on both the river and the sea (Garmonsway 1939, 27–8). It is of course difficult to know how accurate a boys' grammar textbook might be, but it is likely that by the time the Colloquy was composed in the later tenth century both river and sea fishing took place. The late tenth century has been identified as the period in which sea fishing became important as the catches from rivers failed to keep pace with rising demand (Barrett, Locker and Roberts 2004, 618–36). Ælfric's fisherman says that he sells his catch in the town, suggesting that the rising town

population were turning to sea fish as a relatively cheap source of protein. The Somerset coast is singularly devoid of seaside settlements, apart from the ports at Porlock, Watchet and Portishead, and the only fishermen mentioned in the Domesday Survey were at Meare (DB 8.1). Ten of them worked on the lake there. The small size of Somerset towns, even in the eleventh century, may have meant that there was too little demand to stimulate an industry which would have been hazardous and relatively unprofitable in the unforgiving waters of the Bristol Channel.

Mills

Associated with the rising output of grain were the watermills. Watermills are known from archaeological discoveries in many parts of Britain, including a mill at Old Windsor, with no less than three wheels, dated by dendrochronology to the later seventh century (Wilson and Hurst 1959, 183–5) and at a number of other sites scattered across Britain (Lucas 2006, 75). The earliest written record of a mill is in 762 at Wye in Kent, when the community of SS Peter and Paul granted half the use of a mill to the king in exchange for grazing elsewhere (S25). Although there are so many in the Domesday Book, the sites of mills of this period are unknown in Somerset. By 1086 they were very common, but 'mill' place-names are rare. In Somerset Milverton, 'mill + ford + tun', Mells, 'mills' and Milborne (Port) 'the millstream', are the only major place-names of this type. Milborne at least can be understood as the stream which powered the mill attached to the royal site at Kingsbury, only a few hundred metres away. A similar stream name (milborne close, t. 875) exists at Chew Magna, an important ecclesiastical estate. The Mells 'mills' may have belonged to the monastic settlement at Frome and the settlement may have grown from its use as a specialist site belonging to the estate centre. The scanty evidence for mills may not mean that they were few and far between. Work on the use of water-mills in Francia shows that they were in widespread use, particularly on ecclesiastical estates, but also on those of lay magnates in the period from the late sixth to the tenth centuries (McCormick 2002, 23). If the same pattern is true in Wessex the constant re-use of mill sites may have destroyed remains of earlier mills.

However, even the bounds of Anglo-Saxon charters show little evidence. Mills are often found on the edges of estates, since the streams they utilize are often used as boundaries. Only two references occur, in S311 and S345, to *melenburnan* and *mylenburnan* respectively. Both charters relate to lands of the Old Minster at Winchester and both are deeply suspect as documents (Keynes 1994b, 1135). The bounds may well have been added after the Norman Conquest. It may be that the investment in a water-mill was something which only the large estate could justify in the seventh and eighth centuries, but by the tenth century it was coming to be regarded as a normal adjunct of many medium sized places.

The siting of a water-mill was clearly dependent upon a suitable water supply and many of the places which had no mill in 1086 were probably too level to allow the accumulation of a suitable head of water, or did not have a water source beginning high enough to allow for a suitable drop. The Glastonbury manors on the Poldens and some of the manors to the east of Glastonbury were in this situation. In many cases these were communities where the abbey invested in windmills in the thirteenth and fourteenth centuries. Not all the mills were powered by streams. At Weare the Domesday Book records two mills and in the post-Norman period there are references to 'twinmills' which were tide mills (Ross 1959, 13). The site still survives as a field-name, on the moors beside the Axe. On the large estates mills were quite common, but not universal. Somerton, one of the most ancient and most important of royal sites in the county, had no mills. Smaller estates tended not to have mills, presumably because the cost of the investment was too great for the lord to make, either because he was too poor, or because the investment was judged uneconomic. Of Roger Arundel's 26 estates (DB 22), only 12 had mills. Of these, the mill at Raddington was given no value and was described as grinding only for the hall (DB 22.13). The values of the mills varied wildly. On the royal estates the two mills at Queen Camel were worth 20 s per annum between them (DB 1.22), but the royal mill at North Petherton was worth only 15 pence (DB 1.3). The six mills at Milborne Port paid £3 17s 6d, the three at Frome £1 5s and the four at Crewkerne £2. The large number of mills indicates that the siting and technology

used did not allow the construction of very large machines, but the head of water available made it possible to develop several mills on the same stream over a comparatively short distance. These were able to make a profit because they were sited close to the small towns and markets. They probably ground grain marketed in the towns and sold the flour there also. Elsewhere mills with very small values may only have ground for their own manors, or perhaps also one or two others nearby.

Water-mills are clearly at the intersection of production and commerce, turning a bulk agricultural product into a saleable product for household and commercial use, and provide evidence that the agriculture of the tenth and eleventh centuries was becoming part of a market economy. Even where mills ground for local consumption the fact that they returned a money rent shows that the miller got his living by selling the flour made from his toll on grain brought to him to process. He must have sold his product at a market in return for cash. Such a transaction was only a part of what took place. One great stimulus to the commercialisation of the peasants' output was the need to pay the geld.

Throughout the later ninth and tenth centuries English kings were forced to pay off Danish raiders with cash. At first much no doubt came from the accumulated treasuries of the king and the church, but during the tenth century general levies became more common, and by the reign of Æthelræd there was a general tax, the heregeld, which was levied on all taxable lands, suggesting that the ready stock of treasure in the hands of the king and the church was declining or had been exhausted. Large sums of money left the country. The Danes were supposed to have taken out £10,000 in 991, 16,000 in 994, 24,000 in 1002 and 36,000 in 1007, 3000 in 1009, 48,000 in 1012, 21,000 in 1014, 72,000 plus 10,000 from London in 1018 and over 32,000 in 1041. Although Professor John Gillingham has questioned the reality of these payments, the arguments of Dr Lawson seem to me convincing (Lawson 1989, 385–406; Gillingham 1989, 373–83). Dr Metcalf suggests that England had a very favourable balance of payments in the late tenth century and that the geld levied represented only 20% or so of the coin in circulation (Metcalf 1978). The geld was levied until the reign of Edward the Confessor and it was through the sale of surplus produce that the peasant farmers of Somerset paid their taxes.

Conclusions

The word 'revolution' now carries the idea of a complete change in behaviour; new ways of doing things; a social change of a profound nature. We have also become used to a debasement of the word to describe the most trivial of changes in everyday life. But the word was at its most powerful when used to describe radical political and social upheaval – particularly the French Revolution and its offspring the Russian Revolution.

The men of the tenth century would not have understood the concept, but they experienced innovatory changes in the rural economy which profoundly affected their whole society. Change of a drastic nature does not come easily in peasant society and usually needs to be driven by severe pressures, often from outside the system. The later ninth century and the whole of the tenth century, with its dramatic expansion of Wessex into England and then the disaster of the Danish conquest by Swein and his son Cnut, provided the pressure and the necessary setting in which new ideas might take root. The tenth century was a period of radical change and the people who advocated these ideas were probably an elite who had most to gain from changes. Smart young men in the new monasteries of the mid-tenth century would be the obvious people to oversee such changes, but it is also possible that clerks in the households of secular lords might equally well be innovators. The aristocracy grew as the kingdom expanded and it is likely that the numbers of people who regarded themselves as members of the ruling class also grew. The large numbers of charters issued to laymen and women and the range of landed interest demonstrated in the surviving wills of the tenth century are testimony to this. The class of the thegns was also growing. The title concealed yawning disparities between the thegn with perhaps a hide of land or less and the King's thegn with lands scattered across several shires, but even the poorest of these men commanded others and so were part of the landed classes, supported by the peasants' labours. Aristocratic men found new careers in the church and a new class of peasant tenant farmers was growing rapidly. By 1086 Somerset was quite clearly divided into a land owning class, which ranged from men with thousands of acres to others with a virgate or two, below whom were a mass of tenant farmers, with large numbers of unfree workers on the lord's demesne. It is not without significance that the *Rectitudines Singularum Personarum* was composed in the early eleventh century.

Overall, the population growth encompassed all classes and must surely be seen as the result of the changes which had taken place chiefly in the agricultural practice of the tenth century. The new system aimed to exploit the land more fully, by intensifying arable cultivation and integrating animal husbandry into the routine. It introduced the possibility of supporting more people from the same areas of land and functioned best when there were plenty of people to work in it. Such a development favoured the growth of population, but Wessex still lacked people, so that control of the population by legal and customary practices, such as slavery and bond tenures was well worthwhile. Labour was valuable and it was only after the Norman conquest, as population continued to grow, that slavery began to disappear.

It was also natural that English agricultural society should become quite deeply monetized. In practice the rural economy had never been completely 'self-sufficient' and it had probably never been intended to be, but the tenth century saw the appearance of a marketized system oriented towards the production of surpluses which could be exchanged for cash. The demands of taxation, conceived as the response to military defeat and conquest and applied systematically, affected every estate and probably every person. As producers of basic agricultural commodities the lords and peasants of Somerset were able to take advantage of the late tenth century rise in the money supply to trade for the silver they needed to pay their geld. Even humble dwellings might now hold a store of coin as demonstrated by the silver penny of Edward the Confessor, found in the ashes of the hearth in an earth floored hut, built with earth-fast posts at Brent Knoll (Young 2009, 108).

Note

1. A random sample of 121 manors taken from Domesday Book.

7

Early Trade

For the people of early post-Roman Somerset it is likely that nearly all trade was local. Trade and manufacture does not need money. Many societies have used some form of barter which bypassed coin, but the people of the late Roman world were familiar with an economy in which coin was used on an enormous scale. When coins are discovered in archaeological contexts they are almost always Roman coins. Finds of medieval coin of all types are negligible in quantity compared with the abundance of money of the Roman empire. The disappearance of that coin from British sites has always been regarded as a mark of the extreme nature of the social changes which took place in the first half of the fifth century.

Post-Roman activity

As we saw above in the introduction, there is some evidence that coin continued to circulate in diminishing quantities during the early part of the fifth century, but there is an apparent hiatus in coin use in Somerset between the first quarter of the fifth century and the first coins of the early medieval period, which are all dated to the later fifth and the early sixth centuries. It may be that further evidence will bridge the gap more fully and show that coin continued to circulate continuously and that the arrival of good quality Byzantine coin actually dealt a death blow to the surviving clipped siliquae, but the chance of such evidence coming to light looks increasingly remote as new sites are found. We must assume that barter gradually replaced money as the means of exchange in a local rural economy where

necessities were traded and the accumulated store of late Roman objects was used up as things wore out.

The evidence of social contact between south-west Britain and Armorica in the fifth and sixth centuries is very strong, so it is clear that overseas contact was not lost and commercial activity was at least theoretically possible. Clearly there were real difficulties caused mostly by seaborne raiding by the Saxons. They were present as raiders from the continent in the early fifth century and may have used their settlements in south-east England as well as northern Gaul as bases for their attacks after the mid-fifth century (Hayward 1999, 86–8). There is no evidence to show that goods passed to and fro along with people. Trade on any large scale may not have been needed.

The Byzantine coins which mark the beginning of early medieval trade in Somerset and elsewhere in western Britain were of the later fifth and first half of the sixth century and since they were imported there may never have been large numbers of them in Somerset. However, the tiny numbers found probably represent a considerable circulation (Fig. 7.1). The coins are only part of the evidence for the connection with the eastern Mediterranean world of the Byzantine Empire, contact with which was controlled from the defended site at Tintagel on the north Cornwall coast (Thomas 1999, 75). The ruler here was powerful enough to influence contact with the Byzantine traders over most of the south-west peninsula and it has been suggested that this power was based upon control of the production and distribution of tin (Gerrard 2000, 23). As we have seen above in chapter one, an alternative explanation

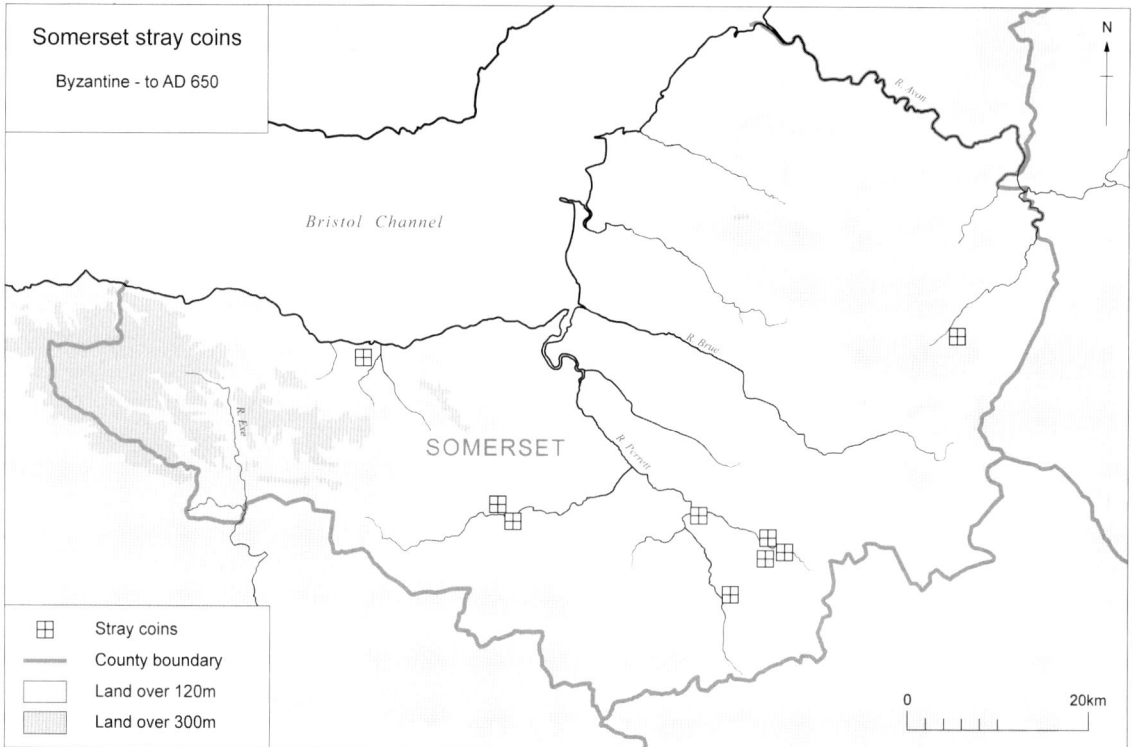

Figure 7.1. Byzantine coins found in Somerset.

would be that the coins along with the pottery are evidence of the wide-ranging diplomatic policies of the Byzantine Emperors, which included encouraging contacts and spreading their influence through many parts of the old Western Empire (Harris 2003, 146–9).

The first coin was one of Anastasius, 491–518. It was pierced for wearing as an ornament and was found at Ilchester. When it was pierced and whether it ever first functioned as a coin in Somerset is unknown and it may have been an exotic arrival which was always an ornament. The find-sites of the others, all coins of Justinian and thus dated to 527–565, are at St Decuman's in the churchyard just outside Watchet, at Taunton, Langport, Ilchester, Ham Hill and at Whatley in the eastern Mendips. It is instructive to compare this distribution with the known distribution of pottery associated with Byzantium. The known prestige sites at Cannington, Cadbury-Congresbury, South Cadbury and Ham Hill

all produced evidence of the consumption of wines, olive oils and other delicacies, but coins are noticeably absent, except at Ham Hill. The same seems to be true for the lesser sites at Glastonbury, Beckery and Athelney (Campbell 2007, 118), suggesting that commerce, which involved the use of coin, and the consumption of prestige material were two separate areas of activity. The prestige goods may have arrived as gifts from the king at Tintagel, while the coin was associated with direct trade, which brought foreign merchants to Somerset, though perhaps only after permission from him.

The only coastal siting of these early coins in Somerset is near Watchet, later to become an important port, perhaps the most important on this coast, during the Anglo-Saxon period. This is where we might reasonably expect a beach-market to have existed, but if there is evidence it may be too deeply buried under the modern town to be recoverable. The place-name is Primitive Welsh in origin and means 'lower wood' (Watts 2004). The retention of the ancient name suggests a strong element of continuity. This alone undermines the idea that Watchet was founded after the abandonment of the *burh* at Dawes Castle. It is clear that the reason for the construction of the *burh* was the existence of an active trading settlement beside the sea. (Any seaside settlement at this period is rare and probably important therefore). It was also part of the large Williton Anglo-Saxon royal estate which has strong associations with the post-Roman cult of St Decuman and it was in his churchyard that the Watchet coin was found. This might suggest a connection between the traders and the religious site, if it was actually at this spot in the sixth century. The natural route inland then takes road travellers along the foot of the Quantocks to Taunton, where there are two more finds and from there on into central Somerset. Associated with the Taunton coins is a Byzantine coin-weight for six nomismata. Now in the British Museum, it was found near Taunton and given to the British Museum by Augustus Wollaston Franks in 1866 (Dalton 1901, 94, no. 453). The weight has a monogram which indicates that it may have come from Constantinople in the sixth century. It carries the inscription 'of Eudaimonos' and a *Eudaemon* was Prefect of Constantinople in 532 (Buckton 1994, 86). This must strongly suggest that travellers from the east ventured well beyond the shore.

An alternative route for traders was up the river Parrett and then along its tributaries to finish at the head of the navigation at Ilchester. There are as yet no coins of this type from the Cannington area, at the mouth of the Parrett, despite its high profile as a centralised estate as indicated by the large post-Roman cemetery there (Rahtz, Hirst and Wright 2000). Such evidence as there is for Cannington comes from the Portable Antiquities Scheme records. A copper alloy rivet mount from Otterhampton is said to be similar to one found in an Anglo-Saxon grave on Chessell down, Isle of Wight (PAS, SOM-DFE383). From the same parish comes a penannular brooch of 490–699 (PAS, SOMDOR-EE1252) and from Fiddington a copper alloy mount, dated AD 500–800 (PAS, SOMDOR-5C2CA7). But this is native British or Anglo-Saxon material, not exotica.

Travelling up the river Parrett system, there is a coin at Langport, a stopping point for the Somerton upland with its concentration of old villa sites and easily worked arable, and then it was possible to reach Ilchester itself by water. The re-used hill-forts in Somerset, Cannington, Cadbury–Congresbury and South Cadbury have not produced coins from Byzantium, despite extensive and exemplary excavation. This is significant. There are no coins at South Cadbury, although Ilchester must have been the place which supplied it with the wine and oil in jars. It looks as if South Cadbury's trade, if there was any, was carried on at Ilchester. It may also be significant that not only are there no coins from Cadbury–Congresbury, but also none from its hinterland either. The only hill-fort with possible coin and pottery material is High Ham (though the evidence is more than a little shaky). The coin far to the north-east at Whatley could be the result of traffic along the Mendips from the sea, going towards Wiltshire, or more likely from Ilchester, up the Fosse Way towards the Bath area. The coins, then, have been found at sites which were later generally connected with ecclesiastical and royal estates of the Anglo-Saxon period, rather than at the princely hill-forts, and this points towards a long term continuity of centres of communication and exchange in the Old Welsh period into the Anglo-Saxon centuries. From this perspective the hill-forts can be seen as ephemeral aberrations in a persistent pattern of communication and trade. Trade did not need to be a princely activity, though doubtless it could not have continued without princely approval.

The conclusion that trade and exchange within Somerset was something which was the result of a policy sanctioned through political and social relationships with Tintagel is reinforced by consideration of the position in Dorset. Here there is only one discovery of a Byzantine coin, near Poole. Despite the existence of the very important post-Roman community at Dorchester which has been extensively studied, there is no sign of either pottery or coins linking the area with the Byzantine traders or emissaries (Sparey-Green 1996, 140). Dorset, in contrast to Somerset, seems not to have enjoyed the contacts, perhaps because it was not dominated by the Dumnonian ruler (Fig. 7.2).

Somerset was cut off from easy contact to the north once the Bath area passed into the hands of the

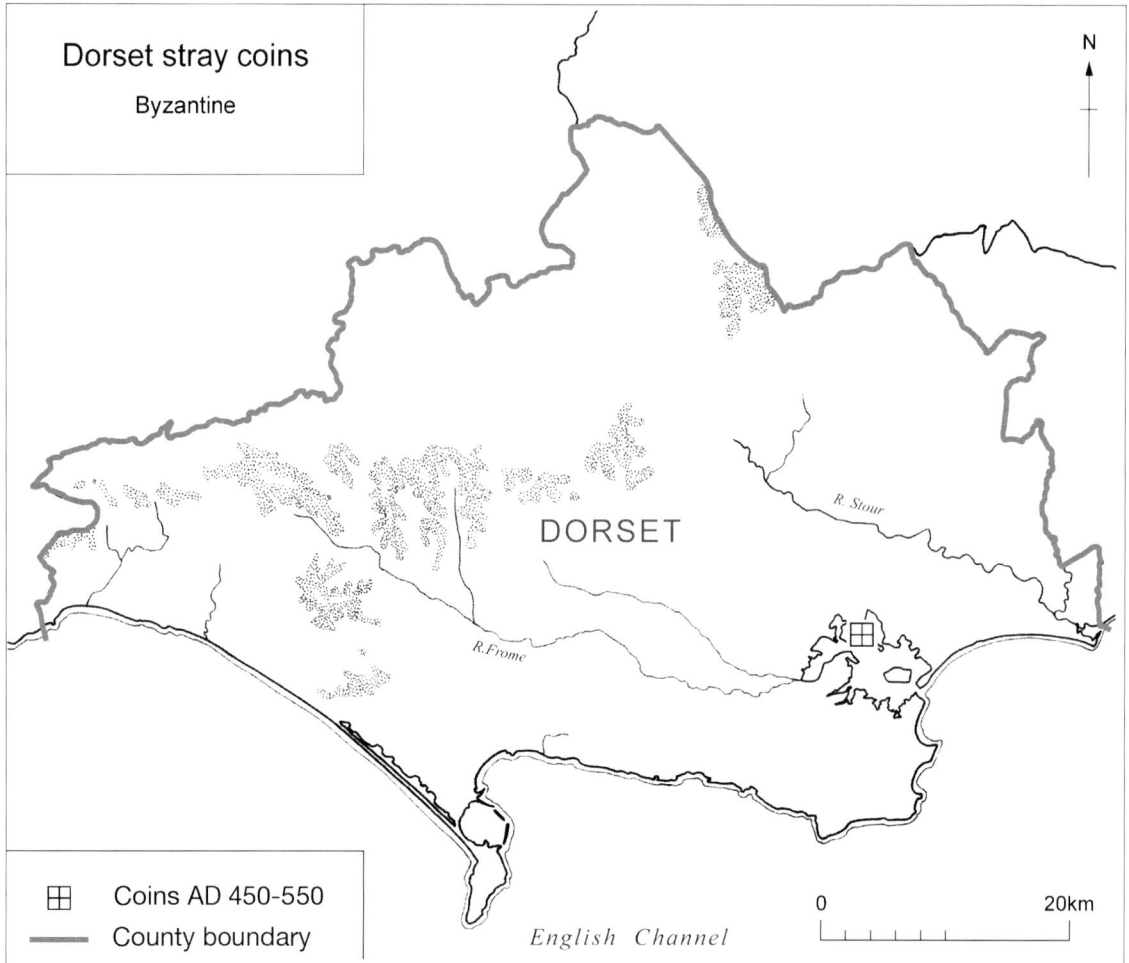

Figure 7.2 Byzantine coins found in Dorset.

Hwicce in the late sixth century. Reduction in contact with the north may have caused the further decline of small communities at Camerton and Charlton on the Fosse Way. Trade with Somerset was therefore much like trade with an island and consequently was mostly carried on by sea.

What was exchanged at Watchet and Ilchester is a mystery. Certainly if coin was being introduced to the countryside, then it seems likely that something was being supplied; something had been produced. Ewan Campbell has suggested that the Somerset concentration of pottery at Cadbury-Congresbury points to the export of lead and silver from the Mendips (Campbell 1996, 88), but there is no evidence for the continuation of the lead mining industry into the later fifth and sixth centuries and the pattern of coin distribution does not indicate that Congresbury was a commercial centre. It is difficult to think of anything that might be produced in the west of Britain, which would be worth carrying as far as the eastern Mediterranean, unless the trade included slaves. Slaves were a very high value commodity and would have been well worth a trade visit to Somerset (McCormick 2001, 752–9). Slave raiding into Anglo-Saxon Wiltshire is not an impossible source of people to be trafficked.

The coins of the Byzantine world do not continue beyond the mid-sixth century and so it looks as if the contact period was relatively short. There is no consensus about the reason for the sudden cessation of this trade. Campbell has suggested that the Byzantine traders brought the plague with them and that the ensuing social disruption destroyed the elite group who controlled the trade in tin (Campbell 2007, 132). While it is true that the plague became endemic in western Europe, including Britain, at this period, it is hard to see why that would have disrupted trade on a permanent basis. The destruction of the elite is unlikely. The evidence from the plague in the fourteenth century suggests that the elite nobility and clergy were the group who suffered least and emerged relatively unscathed from the event. The social and economic conditions of the sixth century were not so different from those of the fourteenth century as to make the comparison implausible. In the fourteenth century economic and therefore social relationships between the elite and the peasant classes were profoundly affected, but in sixth century Dumnonia the disruptive effects would have been smaller among a population which was mainly engaged in pastoral activity and the potential tin trade was available to anyone who could control the local tin production, even if a fall in manpower temporarily reduced output. What seems more likely is that there was a change in demand from the Byzantines which made tin from such a distant source no longer attractive. By the end of the sixth century trade within the late-Roman world was in steep decline and by the end of the seventh century the connections between western Europe and the eastern Mediterranean had all but ceased (McCormick 2002, 27). Loss of the tin trade should be seen as a part of a generalised slowing and restriction of activity throughout the West.

The evidence for overseas trade in the second half of the sixth century and the first half of the seventh century is very elusive. The 'E' ware, which was manufactured somewhere in western France, is widely found around western British shores. This material was clearly the result of a continental trade of a more localised type than the long distance material from the eastern Mediterranean. Only Carhampton has produced evidence of 'E' ware (Campbell 2007, 118), and in the absence of further material we must conclude that such trade as existed was conducted at a low level. Contact with the western Continent, at least as far as trade was concerned, had fallen very low. The trade of the early Anglo-Saxons of Somerset therefore probably owes more to the dislocation of that late Roman world and a re-focusing on the north-west of Europe than it does to any ideas of ethnicity or political shifts. A fall in the level of trade with the continent did not mean that coasting trade ceased. The excavations at Cannington produced some grass-marked pottery which originated in Cornwall (Rahtz, Hirst and Wright 2000, 298). This might suggest that pottery was imported into an area which had no pottery of its own at this time. Alternatively it could be the residue of containers used to import some other materials. It is clear, however, that shipping must have moved along the coast and that Cannington at the mouth of the Parrett was a point of entry for goods.

Discussion of trade concentrates on long distance communication and the supply of luxury items. By implication this is necessarily a discussion of the tastes and habits of an elite which is otherwise almost entirely hidden from us by lack of documentation. It is as if a modern discussion of long distance trade dealt entirely with the importation of Gucci handbags and Porsche cars and the export of luxury yachts and ignored the import of cheap clothes from China and the export of whisky to Japan. We would see mostly London and the Solent and ignore provincial England's shopping centres and Scotland's manufacturing industry in the Highlands.

The things which people used and which survive tell us something about the items of daily life, some of which were probably made locally, some of which were carried or traded into Somerset from distant places. It is impossible to know what the connections are between the items which survive and the coins we find. We need to remember that there were many other items which have perished and which would have been important to people also. Things which have survived come either from finds of objects during archaeological fieldwork or by metal detecting. Common objects of ferrous metal rarely occur in open ground. Instead most survivals are of non-ferrous material, usually copper alloys. This means that the range of objects found, excluding coins, is quite limited.

Figure 7.3. Beads from a grave at Buckland Dinham.

Other items are recovered during excavations, particularly during the excavations of graves. Such material is important in revealing information about the beliefs, cultural affiliations and status of those buried, but they also reveal the type of objects which were common in the community. The range of materials found is more varied and includes items made of iron, glass and bone as well as precious metals and non-ferrous alloys.

Glass beads are among the more durable items found and there is some evidence that there was a local manufacture in the post-Roman period. A good many were found during the excavation of the graves at Cannington. There was a 'local manufacture in a long lingering Romano-British idiom'. There was also a bead manufactured in either Kent or East Anglia between 650 and 700 (Guido 2000, 311). Beads were also present in eight of the graves excavated at Camerton (Horne 1929 and 1934) and there were indications that a female burial at Hincknowle Slait near South Cadbury, had included a beaded necklace (J. Davey, pers. comm.). Beads had also accompanied one of the burials at Buckland Dinham (Horne 1926) (Fig. 7.3). Probably most women wore bead necklaces in the period 410–650 and almost certainly beyond. Although such material survives well, there

must always have been a demand for new beads, both locally made and carried in trade. This was the kind of manufacture and trade which probably produced a steady demand, but which was not of enormous economic value inside the community. We do not have enough examples of 'exotic' beads like the one from Kent or East Anglia to know whether this was a traded item, or whether it was a rare sign of a social contact with the Anglo-Saxon east. It is, however, a marker for many other goods which would be needed or desired and which have perished, some of which had travelled long distances and which may have been part of informal exchange mechanisms. Among the items found at Cannington was a comb (Rahtz, Hirst and Wright 2000, 272–3). Made normally of horn or bone, such items easily decay, so this is representative of an enormous number of other combs which must have employed someone locally in making them. More valuable and less perishable items of jewellery include brooches. Currently four are known dating between 400 and 600 (Fig. 7.4). There was one found at Bishops Hull (PAS, SOM-0B1693) one at Otterhampton (PAS, SOMDOR-AB3955) and one near Wells (PAS, SOMDOR-DEA564). Again these must be representative of an enormous stock of jewellery which would imply the existence

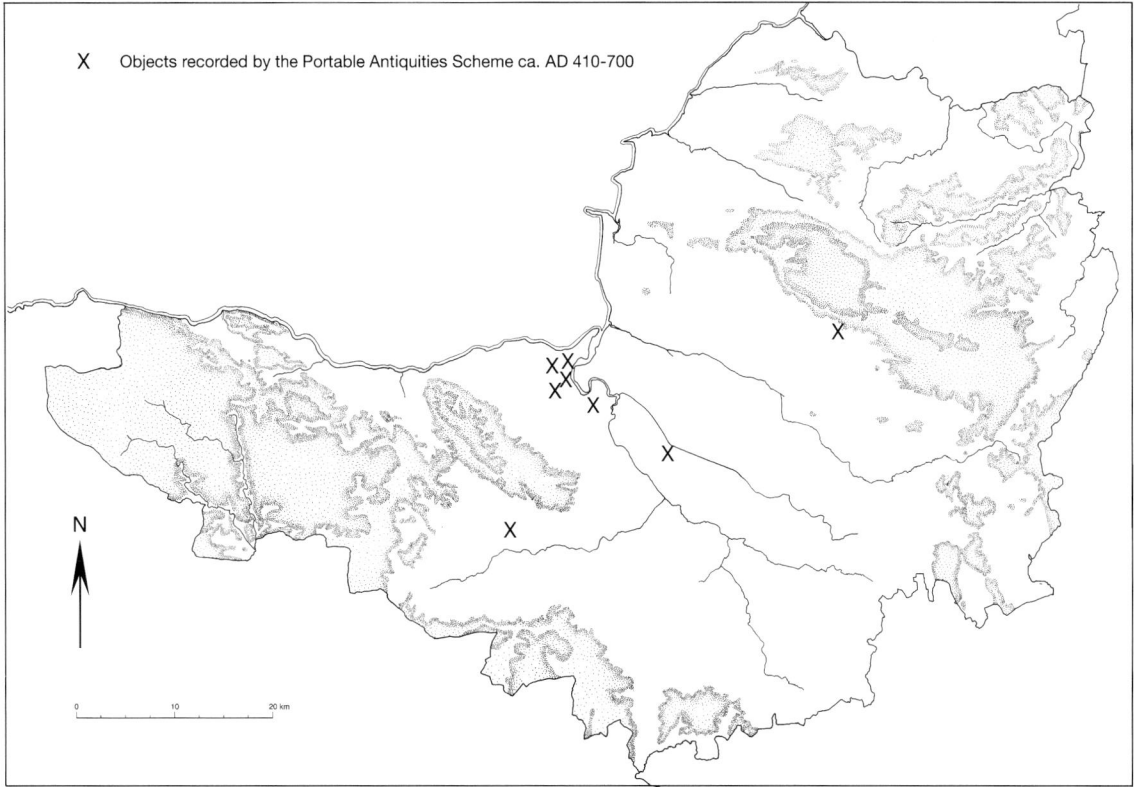

Figure 7.4. Objects recorded by PAS for period 400 to 700 approximately.

of craftsmen able to meet demand and perhaps distributing their manufactures locally. Such men may have worked exclusively for members of the elite as craftsmen tied to them through bond relationships, or they may have moved about the community working where they could find a patron or patroness. The same may be true for smiths who supplied the community with knives. Most burials where there are grave goods include knives. They must have been among the essential accoutrements of everyone in post-Roman society.

A few objects from the Anglo-Saxon world dating from the fifth and sixth centuries suggest that jewellery was traded or carried over some distance. A button brooch of the fifth or sixth century comes from Ham Hill (HER 28625) and a brooch of an Anglo-Saxon type (PAS, SOMDOR-BC1877) was found at Otterhampton. Anglo-Saxon styles were not necessarily spurned by the women of post-Roman Somerset.

The Anglo-Saxons and trade

Writing 30 years ago, Richard Hodges outlined a scheme which was based upon the view that trade was largely controlled and promoted by kings and princes and was directed mostly to satisfying their needs, both for their own courts and for redistribution to followers. Commerce was controlled and directed chiefly through a network of specialised centres, which might be regarded as proto-towns and which dealt mainly with international and long distance trade (Hodges 1981, 213–33). On the continent this led to the appearance of Dorestadt in the east and Quentovic, Rouen and Amiens in the west.

The English reaction to this was the foundation

of the *wics*, from Hamwic eastward (Hodges 1982). The creation of these seaside trading sites served to concentrate trade in the hands of the local ruler at a time when the Anglo-Saxon kingdoms were being consolidated. Thus Hamwic provided the kings of the West Saxons with a port and exchange point close to their principal seat at Winchester.

In comparison with the detailed work which has revealed so much about the post-Roman world in the south-west, the period from the early seventh century up to the mid-to-late ninth century is much more obscure, despite the active approach to trade posited by Richard Hodges. There can be little objection to the idea that money was changing hands, even if by no means all the coins in use were English minted. In his classic paper written as long ago as 1967 D. M. Metcalf argued, successfully I believe, that the early coins were not simply stores of wealth or gifts between the powerful but currency in use for buying and selling (Metcalf 1967). The same position has been adopted more recently by Williams who suggests that coin circulated widely in sixth and seventh century Britain and that both continental and English issues circulated together in the mid-seventh century (Williams 2006, 174). The quantity of coin in circulation – and he suggests at least a million coins issued by Eadbald of Kent, with another million continental issues alongside – shows that the coin was used commercially and not merely for specialised transactions such as wergild payments. As gold ceased to be much used as a medium of exchange in the Merovingian world, large quantities of silver, suitable for use as a trading medium, began to be produced in northern Francia around 670 (Grierson and Blackburn, 1986, 94–5). Spufford, discussing the early pennies, struck in Frisia and here in England as well as in northern Francia, remarks that '*the most common types, like the 'porcupine' type of around 720–740,* (which) *may have been minted in millions*' (Spufford 1988, 29). In Offa's reign there may have been as many as six million coins in circulation (Metcalf 1967, 354). Trade was a major preoccupation of eighth century Anglo-Saxon kings. When Offa and Charlemagne quarrelled trade sanctions were imposed and English merchants were forbidden to enter Gaul (Story 2003, 188). It seems obvious that there was plenty of silver coin about

in the later seventh century and during the eighth century and this money was clearly intended to be used to buy things. However, there is no evidence that coins were struck anywhere in south-western Britain. All the circulating coin came in, ultimately from eastern England or from northern Francia.

This view is amply illustrated if we look at the pattern in Dorset where there is an interesting distribution of early continental coins especially in the east of the county (Fig. 7.5). The Dorchester – Weymouth axis suggests considerable activity, but the busiest area is to the east, where access up the river valleys from Poole Harbour shows a connection with northern Gaul, or south-eastern Britain, which runs north from Blandford, with an outlier at Bere Regis.

Somerset has only two finds of early continental coins, the first at Bicknoller, which would point to the continued use of Watchet, with traffic passing along the route south-west of the Quantocks towards Taunton, which became an important early Anglo-Saxon royal outpost by the early eighth century (ASC, 722 'A'). The second comes from the site of a Roman period building at Bathampton, near Bath (Fig. 7.6). There are no finds as yet from the city, which was, in any case, not inside the area of West Saxon control at this period, being part of Mercia. Merchants from northern Gaul evidently did not penetrate Somerset very often – it was probably too difficult to access by sea and too far overland to make contact worthwhile. What the Frankish and Frisian merchants were buying in Dorset which they did not buy in Somerset is open to speculation, but might already be wool, or woollen goods, coming from north-east Dorset and southern Wiltshire. Early continental coins are much rarer in Wiltshire. There are eleven reported in the Fitzwilliam Museum corpus of which two cannot be localised (www.fitzmuseum.cam.ac.uk/dept/coins/emc). Five of the remaining nine are located in southern Wiltshire and would connect with the Dorset spread.

That there were some Somerset connections overseas is evident from the find of a leaded brass censer of Byzantine type, said to have been found in the early 1980s near Glastonbury Abbey, perhaps in the Silver Street area, and now in the British Museum. A unique import into Britain, it is of the

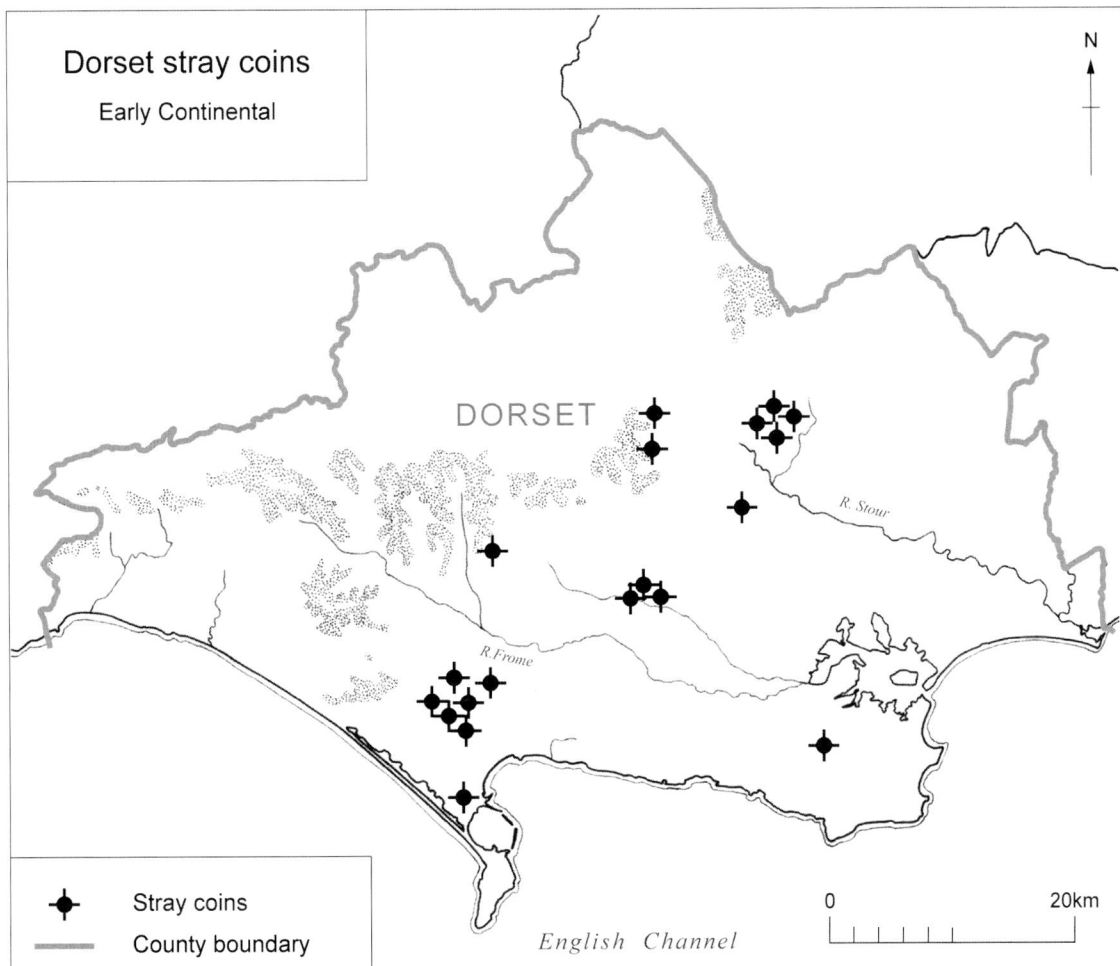

Figure 7.5. Finds of early continental coins in Dorset.

early to mid-seventh century (Buckton, 1994, 105). This must have been connected with the monastic community at Glastonbury, though we cannot know if it was new when it arrived, or by what route it arrived. It is also a reminder that ecclesiastics could be major agents in the distribution of goods. High value objects, like the censer and probably also vestments and manuscripts, were needed by religious communities. The early major monastic sites in Somerset, Glastonbury and Muchelney, were both situated at places which had ready access to water transport and continued the pre-Anglo-Saxon

connection with the outside world via the rivers and the sea.

More significant is the spread of early English coins (Fig. 7.7). There are few enough of them – only thirteen, but the find sites are revealing. Two are located in the Cannington area near the Cannington Hill-fort graveyard site excavated by Philip Rahtz (Rahtz, Hirst and Wright 2000). Cannington first appears in documentary evidence in King Alfred's Will (Keynes and Lapidge 1983) and was an unhidated royal estate of ancient demesne in 1086 (DB). The two finds are actually very close to

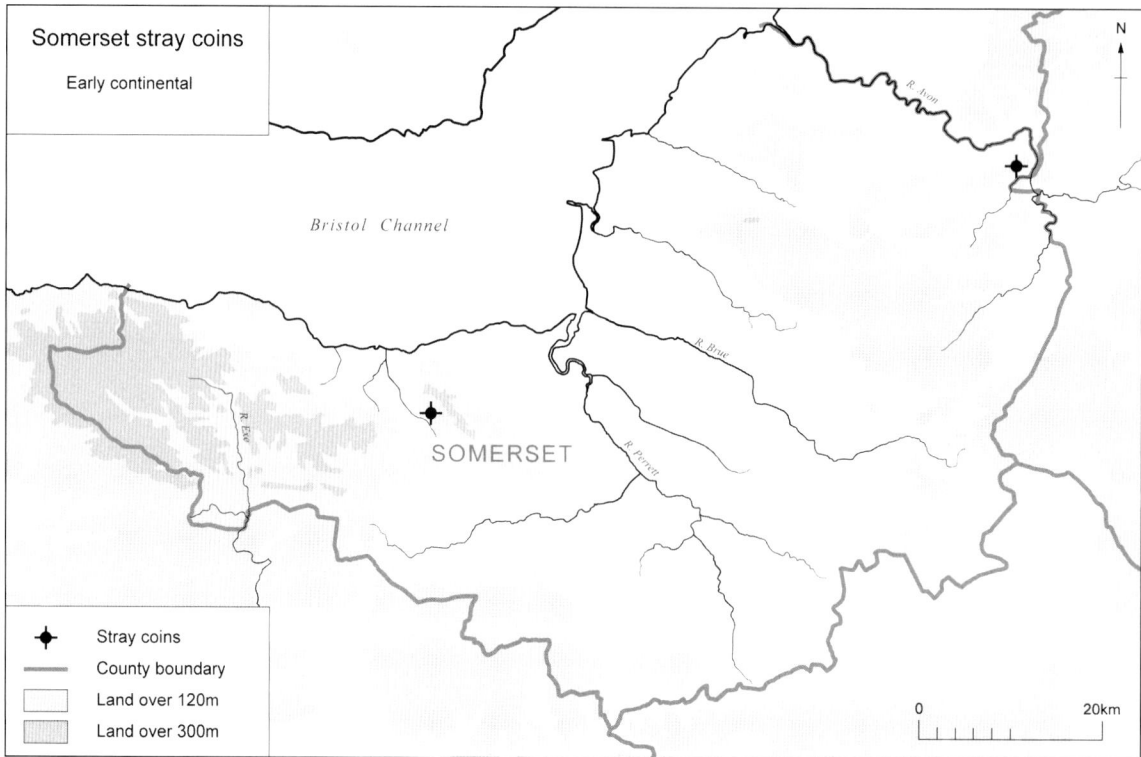

Figure 7.6. Finds of early continental coins in Somerset.

Combwich which is a small port site with Roman antecedents. Combwich is a difficult place-name. Formally it is the *wic* in or at the *cumb*. However, there is no combe anywhere near. Combwich lies on a river bank, on a slight slope above its pill. It may have been named by analogy with other *wics* around the English coast and it seems likely to me that it probably traded with Mercia via the Severn, thus gaining ready access to Gloucester and Worcester. If that is so, then it was the beginning of a local river traffic and trade which lasted until the demise of coastal shipping in the first part of the twentieth century. In view of the comparative lack of evidence it is not possible to regard Combwich as an 'emporium', but it is certainly well placed to be regarded as a port or transhipment point under royal or ecclesiastical control. The coins from this site were late seventh/early eighth century as were other single finds from Congresbury, Portishead, Glastonbury, Wells and Ilchester.

By the early eighth century Ilchester had lost its position as the port for South Cadbury (long since deserted) and probably become a centre for Somerton, the royal estate just to the north.

There is a clear tendency for the coins and therefore the trade to be linked to early important ecclesiastical sites by this early Anglo-Saxon coin group. The sites at Congresbury, Cannington, Ilchester, Cheddar (where the finds are later ninth century), Wells and of course Glastonbury would all fit into John Blair's view of the importance of early minster sites. The Anglo-Saxon Chronicle clearly regards Somerton, another royal site, as primarily a secular stronghold and it has no finds (ASC 'A', 733). It seems unlikely that the trading site at Ilchester, which probably served Somerton, was actually within the walls of the old Roman town, which has produced no evidence of occupation prior to the late Anglo-Saxon period. A site at or close to St Andrew's church, a minster,

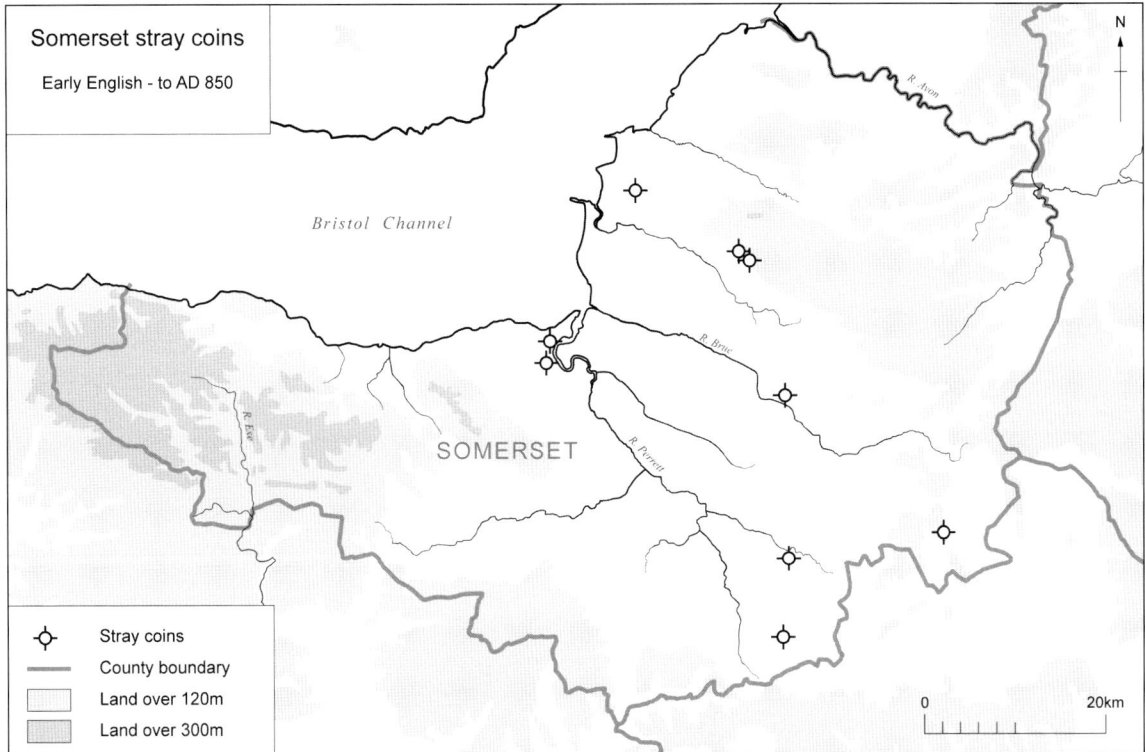

Figure 7.7. Finds of early English coins in Somerset.

at Northover therefore looks more likely. Its position on the Fosse Way, overlooking the river Yeo and very close to the crossing of the river where the old Roman roads diverged, with one going to Dorchester and another towards Exeter, gave it control of both road and river. It is noteworthy that the boundary of the later parish of Northover, which was co-terminous with the church's pre-Conquest estate, diverges from the Fosse Way to run along the river bank. The low-lying area in front of the church and alongside the river may have served as a market site for traders, with the church and its associated building standing on the higher ground to the north-west (Fig. 7.8).

Portishead is close to Portbury, which may have been a defended site, like Congresbury, and has a post-Roman cemetery as well as having the element 'port' in its place-name. It was later to be a royal estate, although it does not fit so well into the minster category, but it does suggest an element of continuity

between the post-Roman era and the early Anglo-Saxon period.

Two other finds are more difficult to fit into an obvious pattern. These are the coins at South Cadbury and at Charlton Mackrell. Both are of the first half of the eighth century and both are in places which were not important royal or ecclesiastical centres. The local context suggests loss in a domestic setting at the end point of some of the trade. At South Cadbury the loss did not occur on the hill-fort, but at its foot at what seems to have been a small settlement. Charlton Mackrell was an estate probably dependent upon Somerton. Connections with Ilchester for Charlton and with Ilchester or Sherborne for South Cadbury might provide possible sources for the coins and serve to suggest that coin could be used (and lost) at sites which were not of first rank importance. One might hazard the guess that only a person of quite high rank would be wealthy enough to hold coin in any

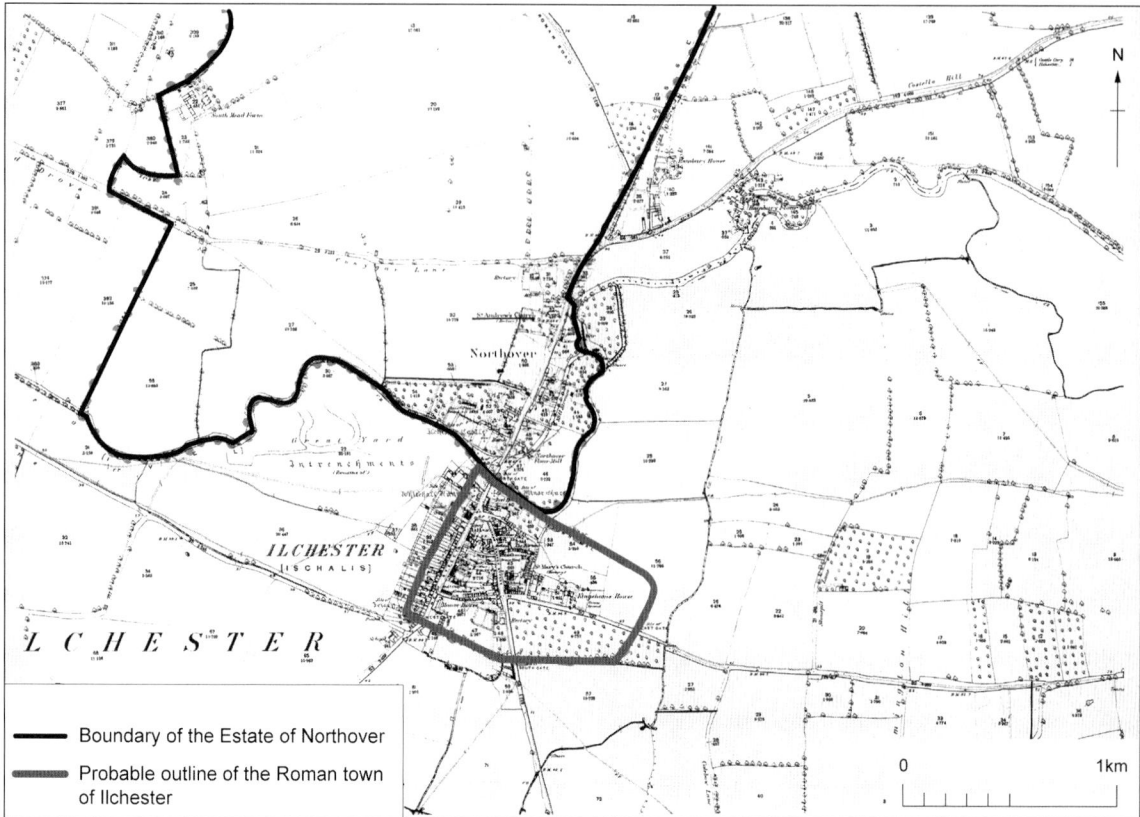

Figure 7.8. Northover and Ilchester.

quantity, but it does not follow that lesser men did not handle and use money as well. In the Laws of the later seventh and early eighth centuries the wergild values and the fines imposed for offences were all expressed in terms of money values and while it seems unlikely that ceorls could raise large sums of cash to pay off fines, nevertheless the law-makers thought this something everyone could understand and use.

Other early English coin finds in Dorset repeat the pattern of early continental finds and connect most closely with a group of coins in south-west Wiltshire. Somerset does not seem to share in the trade across central Wessex, with its clear links to the English Channel and signs of northward connections to Mercia through Wiltshire. Instead, it seems to have looked towards the Bristol Channel, which would have given access to the west of Mercia via the river

Severn and across the Bristol Channel to southern Wales and beyond to Ireland. The pattern set up in the post-Roman era seems to have persisted into the time of the Anglo-Saxons. The presence of monastic sites as important points on this exchange network seems to signal a strong element of continuity from the post-Roman world into Anglo-Saxon Wessex of the seventh and eighth centuries.

How much this trade may have been affected by the increasing severity of Danish pirate activity in the second half of the ninth century is impossible to know, but the Danes attacked Carhampton on two occasions (ASC 'A' AD 833 and 840). They were probably looking for plunder on shore, but must have disrupted sea communications as well. However, we do not know how frequently the Vikings were seen in the area. Their visits may have been very intermittent at first, or they may often have come as traders, since Viking settlement in Ireland began in the 840s. There is nothing improbable in the idea that the Vikings could be both traders and raiders. Slave raiding, which of course became slave trading when they sold their captives elsewhere, was probably only one of their activities. The idea that they were actually frequent visitors to the region is strengthened by the naming of the two islands in the Bristol Channel, Steepholm and Flatholm (Fig. 7.9). Steepholme is 'the steep island' using the Norse word '*holm*' for island and Flatholm is entirely Scandinavian in origin '*flota*' – fleet (of ships) and '*holm*'. This name superseded the older English name 'Bradan Relice' (broad or flat grave yard'). This in turn was from the Old Irish *reilic,* a cemetery. Lundy, much further out in the mouth of the Bristol Channel, also has a Norse name, 'Puffin Island' (Ekwall 1960). It seems very unlikely that these names would have become current unless there was a frequent and considerable Norse presence in the channel. The islands made secure bases from which the Vikings could trade as well as ravage the area.

We can have no real idea what goods these places traded to obtain their coin. Pottery is the great indicator of trade and trade routes, but is generally absent in the south-west. Philip Rahtz thought he could distinguish some fifth to seventh century wares at Cannington cemetery, Cadbury-Congresbury, Pagans Hill, South Cadbury and Glastonbury Tor (Rahtz 1974). Thereafter its absence before the very late ninth century makes tracing trade routes in any detail almost impossible (Blinkhorn 1999, 4–33). Even then there is actually little secure evidence for pottery before the mid-tenth century. For instance the extensive field work and excavation at Shapwick failed to record any pottery between the later fourth century and the mid-tenth. However, the discovery of an Hiberno-Norse weight at Ilchester, also dated to the period 700–899, but more likely late than early, (PAS, SOMDOR-9FE618) adds weight to the view that Ilchester was a place of real importance in the trade of the eighth and ninth centuries, perhaps taking over somewhat from the more distant site at Cannington at the mouth of the Parrett, which was not so well served by overland communications. There are several Viking lead weights known from Scottish sources, a lead weight with an Irish glass bangle embedded, from Clyde Rock, is probably a trader's item (Graham-Campbell and Batey, 98–9), while the lead weight found in the Talnotrie Hoard (in Galloway) (*ibid.,* 227), is probably from a metalworker's stock. Both weights are ninth century objects.

J. Moreland has emphasised the importance of seeing trade in relation to production when discussing the economic activity in 'the long eighth century'. He sees a rise in production across much of eastern and southern Britain and perhaps the south-west as well (Moreland 2000, 98–101). The difficult question which arises is: what were the men of Somerset selling? One possibility is that they sold slaves and a long distance trade certainly existed in King Alfred's time. People were exported as far as Italy, though we cannot be sure that they came from Britain (Pelteret 1995, 74–5). This trade is likely to have had deep roots in local society and relations between the post-Roman and Anglo-Saxon peoples of the fifth and sixth centuries probably involved extensive slave raiding on both sides. Slavery was an adjunct of war and the violent nature of relations between the kingdoms of Britain encouraged the practice. In Somerset a connection with Viking traders from Ireland makes such a trade very likely. Much later Bristol was a major slave market, so that the export of slaves from Somerset to Ireland is not a far-fetched idea (*ibid.,* 76–7). Such a trade is likely to have flourished in the times of warfare and social disruption experienced in the ninth century. This trade would have been over and above the abduction of local people by Viking raiding parties.

Another possibility is worth suggesting, though the evidence is as yet untested. It may be that iron was being produced in some quantity on the Mendips. Recent fieldwork in the Mells and Doulting area, on the high ground of Mendip to the east, near to Frome, has produced evidence of many small-scale smelting sites. There is no physical evidence to connect them with the Roman period and there is nothing in Domesday Book, or in later Glastonbury records, to suggest that these sites were active in the later Old English period or post-Conquest. If this was the case, it is likely that in the eighth century the iron was being produced for the monastic site at Frome, founded by St Aldhelm, and for Glastonbury Abbey, the owner of the lands around Doulting.

Figure 7.9 Steepholm seen from the east.

Ilchester may have been involved in overseas trade to Ireland as much as in the more local trade with the Severn estuary and river valley. Despite its situation at the edge of the post-Roman world, Ireland had enjoyed a vigorous trade with the rest of Europe from the Roman period onward and the Vikings who settled there were merely taking advantage of an already well developed commerce (Doherty 1980, 67–90).

D. M. Metcalf has shown that the finds of coins south of the Humber are so widely scattered that they show that ninth century trade and the use of currency with it was ubiquitous, so that coin was used in trading by large parts of the population, not just the aristocracy (Metcalf 1998, 167–98). The idea of trade in ninth century Somerset particularly is hard to sustain but D. M. Metcalf suggests that the decline in the quantity of coin is relative and that there was still a great deal of money in circulation. A few coins are indicative of a much larger number in use. The apogee of trade on the near continent was reached in the early years of the ninth century and from about 830 was generally in steep decline. Hamwic, for instance, has few coins after c. 820 (Hodges 1981, 215). There are only four coins from this period found in Somerset, if we exclude one from Charlcombe which can be regarded as part of Mercia. Three of those coins come from the Cheddar Palace site (Rahtz 1979) and so might be considered a special case. The fourth was found at

East Coker, part of the royal estate of Coker in the eleventh century. This coin might be connected with Sherborne or with Ilchester. Objects other than coins, mostly found through metal-detecting, are more widely spread than the coins but tend to reinforce the impression that activity was concentrated in the basin of the major rivers. It is noticeable that nothing has been reported from the whole of the northern half of the county and very little from the west. The finds clearly reflect the activities of metal detectorists as well as real deposits, but the finds for the period 410–700 are much more concentrated around the mouth of the Parrett, suggesting that there is a real difference in distribution, with a widening of activity in the eight and ninth centuries. Janet Nelson has ably demonstrated that the importance of Somerset and indeed other parts of Wessex lay less in the possibility of trade and much more with the resources in kind which could be drawn from the estates of king and church (Nelson 1992, 151–63). The trade links so laboriously demonstrated above can have provided only a small addition to the wealth of the community and must have been mostly aimed at satisfying the needs of local people of all classes for items of use for everyday. They were not becoming wealthy through commercial activity.

The weight of evidence provided by the coins leads us inexorably towards the view that trade, at least the

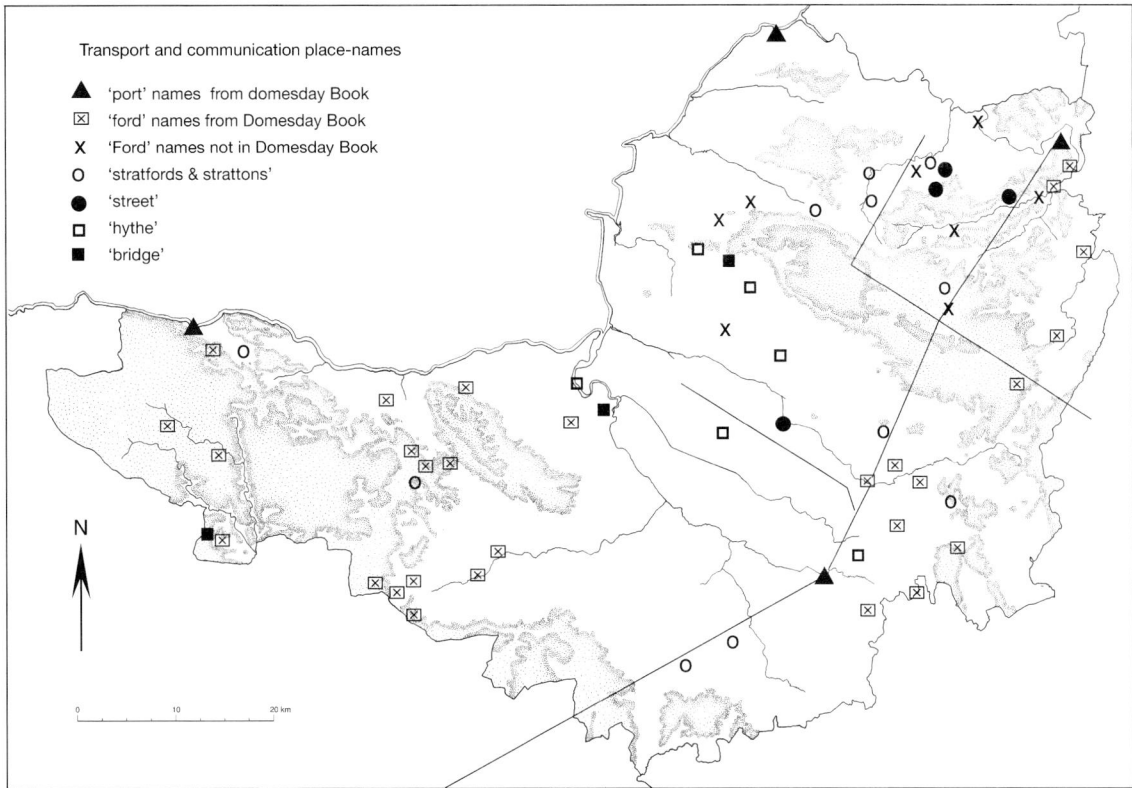

Figure 7.10. Place-names associated with transport and communications.

trade which involved coin, was concentrated upon the central river system of the Parrett and its tributaries. However, there were large areas of the county where rivers did not provide access and communications with the rest of Wessex and with it some trade and exchange. Early information is very sparse and we must turn to place-names and to information in Anglo-Saxon charter bounds for clues.

Communications by land

Amongst the most common of place-names connected with travel is 'ford'. Margaret Gelling points out that it is one of the most common topographical terms used in English place-names (Gelling 1984, 67). Some 550 places in Ekwall's *Dictionary of English Place Names* contain the term (*ibid.*, 67). It is of course, also extremely common as a minor place-name. Settlements which came to be named

from a ford suggest that the ford in question was widely known and used and therefore likely to be indicative of commonly used routes. It is likely also that the element was in use from an early stage in the development of English naming practice, so that 'ford' names may be early in the landscape, especially in Somerset, which cannot have received its English names before the mid-seventh century when English first became the dominant language.

A map of the Somerset place-names which contain the 'ford' element shows a large number of such names in the west, around Exmoor and the Brendon Hills (Fig. 7.10). Many of these may have had more to do with access to the moors for grazing from surrounding settlements than with trade routes. Rivers around the moors would not have been easy to cross, especially with sheep or cattle, and such crossing points must have been identified and used long before, probably in prehistoric times.

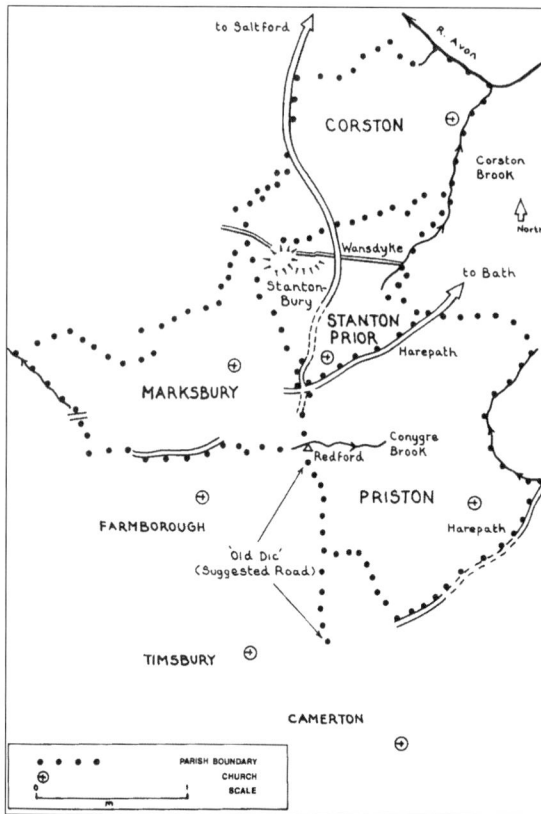

Figure 7.11. Ancient roads in the Stantonbury area.

In the north of the county the ford at Saltford on the river Avon is almost certainly an early example of a marker on an important early trade route. The place-name has been proposed to mean 'the ford at which the river is salty' (Ekwall 1960), a place to which the tides flowed therefore. An alternative might be that it was a point at which salt could be carried across the river. There is certainly some evidence from information in the boundary clauses of Anglo-Saxon charters to support this idea (Costen 1983). North of the river Avon the nearest settlement is Bitton, an important royal manor. To the south of Saltford a modern road leads southwards and forms the boundary between Keynsham and Burnett on the west and Corston in the east (Fig. 7.11). The Corston charter (S746) describes the north-western boundary of the estate as running along '*þone herepaþ*', the main road. Just a little further south this road

was used again by the boundary clause of one of the charters for Stanton Prior (S735). It is described as old road '*ealdan waeg*'. This seems to be the road which runs from Saltford to Marksbury, passing the eastern side of Stantonbury Hill. This same road runs down to the western side of the modern Stanton Prior village where it ends. However, it is continued by a modern footpath and then reappears in the charter for Marksbury where it is '*stanewege*', the stony road, forming part of the eastern boundary. It runs down to a ford on the boundary with Priston. This was *radan ford*. In the Stanton Prior charter (S711) the same boundary, now the western boundary for Stanton, is described as 'the old dyke'. This 'dyke' continues as the western boundary of Priston (S414) where it runs '*norþ andlang þære ealdan dic on readan ford*', north along the old dyke to redford. We thus have a description of a road which was old in the tenth and eleventh centuries when most of these boundary clauses were probably written. It is highly unlikely to post-date the drawing of the bounds of Marksbury, Stanton Prior and Priston, which predate the charter boundary clauses. A road would almost certainly not develop along the boundary. On the contrary, the boundaries were laid out with reference to a pre-existing road, with the ford as an important marker. We cannot be so certain of its course thereafter, but it seems to reappear as Parkway Lane in Camerton and crosses the Cam brook at Camerton to finish at the Fosse Way beside the Camerton roman vicus and very close to the post-Roman cemetery. Such a road might suggest that an early salt trade into Somerset from Mercia followed this route to the Fosse before turning south to cross the Mendips on the old road.

There are no charter bounds to help with the region to the north of Frome. Here there are a succession of 'fords' running northwards (see Fig. 7.12). These run from Somerset into Wiltshire in most cases, indicating that there was plenty of movement east to west as well as north towards Bath.

To the east of Ilchester there are a series of 'ford' names running northwards, to the east of the Fosse Way. Sparkford carried traffic eastwards from Ilchester towards Wiltshire, but further north Lydford, on the Fosse Way and Alford and Ansford all crossed the Brue, facilitating north to south movement across the river Brue. Michael Aston has

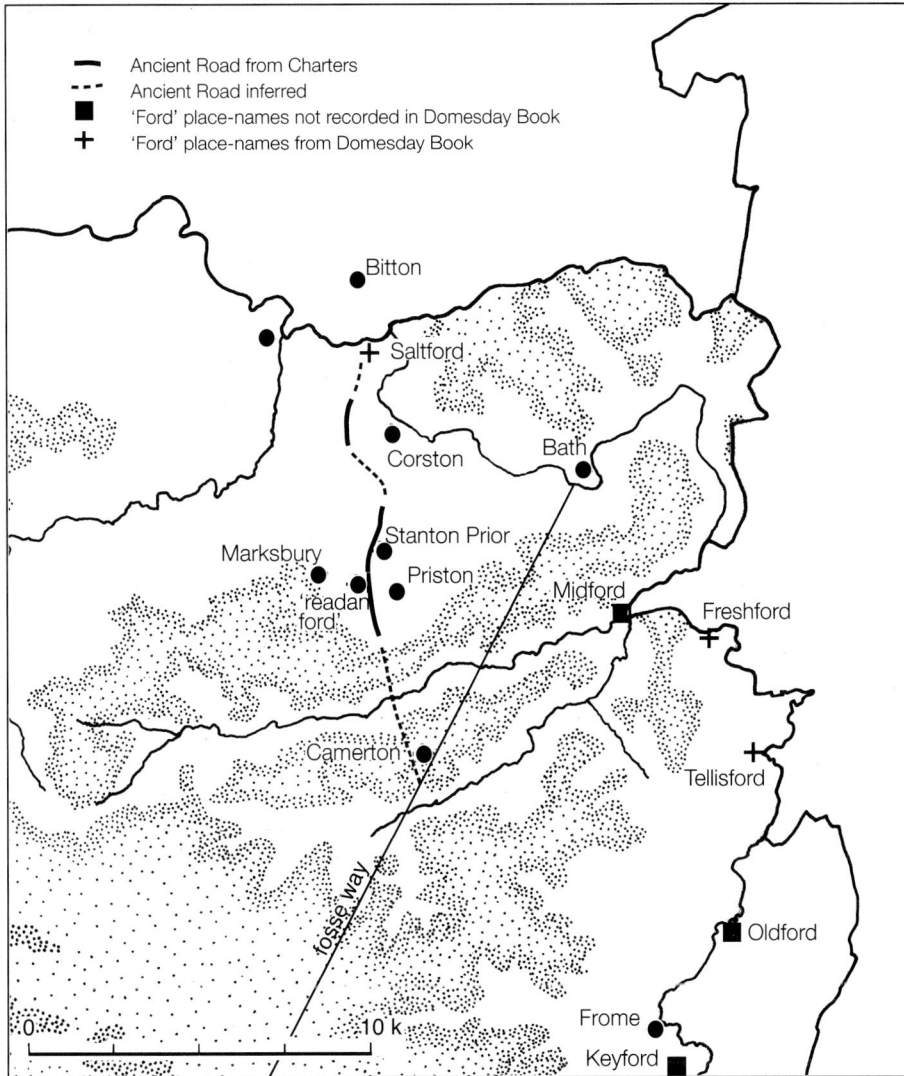

Figure 7.12. Communications in north-east Somerset.

shown that the road system in the Ilchester area contains elements which pre-date the Roman roads and foundation of Ilchester (Aston 1985, 146–8). That seems to be true for the road now generally the course of the A303 and for the series of lanes which run west to east across the landscape to the south of South Cadbury Castle. Roads to and from Ilchester built in the Roman period dominate the local landscape and provide uncompromising

evidence of the continuation of communication along the roads and the importance of Ilchester. Underneath this pattern lies a network of roads running generally north-to-south and clearly linked to the pre-Roman layout of field-systems elucidated by John Davey (2005). That such a system of tracks and paths continued to function shows that they were continually useful in the landscape and points up the underlying continuity of agricultural practice

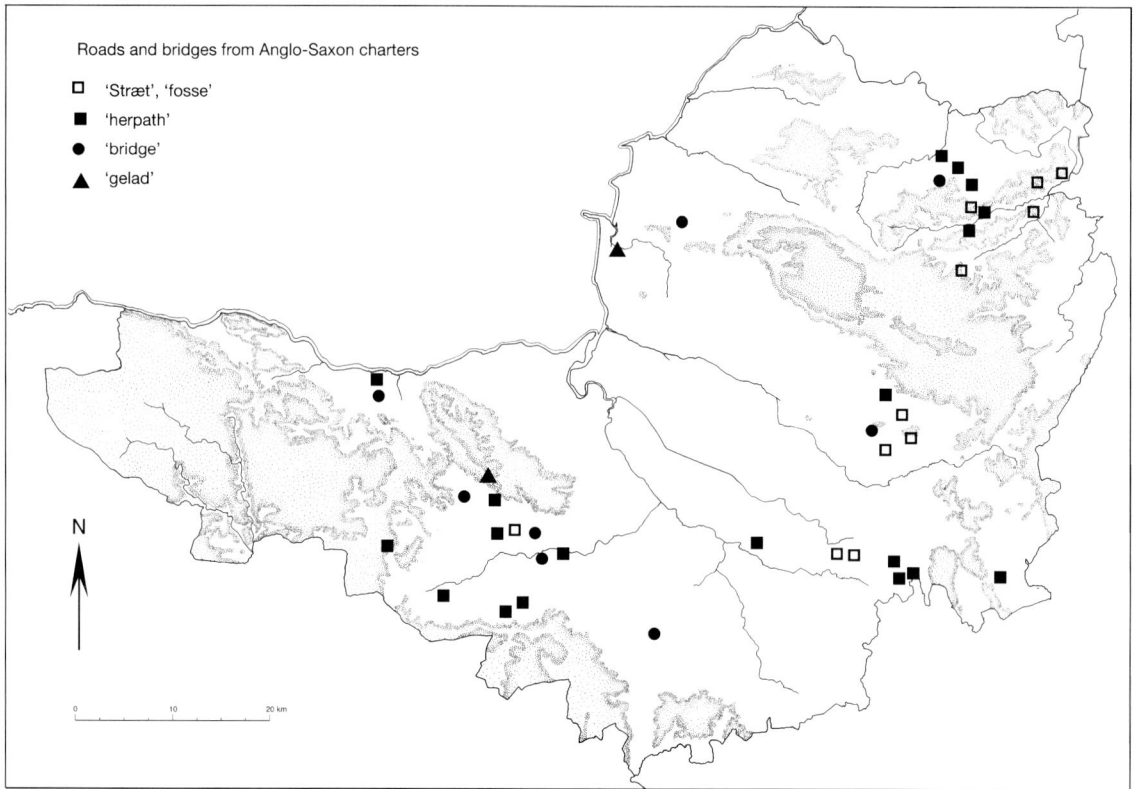

Figure 7.13. Roads and bridges from Anglo-Saxon charters.

and local communication in the landscape over very long periods.

'Stræt' and 'Stratford' and 'Stratton' names are relatively common along the course of the Fosse Way and also in the district north of the Mendips, around Chew Magna (Fig. 7.13). Here a Roman road led from the Avon onto the Mendips to end near the lead workings. Such names are more common along the course of the Fosse Way, both north and south of Ilchester, the most southerly being in Chard parish. This concentration of activity in the south and south-east is strengthened by the finds of metal objects recorded by the PAS (Fig. 7.14).

Finds are concentrated in the basin of the major rivers and they are entirely absent from the whole of the county north of the Brue. Of course the vagaries of detecting and reporting are partly to blame for this, but it is still likely that the map shows where the greatest concentration of activity was in the period up to the end of the ninth century. The objects themselves are generally unremarkable. Most are hooks from garments and strap ends, a reminder that clothing and its accoutrements formed a very large part of all medieval personal possessions. Among the finds from near Ilminster was a die for making plaques, decorative attachments for harness or for items such as book covers (PAS, SOMDOR-D9DEE2). This was an eighth century item and could have belonged to an itinerant craftsman, making decorative material for wealthy clients, both lay and ecclesiastical. The tags, hooks and strap ends were probably made in some quantity, since they would have been used extensively on garments. For the very wealthy they would have been silver, for instance the tag end from Milborne Port (PAS, SOMDOR-18D8F3). Others wore either bronze or even lead tags. Fittings like

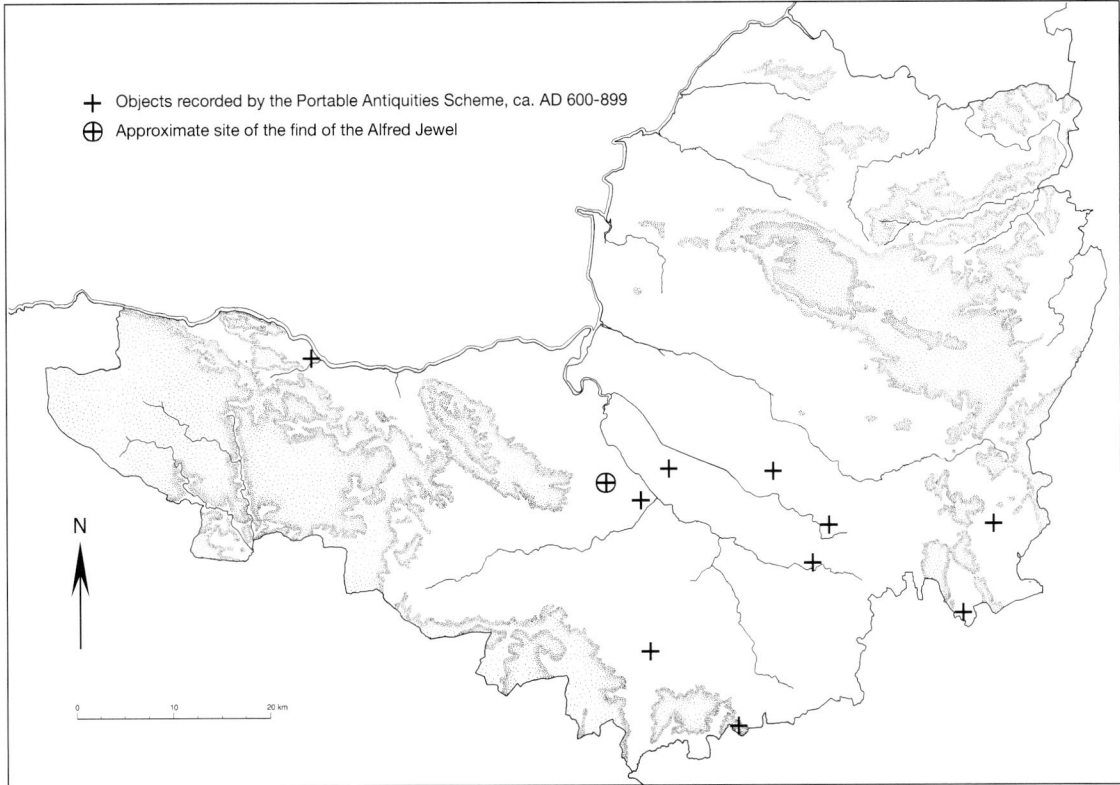

+ Objects recorded by the Portable Antiquities Scheme, ca. AD 600-899
⊕ Approximate site of the find of the Alfred Jewel

N

0   10   20 km

Figure 7.14. Objects recorded by the PAS AD 600–899.

these were probably transferred from one garment to another as they wore out and new garments were made, so that their lives as useful objects may have been quite long. What are missing from local finds, as elsewhere, are items of very high value. The recent discovery in Staffordshire of large quantities of decorative metal work in gold and silver, evidently looted from weapons and armour of the later seventh and early eighth century, makes it clear that warriors could carry or own extensive decorative metalwork. Such material was rarely lost and so is not now often discovered, but it is evidence that great wealth could exist among the elite.

One famous discovery stands out. This is the 'Alfred Jewel', discovered in 1693 in Newton Park by a labourer who was digging peat (Hinton 2008, 11). There has been much controversy concerning the nature of the jewel. It is one of several highly

decorative and outstanding pieces of craftsmanship to have survived, including the Minster Lovell Jewel, the Bowleaze Cove Jewel and the Warminster Jewel, all of which seem to have been similar in function to the Alfred Jewel. Current thinking sees them as the decorative top of an aestel, a pointer used as an aid for reading from the service books during church rituals, or alternatively that they were parts of objects such as reliquaries (Hinton 2008, 36–9). Whatever their purpose, these objects were of high value when they were made and in use. They would have been most closely associated with a religious environment and the Alfred Jewel was found not far from Athelney. However, all these objects have been found in the open, not on ecclesiastical sites, and it seems unlikely that they were all carelessly lost in the course of journeys by clerics. It is much more likely that what we see is the remains of ninth century loot, perhaps stripped from churches by Viking robbers, or given up as part of ransom or tribute. Such objects do not survive in treasuries, so their discovery in this way points to the enormous riches available to the churches and held as ritual objects of all kinds. These were emphatically not items of trade, but probably manufactured within the monastery or church by craftsmen who specialised in this type of work. If there was a trade it was probably in craftsmen, passed from one ecclesiastical or aristocratic patron to another. It is a reminder that trade and industry in the period should be seen inside the hierarchy of Anglo-Saxon society. Objects of the highest value would have been made to order and the trade involved may have consisted of purchase of some raw material, though much of it, gold for instance, might be obtained as a gift through patronage. More everyday objects may have been made and traded locally by craftsmen who travelled and worked for anyone who could afford their labour and others may have hawked objects along the roads between settlements. Behind the surviving objects lay an unseen trade in everyday goods, such as sheep and cattle, wool and iron and salt, which may not always have involved cash, but was the result of barter between peasants.

Conclusion

The whole thrust of the examination of finds and of coins has been to present a picture which strongly suggests that the river system of Somerset dominated trade and exchange.

Ilchester, perhaps through the monastic site at Northover, was clearly a major central place for trade. In the more western parts of the county Taunton controlled access to the major port or exchange point at Watchet, and Cannington maintained its position as a controlling site at the mouth of the Parrett through the post-Roman period and into the seventh and eighth centuries. All four places were controlled by royal estates. Watchet was part of the Williton estate. Taunton was an important royal site mentioned as in existence in the early eighth century. Cannington was a royal estate of ancient demesne and Ilchester stood on the edge of the royal estate at Somerton. This pattern of control of access from the interior to the coast was long lasting and highlights the importance of access to the Bristol Channel and from there perhaps to South Wales, the Severn and the west of Mercia, Devon and Cornwall and further afield to Ireland. Control was exercised by those in positions of power. The pattern of finds and the correspondence with the centres of royal authority strongly suggest that royal interest in traditional trade routes was strong. Anglo-Saxon commerce prior to the tenth century displays considerable continuity with the post-Roman period if the meagre information from the period is to be trusted. The paucity of coin probably reflects a fall in the supply of money – a fall which really precedes the onslaught of the Vikings and may be a contributor to their attacks, rather than a consequence. Kings were just as constrained by the difficulties caused by a depression as were their followers and it would have been difficult to continue to use the supply of moveable goods to followers as a means of control. Being a 'ring-giver' was probably very difficult by the time of King Alfred, despite his putative wealth. No doubt a gift of land was the alternative which the king was forced to make and we should perhaps see part of the reason for the permanent alienation of land in the lack of ready cash and prestige gifts with which to reward loyalty.

What is impossible to know is what the 'balance of trade' was for the county. With so few coins or objects available and the patterns displayed so meagre we cannot know whether material left the county in any quantity to bring in coin. It is possible that there was a reliance upon the import of coin by elite members of society who received it as payment or gift from other parts of the kingdom and perhaps from the king himself and then placed some of the coin into circulation. On the other hand the assumptions made in the Laws, that breaches of the law can be atoned for with cash payments at all levels of society, suggests that groups of people, kin-group members, could raise cash when it was needed. The recent discovery of the Staffordshire Hoard (Leahy and Bland 2009) shows that gold was used extensively in the personal adornment of seventh to eighth century warriors, but it tells us little about the silver coin in circulation, or to what extent men and women who were not of very high rank had access to precious metals. Clearly there is much behind the broken objects and few coins that cannot yet be comprehended.

8

Trade and Town

As with so many other aspects of Anglo-Saxon society, the widening of the rule of the kings of Wessex into the kings of the English – the outcome of the struggle against Danish invasion in the ninth century was accompanied by profound changes in the nature of trade. It is common knowledge that this is the period which sees the rapid expansion of towns and of commercial activity, much of it in eastern England, stimulated by the much closer contacts with Scandinavia and the north-eastern European littoral (Pestell and Ulmschneider 2003). The argument has been advanced that in the later ninth century treasure from churches and monasteries was mobilised to pay off the Danes and that part of the treasure which remained in England was then spent by the army, starting off the new urban economy (Jones 1993). D. M. Metcalf has firmly rejected that idea and shown that for most of the tenth century the coinage in circulation was meagre in comparison with the later tenth and the eleventh centuries and indeed in comparison with the ninth century before 870 (Metcalf 2006, 159–60). He also points out that the later burgeoning of the coin supply must be related to trade and specifically foreign trade and that the phenomenon affected the whole of eastern England, not just the Danelaw. It was not the advent of the Danes which kick-started English trade; on the contrary their activities caused a depression.

J. R. Maddicott is convinced that the Mendips were producing lead and silver by the end of King Alfred's reign (Maddicott 1989, 19) and S. R. H. Jones also makes the same assumption (Jones 1991, 598). If this were so, then a source of exports would

be obvious. There is, however absolutely no evidence to support this view. McCormick is clear that metal production in the western Roman empire was in sharp decline by the fifth century (McCormick 2001, 42–9) and Jones and Mattingley note that the silver content of lead being worked in the Roman period seems to have declined as those ores carrying the most silver, which were near the surface, were worked out (Jones and Mattingley 1990, 189–90). 'Alfredian mining' therefore would have been working ores rather more deficient in silver than in the Roman period and needing a good deal of technical equipment and knowledge to refine. There are no recognisable physical remains. The Domesday survey, nearly two centuries later it is true, does not record any payments or rents in lead or for lead from the Mendip manors. No post-Roman lead workings are known, even for the period after the introduction of pottery in the late ninth/early tenth centuries. If there were silver available we might expect the mints of King Alfred's time to use it and for there to be clear evidence of those coins spreading out from the mint centre, but there is no evidence of silver being coined in the neighbourhood in the later ninth century. Although there is no doubt that King Alfred and his successors made extensive use of Cheddar, the excavations produced only slight evidence for early lead-working (Rahtz 1979, 253), suggesting that industrial production was not a prime concern at the site. There is no evidence that lead and silver were mined and smelted on the Mendips between the late fourth or early fifth century and the Norman Conquest. Somerset during King Alfred's reign and

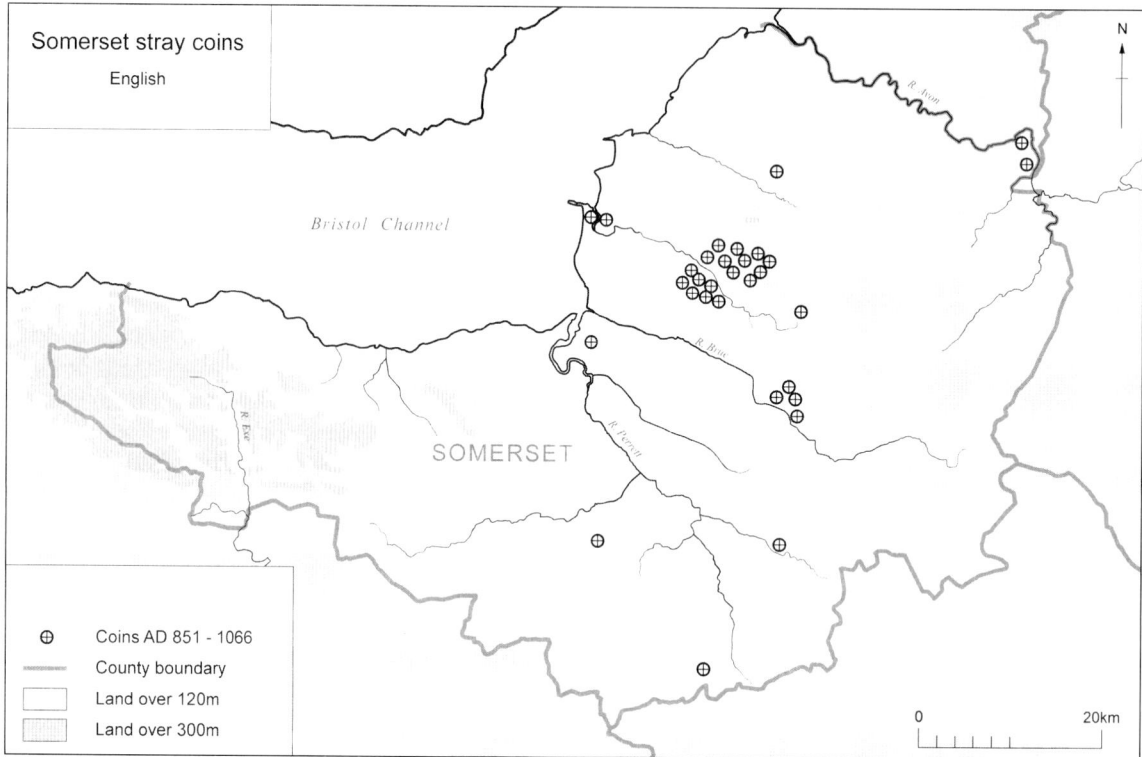

Figure 8.1. Finds of coins 851–1066.

beyond into the reign of his son, Edward the Elder, has little evidence of commercial activity. Although King Alfred's achievements do mark a real turning point in a military and political sense, commercial and trading activity seems to have continued at the same low level as during the ninth century. The real upturn in activity did not occur before the later part of the tenth century.

Somerset, along with other south-western counties, did not experience a growth of population and intense urban activity on a par with that of eastern England. There are as yet no 'productive' sites in the county. However, the provenanced stray coins do add to our picture of economic activity and they do not necessarily conform to the expectations roused by the existence of a large number of small towns at royal sites in Somerset. There are a very large number of finds from Cheddar (Fig. 8.1). The palace site is of course well known. It was first constructed and occupied as a secular royal vill at the end of the ninth

century, during the reign of King Alfred at the latest. Philip Rahtz was prepared to see the first palace or hall as being constructed at Cheddar towards the middle of the ninth century, partly on the evidence of the first two coins on the site, the first of Æthelwulf, probably lost by 845 and the second, of Æthelred, probably deposited between 865 and 875 (Rahtz 1979, 291). However, the bulk of the coin finds are of the tenth and early eleventh centuries. This fits quite well with the known use of the site (Hill 1981, 87–91) but the itineraries of the later Anglo-Saxon kings suggest they spent most of their time in central southern England, rarely venturing into Somerset, despite the extensive royal estates. The coin deposits might therefore be connected with the minster at Cheddar as much as with the palace (Blair 1997, 97–121). Whether this was a primarily a royal palace site or a minster in the ninth and tenth centuries, it was not a *burh*. That was at Axbridge 2 km to the west from which only two coins are known, one found at Axbridge, the other

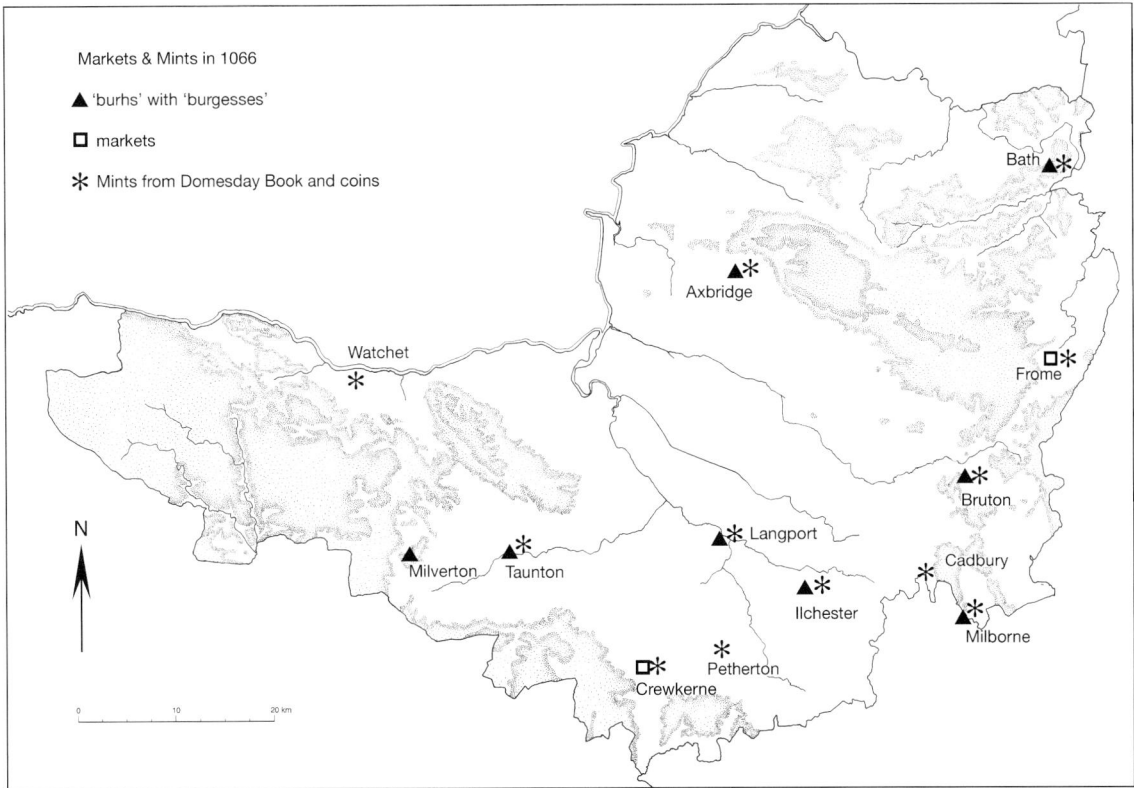

Figure 8.2. Towns, markets and mints.

at Winchester (Fitzwilliam Corpus). The numbers of coins found at Cheddar would certainly suggest trade. The site at Wedmore was a part of the Cheddar estate in 1066 (DB 1.2). Here there is a remarkable series of coins from the churchyard. At first glance this might look like a rural market. However, the coins are from quite distant mints, one from Exeter, two from London and three from Lincoln. No other coins from Lincoln are known in Somerset. The dates of the coins run from the reign of Cnut to King Harold. It must be that this was part of a hoard, buried possibly at the time of the Norman Conquest, perhaps by a clerk since it was in the churchyard. The other site with substantial coin finds is Glastonbury. Here we might expect the reformed monastery to become a centre where a market would take place, if only because it is unlikely that all the monastery's domestic needs could be met locally without resort to trade.

All these sites, and indeed the trade of the whole

area, must to some extent be influenced by the influx of silver from Ottonian Germany in the second half of the tenth century. This came from the new mines at Rammelsberg and produced a flood of silver coin some of which found its way to England (Spufford 1988, 74–5). D. M. Metcalf suggests that the increase in money in circulation in the later tenth century is the result of a triangular trade between Scandinavia, the Low Countries together with the north-western German Empire, and England. The influx of silver is hidden from us by the requirement that foreign coin be exchanged for English currency (Metcalf 2006, 167). Although the total number of provenanced coins found in Somerset is low, the greatest number come from the later tenth century and the first half of the eleventh century. Æthelred's issues number 37 (0.97 coins per year of his reign), and under his successor Cnut there are 31 (1.63 coins per year of his reign). The sudden increase in liquidity clearly provided a stimulus to industry and trade and must surely explain in part how the English of the late tenth and early eleventh centuries were able to pay such huge Danegelds. The coin paid over in this way was only a small part of the total available wealth.

The striking fact about the coin finds is that they do not occur in quantity within the Anglo-Saxon *burhs* or the late Anglo-Saxon towns of Somerset. We must question whether they are to be regarded as the engines of economic expansion (Fig. 8.2).

The towns and markets

A definition of the meaning of 'town' is fraught with difficulties. Writing in 1996 Steven Roskams attacked the use of lists to define the characteristics of an urban centre (Roskams 1996, 263). His view of York is that it was primarily a commercial undertaking and points to the way in which the Anglo-Scandinavian food assemblages show a wider diet than that enjoyed in rural settlements, suggesting access to a broad hinterland and to the sea. He implicitly associates this with urbanisation (*ibid.*, 284–5). I have real sympathy with a view which sees the town as essentially a commercial undertaking, but it seems too restrictive to ignore what contemporaries saw and described at differing times in the Anglo-Saxon period and their view of 'urbanisation' is as legitimate as anyone else's. We might note the frequency with which Bede writing in the early eighth century remarks that a particular place is a 'city'. Canterbury and York were both royal 'cities' (Bede, 57). Clearly the association between the old Roman towns and the Church was strong for him and for other clerics, even if such places were now pale shadows of their former selves. For him cities were religious and administrative foci and we might see the addition of commercial life as a simple extension of that activity. Writing about the tenth and eleventh centuries, Robin Fleming has drawn attention to the important connections between the rural elite and the towns and she goes so far as to dispel the notion that Anglo-Saxon England was inhabited by an aristocratic landowning elite which was country dwelling (Fleming 1993, 3–37). Considering the relatively recent development of the towns it is surprising that the aristocracy seem so deeply embedded in them in the tenth century. We

must ask why they felt it imperative to have residences and holdings in towns. A theoretical model would propose that the elite did whatever was necessary to maintain and expand their power. Just as in the countryside there was a never-ending struggle to extend their landholding, so in the towns they felt the imperative to control the resources peculiar to the urban environment. Towns in the tenth century provided economic opportunities but also access to political and administrative authority.

Writing about the origins of Taunton, Robin Bush and Michael Aston (1984, 75) were reluctant to commit themselves to a site for the early Anglo-Saxon settlement or the later Anglo-Saxon town with so little archaeological evidence available. It is still the case that very little other material has appeared since their publication. Writing in the same volume C. F. Clements suggested that the Anglo-Saxon minster stood within the present castle precincts, perhaps adjacent to or on the site of the later Castle chapel of St Peter which stood close to the southern entrance of the inner ward (Clements 1984, 29). Nearby at Castle Green part of the extensive cemetery of the minster was recorded in the nineteenth century and further burials within the castle itself have also been shown to be part of the same (*ibid.* 28). It was probably also the site of Ine's late seventh century *burh* recorded in the Anglo-Saxon Chronicle (ASC 'A', 722). There is no need to assume that the secular and religious sites were physically distinct. It is more economical to assume that the minster was the central place from which the area was controlled and that it also provided the king and his following with lodging should they visit and that the necessary labour; the slaves and other dependants, lived around the minster.

Eventually the minster at Taunton came under the control of the Old Minster at Winchester, but the date at which this happened is unclear. Many of the charters relating to Taunton are spurious (S254 of 737, Edwards 1988, 138–40. S311 of 854, Keynes 1994b, 1122, n. 1) and the first one which has any validity is probably S373 of 904, a charter of Edward the Elder (Keynes 1994b, 1144–5). The minster was therefore in Winchester hands by the very early years of the tenth century. With it went a huge estate, though the size attributed in Domesday Book of 54 hides and 2½ virgates probably understated its true size and value. The minster stood at a significant point in the west Somerset landscape. It controlled the crossing of the river Tone for traffic coming from the coast along the valley to the south of the Quantocks and the river itself provided water access to the sea via the rivers Tone and Parrett. It was also some way from royal estates which might have provided competition at a time when markets may have been few and far between. The minster stood very close to the Tone, so like the minster at Ilchester it would have controlled a quayside and provided a transhipment site for goods from the estate and probably from a wider area also. It would then be logical to expect the later tenth century town to develop under the Bishop of Winchester's control, close to the minster, perhaps around a market site outside the monastic precinct. The spur to growth was probably the increasing supply of silver in the later part of the century and the bishop's privileged position may have made possible the establishment of the mint in a non-royal town. By 1086 there were 64 burgesses, who paid six pence a year each in rents, a market worth 50 s (£2 10s) a year in dues and a mint which produced the same amount of rent. The bishop's total yearly income from the town was therefore recorded as £6 12s, not a princely sum and a very small part of the total value of the manor which was valued at £154 1s 1d per annum.

Ilchester has no evidence that the old Roman town was occupied before the tenth century. I suggested in the previous chapter that Northover, beside the river and just across the bridge over the Yeo, was the most likely place for the Anglo-Saxon port. In its setting beside a river Northover resembles Taunton. A minster church was at the heart of the enterprise and seems to have been the institution which maintained Ilchester as a commercial undertaking. However, the church did not have a huge estate to support it, unlike Taunton. Its lands at the time of the Norman conquest amounted to only 3 hides and they were valued at £5 per annum. Prior to 1066 it had belonged to Glastonbury Abbey which had leased it to Britric (DB 8.37). We might surmise that the repopulation of the town with burgesses was a deliberate act on the part of the king and that this deprived the minster of much of its importance, so that it fell under the domination of Glastonbury Abbey, which was close enough to be able to exploit the estate by letting it to

a secular supporter. Unlike the situation at Taunton, where the proprietor was a bishop with a distant seat at Winchester and a large estate to manage, for which the minster was a convenient centre, Northover was probably dominated by the king or his agents at Somerton, nearby, for whom the adjacent ruined Roman town of Ilchester with plentiful supplies of building stone from the derelict site and room to expand made for an appropriate location for a new venture. However, administratively it was connected not to Somerton, the nearest major royal manor, but to Milborne Port some miles away (DB 1.10). The new town could capitalise on the Fosse Way and access eastward to Wiltshire as well as its connection to the sea via the river Yeo. By 1086 it had 107 burgesses and was worth £12 per year to the king. The ephemeral mint at South Cadbury was probably the mint from Ilchester removed there as a protective measure during the late tenth century turmoil, rather than any attempt to set up a market or town there.

Bath was assessed in the burghal hidage as needing 1000 hides for its support (Hill and Rumble 1996, 84). That placed it among the largest *burhs* in western Wessex, but nothing like as large as Winchester (2400 hides) or Wareham (1600 hides). It came under the control of King Alfred after 878, and since it stood at an important river crossing and on the Fosse Way it is almost certain that it must have been fortified soon after it fell into the king's hands. By c. 900 coins were being minted there for Edward the Elder (Lyon 2001, 69), so it is likely that the town had been fortified by that time. Like other major towns which were being developed at this time it had a planned layout of streets (Biddle and Hill 1971, 70–85) and the likely layout of the streets has been suggested by Professor Cunliffe (Cunliffe 1984, 348) and Peter Davenport 2002, 46).

The Bath mint has produced the largest number of locally provenanced coins (27), and the number of coins reflects its importance as a nodal point for transport between the south-west and the south central midlands. There are no coin finds from inside Bath itself for the whole period under consideration, despite its size by 1086 (DB 1.31). Its importance as a market centre would seem to be entirely tenth century in origin. Bath's trade may have included some contact with European markets (Grierson and

Blackburn 1986, 314). Bath Abbey had been the refuge of a group of monks expelled from the abbey of St Bertin, at St-Omer in Flanders in 944. They must have provided a contemporary contact between Bath and Flanders. The relics still found at the Abbey in the period just after the Conquest included an interesting group of saints from eastern Francia, including St Remigius, St Bathild, St Austrebert, St Germanus of Auxerre and St Gertrude of Nivelle as well as a relic of St Opportuna, a saint of Normandy and north-western Francia (Hunt 1893, lxxv). Such a trade would have been overland and possibly associated with the second half of the tenth century and the first half of the eleventh century, when relations between England and Flanders were close. A connection with Scandinavian traders is also possible. The relic list contained a relic of St Olaf, but that could, of course, be the result of Danish incomers after the accession of Cnut.

By 1086 Bath produced a substantial income for the king and probably for other interested lords as well. The king took geld from Bath as if it were a 20 hide estate (DB 1.31). He also received £60 in rents and £5 from the mint and £11 from the proceeds of 'the third penny' (a third of the proceeds of justice). The king had only 64 burgesses there, the abbey 24 and other lords 90. The greater part of rental income therefore went to the church and to other non-royal lords. Without the tax revenues the king would have been a minority 'shareholder' in the borough. The lords of a number of other places in Somerset either had the dues from burgesses or held houses in the borough. Eight burgesses belonged to Keynsham (DB 1.28). Another four belonged to Chewton Mendip (DB 1.29). These were royal manors and not too far from the town, but the burgess belonging to Backwell (DB 5.30) shows that there were investors in the borough who lived far away. The burgess paid the manor of Backwell 32 pence each year, so his rent was worthwhile. Other places had houses in the town – Hinton Charterhouse had two (DB 40.1), the manor of Bishopsworth also had two (DB 5.20).

The size of Bath and Ilchester reflects the extent to which commerce had become important in the tenth and eleventh centuries and also the extent to which the king could profit from this relatively new stream of revenue. In the case of Bath, however, he

was sharing the profits with other men and with the monastery. Control of the burgesses by the monastery may have been the result of the expansion of the town onto their lands within the town walls, or simply have been a gift from the king, but the 90 other burgesses belonging to other men showed that other members of the Anglo-Saxon aristocracy saw investment in the towns as a worthwhile venture. Robin Fleming has documented the way in which the aristocracy held property in the towns and has shown that this was true often for many of the poorer thegns as well as the rich and powerful (Fleming 1993). This property gave them access to both the political and economic life of the towns, which, by the later tenth century were the scenes of many of the more important political events. Ilchester did not seem to share in that same relationship with the rural elite and neither did the other small towns of the county. This may be one way in which the rather under-developed character of Somerset urbanism is revealed. However, despite Ilchester's lack of connection with the rural aristocracy, its size clearly placed it outside normal manorial control. It was recorded in the Domesday Book as part of Milborne Port, a royal manor about 20 km away, separated by many other manors. This is highly unusual in Somerset, where manors did not normally have distant dependencies.

As a non-royal town Taunton is clearly in a class of its own in Somerset, but the other towns were much less important and are shown in Domesday Book as adjuncts to royal manors, rather than important centres in their own right. The king's manor of Somerton included the *burgus* of Langport, which had 34 burgesses who paid rent of 15 s per annum (DB 1.1). Langport at this point was clearly a very small town and the rents were a tiny proportion of the £79 10s 7d which the manor provided each year. The town was recorded in the Burghal Hidage as having 600 hides for its support (Hill and Rumble 1996, 33). Its name shows that it was a market 'the long market town' and this is a very interesting name in view of the suggestions put forward about its development as a *burh* in the later ninth and early tenth century. As Michael Aston points out, the area assigned for its support would indicate a defensive earthwork or wall of only 825 yards. The *burh* was almost certainly situated on the higher ground in the eastern part of the modern town (Aston 1984, 182). This was hardly a 'long market town'. However, the later medieval town extended westward on low ground along Bow Street towards the bridge along a causeway. The name of the town strongly suggests that the market already existed when the Burghal Hidage was drawn up and it may be that the *burh* defended an already existing market site alongside the river, which lay outside the ramparts. This would accord with the discovery of a coin of Justinian (550–64) found here and would suggest that the river made it a useful trade site even in the sixth century. Langport functioned as a trading centre and port for Somerton and perhaps for other manors close by.

Milborne Port was larger than Langport, with 56 burgesses. Here there was no suggestion of a *burh*. The town was an especially created dependency just outside the rural manorial centre of Kingsbury, a manor of 50 ploughlands (DB 1.10). It was a tiny planned town with a regular rectangular layout (Fig. 8.3). The church of Milborne Port, an institution with a hide of land in 1086 (DB 1.10), stands inside the town, not in the rural manorial centre. For a new town church to have an estate of this size is extraordinary. Most town churches stood within the parish of a rural church and struggled to achieve independence unless the town was large. The position of the church, on the end of a small promontory, above a stream, is typical of the siting of churches of the later Anglo-Saxon period, so it is possible that the church preceded the town, which was founded around it. The area of the *burh*, still visible today, amounts to about 5.5 hectares and this may be the original precinct of the minster. A triangular market place stood just on the north eastern side of the *burh*, outside the precinct and still traceable today, despite being partly obscured by modern building. This market place lay between the new *burh* and the royal centre at Kingsbury, a few hundred metres further north. The plan is remarkably similar to that of Congresbury (Costen and Oakes 2003). Its position gave the town control of trade passing through Wiltshire into south eastern Somerset and north Dorset. The important monastery and episcopal seat at Sherborne was only 5 km to the west and beyond that lay access to northern Dorset. However, despite its relatively large number of burgesses, the town's mint seems not to have had

a large output and no coins exist from Milborne as single finds (fitzmuseum.cam.ac.uk/dept/coins/emc).

Bruton also had burgesses. There were five of them on the royal manor (DB 1.9) and the lord of Pitcombe controlled another 11 (DB 36.1) and there was one who was a dependant of Castle Cary (DB 24.17). Seventeen burgesses therefore lived at Bruton. There is no mention of a market, which must have existed, but clearly did not produce a worthwhile profit for its owners. Its mint had a very small output and only two coins from it are extant as single finds, neither of which can be located. At Frome there was a market (DB 1.8), but no mention of burgesses and the same was true for Crewkerne (DB 1.20). Watchet had completely disappeared from view in Domesday Book and was part of the royal manor of Williton. However, its mint continued to function and a coin of William I struck between 1083 and 1086 is extant (fitzmuseum.cam.ac.uk/dept/coins/emc) and there are eleven known for the period 978–1035. If the number of coins extant from a mint is a measure of the commercial activity of the community within which it operated, then Watchet was clearly important. As a mint at a sea-port it would have been the point at which foreign merchants would have changed their own money for current English coin. It is regrettable that the find spots of almost all the Watchet coins are unknown, but one was found in London (Fig. 8.4).

There is a danger of regarding each town as an entirely separate and isolated entity, but it is apparent that trading sites of differing kinds could have similar trading profiles. Thus both Ilchester and Porlock, which was not a market or a *burh*, had chapels dedicated to St Olaf, a saint who was popular with the Viking traders of Dublin and Waterford in the eleventh century, suggesting that they both traded with the Viking community in Ireland (for Porlock see Weaver 1983, 283; for Ilchester see Dunning 1974, 198). At Porlock the chapel stood well away from the parish church and close to the harbour site at Porlock Weir, so it is clear that this was the trading place (HER 33926). The place was important enough to be attacked by Vikings in 914 (ASC 'A'). It was also the site of Earl Harold's landing in 1052, during the course of the Godwins' rebellion (ASC 'E'). However, despite its clear importance it did not have a mint,

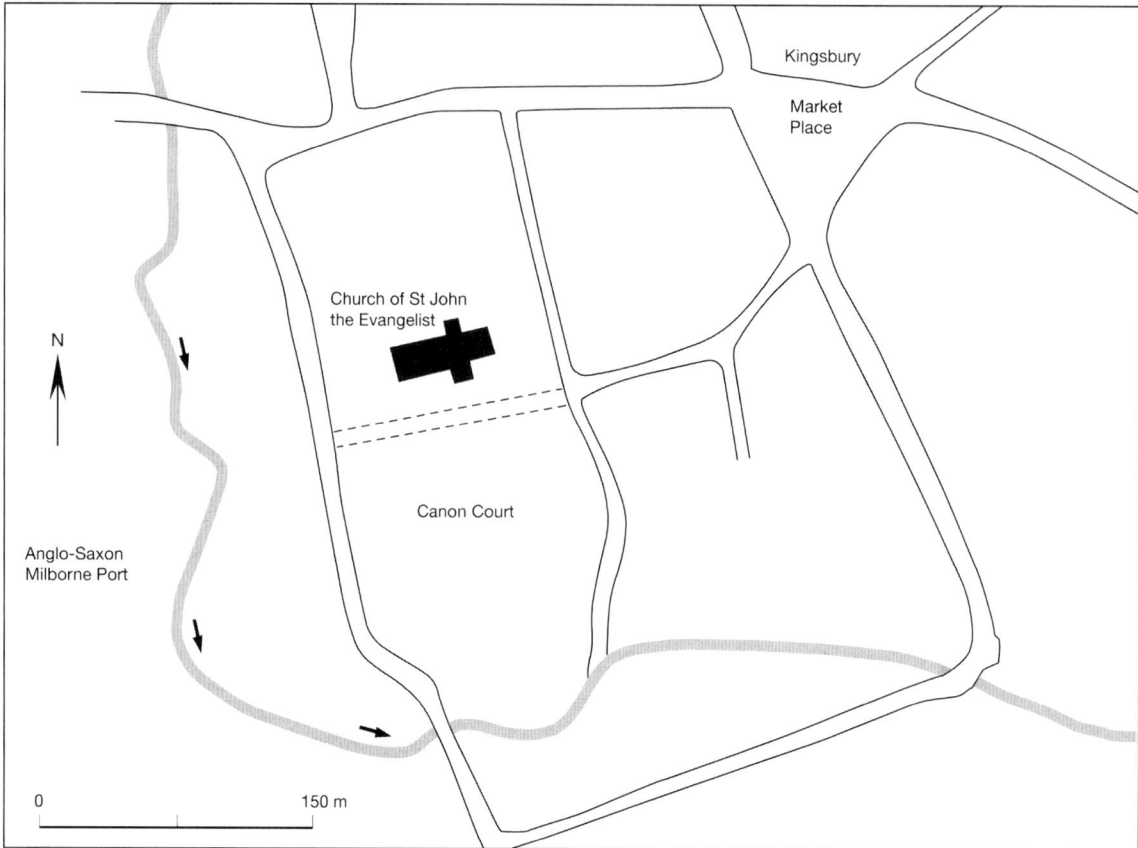

Figure 8.3. Milborne Port; A new town formed from a minster precinct? Note the market site outside the precinct, in the north-east corner.

Figure 8.4. The town of Watchet, seen from the south. (photo Michael Aston).

perhaps because it had no connection with the king or with a major church. How old Porlock is as a port and trading site is difficult to establish. There are no archaeological finds to help establish its age. The name means 'harbour enclosure', and is Old English in origin. It is one of two 'port' names in Somerset, the other being Portishead (Watts 2004). Porlock is first mentioned in the Anglo-Saxon Chronicle, so we cannot be sure if the name is very early, but the dedication of the church to St Dubricius (correctly Dyfrig), a 'Celtic' saint who is attested as working in south Wales in the mid-sixth century, might indicate a very early connection with South Wales. Bath Abbey also had a relic of St Olaf in the later eleventh century which might also suggest that the city had contact with Ireland (Hunt 1893, lxxv). Other trading sites seem to have been linked together. With such an active mint Watchet was more than a local trading point and was almost certainly linked to Taunton. The smaller sites, such as Frome, Bruton, Crewkerne and Milverton, which had a market in 1086 (DB 1.26) were probably local market centres, with little in the way of trade in manufactured items.

Axbridge, which had begun as an Alfredian *burh* (Hill and Rumble 1996, 33), was a river port, like Langport, and similarly stood on the edge of an important royal estate. In the case of Axbridge its lands were carved from the western edge of the Cheddar estate. It was probably not very important or successful in the eleventh century. Although it had a mint in the tenth century it was not recorded in the Domesday Book, suggesting that if it still functioned it returned no significant profit to the king. That in turn would suggest that the value of the town and its trade was low. In 1086 it was worth only 20 s to the king and this probably represented the rents 32 burgesses paid on their house plots (DB 1.2).

Although the king was the dominant lord of the towns it is possible that during the later tenth century other sites began to develop 'market' characteristics. This may be the case for the settlement at Glastonbury Abbey. Michael Aston has suggested that Glastonbury may have been developing a market site in the same way that markets were founded at Ely, Peterborough and St Albans (Aston 1984, 178). Arguments based upon the topography of Wells have also been advanced in favour of the development of a town or market there (Aston and Leach 1977 and Aston 1984, 194). Such a development is unlikely to have happened until after the re-establishment of the canons by Bishop Giso in the mid-eleventh century (Hunter 1840, 4–5). He was an active reformer who acquired lands for his cathedral and the formation of a market would have been well within his capabilities.

River transport

One characteristic shared by many of these towns, both the larger and the smaller, was access to water. Watchet was, of course, beside the sea. Axbridge, Langport, Taunton and Ilchester were all connected to the sea by the Axe and the Parrett river systems, while Bath had river access to the Bristol Channel via

the Avon, and it may be arguable that this was still their most important asset. Glastonbury Abbey also had connections to the Bristol Channel through the river Axe and the Brue which ran into the Axe at this period. Access directly to the abbey by water was made possible in the tenth century by the construction of a canal from the Brue as far as the monastery itself (Hollinrake and Hollinrake 2007, 235–43).

Spread across the Parrett and Axe basins are a number of minor place-names which show that river transport was useful for a wide range of estates (Fig. 8.5). Anne Cole has already documented the landing places, the 'hithes' (Cole 2007, 73). The charter S1253 has '*portam qui dicitur Bledenythe*, the port called Bleadney' (*bleadanythe*, Bledda's landing place) and it stood where the River Sheppey flowed through the gap between the Wedmore island and Bleadney to join the Axe (Williams 1970, 63). The date of the charter, AD 712, is more than a little suspect, but it probably preserves a notice of a real transaction, though the name may well be recorded much later than the supposed charter date. A landing place here would have been useful for the approach to Wells. Another hithe existed at Cheddar, on the river Yeo, which flowed into the Brue. Hithe at Cheddar gave Cheddar access by water, in addition to Axbridge and has been suggested as the site of a Roman port (Rippon 2007, 210–11). Other smaller 'hithes' were situated higher up the Brue valley, at North Wootton (S509) and Butleigh (S270a), where there were three hithes named as points in the bounds. At Podimore, to the north-east of Ilchester, there was another hithe, this time on the river Cary. This landing place gave access on a small river to a small rural settlement belonging to Glastonbury Abbey. The discovery of a landing stage at Weare, deep in the soil of the Axe valley along the ancient course of the Axe is representative of many such places along the rivers (Major 1911, 110–3). The place-name Stathe, in North Curry, (Old English *stæth*, 'a landing place'), probably fulfilled a similar role to the hithes, this time on the Parret and giving access by water to the royal estate there (Lib. Alb 1, c. 1216). There is a Nythe Farm at North Curry which is a name from the Middle English *atten hythe*, which has become *atte n(h)ythe* and from there *at Nythe*. A similar name process can be seen at 'Nythe', between Moorlinch

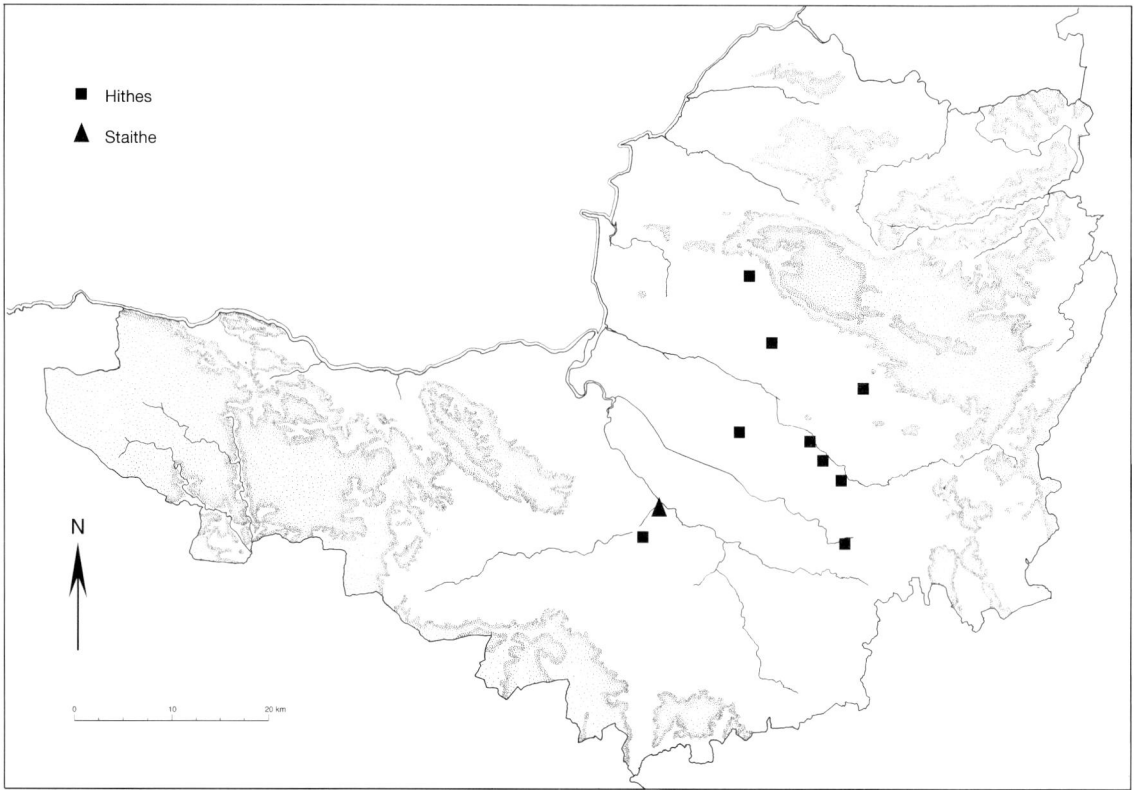

Figure 8.5. Hithes and staithes.

and High Ham. There must have been many other small landing places which are no longer documented. Such facilities made it possible to move both produce and livestock from one manor to another, but also to market.

Implicit in the idea of an active development of towns and markets is the expansion of the road network and the provision of more facilities for transport and travel. Of course improved communications benefited the rural dweller just as much as the new burgesses in the towns and it is likely that most of the developments were the result of monastic, royal and private initiatives to improve access to rural manors or from such places to the new market centres.

The best contemporary evidence we have for the system of roads is provided by the boundary clauses of the Anglo-Saxon charters for Somerset. Most of

these charters are tenth and eleventh century in origin, but we need to treat the boundary clauses with some caution, since some can be shown to be later than the tenth or eleventh centuries. The twelfth century was a period of rapid expansion of communications and it is possible that this is reflected in some of the charter bounds. A further problem is that a charter may tell us of the existence of a road or bridge in the tenth or eleventh century, but it does not tell us how long the road or bridge had already existed when it was used as a boundary point. However, the charter bounds were normally describing an estate which was not new when the survey was made. Where boundaries ran along roads or paths we can be confident that they predate the boundary, since it is unlikely that roads would be deliberately created along pre-existing bounds. In the previous chapter the charter bounds around the estates of Corston, Stanton Prior, Priston

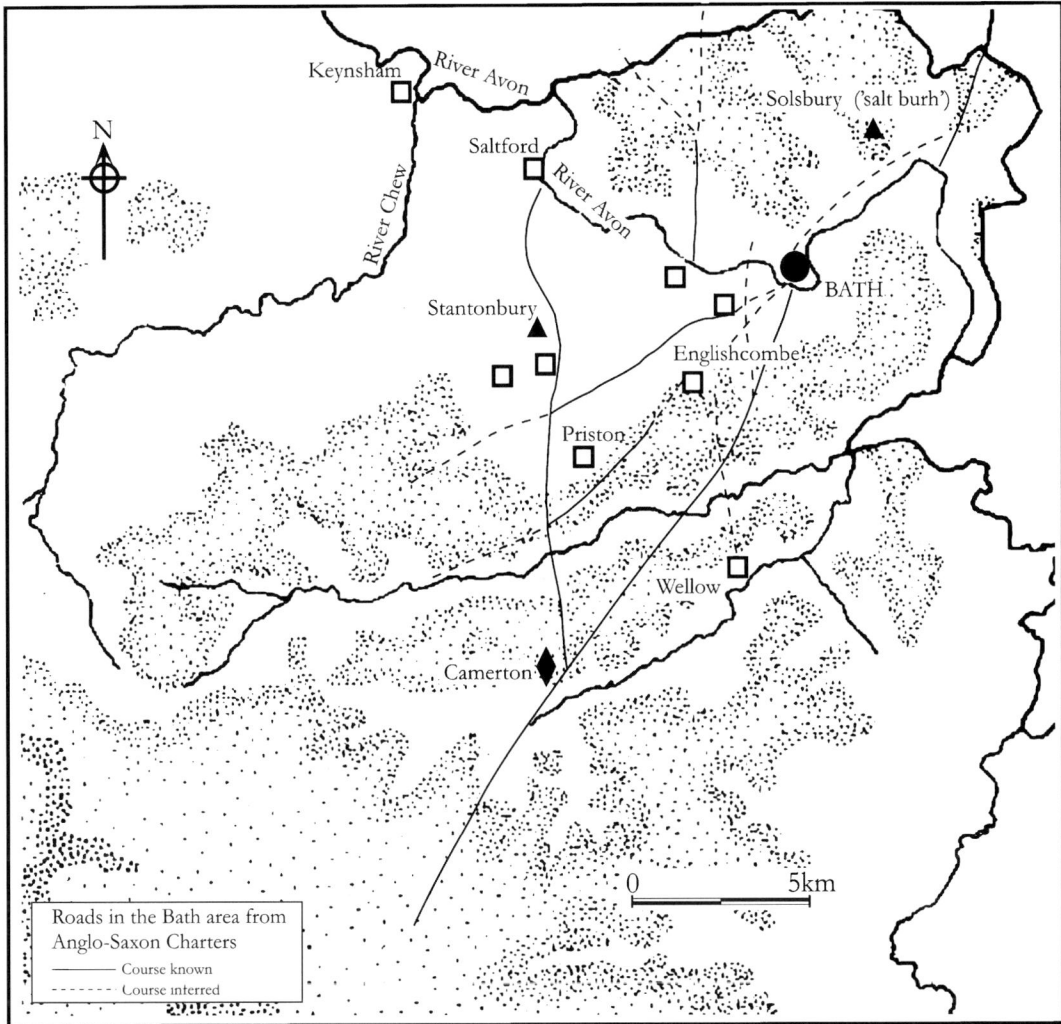

Figure 8.6. Roads in the Bath area in the 10th century.

and Marksbury were used to demonstrate the existence of an early 'salt road' running from the lands of the Hwicce into western Wessex. The same charters also show a system of roads running towards Bath from the south-west (Fig. 8.6). The Stanton Prior charter actually describes the road which forms its southern boundary as the *bað herpað*, the main road to Bath (S711). This road still exists, though as a minor road running towards Newton St Loe, but bypassing that village and running towards Bath through Twerton, suggesting that the 'new tun' post-dates the road. On

the southern side of Priston a similar road described as a '*herpað*' forms the boundary. It is now called 'Blind Lane' and ceases to be a made-up road as it goes south-west, though it continues as a green lane to Tunley Farm and beyond becomes a modern road again. It may be the '*herpað*' mentioned in the bounds of 'Eversy' a lost estate in Dunkerton (S692). The modern road then continues south-westward, probably to the royal manor of Chewton Mendip, which held the rights over four burgesses in Bath (see above). To the north-east it runs as a metalled road

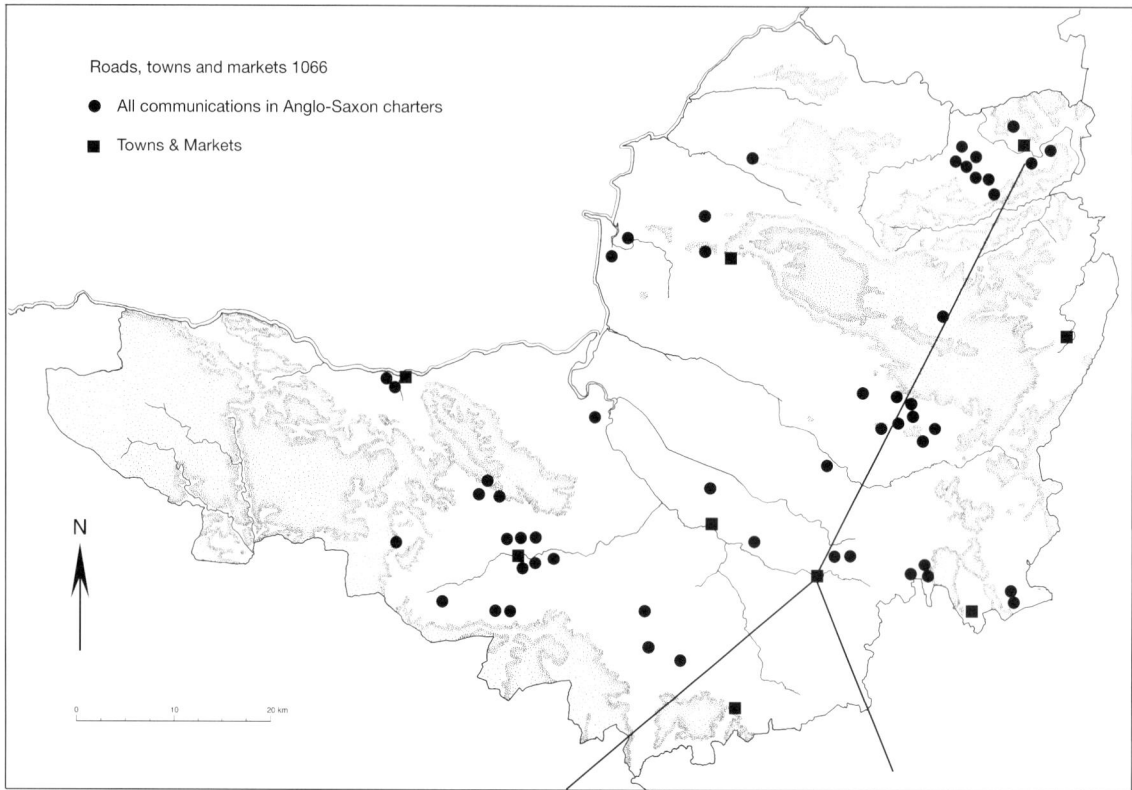

Figure 8.7. Evidence for all towns, roads, fords, bridges etc. *from charters.*

to the village of Englishcombe and can be traced as far as the Fosse Way as small lanes and a footpath. It passes the site of Englishcombe Castle, which was probably sited at this point in the twelfth century because it overlooked the road.

At the other end of Somerset the road along the coast towards Watchet was also a '*herpað*' and there was a bridge somewhere nearby (S1572). Further along the coast Porlock is linked to the ridge-way on the Brendon Hills and from there southwards towards Dulverton and west into northern Devon (Cole 2007, 59). Since the charter material does not cover the county evenly the impression gained from the evidence in them is geographically very partial (Fig. 8.7), but it is clear that if charters with bounds existed for every manor in Somerset the county would be covered with a dense network of roads and that bridges would be frequent by the end of

the tenth century. Two bridges stand out – Axbridge and Bridgwater. These two places stood at the lowest points at which the two most important rivers south of the Mendips, the Axe and the Parret, could be crossed. Axbridge provided a link between the Isle of Wedmore and the Mendips, while Bridgwater allowed traffic along the Polden Ridge, coming up from the Ilchester area by land or across from the eastern parts of the county to reach Cannington and the land along the West Somerset coast. The two bridges may have had another function, that of defence. Bridges proved a way of blocking rivers. In Francia the construction of a fortified bridge at Pont-de-l'Arche, near Pîtres, by Charles the Bald in 865, protected his estates in the Paris region against the Vikings, who turned their attentions to England instead (Nelson 1992, 213). King Alfred as a very young man had seen the fortifications in Charles the

Bald's realm and there is no reason to imagine that other contemporary Englishmen were ignorant of the methods of defence used in Francia. Labour on the construction and maintenance of bridges remained part of the three reserved burdens on all land (Abels 1988, 59–60).

Goods and services

If the greatest political challenge to the late tenth century monarchy was that posed by the Danes, the availability of large sums of cash provided one way of coping with the problem. The marauders could be bought off with some of the new supply of silver which was flooding into England from the continent. Æthelredian coins form the largest group of issues found in Somerset and this is a true reflection of the numbers issued, despite the length of his reign. After the native monarchy's defeat and overthrow the new Danish kings needed money just as much as Æthelred, to pay their warriors upon whom they depended for protection against the native aristocracy. In a previous chapter it was suggested that the levying of the geld from Æthelred's time until near the Norman Conquest was an important stimulus to both lord and peasant, forcing them to produce a surplus which could be sold for silver with which to pay taxes. Although labour services continued to be an important part of the economic and social relationship between lord and man, cash payments increased and the Domesday Book, with its assessment of every manor in terms of its rentable value, showed how far the idea of the money economy had penetrated English consciousness. The miller, for example, made his living by collecting a multure from the grain he ground for the men of the manor. The surplus was sold, probably already converted to flour, in a market and the cash used to pay the lord his money rent. The town proved the setting for some of this exchange of goods for cash, though we cannot know how much was shipped as direct contracts between merchant and producer. The hithes in the marshes of Somerset may have seen wool and grain belonging to monasteries and great men bought by ship-men without the need to involve towns and official markets. The markets and the towns provided a setting for the peasant to buy and to sell, while the

burgesses could trade in the classic medieval luxuries imported from the continent. Ælfric's merchant says; 'I buy valuable goods not produced in this country and I bring them to you with great danger across the sea and sometimes I suffer shipwreck, losing all my goods, scarcely escaping with my life.' He brings 'purple cloth and silk, precious stones and gold, various sorts of clothes and dyes, wine and oil, ebony and brass, tin and brimstone, glass and like products.' (Garmonsway, 1939). Of course Ælfric was writing a text-book, not a social survey, so that we cannot assume that Somerset merchants imported such luxuries as a matter of course, but the Colloquy demonstrates the popular idea of the merchant's activities. Some surpluses were enough to provide such items for the wealthy, while for the peasant the surplus might be enough to pay his geld and buy some salt and other necessities. He probably didn't make his own leather boots or the tack for his horse, if he had one. The late Anglo-Saxon period comb handle found at Bawdrip is of a type distributed from Frisia and most of the few examples found previously were located in the south-east and on the Baltic coast (Hollinrake and Hollinrake 2002, 213). Some goods could travel a long way. Clearly people did not make their own combs either.

By the end of the tenth century and perhaps a little before such men were beginning to buy pottery, though perhaps not in great quantity. A restricted range of pottery has now been found at a variety of sites and probably much more remains to be identified wherever there were dwellings in the tenth and eleventh centuries. At Shapwick a considerable amount of pottery which was dated to the period before 1066 was recovered during extensive field-walking and excavation. The type AA1 was securely dated to the later ninth and early tenth century through its association with the dismantling of a building dated by C^{14} to cal. AD 810–980 (95% probability) (Gutiérrez 2007, 603). Similar pottery has been identified at Taunton and at Ilchester (Pearson 1982, 169–217); at Castle Cary (Gutiérrez 2004, 106–12) and at Puxton (Gutiérrez 2006). Thanks to recent petrographical analysis, the source of this pottery was established as somewhere on the Blackdown Hills, on the border between Somerset and Devon (Dunne 2009, 66). Other pottery of this general period (types AA2 and AA4) was shown to come from the Mendips (Dunne *op. cit.* 41–3) and one solitary sherd from somewhere in West Somerset (Dunne *op. cit.* 44–5). Obviously this pottery was being traded, though we don't know how. We may guess that it was sold in the market places of towns and in other less formal rural markets and that it was carried by pack-horse or cart from the Blackdowns and from the Mendips. This early pottery is of course only part of an ongoing traditional trade which expanded and became much more diverse in its origins as population and wealth grew in the twelfth century. It may be that it was not until the tenth century that the population had grown large enough to support an industry of this nature and that its appearance is a sign of the quickening of activity at all levels of society at this time.

Iron, on the other hand, was an everyday necessity at all levels of society. Its spectacular and extravagant use might be in weapons and armour, but it was also needed for the knives which everyone carried and for farm implements of all kinds, as well as tools for woodworking and stone production. Most of the production of the raw material is invisible, but the Domesday Book shows how it may have been organised. At Cricket St Thomas each freeman was obliged to give a render of one bloom of iron to the king's estate at South Petherton (DB 19.1). There were eleven villeins and bordars. The men of Seaborough paid in the same way to the royal estate at Crewkerne, this time there were twelve men eligible (DB 3.1). A similar render was due from the men of Bickenhall to the king's estate at Curry Rivel (DB 19.27). This time 16 people each owed a bloom. Lexworthy was divided into three small manors, each of which returned two blooms (DB 17.3. 21, 5–76). At Whitestaunton a fixed render of four blooms was owed (DB 19.4) and at Alford, eight (DB 19.65). It is notable that in 1086 four of these manors belonged to the Count of Mortain and that the payment to the royal manors had ceased. Did he appropriate the output for himself?

A reasonable assumption would be that the peasants in these communities enhanced their incomes by iron ore mining and smelting, probably on a seasonal basis. The total output from these workings must have been very small, and source of

the ores was probably small deposits in the greensands, in the Blackdowns, which could be won by shallow quarrying or minor deposits on the Quantocks (Peter Hardy, pers. comm.). The iron ore presumably came from lands which were in some way regarded as part of the royal fisc, probably in the Neroche forest region, or on the open land of the Quantocks, and the producers paid a proportion of their product to the king. Taxation of their output suggests that this was more than a subsistence operation. The rest of the iron could be traded or worked to produce saleable goods for display in the markets at places such as Ilminster or Taunton. It is difficult to be certain how large a bloom was, but excavation of a bowl furnace at West Runton, near Cromer in Norfolk, showed that an eleventh century furnace was no more than 50 cm in diameter, suggesting that the hammered bloom would have been light enough for a man to lift (quoted in Geddes 1991, 170).

Another local industry was quarrying. Throughout the middle ages local quarries, village by village, produced stone for local consumption and the presumption must be that most of the material never became part of a commercial transaction. Local quarries did exist and are sometimes recorded in the bounds of Anglo-Saxon estates. We cannot be certain that the quarry mentioned was being worked and it is possible that some references are to very ancient quarries of the Roman period, but most were probably in the tenth and eleventh centuries. The charter bounds for Bathampton have a reference to quarries which are Roman but the quarry at Charlcombe, just north-east of Bath was probably tenth or eleventh century as were the quarries at East and West Pennard, Bishops Lydeard and Washford. These quarries probably served local needs, but evidence from the few surviving pieces of worked stone from the pre-Conquest period suggest that high quality stone could travel considerable distances. Stone from the Anglo-Saxon period can really only be identified when it has been recovered from an ecclesiastical site. Style of decoration and carving provide guides to dating (Cramp 2006, 133–96). Bath stone, that is stone taken from the beds in the region around Bath and immediately to the east, was very popular. Of the 52 pieces of identified material listed by Professor Cramp, 31 came from the Bath district. The sample is heavily biased by the large number of finds from Bath and Keynsham, but the ninth-century cross shaft from West Camel is of Bath stone as is a fragment at Porlock, which could be of eighth to tenth century date. There are nine examples of worked Doulting stone, the furthest from Doulting being the font at Aller. Almost all these pieces are eleventh century in date, but the inscribed stone from Holcombe is seventh to ninth, so stone from the Doulting area, close by, was in use in that early period. It is most likely that stone travelled by water wherever possible and places such as Porlock or Congresbury could be directly reached by boat, but as we have seen much of Somerset could be supplied by water transport, which must have aided the economics of stone utilisation enormously.

The major question once more is, of course; 'what were the men of Somerset selling which would bring money from outside into the economy?' The answer in part is that it was probably wool. As we have seen earlier, the great royal and ecclesiastical manors around the slopes of the Mendips all ran sheep in great numbers. In fact the crown and church between them controlled nearly all the access to the upland grazing, dominating the plateau from Bleadon in the west to Doulting in the east. The demesne flocks are recorded rather haphazardly in the Exeter Domesday, but Chewton Mendip had a flock of 800 sheep; there were 500 at Pilton; 340 at Doulting; 250 at Bleadon (DB 8.20, 8.23, 2.11). In all Glastonbury Abbey had about 2900 sheep scattered around its estates across the shire. The tenants almost certainly kept sheep as well, perhaps as many again as in the demesne flocks. Glastonbury lands may have supported around 6000 sheep at any one time. The abbey is unlikely to have needed the fleeces of nearly 3000 sheep to clothe its monks and servants. A cash crop is far more likely as an explanation of the numbers. Bath Abbey had fewer sheep, but its endowments were smaller. On the lands around Bath it had nearly 700 sheep recorded (DB 7) and its tenants 750. Although the evidence is post-medieval there is a tantalizing record of the 'Great Flock of Lansdown' which lived on Lansdown during summer in the early sixteenth century (DD\BR\cr\c 1402). This was a flock belonging to the abbey and the abbey estate of Weston has evidence in its Anglo-Saxon charter boundary for the existence of a wall

around the edge of Lansdown which was probably intended to keep sheep out of the cultivated lands below (S508 of AD 946). While it is very doubtful that this boundary clause is really of the tenth century, it may well date from the eleventh and the wall is still visible today. The Great Flock may be the result of a very long established practice. It was noted in chapter six that there was a concentration of large sheep flocks in the region to the north and east of Frome, towards Bath and here the land was mostly owned by laymen, suggesting that they too were interested in commercial production of wool.

The numerous small manors of the Brendons and Exmoor were probably quite haphazard about their reporting of sheep flocks for the survey but the 45 manors of Carhampton Hundred returned 2446 demesne sheep, so there were probably at least 6000 if the tenant flocks are included. In addition many manors which record no livestock nevertheless had impressive pastures. Porlock, with no recorded stock, had 500 acres of pasture. Its sheep were surely omitted. Given the ubiquity of sheep in the Domesday record for the county, much of the crop from the ecclesiastical and royal estates must have been exported for it would have been too much merely to clothe the people of Somerset. Watchet was probably the port of choice, though Porlock should not be overlooked. Ireland, through its Viking traders, was conceivably one of the export markets to which wool was consigned. It is notable that the two recorded attacks on Watchet by Danes in the tenth century were the first in 914 (ASC 'A') part of a great raid from Brittany and in 997 a great expedition from the east which plundered the whole of the south-western peninsula. It was not connected with the Vikings of Dublin who were the likely partners of the Somerset traders (ASC 'E'). The Viking ships even used woollen sails! (Vinner 2002, 27).

A more controversial speculation would suggest the export of grain. Peasant farmers needed to pay their taxes and from the time of Æthelræd II onward heavy taxation – the geld – became a regular feature and continued until Edward Confessor's suspension of the levy in 1051 (ASC 'D'). It was the peasantry on their tenanted land who paid and the Anglo-Saxon Chronicle makes it clear how large were the sums of money raised in tribute to the Danes and

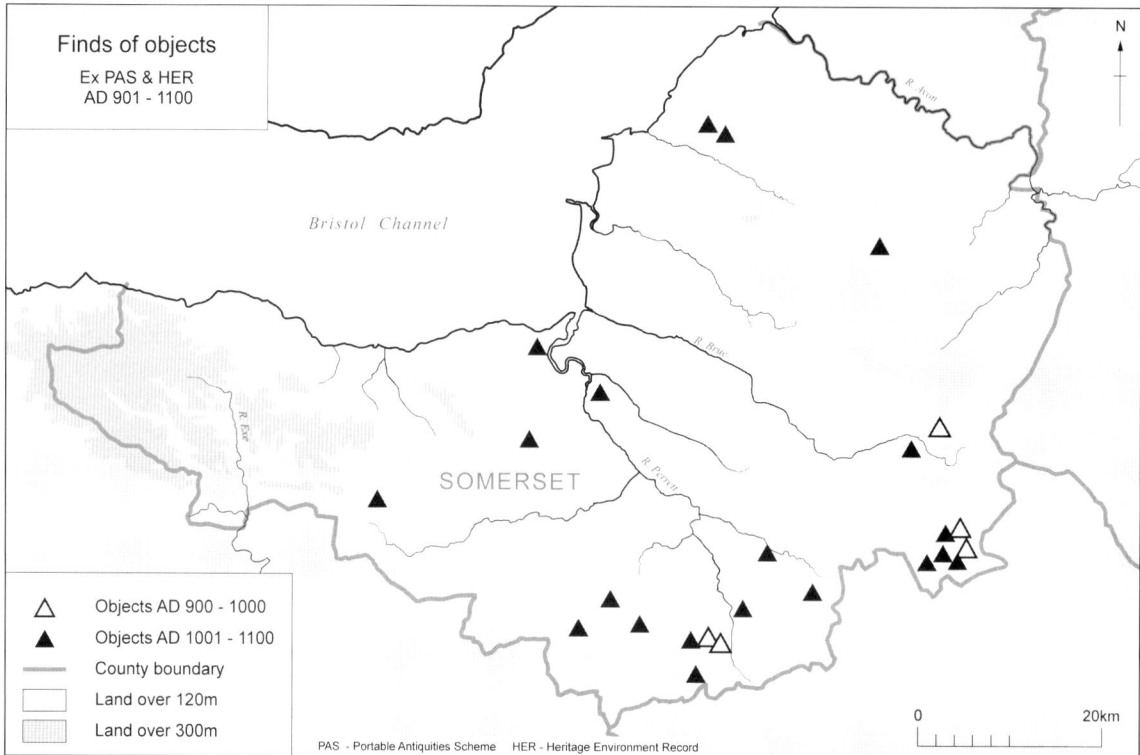

Figure 8.8. Finds of objects (mostly of bronze) dated between AD 901 and 1100.

in taxation. In order to pay the geld the peasants needed to sell their produce. The major crop, apart perhaps from wool, was grain, and although much would have been consumed directly some must have been sold in the markets of the small towns. Town populations were too small to have consumed much themselves and many Somerset towns also had fields which must have produced some crops. In addition the large working demesnes of major landholders, the abbeys, the king's estates, with their slave labour forces could also have produced large surpluses. At Taunton, where the bishop of Winchester had a very large estate of 100 ploughlands, 20 ploughlands of which were untaxed (DB 2.1), there were 70 slaves and 16 freedmen who must have worked the arable estate (Faith 1997, 59–70). The output could not have been used by the bishop or the monks far away in Winchester and must have been sold locally, probably through the market at Taunton. Was the

grain shipped out along the Tone? Was the great royal estate at Somerton, which was mostly arable, shipping grain through Ilchester, or was it using the port at Langport, the site of its ninth/tenth century *burh*? In both cases water transport would have been the only feasible method of carriage, since grain is heavy and expensive to move overland.

It is perhaps worth noting that the spread of finds from the PAS and the county HER between 900 and 1100 is heavily concentrated in the south-east of the county. Most of the finds are of horse harness or strap ends and tags from clothing (Fig. 8.8). It has been suggested that the use of horses as riding animals expanded rapidly towards the end of the Anglo-Saxon period among the aristocratic elite. This was the result of influence by the Scandinavian settlers. The resulting horse-furniture was heavily influenced by their tastes and of course the quantities found reflect the spread of this fashion (Graham-Campbell 1991).

What evidence there is for metal-working suggests that this industry was urban. Cheddar is the only place in Somerset to have produced evidence of metal working and that was connected with the palace. Otherwise the horse furniture and strap ends were made in eastern England, though there was also metal working in Winchester (Bayley 1991). The Somerset finds were imported into the county. It is noticeable that the finds still tend to be concentrated close to important royal estates, rather than in the towns. They are also distributed away from the concentration of ecclesiastical estates in the centre of the shire, towards an area of secular lands. There is a possibility that distribution may reflect the areas which have modern arable cultivation where metal-detecting is prevalent, but it might also be the result of the spread of modest luxury among the middling gentry who emerged from the royal and aristocratic demand for followers and soldiers in the tenth and eleventh centuries.

Conclusions

The patterns of distribution of different coins over the long period of this study betray a surprising geographical continuity throughout the whole period. The central levels, with Ilchester at their eastern end, seem to be the focus of activity from the later fifth century through to the mid-eleventh. Sites of importance in the sixth century, such as Portbury and Congresbury along the north coast, did not maintain their status into the period after 900 and their hinterland is notably lacking in finds. However, Watchet, on the west Somerset coast, did remain important and control of the communications from the port to the hinterland was secured early on by the foundation of Taunton, which was in royal hands by c. 730 (ASC). Trade and communication as disclosed by coins seems to have been with far away places in the sixth century, though we cannot know how much other trade with the near continent also existed. The lives of the Welsh saints, in so far as they can be trusted, certainly demonstrate close relations with western Gaul, but finding trade is more difficult and in any case it may not have affected Somerset very much. Connection with Exeter does not seem to have been strong, despite the continued existence of the Fosse Way.

The distribution of early English coin reveals the same general pattern of trade, concentrated on the central lowlands, with the kings' great Cannington estate at the mouth of the Parrett as a gatekeeper for the system. The region seems to turn its back on its neighbours, Dorset and Wiltshire, and to look westward, to Wales and perhaps also to Ireland, and this connection seems to have continued into the tenth century, by which time the traders from Dublin were Christians. During the period prior to the Danish wars of the mid-ninth century and later, the influence of the sites of *monasteria* cannot be ignored, though by no means all of them have produced evidence of trade. Congresbury, Carhampton, Northover, Glastonbury and Cheddar all feature as sites of this type, though it is hard to distinguish the influence of secular royal interests from those of the Church. It is speculation to suggest that the great royal estates and those of the church stimulated trade and were at the centre of the production which made exchange possible. It is noteworthy that many of these centres were placed so that they could take advantage of water transport and we would do well to make more effort in Somerset to look for evidence to support this line of enquiry.

The tenth century saw a re-orientation with the growth of the market sites at towns, but this change may be more apparent than real. The connection with the sea through the river systems continued and was to develop further in the post-Conquest period, with the rise of ports such as Bridgwater. The inland towns, most of which remained small in comparison with trading centres further east in England, and the markets were far from being uniform, either in their creation or their functions. While it is clear that royal interest in them was strong, since so many were royal property and since the king probably hoped for substantial income from them at some point, other men and institutions also had substantial interests in them. The Church and the local aristocracy were beginning to take an interest in the towns as possible sources of income and perhaps political interaction. However, the towns may be grafted on to an existing system rather than providing something novel. There are hints of a market system which ignored the official *burhs* and which was adapted to local demands. Here we might see the cracks developing in the close relationship between the king and the estate system.

Rising populations along with rising wealth gave opportunities for men at all levels to exercise choices themselves. Slaves with newly earned cash might buy themselves and their families freedom. Rich thegns might buy silks for their wives to wear. The king could not control this activity, all he could hope to do was to profit from it by collecting tolls and rents at markets and in the towns and above all to tax his subjects through the land-tax. With the advent of the burgesses in the towns there is the prospect of a link between urban manufacturing and rural production of the materials for that activity, but in Somerset the beginnings of such activity were stunted by distance from potential markets. The great trade was on the eastern side of Britain, with the near continent and thence into the Germanic and Scandinavian polities, and compared with that the west had little to offer.

Inescapable is the fact that Somerset's trade with other parts of the kingdom was a relatively minor matter when compared with the activity of great centres in eastern England, such as York, Lincoln or Norwich. Of the 135 coins in my sample which covers all the coins for the period 410 to 1066 found in the county and which were casual losses, the minting place of 105 is known. Of these 105 just 22, 21% came from outside the county; one each from Cambridge and Wallingford, two each from Oxford, Wilton and York, three each from Exeter and Winchester and four each from Lincoln and London. 78% were local coins and it is likely that further discoveries will simply reinforce that trend. Had the coins of the great mints of London and the east been more widely represented it would be obvious that trade with those places was commonplace. Instead the provenance of the coins shows that most trade was local. This alone must have kept the towns small and underdeveloped.

Coins from the *burhs* show that the seaward orientation towards the west, including Ireland, continued. However contacts with the east and northwards through Bath also grew and the importance of the mint at Bath is shown by the numbers of Bath coins recovered. Some of this re-orientation must be due to the political changes of the tenth century, which broke down the barrier between the south-west of Wessex and the west Midlands. Bath became part of Somerset, although its connections were much more with Mercia to the north. Because of that trade into the Midlands had become important, as had flows of goods from southern Wiltshire through Milborne Port and Sherborne and into south-east Somerset, as revealed by the spread of metal-work. The increase in the rate of economic activity must be related to the increasing demands of royal taxation, as well as the growth of the warrior elite with their need for weapons and luxuries. The men of Somerset, like other Anglo-Saxons, were fortunate that there was demand for their output and the silver to pay for it. Somerset, it is suggested, met this demand through the export of wool and grain, using the rivers as highways. What we do not have from the Anglo-Saxon centuries is the hull of a ship, used to carry the goods. There must have been many.

Old Religion

The post-Roman church

There is no doubt that the meaning of the word 'Christian' has changed dramatically over the centuries and it is all too easy for people in the early twenty-first century to project ideas about modern Christianity on to the people of the early middle ages. We do not know how the early medieval inhabitants of Somerset imagined the world round about them or how they saw their place in it. What we know about the internal life of Christians of this period comes mainly from a literate and educated continental minority who often held high office in the Church and so may not connect at all well with the internal lives of the peasantry of the post-Roman countryside of western Britain. The religious landscape of the Somerset peasants and their social betters was probably still closely connected with the pagan world they had recently left behind. Charles Thomas thought that the evidence for Christianity in late Roman Somerset was rather weak as compared to further east and south, and his map of the comparative strength of evidence shows north and eastern Somerset as carrying only the second level of weighting, while western Somerset has no evidence at all (Thomas 1981, 139). In contrast

Figure 9.1. Glastonbury Tor from the south-east.

Somerset in the mid-fourth century was dotted with temples which were clearly connected with the rural estates round about and which suggest a vigorous continuing interest in the traditional pantheistic cults of the western Empire.

There are three stages in the development of the post-Roman church apparent in Somerset. Broadly these are: firstly the period during which the temples ceased to function as religious foci, then came the spread of private chapels and churches catering for the local population, and finally from the mid-sixth century onward the establishment of monasteries, modelled upon the example of those of western Gaul. The evidence for these changes is characteristically ambiguous and disparate. Interpretation of the material needs caution but the model, for all its failings, makes rather more sense than the alternative.

Temples

The temples at Brean Down, Lamyatt Beacon, Henley Hill and Chew Stoke were all in use during the fourth century (see ApSimon 1965, Leech 1986, Watts and Leech 1996, and Rahtz and Harris 1957). Other temples may have existed at Brent Knoll, Cadbury Castle, Worlebury and Pedwell. The Lamyatt temple continued in use until the early fifth century, suggesting that native cults were still active at the time of the collapse of Roman administration (Leech 1986). At Brean Down the temple may have ceased to be used in the second half of the fourth century (ApSimon 1965, 230), though there was activity on the hill into the fifth century. At Pagans Hill the presence of a coin of Arcadius (383–408) showed that the site was still in use at the end of the fourth century (Rahtz 1951, 118) and as we have seen the other buildings on the site continued to be used in some fashion for several centuries more. The temple at Henley Wood was also still in use at the end of the fourth century.

The disuse of the temples in the first part of the fifth century is the most important indicator we have of the disappearance of pagan cult practices. Temples might decay as the well-to-do who maintained them became poorer with the changes in the early fifth century economy, but there is no trace of anything which might have replaced the temples on their

sites, which were likely to have remained associated with the cults. A later burial cut through the temple at Henley Hill certainly suggests that the site was thoroughly disused and not regarded as 'sacred'. It is not a coincidence that the replacement of pagan beliefs and activity seems to have taken place in the first half of the fifth century. The destruction of the old order of the Roman world must have weakened allegiance to traditional belief systems, and Christianity with its offer of a new rationale for catastrophic contemporary events, as well as a new paradigm for the organisation of social life, was able to make headway in the countryside, just as it did in other parts of the western Roman world at this period. In Gaul, Hispania and Italia the survival of the towns, the stronghold of Christian organisation and culture, provided a base from which the cult could spread and this was strengthened by the adherence of the surviving aristocracy who often lived on their country estates and controlled episcopal office. Here the cult did not have those advantages, but may still have had supporters among the new elite which came to control the countryside and their influence may have helped the cult to spread among the 'pagani'. The Christianisation of Somerset in the fifth century should be seen as the result of local, indigenous activity, not from missionary work from outside, and the idea that the activities of 'pilgrim saints' were important in spreading Christianity by missionary activity from South Wales as propounded by Canon Doble (Doble in Attwater 1960–70 and Evans 1984), Radford (1963, 31–6) and Bowen (1977) in this area has long been superseded (Pearce 1973).

Alan Thacker has shown that although the cult of the saints was beginning to develop in Britain by the early years of the fifth century there is little evidence that it became widespread (Thacker 2002, 31–2). There is nothing like the cult of St Alban anywhere here. A model for the development of the Church might suggest the appearance of Christian communities with churches in the towns in the fourth century and since the cult had the strong backing of the Roman State we might expect there to be many well-to-do and politically powerful members of the churches. These would be the people whose financial support would underpin the cult. With the collapse of urban communities, survival for the Church meant moving to the countryside and adapting to the

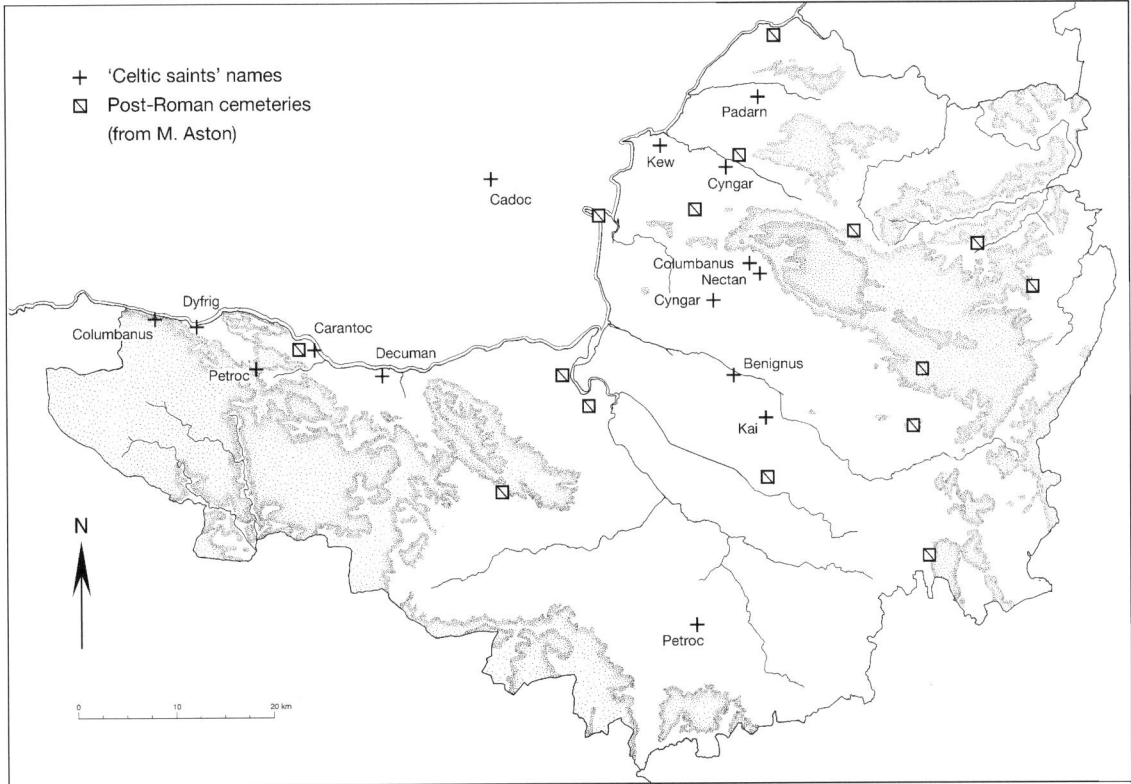

Figure 9.2. Saints and cemeteries.

new social structure which was appearing. Outside Somerset, in Dorset for instance, there is evidence that some villa proprietors had already adopted Christian symbolism and so perhaps some Christian practices before the collapse. Rural churches to serve such people and perhaps the peasantry round about might be the first signs of Christian acceptance in the countryside during the early part of the fifth century. Knight has drawn parallels with the situation in fifth century Gaul, where pastoral care was the main focus of attention in the fifth century and was a secular activity (Knight 1992, 48). Monastic activity seems to be a later development in the sixth and seventh centuries.

The saints

A good deal has been written about 'celtic' dedications in Somerset in this early period, and it is difficult to sift the evidence when so much is ambiguous or tenuous (Fig. 9.2). Ian Burrow, while accepting Susan Pearce's strictures, was inclined to see a few, mostly coastal dedications as indicating missionary activity (Burrow 1981, 47–63). He adduced Dubricius at Porlock, Carantoc at Carhampton, Decuman at Watchet, Cyngar at Congresbury and Badgworth, Paternus (Padarn) at Nailsea, Kew at Kewstoke and Kai at Street. To this list might be added Cadoc, on Steep Holm, Benignus at Meare, Columbanus and Nectan at Cheddar and Petroc at Timberscombe and at Shepton Beauchamp, as well as Gildas at Street. From among these disparate saints one group falls squarely within the post-Roman period, even if they are not fifth century, and they are nearly all associated most closely with southern Wales and in some cases also with Cornwall and Brittany.

Carantoc was a monastic of the sixth or early seventh century whose cult was also strong in Cornwall and Brittany. David Farmer accepts the tradition that he founded a monastery at Carhampton (Farmer 1987, 74). There was certainly a chapel dedicated to him at Carhampton which may have stood in the churchyard or elsewhere nearby and which was still standing in 1533 when it was seen by the antiquarian and traveller, Leland (Chandler 1993, 426). However, excavations at Carhampton have produced material which suggest that this was a high status site before Carantoc's time. Metal-working furnaces and sherds of B-ware amphora might indicate that this was a site in use in the later fifth and early sixth century, contemporary with Cadbury–Congresbury and South Cadbury, but not defended. Burials around Eastbury in Carhampton, well away from the current parish church, are also evidence of religious activity at the site, though they seem to be later in date than either the metal-working or the saint (HER 33449). A site with metal working and amphorae does not have to be secular and it may be that a religious community of some kind was present here before the connection with Carantoc was established.

The parish which serves the royal estate of Williton is St Decumans. He is regarded as a sixth century Welsh monk who has dedications in Cornwall (Farmer 1987, 116). St Decuman's church stands on the higher ground above the town of Watchet, in the countryside, above a valley at the bottom of which is St Decuman's Well. It has been suggested that there was a church site prior to the present one, on the other side of this valley, close to the *burh* (Dunning 1985, 165), but Michael Calder has made a strong case for the removal of the church and perhaps its saint, back to an original site, close to the holy well (Calder 2004, 18). As at Porlock, it is probable that the dedication is the result of a connection with Wales through the early and active trading site at Watchet. It may be that there were monks and traders passing through the port regularly bringing the cult with them, or that the community received relics of the saint. It is notable that the cult of Decuman did not spread far in Somerset. He had a place in the kalendar of Muchelney Abbey, but not at the cathedral or other monasteries of the pre-Norman period (Scholfield 1927, 137). It looks unlikely, therefore, that a monastic or episcopal interest influenced the dedication as may have happened

for Columbanus at Cheddar. This may have been a church serving the local population rather than a monastic community.

Elsewhere along the coast the cult of Dyfrig (Dubricius) occurs at Porlock, another major seaside focus. Dyfrig died c. 550 and lived and worked mostly in the Hereford-Gwent area (Farmer 1987, 124–5). His cult was certainly attested at Porlock before the Reformation in 1527 (Weaver 1983, 268) but there is nothing to suggest that he came to the area. It is much more likely that his cult is evidence of the strength of the connection between the port of Porlock and southern Wales from the fifth century onwards and his cult may have resulted from the arrival of a relic of the saint. This is more likely in the pre-English period than later, simply because of the tendency of the English Church to look towards the continent and the established Gallic traditions rather than to the Celtic Church in the west. However, a post-AD 650 date cannot be totally excluded.

The 'Columbanus' at Culbone in West Somerset is not so easy to explain. Culbone is derived from Columban(us). However, in 1086 the name of the settlement was *Kitenore*, 'the kite's hillside' (Ekwall 1960). The present settlement beside the church is tiny and is situated in a deep valley just above the sea. In the Domesday Book Culbone was an estate of just 1 hide and 1 virgate and had a population of two villagers, one smallholder and a slave. There was no demesne (DB 5.7). However, this tiny settlement may have had a church. The existing structure has features that suggest a pre-Conquest origin and given its location in a remote combe near the sea, it may have started as a hermit's cell. Columbanus, who died in 615, was not, of course, a Welsh saint, but Irish. His long career as a monastic leader and the founder of Luxeuil and Bobbio made him widely known and he was respected throughout Europe as an 'exile for God'. Consequently it may be that a solitary used his name in the dedication of an oratory. This need not have been in the immediate post-Roman period.

The dedication to St Cadoc on Steep Holm was certainly in place by 1147–83 (Walker 1998, 27) and the location is typical of those chosen by eremites of the western Church, especially those of the western British Isles. With its dedication to a priest from southern Wales who had many dedications there, it was clearly within the saint's penumbra and could have been established at any time after the mid-sixth century, but before the advent of the English Church (Farmer 1987, 67).

A minor place-name, that of 'St Hernin' at St Erne's Well in the parish of Upper Weare, may represent a lost dedication (Costen 1978). It preserves the name of another saint from South Wales and may be understood as an importation to a place which lay beside the river Axe and had direct connection to the Bristol Channel.

St Kew at Kewstoke is more difficult, in that he is located by the place-name, rather than a dedication. Unfortunately the place-name is not attested until 1086 when it was *Chiwestoch* (DB 42.1). This is 'Kew's holy place or cell' (Ekwall 1960). Michael Calder has made the case for a church of a type similar to Lantokay at Street (Calder 2004, 13–16). However there are no charters or other evidence to show that this church ever held lands sufficient to support a monastic community. Not far away, on the other side of the Yeo river, lies Banwell. More will be said about this place later in this chapter, but it is apposite to suggest that like Congresbury it may have had a monastery in the post-Roman period. Like Congresbury it had a substantial post-Roman community and a hill-fort nearby, though since it has never been satisfactorily investigated it is not known whether it was re-occupied in the later fifth century. Like Congresbury it was given by King Alfred to Bishop Asser. In Asser's 'Life of King Alfred', he relates that the king gave him the monasteries 'called Congresbury and Banwell in English' (Keynes and Lapidge 1983, 97). The 'Life' was written in 893 and the gift must therefore have taken place shortly before, perhaps in 886 (Keynes 1999, 49). Banwell takes its name from the powerful spring (now channelled away) close to which the monastery stood. The place-name is derived from the Old English '*bana*', 'something which destroys or slays' plus Old English '*weall*', a 'spring'. Like Wells a powerful spring may have attracted a cult before the advent of Christianity, and would certainly have been appropriated by the Christians as part of their drive against pagan practices from the fifth century onwards. The foundation of the two monasteries might have reduced the church at Kewstoke to the status of a cell, even if it had started as a more important site.

The earliest forms of the place-name Congresbury are *Cungresbyri*, c. 893 (Asser), *Cungresbyrig*, c. 1031 (Rollason 1978, 61–94), *cungresberia*, 1084, (Geld Rolls) and *Cungresberie*, 1086 (DB). The saint's name is an anglicised version of the Old Welsh name Cyngar which has had the English genitive case added to it together with the dative case of the Old English *burh* – *byrig*. *Burh/byrig* place names of this type have long been recognised as forming a distinctive category, among which in the west of England are Tewkesbury, Glastonbury, Malmesbury and Amesbury where the sites referred to are not the more common hill-fort but monastic sites. 'St Cyngar's monastery' therefore is the best meaning. As we shall see later, the present church occupies a site probably chosen for it in the later seventh or early eighth century. The legend of St Cyngar was studied by Canon Doble in 1945 (Doble 1945, 32–43 and 85–95). He suggested that Cyngar was one of a group of Old Welsh missionaries who worked in the west of Britain in the later fifth and early sixth centuries and that the Cyngar commemorated in north Wales is a different saint, since he does not share a feast with the Somerset Cyngar (27th November). The Somerset Cyngar does not have a cult outside the shire, since he is not mentioned in Breton and Cornish Kalendars. There is another dedication to St Cyngar in Somerset at Badgworth, on the edge of the Wedmore island, but there is nothing to suggest that this low-status community had a very early church site and so this may be a secondary dedication. While it is difficult to accept the Canon's view that he was one of a group of missionaries, it is clear that like Carantoc, Decuman and Dyfrig his cult may be the result of the influence of travellers between south Wales and Somerset and more specifically in the case of Cyngar the arrival of relics of the saint. As we shall see in the next chapter, Congresbury was the setting for an important pilgrimage to Cyngar's relics in the tenth and eleventh centuries.

Two of these saints, Carantoc and Cyngar, would seem to be connected with important religious centres, which may have functioned as monasteries in the sixth and seventh centuries. Later each was to become patron of a minster church and in both cases, Congresbury and Carhampton, there is clear evidence of a high status community of the later fifth century very close by. Patterns of trade in the later fifth and early sixth centuries tie high status activity mostly to the coastal belt and the known post-Roman cemeteries in the same region reinforce the impression of coastal communities which dominated the interior. It might be considered only natural that major religious activity should be similarly disposed.

The Glastonbury Abbey charter S1249 mentions the gift to the abbey of an estate called 'Lantokay'. This charter, which Lesley Abrams has discussed at some length, is dated to AD 680 and as it now exists it must be suspect (Abrams 1996, 153–4). While the authenticity of the grant as late seventh century may be in question, there is little doubt that the place-name itself has a genuine pre-Conquest history, since the charter is mentioned in the *Liber Terrarum*, which was compiled between the end of the tenth century and the early part of the twelfth century (Abrams 1996, 14–18). As a Welsh place name of the '*llan*' type, meaning the 'church of Cai', it is likely to preserve a place-name of a type very common in Wales and in Welsh borderlands, as well as appearing regularly in Cornwall, but which must have been very rare in Somerset. '*Llan*' ('an enclosure', 'a church') as a place-name element had a long history in Wales and so its existence as a place-name in Somerset does not imply very great antiquity. The earlier element '*merthyr*' a borrowing from the Latin '*martyrium*', 'the grave of a martyr', which was sometimes replaced by '*llan*' does not occur (Roberts 1992, 42–4). On the other hand a coining after the mid-seventh century seems very unlikely on both political and linguistic grounds. It might therefore be a site of a church of the sixth or early seventh century. The place itself has been identified as Leigh near Street since it was given as *Lantokay id est Leghe* in the *Liber Terrarum* and since Leigh was part of Glastonbury's possessions in 1086 (Robinson 1921, 48). Street does not appear in the Domesday survey and it is clear that the whole estate was then included under the *Lega* name (DB 8.16). It is probable therefore that the church referred to is the church at Street. Work by Michael Calder has strengthened this identification and he has shown that the graveyard of the church fits well with other similar '*llan*' sites in Wales and Cornwall (Calder 2004). The 3 hides mentioned in the charter would therefore be the existing endowment of the church when it was transferred to Glastonbury's ownership.

Petts (2002) has argued that '*llan*' names did not refer to graveyards until the tenth century and that churches with such names should be considered as possible early monasteries. Calder also thinks this may have been the position at Street, in which case a 'celtic' monastery was gobbled up by its more powerful Anglo-Saxon neighbour.

The more we examine these saints, the more it becomes apparent that what is important is the location rather than the dedication itself. If important sites, those used by an elite in the later fifth and early sixth century, are often close to the coast, we should not be surprised to see the dedications also appearing close to them. Contact with southern Wales and further abroad was clearly an important part of the social and political network of the Somerset elite and the bias towards the coast reflects this. A cultural drift, with a penetration of local cults, was therefore a natural development.

Other 'celtic' dedications are probably the result of later local interest and patronage and are probably post-Conquest in origin. The church at Street later bore a dedication to St Gildas, although there is nothing to suggest that it is very ancient and it may be possible to exclude him as a product of Glastonbury's interest in the eleventh and twelfth centuries in possible local saints. The same argument might apply to the cult of Benignus at Meare. In 1323 the parish church there was dedicated to The Blessed Virgin, All Saints and St Benignus (Hobhouse 1887, 219). The triple dedication suggests several rebuilds and re-dedications of the church. The *Vita* of the saint as given by John of Glastonbury makes him an Irish saint of the fifth century, a disciple of Saint Patrick, who worked, lived and died at Meare where he was buried. He tells us that Benignus was translated to Glastonbury from Meare where he was re-interred during the time of William Rufus, in 1091 (Carley 1978, 88). Clearly the abbey had an interest in promoting Benignus since it also claimed the relics of St Patrick himself. Significantly the saint does not appear in the abbey's tenth century kalendar, suggesting that his cult was not particularly old at his translation. The cult may well be eleventh century.

Columbanus at Cheddar may be the result of patronage and interest by a major church, in this case Wells. The saint was commemorated in the eleventh century kalendar of the cathedral, which may explain the dedication at Cheddar where the chapter had important interests in the post-Conquest period (Wormald 1988, 109). Similarly the dedication of an altar to St Nectan in the parish church may be connected to his commemoration at Wells. We are left with a dedication to Petroc at Timberscombe and a medieval fair at Shepton Beauchamp on St Petroc's feast. There is no evidence that the dedication at Timberscombe pre-dates the Norman Conquest and the fair at Shepton Beauchamp on fourth of June may simply have been a summer fair, rather than an indication of an ancient dedication of the church.

One further view about the nature of the early Church in western Britain deserves some examination in a Somerset context. Susan Pearce has argued that in the West Country in the fifth century villas were turned into religious centres. This of course happened many times in Gaul and elsewhere in western Europe and so it seems appropriate here also. A counter argument would say that there is too little evidence of continuing occupation of the villas in the fifth century to make them likely to be used in this way. Certainly the standard of living of the villa owners in the mid-fifth century had fallen dramatically, but that may not have stopped the buildings being re-used or converted. Both Banwell and Cheddar might therefore be suitable candidates for such institutions, carrying a religious presence through from the fifth century into the Anglo-Saxon period and even down to our own day. At Cheddar the present church lies close to the villa site and the same is true at Banwell, though there the church was probably built for the local people by the bishop in the post-Conquest period. We do not know where the post-Roman monastery lay (Pearce 1982, 117).

The physical evidence

Elsewhere in Wales and the South-West, inscribed memorial stones are another important source of evidence for early Christian activity. Somerset has only two examples, the 'Caractacus' stone on Winsford Hill and the Culbone stone (Fig. 9.3). For the first of these there is dispute over the correct reading of the inscription, though no-one doubts that this is a post-Roman inscription on a memorial

stone and all seem to agree that that it is probably standing in its original position. Okasha (1993) doubts that the inscription is complete, but reads it as *CARAACI NEPUS*, probably 'the descendant of Caractacus' and thinks that it could be dated at any time from the fifth century to the eleventh. The compilers of the Historic Environment Record (HER) are more positive in suggesting a 'sixth century type' inscription. The stone was in its present position in the twelfth century, when it was referred to as the 'Langestone' and was a marker for the bounds of Exmoor Forest (HER 34225). It stands near a point at which many medieval tracks pass; it was not therefore in an obscure position, but there was no burial associated with it. To suggest that the stone has not been moved seems very questionable. The lack of an associated burial would make it a cenotaph, when Christian memorials are almost always placed close to the reputed grave. It may have been moved to make a marker for the forest bound, which was its function in the twelfth century.

The Culbone stone carries an incised wheel cross and might date from the seventh to ninth centuries (Grinsell 1970, 126), though more recently this has been questioned and it has been suggested that it could be of any period, even post-medieval (Cramp 2006, 191). Again one must question whether this simple memorial or marker is in its original position. It stands very close to Culbone parish boundary, so it may have been moved once its significance was lost, to be used as a boundary marker.

Further physical evidence of possible early churches comes from the hill-fort at Lamyatt Beacon where Roger Leech recorded a small cemetery of 16 burials, nearly all female, above average height and showing few signs of hard manual labour. There is a strong possibility that this was the cemetery of a community of religious women. Carbon dating ranging between AD 559 and 782 would place this establishment firmly in the sixth and early seventh centuries (Leech 1986, 259–328). At Brean Down, as mentioned in Chapter 3 above, there is a real possibility of a small late-Roman or post-Roman chapel or church on the hill-top, beside the ruined temple (Leech 1980, 349–50). Like Lamyatt Beacon, this might represent a small monastic community.

At Wells Dr Rodwell has proposed that the

Figure 9.3. The 'Caractacus' stone.

remains of a small chamber marked the existence of a late-Roman mausoleum, over which a substantial building stood. Extensive comparisons with sites elsewhere in western Europe suggest that this mausoleum could have formed the basis for a later use of the site for Christian religious purposes. 'Whatever religion prevailed at the time of its initial construction, it is inescapable that the Wells mausoleum must have acquired sanctity within a Christian milieu before it became enveloped by the Anglo-Saxon minster church' (Rodwell 2001, 47). Thus Dr Rodwell makes the point that there must have been some continuity of use or knowledge of the religious importance of the mausoleum, from the late-Roman period to the seventh and eighth centuries. However, Professor Blair has reviewed the evidence provided by the excavations and suggested that the structure was not as early as Dr Rodwell claims and that it was no more than a damp proofing structure for the building above (Blair 2004, 134–7). There is no need then to posit a continuous history

for Wells and its churches before the seventh or eighth centuries.

The idea of a three stage development of the church in the post-Roman period has much to commend it. In the fifth century we might expect there to have been churches with priests serving the communities whose existence is revealed by the known open cemeteries (Fig. 9.2). These are now well documented across much of the county, but provide us with evidence of the existence of communities, not of their religious habits, apart from the mode of burial, which is that common to the western Christian world of this period. Certainly the larger and longer lived communities at Cannington and Banwell would have had a chapel of some kind. However, the smaller cemeteries probably represent very small groups living in hamlets, or isolated farmsteads. They would not have had their own chapels. Some churches serving the laity may have modern successors at Porlock, Watchet, Street and perhaps Kewstoke. This last, along with Kai's church at Street, were captured by the developing monasteries, Kewstoke by Banwell and Street by Glastonbury. There is also a tantalisingly oblique glimpse of a possible church at Bleadon. The Anglo-Saxon charter bounds have a reference to a *cyric stæd*, 'the site of a church' (S606 of 956). This seems to have stood somewhere along the top of Bleadon Hill, perhaps close to a track running along the Mendips to Uphill and possibly to Brean. This would have been an early church built to serve scattered groups at farmsteads and hamlets, in a landscape without villages or towns.

All four of the possible post-Roman monasteries are associated with hill-forts or with high-status settlement. The settlement at Cadbury–Congresbury would have attracted clerics and possibly there were chapels to suit the aristocratic clientele. When the fort was abandoned in the mid-sixth century it may have been handed over to a group of monks. A similar process may have occurred at Banwell, but South Cadbury, an obvious choice for such a venture, has nothing. Perhaps the possible early site at Sherborne precluded such a development. At Carhampton also, a successor to a high status secular settlement seems to have been a monastic community. This brings us inevitably to a consideration of the place of Glastonbury, the last of these communities for which we have some evidence.

The archaeological work carried out on Glastonbury Tor by Professor Rahtz makes it abundantly clear that the Tor was a high status site. Classic Mediterranean wares of the sixth century, found there, together with extensive animal remains show that the site was in use in the post-Roman period (Rahtz 1971, 65). Evidence of timber structures was recovered as well as burials. Professor Rahtz initially viewed this as a high status post-Roman secular site, on a par with South Cadbury or Cadbury-Congresbury, but finally decided that it might well have been a monastic Christian site (Rahtz 1993, 59).

If we look at the fragmentary evidence for churches and monasteries in the post-Roman period it should not be too much of a surprise to find a loose correlation with the known settlement pattern. If the society of Old Welsh Somerset was as well organised as that across the Severn in south-east Wales, then there were plenty of local churches in existence by the first half of the seventh century (Pryce 1992, 58–9). Somewhere behind the rather disparate data must lie a bishop or bishops and some sort of organisation of the local church. Any statement about where he might have been seated or what pattern of authority existed would be pure conjecture, but we should not be surprised if it were to appear as a rather loose structure, mostly reflecting the rather dispersed nature of Somerset's Old Welsh society which seems to have developed in the course of the sixth and early seventh centuries. The pattern consisted of a spread of local churches, now mostly lost to us, and the emergence of a number of monastic churches mostly linked to former high-status secular settlements. We should be careful, however, to remember that in this context 'monastic' should not necessarily lead us to imagine a community of regular monks, but perhaps something much more like the 'minsters' of the Anglo-Saxon church. By the time the Anglo-Saxon rulers took over that pattern was probably quite well developed, but because of the loose structure was easily adapted and overlain by the much more comprehensive organisation the Anglo-Saxons put in place.

The Anglo-Saxon church: the first minsters

The coming of the Anglo-Saxon kings and their followers, religious as well as lay, meant that there was a group of men who had made their lives in the new church and were anxious to colonise the newly seized territory, in much the same way as their warrior brothers. There can be little doubt that the clerical newcomers were able to take over the existing church, just as the laymen took over existing estates and that the king, in alliance with his bishops, was prepared to re-mould the church in these new lands to suit the new society he introduced and to promote his own control. The result was a new structure for the church in Somerset, but one which utilised existing communities where that was advantageous or necessary.

Professor Blair has suggested that the explosion in the foundation of Anglo-Saxon minsters in the late seventh century is partly to be explained by the rapid expansion of the money supply and the burgeoning resources available to elite groups in Anglo-Saxon society (Blair 2005, 84–5). In Wessex that included the acquisition of enormous new territories which doubled the size of Wessex in no more than fifty years. This was a 'free' injection of resources, both of land and manpower. The English experience and by implication the Somerset experience is only part of what was actually a western European-wide phenomenon. However, there can be little doubt that the decisions kings took about how to use their wealth, which led to the foundation of so many new churches, were based upon both religious and ideological considerations. The monks and clerks formed a natural group of allies for the king, and his ability to choose the head of a minster, often of course, a relative, further enhanced the power and status of his kin. The dynasty (on shaky foundations at this point) could also benefit from alliance with the new God and His saints who would bolster their claims to legitimacy and ensure their path to the world to come.

Wessex in the second half of the seventh century had not long begun to adopt the new religion, though contacts with their western neighbours and with northern Gaul must have long familiarised members of the aristocracy with the general outlines of Christianity. As it was, the first major contact with the Frankish church came when Birinus arrived from Gaul in 634 and set about converting the Gewisse. King Cynegils adopted the new religion, probably because it was politically expedient to ally himself with the Christian Oswald of Northumbria (Bede, 112–3). Cynegils's son Cenwalh was a pagan and was initially allied to Penda of Mercia until he put away his wife, Penda's sister. In the ensuing war Cenwalh was driven from Wessex and took refuge in East Anglia where he was converted and when he returned to Wessex he appointed another Frank, Agilbert, as bishop. Eventually Cenwalh decided to divide the church in his kingdom into two dioceses, appointing a new native-born bishop named Wine, with his seat at Winchester and leaving Agilbert at Dorchester on Thames. This was supposedly because the king found Agilbert's Frankish unintelligible, but probably because Mercian expansion in the Thames valley made Dorchester untenable for the West Saxons, so that in effect Winchester became the seat of a reconstituted diocese (Yorke 1995, 172). Agilbert thereupon returned to Gaul where he became bishop of Paris. Wine also left to join Wulfhere of Mercia and purchased the see of London from him. Although Agilbert refused to return, his nephew Leuthere was appointed to the reunited see in 670. Stability had at last been achieved and Leuthere ruled until his death, to be succeeded by the Anglo-Saxon Hædda, a frequent witness of Ine's charters. Hædda found himself the bishop of an enormous diocese which had expanded during the second half of the century as Wessex was established as a state. It is from this point that we begin to see the growth of monastic establishments in Somerset and it seems likely that serious attempts to reshape the church in Somerset to suit the needs of the kings and their followers were only possible once the see was firmly established.

The Anglo-Saxon church of the seventh and eighth centuries was built upon a system of major churches, the minsters, which came to form a network covering the countryside.[1] Patronage of these houses in Somerset was firmly in the hands of the king and his family. It is a mark of the importance of these institutions that in the eighth century there are signs that when the Mercian kings became the dominant rulers in southern Britain they exerted and consolidated their power by exercising control over the minsters. In the charter S1410 King Athelbald of Mercia is shown overseeing the purchase of land

by Glastonbury. A generation earlier King Ine had approved a grant of land at Brent to Glastonbury (S238 of 693). Some years later the same charter was confirmed by King Athelbald. It seems probable that this Mercian influence extended across the whole of Somerset in the mid-eighth century.

As institutions the minsters varied between churches which followed a rule akin to the Benedictine system as it existed in Gaul, double houses of monks and nuns, and probably minsters served by a group of canons who might vary in number according to the resources available to support them. All types of minster seem to have had contact with the laity outside, so that the later more rigid distinction between communities following a monastic rule of enclosure and more or less cut off from the world, and groups of canons and priests serving the laity, is not apparent. The term 'minster' in the Anglo-Saxon world was adopted from the Latin '*monasterium*' but this one word covered a multitude of differing establishments. Sarah Foot has made the point that the minster consisted of a 'religious congregation … engaged in non-secular pursuits' (Foot 1999b, 39), which gives much latitude for understanding them. They could consist of houses of men or women or both, who were understandably 'monks' or 'nuns', and others where there was a community of secular priests. They also varied wildly in size and status (Blair 2005, 82–3). Probably for the average lay observer of the early eighth century the major distinction between churches was the size of the religious community. Glastonbury and Muchelney, which we see as monasteries, may not have seemed so much out of the ordinary to seventh and eighth century observers therefore. It may be that only the increasing size of their endowments marked them out, and that to a contemporary churches which are now quite obscure may have been just as important in the everyday life of the people as those we would regard as prominent. Perhaps most important was an understanding of the social connections of the individual minster. Those in Somerset seem to be most closely aligned with royal estates and centres and thus provided the king with a series of institutions which he could use as part of his control and governance of the new part of his kingdom. Both socially, as examples of the Anglo-Saxon aristocratic household, and as expressions of the particular continental religious structure which the kings of Wessex had adopted, they were admirably suited for integrating his new Welsh followers into the Anglo-Saxon kingdom of Wessex.

Philip Rahtz has proposed that the monastery site at Glastonbury was first occupied by a Celtic religious community which moved down from the Tor in the early seventh century and that the wooden church was built by that group (Rahtz 1993, 72). An alternative view might be that the Celtic community continued to function on the Tor until the coming of the Anglo-Saxons in the mid-seventh century when it was moved to its present site as part of a programme of Anglicisation. The wooden church would thus be the first 'English' church on the site, followed some years later – perhaps half a century – by the stone church, built by Ine. At this point one should add the observation that an Anglo-Saxon model for early Glastonbury does not mean that it was necessarily a 'monastery' in the sense usually understood today. Glastonbury here will be referred to as a 'monastery', principally because the scale of its endowments by the early years of the eighth century suggests that it had moved beyond being a house of lay clerics and had become a larger and more complex establishment with monastic aspects to its life.

Despite the extensive archaeological work carried on at the abbey for about a century we still lack precise information concerning its early history (Fig. 9.4). The oldest structure of which we have knowledge, though entirely from literary sources, is the *Vetusta Aecclesia*, the old church, which was wooden. It still stood when William of Malmesbury visited the abbey (Mynors, Thompson and Winterbottom 1998, 804–5) and it survived until the disastrous fire of 1184 (Rahtz 1993, 71). The *vetusta aecclesia* was probably the first building on the new monastic site. Rahtz (1993, 72) proposed that it was a seventh century building and William of Malmesbury tells us that King Ine's stone church, constructed in the early eighth century, was secondary to it.

The monastery occupied one of the largest 'islands' in the Levels which stood in a prominent and potentially powerful position. Glastonbury island itself was large enough to have extensive arable lands. The Fosse Way, with connections north and south, lay only 10 km to the east and to the west there

was ready access to the Brue and Axe, providing a water way to the Severn Estuary. Other islands also belonged to Glastonbury from an early date. The *De Antiquitate* of William of Malmesbury (Scott 1981, 91) claims that King Cenwalh (642–672) gave the monastery the islands of Andreyseie (now Nyland), Marchey, Beckery and Godney. This is a suspect claim (Abrams 1996, 46), but it may be that they were islands already connected with Glastonbury before any formal grants were made and that the claim was intended to regularise an ancient position which had no documentation. Andreysie was supposedly so called because there was a chapel dedicated to St Andrew on it (Scott 1981, 152) (Fig. 9.5). However, the spelling in the Domesday Book would indicate that it was originally 'Eadred's Island' (Ekwall 1960). With that in mind it may be that the 'Andrew' dedication was the result of a connection with Cheddar, not Glastonbury. Nyland may not have come to Glastonbury until later in the Anglo-Saxon period. The grant of 'Ætheresig' by King Edgar to Ælswith appears in the Liber terrarum (S1761). However, the grant appears to have been only half a hide, whereas the Domesday entry has 2 hides. This must have covered the adjacent farmland stretching up onto the Mendips and embraced by the parish of Batcombe cum Nyland. Marchey had a chapel dedicated to St Martin; the name means 'Martin's island' (Scott 1981, 91). Both settlements could have survived by farming cattle on the marshes and by water-fowling and fishing, but the existence of chapels in such remote places strongly suggests that they were primarily religious sites, inhabited by small groups of hermits; in the case of Nyland, hermits from Cheddar. Without firm evidence that these places had chapels in the early sixth century we cannot safely claim that they were 'celtic', but we should see them as the type of religious retreat where men might wrestle with the devil amidst the floods and mists of the moors.

At some early date also, the island of Beckery, close to Glastonbury, provided the setting for a chapel, which Philip Rahtz thought might be of the seventh century. Here there was a community of men, enough to fill a cemetery of at least 100 people. This would represent a small community of monks or hermits over a period of several centuries (Rahtz and Hirst 1974). This was certainly part of the Glastonbury

Figure 9.4. Modern Glastonbury ruins seen from the south-east. The early minster on this site was tiny compared to the post-Norman developments and seems to have used a quite different layout for its precinct. However, the Romanesque chapel to the left of the picture lies over the Vestusta Aecclesia and part of Ine's early church.

Figure 9.5. Nyland (Andersie) from the south-east.

possessions by 1066 and had probably always been part of the abbey's endowment.

Glastonbury island, which the monastery inherited from its predecessor, was limited only by the surrounding moor land to which it had ready access.

The island itself was said to have been first formally granted by Centwine in 678, when he appointed an abbot for the house (Carley 1978, 110). This was a grant of 6 hides and probably represents the real size of the Glastonbury island estate. Since the record

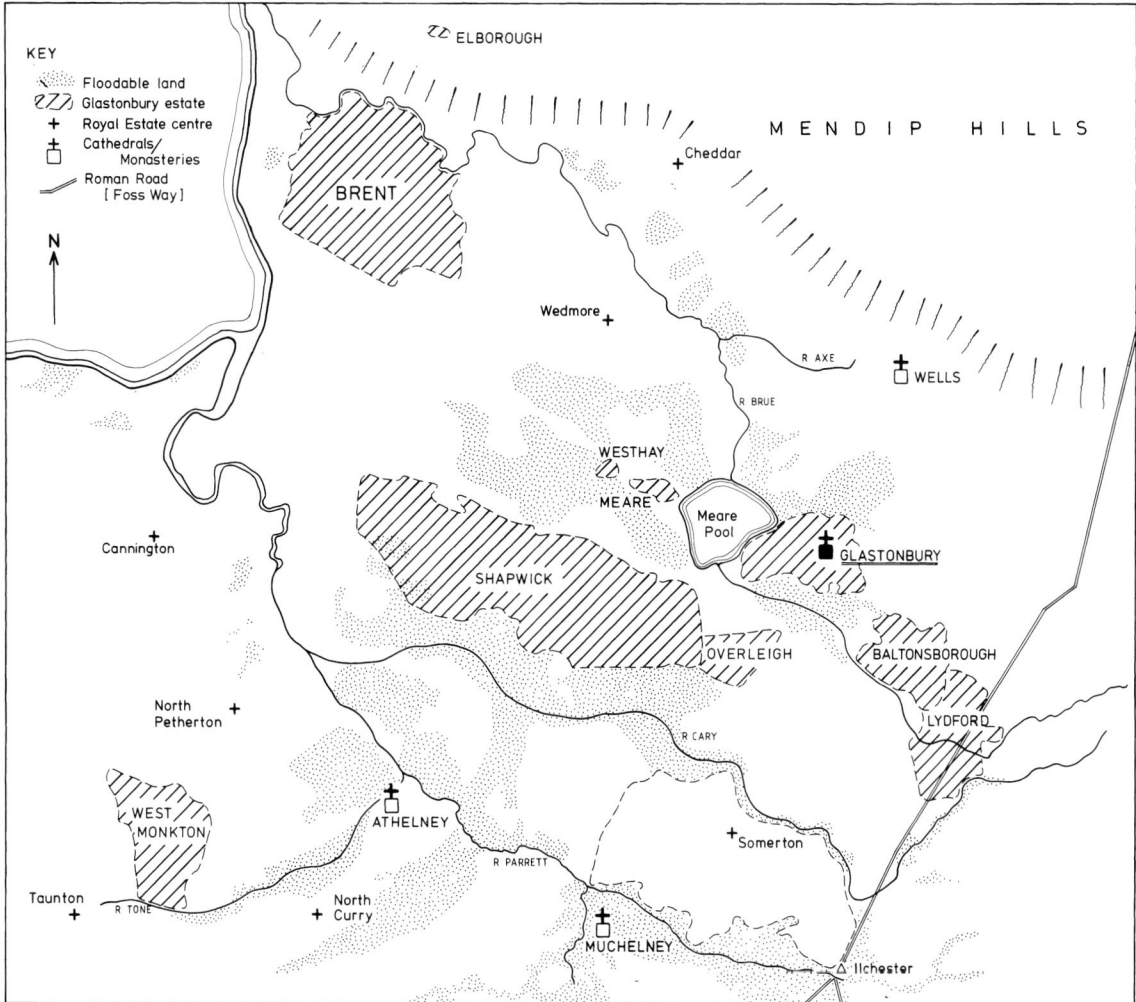

Figure 9.6 Glastonbury's early estates.

of this grant does not survive as a charter, but only in later accounts of the history of Glastonbury, it is difficult to be sure that this is authentic. Certainly, the accompanying statement that the monks were to elect the own abbots and to follow the Rule of Benedict looks like propaganda inserted at a much later date. Other grants were chiefly on the higher ground to the east and west of Glastonbury and provided it with a ready extension of the home estate. There were, however, outlying lands, land 'at the foot of mendip', at Monkton near Taunton and at Sowy, in the marshes, closer to the mouth of the Parrett. From the later part of the seventh century it began to acquire property from its secular overlords, both noblemen and from the king. As we saw in chapter two above, the first recorded grant outside Glastonbury, made by the bishop of Wessex, Hædda, was of the land and probably the church also at Street and at Meare (S1249) in about 680. King Centwine gave land at Creechbarrow and West Monkton near Taunton in c. 682 (S237) (Fig. 9.6). Thereafter there was a series of grants by Ine which probably enabled the monastery to expand its personnel. The men who attested the grants often included Aldhelm, probably the most influential churchman in Wessex in the later years of the king's rule, who, along with many other abbots, was a regular witness of the grants. As members of the king's councils they clearly played an important part in holding the fragile new kingdom together. Enhancement of the monasteries' power was intended to strengthen the king's authority by counterbalancing the power of the king's warrior followers in the shire. Glastonbury was probably chosen for this role because it stood closest to the royal estate at Somerton. Muchelney, further south, and also built upon an island in the marshes, was the second focus of royal attention.

Professor Aston has recently made a study of the origins of Muchelney and suggested that it began as a hermitage in the marshes, which was elevated to the status of a monastic community by the grant of a number of islands (Aston 2007, 63–71). Like Glastonbury it then received endowments on the 'mainland' which were much more productive than the islands and would enable it to support a growing community. As so often the earliest grants are difficult to assess, since the charters survive only at second or third hand and have suffered much emendation of one sort and another (Fig. 9.7). Muchelney was never as grand and as successful a house as Glastonbury and its chartulary is much sparser than Glastonbury's (Bates 1899). Unlike Glastonbury, the correspondence between its early endowments and the picture in the Domesday Book in 1066 is feeble. The original islands in the marshes have no charter but are in the Domesday Book. Muchelney, Midelney and Thorney were not hidated and Professor Aston has shown that they were taken out of the royal estate of Martock, which probably had the Parrett and Yeo as boundaries on this western side (Aston 2007, 67). Most of this ground was floodable marshland, so the islands were really isolated and outlying portions of the larger estate. The first substantial grant of dry land, which could presumably give a return as farmland, was granted by Ine in 693 (S240). This consisted of 40 hides of land, '37 hides of land on the eastern bank of the river Isle and on either side of the public highway and three on the western side of the Isle together with a wood called Stretmerch'. This land is not now identifiable with estates held by the monastery much later in 1066. It was not until 762 that another

substantial grant was recorded (S261). This gave land to the west of Castle Neroche, well to the south of the monastery and probably mostly woodland at that time. Again the description of the land is too vague for us to be sure exactly where it was and it does not seem to correspond with anything held by the abbey in 1066. The name used for the area is *duun meten,* an Old Welsh name containing the word for a hill-fort, '*din*'. This must refer to the modern Castle Neroche, which now contains the remains of a Norman castle built inside an Iron Age hill-fort (Prior 2006, 70–3). Professor Aston has made a detailed attempt to reconstruct this early landholding and has suggested that it consisted of a block of land around the present day Isle Abbots, which was then extended into a large semi-coherent estate stretching from Earnshill in the north to Cricket Malherbie in the south and from Whitelackington in the east to Ashill and Steweley to the west (Aston 2009, 84–5).

Unlike Glastonbury, there is nothing at Muchelney which could plausibly be interpreted as suggesting a pre-English origin for this monastery. It may well have been constructed simply from a grant to a group of pioneering English hermits. Writing in the twelfth century, William of Malmesbury knew nothing of its early foundation and thought of it as a tenth century monastery. He did characterise its situation however, saying 'Muchelney is difficult of access. In summer it is generally approached on foot or by horse. In winter there are no visitors' (Preest 2002, 133). What Muchelney lacked in later days was the ability to attract enough secular patronage to allow it to build up substantial estates and to construct a plausible foundation myth.

Glastonbury and Muchelney are perhaps special cases, since they survived to be re-founded as monasteries in the tenth century, and this may be because they always maintained a presence which was more overtly 'monastic' than most of the other churches of the shire. Certainly they were the only early Anglo-Saxon foundations (apart from Bath) which preserved a chartulary, however garbled and corrupt. It is always possible that other early foundations also held charters showing their entitlement to their endowment. Frome gives us a clue as to how these much more anonymous establishments functioned. Sometime between 687 and 701 Aldhelm, then the

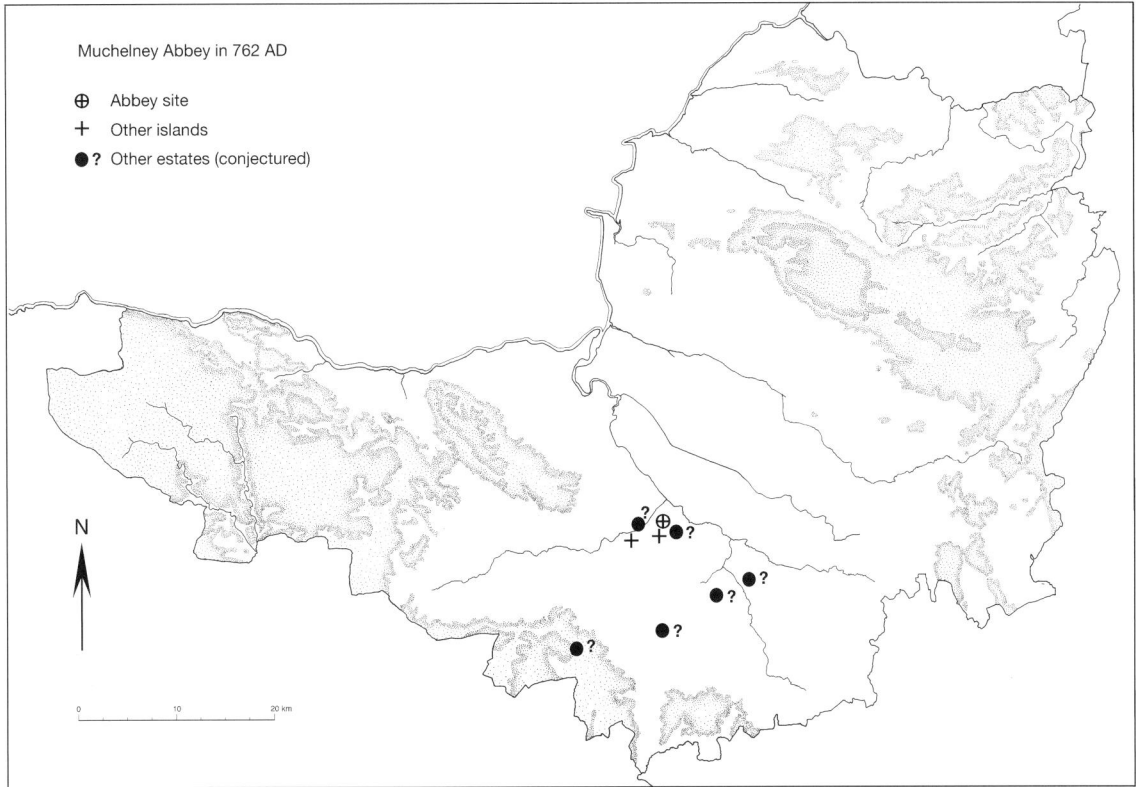

Figure 9.7 Muchelney and its early estates.

abbot of Malmesbury, obtained a papal privilege from Pope Sergius I, probably while he was on a visit to Rome. The privilege exists only in a late and reconstructed copy, but contains a grant to Aldhelm for the monasteries of St Peter and St Paul at Malmesbury, and of St John the Baptist by the river Frome (Edwards, 1988, 100–2). There seems little reason to doubt that he had founded a *monasterium,* possibly as a dependency of Malmesbury (Preest, 2002, 235–6; Winterbotom 2005, 105)). In 1086 the royal manor of Frome had 50 un-taxed ploughlands and the church of St John held an estate of 8 carucates (DB 1.8 and 16.1). Significantly, un-taxed lands, sometimes described in carucates, are a feature of the Domesday description of some ecclesiastical estates. Muchelney held four un-taxed carucates, as the nucleus of its lands. Other churches had lands which were hidated but had never been taxed. This

was true for Glastonbury, which had the 12 hides of Glastonbury itself (perhaps 6 originally) (DB 8.1), 2 hides at Andersey (DB 8.1), 20 ploughlands at Shapwick DB 8.5) and 20 at Pilton (DB 8.20) all of which had never paid tax. The other ecclesiastical establishment with un-taxed lands was Taunton, where the bishop had 20 un-taxed ploughlands (DB 2.1). It looks as if the early grants of estates were un-hidated, perhaps because they had come directly from the king and had been part of his un-hidated lands. The nucleus of each estate retained that status, since it was part of the inland of the monastery, while other land was probably already hidated when it was granted.

Taunton only became a possession of the Bishop of Winchester quite late in the Anglo-Saxon period. The claim that it was given by King Æthilheard in 737 (S254) is absolutely false. The charter is a late tenth century fabrication by the monks of Winchester (Edwards 1988, 138–40). The earliest authentic documentation for their claim would seem to be two charters of 904, issued by King Edward the Elder. They both concern a grant to the bishop of Winchester of privileges for the minster at Taunton. This seems to have been a commercial transaction since the bishop gave up property at Crowcombe, Compton Bishop, Banwell and Stoke near Shalbourne in Hampshire (S373 and S1286). As we have already seen in chapter one, Taunton was an early royal possession in an important strategic position. However, it was not mentioned in King Alfred's Will, despite its huge size and importance (Keynes and Lapidge 1983), so it had probably passed into Winchester's hands by the later ninth century. It may have been considered appropriate to grant the Taunton estate to Winchester because it included an important church with lands.

We have so far considered four prominent churches which have claims to some antiquity. Other minsters were probably founded during this same period. Aldhelm was credited with founding Bruton and this was possibly intended to be another house much like Frome. An abbot of high status, as Aldhelm was, could rule a number of houses, building up a network of followers and communities all owing him allegiance, much like the estates and followers of a great secular lord. Aldhelm became the first bishop of western Wessex, when the diocese of Winchester was divided, so that Somerset, Dorset and Devon formed a see based at Sherborne. Teresa Hall has summarised the arguments for Sherborne as an early Anglo-Saxon foundation close to a previous 'celtic' church of 'Lanprobus' (Hall 2005, 133–48). Aldhelm can be seen exercising power along the western side of Wiltshire and the eastern border of Somerset, through his string of foundations, and his activity provides a model for the dynamics of church foundation in the west of Wessex in the seventh and early eighth centuries.

There is an unspoken assumption that these minsters housed men and in many cases that was almost certainly true. We have no certain knowledge of whether any of the early minsters housed religious women. This could have been in double houses or in single sex institutions. In 744 a nun called Lulle

sold land at Baltonsborough to Glastonbury Abbey and placed some of her land at the disposal of King Athelbald of Mercia (S1410). Professor Barbara Yorke has suggested, very plausibly, that this nun came from and probably ruled a house somewhere close by (Yorke 1998, 160). The foundations by Aldhelm, at Bruton or Frome, might well be candidates. Both seem to have had Aldhelm as their first abbot, an office he continued to hold during his lifetime, together with control of Malmesbury and eventually his bishopric at Sherborne. Most of these minsters were in some sense family minsters, where the abbacy and probably other posts became the preserve of a single powerful family. This may well have happened at one of the minsters in eastern Somerset, with headship of the institution passing to a female member of the family as part of its inheritance customs. However, that is merely speculation and for the moment we cannot know where Lulle ruled.

Minster plantation

Other minsters have no named founders, but we can assume that the important decision to found a church, with all that implied, was not taken without consultation between king and bishop or king and abbot. Churches with a well documented history are easy enough to place as early examples. It is harder to make judgements about the possible early history of churches which have much more meagre evidence. Teresa Hall's important work on the minsters of Dorset examined their physical settings, categorising their attributes, and this approach is a useful starting point for looking at the possible Somerset minsters (Hall 2000). Appendix one is my table which lays out the names of a group of possible minsters and a set of scores based on a series of questions. The higher the score, the more securely we might view the likelihood of the antiquity of the church (Fig. 9.8).

The first of these questions concerns the land held by each church. Since the compilers of the Domesday Book were so meticulous about recording the extent of estates it seems likely that few churches with lands escaped their scrutiny. The lands held in 1086 were often a shadow of the lands held earlier and John Blair has shown that often the large estate around a church, held by a secular lord in 1066, was land

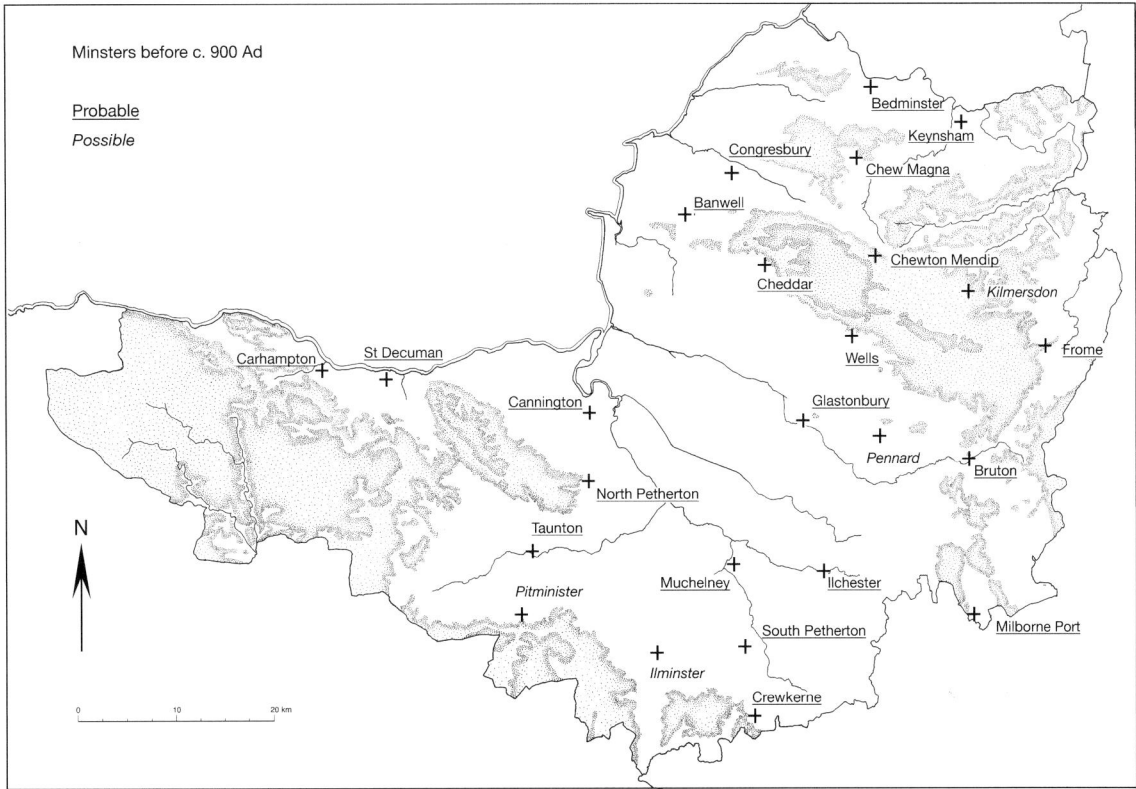

Figure 9.8. Minsters before AD 900.

which had been lost by the church at some earlier time. Congresbury illustrates the process very well. In 1066 the estate of 20 hides had been the property of King Harold, while the church of Congresbury held a half hide. The first certain mention we have of Congresbury comes from Asser's 'Life of King Alfred', where he relates that the king gave him the monasteries 'called Congresbury and Banwell in English' (Keynes and Lapidge 1983, 97). The 'Life' was written in 893 and the gift must therefore have taken place shortly before, perhaps in 886. It is assumed that Congresbury then went with the bishop when he was elevated to the see of Sherborne between 892 and 900. He died in 909 and after his death the old diocese 'West of the Wood' was divided into the three dioceses of Wells, Crediton and Sherborne (Stenton 1947, 433). The exact date of the division of the see is not entirely certain (see Chapter 10).

Congresbury may have gone to the new Bishop of Wells, along with other property in Somerset formerly held by Sherborne, but there are no charters extant for the land and no mention of Congresbury in documents from Wells in the tenth century (Armitage Robinson 1918). At some time in the tenth century, perhaps quite early, at Asser's death, the estate passed back into royal hands. Early in his reign King Edward the Elder (904) is supposed to have recovered Banwell, along with Compton Bishop with which it was always linked, from the bishop and clergy of the cathedral at Winchester. If this is a genuine transaction, it suggests that Asser's properties, Congresbury included, were dispersed at his death (see Sawyer 1968, no. 373 of 904). H. P. R. Finberg thought that the transaction actually recorded the point at which Taunton first passed to Winchester. Banwell and Compton Bishop were subsequently exchanged by King Edward for the estate at Carhampton, then held by the church of Cheddar, according to a lost charter (see H. P. R. Finberg, 1964b, 424 and 427). The implication must be that the land which we see in the Domesday Book as the estate at Congresbury was originally the land which supported the minster and that during the tenth century the land and minster together formed a royal estate.

The priest Dudoc, who became bishop of Wells in 1033, was given Congresbury by King Cnut before he became bishop (Armitage Robinson 1918, 53). He had been a clerk in the royal house and the gift of a monastery or minster church and its estate would have been a suitable reward for such a man. When he died in 1060 he left Congresbury and its lands to his cathedral but Archbishop Stigand and Earl Harold persuaded King Edward to annul Dudoc's will in 1061 and the estate and the minster came back into royal hands from whence it passed to Earl Harold. This was no doubt the intended aim of the manoeuvre (Barlow 1979). We can see how the church of Congresbury, with its lands, passed back and forth between lords. To begin with it was clearly regarded as something which might be granted by the king, Alfred, to a clerical favourite. The later gift of the church and its lands to the bishop Dudoc shows how a substantial independent minster might fall under the domination of a larger and more powerful institution. The last phase of its pre-Conquest history seems to show that eventually the church, with a small endowment, was passed to a cleric, Bishop Maurice (DB 1.21) while the rest of the land remained with the king. This arrangement was probably the result of Harold's intervention. Some other Somerset minsters may have followed a somewhat similar, though undocumented, trajectory.

St Bartholomew's, Crewkerne, on the other hand, held a 10 hide estate at Misterton in 1086 (Dunning, 1978, 28). The name of the settlement means 'minster tun', the minster's estate (Ekwall, 1960). It is impossible to tell if this was the original endowment of the church, or whether it was a grant of a substitute estate made when the Crewkerne estate, un-hidated, but having 40 ploughlands in 1086 (DB 1.20), was taken over by the crown, perhaps in the ninth century.

The grandest of all Somerset minsters was St Andrew at Wells. There is no certain proof of the antiquity of Wells as a minster site. The charter of AD 774 (S262), the first in the Wells Chartulary, was almost certainly a grant to Sherborne of land at Wellow, which was later amended to meet the needs of Wells in the tenth century after the minster had been elevated to the status of a bishop's seat and endowed with the Somerset possessions of Sherborne (Edwards 1988, 259–61). By the time of the Domesday Book the bishop and his cathedral held a large estate around Wells which later appeared as the parish of Wells Without, though with some peripheral losses, and this seems to have been the original endowment of the minster church, which survived the depredations of the ninth century largely because the minster was part of the possessions of the bishop at Sherborne.

Almost all the potential minsters are documented in the Domesday Book as churches. Only Chew Magna and Kilmersdon do not have churches named, though in some cases it is only the place-name which makes it clear that a church did exist. This is the case for Bedminster, Pitminster and Ilminster, respectively 'Beda's minster', 'Pipa's minster' and the 'minster by the River Isle' (Ekwall 1960). East Pennard was also named as *Pengeard mynster* (S236), though this is probably a tenth century charter and is certainly not seventh century as it purports to be (Abrams 1996, 126). That it is a blatant forgery does not invalidate a tenth century name for the estate, but it does preclude the idea that it was a minster in the seventh. Generally the churches with 'minster' names do not score highly in my table. We should perhaps regard them as late minsters, part of a second wave of foundations and not expect that they are earlier than the later eighth or even the ninth century.

Churchyard chapels are a less straightforward criterion. However, it is noticeable that many churches at the centre of large and important estates have churchyard chapels in the later Middle Ages. Of course it is impossible to connect these chapels with the pre-Conquest period, but it is possible that this is a remnant of the early medieval practice where several small churches might surround the main church, providing special functions for the associated community. Some of the later medieval chapels are chantries, but most are simply described as 'chapels' and in some cases as 'free chapels', emphasising their status as buildings with a major function of their own. Nine of the 25 considered had chapels. At Congresbury there was a chapel dedicated to St Michael standing in the churchyard (Weaver 1901, 23). This was probably a funerary chapel: St Michael was regarded as the guide of the souls of the dead. At South Petherton there was a free chapel dedicated to St John the Baptist, perhaps similar to the one recorded at Glastonbury and used as a baptistery (Green 1888, 8), while Bedminster had a churchyard chapel with an unknown dedication in 1548 (Green 1888, 92).

Archaeology at the various churches covers a wide range of evidence. At Glastonbury excavation has been ongoing for a century and has produced extensive plans of buildings (Rahtz 1993, 77). Just outside Ilchester the Church of St Andrew at Northover had a 3 hide estate in 1066. As we saw in an earlier chapter, there is a strong possibility that the post-Roman and early Anglo-Saxon trading site at Ilchester was close to the church, not in the town. The church stands on a low eminence close to the river and to the north-east of the town. Stretching south-west from the church to the river bank is an extra-mural cemetery of the Roman town. This was a relatively large burial ground, with an enclosure bank, which is estimated to have held at least 1500 graves. There were the foundations of two buildings and the burials spilled over outside the original fourth-century enclosure. The opinion of the excavators was that this was a Christian cemetery in use in the fifth century and they invited comparison with the cemetery at Poundbury, near Dorchester (Burrow, Minnitt and Murless 1983, 21–2). Dr Dunning has also suggested that the position of the church may have been influenced by the presence of the cemetery (Dunning 1975, 44–50). The positioning of this church is very similar to that of many European churches which stand in or beside Roman and post-Roman cemeteries. However, it is also always possible that the site was chosen as a non-flooding position close to the waterway and suitable for landing and loading goods once the town of Ilchester had ceased to function. Ilchester was not the hundred centre, which was at Somerton, the royal estate to the north.

Another source of archaeological data is the surviving monumental fragments, which have been art-historically dated (Cramp 2006, 135–90). Keynsham, a place that is almost silent before the Conquest, has several fragments of stonework, some of which are from the eighth century and other material of the very early ninth, tenth and eleventh centuries. A stone-built church was here from at least c. 800 at the latest and probably earlier. Wells, with no authentic documentary evidence from a date before the tenth century, has eighth and ninth century fragments of stonework.

Fifteen of the 25 possible minsters are close to significant bodies of water, either rivers or springs. The importance of 'holy' wells is well known across western Europe. The belief in the importance and sanctity of springs was widespread and still quite strong today. Britain has many such springs, often of dubious authenticity, and Somerset has many which probably do not pre-date the romantic movement of the later eighteenth and early nineteenth centuries. However, the siting of the church at Wells is closely related to its proximity to St Andrew's Well, which would have been a cult site in the pre-Christian period.

At Banwell the 'well' is a powerful spring close to the former monastic site and the present church. It was described in the late eighteenth century as 'a spring of excellent water formerly esteemed for its efficacy in scrophulous disorders. At a small distance it forms a large pond and turns a grist-mill below the church' (Collinson 1791, vol. 3, 568). The place takes its name from the spring, 'the spring that slays', Old English *bana* a killer or destroyer (Watts 2004). Margaret Gelling (Gelling and Cole 2000, 33) thought that it might be a reference to contamination of the water, but this seems rather unlikely, since the contamination would need to be more than temporary to produce a lasting place-name. The pool may have been used as a bath for the administration of the ordeal by water. St Decuman's church stands just above a spring called St Decuman's Well, which is ancient enough to be mentioned in the apocryphal medieval life of the saint (Horstman 1901, I, 263–5). At Crewkerne there is a series of springs just to the west of the church. Elsewhere, at Congresbury, Bruton, Taunton, Ilchester, Chew Magna and Cheddar, the churches all stand (or stood) close to a river and at Frome the water is close by at the bottom of the hillside on which the church stands.

Sometimes this river would have been navigable, as at Taunton and Ilchester, but that is not the case for Chew Magna, Cheddar or Frome, for example, so the connection with water is much more likely to be spiritual in intention.

Writing about Dorset minsters Teresa Hall draws attention to the topographical characteristics of these settlements as follows:

a.   a waterside settlement, often at the confluence or in a bend in the river; occasionally sited at a spring
b.   a central church within the rectilinear area
c.   east–west, north–south alignment of roads and boundaries over a large area up to about 300 m (e–w) by 400 m (n–s)
d.   the presence of a fixation line along what may have been the precinct enclosure
e.   the presence of suburbs and/or a market outside the rectilinear area (Hall 2000, 66).

We have already noted the presence of water. Rectilinear enclosures are more difficult to find, given modern development. The monastic sites and the cathedral obviously have enclosures, but these are in essence post-Norman and except at Glastonbury traces of any earlier enclosures have disappeared. However at Congresbury it was possible to reconstruct the likely area of the early enclosure which still survives on early maps and much of which is still visible today (Costen and Oakes 2003). At Crewkerne the outline of the ancient precinct may be preserved in the central part of the town. The current graveyard is clearly too small to have held the church, a chapel and a hermitage dedicated to St Edmund (Holmes 1899, 37) and it is likely that much of the graveyard was covered with domestic buildings after the Reformation. A market place outside the rectilinear area exists at both Congresbury and Crewkerne. At Milborne Port, it is possible that the *burh* was built inside the precinct of the church. The market place is again just outside the limits of the *burh*. Cannington still has part of the precinct wall from its later house of canonesses suggesting an enclosure with sides of about 200 m square.

Many minsters retained some corporate life into the mid-eleventh century and the new Norman owners were often uncomfortable with this arrangement (which may have involved married clergy) and founded houses of canons to replace them. At Bruton

a house of Augustinian Canons was founded in 1142 by William de Mohun (Currie and Dunning 1999, 18–42). This replaced an earlier arrangement which is undocumented. Here the church was reputed to have been founded by Aldhelm and there is no good reason to doubt this. William of Malmesbury claims that there were two churches here in the twelfth century, one of which, SS Peter and Paul, was the convent church and probably the original minster, while the other was dedicated to the Virgin and used by the town. This seems a very likely arrangement, so that the present church is the successor of the chapel mentioned by William, while the monastic church lies under the school playing fields (Preest 2002, 254). At Cannington the clerks of the Anglo-Saxon period were replaced by a house of Benedictine nuns c. 1138 (Dunning 1992, 76).

At Taunton the minster controlled by the Old Minster at Winchester was replaced by the bishop, Walter Gifford c. 1115, by a priory of Augustinian canons (Page 1911, 141–4). The bishop's estate as detailed in the Domesday Book was huge and it seems reasonable to assume that this was the estate the minster held when it passed to Winchester, perhaps late in the ninth century or early in the tenth. The bounds attached to the spurious charter S311 of 854 describe an enormous area around Taunton which was under the control of the Old Minster at Winchester in the years after the Norman Conquest. The bound probably dates to the time of the forgery and may be either tenth century or more probably eleventh. There is no reason to assume that it differed from the early estate in more than detail.

Both Crewkerne and St Decumans continued as collegiate churches for some time after the Conquest. The land at Misterton which belonged to Crewkerne Church in 1086 was given with the tithes of the whole Crewkerne parish to the abbey of St Stephen in Caen (Dugdale 1817–30, vi, 1070). In the later thirteenth century the living was divided into three parts, the Rector's, the Deacon's and the Sub-Deacon's and this may be a remnant of the pre-Conquest system (Dunning 1978). At Watchet the living of St Decumans had a dean and two chaplains in the mid-twelfth century (Bird 1907, i, 45), so that it was very similar to Crewkerne, though it had no land attached to it by 1086 (DB 1.6).

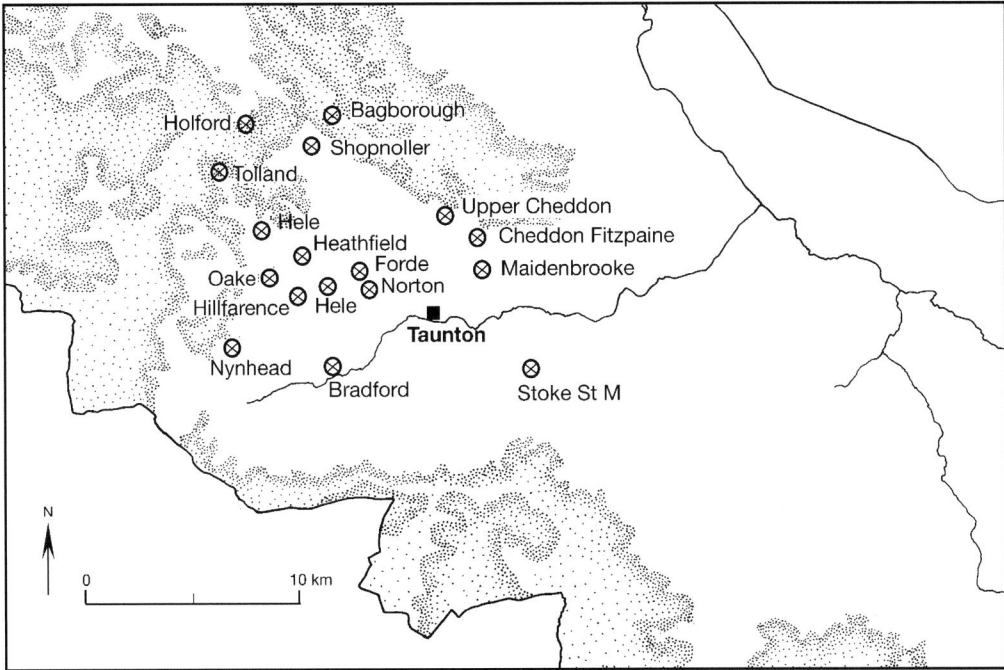

Figure 9.9. Parochial dependants of Taunton minster in 1066.

Minsters normally controlled a large parish, and of the 25 churches examined 20 had dependent churches or chapels in the post-Conquest period, perhaps reflecting remnants of that primitive system. In theory at least, each minster was surrounded by a very large area (often now referred to as its *parochia*), so that the boundaries of these jurisdictions touched one another, leaving the whole shire covered. Whether that was true in practice seems unlikely. Areas of extended woodland and upland moors were probably outside the system. This book is not the place to undertake a reconstruction of that system in its entirety, but the next chapter will look at the possible *parochia* of the Cheddar minster in the context of the foundation of local churches in the region. The minster *parochia* at Taunton is however, a good example, since its dependencies were enumerated in the Domesday Book survey (DB 2.1). Taunton held the right to collect Peter's Pence and Churchset from a long list of local estates of which the lords were obliged to be buried at Taunton, presumably as a recognition that Taunton had once buried all the people of the

surrounding estates. Sixteen vills were listed in this way, while Bagborough was not obliged to bury its lord at Taunton, but owed the dues and taxes. This was an obligation which covered a wide area, the ancient estate of the minster, and probably shows the extent of the primitive *parochia* also (Fig. 9.9).

A similar exercise for other minsters is not so easy, though the parish of St Cuthbert Without, with the addition of Westbury sub Mendip, Wookey and Dinder, probably shows the extent of the minster's *parochia* at the time it became the bishop's seat. At the time of the Reformation South Petherton still controlled the chapels at Lopen, Chillington, Dinnington and Seavington St Mary. Chillington was dedicated to St James. This was probably St James the Great and since his pilgrimage did not become popular in England until the twelfth century the chapel is unlikely to be earlier. Similarly, the dedication of Dinnington to St Nicholas indicates that the church was eleventh century or later, since St Nicholas did not become popular in England until after the translation of his relics to Bari and the dedication of the new church there by Pope Nicholas II in 1089 (Geary 1978, 98). It is unlikely that the primitive *parochia* failed to include Seavington St Michael but that church had become independent by 1285 at the latest (Cal Pap. 1, 481). Some of these chapels may have existed before 1066; in particular Seavington St Michael may have had a graveyard from an early time, unlike the other chapels, and hence the dedication from an early period, but the existence of the chapels before or after 1066 is not material. All the territory was included inside the ancient *parochia*.

The Crewkerne *parochia* has been documented by the Victoria County History (Dunning 1978). It covered at least the ancient parish of Crewkerne and also Misterton, Wayford and Seaborough, later in Dorset. The hundred of Crewkerne also included Hinton St George and Merriott, so it is possible that they too were originally included inside Crewkerne's *parochia*.

Nearly all the candidate minsters pass the 'hundred centre' test, 18 of the 25. There can be little doubt that minsters were generally founded at estate centres which were either royal estates, or were estates granted to the newly founded church by the king. Although he would lose control of the immediate revenues from such places, they were by no means totally lost to him. Communities such as Glastonbury might feel relatively independent with their charters, but for the smaller minster, with no obvious written proof of their entitlement to their lands, the king would have appeared as a dominant patron with rights over the church and its men which could not be gainsaid. He would expect their hospitality whenever he passed through a region. The church with its surrounding buildings constructed for the religious community would have provided the king with somewhere suitably large for his lodging and the surrounding estate would feed him and his entourage. The needs of the religious community, though it might not be very large, would also ensure that the estate was cultivated to produce a surplus which the king and his followers could eat when they passed through. It was perhaps only once the king's court became very large that he began to require purpose built accommodation and the palace complex at Cheddar, built alongside the minster church, is the only known example in Somerset (Rahtz 1979). As yet there is no evidence of any buildings which might be a king's hall at any

of the other hundred centres and so ecclesiastical buildings must have been the largest on the estate.

Lesser churches

We know little about the existence of other, lesser churches in the period before the tenth and eleventh centuries. It is possible that noblemen and churchmen founded chapels on their estates for the benefit of their men. St Aldhelm is reputed to have died in the wooden church he had had constructed at Doulting in 709 or 710 (Preest 2002, 260). As a probable outlying estate of the monastery at Frome, Doulting could well have been provided with a church by the abbot and the same may be true of many other places held by the religious.

Although Bedminster was royal property in 1066, the name suggests that it was originally a private foundation. Pitminster, also, has a personal name in its place-name. It seems likely that such churches might be founded by private individuals in the course of the eighth century. Bede, writing about his own day, talks of the scandal of 'minsters' founded in order to remove the public burdens normally borne by private property (Plummer 1896, 414–6). Secular individuals bought or were granted an estate from the king with the claimed intention of founding a 'minster', but then continued to enjoy the property as a secular estate, thus depriving the kingdom of land which might be available to support warriors for the king. Worse still in Bede's eyes was that the founders of these establishments recruited men to be monks in their minsters. Thus these were minsters with lay-abbots or indeed abbesses. Professor Blair has argued that the situation was more complicated than Bede's strictures suggest (Blair 2005, 100–6). In many cases the minsters thus founded were genuinely religious establishments and their lay abbots were following a practice which was becoming widespread in western Europe in the eighth century, of churches which were ruled by a lay-abbot who founded a dynasty of family rulers, passing on the minster to sons or daughters. Both Bedminster and Pitminster may have started as churches of this kind. Ilminster also, may be a similar minster, but one which failed to adopt the name of its founder and ended by being absorbed by its more powerful neighbour, Muchelney. Muchelney later produced a concocted charter to explain how it came to hold something for which it otherwise had no written authentication (S249). This must have happened before 995 when King Æthelraed confirmed the monastery in its possession of both Ilminster and West Camel (S884).

As part of the programme of Anglicisation of the Church in Somerset, everyone, Welsh or English, was to be buried at their respective minster. The lack of extensive early cemeteries beyond those found at the minsters suggests that this was generally the case. It has long been considered that churchyard burial was rare before the eighth century and that seems to be the case here, since the earliest burials were probably at the minsters at that time and burials in village churchyards followed much later (Morris 1983, 49–62). However, at Holcombe, near Frome, there is a stone, reused in the Romanesque doorway of the church, which bears a fragmentary inscription (Fig. 9.10). It has been suggested that the stone was reused from the nearby Roman villa and that it may have been a stone incorporated into a church and therefore perhaps carrying a dedicatory inscription. Another possibility is that this was part of an inscription from the post-Roman period, perhaps from a monument similar to the 'Caractacus' stone (Foster 1988). An alternative is that it was part of a grave marker (Cramp *et al.* 2006, 160–3). If that is the case then it is considered to be of the seventh to ninth centuries.

The inscription is too incomplete to be understood, but its existence raises two possibilities. The first is that there was a stone church on the site in the period after the coming of the Anglo-Saxons. This is possible, but unlikely if the church at Doulting, not far away, was wooden in the early eighth century. The alternative of a burial ground without a church, or with a wooden church seems more likely. Holcombe was probably a dependency of Frome, the nearest minster. We have seen that the minster at Taunton expected the lords of its dependent settlements to be buried at the mother church, leaving the rest of the villagers to be buried elsewhere. The implication is that they were buried in their own settlements, but it is not necessarily the case that they had churches with enclosed yards in which they might be interred. We do not know when the villagers around Taunton began to be buried in their own settlements. It may well have been an initial requirement that they should

all be carried to Taunton, but with an expanding population on a large tenth century estate this may have become impractical. At this point there may have been graveyards provided, perhaps at chapels already existing, with the proviso that the lord should be buried at Taunton to acknowledge the superior rights of the mother church. The burial rights of minster churches probably varied widely as new estate churches were established and some of their builders were powerful enough to demand the right for their new establishment. Holcombe may have gained this right quite early, while the churches around Taunton were more constrained by the powerful minster.

Clergy and laity

By the end of the ninth century the county was probably supplied with enough churches for most people in the well populated parts to be within 7 to 10 km of a minster and many may have had a chapel or church fairly close at hand somewhere within their own settlement. It is likely that many wooden churches underlie modern parish churches, but some may remain to be recognised in deserted settlements. To what extent the 'Christianity' of most people resulted in regular observance or extensive understanding of Christian tenets is impossible to tell. The bishop was at first the person expected to preach to the people, but his work was quickly supported by the ordination of priests. Bede writing about Northumbria in the early eighth century expected many priests and monks to be ignorant of Latin and therefore unable to read the Scriptures or other religious texts necessary for the performance of the divine offices, so their care of the faithful was probably quite variable in quality (Whitelock 1955, 737).

The Church had taken over and adapted many practices from the popular beliefs of their flock. The widespread belief in the sanctity and power of springs was deeply engrained in early Christianity, a result of the early adoption of the rite of Baptism for the faithful, following Biblical precedent. We have already seen how readily the Anglo-Saxon Church adapted itself to this view and placed churches beside rivers, or adopted springs, such as those at Watchet, Wells and Banwell, probably taking over pre-existing church sites. Holy wells were widespread and suggest informal practices which were only loosely connected

Figure 9.10 The partial inscription at Holcombe.

with official belief, while named wells, which are probably a sign of priestly control of a cult are rare. Dedications such as St Anthony (Bathford), St George (Brompton Regis) and St Leonard (Dunster), all saints associated with the later eleventh and twelfth centuries, suggest that the post-Norman Church moved to take over and regularise popular cults which probably conferred fertility on women and cattle, cured sick cows and put right children's squints. Elsewhere the place-name Hallatrow, 'holy tree' and the existence of a 'holy ash' in the bounds of Taunton (S311) are a reminder that traditional beliefs were not entirely driven out by Christianity and survived alongside the official cult throughout the whole period. King Alfred proclaimed that women who were in the habit of receiving wizards, sorcerers and magicians should not be suffered to live (Whitelock 1955, 373). The charter bounds for Bleadon have a reference to *wiccan stanas*, the 'wizard's stones' (S606 of 956).

Conclusions

The growth of the Church in Somerset between c. 410 and c. 900 was certainly not one of a smooth and continuous spread of Christianity, neither was it one with a sudden break and wrench from a 'Celtic' Church to an Anglo-Saxon 'Catholic' Church. The differences between the newly Christian Anglo-Saxons and their Old Welsh neighbours were political and social rather than religious and in the understanding and acceptance of Christianity the resident Old Welsh of Somerset must have been well in advance of the incomers. The early seventh century natives of Somerset had grown up with a church which was loosely organised probably around monastic churches with outlying hermitages and chapels. It was decentralised, much like the society within which it operated, and was probably not endowed with extensive estates. Together with their close allies, the bishops, the kings of Wessex set out to provide the church in Somerset with a structure which would reinforce the king's authority by linking places of religious significance with the king's own estates and would be well adapted to the deeply hierarchical nature of Wessex society in the seventh and early eighth centuries.

The new Church was perfectly prepared to accommodate the existing post-Roman churches where they were relevant, so that elements of the pattern of early settlement and their religious functions were preserved at places such as Wells, Glastonbury and Congresbury. That so many of these ancient sites were well sited and economically important was only to be expected and it was natural that the incomers should also be attracted to them. The pre-Anglo-Saxon landscape still shows through at the ecclesiastical level, strengthening the evidence for continuity provided by royal estates and trading patterns. However, the minsters were founded with due regard for the interests of the king and his followers. Thus minsters were also provided at the centres of royal estates, regardless of their antecedents. They were not planted from concern for the souls of the peasantry – had that been the case there would have been minsters in the north-east of Somerset besides Frome, and the far west, sparsely populated as it was, might have had more provision than Carhampton, on the coast. Rather they were placed at sites which made them economically viable or politically important.

Of course, once the pioneering work was done the system matured. Scattered among the king's minsters were churches which were the estate centres of properties belonging to the bishop at Sherborne. His diocese stretched through Dorset, Somerset and Devon, so that relative to the minsters his position was rather distant and it is likely that they pursued their spiritual and economic interests without much reference to him, except where necessary for religious purposes. We do not know how many subsidiary churches were built by churchmen and lords during the eighth and ninth centuries, though there is evidence for the development of some personal minsters. The elaboration of a network of rural churches was to be the work of the next century and a half.

Note

1. For discussion of the constitution of minster churches, especially in the seventh and eighth centuries, see A. Thacker, 'Monks, preaching and pastoral care in early Anglo-Saxon England', in J. Blair and R. Sharpe, eds *Pastoral Care Before the Parish*, Leicester, (LUP, 1992), S. Foot, 'Parochial ministry in early Anglo-Saxon England: the role of the monastic communities', in *Studies in Church History* XXVI (1989), 43–54, J. Blair *The Church in Anglo-Saxon Society*. Oxford, (OUP, 2005)

The Church Reformed

Introduction

The lessening in the severity of attacks by the Northmen and their steady assimilation into European society removed the outside pressure which had done so much to disrupt communities in the ninth century. On the continent the decline in the authority and power of the Carolingian monarchs led to a concomitant rise in the autonomy and activity of the regional rulers, the counts and the dukes, who were often forceful leaders and who oversaw the reorganisation of relations, along increasingly militarised paths, among their lesser nobility. Here among the English, the tenth century saw the widening of the power of the kings of Wessex until they exercised effective hegemony over most of lowland Britain, but again at the cost of a much more militarised society, re-organised socially and economically for the support of the warriors the king demanded.

It was not surprising that the Church took part in these changes, and that its renewal was such an early manifestation of the improving social and economic climate. For everyone in the tenth century the Church was the section of the community most closely associated with the transmission of society's normative beliefs and behaviour, offering order and stability in a changing world. Nominally it looked back to the golden age of early Christianity and to the culture of the late antique world of which it was the guardian. Any attempt at renewal would necessarily come through a return to early exemplars and since these were transmitted chiefly by monks it was a revival and dramatic expansion of monasticism,

particularly the monasticism of St Benedict, which began the process. In practice the reformers developed a new form of monasticism which took advantage of the expanding economy to rework its rituals and Rule on a much larger scale than anything seen before. Just like the growing aristocratic warrior class, the monks both stimulated the economy and diverted the surplus into their own specialised activities.

The monasteries

This chapter begins with the reform of the monasteries of Somerset, since they dominated the spiritual life of the county in the tenth and eleventh centuries and became enormously powerful as lords and landowners during the same period. During the course of the century the distinction between those minsters which housed men and women who had taken vows of chastity and obedience and came to live by a monastic Rule and those minsters which retained their secular clergy, often married, finally became clear. It was the houses of the Regulars which benefited from the generosity of the laity and the differences between the regular and secular clergy came to be marked by wide differences in the property they owned and incomes at their disposal. Between them, Glastonbury, Muchelney, Bath, Winchester and Athelney owned almost 24% of the county by 1066 and that seems a potent reason to treat the whole movement with the utmost seriousness.

The traditional view of the nature of the reforms has tended to see the monasticism in the shire prior to Dunstan's work as benighted and shrunken into decadence after a century or so of neglect and depredation (Knowles 1963, 32–3). Bishop Asser, writing in 893 stated that 'for many years past the desire for the monastic life had been totally lacking in that entire race (and a good many other peoples as well), even though quite a number of monasteries which had been built in that area still remain but do not maintain the rule of monastic life in a consistent way' (Keynes and Lapidge 1983, 103). King Alfred did, of course, work to reinstate learning, that is access to the written world of Latin learning, getting help from the continent and importing monks to set up his monastery at Athelney. However, William of Malmesbury, writing in the twelfth century, thought that Glastonbury had been without monks since the time of the Danish raids into the area in King Alfred's day (Preest 2002, 131). Whatever the situation was at Glastonbury in the first half of the tenth century it would be wrong to dismiss it as a totally failed or decayed institution. After all, it was able to offer the young Dunstan an education which was good enough to enable him to enter holy orders (Stubbs 1874, 7). There were evidently many other young men, some his relatives, also studying there, so it looks as if it provided a school for boys. Glastonbury had probably become a proprietary minster belonging to the royal house. It would be foolish to regard the catastrophes of the later ninth century as anything but serious for the minsters and for the church generally, but Somerset never suffered the collapse of church organization and episcopal oversight evident in eastern England. On the contrary, c. 909 the shire was invigorated by the establishment of the new bishopric of Wells, part of a reorganization by Edward the Elder, when Bishop Asser died. Devon and Cornwall, and Dorset each received their own bishops also (Stenton 1947, 433). This initiative is a timely reminder that the kings of Wessex never lost a sense of their responsibility for the governance of the Church. In this they were much like their contemporaries in mainland Europe, where church and monastic reform was frequently sponsored and supported by lay rulers (Wormald 1997, 25–6).

Everywhere in western Europe in the tenth century there were stirrings of change within the Church and they were felt even in Somerset. This urge to reform the Church and its life through the agency of the monasteries was manifested most famously in Burgundy where the monastery of Cluny, founded in 910, became the standard bearer for the new movement. At Cluny the Duke of Aquitaine was the lay patron who founded the new monastery and encouraged it to develop as an independent institution, free from interference by outside powers whether secular or episcopal. Through the example of Cluny, but normally also with the encouragement and support of powerful secular rulers, many other monasteries throughout Francia were reformed to follow the Rule of St Benedict as developed at Cluny. The monastic life became the highest form of the spiritual life open to the faithful during the tenth century and attracted the patronage of rulers and landed noblemen everywhere. By the 940s there were many houses in northern Francia which had been reformed or had been refounded and which were relatively accessible to Englishmen. Independently of the Cluniac movement, Gérard de Brogne had founded a monastery on his own lands near Namur and he was then invited in 941 by Count Arnulf of Flanders to reform St Peter's in Ghent and three years later St-Bertin (Wormald 1988, 25–6). Odo of Cluny pushed through the reform of Fleury c. 930 with the support of Count Hugh the Great (Verdon 1979, 50). Reform or renewal nearly always needed secular support if it was to succeed. King Athelstan was in regular communication with the courts of both the eastern and western parts of the Frankish empire as well as with the Count of Flanders. In 929 Bishop Cenwald of Worcester visited the monastery of St Gallen, apparently on a fact finding tour of German monasteries on behalf of the king, and both he and the king henceforth appeared in the Confraternity Book of the abbey (Bullough 1975, 21). Athelstan was widely viewed as an important and powerful ruler and he was well connected, both diplomatically and through family affiliations. He had married his half-sister, Eadgyth, to Otto the heir of the German emperor, Henry the Fowler, and later emperor himself. Later Eadgyth's sister Ælfgifu married Konrad of Burgundy and at the end of Athelstan's reign a third half-sister, Eadgifu, married Louis the Blind of Aquitaine (Sharp 2001, 86). All this was part of a campaign to counter the rising power of the Capetians and such extensive alliances attracted a stream of noblemen and scholars, some from as far away as Italy, who brought news of the development of the Reform movement and manuscripts to make up local deficiencies (Wood 1983, 250–72). Naturally enough the Reform in England was closely bound to the movement as it developed in Lotharingia, Flanders and the northern counties of Francia (Cubitt 1997). It must have been through this medium that Dunstan and his friend and fellow priest Æthelwold were fired to move at least to an interest in the monastic life and later towards a reform of the monasteries of Wessex.

Both young men had been consecrated as priests and also become 'monks', under the influence and at the hands of Bishop Ælfheah of Winchester, who was claimed to have been a relative and whose patronage was invaluable (Brooks 1992, 4). Interestingly, the author of Dunstan's *Vita*, known to us as 'B', thought that Dunstan had been initially reluctant to accept the calling as a monk because it would involve renouncing the possibility of marriage. He had presumably been thinking of a life as a married canon at a minster (Stubbs 1874, 13). He therefore made a radical choice by opting for celibacy which seems to have been the practical result of becoming a 'monk'. When he left the bishop's household the young Dunstan clearly needed a patron or protector, suggesting that he had no means of support for himself. As a younger son he evidently needed to make his own way in the world and Ælfheah had done his part by extending the young man's education. Dunstan went to the household of a noble lady, Æthelflæd, to whom he may have been distantly related, who lived close to Glastonbury Abbey (Stubbs 1874, 17). She had built a house '*in affinitate sacri templi ad plagam occidentalem*' – on the western side of the church. This might have been somewhere within the precinct of Glastonbury Abbey. Other noble ladies also played a part in his rise. A lady called Æthelwynn asked him to make a design for a stole which she intended to make (Stubbs 1874, 21) He clearly spent time with her also. It was probably through Æthelflæd's family connection with King Athelstan and the royal household that Dunstan entered the circle of nobility around the king. However, it was not until the reign of his successor, Eadmund, that Dunstan became an important member of the king's household (Brooks

1992, 10). It was Eadmund who made him Abbot of Glastonbury sometime round about 940. The story of the projected expulsion from the court during a stay at Cheddar (Stubbs 1874, 23) and the king's dramatic change of mind as a result of nearly riding over the edge of Cheddar Gorge, probably hides a series of intrigues at court, perhaps related to agitation for religious change by Dunstan. Dunstan was a man who made enemies, as his time at Eadwig's court was to show again, and a move to disgrace him suggests that he had antagonized people of influence.

The reforms which Dunstan introduced to his house were by no means as radical as reforms elsewhere. It does not seem to have involved the expulsion of clerks from the house and neither does the monasticism which he introduced seem to have been particularly 'strict'. 'B' chiefly remarks upon the education Dunstan offered, which produced a string of abbots and bishops (Stubbs 1874, 26). His friend Æthelwold had joined him at Glastonbury but eventually left and was given the derelict monastery of Abingdon which he rebuilt as a reformed institution, using monks from Glastonbury and sending one of them to Fleury to study the new Cluniac practices at first hand (Yorke 1988, 2). He was to become the major proponent of Benedictine reform in Wessex, first as abbot at Abingdon and then as Bishop of Winchester. He evidently did not find the reformed life of Glastonbury rigorous enough to satisfy him and his work at Abingdon probably produced a monastery more closely aligned to the practice of the Cluniac houses of Francia than to Glastonbury. It seems unlikely that the reform of other monasteries in Somerset was the direct result of Dunstan's activity. Nor is there much evidence that Dunstan was at the forefront of the Reform movement once he became Archbishop of Canterbury, though he was certainly not its opponent (Robertson 2006, 153–67). Glastonbury did of course participate in the movement towards a general uniformity of practice brought about by the adoption of the Regularis Concordia, a rule deeply influenced by the observances of Fleury, with which Oswald, Æthelwold and Dunstan had close ties.

Dunstan was driven into a brief exile soon after the accession of the young Eadwig in 955. Ostensibly the trigger for Dunstan's fall from royal favour was his action in retrieving the king who had strayed from his coronation feast into the arms of two loose (though very aristocratic) ladies, mother and daughter (Stubbs 1874, 32–3). Later, Eadwig married the younger woman, Ælfgifu, but presumably Dunstan had managed to cross her family which was descended from King Æthelred 1st and included her brother Æthelweard, later ealdorman of Devon, Dorset and Somerset. Dunstan's exile lasted about a year and he settled at St Peter's in Ghent at the invitation of Count Arnulf. Eadwig's reign was very short and his brother Edgar who succeeded him soon recalled Dunstan. Thereafter Dunstan's career was primarily at the English court and at Canterbury as Archbishop, but he maintained his interest in Glastonbury and remained abbot until at least 974 (Brooks 1992, 22). His patronage and protection was therefore of the greatest importance for the abbey and it is notable that it was to become one of the richest of all pre-Conquest monasteries. It is likely that it was able to build upon a long connection with the kings of Wessex and their great aristocracy. Glastonbury island itself was described by 'B' as the royal island (Stubbs 1874, 6–7) and Nicholas Brooks has suggested that the land around the monastery was in royal hands and only returned when Dunstan became abbot (Brooks 1992, 11). The presence of 'holy women', mostly aristocratic widows, at Glastonbury, and the burial of kings Eadmund and Edgar there, does suggest that the kings of the mid-tenth century regarded Glastonbury as their royal monastery and so its rise to wealth may not be too surprising.

The author of the first life of St Dunstan, 'B', was an Englishman who had himself known Glastonbury and knew Dunstan very well (Lapidge 1992, 247–9). Although the chronology is not at all clear, 'B' tells us that one of the things which Dunstan did was to rebuild his monastery (Stubbs 1874, 25). It certainly looks as if this was an early part of his endeavours and it was of course an important part of the Reform movement to construct appropriate buildings so that the Rule might be followed more closely. He rebuilt and extended the existing church, leaving the '*vetusta ecclesia*', to the east and adding a further chapel of St John the Baptist on the western side of the Old Church (Rahtz 1993, 77). He presumably intended this as a specialised baptistry. It was probably at this time, near the middle of the tenth century, that

Glastonbury was first provided with a substantial stone cloister to the south of the churches so that the monks could live the enclosed life normally required (Rahtz 1993, 91). As the monastery became an active landlord, with very large estates to administer, it seems reasonable to assume that the precinct also contained the extensive farm buildings, workshops and stores necessary to maintain a large agricultural enterprise.

Glastonbury's estates

What we know of Glastonbury's estates comes from three main sources. Firstly there are the charters in the cartulary of the Abbey (Watkin 1947–56). This was probably compiled c. 1343 (Davis 1958, 49–50). Secondly there is the extant contents list of the *Liber Terrarum*. This was an earlier cartulary of the monastery which has been lost, but which was compiled before c. 1129. Lastly there is the *Index Chartarum,* a series of mid-thirteenth century lists of charters. The last two have never been printed (Abrams 1996, 10–17). Neither the Chartulary, nor the *Liber* and *Index* lists can be taken at face value and they contain between them much contradictory material. The estate at Doulting, for example was listed in the *De antiquitate* of William of Malmesbury as a gift to the abbey by King Ine (Preests 2002, 260). However, the charter S247 of 705, does not name Doulting, but rather the river Duluting, now the Sheppey, so that there is no reference in this early source to the estate. In any case, it is unlikely that the abbey would have held Doulting at this date. St Aldhelm died in 709 or 710, in the church there which he had built a few years before. He would not have built a church on Glastonbury lands and it is much more likely that he built the church there because Doulting was part of the lands of the monastery he had founded at Frome. The history of the acquisition of Glastonbury's estates has been analysed in detail and with great skill by Dr Abrams (1996) and the figures which follow are based on material extracted from her work.

In the Domesday Survey we can see the size of the abbey's estates in 1066. They amounted to about 828 hides of land, spread across Somerset, Gloucestershire, Berkshire, Wiltshire, Dorset and Devon. Of that hidage some 445 hides were in Somerset. Most of the estates had come to the abbey during the tenth

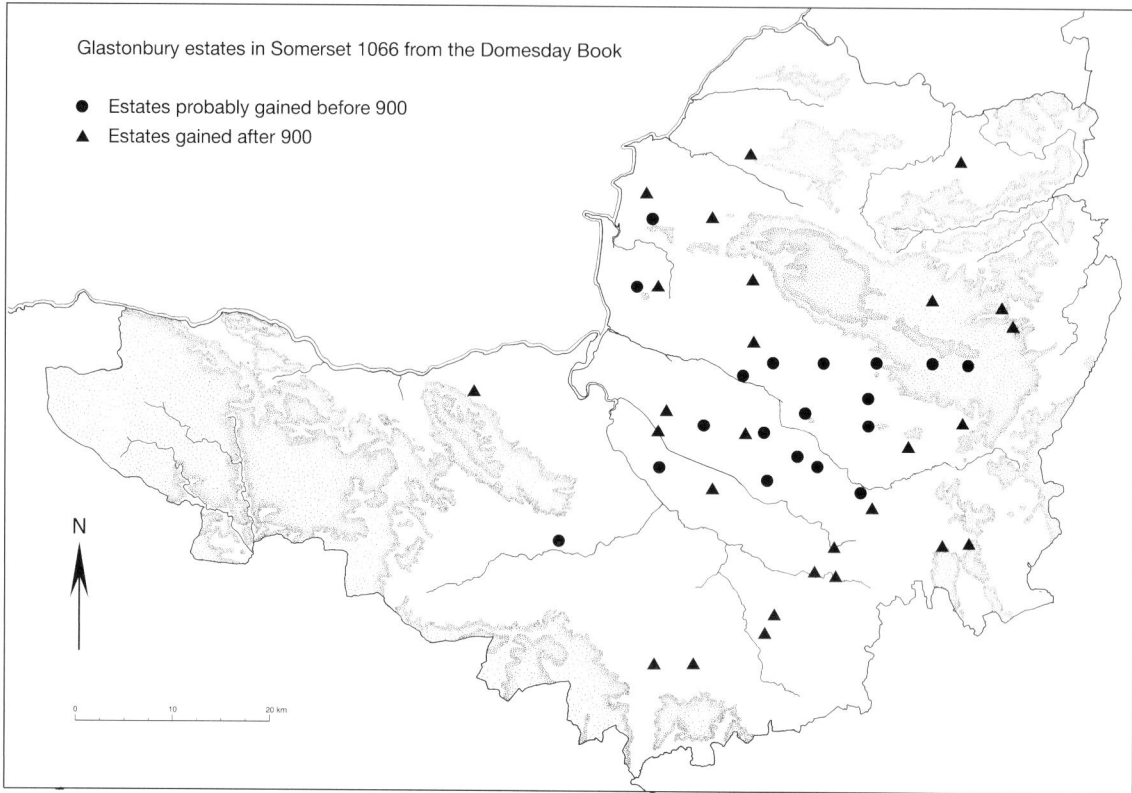

Figure 10.1. Glastonbury's Somerset estates in 1066.

century, after the Reform of the abbey, and were received as gifts from the laity. Both men and women hoped to gain grace for themselves and their families by a pious gift, often made through a will. Thus the ealdorman Ælfheah left a very long list of estates in his will, made between 968 and 971 (S1485). Amongst the bequests was one for Batcombe which he left to Ælfswyth his wife, for her life, with a reversion to Glastonbury Abbey. In the Glastonbury Chartulary is a charter for Batcombe, S462, by King Edmund, which is much earlier, 940, and which grants Batcombe to Ælfswyth, his faithful kinsman and minister. Ælfswyth is of course a woman's name and she is clearly the wife of ealdorman Ælfheah, who must have been named on the original grant as well. The sequence of events was probably that when Ælfswyth died, sometime after 971, the provisions of her husband's will were implemented and Batcombe

passed to Glastonbury. With the land went the charter, the proof of the abbey's entitlement to the land. This was then copied at some point, perhaps when it was inserted into the cartulary or even earlier, and Ælfheah's name was omitted from the copy. Glastonbury therefore received the land towards the end of the century and not in or soon after 940, as the charter might imply. This course of events can only be traced because the will was copied into the cartulary of the Old Minster at Winchester, which also received a bequest (BL Add. 15350, 95v–96r). Many other gifts were similarly the result of bequests and the charter recorded is often that which gave the land to the noblemen and women who subsequently passed it on to Glastonbury. This type of arrangement meant that grants made initially to private individuals often did not find their way to Glastonbury for many years after the issue of the charter. Of the 55 charters made for places which belonged to Glastonbury in 1066, 30 are to named laypeople. Some of the 55 grants are only known through the lists, which often do not specify the grantee, so that some of them also may be charters from laypeople. Direct grants from the king to the monastery were therefore a minority of the benefactions it received.

Similar circumstances existed at other institutions. The very influential Old and New Minsters at Winchester received numerous grants from the aristocracy in the tenth century. The will of Brihtric preserved in the records of the Old Minster (S1512), shows that not only did he leave his estate at Rimpton to the Old Minster, but he also mentioned the charters for the estate as included in the bequest and they also are recorded in the cartulary (S441 of 938 at BL Add. 15350 fo. 53rv and S571 of 956 at BL Add. 15350 fo. 52 rv). The transfers of property from the laity to the monasteries were astonishing. Between 900 and 1066 Glastonbury received at least 372 hides directly from lay benefactors. Some of the lay charters which were dated before 900 may well have come to the monastery in the course of the tenth century. That was almost certainly the case for Ditcheat, the charter for which was issued to Eanwulf in 842, but probably came to Glastonbury, with the land, through his descendants in the tenth century. The true tally of land obtained in the tenth century is almost certainly therefore higher than would appear at first sight, if it is recognised that the grant of the charter and the receipt of the land were events often separated by many years. The bulk of the grants were probably received by the monastery in the later part of the century.

Bearing in mind the examples already put forward regarding Glastonbury's exploitation of its estates, it seems reasonable to assume that the abbey was not a passive recipient of aristocratic largesse, but rather sought to expand its estate in a rational way where possible (see Fig. 10.1). The monks may have actively solicited particular grants, perhaps many years before the policy came to fruition. The estates on the Mendips, at Mells, Whatley, Stratton on the Fosse and around the edge of the high ground to the south of the Mendips, at Batcombe for example, were probably intended to extend the abbey's sheep flocks,

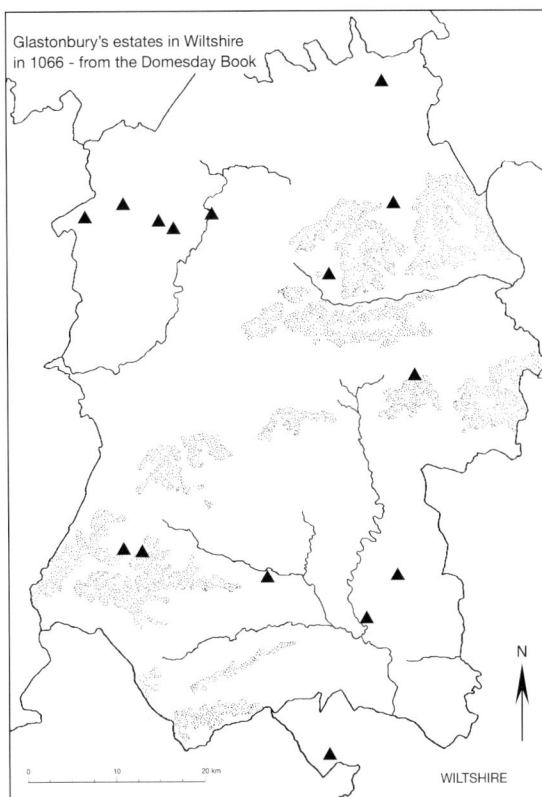

Figure 10.2. Glastonbury's lands in Wiltshire in 1066.

and Wrington and Winscombe may have served the same purpose. The smaller estates scattered along the southern part of the Fosse Way, south of Ilchester, were on fertile well drained soils and were heavily farmed as arable. They probably produced commercial crops to sell in the markets at Ilchester and Crewkerne, while the core estates, such as the land on the Poldens, provided the grain, livestock, timber and stone the abbey needed for immediate consumption. The Domesday detail of estates in Wiltshire, where the abbey became a substantial landowner in the course of the tenth century, shows the same mix of land exploited directly by the abbey and substantial areas of thegnland, enabling the monastery to maintain its following of armed retainers (Thorn and Thorn 1979, chap. 7) (Fig. 10.2).

Bath Abbey

The minster at Bath looked towards Mercia for most of its early existence. It was founded in the late seventh century and has a foundation charter which modern authorities regard as substantially genuine (Sims-Williams 1975, 29–30). The foundation was ascribed to the king of the Hwicce, Osric, in 675 (S51) and the grant he made was of 100 hides around Bath and was made to an abbess, Bertana. Her name indicates that she was Frankish and there is other evidence from charters to show that the Frankish influence at Bath in the seventh century was strong. It has been suggested that it was essentially a Frankish monastery staffed in part by Frankish nuns from the Paris area (Sims-Williams 1975, 6–7). The new minster was ruled by an abbess and therefore was a 'double' house, with both nuns and men, each within their own precinct. The charter states that the houses for men and for women should be separated, but clearly intended the abbess to be the ruler of the community. However, double minsters, which were a peculiarity of northern Frankish and English Churches, did not last very long. By the mid-eighth century a charter (S265) was addressed to an abbot and the house seems always to have been a house of men thereafter.

By the time of King Offa of Mercia the minster belonged to the Bishop of Worcester. He was forced to hand it over to the king along with much other property as part of the settlement of a dispute and the house became a minster under the direct control of the Mercian kings (S1257 of 781). This has been interpreted as part of a policy by Offa, both to control land for his family and in the case of Bath to provide the king with control of a strategic site (Edwards 1988, 226; Sims-Williams 1990, 161: Cubitt 1995, 226). It has been suggested that early Bath had been the centre of a Roman 'provincia' (Basset 1992, 26), but by the time of Offa, the estate which surrounded the minster consisted of 90 hides of land (presumably surrounding the monastery to the north of the Avon) and another 30 hides to the south of the river, which the bishop had bought from the West Saxon king Cynewulf (S1257). Thereafter Bath remained closely tied to the royal houses, first of Mercia and then of Wessex, as a proprietary minster.

Bath was not closely connected with any of the great monastic reformers. Instead, in 944 King Eadmund settled a group of monks from the monastery of St-Bertin, near St-Omer, in Flanders, who had been ejected from that monastery in the course of the reforms of Gérard de Brogne (Whitelock 1955, no. 26). As has been pointed out, if nothing else this shows that the king was far from blinkered about Reform and clearly thought that monasticism could take several forms (Dumville 1992, 176). Perhaps, like later secular patrons, he was more concerned with the quality of life displayed by a house than with its particular form of observance. It would not be too fanciful to imagine that such a group would want little to do with the reforms of Æthelwold, at least while members of the original group were still alive. Did Eadmund, or any of his advisers, know of the earlier close connections between the Bath minster and its continental counterparts (Sims-Williams 1990, 204–5)? It certainly suggests that the king did not see changes in the English Church as part of a systematic plan of reform along strict new lines.

On Whit-Sunday in 973 King Edgar's long delayed coronation took place in Bath abbey. Many abbots, abbesses, monks and nuns were present for the service and were entertained to a feast by the Queen after the ceremony (Knowles 1963, 52). Bath had received the young monk Ælfheah from Deerhurst and he became abbot of the monastery at the instigation of Dunstan. He was still abbot at the time of Edgar's coronation and remained there until appointed bishop of Winchester in 984 (Preest 2002, 112). It would seem unlikely that Bath would have been singled out as the setting for the coronation if the brothers at Bath had not yet adopted the provisions of the *Regularis Concordia* or failing that, were not living a regular communal life, so some changes had occurred during the 29 year period between the introduction of the Flemish monks and the coronation. No doubt Ælfheah, who went on to become first bishop of Winchester and then archbishop of Canterbury and of course died at the hands of the Danes in 1011, was a strong enough personality to reform his house (ASC 'E'). The relic list of the abbey, already alluded to in chapter eight, with its strong connections with Flanders, north-eastern Francia and Lotharingia, shows that contact between the exiled monks and their homeland had remained strong.

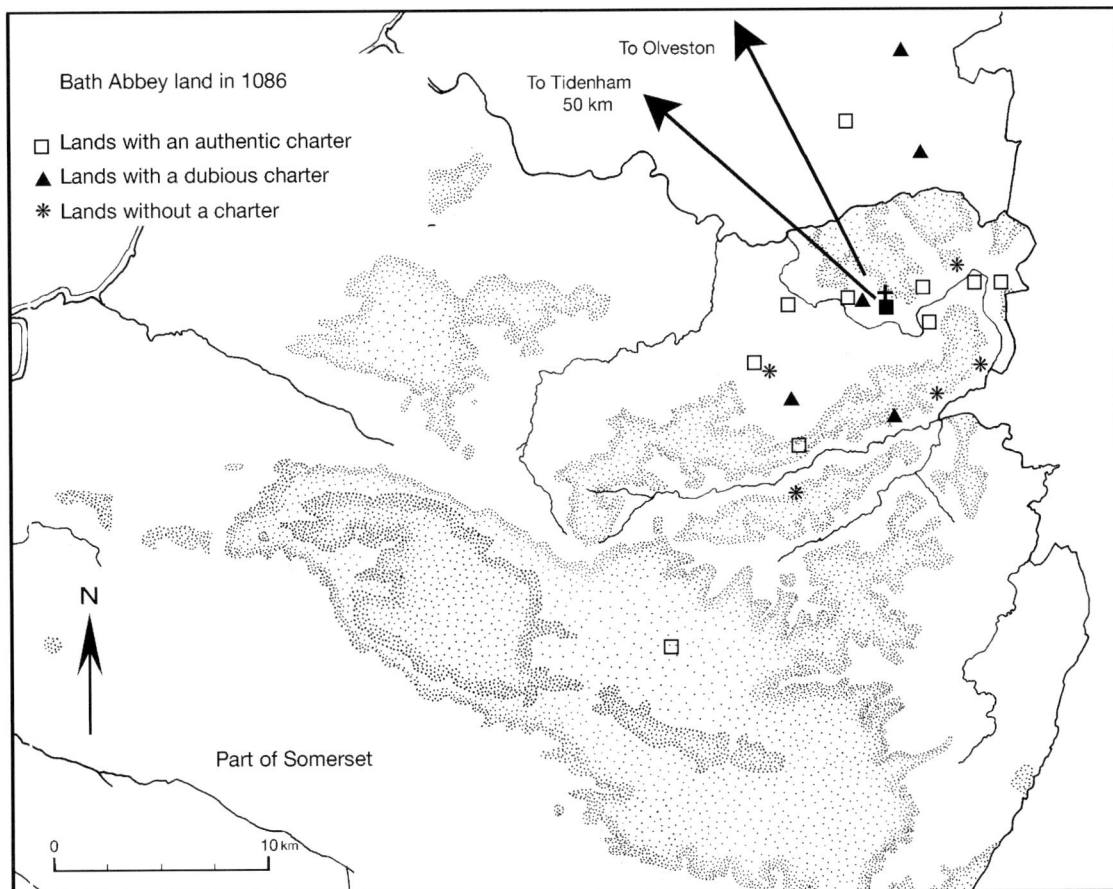

Figure 10.3. Bath Abbey estates in 1086.

The list of lands held by Bath at the time of the Domesday Book is quite small compared with that of Glastonbury and the cartulary is similarly briefer (Fig. 10.3). However, this does not mean that there are no problems in understanding the monastery's land holdings. While it is possible to make an estimate of the lands which Glastonbury may have held at the time of the reform it is much more difficult to do the same for Bath.

One result of the inclusion of Bath within Somerset was that many of the lands acquired by the abbey in the tenth century were south of the Avon. Dr Frank Thorn has demonstrated the distribution of the abbey's estates in 1086 and shown how their holdings dominated the hundred of Bath, with the settlements around the *burh* showing evidence in their place-names of being closely tied to it (Thorn 2005, 9–27). Thus the 'Stokes', North and South, were dependencies of Bath and both Weston and (Bath)easton were named from their relationship to the *burh* or to the minster. The settlement pattern has a distinctly ancient look to it and this suggests that there was very little opportunity for the division of lands and the granting of independent estates to thegns, with concomitant failure of the development of settlements with names of the 'personal-name plus tun' type discussed in earlier chapters.

The king would seem to have been the greatest landowner around Bath in the first half of the tenth century. At Bathampton (S627 of 956) a grant was made to Hehelm by the king and the land probably came to Bath Abbey through a death-bed gift or a will. Further south of Bath, land in Freshford (probably at the lost settlement of Woodwick) came to Bath through the will of Wulfwaru between 984 and 1016, though, it seems, without a charter (S1538). The rest of Bath's tenth century acquisitions came from the king. The monastery also had a substantial stake in the *burh* at Bath with 24 burgesses and a mill. Where Glastonbury was able to call upon the Somerset aristocracy for gifts of land during the revival, Bath was largely dependent upon royal patronage and it never developed the financial base which Glastonbury had. Its setting, within an important market town, was different also, although it did not dominate the town. The king had 64 burgesses and 'other men' 90 (DB 1.31) and it also paid geld as if it were a 20 hide rural estate. The town may have farmed this geld itself, so there is every reason to see the abbey as an important part of town life, but not its dominant feature.

Muchelney

As far as William of Malmesbury was concerned Muchelney had been founded by King Athelstan and he remarks on the difficulty of access, which he thought made devotion easier (Preest 2002, 133). Muchelney functioned as a religious establishment before St Dunstan's time, since King Athelstan's charter of 934–9 (S455) shows him granting land at Stowey, near Curry Rivel, to the abbey, though it did not hold it in 1066. In 964 King Edgar granted them the privilege of electing their own abbots (S729). It is probably significant that this privilege was only to be available to the monks after the death of the then bishop of Sherborne, Ælfwald. This strongly suggests that the bishop of Sherborne exercised a right to nominate the abbot of Muchelney. He was almost certainly exercising a traditional right which had belonged to the bishop before the creation of the new diocese after 909. The privilege must have been the result of a request from the monks and that desire to break free from the bishop's control may well mark the moment when the *familia* at Muchelney decided to adopt the Rule.

Not much can be said about Muchelney as a monastery before the Norman Conquest. Its kalendar

names a list of English and local saints. Edith of Wilton (translated 997) and Ælfheah, martyred in 1011, were west country regional saints who must have entered the kalendar soon after the beginning of the eleventh century. Æthelwine of Athelney could have been a much older cult and Edwold of Cerne, Egwin of Worcester, along with St Decuman and St Bridget, point to some continuity with the earlier Muchelney.

Muchelney had been a poor house before the tenth century and that relative poverty continued until the Norman Conquest. Apart from the four carucates at Muchelney the community held Ilminster, a 20 hide estate, Drayton, another 20 hides and West Camel, 10 hides. At Chipstable they held 2½ hides in 1086 which had been held by Ceolric in 1066, but he may well have been a tenant. The grant of Stowey had clearly come to nothing. Ilminster had been a source of contention and the abbey had a charter of King Ine dated 725, which was forged, with which to try to prove its ownership. However, the abbey owned Ilminster in 1066 and another charter of 995, issued by King Æthelræd, shows that the monks did own it and had recovered the estate after it had been leased for three lives to a layman. An attempt to convert the lease into an hereditary title had been thwarted and the king confirmed title both for Ilminster and for West Camel for which there was also no charter (S884). The charter makes it clear that West Camel had come to the monastery partly as a result of a purchase by Abbot Leofric, using money given him by King Æthelræd, and partly as the result of a donation by the ealdorman Æthelmaer. There seems not to have been a landbook and so the king's charter of confirmation provided security of title.

Athelney

Athelney claimed King Alfred as its founder. Bishop Asser, in his biography of King Alfred, tells us categorically that Alfred not only founded the abbey on land close to his fort at Athelney, but that he also staffed it with an abbot, John, who was an Old Saxon and with other clerics from abroad. He also reports that there was a young man of Viking origin in the community and that the king had imported or somehow acquired people (presumably slaves) from

Gaul whose children he ordered to be educated at the monastery and then enrolled as monks (Keynes and Lapidge 1983, 103). Asser also says that the king abundantly endowed the monasteries he had founded. It is possible that the king chose Athelney as the site for his monastery, not only because of its importance to him as a refuge during his most difficult time, but also because of the story of Æthelwine. His cult was undoubtedly important by the time of William of Malmesbury who reports on the saint (Preest 2002, 133) and the abbey had included him in its dedication by 1174–91 (Bates 1899, 135). The legend claimed him as the brother of King Cenwalh, (643–74), and the name 'Athelney' does mean 'the island of the prince'. He may have been a hermit using the island as others did, well before the monastery was founded, or the story may be a way of explaining the name.

The earliest charter directed to the monastery was S343. This was a grant of the 10 hide estate of Long Sutton, which the abbey still held in 1066 and which was its largest single holding. The charter cannot be genuine in its present form, but Professor Keynes has said 'there is every reason to believe that an authentic charter of the 870s, of standard 'West Saxon' type, lies not far behind it' (Keynes 1994b, 1134). Long Sutton had been part of the Somerton royal estate, and it was a natural grant to make to the king's new monastery which was not far away. A community still existed in the time of King Athelstan who made a grant of land close to the monastery at Lyng (S432 of 947). It may be that this grant, of a single hide, with relief from taxation which it still enjoyed in 1066, was of the land immediately around the monastery and may have been in its possession since its foundation. Also in King Athelstan's reign the abbey received a grant from a Cornish prince Count Maenchi at a place called 'Lanlovern', though they did not hold the land in the later middle-ages (Bates 1899, 156; Davies 1982, 260, n. 8). Thereafter the monastery attracted little patronage compared with other Somerset abbeys. By 1066 it held land at Ilton, for which it had no charter, at Seavington, at Hamp, at Long Sutton, at Lyng, at Bossington and at Ashill. It held 25 hides in all. Although Ilton may have been a gift or bequest from a layman there is nothing to suggest that the abbey attracted much interest from local thegns. Perhaps the early establishment of foreigners

had meant that the abbey had not integrated well into the local community. We know nothing of how or when the community adopted the Rule.

Two other monastic landowners in Somerset deserve some mention. The Old Minster at Winchester was the owner of the estate at Taunton with the minster at its centre. During the tenth century that landholding was extended by the addition of land at Pitminster, Bleadon and Rimpton. Over in the far eastern corner the nuns of Shaftesbury held an estate at Abbas Combe, but otherwise had no interest in the shire (DB 14.1).

Any impact the monasteries, and to a lesser extent the cathedral, had upon the spiritual life of the shire is now practically invisible to us. To contemporaries they probably stood out as the guardians of the relics of the saints. All across Europe the cult of the saints, always strong from the time of the later Roman Empire onwards, became a popular and unifying force. Custody of the bodies of the saints, always of importance to any church, became an increasingly important sign of its spiritual authority, to which even kings might defer (Abou-el-Haj 1997; Brown 1981). The saints were intermediaries between God and men and women and whoever controlled the saints controlled access to God Himself. In earlier times pilgrimage had been the almost exclusive preserve of clerics, but increasingly lay men and women were beginning to journey to the bodies of the saints, seeking spiritual comfort and remission of their sins. Monasteries and churches such as cathedrals therefore became increasingly interested in their own dead and in the possibility of gaining control of the relics of saints from other places. Tenth century Glastonbury, with its royal connections, chose to concentrate on saints with a 'Celtic' connection, perhaps because it was already anxious to emphasise its antiquity and thus its legitimacy as an institution. St Patrick the evangelist and patron of the Irish was of particular interest to the abbey, perhaps because the Irish connection through the chapel at Beckery was strong and predated the Reform, and they claimed to have his body. The abbey claimed that Patrick had been an early abbot of the monastery as part of their campaign to push the origins of their house back to the distant past of early Christianity (Scott 1981, 55). David Rollason has suggested that Glastonbury may have confused Patrick with Petroc and that may be the case, but it did not hinder the community in its drive to promote the saint and themselves (Rollason 1989, 204). They claimed the relics of St David, again citing an ancient connection, but may have gained such relics in the tenth century, possibly through the agency of King Edgar (Rollason, *op. cit.* 204). They also promoted the cult of other, quite obscure local saints. St Indracht was another supposedly Irish saint, martyred close to Glastonbury (Lapidge 1982, 179–212). He lay buried beneath a 'pyramid' on the north side of the high altar in the abbey Old Church of St Mary, complementing the supposed remains of St Patrick on the south side. He was supposedly martyred in the marshes of Somerset along with his followers, while returning from a pilgrimage to Rome. There is no evidence that his cult was of importance at Glastonbury in the tenth century, since he does not occur in the earliest kalendar of the monastery c. 970 (Wormald 1988), but first appears in a manuscript from Winchester copied in the second quarter of the eleventh century (Lapidge 1982, 184). Indracht was being cultivated in the later tenth or early eleventh centuries. Interestingly, Glastonbury never claimed the relics of any of the great biblical saints, as some continental churches did, but was keen to cultivate an interest in saints of the locality or of western Britain, as well as a connection with Ireland. Bath had a collection of relics which reflected its continental connections and was therefore much more international. The list contained relics of St Germanus of Auxerre, St Gertrude of Nivelle, St Wulfram of Sens, St Wulmar of Ghent and St Remigius of Reims (Hunt 1893, lxxv). It seems to have been less interested than Glastonbury in promoting itself as an ancient house with connections with a post-Roman past.

Between them these houses provided the opportunity for a considerable number of men (for Somerset had no houses for women that we know of) to enter the monastic life. Some of the monks were mature men, with important public lives behind them, who retired into a monastery. Athelstan 'Half-king', who gave land at Mells to Glastonbury, retired there in 957, towards the end of his life (S481). Most were the sons of the nobility of the region, for whom life as a monk offered security, prestige and the real promise of salvation. The web of connections between monks and local landowners integrated the monastic community into wider society and as we have seen in other chapters, the monastery, as one of the greatest landowners, also acquired its own very large group of retainers, many of them warriors, who gave the monastery a pre-eminent 'interest' in the shire. As both farmers themselves and as agricultural landlords, as lords with jurisdiction over hundreds of families, as lords of several hundred warriors and above all as the keepers of the relics of the saints in Somerset the monasteries outshone every one but the king himself.

The secular church

Writing in some detail about the church in Wessex in the tenth and eleventh centuries, P. H. Hase has described the way in which the older minster system began to change, in a direction which led eventually to the parish system which has survived until the present (Hase 1994, 62–69). Pressure from the laity upon the old system was probably the chief factor in bringing change. The social structure of Somerset was changing and the newly revived interest in religious practice which impelled the greater aristocracy to make grants to the reformed monasteries must have also affected laymen further down the social scale. Social pressures inside Anglo-Saxon society were particularly strong in the tenth and eleventh centuries since this was a period of such immense change. The thegns who appear in the tenth century as landowners needed to show that they were willing to integrate themselves into aristocratic society, even if their lordship was only over a small group of peasants. When men were establishing their position in a world where the old hierarchies were being challenged and new ones were emerging, involvement with the Church offered a signifier of status. Kings might patronise Glastonbury or Bath, the owner of a single manor might look to build a church on his estate to which his peasants might come and where he might exercise the role of patron and gain grace through his support of the altar he had endowed.

The Bishop of Wells and his see

As we have also seen, early in the tenth century, the shire became a diocese with the new bishop's seat at

Wells. Nicholas Brooks has pointed out that there is no direct evidence for the usual date, 909, as the date for the creation of the see. Asser, the bishop of Sherborne, did die in that year (ASC 'A', 908 for 909), but the see could have been erected at any time up to the death of the bishop Wearstan of Sherborne in 918 (Brooks 1988, 210–12 and Rumble 2001, 242). Dr Rodwell's excavations at the Cathedral allowed him to suggest that by the time the minster became the diocesan seat there was a church where the modern cloister stands and that it was part of an emerging group of buildings demonstrating the linear pattern so frequently found at major Anglo-Saxon church sites as chapels and other sacred buildings were constructed, standing one behind another (Rodwell 2001, vol. 1, 83–6). It is also linked to the church at the southern end of the town, now St Cuthbert's, which stands along the same axis as the minster group. Despite the likelihood that this was the church of a secular settlement, we cannot ignore the possibility that it was integrated into a liturgical pattern which extended well beyond the minster precinct.

In the post-Conquest period, by the later twelfth century, the canons were ignorant of the origins of their church and in the '*Historiola*' the writer put forward the view that the see of Wells had originally been sited at Congresbury and that it had existed continuously until transferred to Wells (Hunter 1840, 10) (Fig. 10.4). There is of course no truth in this idea, but it serves to show that Congresbury was clearly linked in the minds of the Chapter with the cathedral. It might also preserve some genuine tradition linked either to early 'Celtic' bishops or perhaps to a suffragan working on behalf of the bishop at Winchester in the early days and later for Sherborne.

Like Glastonbury Abbey, Wells was interested in the cult of the saints, but it had few of the advantages of its neighbour. It could not lay claim to a very ancient ancestry, but in its promotion of the cult of

Figure 10.4. The minster at Congresbury. The remains of part of the precinct show as two sides of a rectangle of ditches to the south and west of the church. The rest of the precinct has been covered by modern building in the foreground.

Figure 10.5. The bust of Christ from the shrine at Congresbury.

St Cyngar at Congresbury it indirectly linked itself to the post-Roman past (Costen and Oakes 2003). The shrine of the saint was probably built by Bishop Duduc, a protegé of King Cnut, and was important enough to have national recognition (Rollason 1978, 61–94). However, the shrine was not at Wells, but some 20 km away. It was sufficiently important to the bishop and his clergy for them to devote considerable resources to the construction of the shrine. The surviving fragments show a high degree of craftmanship and a knowledge of the best of local contemporary style. It was certainly not 'rustic' or provincial (Fig. 10.5). This makes the later remarks of Bishop Giso about the poverty and backwardness

of his cathedral and its chapter only a few years later quite remarkable. Perhaps his comparison with what he was used to at home in Lorraine coloured his outlook.

Closer to home, the church which was possibly built for the secular settlement at Wells (Rodwell 2001, vol. 1, 120–1), contained relics of St Cuthbert. The most likely source of the cult is the interest in St Cuthbert generated by Athelstan's campaigns in northern Britain from 927. In 934, on his expedition to Scotland, he presented a copy of the Gospels, probably written at Glastonbury, to the saint's shrine at Durham (Robinson 1919). The circumstances of the gift have been discussed by Luisella Simpson and she has demonstrated how the community at Chester-le-Street had an interest in the support of the rising power of the royal house of Wessex in Athelstan's time and how the king replied with devotion to the saint (Simpson 1989, 397–411). The king may have given the relic to the cathedral and from there it passed to the local church and this may have been the result of an intimate link between the minster and its outlier. The cathedral also remembered the saint in its kalendar in the later eleventh century (Wormald 1988, 102). This, though, was hardly the stuff of pilgrimages.

At the time of the division of the diocese the monastery at Sherborne and the bishop seated there held extensive lands in Dorset, Somerset and Devon. Land near Priddy, 'aput Menedip', Congresbury, Wellow, 'iuxta Pedridun', Chesterblade and Chard (Somerset) or Chardstock, in Devon, are all mentioned in the two fourteenth century lists from Sherborne (O'Donovan 1988, xxxvii–xlvii). These lands in Somerset, formerly held by Sherborne, seem to have passed to the new bishopric at Wells as its endowment. There are no charters extant for most of the land and it may be that none were ever made to authenticate grants which had been made initially to Sherborne, perhaps at the beginning of the eighth century (Robinson 1918). However, the estates recorded as belonging to the Bishop of Wells and to his chapter in 1066 were extensive and deserve examination. The bishop's lands were set out in the charter S1042 of 1065 and this document, which cannot be reconciled with the property detailed in the Domesday Book, has been accepted as a post-

Conquest forgery. Simon Keynes has suggested that too should be seen as part of the campaign by Bishop Giso to recover the estates which he believed the Church of St Andrew at Wells should rightly hold (Keynes 1997, 203–271) .

Wells itself has no authentic early evidence of its existence. It is named in the charter of 766 X 774, S262, but this is probably a later, tenth or eleventh century reworking of an earlier charter issued to Sherborne (Edwards 1988, 259–61; Levinson 1946, 242). Assuming that such a reworked charter dates from some time in the tenth century, it is clear that the dedication of the minster to St Andrew was already established by that time. If the Wells estate itself had originally belonged to Sherborne and probably came to it at the time of the creation of the diocese 'West of the Wood', it is likely that the minster was established early. It was at the centre of a very large estate, which was still a 50 hide unit in 1086 (DB 6.1). Westbury, a manor of 6 hides, abutted the estate of Wells on the west side and may once have formed part of it.

By 1066 there were other major estates scattered across the shire. Kingsbury Episcopi was a 20 hide estate in 1086 (DB 6.3), and was probably part of the ancient endowment, although it does not appear in early documentation at Sherborne (O'Donovan 1988, xxxix). It is only mentioned otherwise in the charter S1042, while the bounds only survive in the Chartulary of Muchelney Abbey, and are clearly late medieval in their form (Bates 1899, 99). Although only an 8 hide estate in 1086, Chard was a substantial property throughout the Middle Ages. Again this manor was probably part of the endowment of 909 (O'Donovan 1988, xxxix), as was Wiveliscombe, a manor of 15 hides. The 14 hide estate at Wellington also included the manor of West Buckland (DB 6.7) and not far away was the estate at Bishops Lydeard. The charter S380 of 899 X 909 is a grant by King Edward the Elder to Asser, bishop of Sherborne, in which the estates at Wellington, West Buckland and Bishops Lydeard were exchanged for the minster at Plympton in Devon. This does appear to be a charter which has a genuine basis, although the property does not appear in King Alfred's Will (Keynes and Lapidge 1983). The 20 hide estate at Evercreech held by the bishop in 1066 was almost certainly part of the ancient endowment, since there are no references

to it except in the charter S1042 and there is no sign that it ever passed into other hands before the Conquest. Chew Magna was a large estate of 30 hides, with land for 50 ploughs in 1066 (DB 6.3). It too is included in the charter S1042 and had probably been an endowment of the church at Wells from its foundation and a property of Sherborne before that (O'Donovan 1988, xxxix).

The endowment Wells received was therefore quite substantial. Some of the estates had probably been granted to Sherborne as soon as the bishopric was established under St Aldhelm and were lands granted from estates either seized from the Old Welsh by the West Saxon kings or built up by them in the first half century after the conquest of Somerset. They would have provided the bishop both with income and with property which he could visit during his travels around his vast diocese. The minster benefited from Asser's exchange of lands with the king in which he had received Wellington and Bishops Lydeard. However, as we have seen, the gift of Banwell and Congresbury which he had received from King Alfred did not last beyond his death and it is very unlikely that the estate passed to the new bishop of Wells after 909.

During the tenth century the bishop and the Head Minster at Wells failed to expand their estates. They were not favoured as part of the monastic reforms and there is no suggestion that they were interested in the kind of changes which had introduced monks to the Old Minster at Winchester and to Canterbury. It was not until the early eleventh century, with the introduction of foreign prelates by Cnut, that the new continental ideas about the reform of cathedral chapters and the introduction of colleges of canons began to take place. As noted earlier, the priest Dudoc, who became Bishop of Wells in 1033, was probably a Saxon or a Thuringian. His successor suggested that he left the diocese in poor shape, but he may have been a man who cared about his cathedral, for when he died in 1060 he tried to leave it vestments, relics, altar vases and books as well as his estate at Congresbury and Banwell. Earl Harold got his hands on the land and it was only after the Norman conquest that bishop Giso recovered the land and the church which went with it. This is a documented example of the way in which the lands of churches could be vulnerable to the pressures exerted by the politically powerful and also makes more comprehensible the enthusiasm with which later bishops embraced the Gregorian Reforms of the later eleventh century.

The last bishop of the Anglo-Saxon period was Giso, another Lotharingian and chaplain to Edward the Confessor. He was not at all impressed by the seat he had inherited, remarking that the church was very ordinary, that there were only four or five clerks and that there was no cloister or refectory (Hunter 1840, 16–17). He set to work to remedy this, evidently regarding the endowments of the church as insufficient to enable it to function as he wished and proceeded to solicit gifts of land from the king (Edward the Confessor) and from Queen Edith.

He gathered his canons together and made them live a communal life using the dormitory, refectory and cloister he had built for them. This would have enabled him to introduce a regular liturgical life in the cathedral and separate the cathedral staff from the episcopal household. He was also relentless in his pursuit of lands he thought had been lost to his cathedral and in seeking additions to the patrimony. The bishop certainly held a part of Wedmore in 1086 and the land had been the subject of a grant to Giso by Edward the Confessor (S1115 of 1061–6). This had been royal land, unhidated and untaxed prior to King Edward's gift, and although it had slipped from Giso's grasp after the Conquest it was restored between 1068 and 1083 by a writ of Queen Mathilda (Lib.Alb. I, 1, 66). Similarly Giso obtained land at Winsham, which he said was actually the property of Wells which had not been returned after a lease (Hunter 1840, 17), and at Yatton and Milverton, some of it from lay-landowners, some from royal gifts. It was the income from this property which enabled Giso to regulate his canons so that they lived a collegiate life and this in turn would have enabled the regular liturgy of the cathedral to be instituted. However, there is little to suggest that he changed the fundamental structures of his diocese. This remained a loose confederation of churches, the greater minsters needing the bishop only for his liturgical monopolies and the lesser ones dependent either upon minsters or upon lay-people who endowed and owned them.

Somerset Churches

During the time between the death of King Alfred and the death of King John, the parish system, remnants of which we still see today, was finally set up. It is therefore the important period for the establishment of the predecessors of many of the existing churches in Somerset. The first task is to try to establish what churches existed in Somerset by 1066. We may then be in a position to see how the pattern of foundations developed in the last century and a half of Anglo-Saxon Somerset (Fig. 10.6).

It is possible to divide the evidence for the existence of churches at particular sites into a number of groups, reflecting the quality of the evidence available (see Appendix 1 for details). The first group consists of minster churches at important centres, most of which have already been discussed in the previous chapter. They almost all have written evidence, either from before 1066, or from the Domesday Book. Keynsham is not mentioned in Domesday Book, or any other pre-Conquest written source. However, the impressive list of architectural and sculptural fragments from the eighth to the eleventh centuries listed in Professor Cramp's 'Corpus' make it obvious that a major church stood there throughout the Anglo-Saxon period (Cramp 2006, 164). St Decuman's church is not mentioned in the Domesday Book either, but can be inferred from the dedication. As we have already seen these are the major churches at important sites and the evidence is very strong.

The next group of churches are more disparate, but are nevertheless very important in beginning to fill the countryside with churches at settlements which were not of the first rank. Aller was the site of Guthrum's baptism in 878 (ASC, 'E' 878). It seems likely that the christening took place in a church. Guthrum's chrism loosening took place a week later at Wedmore. Again, this ceremony is likely to have taken place in a church. Some churches which were not minsters are mentioned in Domesday Book, so that evidence is strong. Some others have no written record, but have architectural or sculptural fragments surviving and found on site which make it clear that a church stood there, as at West Camel, where the carving on the remaining cross shaft is in such good condition that it cannot have stood outside (Cramp 2006,

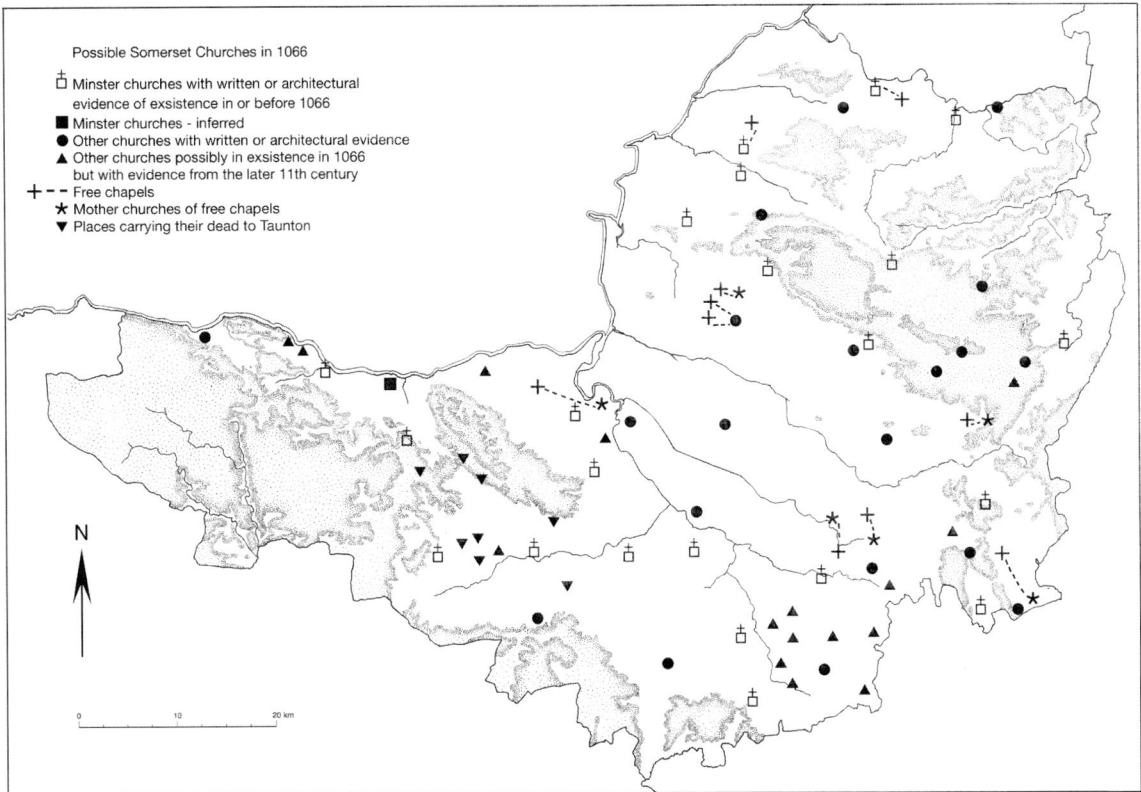

Figure 10.6. Probable and possible churches in Somerset in 1086.

178). Two other places have 'minster' place-names, Ilminster and Pitminster. These must be references to churches.

The next group consists of possible churches the existence of which can be inferred from post-Conquest documentation. Here we are on much less substantial ground and we cannot be certain that the churches were not built in the period between the Norman Conquest and the beginning of the twelfth century. Much of this evidence comes from the cartulary of Montacute Priory, which was founded in 1102 (Two Cartularies 1894, 119–20). The foundation charter lists a number of churches which were given to the new House. Their existence at the end of the eleventh century does not, of course, mean that they were *in situ* in 1066, but it seems at least possible that they were. Most of the grants were actually made by the military tenants of the count, who held the estates

named and who acted as witnesses to the charter (see EEA BandW, 106). Although they may all have set to building churches on their lands, it does seem more likely that most of the churches were there by 1066.

Next comes a category of church which may preserve traces of the organisation of the churches of the tenth century. These are the 'Free chapels'. These churches were recorded throughout the post-Conquest period and most had some mention at the time of the seizure and dissolution of chantries and chapels in 1548 (Green 1888). Others occur in medieval wills. The distinguishing feature of these churches was that, although they had no burial or baptismal rights, and for that reason were chapels, they did control their own tithes and the incumbent was normally a rector and not a chaplain appointed by the parish incumbent. They therefore had parishes of their own despite their lack of a graveyard. This was a feature of the 'field churches' of the tenth century mentioned in the Laws of Edgar in his 'Andover' code.

> And all payment of tithe is to be made to the old minster, to which the parish belongs, and it is to be rendered both from the thegn's demesne land and from the land of his tenants according as it is brought under the plough.
>
> If however, there is any thegn who has on his bookland a church with which there is a graveyard, he is to pay the third part of his own tithes into his church.
>
> If anyone has a church with which there is no graveyard, he is then to pay to his priest from the remaining nine parts what he chooses (Whitelock 1955, 395).

Edgar's simple hierarchy looks too neat to be true. The reality was probably much messier and very difficult to police. At Alston Sutton there was a free chapel at what looks to have been a planned settlement of the tenth or early eleventh centuries. The chapel, which in 1548 was described as 'utterly decayed' (Woodward 1982, 58), stood next to the manor house as a part of the settlement. It must cetainly be a foundation which predates the mid-twelfth century regularisation of parishes. No incumbent after that time would have allowed tithes to escape from his control, or grant a chapel 'free' status. It may well be that it represents the field-church of the thegn of the new development of Alston Sutton, taken out of lands formerly part of the settlement of Weare, which he was able to remove also from the grasp of the church, although he never got the burial rights. It is notable that the other manor also within Weare parish in 1066, Stone Allerton, never gained its own church or chapel (Whitelock 1955, 395).

The chapels included in the appendix are only those Free Chapels which stand within a manor defined in Domesday. Among the free chapels was that at Claverham, near Yatton. It was within Yatton parish and it was dedicated to St Swithun. This is an unusual dedication in Somerset, the only other ancient dedication being at Bathford. Swithun was translated in 971 and his cult became popular after that time. Claverham is unlikely to have received its dedication before the late tenth or early eleventh century. The existence of the free chapel would suppose that there was a superior church at hand, so churches may also have existed at the parish centre by 1066.

The final category are those manors which lay within the jurisdiction of the minster at Taunton. As we saw above, the Domesday entry for Taunton lists subsidiary manors whose lords were obliged to be buried at Taunton. The tenants of these manors were not so obliged and we must presume that they were buried closer to home, in their own churchyards. The churches shown are therefore those where a parish existed after 1066.

Not included in this discussion are the possible churches on monastic estates. The remains of the cross-shaft at West Camel show that there was a church there in the tenth century and the manor belonged to Muchelney Abbey. There is evidence for the existence of Doulting church from the early eighth century. This supposedly began as a church provided by St Aldhelm, since Doulting was then a possession of his monastery at Frome. This might lead us to suppose that many estates owned by monastic overlords, at least if they were kept in hand and not let to tenants, would have had a church by the eleventh century.

Finally, mention needs to be made of the one church in Somerset with a real claim to have surviving structural remains from the pre-Conquest period. At East Coker, the present parish church contains evidence of standing walling which indicates a substantial structure. This may well have been an estate church, the first with extant masonry to be recognised in Somerset (Gittos and Gittos 1992, 107–12). East Coker was the property of the Queen in 1066 (DB 1.23), but it was only part of the 'Coker' estate and was not separately described. It is likely that East and West Coker were already two separate estates, but this was not yet recognised for tax purposes. There is no indication of when the Cokers passed into crown hands, but they were not ancient demesne, although the Queen paid tax on only seven of the 15 hides. It may be that construction of a stone church was the result of royal ownership. The church is dedicated to St Michael, which underlines its burial rights and hence its status as a major church, but it may not have been the oldest church on the estate, since the church at West Coker is dedicated to St Martin, a rare dedication in Somerset and normally regarded as very early.

It must be understood that this is a reconstruction

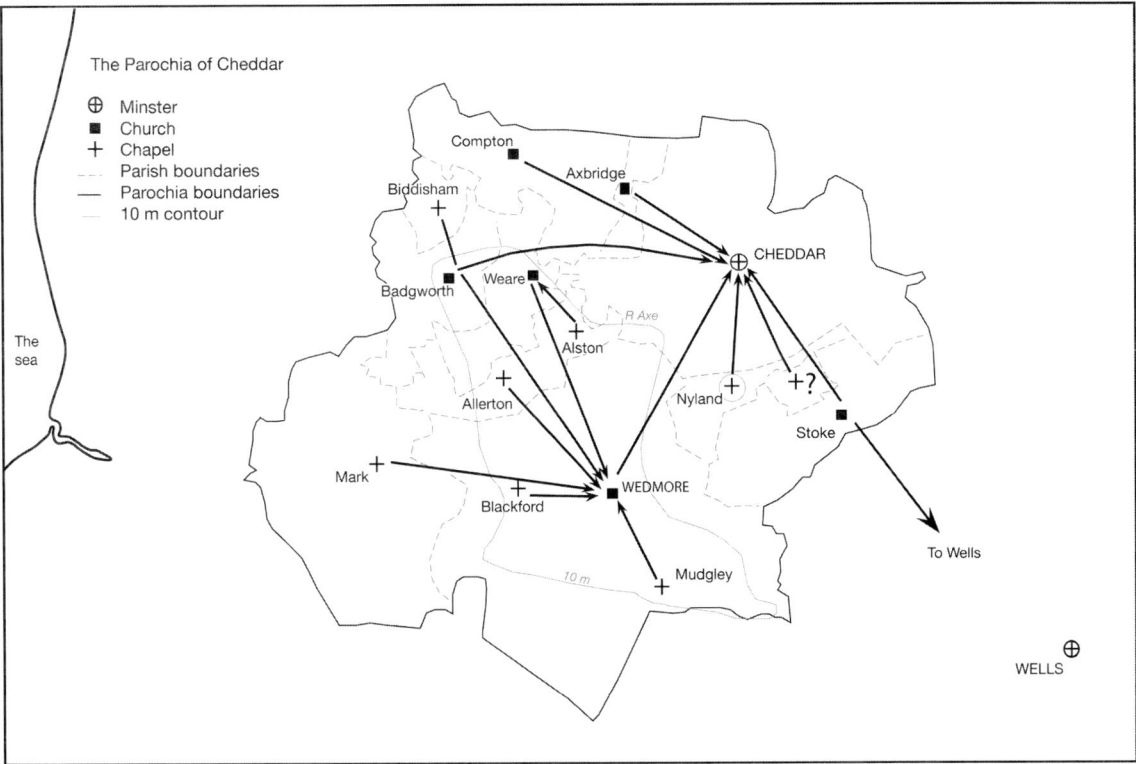

Figure 10.7. Reconstruction of the possible Cheddar Parochia.

which is tentative, since the evidence varies so much in quality. It is not, naturally, a description of church organisation in the eleventh century, but merely an attempt to show how widely churches had spread by the end of the Anglo-Saxon period. The map in Figure 10.6 shows many possible church sites in south-east Somerset, but this is merely a result of the many churches conjectured from the gifts of the Count of Mortain and his *fideles* to the newly founded priory of Montacute. If there is any approximation to reality here, it is likely that churches were as widespread throughout the populated areas.

There was, almost certainly, a very disparate pattern of organisation. The later apparent uniformity of parishes turns out on closer inspection to be nothing of the sort. Churches with dependent chapels were extremely common, for example, and in some cases this must be the result of a failure on the part of subordinate churches and chapels to break free

from mother churches. The ghost of the hierarchy described by Edgar continued to hover long into the post-Norman world.

The parochia of Cheddar

A hypothetical reconstruction of the *parochia* of Cheddar Minster may demonstrate how the spread of provision is likely to have developed (Fig. 10.7).

1. The minster church of St Andrew at Cheddar was certainly in existence in the later ninth century when King Alfred made his will, asking the community at Cheddar to choose his son (Edward the Elder) 'on the terms we have previously agreed' (Keynes and Lapidge 1983, 174). There has been a suggestion that Cheddar may have been a house which provided for women as well as men (Foot 2000, II, 59). The charter S608, a possibly spurious confirmation of the liberties of Taunton minster, mentions '*famulis*

famulabusque Domini . on Ceodre'. 'the male and female households of the Lord at Cheddar'. If this were genuine it would be the only example of female monastics in a community in Somerset, either before or after the Viking period. It may be that the scribe at Winchester who was compiling this probably fraudulent charter knew nothing about Cheddar and covered himself by including both sexes.

At this point it may be worthwhile to look at the dedication of the church 'St Andrew' and try to place it in context. It is sometimes assumed that the frequency of the dedication to Andrew in Somerset is a consquence of the dedication of the Cathedral church to him. While this may be true for some later churches, it is not necessarily true of many of the early and more important. Chew Magna with its church dedicated to St Andrew was part of the lands given to Wells, which had previously belonged to Sherborne. The later additions to the patrimony of Wells, at Banwell and Congresbury, long claimed by bishop and chapter, were indeed dedicated to St Andrew. The existence of four great church centres, on large estates, with the same patron, so close to one another certainly points to some co-ordination of dedication. There is every possibility that all four sites were possessions of the West Saxon kings before they became the property of Sherborne, since both Banwell and Congresbury belonged to King Alfred in the later ninth century (see above), and Wells and Chew were probably very early grants to Sherborne by the West Saxon kings or royal grants to the Bishop Aldhelm when the new diocese 'West of the Wood' was created in 706. The *St Andrew* examples therefore stand out as unusual and the roots of those dedications must lie in a period before the creation of the diocese. The monastery of Sherborne and its bishop seem not to have had dependent churches dedicated to Andrew outside Somerset. *St Peter, SS Peter and Paul, St Mary* and *St Matthew* were all dedications associated with Aldhelm (Levinson 1946, 259–6*),* who in any case seems not to have worked much in Somerset apart from along the eastern border (Preest 2002). He does not seem to have been associated with 'Andrew' dedications. It may be that instead we should look to the early West Saxon kings and their clerical advisers as major influences. Other major royal estates in Somerset also had churches

dedicated to *St Andrew.* These were at Curry Rivel, and at Old Cleeve, all places named as royal land in Domesday Book. A major church dedicated to *St Andrew* existed at Northover, just outside Ilchester, and in 1066 it belonged to Glastonbury Abbey. It has been suggested that it came to Glastonbury as a gift from the West Saxon kings and that it started as a part of the Somerton estate (Dunning 1974, 224–9). This church was the mother church for the estate, although it lay far from the estate centre. Dr Dunning has suggested that this church may have started as an extramural church for the Roman town of Ilchester, just outside which it stands, close to an extra-mural cemetery. Another candidate would be the church at Aller, where Guthrum famously took his oath to Alfred and received baptism. This site may have been chosen for the ceremony because it was a royal estate, although this was no longer the case by 1066. The church here is also dedicated to *St Andrew.* Finally, the early church at Shapwick, almost certainly pre-Conquest in origin, was also dedicated to *St Andrew.* Cheddar therefore joins this group and is probably best understood alongside the four church estates of Wells, Chew Magna, Congresbury and Banwell.

If these dedications do indeed have a common origin it must lie in the period before the creation of the see of Wells and indeed at the very beginning of the Anglo-Saxon rule in Somerset. St Andrew at Cheddar would therefore have a claim to be as old as St Andrew at Wells, and perhaps as distinguished in its ancestry, with a Roman villa lying close to the church and along with many other signs of Roman period occupation (HER 11141).

2. Stretched along the foot of the Mendips are a series of settlements, each with a church, which are probably daughters of Cheddar. Nyland, which formed part of the ancient parish of Nyland cum Batcombe, had a chapel of St Andrew, already referred to in the previous chapter. The Andrew dedication is probably an offshoot of the mother church at Cheddar.

3. Next is Draycott, a tiny manorial dependency of Cheddar in 1066 (DB 47.15). The church here is dedicated to St Peter, but nothing is known of its early history.

4. Finally, most distant along the foot of the Mendips is Rodney Stoke. This is the settlement on the periphery

of Cheddar. Beyond it lies Westbury, which was part of the Wells minster lands. Its 'stoke' name implies that it was a dependent settlement and the abstraction of Draycott, which belonged to Cheddar, from Stoke suggests that Stoke was a Cheddar dependency. The church was dedicated to St Bernard in c. 1200 (Bird 1907, 480). Since St Bernard was not canonised until 1174 it is likely that the church had not long been built and consecrated.

5. To the west of Cheddar, the *burh* of Axbridge has a church dedicated to St John Baptist. This cannot be older than the *burh* and thus must post-date the beginning of the tenth century.

6. Further west still is Compton Bishop. Compton Bishop is mentioned in 904, in the charter S373. There it is named alongside Banwell, but is probably originally part of the lands of Cheddar. The ridge along the top of Wavering Down forms a firm boundary between Banwell and Compton, while the boundary with Cheddar is less clearly defined. In the post-Conquest charter for Compton it has a typically late boundary, skirting Axbridge, while its bounds on the north and the west are formed from natural features, hill-ridges and streams, and are likely to be older. In 904 Compton belonged to the Old Minster at Winchester, along with Banwell, and was taken back by the king in exchange for a grant of privileges to Taunton minster. It remained with the king until 1068 when King William granted it to the Bishop Giso of Wells (Lib.Alb. II f. 246). The church has a medieval dedication to St Andrew (Weaver 1903, 270). This too could have been a dependency of Cheddar at an early date, but was transferred to Wells when the ownership of the estate changed.

7. Wedmore was also royal land in 1066 and was named as part of the Cheddar estate at that time (DB 1,.2). It was clearly also part of King Alfred's lands in 878 when Guthrum's chrism loosening took place there (ASC 'A' 878). Such a ceremony would have taken place in a church. Wedmore was probably, therefore, the eldest daughter of Cheddar. It certainly had its own burial ground and must have begun as the church for the Isle of Wedmore. It was dedicated to The Blessed Virgin.

8. Wedmore in its turn had a number of daughter churches. The earliest of these was probably Weare, at the northern end of the island, dedicated to St George, though now St Gregory (Cart Aug, 1150–93). It was suggested above that Alston Sutton free chapel was in origin a field church of the tenth century, dependent upon Weare for baptism and burial (Costen 1991, 51).

9. Alston Sutton was therefore a grand-daughter of Wedmore and a great-grand-daughter of Cheddar.

10. Wedmore had a string of chapels dependent upon it.

> 10a. Mark. This was described as a chapel of Wedmore in 1176 (Lib.Alb. I, 534) and as 'lately dedicated' in 1254 (Lib.Alb. I, 105).
> 10b. Mudgeley. A chapel of Wedmore in 1176 (Lib.Alb. I, 534).
> 10c. Blackford was a chapel of Wedmore in 1176 (Lib.Alb. I, 534) and a free chapel in 1548 (Woodward 1982, 52).
> 10d. Biddisham was a chapel of Wedmore in 1176 (Lib.Alb. I, 534).
> 10e. Chapel Allerton was a chapel of Wedmore in 1176 (Lib.Alb. I, 534).

11. The only remaining church on the Isle of Wedmore is Badgworth. Here the church was dedicated to St Cyngar. This church was not a dependency of Wedmore and the manor was the only member of the hundred of Winterstoke on the Isle of Wedmore, all the other manors being part of the Bempstone Hundred which had its meeting place in Chapel Allerton. Cheddar, however is also in the Winterstoke hundred, so it looks as if some lost event placed Badgworth with Cheddar, on the other side of the river Axe. The dedication of the church might therefore be a result of the later Wells interest in St Cyngar, through their connection with Congresbury, though since they did not regain possession of Congresbury until the reign of King John, the dedication may well be late and reflect a rebuilding of the church.

There can be no certainty about this reconstruction, but it may show how the pattern of churches developed over a long period. The dating is the most uncertain factor of all and there is no suggestion that all the churches and chapels pre-date the Norman Conquest. However, it is the structure or pattern which the early *parochia* provided which directed the course of church foundation over the tenth to twelfth centuries. Its division into the parishes existing in the Middle Ages and modern times broadly reflects the appearance of the smaller estates and manors as independent units, mostly before 1066. Thus those estates which were held by laymen in 1066 were those which gained their own parish churches, while the lands of the Cathedral on the Isle of Wedmore either remained chapels, as at Mudgeley and Blackford, or gained parochial status rather late, as in the case of Mark (probably in 1254).

Conclusions

We have seen that one reaction to the external pressures of the Northmen was the recruitment of more soldiers and the more thorough militarisation of late Anglo-Saxon society as the kings of the English sought to protect their domains against outside attack. The kings of Wessex also used that military might to become lords of most of the English speaking parts of Britain. It was also a time of great social and economic turmoil as the the economy moved towards a substantial degree of monetisation. In the countryside important changes were affecting the lives and status of the mass of the people and the warrior-landowners were becoming a fixed part of the rural landscape. It was not surprisng therefore that men and women at all levels of English society looked to a renewal of their religious and spiritual lives. As the century advanced and the bad old days of Viking incursions were put behind them, England became increasingly wealthy and had money to spend on what almost everyone amongst the aristocracy regarded as important, the building of churches.

Intellectual currents from the continent were enormously important in providing the impetus for the renewal, which first affected the monastics. It was at the courts of kings such as Athelstan and Edgar that the new ideas about monasticism were first propounded and as we have seen the reform in Somerset was the result of the ideas enthusiastically taken up by Dunstan and Æthelwold and supported by influential and powerful laymen and women. The kings of the English were generally wholehearted in their support for the movement and they and their

aristocracy used the new surpluses of wealth they had accumulated to invest in their own and the nation's spiritual welfare through the donation of land. This transfer of wealth made it possible to create a new sort of monasticism which needed substantial capital and continuing revenues to support a system of life devoted almost exclusively to prayer and study and in which many members of the ruling class were engaged. As a result in Somerset one monastery, graced with great patronage, acquired a huge estate, one which did not substantially increase during the rest of its existence. Between them Glastonbury, Bath, Muchelney and Athelney represented a new sort of landlord. Even more than the great crown estates, which came and went as kings donated, sold or acquired lands, these estates tended to stay together and were worked together according to a policy which made use of the strengths of each unit. They were well positioned to adopt new ways of organising their estates to increase their incomes and so were progressive landlords who helped to drive forward the agricultural and social changes which made the Somerset landscape within which we still live today. Since the abbey could not go to its estates as kings and ealdormen did, it had to adopt an integrating policy which made the abbey the central collecting point for goods and services, but also made it happy to collect cash where lands were distant. It was this new view of the lands of the monasteries which made it possible in later times for abbeys to embark on long-term projects, such as drainage of marshes and diversion of rivers. They were permanent landlords with centuries in view.

As lords the monasteries were bound up in the politics of their county and of the country. Through the substantial numbers of retainers to whom they had granted estates for service they controlled a large body of thegns who were readily available to the king, providing him with a useful counterbalance to the strength of his great noble followers.

Less tangible for us is the way in which the abbeys offered a new spiritual life for many men, not always young, from the burgeoning aristocracy. As they entered the religious life they made it possible for their lay relatives to take part vicariously in the life of the community and bound them into its spiritual world. We should not ignore this as a 'civilising' influence upon a violent world. In Somerset at least that path was not open to women. The nearest houses for women in Wessex were at Shaftesbury in Dorset and at Wilton. As elsewhere in Europe the new monasteries provided a new ideal of the 'city of God' and also provided the major avenue for the production and transmission of learning, as well as being the major patron for art and architecture, with probably the largest collection of stone buildings anywhere in the region.

Where the laity held much more sway was in the development of the secular church, which provided them with most of their daily religious experiences. Again the growing wealth and numbers of the landlords made it possible for them to begin to take to themselves control of their own religious lives by building churches on their estates. Substantially unregulated, this led to a major expansion of church ownership by the laity and from there to an appropriation of the tithes of the lands and people on their own estates. We can see the reverse process at work as the later Norman aristocracy, touched by the fear of the consequences of the ownership of church property, began to donate both tithes and the churches they owned to monasteries and cathedrals from the late eleventh century onward. The scale of those gifts over the next two centuries is testament to the size of the take-over of the secular church by the laity of the tenth and early eleventh centuries.

Appendix

Somerset Churches in 1066. They are listed in descending order of evidential strength.

1. Minster Churches with written or architectural evidence of existence in or before 1066

Banwell (Keynes and Lapidge 1983, 97; Cramp 2006, 135)
Bedminster name (DB 1.7)
Bruton, St Aldhelm (Preest 2002, 254)
Cannington (DB 16.3)
Carhampton (DB 16.6)
Cheddar, King Alfred's Will (Keynes and Lapidge 1983, 175)
Chewton Mendip (DB 1.29)
Congresbury (Keynes and Lapidge 1983, 97; DB 21.1; Cramp 2006, 149)
Crewkerne (DB 12.1)
Curry Rivel (DB 16.11)
Frome (Preest, 2002, 235–6; Winterbottom 2005, 105; DB 16.1; Cramp 2006, 152)
Keynsham (Cramp 2006, 164)
Milborne Port (DB 1.10)
Milverton (DB 16.4)
North Curry (DB 1.19)
Northover (DB 15.1)
Petherton N. (DB 16.7)
Petherton S. (DB 16.5)

Stogumber (DB 16.2)
Taunton (DB 2.1)
Wells (DB 6.1)
Yatton (DB 6.14)

Minster churches inferred
St Decuman, from the dedication

Other churches with architectural or written evidence for existence in 1066

Aller, site of Guthrum's baptism (ASC, 878)
Doulting (Preest 2002, 260)
East Coker (Gittos, B and M 1991, 107–11)
East Pennard, place-name (S 563)
Henstridge (Cramp 2006, 159)
Holcombe (Cramp 2006, 160)
Ilminster, place-name
Kelston (Cramp 2006, 163)
Kilmersdon (DB 16.14)
Long Ashton (DB 5.34)
Maperton (Cramp 2006, 171)
Nunney (Cramp 2006, 173)
Pignes (DB 46.7)
Pitminster, place-name

Porlock (Cramp 2006, 174)

Rowberrow (Cramp 2006, 175)

Shapwick (Costen 1989, 77–9)

Wedmore, Guthrum's Chrism loosening (ASC, 878)

West Camel (Cramp 2006, 178)

Wells, St Cuthbert. Possible relic of St Cuthbert. See Chapter 10 above.

Possible churches in 1066, but with evidence from the later 11th century

Bridgwater Church. Given to Bath Abbey c. 1086. See Egerton 3316 for gift of Bridgwater church by Walter of Douai to Bath Abbey.

Chiselborough. Half tithes given to Montacute Priory by Count of Mortain 1091–1106 (Montacute Chartulary, p. 119).

Cloford. Half tithes given to Montacute Priory by Count of Mortain 1091–1106 (Montacute Chartulary, p. 119).

Closworth. Church of All Saints given to Montacute Priory by Count of Mortain 1091–1106 (Montacute Chartulary, p. 119).

Dunster. St George, Church and tithes given to Bath Priory 1086–1100 (Hunt 1893, 38)

East Chinnock. Church given to Montacute Priory by Count of Mortain 1091–1106 (Montacute Chartulary, p. 119).

Houndstone. Church given to Montacute Priory by Count of Mortain 1091–1106 (Montacute Chartulary, 119).

Kilton. Church of St Nicholas, Wm de Mohun gave tithes to Bath Priory 1090–1100 (Hunt 1893, 38).

Marston Magna. Tithes of the demesne given to Montacute Priory by Count of Mortain 1091–1106 (Montacute Chartulary, p. 119).

Martock. Probably given by Wm Ist before 1086. Owned by Mont St Michel by 1156, but was restored to them in that year by the Bishop of Winchester (VCH)

Meare. St Benignus recorded as translated from there to Glastonbury Abbey in 1091 (Scott 1983, 63).

Minehead. Half the tithes given to Bath Abbey 1086–1100.

Montacute. Church of St Peter; given to Montacute Priory by Count of Mortain 1091–1106 (Montacute Chartulary, p. 119). Suggestion that Glaston had founded a church here by 854. See VCH III p. 220

and Stubbs, *Foundation of Waltham Abbey*, 4. The church of St Peter was the monastic church. The chapel of St Catherine in the monks graveyard between 1174–80 eventually became the parish church.

Mudford. Church given to Montacute Priory by Count of Mortain 1091–1106 (Montacute Chartulary, p. 119) Though actually given by William of Mudford, a follower of the Count of Mortain, see EEA BandW p. 106.

Norton Fitzwarren. Half the tithes given to Montacute Priory by Count of Mortain 1091–1106 (Montacute Chartulary, p. 119).

Tintinhull. Church of St Margaret given to Montacute Priory by Count of Mortain 1091–1106 (Montacute Chartulary, p. 119).

Yarlington. Church given to Montacute Priory by Count of Mortain 1091–1106 (Montacute Chartulary, p. 119).

Free chapels and the churches to which they carried their dead. Only those where the manor appears in Domesday Book are included.

Allerton (Wedmore)

Alston Sutton (Weare)

Blackford (Wedmore)

Foddington (Babcary)

Forde (Bawdrip)

Idstock (Chilton Trinity)

Knowle (Bedminster)

Lytes Cary (Charlton Adam)

South Cheriton (Henstridge)

Spargrove (Batcombe)

Claverham (Yatton)

Places named as carrying their lords to Taunton for burial (DB 2.1). Only those with a later parish church are included.

Tolland

Oake

Holford

Cheddon Fitzpaine

Hillfarence

Heathfield

Stoke St Mary

Bagborough

11

Conclusions

A theme or thread which can be traced throughout this study is the way in which the elite in these two societies, first the post-Roman Somerset of the fifth and sixth centuries and then the new grouping created by absorption into Anglo-Saxon Wessex from the mid-seventh century onwards, organised the world around them to best enable them to maintain themselves both within Somerset and against their external enemies. Of course there is nothing novel about such an idea, but in a larger and more sophisticated society such action is more difficult to track. In a small and really quite simple rural society like Somerset and in a situation where the information we have is relatively limited it is easier to discern.

Status

The withdrawal of Roman administration at the beginning of the fifth century was the signal for a major restructuring of a society which had lost its medium of exchange and which initially needed to respond to a severe contraction in the economy. The decline of the small urban settlements, Ilchester, Camerton and above all Bath, which probably provided market and local administrative services, and the relative impoverishment of the local rural elite shown by the decay or debased occupation of their Romanised 'villa' dwellings, probably drove the survivors into creating a truncated version of the late Roman system of governance they had known. Local self-government was, after all, a strong tradition everywhere in the later Roman Empire. Distances were too great for the minutiae of everyday life to

be directed from afar and the local decurions must have had considerable autonomy in their day to day activities. This may have made it relatively easy to adapt existing systems of governance to fit the new situation. They certainly seem to have continued to exercise power for the first few years of the fifth century. St Patrick, for example, came from just such a background – one in which a quite advanced education was still possible. We should probably imagine the local aristocracy as running their affairs from their rural estates and becoming as self-sufficient as possible as trade contracted and money became increasingly scarce. The advent of the mid-fifth century plague was probably a destabilizing blow. By analogy with the later fourteenth century outbreak it is likely that the plague disproportionately affected the peasant farmers and their servants and slaves more than it affected the better-housed ruling groups. The result would have been a change in the balance of power between the two groups, with the peasant farmers becoming more powerful and better able to resist economic demands by their rulers.

The elite were saved by the advent of the English. After the mid-fifth century crisis the countryside was ruled by tyrants who were probably able to adapt their Roman style *familiae* to a more war-like way of life. The retreat to the hill-top forts not only gave security; it also enhanced their social position as they gathered followers and formed a warlike group, while the reconstruction of the forts, which must have been effected by the labours of peasant cultivators, perhaps with the promise of protection for themselves and their livestock, helped to cement their position of superiority. Once the elite had become a warrior group they became impossible to dislodge from within and could adapt their surroundings to suit themselves. The refortification of South Cadbury and perhaps of other hill-tops took place before the appearance of Mediterranean luxuries, signalled by the remains of Eastern Mediterranean pottery at a number of centres. Those imports were probably the direct result of merchants voyaging from the Byzantine Empire seeking tin from the south-western peninsula. Close to the tin source a local magnate, whose power sprang from his control of the production and export of the tin to the Byzantine Empire, was able to control the trade and through the acquisition of both goods and gold make himself the dominant ruler. In true barbarian style he stood as the door-keeper between the rich outside world and the comparatively poverty stricken south-west of Britain, exercising influence through control of the flow of exotic goods.

Whether or not the magnates of Somerset in their turn became his subordinates is impossible to know. It may well be that they were prepared to acknowledge some kind of overlordship in return for access to goods, and the person who controlled Cadbury-Congresbury may have been the gate-keeper through whom largesse flowed into the locality. It is likely that a well-organised society developed, but it is not clear how large this militarised ruling group became. Nothing remains – as yet – to confirm their warlike stance. We do not have elaborate dress materials, such as brooches and clasps and the like. Neither do we have elaborate horse trappings or any trace of arms and armour apart from the odd spear. In death as in life, these people left little overt sign of their status or their role in their communities.

When demand for the tin declined, along with most trade in the Byzantine Mediterranean world in the mid-sixth century, the ruler at Tintagel saw his influence decline and it seems likely that the same fate overtook many of the local Somerset rulers. The threat posed by the Anglo-Saxons to the east seems to have declined also at about the same time and so the status and function of the elite groups were seriously undermined. The hill-fort at South Cadbury was abandoned and the former occupants and their successors went elsewhere. They probably retreated to halls and farmsteads around the hill-fort, but there

is as yet no evidence of where they may have lived. The same is true for other prestige sites. Clearly their status was not reflected in their daily lives, which have left few traces. Somerset in the second half of the sixth century and the first half of the seventh was probably largely a society of peasant farmers with a few more affluent land-owners among them with a higher status and general positions of authority. This did not matter as long as the society to the east in what is now Wiltshire had a very similar structure, even if it did consist of people who spoke English rather than Old Welsh. As we have seen, there is some reason to believe that contact and cultural exchange was not uncommon. John Davey's find of two burials at Hincknoll Slait produced the remains of a young male, buried with a knife, analysis of whose teeth suggested that he was a local man. The same was true for the young woman also recovered from the same site (Davey 2005, 117).

The Anglo-Saxon group which usurped power in Somerset in the mid-seventh century was organised in a different way, which explains its rapid success. This was a much more stratified and hierarchical warrior society. The Laws of the earliest Anglo-Saxon kings, beginning with those of Ethelbert of Kent in the first half of the seventh century, are permeated with a consciousness of rank. A nobly born woman could be of the highest class or of the second, third or fourth – and all in a society which was numerically tiny by most standards (Whitelock 1955, 357–9). Of course it unlikely that everyday life in seventh and eighth century Wessex tallied very closely with an ideal construction, probably laid out by bishop or priest at the king's court, but clearly it touched salient points or it would not have survived in the Laws. The Laws of Ine, over half a century later, betray the same concern for status and rank, with the close attention to the detail of the wergild for everyone in Wessex society from Archbishop and king to Welsh slaves. An enormously complicated hierarchy had been generated and probably in no more than a hundred years. This emerging system of ranking was closely tied to the construction of an Anglo-Saxon consciousness and to the forging of the kingdom of Wessex. As Wessex grew its population was increasingly differentiated into nobly born, free and slave. At first it was also divided into

Anglo-Saxon and Welsh, with a much lower status accorded the now subject population. How long that distinction remained is unclear, but King Alfred included it in his recension of King Ine's Laws, so he clearly thought it still relevant at the end of the ninth century.

Elsewhere in Britain the rise of kings and their nobility generated a number of ostentatious burials, but none have been discovered in Wessex. It may be that the norms of Christian burial had spread too deeply into Wessex society as it expanded for burials of that type to take place, but it was more likely the rapid expansion of Wessex and the opportunities that it provided for plunder and for military success, which diverted attention away from the need for display in death.

Wessex was built upon a warrior-led extension of territory which continued into the eighth century. Somerset was a part of a warrior society which was ultimately organised to support its fighting men. Around him the king had gathered an aristocratic warband, dominated by ideas of warfare and plunder, which quickly developed an ethos which called for absolute loyalty, to the death if necessary, as the account in the Anglo-Saxon Chronicle of the death of Cynewulf shows (ASC, 755). However, bearing in mind the way that the warriors on that occasion were offered financial inducements to stop fighting it seems right to conclude that buying off the rebellious was common and there is plenty of evidence in the Anglo-Saxon Chronicle to show that bloody struggles for power were an everyday occurrence, so that aristocratic loyalty was actually a fickle thing. The king needed a steady supply of material wealth and of land to command the continuing loyalty of his aristocratic followers. They needed a sense of superiority and a unifying ideology of warrior behaviour to hold the group together in the face of almost incessant fighting and violence. The westward drive which brought Somerset into being as an English shire was the product of this hierarchy and its needs. Expansion provided the king with the plunder and the land to maintain the loyalty of his followers and diverted dissident members of the band from turning to internal intrigue and rebellion. It also cemented a sense of unity out of which emerged the West Saxon identity. Without the inclusion of Somerset

within Wessex the kingdom would have been a very different entity. As we now know this aggressive 'Englishness' emerged among a population within which 'Anglo-Saxon' genes were actually quite rare. Inevitably a society built upon a warrior hierarchy was a competitive society and the position most eagerly sought was probably that of the king himself. The kings of Wessex were rarely succeeded by a son and few died in their beds, unless they were exiles.

In exchange for his specialised warrior status, the gesith-born man looked to the king for his reward. There were evidently plenty of young warriors in Wessex society who did not have hereditary lands and the gift or loan of land was what they sought and what eventually bound them to the king. We do not fully understand the relationship between the gesith and the land he occupied, but it seems fair to accept the views of those scholars who regard so many of this class as landless. We do not know whether the accession of so much extra land to the king in Somerset after c. 650 resulted in an increase in the number of warrior nobles. It is always possible that the focus on the status of individuals and the emphasis on birth actually conceals a rapidly changing situation in which men who fought as ceorls became warrior nobles by the grant of loanland. Somerset society may have been more fluid than the rigid Laws allowed. However, there are good reasons from a study of the place-names to think that the personal ownership of estates was quite unusual in the seventh and eighth centuries. Personalised place-names are rare in Somerset in early documents, suggesting that individuals rarely became closely associated with the land. The gesith class may indeed have rarely been able to settle real roots into the countryside long enough for son to follow father. This was in strong contrast with the position of the ceorl who seems to have enjoyed security of tenure in return for his renders. The '*buckland*' place-names record an era when land with a charter and thus with security of ownership and the rights of inheritance was comparatively rare enough to warrant special attention.

No hierarchy lasts unchanged for long and shifts in the relationship between the king and his nobles also caused changes in the way in which the land was used and held. In the eighth century what one might almost call 'private property' began to appear. The '*bucklands*' were one sign of this, but only sporadic chance survivals of charters enable us to see the shift by which land moved permanently out of royal control and into the hands of the noble class, aided by the device of the charter. How widespread this process was is impossible to gauge. Undoubtedly the king remained by far the greatest secular landowner, but the rise of the landed nobleman meant a change in their relationship with the king and his court. Men with property could be more independent socially and politically and so had less need to please.

The men and women who were anomalous were those who had adopted a religious life. This included the bishops and priests and abbots and their monks and also those noble women who became nuns. They seem to have been drawn from among the nobility, and like the gesith-born followers of the king held no property of their own. However they were able to command considerable landed resources through their alliance with the king and in Somerset it is possible that places such as South Petherton, Cannington, Wells, Cheddar, Chew, Chewton and Carhampton and a good many others were primarily church settlements. The households of the clerks, monks and nuns were very like those of the lay nobility, and as nearly permanent institutions they filled a similar place in the landscape to the great estates of the king. It is not surprising that the gesith class saw the churches as a way to command resources of land and men which might enable them to establish families in one place for long periods.

Behind the apparently simple structure of the top of Somerset society lie some unanswerable questions. How did Lulle the nun come by her property? Did her family own it? Had she inherited it from a relative? Why did she need the king's permission to grant it away? It seems possible that she had inherited family land and needed special permission to alienate it and place it outside her family. She may be representative of many noblemen and women who held family land, not received as a reward and which they could not dispose of.

Somerset was not immune from the pressures imposed by the internecine warfare between the early Anglo-Saxon kings, and the domination of Wessex by the Mercians during much of the eighth century included incursions into Somerset. How these

affected the nobility we do not know. Much greater pressures from outside were imposed by the Vikings during the ninth century. The shire levy shows that the local warriors were organised beyond the king's immediate war-band into groups under the command of his deputy in the shire, the ealdorman. The shire itself probably owes something to the existence of this levy system. As long as the Danes simply raided in warbands of perhaps one to two thousand men, the local warriors, estate owners and their ceorl followers could keep them at bay. The great army was a much more formidable opponent and in the end King Alfred needed to fall back on Somerset and his fort at Athelney. This stronghold was described in the bounds of a charter as 'the old herworth' in a boundary which purports to be tenth century, but which is almost certainly many centuries younger as we know it (S432 of 937). His enormous personal reserves of land and men in Somerset, the difficulty of approaching Athelney in winter, as well as his ability to call on the shire levy, were what enabled him to raise a new army against the Danes, but it was a close call. Once the great army over wintered the weakness of the system was exposed. Alfred and his successors needed to be able to call on many more men and they needed some way of reinforcing the landowners' loyalty to the king and the kingdom when times were hard.

From the later part of the ninth century and throughout the tenth century the kings of Wessex followed a new path forced upon them by the escalation of the size of armies and by the lengthening of campaigns. During the later part of the ninth century it seems as if the nobility had already begun to extract from the king substantial grants of bookland. Some charters survive in the cartularies, particularly that of Glastonbury, which were clearly issued to laymen in the ninth century and then passed on to the monastery in the later tenth century, when land was bequeathed. Ditcheat was quoted as one example and Wrington shows the same kind of history. Only during the tenth century do we begin to see the Wills of important people, often showing landed possessions spread across many shires and bequeathed to monasteries and churches as well as to sons, daughters, relatives and *fideles*. We can recognise a landed aristocracy emerging with inherited lands to be passed on to children. Those we see have lands scattered widely, but it is likely that below them were more modest landowners whose bookland was concentrated mostly in Somerset. If the men who wrote the lives of Dunstan are correct and not simply reproducing an appropriate topos for a great churchman of the tenth century, then his family was relatively modestly endowed, though well connected. The day of the landless gesith looking to his lord for preferment was probably over. Once land could be bought and sold freely membership of the thegnly class came from ownership of land. The gulf in the hierarchy was now between the peasant with his unwritten customary tenure of his farm and the man or woman who held rights over him and his land by virtue of having a book for his estate and with it all the rights of lordship.

The king's response to this development was to demand that everyone who held bookland should do military service when called upon. Great men and the monasteries which were great landholders also had to provide soldiers off their estates as well as doing personal service. As a result a body of soldiers, the thegns who are not often named in the Domesday Book, had come into existence. Often living on no more than a single hide of land, sometimes less, they may have replaced the ceorls who followed their lords in previous centuries. There were several hundred of these men in Somerset who can be traced through the Domesday Book. There were probably many others living on the estates of King's Thegns without the formality of a separate holding. The shire could easily raise a force of a thousand well armed men by the mid-tenth century. It was this increase in the numbers of well-armed men which enabled the king to expand his kingdom from Wessex into the kingdom of the English in no more than half a century. Once more, however, the system was unable to cope with a well equipped and mobile army from Denmark which could seize the initiative. The men of Somerset submitted to Swein at Bath, suggesting how much the system depended upon good leadership to be effective.

The landscape

By the end of the period of study it is the case that the outlines of the social geography of Somerset as we see it today were already firmly in place, but we still see only a very partial picture of what the landscape of Somerset was like in the fifth century. However it does at least appear that after the retreat of the extensive villa culture and the fall in the population in the mid-fifth century, there was a shift to a predominantly pastoral economy, but one which continued to use the bones of the old landscape for its setting. Many settlements disappeared, probably as population fell, but some continued to function, though probably at a lower level than before. Apart from the dramatic but rather ephemeral re-occupation of the hill-forts it is hard to tell where the elite centres were, except that the survival of some religious settlements, Carhampton, Banwell and Cannington for example, through into the seventh century, and their re-invention by the Anglo-Saxon Church as part of their minster system, makes it likely that many of the later Anglo-Saxon centres of power were of major significance in the post-Roman period. This analysis cannot be carried too far however. The large cemetery at West Harptree is not immediately tied to a nearby settlement centre, unless it belonged to the rather distant Chew Magna, and some of the smaller burial sites are clearly part of a small scale rural settlement system, at Buckland Dinham for example. The picture which emerges is of a small scale world, in which places which had been important in the countryside in the fourth and early fifth century continued to function as elite centres, often marked by large centralised cemeteries, up to and beyond the coming of the Anglo-Saxons. Some of these sites may have been clerical centres with quite large numbers of people working to support a group of priests who occupied what may once have been a secular centre. Congresbury may have been something of the kind. However, there seems to be little in the way of a hierarchy of settlement beyond these places, with most people living in very small communities. Lack of pressure on physical resources allowed a retreat from arable, so that the mixed farming, using valleys and hill-tops, characteristic of West Somerset and the parts of Devon around Exmoor, is probably the appropriate model for most of the region. In a society with little access to coin or any other treasure source cattle would have been the chief marker of wealth and authority, reinforcing the tendency towards small scattered settlements.

The coming of the Anglo-Saxons profoundly changed the way the countryside was used. Both the size of the king's following and the need to provide well for his companions deeply affected the way in which the king organised his estates and it is likely that the same issues influenced his greater nobility as well. The most striking feature is the appearance of the great centralised estates, which I have argued are the result of the need to provide for a large group, whether of companions for the king or clerics for the Churches. The surviving depictions of the life of kings and noblemen always emphasise their importance as providers of food, a lord was, after all, literally 'a loaf giver', and the provision of great feasts was clearly an important part of the king's role. We should not underestimate the scale of the supplies needed for this type of lavish display, and the centralised estate gave the king or other great lord sufficient control over production by his servants and slaves to guarantee supply.

Anglo-Saxon society, with its much greater and more well-defined superstructure, needed more resources than extensive pastoralism could easily supply. Existing major centres were remodelled to become the hubs of an estate system which was geared to providing support for a large body of non-productive people, both lay and clerical. At its centre lay a royal hall or a major church complex, with the unfree tenants grouped around. They worked fields adjacent to the estate centre. Beyond the core of the estate were smaller settlements, often tributary to the core, some occupied by individual ceorls, others by small groups of semi-free men, most of whom were bound to the estate and its lord by having accepted land and a dwelling in return for rents and services. It seems likely that part of the immediate impact of the incomers on the landscape was that there were a considerable number of ceorls who moved in behind the king or some other lord. They were able to fill spaces in a pastoral landscape, found new farms, and turn to arable cultivation in order to meet the tribute requirements of the lord. At the same time it probably bound some ceorls closer to the lord. They now found themselves becoming integrated into the great estate system, even if only as rent payers or as tribute payers on lands distant from the great hall. As a result we see the appearance of settlements such

as Shepton Beauchamp or Shepton Mallet, places which provided a special render of sheep to the great hall, or the Charltons, Charlton Adam, or Charlton Musgrove, settlements where a group of ceorls farmed together, paying tribute to the central place. Such a system did not at first completely obliterate the old post-Roman landscape, so that many individual farmsteads or hamlets remained and the 'walcots' and 'waltons' are probably a reminder of what was once a landscape in which incoming Anglo-Saxon ceorls lived among the pre-existing post-Roman Old Welsh speaking population.

However, these great estates did not fill the landscape, there were always lands which fell outside this system. It is likely that many of the settlements of the highland zones and of the woodland areas were semi-independent. The *cotts* and the *wyrths* around Exmoor and the Brendons were surely occupied by men who had lords to whom they paid tribute, but who were otherwise left to their own devices. Other forest areas existed all around the edges of the shire and there intensification of exploitation is marked by the appearance of the '*leah*' place names, which occur in significant numbers, often in landscapes which have now lost their trees. Many of these areas of managed wood-pasture had names which reflect the existence of individual owners or tenants. These were probably the areas where ceorls were relatively free from lordly pressures, though the regulations in Ine's Laws concerning the destruction of trees (by burning) suggests that in the eighth century assarting of woodland was increasing and that there was a conflict of interest developing between the peasants and the aristocratic hunters.

Elsewhere there were estates which were tributary to the great centres, but which could be loaned to the nobly born warriors and to the king's or lord's greater servants. The problem here is that we do not know if the boundaries of these estates were already fixed as early as the seventh or the early eighth centuries. A great estate granted to Glastonbury, such as Brent, had a boundary which may have reflected the reality of the late seventh century, but it was hardly a realistic reflection of the type of grant to be made to a servant. Hornblotton, 'the tun of the hornblower' is clearly the result of a grant to a ceremonial servant. But we do not know if the boundaries of Hornblotton as they appear in the post-Conquest period reflect a seventh or eighth century reality, or a post-Norman construction.

Already in the eighth and ninth centuries there were an increasing number of estates which were outside any major tributary system. Some were lands which had formed part of the tribute system of the king, others were part of the estates of minster churches which had been appropriated by the king. These were the lands now held as bookland, which could not normally return to the melting pot of royal property, and the landscape is increasingly marked by the appearance of estates with personal names as part of their identifiers, the 'ingtuns' for instance. Fragmentation of the landscape had probably begun so that places such as the Harptrees or East and West Lydford were distinguishable, but the greatest changes came in the tenth century. The forces which acted upon the landscape were the king, with his need for warriors, the greater nobility who pressed upon it because they too needed followers, resources and income, and the new monasteries, who from the mid-tenth century exhibited the same needs as the greater nobility. By the end of the century universal taxation had replaced customary tribute and probably *ad hoc* levies to pay off the Danes and the need for ready money was an immense spur to change and to intensification of the exploitation of the landscape. The plough was the engine which made the changes possible, and its extensive use changed the look of the landscape by encouraging the growth of common fields and intensifying the drive towards arable cultivation. By 1086 the Domesday commissioners reckoned the taxable value of an estate in terms of its ploughlands and plough-teams and Somerset had 4815 ploughlands and 3924 plough-teams (Darby 1977, 336). Many smaller estates were almost completely arable by 1086 and probably had been for nearly a century. The re-arrangement of lands into great fields necessitated the relocation of peasant farmsteads into the system of cultivation in furlongs and the nucleation of these small settlements was a by-product of the new system.

As the king and lords rewarded followers by planting them on their own lands in return for their service they sometimes needed to create new settlements and thereby encouraged the break-up of the landscape into smaller units. Some of these new settlements took new names from their new lords, giving us names of the 'Allerton' or 'Houndstone' type. Hitherto insignificant settlements were developed as independent units, to appear in the Domesday Book as manors. Thus Badgworth near Wedmore or Ashcott on the Glastonbury estate became manorial centres.

All this describes the landscape of arable. There were of course many other landscapes. Those estates which still remained largely wood-pasture, on the steep hill-slopes or in combes, could not easily be adapted to the common-field system. Their arable remained scattered around multiple small settlements and cattle and sheep rearing probably remained central to their activities. Such places are not easily distinguished in fiscal and tenurial records, such as Domesday Book, but need to be revealed by modern field-work.

It was the interaction of these pressures which encouraged the population to grow, especially during the tenth century, though I do not discount the likely effects of the cessation of the plague, which seems to have become much less of a problem by the end of the eighth century. The old extensive system of settlement and agriculture did not encourage population expansion. There is nothing to suggest that the *ceorlisc* men were able to split their lands for inheritance purposes. Had that been possible we might have seen the endless division and re-division of peasant lands that characterised some of the territories of southern Gaul in the ninth and tenth centuries and which resulted in the abandonment of land and its seizure by lords and by churches. In a world where a workable farm was a necessity for a peasant if he wished to marry, the old system offered little opportunity for expansion, except on those lands where asserting into communal woodlands was possible. The introduction of the new system of agriculture reduced his independence, but enabled the peasant to expand his numbers by adding to the common fields. It meant there were more families to contribute to the geld, but also more men to work the lord's demesne.

Unfreedom in the landscape

Unfreedom is a common theme throughout the whole

period. Slavery was the most extreme form of this state and although it undoubtedly had an important role as part of the differentiation within the social hierarchy, in the end the purpose of slavery was economic. Labour was scarce and slavery provided a way of getting work done at a minimum cost and, just as importantly, without the need to pay people in a world with little or no ready money. By the later eleventh century the institution of slavery showed a considerable duality. On the one hand the numbers of slaves were quite closely aligned to the ploughland capacity of the shire. The economic role of the slave is clear. Compared with other Wessex shires Somerset does not stand out as especially 'unfree'. These were slaves who were very much part of the stock of the average arable estate. On the other hand the tiny estates in western Somerset were often inhabited solely by a slave. As the farmer of the whole manor he must have had considerable autonomy in his day to day life, so that his slavery lacked the quality of personal oversight one would expect of the condition. His status was social, with the stigma attached to it, rather than economic. Such a man might hope to make enough money of his own to buy freedom for himself and his family. The position of the cottars and the bordars who appear in the 'cott' place-names was little better than those of the slaves. They probably arrived with their lords as part of the stock of the newly expanded estate system, and as Dr Faith has shown, mostly filled specialist roles in agriculture. However, by the mid-eleventh century they were mainly differentiated from their villein neighbours by the possession of smaller farmsteads or tiny plots of land and so the probable need to work for others, including the lord, to supplement their incomes. The peasant farmers who appear in the Domesday Book as villeins were also only semi-free. Most of them were probably the descendants of the ceorls and had become bound closely into the new agricultural system. By the time of Domesday, Somerset, in common with other south-western counties, had no freemen recorded. Although this may be due to the vagaries of the recording methods employed by the commissioners in the south-west, it does look as if the concept of a 'freeman' below the rank of thegn had disappeared in Somerset. Everywhere the labour services demanded from the unfree and the semi-free had been regularised,

although the development of custom meant that the services and allowances varied to some extent from one manor to another. At Shapwick the fourteenth century peasants were obliged to 'go with the bailiff of the hundred wherever it is necessary to summon and distrain *everywhere in the west of the hundred*' (BM Egerton 3321). The hundred Egerton referred to was the hundred of Whitley, which was a twelfth century amalgamation of the two pre-Domesday hundreds of Ringwoldesway and Loxley (DB 376). Loxley, named from Loxley Wood in Shapwick, was the western half of the hundred. The villeins of Shapwick had been burdened with this duty in the Anglo-Saxon period. The system was flexible and when after the Norman conquest the abbot constructed his park of Pilton he was able to impose on all his Somerset peasants the burden of ditching and fencing and maintenance there. A similar ability to vary conditions of tenure had probably existed in earlier times.

Money

This book began with the virtual disappearance of money and it ends with a countryside geared to provide money for its lords and for the king. It is the collapse of the currency system and the disappearance of coin which explains in part at least the way in which the post-Roman polity developed. Somerset was a society which had little which could be used for exchange. No silver was extracted from lead locally, or it would surely show in the production of local currency substitutes, and there was little else which could be used for exchange. There are no hoards of precious metals or coin after the first quarter of the fifth century. Nor is it at all clear what the region had to offer for trade. Slaves and cattle seems the likely answer, which makes the influx of coin and luxury goods at the end of the fifth century and in the early sixth century an unusual interlude, driven by diplomatic and trade activity initiated in faraway Byzantium.

What this event reveals is the extent to which the region turned its back upon the east and the north and looked towards the sea and the south-west. The string of post-Roman sites extending along the coast from Portishead, via Cadbury-Congresbury to Watchet, Carhampton and perhaps to Porlock are evidence of the importance of the coast and the river system which gave access to the interior. Although Anglo-Saxon Somerset was tied to the east as part of the kingdom of Wessex the rivers remained immensely important as a means of transport and also as a source of food. Hythes and staithes along the rivers as well as inland ports, such as Langport or Ilchester, provide evidence of activity over a long period. The most interesting place is Watchet. Here was a site which had connections with trading activity from the later fifth century and retained its Old Welsh name as evidence of continuity of occupation. It is not a coincidence that it was brought within the Anglo-Saxon estate of Williton and that it retained its post-Roman religious connection with south Wales. Nor is it chance that it was a target of Viking attack and defended by a *burh*. It was still an important mint site in the later eleventh century, a sign of its overseas trade links. Watchet provided access to much of western Somerset and offered a port for trade with Wales, Ireland and western Francia.

Eventually Watchet was eclipsed by a reversal of focus from West to East which coincides with the growth of a real money economy in the later tenth century. Somerset was able to look east and also north towards Mercia as Wessex expanded into England. Bath provided the gateway through its position on the edge of Mercia and in control of land communications. Somerset was always at the edge of the growth of trade and manufacturing which was so important in eastern England at this time, but it too was warmed by the glow of silver from Germany and the Low Countries. Although the details are elusive Somerset paid its taxes in silver and as elsewhere the novel demand for regular taxes, as opposed to customary tributes and renders, helped to drive the expansion of agriculture. There is no evidence that Somerset had anything to offer beyond agricultural produce with which to pay its way. The extensive arable of the eleventh century and the widespread sheep grazing can only be understood as the result of a need for cash crops. Great monasteries and royal estates ran very large flocks of sheep, and there were also large flocks on private lands, especially in the north-east of the shire, suggesting that wool was being exported eastward and northward, as well as by sea by the mid-eleventh century.

Long distance trade began as a response to the desires of the elite for goods not available at home and elite exchange was always a driver of trade and transport, whether it was for warrior lords or for monks and clerks. By the end of the period the rise in the numbers of local 'gentry', the lesser owners of bookland, increased the demand for personal goods, the results of which show in some of the casual finds of horse-harness, straps ends and buckles. Behind these durable objects must have been much material now decayed and lost, but valuable at the time. This helps to explain the growth of the markets in the tiny towns, but behind it all must have been the continuing need to find the money to pay the geld.

Belief

It might appear to be a little cynical to describe the Christianity of the whole period as prospering because it was useful, but nevertheless this must be true. Christianity provided a belief system which helped to hold both the post-Roman and the Anglo-Saxon societies together. It is not fortuitous that the end of paganism and the spread of Christianity coincide with the emergence of the post-Roman polity and of course the same is true for the growth of Wessex and the conversion of the Anglo-Saxons. For the post-Romans an element of continuity in the landscape may have been preserved by the establishment of Christian cult centres at or close to the late Roman temples at Lamyatt Beacon and at Brean Down. At Cannington the great cemetery progresses smoothly from paganism to Christian burial without a break in continuity and the same might be true of other smaller cemeteries. The establishment of what look like churches at or very near to centres of power at hill-forts, such as Banwell or Congresbury or hill-tops like Glastonbury, also suggests that the church moved in to fill the spaces left by the retreat of the elite after the mid-sixth century. There is no doubt either, that the post-Roman church was at its strongest close to the coast, where so much of the secular power was also concentrated. Whether it also filled a political vacuum we cannot tell, but the emergence of Anglo-Saxon minster churches at so many of these sites points to an element of continuity into the Anglo-Saxon period, which is necessarily missing on the lay side of Somerset society.

The early Anglo-Saxon church in Somerset was an expensive undertaking. The system of minster churches mirrored the great estates established by the Wessex kings and their followers since the minsters could resemble a great lay household with their priests or monks surrounded by servants. Aldhelm, son of a king, founder of churches, multiple abbot and finally bishop exemplifies this. The minster system must therefore be seen as an integral part of the social and political structure of Somerset in the seventh and eighth centuries. It served to dominate the church which already existed and made it possible to subsume it within the new Anglo-Saxon church. In Somerset, where the king controlled so much of the land, it was not surprising that some churches soon attracted special patronage. Glastonbury seems to have already been an important religious centre in the mid-seventh century and its siting made it an easy choice as a possible royal monastic retreat.

The transfer of so much land to the new church provided a potential counterbalance for the king to the power of his great men and it also had visible effects upon the landscape. Glastonbury, as the greatest of these churches, was able to get and hold land continuously throughout the whole period and in some cases right down to the dissolution of the abbey. This stability of tenure was one reason why some parts of the Somerset landscape remained divided into large estates and was never cut up into very small units. There was no division among heirs. Such divisions as did take place were aimed at making the land more productive and never proceeded very far. Places like Batcombe, Ditcheat or Pilton remained large. However, the rejuvenated monasteries were not slow to adopt the new farming ways of the tenth century and the size and diversity of land types of their estates probably made the introduction of the new methods much easier than for the smaller landowner.

We know little about the how the church affected the lives of ordinary peasants, or indeed of the thegns at any period, and it is likely that for much of the time and for most of them the rituals of the church were something which was well removed from their daily lives, though rules about baptism, burial, marriage and tithes affected their personal relationships. They were also affected by the Church's involvement in administrative and judicial activities, such as the administration of ordeals and particularly with regard to the oaths needed on so many occasions. At the beginning of the period the church for most people was physically well removed, 7–10 km distant, so it was hardly a daily presence in their lives. Over the next three centuries the numbers of churches multiplied, especially in the later tenth and in the eleventh centuries, and by the time of the Norman Conquest most larger communities had a church of their own. A resident priest became a normal feature of village life, but might be seen as often an extension of the lord's authority further into the lives of his peasants, especially as he had built the church, owned it and often collected the tithes as well. The Gregorian Reforms of the next two centuries included a determined attempt to bring the Church and its teachings much more deeply into the lives of the laity. It set out in some sort, to 'Christianize' them, to alter their internal lives. This could not have happened without the provision of the network of community churches, with their priests, largely put into place by the mid-eleventh century, which was to develop into the parish system. The monks particularly were in a unique position to foster religious life across their estates and by the end of the tenth century most of their larger properties had churches. By the time that St Benignus was translated to Glastonbury Abbey in 1091 popular devotion to the saint was clear. The cult of the saints was of course central to early medieval devotion and it is likely that there were other examples of popular religion of this type of which we know nothing unless they were swallowed up by an institution such as a monastery or cathedral. Cyngar may well have begun in the same way, but the quality of the surviving stonework from his shrine shows that he had been captured by the Cathedral at Wells by the early eleventh century.

The reformed monasticism of the tenth century at last made the distinction between the regular and the secular clergy clear. The movement began as a reaction to the control of ecclesiastical property and office by the laity, which was seen by both churchmen and devout laymen as the root cause of the decay of monasticism. Glastonbury was among the first monasteries to benefit from this new path and with royal support attracted the enthusiastic patronage of many of the great families of the region. The new monasticism was on a scale which dwarfed previous institutions, with extensive property across Wessex, though the bulk was in Somerset. As great as the impact of the monastery as a landowner was, it was even more important as a part of the social structure of Somerset. It provided an entrée to a career for the younger sons of the local 'gentry' at a time when that class was rapidly expanding. It offered an alternative to a career as a warrior for the young man of good family, indicating perhaps the beginnings of a change in the nature of the aristocratic class. Daughters had nowhere to go in the shire and must have entered somewhere such as Shaftesbury or even Wilton. Through such familial connections local families could enter into a relationship with Glastonbury, Bath or another house which provided spiritual benefits. If nothing else it provided them with a view of the ideal of the 'City of God', which was how the monks themselves so often saw their monastic endeavours and for which Glastonbury, with its rebuilt churches and enclosure, was an exemplar. Elsewhere on the Continent the eleventh century saw a determined effort on the part of the Church to draw the knightly class into a social and spiritual relationship, partly through the 'Peace of God'. Here the lawlessness the Church so often faced elsewhere seems less obvious, but the tight knit nature of local communities may have worked in much the same way in Somerset once the monasteries became influential institutions. Glastonbury, of course, became one of the revived centres of learning, but how much of that rubbed off on the local laity is unknowable.

This book has concentrated on one small corner of Wessex, but it is pertinent to remember that the shire was far from isolated, despite its rather inward looking geography and history. The influences of the outside world were everywhere to be seen, even if not always appreciated. Changes in social structures and in the way in which agriculture and the countryside were organised can be traced in other western European communities. The use of great estates, organised along quite centralised lines, may well owe something to the practices of the north-east of Merovingian Gaul. The effects of the policies of kings also showed in the foundation of the *burhs*, with their obvious connections with the defence policies of the Carolingian kings in Gaul. Unwelcome intrusions by raiders and pirates from abroad, the Vikings both from Scandinavia and Ireland and the Danes in the late tenth and early eleventh centuries were serious and damaging. Eventually a Danish king ruled England, but had little permanent effect in Somerset, though no doubt his financial exactions were much resented at the time. The Scandinavians, as Norman Frenchmen, of course conquered England once more and this time replaced the ruling warrior class almost completely, as they had not done when Swein and Cnut conquered the English. The 'warrior' state of the Anglo-Saxons failed, despite its elaborate mechanisms for the support of its elite. The reasons for that traumatic event and the profound changes it introduced, even in Somerset, were not the subject of this book.

The Anglo-Saxon period has given Somerset its basic 'shape', the pattern of villages and towns, the direction of communications, even the broad appearance of its fields and woods. These physical remains outlived the catastrophe which engulfed the late Old English state. Little remains of ecclesiastical buildings in Somerset to bear witness to the church's profound impact on both people and their surroundings. More important was the continuity of written words, the learning of the distant past, the rituals of the Church, the structure of its buildings, its beliefs and teachings about the nature of the world, of the nature of history and of mankind, which were common to all of Europe, from Constantinople to Dublin. Somerset's history is part of a much greater continuum.

Abbreviations, Manuscript Sources and Bibliography

Abbreviations and manuscript sources

't'. Tithe award numbers from the tithe maps of the appropriate parish.

ASC. Swanton, M. (ed. and trans.). *The Anglo-Saxon Chronicles*. London, (Phoenix Press, 2000). References are to manuscripts and dates of entries.

Asser. 'Asser's Life of King Alfred', in Keynes S. and M. Lapidge, trans. and eds *Alfred the Great; Asser's Life of King Alfred and other contemporary sources*. London, (Penguin Books, 1983). References are to page numbers.

Bede 170. 'Letter of Bede to Archbishop Egbert, AD 734', in D Whitelock, ed. *English Historical Documents c. 500–1042*, 1st ed. London, (Eyre and Spottiswoode, 1955) 735–745.

BL Add. ms 22934. British Library manuscript, copies of grants and other instruments relating to Glastonbury Abbey; circa 1230–1312.

BL Egerton 3034 of 1507–27, British Library Manuscript, terrier of the Somersetshire estates of Glastonbury. Abbey; 1514–1517.

BL Egerton 3316. Cartulary of the Benedictine cathedral priory of Bath, second half of the fourteenth century.

BL Egerton 3321 of 1327, British Library Manuscript, survey of the estates of Glastonbury Abbey.

Cal. Pap. *Calendar of entries in the Papal registers relating to Great Britain and Ireland*. 17 vols. London, (HMSO, 1897–1989).

CCC 111. Corpus Christi College, Cambridge Ms. s.xii, ff. 94–.

DB – Thorn C. and Thorn F. (trans. and eds) (1980) *Domesday Book – 8 – Somerset*. Phillimore, Chichester

D\D/Rt/A/221, tithe apportionment for Pilton, Somerset Record Office.

D\D/Rt/A/364, the tithe award for East Pennard, 1840–42, Somerset Record Office.

D\D/Rt/A/53, tithe apportionment for Flax Bourton, Somerset Record Office.

D\D/Rt/M/201, the tithe map for Withycombe, Somerset Record Office.

D\D/Rt/M/364, the tithe map for East Pennard, 1840, Somerset Record Office.

D\D\Rt/M/277, the Tithe map for Carhampton, Somerset Record Office.

D\P\ban – Banwell Parish Records, Somerset Record Office.

Eckweek. *Eckweek; report (Avon 2296) of an unpublished excavation*, County of Avon, (now Bath and North-East Somerset Unitary Authority), 1989–90.

EEA Band W = *English episcopal acta.10, Bath and Wells, 1061–1205*. (ed.) Frances M. R. Ramsey. Oxford (Published for the British Academy by Oxford University Press, 1995).

Fitzwilliam Corpus = Fitzwilliam Museum, Cambridge, Early Medieval Corpus of Coin Finds at http://www.fitzmuseum.cam.ac.uk/dept/coins/emc/

Geld Rolls; The Geld Roll of 1084 in *Libri censualis vocati Domesday-Book. Additamenta ex codic. antiquiss.* vol 3, ed. Sir H. Ellis, London, (G. Eyre and A. Strahan, 1816)

Lib(er). Alb(us). Vol. 2, Wells Cathedral Dean and Chapter Library. See also *Calendar of the Manuscripts of the Dean and Chapter of Wells*, ed. W. H. B. Bird, 2 vols., Historical Manuscripts Commission 12. 2–3 (London, 1907–14).

Longleat 10683, Glastonbury Abbey Court Rolls, 1284 or 1300 at Longleat House, Wilts.

MAP\DD\WG\MAP2, map, part of survey of Chewton Mendip, c.1766, Waldegrave Papers, Somerset Record Office.

MBN 1661 and MBN 2008 = Bath and North East Somerset HER

T/PH/Vch 38, a copy in Somerset County Record Office of a survey of Edward Seymour's estates, 1536, in Longleat House, Wilts.

T/PH/dcl/10–11, a copy of a Survey and map of Englishcombe, 1792, Somerset Record Office.

Bibliography

Abdy, R. (2006) After Patching: Imported and Recycled coinage in Fifth and Sixth Century Britain. In *Coinage and History in the North Sea World, c. AD 500–1250; Essays in Honour of Marion Archibald.* eds B Cook and G Williams, Leiden, Brill.

Abels, R. P. (1988) *Lordship and Military Obligation in Anglo-Saxon England.* London, British Museum.

Abels, R. P. (1998) *Alfred the Great: War, Kingship and Culture in Anglo-Saxon England*. London and New York, Longmans.

Abou-El-Haj, B. (1997) *The Medieval Cult of Saints; Formations and Transformations.* Cambridge, Cambridge University Press.

Abrams, L. (1996) *Anglo-Saxon Glastonbury: Church and Endowment.* Woodbridge, Boydell Press.

Alcock, L. (1972) *'By South Cadbury is that Camelot…'; Excavations at Cadbury Castle 1966–70.* London, Thames and Hudson.

Alcock, L. (1987) *Economy, Society and Warfare among the Britons and Saxons.* Cardiff, University of Wales Press.

Alcock, L. (1988) Potentates in Celtic Britain, AD 500–800: a positivist approach. In S. T. Driscoll and M. R. Nieke (eds), *Power and Politics in Early Medieval Britain and Ireland.* Edinburgh, Edinburgh University Press, 22–39.

Alcock, L. with Stevenson, S. J. and Musson, C. R. (1995) *Cadbury Castle Somerset; The Early Medieval Archaeology.* Cardiff, University of Wales Press.

Allott, S. (1974) *Alcuin of York c. AD 732 to 804: his life and letters.* York, Wm Sessions.

ApSimon, A. M. (1965) The Roman Temple on Brean Down, Somerset. *Proceedings of the University of Bristol Spelæological Society* 10, no. 3, 195–258.

Archer, S. (1979) Late Roman Gold and Silver Coin Hoards in Britain: a gazetteer. In P. J. Casey (ed.) *The End of Roman Britain,* 29–64. Oxford, BAR British Series, 71.

Arnold, C. J. (1984) *Roman Britain to Saxon England.* London, Croom Helm.

Aston, M. (1984) The Towns of Somerset. In J. Haslam (ed.) *Anglo-Saxon Towns in Southern England,* 167–201. Chichester, Phillimore.

Aston, M. (1985) *Interpreting the Landscape.* London, Batsford.

Aston, M. (2007) An Archipelago in Central Somerset: The Origins of Muchelney Abbey, *Proceedings of the Somerset Archaeological and Natural History Society* 150, 63–71.

Aston, M. (2009) An Early Medieval Estate in the Isle Valley of South Somerset and the Early Endowments of Muchelney Abbey, *Proceedings of the Somerset Archaeological and Natural History Society,* 152, 83–103.

Aston, M. and Costen, M. (2008) An Early Medieval Secular and Ecclesiastical Estate: the origins of the parish of Winscombe in north Somerset, *Proceedings of the Somerset Archaeological and Natural History Society* 151,139–58.

Aston, M. and Leech, R. (1977) *Historic Towns in Somerset: archaeology and planning.* Bristol, Committee for Rescue Archaeology in Avon, Gloucestershire and Somerset.

Attenborough, F. L. (trans. and ed.) (2000) *The Laws of the Earliest English Kings.* Felinfach, Llanerch Publishers, facsimile reprint.

Attwater, D. (ed.) (1960–70) *The Saints of Cornwall.* Truro, Federation of Old Cornwall Societies.

Badan, O., Brun, J.-P. and Congès, G. (1995) Les bergeries romaines de la Crau d'Arles; Les origins de la transhumance en Provence. *Gallia* 52, 263–310.

Barker, K. (1982) The Early History of Sherborne. In S. M. Pearce (ed.) *The Early Church in Western Britain and Ireland,* 77–116. BAR British Series, 102, Oxford.

Barlow, F. (1979) *The English Church 1000–1066,* 2nd edn. London, Longmans.

Barnwell, P. S. (1996) *Hlafæta, ceorl, hid* and *scir*: Celtic, Roman or Germanic? In D. Griffiths (ed.) *Anglo-Saxon Studies in Archaeology and History 9,* 53–62. Oxford, University Committee for Archaeology.

Barrett, J., Locker, A. M. and Roberts, C. M. (2004) "Dark Age Economics" Revisited: the English fish bone evidence AD 600–1600. *Antiquity* 78, 618–636.

Barrowman, R. C., Batey, C. E. and Morris, C. (2007) *Excavations at Tintagel Castle, Cornwall, 1990–1999.* London, Society of Antiquaries.

Bartholomew, P. (2005) Continental Connections: Angles, Saxons and Others in Bede and Procopius. In S. Semple (ed.) *Anglo-Saxon Studies in Archaeology and History 13,* 20–30.

Bassett, S. (1992) Church and Diocese in the West Midlands: the transition from British to Anglo-Saxon control. In J. Blair and R. Sharpe (eds) *Pastoral Care Before the Parish,* 13–40. London, Leicester University Press.

Bates, E. H. (1899) *Two Cartularies of the Benedictine Abbeys of Muchelney and Athelney in the County of Somerset.* Somerset Record Society 14, Taunton.

Batt, M. (1975) The Burghal Hidage: Axbridge. *Proceedings of the Somerset Archaeological and Natural History Society* 119, 22–5.

Bayley, J. (1991) Anglo-Saxon Non-ferrous Metalworking: A Survey. *World Archaeology* 23, no. 1, Craft Production and Specialization Jun., 115–130.

Bede, the Venerable. (1958) *Ecclesiastical History.* London, Dent.

Bell, M. (1990) *Brean Down Excavations 1983–1987.* London, English Heritage Archaeological Report 15.

Biddle, M. and Hill, D. (1971) Late Saxon Planned Towns. *Antiquaries Journal* 51, 70–85.

Bird, W. H. B. (ed.) (1907 and 1914) *Calendar of the Manuscripts of the Dean and Chapter of Wells*, 2 vols. London, Historical Manuscripts Commission.

Blair, J. (1997) Palaces or Minsters? Northampton and Cheddar Reconsidered. *Anglo-Saxon England* 25, 97–121.

Blair, J. (2004) Wells: Roman mausoleum or just Anglo-Saxon Minster? *Church Archaeology* 5 and 6, 134–7.

Blair, J. (2005) *The Church in Anglo-Saxon Society.* Oxford, Oxford University Press.

Blinkhorn. P. (1999) Of Cabbages and Kings: production, trade and consumption in middle-Saxon England. In *Anglo-Saxon Trading Centres; Beyond the Emporia*, 4–23. Glasgow, Cruithne Press.

Bosworth, J. and Toller, T. N. (1882–1921) *An Anglo-Saxon dictionary based on the Manuscript collection of the late Joseph Bosworth*, edited and enlarged by T. Northcote Toller. Oxford, Oxford University Press.

Bowen, E. G. (1977) *Saints, Seaways and Settlements in the Celtic Lands.* Cardiff, University of Wales Press.

Branigan, K. (1976) Villa Settlement in the West Country. In K. Branigan and P. J. Fowler (eds) *The Roman West Country; Classical culture and Celtic Society*, 120–41. Newton Abbot, David and Charles.

Branigan, K. (1977) *Gatcombe Roman Villa.* Oxford, BAR British Series 44.

Breeze, A. (2004) The Anglo-Saxon Chronicle for 614 and Brean Down, Somerset. *Notes and Queries* 51:3, 234–35.

Brooks, N. (1971) The Development of Military Obligation in Eighth and Ninth Century England. In P. Clemoes and K. Hughes (eds) *England before the Conquest; Studies in primary sources presented to Dorothy Whitelock*, 69–84. Cambridge, Cambridge University Press.

Brooks, N. (1979) England in the Ninth Century: The Crucible of Defeat, *Transactions of the Royal Historical Society,* 5th ser. 29, 2–11.

Brooks, N. (1988) *The Early History of the Church of Canterbury.* Leicester, Leicester University Press.

Brooks, N. (1992) The Career of St Dunstan. In N. Ramsey, M. Sparkes and T. Tatton-Brown (eds) *St Dunstan; His Life, Times and Cult*, 1–24. Woodbridge, The Boydell Press.

Brooks, N. (1996) The Administrative Background to the Burghal Hidage. In D. Hill and A. R. Rumble (eds)

The Defence of Wessex: The Burghal Hidage and Anglo-Saxon fortifications, 128–59. Manchester, Manchester University Press.

Brown, P. (1981) *The Cult of Saints.* Chicago, Chicago University Press.

Brown, P. (ed.) (1984) *Domesday Book, 33, Norfolk.* Chichester, Phillimore.

Buckton, D. (ed.) (1994) *Byzantium: Treasures of Byzantine Art and Culture.* London, British Museum Press.

Bullough, D. A. (1975) The Continental Background of Reform. In D. Parsons, (ed.) *Tenth-Century Studies; Essays in commemoration of the Millenium of the Council of Winchester and Regularis Concordia*, 20–36. Chichester, Phillimore.

Burnett, A. (1984) Clipped Siliquae and the End of Roman Britain. *Britannia* 15, 163–85.

Burrow, I. (1981) *Hillfort and Hill-top Settlement in Somerset in the First to Eighth Centuries A.D.* Oxford, BAR British Series 91.

Burrow, I., Minnitt, S. and Murless, B. (1983) Somerset Archaeology 1982. *Proceedings of the Somerset Archaeological and Natural History Society* 127, 13–31.

Bush, R. J. E. and Aston M. (1984) The Town; History and Topography. In P. Leach, (ed.) *The Archaeology of Taunton*, 59–63. Gloucester, Western Archaeological Trust.

Calder, M. J. (2002) *The Identification of Early Ecclesiastical Sites in Somerset.* Unpublished MA dissertation, University of Bristol.

Calder, M. J. (2004) Early Ecclesiastical Sites in Somerset: three case studies, *Proceedings of the Somerset Archaeological and Natural History Society* 147, 1–28.

Campbell, A. (ed. and trans.) (1962) *Chronicon Æthelweard; The Chronicle of Æthelweard.* London, Thomas Nelson and Sons.

Campbell, E. (1996) Archaeological Evidence for external contacts: Imports, trade and economy in Celtic Britain A.D. 400–800. In K. R. Dark (ed.) *External Contacts and the Economy of Late Roman and Post-Roman Britain*, 83–96. Woodbridge, Boydell Press.

Campbell, E. (2007) *Continental and Mediterranean Imports to Atlantic Britain and Ireland, AD 400–800.* York, CBA Research Report 157.

Campbell, J. (2000) *The Anglo-Saxon State.* London and New York, Hambledon and London.

Capelli, C. *et al.* (2003) A Y Chromosome Census of the British Isles. *Current Biology* 13, 979–984, May 27.

Carley, J. P. (ed.) (1978) *John of Glastonbury 'Cronica'.* Oxford, BAR British Series 47.

Casey, P. J. (ed.) (1979) *The End of Roman Britain.* Oxford, BAR British Series 71.

Chandler, J. (ed.) (1993). *John Leland's Itinerary; Travels in Tudor England*. Stroud, Alan Sutton Publishing.

Clark Hall, J. R. (with a supplement by Herbert D. Meritt) (1960). *A Concise Anglo-Saxon Dictionary*. Toronto, University of Toronto Press.

Clarke, H. B. (1999) The Vikings. In M. Keen, (ed.) *Medieval Warfare*, 36–58. Oxford, Oxford University Press.

Clarke, P. A. (1994) *The English Nobility under Edward the Confessor*. Oxford, Clarendon Press.

Clements, C. F. (1984) The Inner Ward and Outer Bailey. In P. Leach, (ed.) *The Archaeology of Taunton*, 26–36. Gloucester, Western Archaeological Trust.

Coates, R. (1999) New Light from Old Wicks: the progeny of Latin *vicus*. *Nomina* 22, 75–116.

Coates, R. (2000) Idover, Eleven Times Over. In R. Coates, A. Breeze and D. Horovitz, (eds) *Celtic Voices English Places: Studies of the Celtic Impact on Place-Names in England*, 95–6. Stamford, Shaun Tyas.

Cole, A. (2007) The Place-Name Evidence for Water Transport in Medieval England. In J. Blair (ed.) *Waterways and Canal-Building in Medieval England*, 55–84. Oxford, Oxford University Press.

Collins, R. and J. Gerrard (eds) (2004) *Debating Late Antiquity in Britain AD300–700*. Oxford, BAR British Series 365.

Collinson, The Revd. J. (1791) *The History of Somersetshire*, 3 vols, Bath.

Corcos, N. (1982/3) Early Estates on the Poldens and the Origin of the Settlement at Shapwick. *Proceedings of the Somerset Archaeological and Natural History Society* 127, 47–54.

Corcos, N. (2002) *The Affinities and Antecedents of medieval settlement; topographical perspectives from three of the Somerset hundreds*. Oxford, BAR British Series 337.

Corney, M. (2003) *The Roman Villa at Bradford on Avon: the investigations of 2003*, Bradford on Avon, Ex Libris Press.

Costen, M. (1978) A Celtic Saint's Well. *Somerset and Dorset Notes and Queries*, Taunton.

Costen, M. (1983) Marksbury and District in the Old English Period. *Bristol and Avon Archaeology* 2, 25–35.

Costen, M. (1988) The Late Saxon Landscape; The evidence from charters and place-names. In M. Aston (ed.) *Aspects of the Medieval Landscape of Somerset*, 33–49. Taunton, Somerset County Council.

Costen, M. (1989) The Origins of the Rectorial Manor of Shapwick. In M. Aston and M. Costen (eds) *The Shapwick Project; A Topographical and Historical Study, 1989, (2nd) Report*. Bristol, University of Bristol, Continuing Education Department.

Costen, M. (1991) Evidence for New Settlements and Field Systems in Late Anglo-Saxon Somerset. In L. Abrams and J. P. Carley (eds) *The Archaeology and History of Glastonbury Abbey; Essays in Honour of the Ninetieth Birthday of C. A. Ralegh Radford*, 39–55. Woodbridge, The Boydell Press.

Costen, M. (1992) *The Origins of Somerset*. Manchester, Manchester University Press.

Costen, M. (1992b). Huish and Worth: Old English Survivals in a later Landscape. In W. Filmer-Sankey (ed.) *Anglo-Saxon Studies in Archaeology and History* 5, 65–84. Oxford, Oxford University Committee for Archaeology.

Costen, M. (1994) Settlement in Wessex in the Tenth Century: The Charter Evidence. In M. Aston and C. Lewis (eds) *The Medieval Landscape of Wessex*, 97–114. Oxford, Oxbow.

Costen, M. (2007) Anonymous Thegns in the Landscape of Wessex 900–1066. In M. Costen (ed.) *People and Places; Essays in Honour of Mick Aston*, 61–75. Oxford, Oxbow.

Costen, M. (2011) Early settlement around the Mendips; place-names and local history. In J. Lewis (ed.) *The Archaeology of the Mendips: 500,000 years of continuity and change*. Oxford, Heritage Publications.

Cramp, R. *et al.* (2006) *Corpus of Anglo-Saxon Stone Sculpture, volume VII, South-West England*. London, British Academy.

Croft, R. A. (1988) Bridgwater, Wembdon Hill. *Proceedings of the Somerset Archaeological and Natural History Society*, 132.

Croft, R. A. and Woods, H. M. (1987) Wembdon, Wembdon Hill. *Proceedings of the Somerset Archaeological and Natural History Society* 3, 131.

Crumlin-Pedersen, O. (1972) The Vikings and the Hanseatic Merchants 900–1450. In G. W. Bass (ed.) *A History of Seafaring*, 182–207. London, Thames and Hudson.

Crumlin-Pedersen, O. (1981) Viking Ship-building and Seamanship. In H. Bekker-Nielson *et al.* (eds) *Proceedings of the 8th Viking Conference*, 271–86. Odense.

Crumlin-Pedersen, O. (1997) Large and small warships of the North. In A. Nørgård Jørgensen and B. L. Clausen (eds) *Military Aspects of Scandinavian society in a European Perspective, AD 1–1300*, 184–94. Copenhagen, PNM.

Cubitt, C. (1995) *Anglo-Saxon Church Councils c. 650– c. 850*. London, Leicester University Press.

Cubitt, C. (1997) Review article: The tenth-century Benedictine Reform in England. *Early Medieval Europe* 6(1), 77–94.

Cunliffe, B. (1984) Saxon Bath. In J. Haslam (ed.) *Anglo-Saxon Towns in Southern England*, 345–58. Chichester, Phillimore.

Cunliffe, B. (1995) *The English Heritage Book of Roman Bath*. London, English Heritage.

Currie, C. R. J. and Dunning, R. W. (eds 1999) *The Victoria History of the County of Somerset* 7, London, Institue of Historical Research.

Dalton, O. M. (1901) *Catalogue of Early Christian Antiquities and Objects from the Christian East in the Department of British and Medieval Antiquities and Ethnography of the British Museum*. London, British Museum Publications.

Darby, H. C. (1986) *Domesday England*. Cambridge, Cambridge University Press.

Dark, K. R. (1994) *Civitas to Kingdom: British political continuity 300–800*. Leicester, Leicester University Press.

Dark, K. R. (ed. 1996) *External Contacts and the Economy of Late Roman and Post-Roman Britain*. Woodbridge, Boydell Press.

Dark, K. (2000) *Britain and the End of the Roman Empire*. Stroud, Tempus Publishing.

Dark, P. (2000) *The Environment of Britain in the First Millennium A.D.* London, Duckworth.

Davenport, P. (2002) *Medieval Bath Uncovered*. Stroud, Tempus Publishing.

Davey, J. E. (2004) The Environs of South Cadbury in the Late Antique and Early Medieval periods. In R Collins and J Gerrard, (eds) *Debating Late Antiquity in Britain AD 300–700*, 43–54. Oxford, BAR British Series 365.

Davey, J. E. (2005) *The Roman to Medieval Transition in the Environs of South Cadbury Castle, Somerset*. Oxford, BAR British Scrics 399.

Davey, J. (2010) Rectilinear Field Systems and Dispersed Settlement in South Somerset and Dorset. In *Landscape Enquiries, The Proceedings of Clifton Antiquarian Club* 10.

Davies, W. (1982) The Latin Charter Tradition in Western Britain, Brittany and Ireland in the Medieval Period. In D. Whitelock, R. McKitterick and D. Dumville (eds) *Ireland in Early Medieval Europe; Studies in memory of Kathleen Hughes*, 258–80. Cambridge, Cambridge University Press.

Davis, G. R. C. (1958) *Medieval Cartularies of Great Britain*. London, Longman, Green.

Dewing, H. B. (1914–18) *Procopius: History of the Wars*. London, Heineman.

Doble, G. H. (1945–6) Saint Congar. *Antiquity* 19, 32–43 and 85–95.

Dodgson, J. McN. (1996) A Linguistic Analysis of the Place-names of the Burghal Hidage. In D. Hill and A. R. Rumble (eds) *The Defence of Wessex: The Burghal Hidage and Anglo-Saxon fortifications,* 98–127. Manchester, Manchester University Press.

Doherty, C. (1980) Exchange and Trade in Early Medieval Ireland. *The Journal of the Royal Society of Antiquaries of Ireland* 110, 67–90.

Down, T. and Carter, R. W. (1990) Tatworth Middle Field. *Proceedings of the Somerset Archaeological and Natural History Society* 133, 103–124.

Draper, S. (2002) Old English *wic* and *walh*; Britons and Saxons in Post-Roman Wiltshire. *Landscape History* 22, 39–43.

Draper, S. (2008) The Significance of Old English *Burh* in Anglo-Saxon England. In S. Crawford and H. Hamerow (eds) *Anglo-Saxon Studies in Archaeology and History* 15, 240–53. Oxford, Oxford University School of Archaeology.

Dubber, J. (2006) *Woolston Manor Farm; An analysis of preliminary fieldwork and documentary research results*. Unpublished MA dissertation, Bristol University.

Dugdale, Sir W. (1817–30) *Monasticon Anglicanum etc.* enlarged edition, 6 vols. in 8. London.

Dumville, D. (1992) *Wessex and England from Alfred to Edgar; six essays on political, cultural and ecclesiastical revival*. Woodbridge, The Boydell Press.

Dunne, J. (2009) *A Petrographical Analysis of the Early Medieval Pottery Assemblages from Shapwick, Somerset*. Unpublished undergraduate dissertation, University of Bristol.

Dunning, R. W. (1974) Northover. In R. W. Dunning (ed.) *A History of the County of Somerset*, 3, 224–30. London, Institute of Historical Research.

Dunning, R. W. (1975) Ilchester: a study in continuity. *Proceedings of the Somerset Archaeological and Natural History Society* 119, 44–50.

Dunning, R. W. (ed.) (1978) *The Victoria History of the County of Somerset*, 4. London, Institute of Historical Research.

Dunning, R. W. (ed.) (1985) *The Victoria History of the County of Somerset*, 5. London, Institute of Historical Research.

Dunning, R. W. (ed.) (1992) *The Victoria History of the County of Somerset*, 6. Oxford, Oxford University Press for the Institute of Historical Research.

Dyer, C. (1996) St Oswald and 10,000 West Midland peasants. In N. Brooks and C. Cubitt (eds) *St Oswald of Worcester: Life and Influence*, 173–94. London, Leicester University Press.

Eagles, B. (1994) The Archaeological Evidence for Settlement in the Fifth to Seventh centuries AD. In

M. Aston and C. Lewis (eds) *The Medieval Landscape of Wessex*, 23–4. Oxford, Oxbow.

Eagles, B. (2001) Anglo-Saxon Presence and Culture AD c. 450–c. 675. In P. Ellis (ed.) *Roman Wiltshire and After; Papers in Honour of Ken Annable,* 199–233. Devizes, Wiltshire Archaeological Society.

Eagles, B. (2004) Britons and Saxon on the Eastern Boundary of the Civitas Durotrigium. *Britannia* XXXV, 234–39.

Edwards, H. (1988) *The Charters of the Early West Saxon Kingdom.* Oxford, BAR British Series 198.

Ekwall, E. (1936) *Studies in English Place-Names.* Stockholm.

Ekwall, E. (1960) *The Concise Oxford Dictionary of English Place-Names* (4th ed.). Oxford, Clarendon Press.

Ellis, P. (1978) Archaeological Watching Briefs in Avon and Somerset, 1977. *Proceedings of the Somerset Archaeological and Natural History Society* 122, 103–111.

Ellis, P. (ed.) (2001) *Roman Wiltshire and After; Papers in Honour of Ken Annable.* Devizes, Wiltshire Archaeological Society.

Esmonde Cleary, A. S. (1989) *The Ending of Roman Britain.* London, Batsford.

Evans, D. S. (1984) *The Lives of the Welsh Saints.* Cardiff.

Everett, S. (1968) The Domesday Geography of Three Exmoor Parishes. *Proceedings of the Somerset Archaeological and Natural History Society* 112, 54–60.

Fabech, C. (1999) Organising the Landscape: a matter of production, power and religion. In T. Dickinson and D. Griffiths (eds) *The Making of Kingdoms; Anglo-Saxon Studies in Archaeology and History* 10, 37–48. Oxford, Oxford University Committee for Archaeology.

Faith, R. (1997) *The English Peasantry and the Growth of Lordship.* London, Leicester University Press.

Farmer, D. H. (1987) *The Oxford Dictionary of Saints,* 2nd ed. Oxford, Oxford University Press.

Faulkner, N. (2000) *The Decline and Fall of Roman Britain.* Stroud, Tempus.

Faulkner, N. (2004) The Case for the Dark Ages. In R Collins and J. Gerrard, (eds) *Debating Late Antiquity in Britain AD 300–700,* 5–12. Oxford, BAR British Series, 365.

Finberg, H. P. R. (1964) *Lucerna.* London, Macmillan.

Finberg, H. P. R. (1964b) *The Early Charters of Wessex.* Leicester, Leicester University Press.

Fleming, R. (1985) Monastic Lands and England's Defence in the Viking Age. *The English Historical Review* 100, no. 395. (April) 247–65.

Fleming, R. (1993) Rural Elites and Urban Communities in late Anglo-Saxon England. *Past and Present* 114, (Nov.), 3–37.

Foot, S. (1989) Parochial Ministry in Early Anglo-Saxon England: The role of the monastic communities. *Studies in Church History* XXVI, 43–54.

Foot, S. (1999) Remembering, Forgetting and Inventing: Attitudes to the Past in England at the end of the First Viking Age. *Transactions of the Royal Historical Society,* sixth ser. IX, 185–200.

Foot. S. (1999b). The Role of the Minster in Earlier Anglo-Saxon Society. In B. Thompson (ed.) *Monasteries and Society in Medieval Britain; Proceedings of the 1994 Harlaxton Symposium,* 35–58. Stamford, Paul Watkins.

Foot, S. (2000) *Veiled Women; The Disappearance of Nuns from Anglo-Saxon England, I and II.* Aldershot, Ashgate.

Foster, S. (1988) Early medieval inscription at Holcombe, Somerset. *Medieval Archaeology* 32, 208–11.

Fowler, P. (ed.) (1970) *Archaeological Review for 1970.* No. 5. Bristol, Department for Extramural Studies.

Fowler, P. (1975) Continuity in the Landscape? Some local archaeology in Wiltshire, Somerset and Gloucestershire. In P. Fowler (ed.) *Recent Work in Rural Archaeology,* 121–36. Bradford on Avon, Moonraker Press.

Fowler, P. (1978) Pre-Medieval Fields in the Bristol Region. In H. C. Bowen and P. J. Fowler (eds) *Early Land Allotment in the British Isles; A survey of recent work,* 29–48. Oxford, BAR British Series 48.

Fowler, P. (2001) Wansdyke in the Woods: An unfinished Roman military earthwork for a non-event. In P. Ellis (ed.) *Roman Wiltshire and After; Papers in Honour of Ken Annable,* 179–198. Devizes, Wiltshire Archaeological Society.

Fowler, P. (2002) *Farming in the First Millennium AD.* Cambridge, Cambridge University Press.

Fox, A. and C. (1960) Wansdyke Reconsidered. *The Archaeological Journal* 115, 1–48.

Fox, H. (2006) Fragmented Manors and the Customs of the Anglo-Saxons. In S. Keynes and A. P. Smyth, (eds) *Anglo-Saxons; Studies presented to Cyril Roy Hart,* 78–97. Dublin, Four Courts Press.

Francis, P. D. and Slater, D. S. (1990) A Record of vegetational and land use change from upland peat deposits on Exmoor. Part 2: Hoar Moor. *Proceedings of the Somerset Archaeological and Natural History Society* 134, 1–26.

Francis, P. D. and Slater, D. S. (1992) A Record of vegetational and land use change from upland peat deposits on Exmoor, Part 3: Codsend Moors. *Proceedings of the Somerset Archaeological and Natural History Society* 136, 9–28.

Fulford, M. C. (1989) Byzantium and Britain: A

Mediterranean Perspective on post-Roman Mediterranean Imports in Western Britain and Ireland. *Medieval Archaeology* 33, 1–6.

Garmonsway, G. N. (ed.) (1939) *Aelfric, Abbot of Eynsham.: Aelfric's Colloquy.* London, Methuen.

Galliou, P. and Jones, M. (1991) *The Bretons.* Oxford, Blackwell.

Geake, H. (1997) *The Use of Grave-Goods in Conversion-Period England c.600–c.850.* Oxford, BAR British Series 261.

Geary, P. J. (1978) *Furta Sacra: Thefts of Relics in the Central Middle Ages.* Princeton, Princeton University Press.

Geddes, J. (1991) Iron. In J. Blair and N. Ramsey, (eds) *English Medieval Industries,* 167–88. Hambledon and London, The Hambledon Press.

Gelling, M. (1967) English Place-names Derived from the Compound *Wicham. Medieval Archaeology* XI, 87–104.

Gelling, M. (1977) Latin Loan-words in Old English Place-names. *Anglo-Saxon England* 6, 1–13

Gelling, M. (1978) *Signposts to the Past,* London, J. and M. Dent.

Gelling, M. (1984) *Place-Names in the Landscape.* London, J. and M. Dent.

Gelling, M. and A. Cole. (2000) *The Landscape of Place-Names.* Stamford, Shaun Tyas.

Gerrard, C. and Aston, M. (2007) *The Shapwick Project, Somerset. A Rural Landscape Explored.* London, Society for Medieval Archaeology, Monograph 25.

Gerrard, J. (2004) How late is late? Pottery and the fifth century in southwest Britain. In R. Collins and J. Gerrard (eds) *Debating Late Antiquity in Britain AD 300–700,* 65–76. Oxford, BAR British Series 365.

Gerrard, J. (2005a) Bradley Hill, Somerset, and the end of Roman Britain: a study in continuity? *Proceedings of the Somerset Archaeological and Natural History Society* 148, 1–9.

Gerrard, J. (2005b) A Possible Late Roman 'Hoard' from Bath. *Britannia* 26, 271–3.

Gerrard, J. (2007) The Temple of Sulis Minerva at Bath and the End of Roman Britain. *The Antiquaries Journal* 87, 148–64.

Gerrard, S. (2000) *The Early British Tin Industry.* Stroud, Tempus.

Gillingham, J. (1989) "The most precious jewel in the English crown": Levels of Danegeld and Heregeld in the Early Eleventh Century. *English Historical Review* 104, 373–83.

Giot, P., G. Bernier G. and L. Fleuriot (1982) *Les Premiers Bretons: la Bretagne du Ve siècle à l'an mil.* Chateaulin, Editions JOS.

Gittos, B. and M. (1991) The Surviving Anglo-Saxon Fabric of East Coker Church. *Proceedings of the Somerset Archaeological and Natural History Society* 135, 107–11.

Gover, J. E. B., Mawer, A. and Stenton, F. M. (1931–2) *The Place-Names of Devon,* 1 and 2. London, English Place Name Society.

Graham-Campbell, J. (1991) Anglo-Scandinavian Equestrian Equipment in Eleventh Century England. *Anglo-Norman Studies* 14, 77–89.

Graham-Campbell, J. (ed.) (1994) *Cultural Atlas of the Viking World.* Abingdon, Andromeda Oxford Ltd.

Graham-Campbell, J. and Batey, C. E. (1998) *Vikings in Scotland; An Archaeological Survey.* Edinburgh, Edinburgh University Press.

Gray, H. St G. (1913) Trial Excavations at Cadbury Castle 1913. *Proceedings of the Somerset Archaeological and Natural History Society* 59, 1–24.

Green, E. (ed.) (1888) *The Survey and Rental of the Chantries, Colleges, and Free Chapels, Guilds, Fraternities, Lamps, Lights, and Obits in the County of Somerset: as returned in the 2nd year of the reign of King Edward VI. A.D. 1548.* Somerset Record Society 2, Taunton.

Green, T. (2007) Trade, Gift-giving and Romanitas: A Comparison of the Use of Roman Imports in Western Britain and Southern Scandinavia. *The Heroic Age: A Journal of Early Medieval Northwestern Europe,* Issue 10, May (eds) C. Chazelle and D. Forsman.

Grierson, P. and M. Blackburn (1986) *Medieval European Coinage,* 1 *The Early Middle Ages (5th–10th centuries).* Cambridge, Cambridge University Press.

Grinsell, L. V. (1970) *The Archaeology of Exmoor.* Newton Abbot, David and Charles.

Groves, C., Locatelli, C. and Nayling, N. (2004) *Tree Ring Analysis of Oak Samples from Stert Flats Fish Weirs, Bridgwater Bay, Somerset.* Portsmouth, English Heritage, Centre for Archaeology Report, 43/2004.

Guido, M. (1982) The Glass Beads. In R. Leech, *Excavations at Catsgore 1970–73; A Romano-British Village.* Western Archaeological Trust, Excavation Monograph No. 2, Bristol.

Guido, M. (2000) The Glass Beads. In Rahtz, P., Hirst S. and Wright S. M. *Cannington Cemetery.* Britannia Monograph Sr. No. 17, London, Society for the Promotion of Roman Studies.

Gutiérrez, A. (2004) The medieval pottery. In P. Leach and P. Ellis (eds) Roman and Medieval Remains at Manor Farm, Castle Cary. *Proceedings of the Somerset Archaeological and Natural History Society* 147, 81–128.

Gutiérrez, A, (2006) The Medieval and later pottery. In S. Rippon *et al.* (eds) *Landscape, Community and*

Colonisation: The North Somerset Levels during the 1st to 2nd millennia AD. CBA Research Report 152, York.

Gutiérrez, A. (2007) Medieval and Later pottery. In C. Gerrard and M. Aston (eds) *The Shapwick Project, Somerset. A Rural Landscape Explored,* 601–71. Society for Medieval Archaeology, Monograph 25, London.

Haddan, A. W. and Stubbs, W. (eds 1869–78) Penitential of Theodore. In *Councils and Ecclesiastical Documents relating to Great Britain and Ireland,* 172–213. 3 vols. London.

Hadley, D. (1996) Multiple Estates and the Origins of the Manorial Structure of the Northern Danelaw. *Journal of Historical Geography* 22, 3–15.

Hagen, A. (1995) *A Second Handbook of Anglo-Saxon Food and Drink Production and Distribution.* Hockwold cum Wilton, Norfolk, Anglo-Saxon Books.

Hall, D. (1995) *The Open Fields of Northamptonshire.* Northampton Record Society XXXVIII. Northampton.

Hall, T. (2000) *Minster Churches in the Dorset Landscape.* Oxford, BAR British Series 304.

Hall, T. (2005) Sherborne: Saxon Christianity be Westanwudu. In K. Barker, D. Hinton and A. Hunt (eds) *St Wulfsige and Sherborne: essays to celebrate the millennium of the Benedictine Abbey, 998–1998,* 133–48. Oxford, Oxbow Books.

Härke, H. (1990) "Warrior Graves"? The Background of the Anglo-Saxon Burial Rite. *Past and Present* 126, 22–43.

Härke, H. (2002) Kings and Warriors: Population and Landscape from Post-Roman to Norman Britain. In *The Peopling of Britain: The Shaping of the Human Landscape,* 145–75. Linacre Lectures 1999. Oxford, Oxford University Press.

Härke, H. (2007) Invisible Britons, Gallo-Romans and Russians: Perspectives on culture change. In N. Higham (ed.) *Britons in Anglo-Saxon England, 57–67.* Woodbridge, The Boydell Press.

Harris, A. (2003) *Byzantium, Britain, and the West: The Archaeology of Cultural Identity AD 400–650.* Stroud, Tempus.

Harvey, P. D. A. (1993) Rectitudines Personarum Singularum and Gerefa. *English Historical Review* 108, no. 426, 1–22.

Harvey, S. P. J. (1983) The Extent and Profitability of Demesne Agriculture in England in the later Eleven Century. In T. A. Aston, P. R. Coss, C. Dyer and J. Thirsk, (eds) *Social Relations and Ideas; Essays in Honour of R. H. Hilton,* 45–72. Cambridge, Cambridge University Press.

Hase, P. H. (1994) The Church in the Wessex Heartlands. In M. Aston and C. Lewis, (eds) *The Medieval Landscape of Wessex,* 47–82. Oxford, Oxbow.

Haslam, J. (ed.) (1984) *Anglo-Saxon Towns in Southern England.* Chichester, Phillimore.

Haywood, J. (1999) *Dark Age Naval Power: A Reassessment of Frankish and Anglo-Saxon Seafaring Activity.* 2nd ed. Hockwald-cum-Wilton, Norfolk, Anglo-Saxon Books.

Higham, N. (1990) Settlement, Land Use and Domesday Ploughlands. *Landscape History,* 12, 33–44.

Higham, N. (1992) *Rome, Britain and the Anglo-Saxons,* London, Seaby.

Hill, D. (1981) *An Atlas of Anglo-Saxon England.* Oxford, Basil Blackwell.

Hill, D. (1996) The Calculation and the Purpose of the Burghal Hidage. In Hill, D. and Rumble, A. R. (eds) *The Defence of Wessex; The Burghal Hidage and Anglo-Saxon fortifications,* 92–7. Manchester, Manchester University Press.

Hill, D. (2000) Sulh – the Anglo-Saxon Plough c.1000 AD. *Landscape History* 22, 5–20.

Hill, D. and Rumble, A. R. (eds) (1996) *The Defence of Wessex; The Burghal Hidage and Anglo-Saxon Fortifications.* Manchester, Manchester University Press.

Hinton, D. (2008) *The Alfred Jewel and other late Anglo-Saxon decorated metalwork.* Oxford, The Ashmolean Museum.

Hobhouse, E. (Bishop Hobhouse) (ed.) (1887) *A Calendar of the Register of John de Drokensford, Bishop of Bath and Wells, AD 1309–1329.* Somerset Record Society 1, Taunton.

Hodges, R. (1981) Trade and Market Origins in the Ninth Century: An archaeological perspective of Anglo-Carolingian Relations. In M. Gibson and J. Nelson (eds) *Charles the Bald: Court and Kingdom,* 203–23. Oxford, BAR International Series 101.

Hodges, R. (1982) *Dark Age Economics: The origins of towns and trade 600–100.* London, Duckworth.

Hodges, R. (1989) *The Anglo-Saxon Achievement.* London, Duckworth.

Hodges, R. (2006) *Goodbye to the Vikings?; Re-Reading Early Medieval Archaeology.* London, Duckworth.

Hollinrake, C. and Hollinrake, N. (1989) Bridgwater, Wembdon Hill. *Proceedings of the Somerset Archaeological and Natural History Society* 133, 171.

Hollinrake, C. and Hollinrake, N. (2002) A Late-Saxon Comb Handle from Bawdrip. *Proceedings of the Somerset Archaeological and Natural History Society* 144, 213–4.

Hollinrake, C. and Hollinrake, N. (2007) Glastonbury's Anglo-Saxon Canal and Dunstan's Dyke. In J. Blair (ed.) *Waterways and Canal Building in Medieval England,* 235–43. Oxford, Oxford University Press.

Holmes, T. S. (ed.) (1896) *The Register of Ralph of Shrewsbury, Bishop of Bath and Wells, 1329–1363.* Somerset Record Society 9 and 10, Taunton.

Holmes, T. S. (ed.) (1899) *The Registers of Walter Giffard, Bishop of Bath and Wells, 1265–6 and of Henry Bowet, Bishop of Bath and Wells, 1401–7*. Somerset Record Society 13, Taunton.

Hooke, D. (1981) Open Field Agriculture. In R. T. Rowley (ed.) *The Origins of Open-Field Agriculture*, 39–63. London, Croome Helm.

Hooke, D. (1989) Early Medieval Estate and Settlement Patterns: The Documentary Evidence. In M. Aston, D. Austin and C. Dyer, (eds) *The Rural Settlements of Medieval England*, 9–30. Oxford, Blackwell.

Hooke, D. (1998) *The Landscape of Anglo-Saxon England*. London, Leicester University Press.

Horne, Dom E. (1926) Saxon cemetery at Buckland Denham, Somerset. *Antiquaries Journal* 6, 77–8.

Horne, Dom E. (1929) Saxon Cemetery at Camerton, Somerset. *Proceedings of the Somerset Archaeological and Natural History Society* 74, 61–70.

Horne, Dom E. (1933) Anglo-Saxon Cemetery at Camerton, Somerset, Part II. *Proceedings of the Somerset Archaeological and Natural History Society* 79, 39–63

Horstman, C. (1901) *Nova legenda Angli: as collected by John of Tynemouth, John Capgrave and others, and first printed with new lives, by Wynkin de Worde, a.d. MDXVI: now re-edited with fresh material from MS and printed sources*. Oxford, Clarendon Press.

Hunt, W. (1885) *History of the diocese of Bath and Wells*. London, SPCK.

Hunt, W. (ed.) (1893) *Two Chartularies of the Priory of St Peter at Bath*. Somerset Record Society 7, Taunton.

Hunt, J. W. (1964) Notes on the Trial Trench Excavation, Chapel close, Winthill, Banwell, 1954–55. *Journal of the Axbridge Caving Group and Archaeological Society*, 1963, 35–42. Axbridge.

Hunter, J. (ed.) (1840) Historiola de Primordiis Episcopatus Somersetensis. *Ecclesiastical Documents,* 3–41. Camden Society 8, London.

Iles, R. and Stacey, M. (1984) Bleadon. *Bristol and Avon Archaeology* 3.

John, E. (1966) *Orbis Britanniae*. Leicester, Leicester University Press.

Jones, B. and Mattingley, D. (1990) *An Atlas of Roman Britain*. Oxford, Blackwell.

Jones, S. R. H. (1991) Devaluation and the Balance of Payments in Eleventh-Century England: An Exercise in Dark Age Economics. *The Economic History Review* 44, 594–607.

Jones, S. R. H. (1993) Transaction Costs, Institutional Change, and the Emergence of a Market Economy in Later Anglo-Saxon England. *The Economic History Review* 46, 658–78.

Kain, R. J. P. and Oliver, R. R. (2001) *Historic Parishes of England and Wales; Electronic Map – Gazetteer –Metadata*. Colchester, History Data Service, UK Data Archive.

Keen, L. (1984) The Towns of Dorset. In J. Haslam (ed.) *Anglo-Saxon towns in Southern England*, 203–47. Chichester, Phillimore.

Kemp, B. R. and Shorrocks, D. M. M. (1974) *Medieval Deeds of Bath and District*, Somerset Record Society 73, Taunton.

Kent, J. P. C. (1979) Coinage and the End of Roman Britain. In P. J. Casey (ed.) *The End of Roman Britain*, 21–2. Oxford, BAR British Series 71.

Keynes, S. (1994) The "Dunstan B" Charters. *Anglo-Saxon England* XXIII, 165–93.

Keynes, S. (1994b). The West Saxon Charters of King Æthelwulf and his sons. *The English Historical Review* 109, 1109–49.

Keynes, S. (1997) Giso, Bishop of Wells, (1061–88). *Anglo-Norman Studies* 29, 203–71, Woodbridge, Boydell.

Keynes, S. (1999) Asser. In M. Lapidge, J. Blair, S. Keynes and D. Scraggs (eds) *The Blackwell Encyclopedia of Anglo-Saxon England*, Oxford, Blackwell, 48–50.

Keynes, S. and Lapidge, M. (trans and eds) (1983) *Alfred the Great; Asser's Life of King Alfred and other contemporary sources*. London, Penguin Books.

Kidd, A. and Young, A. (ND) *Eckweek in Wellow: A Case Study in the Organisation and Origins of the Medieval Landscape and Society of Somerset*. Bristol, Avon County Council.

Kirby, D. P. (1991) *The Earliest English Kings*. London, Unwin Hyman.

Knight, J. (1981) In tempore Justini Consulisi; contacts between the British and Gaulish churches before Augustine. In A. Detsicas (ed.) *Collecteanea: Essays in Memory of Stuart Rigold*, 54–62. Maidstone, Kent Archaeological Society.

Knight, J. (1992) The Early Christian Latin Inscriptions of Britain and Gaul: Chronology and Context. In N. Edwards and A. Lane (eds) *The Early Church in Wales and the West: Recent work in Early Christian Archaeology, History and Place-Names*, 54–60. Oxbow Monograph 16, Oxford, Oxbow.

Knight, J. (2003) *The Landscape Archaeology of the Ancient Woodlands of Northern Somerset*. Unpublished PhD thesis, University of Bristol.

Knowles, D. (1963) *The Monastic Order in England: A History of its Development from the Times of St Dunstan to the Fourth Lateran Council, 940–1216*, 2nd ed., Cambridge, Cambridge University Press.

Kurath, H. and Kuhn, S. (1954) *A Middle English Dictionary*. Michigan, University of Michigan Press.

Lane, T. and Coles, J. (eds) (2002) *Through Wet and Dry; Essays in honour of David Hall*. Exeter, Wetlands Archaeological Research Project.

Langdon, M. (1986) Wembdon, Wembdon Hill. *Proceedings of the Somerset Archaeological and Natural History Society* 130.

Lapidge, M. (1982) The Cult of St Indract at Glastonbury. In D. Whitelock, R. McKitterick and D. Dumville (eds) *Ireland in Early Medieval Europe: Studies in Memory of Kathleen Hughes,* 179–212. Cambridge, Cambridge University Press.

Lapidge, M. (1984) Gildas's education and the Latin culture of sub-Roman Britain. In M. Lapidge and D. N. Dumville (eds) *Gildas: new approaches* (Studies in Celtic history 5), 27–50. Woodbridge, The Boydell Press.

Lapidge, M. (1992) C. and the Vita S. Dunstani. In N. Ramsey, M. Sparks and T. Tatton-Brown (eds) *St Dunstan; His Life, Times and Cult*, 247–60. Woodbridge, The Boydell Press.

Lapidge, M. (2007) The Career of Aldhelm. *Anglo-Saxon England* 36, 15–69.

Lapidge, M., Blair, J., Keynes, S. and Scragg, D. (eds) (1999). *The Blackwell Encyclopaedia of Anglo-Saxon England*. Oxford, Blackwell.

Lawson, M. K. (1989) 'These stories look true': Levels of Taxation in the Reigns of Aethelred II and Cnut. *The English Historical Review*, 104, no 411, 385–406.

Leach, P. (ed.) (1982) *Ilchester, Volume1; Excavations 1974–5*. Bristol, Western Archaeological Trust.

Leach, P. (1987) The Hinterland of Ilchester: Archaeology, Alluviation and the Environment. In N. D. Balaam, B. Levitan and V. Straker, (eds) *Studies in Palaeoeconomy in South West England*. Oxford, BAR British Series 181.

Leach, P. (2003) Shepton Mallet: a roadside settlement on the Fosse Way. In Pete Wilson (ed.) *The Archaeology of Roman towns; Studies in honour of John S. Wacher*, 137–44. Oxford, Oxbow Books.

Leach, P. with Evans, J. (2001). *Excavations of a Romano-British Roadside Settlement in Somerset: Fosse Lane Shepton Mallet 1990*. Britannia Monograph Series No. 18. London, Society for the Promotion of Roman Studies.

Leahy, K. and Bland, R. (2009) *The Staffordshire Hoard*. London, The British Museum Press.

Leech R. H. (1976) Romano-British and medieval settlement at Wearne. *Proceedings of the Somerset Archaeological and Natural History Society* 120, 45–50.

Leech, R. H. (1980) Religion and Burials in South Somerset and North Dorset. In W. Rodwell (ed.) *Temples, Churches and Religion: Recent Research in Roman Britain*, 329–66. Oxford, BAR British Series 77 (i).

Leech, R. H. (1981) The Excavation of a Romano-British farmstead and cemetery on Bradley Hill, Somerton, Somerset. *Britannia* 12, 177–252.

Leech, R. H. (1982) *Excavations at Catsgore 1970–1973; A Romano-British Village*. Bristol, Western Archaeological Trust.

Leech, R. H. (1986) The Excavation of a Romano-Celtic Temple and a later Cemetery on Lamyatt Beacon, Somerset. *Britannia* 17, 259–328.

Levinson, W. (1946) *England and the Continent in the Eighth Century*. Oxford, The Clarendon Press.

Levitan, B. (1990) Excavation of the cCemetery and the Human Bone Evidence. In M. Bell (ed.) *Brean Down Excavations, 1983–1987, 73–7*. London, English Heritage.

Lewis, C., P. Mitchell-Fox, P. and Dyer, C. (1997) *Village, Hamlet and Field; changing medieval settlements in central England,* Manchester, Manchester University Press.

Little, L. K. (2007) Life and Afterlife of the First Plague Pandemic. In L. K. Little (ed.) *Plague and the End of Antiquity; The Pandemic of 541–750,* 3–32. Cambridge, Cambridge University Press.

Lucas, A. (2006) *Wind, Water, Work: Ancient and Medieval Milling Technology*. Leiden, Brill.

Lyon, S. (2001) The Coinage of Edward the Elder. In N. J. Higham and D. H. Hill (eds) *Edward the Elder; 899–924,* 67–78. London and New York, Routledge.

Maddicott, J. R. (1989) Trade, Industry and the Wealth of King Alfred. *Past and Present* 123, 3–51.

Maddicott, J. R. (1997) Plague in Seventh Century England. *Past and Present* 156, 7–54.

Major, A. F. (1911) Report on Excavation work at Brinscombe, Weare, Somerset. *Proceedings of the Somerset Archaeological and Natural History Society* 62, 110–3.

Margery, I. D. (1955) *Roman Roads in Britain*. London, Phoenix House Ltd.

McCormick, M. (2001) *Origins of the European Economy; Communications and Commerce AD300–900*. Cambridge, Cambridge University Press.

McCormick, M. (2002) New Light on the 'Dark Ages': How the Slave Trade Fuelled the Carolingian Economy. *Past and Present* 177, 17–54.

McCrone, P. (1994) Carhampton, Eastbury Farm. *Proceedings of the Somerset Archaeological and Natural History Society* 137, 144.

McCrone, P. (1995) Carhampton, Eastbury Farm. *Proceedings of the Somerset Archaeological and Natural History Society* 138, 177.

McKitterick, R. (1997) Constructing the Past in the Early Middle-Ages: The Case of the Royal Frankish Annals *Royal Historical Society Transactions,* 101–30.

Metcalf, D. M. (1967) The Prosperity of North-Western

Europe in the Eighth and Ninth Centuries. *The Economic History Review*, New Series, 20, 344–57.

Metcalf, D. M. (1978) The Ranking of Boroughs: numismatic evidence from the reign of Æthelred II. In D. Hill (ed.) *Ethelred the Unready*. Oxford, BAR British Series 59.

Metcalf, D. M. (1998) The monetary Economy of Ninth-Century England South of the Humber. In D. M. Metcalf and D. Dumville (eds) *Kings, Currency and Alliances: History and coinage of Southern England in the ninth Century*, 167–98. Woodbridge, Boydell Press.

Metcalf, D. M. (2006) Monetary circulation in the Danelaw, 973–1083. In S. Keynes and A. P. Smyth, (eds) *Anglo-Saxons; Studies presented to Cyril Roy Hart*, 159–87. Dublin, Four Courts Press.

Moore, J. S. (1964) The Domesday Teamland: A Reconsideration, *Transactions of the Royal Historical Society* 14, 109–30.

Moore, J. S. (1989) Domesday Slavery. In R. Allen Brown (ed.) *Anglo-Norman Studies 11, Proceedings of the Battle Conference 1988*, 191–220. Woodbridge, Boydell Press.

Moorhead, T. S. N. (2001) Roman Coin Finds from Wiltshire. In P. Ellis (ed.) *Roman Wiltshire and After; Papers in Honour of Ken Annable*, 199–233. Devizes, Wiltshire Archaeological Society.

Moreland, J. (2000) Ethnicity, Power and the English. In W. O. Frazer and A. Tyrrell (eds) *Social Identity in Early Medieval Britain*, 23–51. London and New York, Leicester University Press.

Moreland, J. (2000) The Significance of Production in Eighth Century England. In I. L. Hansen and C. Wickham (eds) *The Long Eighth Century*, 69–104. Leiden, Brill.

Morris, R. (1983) *The Church in British Archaeology*. Research Report 47. London, Council for British Archaeology.

Muir, B. J. (ed.) (1994) *The Exeter Anthology of Old English Poetry; An edition of Exeter Dean and Chapter Ms. 3501, vol. 1 Texts*. Exeter, Exeter University Press.

Munby, J. (1982) *Domesday Book, 4, Hampshire*. Chichester, Phillimore.

Mynors, R. A. B., Thomson, R. M. and Winterbottom, M. (eds and trans) (1998) *William of Malmesbury, Gesta Regum Anglorum, The History of the English Kings*, vol 1. Oxford, Clarendon Press.

Nelson, J. (1983) The Church's Military Service in the Ninth Century; A Contemporary Comparative View? In W. J. Sheils, (ed.) *The Church and War, Studies in Church History* 20, 128–42. Oxford, Basil Blackwell.

Nelson, J. (1992) Debate – Trade, Industry and the Wealth of King Alfred. *Past and Present* 135, 151–63.

Nelson, J. (1992) *Charles the Bald*. London and New York, Longman.

Nelson, J. (2003) England and the Continent in the Ninth Century: II, The Vikings and Others. *Transactions of the Royal Historical Society*, sixth ser., 13, 1–28.

Newman, C. (1992) A Later Saxon Cemetery at Templecombe. *Proceedings of the Somerset Archaeological and Natural History Society* 136, 61–72.

O'Donovan, M. A., (ed.) (1988) *Charters of Sherborne*. Oxford, British Academy.

Oakes, C. and Costen, M. (2003) The Congresbury Carvings: An Eleventh-century Saint's Shrines. *The Antiquaries Journal* 83, 281–309.

Okasha, E. (1993) *Corpus of Early Christian Inscribed Stones of South-west Britain*. London, Leicester University Press.

Oosthuizen, S. (2007) The Anglo-Saxon Kingdom of Mercia and the Origins and Distribution of Common Fields. *The Agricultural History Review* 55, II, 153–80.

Orosius, P. (1767) *Adversus paganos historiarum libri septem*. Leiden.

Page, W. (1911) *The Victoria County History of Somerset*, 2. London, Constable.

Pearce, S. (1973) The Dating of Some Celtic Dedications and the Hagiographical Traditions of South Western Britain. *The Devonshire Association Report and Transactions* 105, 95–120.

Pearce, S. (1978) *The Kingdom of Dumnonia; Studies in History and Tradition in South-Western Britain A.D. 350–1150*. Padstow, Lodenek Press.

Pearce, S. (1982) Estates and Church Sites in Dorset and Gloucestershire: The emergence of a Christian Society. In S. Pearce (ed.) *The Early Church in Western Britain and Ireland; Studies presented to C. A. Ralegh Radford*, 117–138. Oxford, BAR British Series 118.

Pearson, T. (1982) The Post-Roman Pottery. In P. Leach *et al. Ilchester, Volume 1; Excavations 1974–5*, 169–217. Bristol, Western Archaeological Trust Excavation Monograph 3.

Pelteret, D. (1985) Slavery in Anglo-Saxon England. In J. D. Woods and D. A. E. Pelteret (eds) *The Anglo-Saxons; Synthesis and Achievement*, 117–33. Waterloo, Ontario, Wilfred Laurier University Press.

Pestell, T. and Ulmschneider, K. (2003) *Markets in Early Medieval Europe: Trading and 'Productive' Sites, 650–850*. Oxford, Windgatherer Press.

Petts, D. (2002) Cemeteries and Boundaries in Western Britain. In S. Lacy and A. Reynolds (eds) *Burial in Early Medieval England and Wales*, 24–46. London, The Society for Medieval Archaeology.

Plummer, C. (ed.) (1896) Epistolam ad Ecgbertum. In

Venerabilis Baedae, Opera Historica. tom.1. Oxford, Clarendon Press.

Ponsford, M. (1979) Human Remains from a sub-Roman Cemetery at Station Road, Portishead, Avon. In N. Thomas (ed.) *Rescue Archaeology in the Bristol Area* 1, 7–14. Bristol, City Museum and Art Gallery.

Preest, D. (trans.) (2002) *William of Malmesbury: The Deeds of the Bishops of England*. Woodbridge, The Boydell Press.

Pretty, K. B. (1969) Portishead. In P. J. Fowler (ed.) *Archaeological Review for 1969*. Bristol, Dept. of Extra-Mural Studies.

Prior, S. (2006) *A Few Well-Positioned Castles; The Norman Art of War*. Stroud, Tempus.

Prior, S. (2007) Strategy, Symbolism and the Downright Unusual. In M. Costen (ed.) *People and Places; Essays in Honour of Mick Aston,* 76–89. Oxford, Oxbow.

Pryce, H. (1992) Pastoral Care in Early Medieval Wales. In J. Blair and R. Sharpe, (eds) *Pastoral Care Before the Parish,* 41–62. Leicester, Leicester University Press.

Rackham, O. (1980) *Ancient Woodland: Its History, Vegetation and Uses in England*. London, Edward Arnold.

Radford, C. A. R. (1963) The Church in Somerset Down to 1100. *Proceedings of the Somerset Archaeological and Natural History Society* 106, 28–45.

Rahtz, P. (1951) The Roman Temple at Pagans Hill, Chew Stoke, North Somerset. *Proceedings of the Somerset Archaeological and Natural History Society* 96, 45–72.

Rahtz, P. and Harris, L. G. (1956–7) The Temple Well and Other Buildings at Pagans Hill, Chew Stoke, North Somerset. *Proceedings of the Somerset Archaeological and Natural History Society,* 101–2, 15–51.

Rahtz, P. (1971) Excavations on Glastonbury Tor, Somerset, 1964–66. *Archaeological Journal* 127, 1–81.

Rahtz, P. (1974) Pottery in Somerset AD400–1066. In V. Evison, H. Hodges and J. G. Hurst (eds) *Medieval pottery from excavations: Studies presented to Gerald Clough Dunning,* 95–126. London, J. Baker.

Rahtz, P. (1977) Late Roman Cemeteries and Beyond. In R. Reece, (ed.) *Burial in the Roman World*, Research Report 22. London, Council for British Archaeology.

Rahtz, P. (1979) *The Saxon and Medieval Palaces at Cheddar*. Oxford, BAR British Series 65.

Rahtz, P. (1993) *Glastonbury.* London, English Heritage.

Rahtz, P. and Hirst, S. (1974) *Beckery Chapel Glastonbury 1967–8.* Glastonbury, Glastonbury Antiquarian Society.

Rahtz, P. *et al.* (1992) *Cadbury Congresbury 1968–73: A Late/post-Roman hilltop settlement in Somerset*. Oxford, BAR British Series 223.

Rahtz, P., Hirst, S. and Wright, S. M. (2000) *Cannington Cemetery*. Britannia Monograph No. 17, London, Society for the Promotion of Roman Studies.

Rahtz, P. and Fowler, P. (1972) Somerset A. D. 400–700. In P. Fowler (ed.) *Archaeology and the Landscape: Essays for L. V. Grinsel,* 187–221. London, John Baker.

Rahtz, P. and Watts, L. (1989) Pagans Hill Revisited. *Archaeological Journal* 146, 330–71.

Raleigh Radford, C. A. (1928) The Roman site at Westland... *Proceedings of the Somerset Archaeological and Natural History Society* 74, 122–43.

Ralegh Radford, C. A. (1975) *The Early Christian Inscriptions of Dumnonia*. Truro, Institute for Cornish Studies.

Rawlings, M. *et al.* (1992) Romano-British Sites Observed along the Codford-Ilchester water pipeline. *Proceedings of the Somerset Archaeological and Natural History Society* 136, 29–60.

Reece, R. (2002) *The Coinage of Roman Britain*. Stroud, Tempus.

Reuter, T. (1997) The Recruitment of armies in the Early Middle Ages: what can we know? In A. N. Jørgensen and B. L. Clausen (eds) *Military Aspects of Scandinavian Society in a European Perspective, AD 1–1300,* 32–7. Copenhagen, National Museum of Denmark.

Reynolds, A. and Langlands, A. (2006) Social Identities on the Macro Scale: A Maximum View of Wansdyke. In Davies, W., Halsall, G. and Reynolds, A. (eds) *People and Space in the Middle Ages, 300–1300,* 13–42. Turnhout, Brepols.

Reynolds, S. (1992) Bookland, Folkland and Fiefs. In M. Chibnall, (ed.) *Anglo-Norman Studies XIV,* 211–27. Woodbridge, The Boydell Press.

Rippon, S. (1997) *The Severn Estuary; landscape evolution and wetland reclamation*. London, Leicester University Press.

Rippon, S. (2006) *Landscape, Community and Colonisation: The North Somerset Levels during the 1st to 2nd millennia AD*. Research Report 152, York, Council for British Archaeology.

Rippon, S. *et al.* (2000) The Romano-British Exploitation of Coastal Wetlands: Survey and Excavation on the North Somerset Levels 1993–7. *Britannia* 31, 69–200.

Rippon, S., Fyte, R. M. and Brown, A. G. (2006) Beyond villages and open fields: The origins and development of a historic landscape characterised by dispersed settlement in south-west England. *Medieval Archaeology* 50, 31–70.

Rippon, S. (2007) Waterways and Water Transport on Reclaimed Coastal Marshlands: The Somerset Levels and Beyond. In J. Blair (ed.) *Waterways and Canal-Building in Medieval England*, 207–27. Oxford, Oxford University Press.

Roberts, T. (1992) Welsh Ecclesiastical Place-Names and Archaeology. In N. Edwards and A. Lane (eds) *The Early Church in Wales and the West,* 41–4. Oxbow Monographs 16. Oxford, Oxbow.

Robertson, A. S. (eds R. Hobbs and T. V. Buttrey) (2000) *An Inventory of Romano-British Coin Hoards.* London, Royal Numismatic Society Special Publication, 20.

Robertson, N. (2006) Dunstan and Monastic Reform: Tenth-Century Fact or Twelfth-Century Fiction? In *Anglo-Norman Studies XXVIII,* 153–67. Woodbridge, Boydell Press.

Robinson, J. Armitage (1918) The Early Endowment of the See of Wells. In *The Saxon Bishops of Wells, A Historical Study in the Tenth Century.* London, British Academy supplemental papers, IV.

Robinson, J. Armitage (1919) A Fragment of the Life of St Cungar. *Journal of Theological Studies* 20, 97–108.

Robinson, J. Armitage (1921) *Somerset Historical Essays.* London, British Academy.

Rodwell, W. *et al.* (2001) *Wells Cathedral: Excavations and Structural Studies 1978–93.* London, English Heritage Archaeological Reports 21.

Rollason, D. (1978) Lists of saints' resting-places in Anglo-Saxon England. *Anglo-Saxon England* 7, 61–94.

Rollason, D. (1989) *Saints and Relics in Anglo-Saxon England.* Oxford, Basil Blackwell.

Roskams, S. (1996) Urban transition in early medieval Britain: The case of York. In N. Christie and S. T. Loseby (eds) *Towns in Transition: Urban Evolution in Late Antiquity and the Early Middle Ages,* 262–88. Aldershot, Scolar.

Ross, C. D. (ed.) (1959) *Cartulary of St Mark's Hospital Bristol.* Bristol, Bristol Record Society.

Rumble, A. R. (1987) Old English Boc-land as an Anglo-Saxon Estate-Name. *Leeds Studies in English* 18, 219–30.

Rumble, A. R. (1996) An Edition and Translation of the Burghal Hidage, Together with Recension C of the Tribal Hidage. In D. Hill and A. R. Rumble (eds) *The Defence of Wessex; The Burghal Hidage and Anglo-Saxon fortifications,* 14–35. Manchester, Manchester University Press.

Rumble, A. R. (2001) Edward the Elder and the Churches of Winchester and Wessex. In N. J. Higham and D. H. Hill (eds) *Edward the Elder 899–924,* 230–47. London and New York, Routledge.

Ryan, N. S. (1988) *Coin Finds from Roman Britain; A computer analysis.* Oxford, BAR British Series 183.

Salway, P. (1981) *Roman Britain.* Oxford, Clarendon Press.

Sawyer, P. H. (1968) *Anglo-Saxon Charters; An annotated list and bibliography.* London, Royal Historical Society.

Sawyer, P. H. (1971) *The Age of the Vikings,* 2nd ed. London, Edward Arnold.

Sawyer, P. H. (1973) Anglo-Saxon Settlement: the documentary evidence. In T. Rowley (ed.) *Anglo-Saxon Settlement and Landscape,* 106–19. Oxford, BAR British Series 6.

Sawyer, P. H. (1983) The Royal *Tun* in Pre-conquest England. In P. Wormald, D. Bullough and R. Collins (eds) *Ideal and Reality in Frankish and Anglo-Saxon Society,* 273–99. Oxford, Basil Blackwell.

Schofield. B. (ed.) (1927) *Muchelney Memoranda; edited from a Breviary of the abbey in the possession of J. Meade Falkner.* Somerset Record Society 42, Taunton.

Scott, J. (ed. and trans.) (1981) *The Early History of Glastonbury. An Edition and Translation of William of Malmesbury's 'De Antiquitate Glastonie Ecclesie'.* Woodbridge, Boydell.

Sharp, S. (2001) The West Saxon Tradition of Dynastic Marriage. In N.J. Higham and D. H. Hill (eds) *Edward the Elder; 899–924,* 79–88. London and New York, Routledge.

Simpson, L. (1989) The King Alfred/St Cuthbert Episode. In G. Bonner, D. Rollason and C. Stancliffe (eds) *St Cuthbert, His Cult and His Community to AD 1200,* 397–411. Woodbridge, Boydell Brewer.

Sims-Williams, P. (1975) Continental Influence at Bath Monastery in the Seventh Century, *Anglo-Saxon England* 4, 1–10.

Sims-Williams, P. (1983) The Settlement of England in Bede and the 'Chronicle', *Anglo-Saxon England* 12, 1–41.

Sims-Williams, P. (1990) *Religion and Literature in Western England, 600–800.* Cambridge, Cambridge University Press.

Scott Holmes, T. (ed.) (1899) *The Registers of Walter Giffard, Bishop of Bath and Wells, 1265–6 and Henry Bowet, Bishop of Bath and Wells, 1401–7.* Somerset Record Society 13, Taunton.

Sitwell, G. (trans.) (1958) *The Life of St Odo of Cluny by John of Salerno,* London, Sheed and Ward.

Smith, A. H. (1970) *English Place-Name Elements,* parts I and II, Cambridge, Cambridge University Press.

Smisson, R. (2004) *The Relationship between Villages and Upland Grazing Areas on and Around Western Mendip from Shute-Shelve to Priddy in the Period from the Early 5th Century to 1086.* Unpublished dissertation, University of Bristol.

Sparey-Green, C. (1996) Poundbury, Dorset: Settlement and Economy in Late and Post-Roman Dorchester. In K. R. Dark (ed.) *External Contacts and the Economy of Late Roman and Post-Roman Britain,* 121–52. Woodbridge, The Boydell Press.

Sparey-Green, C. (2004) Living Amongst the Dead. From Roman cemetery to post-Roman monastic settlement at Poundbury. In R. Collins and J. Gerrard (eds) *Debating Late Antiquity, AD 300–700,* 103–111. Oxford, BAR British Series 365.

Spufford, P. (1988) *Money and its Use in Medieval Europe.* Cambridge, Cambridge University Press.

Stenton, F. M. (1947) *Anglo-Saxon England.* (2nd ed.) Oxford, Clarendon Press.

Stokes, P. (1995) Buckland Dinham, Orchardleigh, *Proceedings of the Somerset Archaeological and Natural History Society* 138, 175.

Story, J. (2003) *Carolingian Connections; Anglo-Saxon England and Carolingian Francia, c. 750–870.* Aldershot, Ashgate.

Straker, V. (2008) Early Medieval Environmental Background. In C. J. Webster (ed.) *The Archaeology of South West England,* 189–94. Taunton, Taunton County Council.

Stubbs, W. (1874) *Memorials of Saint Dunstan; Archbishop of Canterbury.* London, HMSO.

Swanton, M. J. (1999) King Alfred's Ships: Text and Context, *Anglo-Saxon England* 28, 1–22.

Swanton, M. (ed. and trans.) (2000) *The Anglo-Saxon Chronicles.* London, Phoenix.

Sykes, N. J. (2006) From *Cu* and *Sceap* to *Beffe* and *Motton;* the management, distribution and consumption of cattle and sheep in medieval England. In C. M. Woolgar, D. Serjeantson and T. Waldron, (eds) *Food in Medieval England* 56–71. Oxford, Oxford University Press.

Tabor, R. (2008) Woolston Manor Farm, North Cadbury: An outline report of fieldwork in 2006–7 by the South Cadbury Environs Project. *Proceedings of the Somerset Archaeological and Natural History Society* 151, 83–96.

Taylor, R. F. (1967) An Anglo-Saxon Cemetery at Compton Pauncefoot. *Proceedings of the Somerset Archaeological and Natural History Society* 111, 67–9

Thacker, A. (1992) Monks, preaching and pastoral care in early Anglo-Saxon England. In J. Blair and R. Sharpe (eds) *Pastoral Care Before the Parish,* 137–70. Leicester, Leicester University Press.

Thacker, A. (2002) Loca Sanctorum: The Significance of Place in the Study of the Saints. In A. Thacker and R. Sharpe (eds) *Local Saints and Local Churches in the Early Medieval West,* 1–44. Oxford, Oxford University Press.

Thomas, C. (1979) St Patrick and fifth century Britain: An historical model explored. In P. J. Casey (ed.) *The End of Roman Britain,* 81–101. Oxford, BAR British Series 71.

Thomas, C. (1982) East and West: Tintagel, Mediterranean Imports and the Early Insular Church. In S. M. Pearce (ed.) *The Early Church in Britain and Ireland; Studies presented to C. A. Ralegh Radford,* 17–34. Oxford, BAR British Series 102.

Thomas, C. (1981) *Christianity in Roman Britain to AD 500.* London, Batsford.

Thomas, C. (1999) *Celtic Britain,* London, Thames and Hudson.

Thomas, M. G., Stumpf, M. P. H. and Härke, H. (2006) Evidence for an Apartheid-like Social Structure in Early Anglo-Saxon England, *The Proceedings of the Royal Society,* B, 273, 2651–7.

Thompson, E. A. (1956) Zozimus on the end of Roman Britain, *Antiquity* 30, no. 119, 163–7.

Thorn, C. and Thorn, F. (eds) (1979) *Domesday Book 6 Wiltshire.* Chichester, Phillimore.

Thorn, C. and Thorn, F. (eds) (1980) *Domesday Book 8 Somerset.* Chichester, Phillimore.

Thorn, C. and Thorn, F. (eds) (1985) *Domesday Book 9 Devon.* Chichester, Phillimore.

Thorn, F. R. (2005) The Hundred of Bath and Before, *Bath History* 10, 9–27.

Thornton, C. C. (1988) *The Demesne of Rimpton, 938–1412: A Study in Economic Development,* Unpublished PhD thesis, University of Leicester.

Thorpe, L. (trans.) (1974) *Gregory of Tours. The History of the Franks.* London, Penguin.

Turner, S. (2004) Coast and countryside in 'Late Antique' southwest England, c. AD 400–600. In R. Collins and J. Gerrard (eds) *Debating Late Antiquity in Britain AD300–700,* 25–32. Oxford, BAR British Series 365.

Turner, S. (2006) *Making a Christian Landscape; The countryside in early medieval Cornwall, Devon and Wessex.* Exeter, University of Exeter Press.

Two Cartularies of the Augustinian Priory of Bruton and the Cluniac Priory of Montacute in the County of Somerset. (eds) (1894) 'Members of the Council', Somerset Record Society 8, Taunton.

Verdon, J. (1979) *La Chronique de Saint Maixent, 751–1140.* Paris, Société d'édition les belles letters.

Verhulst, A. (1991) The Decline of Slavery and the Economic Expansion of the Early Middle Ages, review, *Past and Present* 133, 195–203.

Verhulst, A. (1992) Genèse du regime domanial classique en France au haut moyen âge. In *Rural and Urban Aspects of Medieval Northwest Europe.* I, 135–60. Aldershot, Variorum.

Vinner, M. (2002) *Viking Ship Museum Boats.* Roskilde, Roskilde Amtsmuseumsråd.

Walker, D. (ed.) (1998) *The Cartulary of St Augustine's Abbey Bristol.* Bristol, Bristol and Gloucester Archaeological Society.

Walters, B. (2001) A perspective on the social order of Roman villas in Wiltshire. In Ellis, P. (ed.) *Roman Wiltshire and after: papers in honour of Ken Annable*, 127–46. Devizes, Wiltshire Archaeological Society.

Watkin, Dom A. (1947–56) *The Great Chartulary of Glastonbury*, vols I–III, Somerset Record Society 59, 63, 64. Taunton.

Watts, L. and Leach, P. (1996) *Henley Wood, Temples and Cemetery*, CBA Research Report 99, London, Council for British Archaeology.

Watts, V. (ed.) (2004) *The Cambridge Dictionary of English Place-Names*, Cambridge, Cambridge University Press.

Weale, M. *et al.* (2002) Y Chromosome Evidence for Anglo-Saxon Mass Migration, *Molecular Biology and Evolution,* 19, no.7, 1008–21.

Weaver, F. W. (1983) *Somerset Medieval Wills*. Gloucester, Alan Sutton Publishing. A microprint edition of the three volumes published by the Somerset Record Society in 1901, 1903 and 1905.

Webster, C. J. and Brunning, R. A. (2005) A Seventh Century AD Cemetery at Stoneage Barton Farm, Bishop's Lydeard, Somerset and Square-Ditched Burials in Post-Roman Britain. *Archaeological Journal* 161, 54–81.

Wedlake, W. J. (1958) *Excavations at Camerton, Somerset.* Bath, Camerton Excavation Club.

Whitelock, D. (ed.) (1955) *English Historical Documents, c. 500–1042*. London, Eyre and Spottiswood.

Whitfield, M. (1981) The Medieval Fields of South-East Somerset, *Proceedings of the Somerset Archaeological and Natural History Society* 125, 17–29.

Williams, A. and Martin, G. H. (eds) (2002) *Domesday Book; A Complete Translation*. London, Penguin Books.

Williams, G. (2006) The Circulation and Function of Coinage in England AD 580–675. In B. Cook and G. Williams (eds) *Coinage and History in the North Sea World, c. AD 500–1250; Essays in Honour of Marion Archibald*, 145–92. Leiden, Brill.

Williams, M. (1970) *The Draining of the Somerset Levels*. Cambridge, Cambridge University Press.

Wilson, D. M. and Hurst, J. G. (1959) Medieval Britain in 1957, *Medieval Archaeology* 2, 147–71.

Winterbottom, M. (trans. and ed.) (1978) *Gildas: The Ruin of Britain and other Works*. Chichester, Phillimore.

Winterbottom, M. (2005) An Edition of Faricius, *Vita S. Aldhelmi, Journal of Medieval Latin* 15, 93–147.

Wood, M. (1983) The Making of King Athelstan's Empire: an English Charlemagne? In P. Wormald, D. Bullough and R. Collins (eds) *Ideal and Reality in Frankish and Anglo-Saxon Society*, 250–72. Oxford, Basil Blackwell.

Wooding, J. M. (1996) *Communication and Commerce along the Western Sealanes; AD 400–800*. Oxford, BAR International Series 654.

Wooding, J. M. (1996) Cargoes in Trade along the Western Seaboard. In K. R. Dark (ed.) *External Contacts and the Economy of Late Roman and Post-Roman Britain*, 67–82. Woodbridge, The Boydell Press.

Woods, H. M. (1990) Bridgwater, Wembdon Hill, *Proceedings of the Somerset Archaeological and Natural History Society* 134.

Woodward, G. H. (ed.) (1982) *Calendar of Somerset Chantry Grants, 1508–1603*. Somerset Record Society 77, Taunton.

Woolf, A. (2000) Community, Identity and Kingship in Early England. In W. O. Frazer and A. Tyrrell (eds) *Social identity in Early Medieval Britain*, 91–109. London, Leicester University Press.

Woolf, A. (2003) The Britons: From Romans to Barbarians. In H-W. Goetz, J. Jarnut and W. Pohl (eds) *Regna and Gentes; The Relationship between Late Antique and Early Medieval Peoples and Kingdoms in the Transformation of the Roman World*, 345–80. Leiden, Brill.

Wormald, F. (1988, [originally 1934]) *English Kalendars before 1100*. Woodbridge, The Boydell Press for the Henry Bradshaw Society.

Wormald, P. (1997) Æthelwold and his Continental Counterparts. In B. Yorke (ed.) *Bishop Æthelwold; His Career and Influence*, 13–42. Woodbridge, Boydell Press.

Wormald, P. (1999) *The Making of English Law: King Alfred to the Twelfth Century*. Volume I; *Legislation and Limits*. Oxford, Blackwell.

Wyatt, D. (2001) The Significance of Slavery: Alternative Approaches to Anglo-Saxon Slavery, *Anglo-Norman Studies; XXIII Proceedings of the Battle Conference 2000*, 327–47. Woodbridge, The Boydell Press.

Yorke, B. (ed.) (1988) *Bishop Æthelwold; His Career and Influence*. Woodbridge, Boydell Press.

Yorke, B. (1989) The Jutes of Hampshire and Wight and the origins of Wessex, in S. Bassett (ed.) *The Origins of Anglo-Saxon Kingdoms*, 84–96. London, Leicester University Press.

Yorke, B. (1995) *Wessex in the Early Middle Ages*. London, Leicester University Press.

Yorke, B. (1998) The Bonifacian Mission and Female Religious in Wessex, *Early Medieval Europe* 7 (2), 145–72.

Young, D. E. (2009) Excavation of an Early Medieval Site at Brent Knoll, Somerset, *Proceedings of the Somerset Archaeological and Natural History Society* 152, 105–37.

Index

Abbots Leigh 63
Abingdon abbey 204
Ælfgifu, wife of Konrad of Burgundy 203
Ælfheah, abbot of Bath 208
Ælfheah, bishop of Winchester 204
Ælfheah, ealdorman 87, 206
    Ælswith, his wife 87, 206
Ælfric's Colloquy 136
Ælfstan of Boscombe 89
Æscwine 27
Æthelbald, king of the Mercians 68
Æthelflæd, a noble lady 204
Æthelmær, ealdorman of Devon 48
Æthelred, king 47, 160–1
Æthelhelm, ealdorman 42
Æthelstan, ealdorman 64
Æthelstan's Laws 120
Æthelweard, ealdorman 205
    Chronicle 38
Æthelwold, abbot of Abingdon, bishop 204
Æthelwulf, king, fights Vikings 39, 65, 160
Æthelwynn, a noble lady 204
Aetius 17
Agilbert, bishop of the West Saxons 186
Alcuin 38
Aldwick 49
Alfred Jewel 157
Alfred, king 26, 43–5, 47, 91–2, 101, 109, 159, 170, 181, 200, 203, 210, 219
Alhampton 65
Aller 44, 216
Allercott 80
Alston Sutton 218, 221
Alstone 72
amphorae 17, 180
Andersey, Andreyseie 187, 191
Anglo-Saxon Chronicle 1, 9, 12, 22, 25–8, 33, 38, 45, 148, 162
Anglo-Saxon polity 25
Anglo-Saxon settlers 12
Anglo-Saxon Wiltshire 142
Animal husbandry 96
Aquae Sulis 8, 21

Arcadius, emperor 4, 6
ard 119–20
armies
    Danish 44
    Great Army 42
    Roman 3, 40, 42
    seventh and eighth centuries 34
    tenth century 49
Armorica 7, 139
    emigration to 15
    émigrés in 16
Ashcott 82
Ashdown 33
Ashill 69
assarting 112
Asser, bishop of Sherborne 1, 38, 109, 181, 193, 203, 211, 213, 215
Athelbald, king of Mercia 186, 192
Athelney island 17, 46, 92, 101, 114, 140
    abbey 37, 64, 68, 202–3, 210–11
    fort 45
Athelstan 'Half-king' 212
Athelstan, king 47–8, 88, 203–4, 210–11
    expedition to Scotland 214
Augustinian canons 196
Avon valley 3
    river 13, 15, 154
Axbridge 45, 46, 160, 167, 170, 221
Axe valley 56
    river 3, 46, 107, 137, 167, 170, 181, 187

b-ware 18
Babington 42
Backwell 63, 164
Badbury Rings 13
Badgworth 106, 179
Baldred, underking 32, 33
Baltonsborough 192
Bantham, Devon 18
Banwell 20, 44, 54, 58, 61, 71, 82, 181, 183–4, 195, 221
baptism 44
    rights 217
baptistery 15

barbarian polity 15
Barrington 42
Bath 6, 8, 9, 13, 15, 24, 45, 47–8, 110, 141, 163, 169, 225
    St Peter's abbey 44, 91, 202, 208–10
   stone 172
   town plan 163
   trade 164
Bathampton 210
Batheaston 210
Bathford 111–12
beach-markets 18
beads 24, 144
Beckery 17, 97, 140, 187, 211
   cemetery at 187
   chapel 187
Beckington 42
Bede 25, 36, 37, 162, 198–9
Bedminster 64–5, 194
Beercrocombe 69
Bempstone hundred 221
Benedictine nuns 196
Beorhtric, king 33, 37
Beorhtwald, abbot of Glastonbury 75
Berkshire 48
Berrow 44
Bertana, abbess of Bath 208
Berwald, abbot 32
Biddisham 57, 221
Birinus 185
bishops
   post-Roman 8–9
   of Sherborne 65
   of Wells 65, 213–6
   of Winchester 192, 163
Bishops Lydeard 106, 215
   post-Romano-British cemetery 51
Blackdowns 172
Blackford 86, 221
Blackmore Vale, Dorset 97
Blagdon 132
Bleadon 113, 136, 173
   possible early church at 184
boats 20
Bobbio 180
Bokerley Dyke 15
bookland 37, 38, 49, 72, 90
Bossington 43
boundaries 12–13, 15, 34
   Mercia-Wessex 47
Bourton in Compton Bishop 82
Bowleaze Cove Jewel 157

Bradford-on-Avon 15
Bradley Hill, Roman settlement 6, 10, 55–6
Brean cliff, post-Romano-British cemetery 51, 53
Brean Down, battle 25
   temple 178
Brendon Hills 80, 96, 109, 113, 153, 170
Brent 32, 44, 96, 138
Brent Knoll 178
Brewham 65
bridges 168
bridgework 171
Bridgwater 170
Bridgwater Bay 106
Brihtric Grim 72, 88
Bristol Channel 13, 32, 150
Brittonic names 15
brooches 144
Brue, river 154, 156, 187
Bruton 29, 64–6, 196
   minster 192
'buckland' 36, 38
Buckland Dinham 38, 55, 144
   post-Romano-British cemetery 51, 53
Buckland St Mary 38, 69
buildings
   dismantled 8
   re-use 9
burgesses
   at Axbridge 167
   at Bath 164, 210
   at Ilchester 163
   at Langport 68, 164
   at Milborne Port 165
Burghal Hidage 45, 47–8, 163–5
burhs 29, 38, 44, 48, 65, 68, 141, 160, 164–5
   garrisons 48
burials 9, 24
   at temples 178
   repair 48
Burnham 96
Burtle 5
Butcombe 88
Butleigh 109, 111
Byzantium 17, 18, 19, 25
   coin 139, 143
   coin-weight 141
   diplomatic contacts 19
   empire 139
   traders 143

Cædwalla 27

Cadbury, Shropshire 18
Cadbury-Congresbury hill-fort 9, 17, 18, 19, 20, 55, 62, 140–1, 184
Cadbury Farm, Hants 18
Cadbury-Tickenham hill-fort 17, 18
Camelar river 64
Camerton 9, 49, 55, 64, 142, 144, 154, 225
    cemetery 23–4, 51, 53
Cannington 17, 29, 43, 58–61, 63–4, 97, 105, 108, 140–1, 143, 147, 170, 184, 196
    cemetery 24, 51, 53, 55, 59, 151
    church, lands of 59
canons of Wells 213
Capland 69
'Caractacus' stone 183
Carhampton 18, 29, 45, 47, 60, 63, 65, 143, 150, 179, 180–1, 184, 193
    battles at 39
Carlingcott 80
cartularies
    of Bath abbey 209
    of Glastonbury abbey 38
    of Montacute Priory 217
Castle Green cemetery, Taunton 162
Castle Neroche 190
Catcott 82
Catsgore, Roman settlement 10, 53
cattle 57
Celtic dedications 179
cemeteries
    Anglo-Saxon 22
    extra-mural cemetery at Ilchester 195
    on Brean Down 184
    on Lamyatt beacon 184
    post-Roman 51
Centwine, king 27, 32, 188–9
Cenwald, bishop of Worcester 203
Cenwalh, king 27–8, 186
ceorls 34, 35, 82–4, 87, 105–6
    as slave owners 79
Chapel Allerton 221
Chard 215
Charlcomb 91
Charlton (Shepton Mallet) 9, 142
    post-Roman-British cemetery 51, 54–5
Charlton Horethorne 71
Charlton Mackrell and Adam 122
Charlton Mackrell 5, 68, 149
Charlton Musgrove 67
'charltons' 35
charters 13, 32, 89, 91, 109, 168–9, 154

bounds 21, 85, 101, 111, 113, 121, 153, 170, 184, 200
Charterhouse on Mendip 13
Cheddar 29, 44, 46, 65, 71, 80, 159–61, 179, 183, 193, 221
    Gorge 204
    nuns at 219
    palace 70, 152, 160, 198
    parochia 219
    Roman villa 220
Chelvey 9
Chew Magna 65, 67, 100, 156, 194
Chew Stoke 68, 100
    temple at 178
Chew Valley 3
Chewton Mendip 49, 64, 78, 85, 103, 106, 164, 169, 173
    church 106
    chapels of 68
Chillington 42
Chinnocks, the 71, 121
Chippenham, Wilts 44
Christon 62
Churchill 62
church estates 34
churches, rural 179
    post-Roman development 184
churchyard burial 199
    chapels 194
Cirencester 15, 25
civitates 15
Clapton-in-Gordano 63
Claverton 88
Clevedon 63
Clifton 13
Cluny, abbey (dep. Saône et Loire, France) 203
Cnut, king 161, 214
Codsend Moor 96
coin 3, 4, 6, 7, 8, 139–40, 142, 146, 148–9, 152, 160, 163
    of Æthelred 171
    of Arcadius 9, 10, 178
    Byzantine 19
    clipped 5–6
    distributions 175–6
    early English 147
    English 150, 165
    finds 160
    foreign 161
    hoards 9
    of Honorius 10, 20
    of Justinian 165
    Roman 5
    supply 159
combs 144

Combwich 60, 147–8
commendation 34, 89, 90
common-fields 105, 119–23, 125, 127–8, 132, 134, 136
    at Overstowey 121
    at Stocklinch, Ottersey and Magdalen 121, 130
common meadow 105
Compton Bishop 44, 221
Compton Durville 103
Congresbury 21, 62, 148, 179, 181, 193–4, 196, 213
Constantine III 3
Constantine of Dumnonia 16
Constantius 16
Cornwall 13, 179
Cothelstone 51
cott place-names 80, 113
cottars and bordars 80
Count of Mortain 64, 219
Creech St Michael 43
Creechbarrow 32
Crewkerne 29, 64–5, 102, 132, 137, 172, 196, 207
    parochia 198
Cricket Malherbie 190
Crowcombe 44
Culbone 180
    stone 183–4
cult of the saints 178, 211, 213
currency 6, 152
    early 146
    English 161
Curry 46, 65, 68
Curry Mallet 69
Curry Rivel 6, 64, 102, 112, 172
customary tenement 121
Cutcombe 96
Cuthred 33
Cuthwine and Ceawlin 9
Cynegils and Cwichelm 25
Cynegils, king 27, 185
Cyneheard 33
Cynewulf, aetheling 33
Cynewulf, king of the West Saxons 33, 207

Danes 38, 42, 137, 150, 159
    Danegeld 162
    raids 203
    tribute to 173
defence of Wessex 44–8
demesne agriculture 128
Denmark/Schleswig-Holstein 26
Devon 13, 16, 18, 30, 33
Dillington 42

Dinas Powys 17, 18, 20
Dinnington 42, 49
Ditcheat 65, 93, 207
Dodington 72
Domesday Book 48, 49, 60, 72, 133, 136, 152, 159, 164
    Exeter Domesday 49
Donyatt 69
Dorchester, Dorset 13, 15, 20, 24, 29, 38, 104, 141, 149
Dorset 13, 15, 29, 150
    boundary with 34
Doulting 65, 152, 205
    stone 173
    wooden church 198
Downend 47
Draycott 80, 220
Drayton 69, 102
Dublin 165
Dubonnic polity 21
Dudoc, bishop of Wells 194, 214
Dulcote 82
Duluting river 65
Dulverton 91
Dumnonia 12, 22, 109, 141
Dunball 13
Dunster 63

Eadgifu, wife of Louis the blind of Aquitaine 203
Eadgyth, empress of the Germans 203
Eadmund, king 204, 208
Eadred, king 38
Eadwig, king 204–5
Ealdberht 33
Ealdormen 33–4
Eanwulf, ealdorman 42, 65, 87, 93, 207
Earnshill 69
East Anglia 39
East Brent 106
East Chinnock 49
East Coker, Anglo-Saxon church 218
East Harptree 49
East Pennard 112, 194
Easton-in-Gordano 63
Ecgberht, king 33
Eckweek 133–4
Edgar, king 44, 212
    crowned at Bath 208
Edington, Wilts 44
Edmer Ator 49, 121–2
education 12, 16
Edward the Elder, king 38, 43, 47, 48, 64, 160, 163, 193, 203, 215

Edward's Laws 120
eels 109
Egbert, king 38
	fights Vikings 39
Egford 42
Ellendun, battle 33
Emigration to Armorica 15
English, identity 26
	language 27
	merchants 146
Englishcombe 21, 170
Exeter 13, 20, 48, 161
	cemetery 24
Exford 96
Exmoor 4, 80, 96, 109, 153

Farmborough 43
Faulkland 36
Faustus of Riez 16
Ferrameare 32
Fiddington 43, 60
field churches 218
fields
	arable 98
	early 98, 100
	fallow 120, 134
fisheries, and fish-traps 106–9, 136
Fivehead 69
Flanders 204, 208
Flatholm 151
Flax Bourton 63, 82
fleets, Viking 40, 42
Fleury 204
folkland 36
fords 153, 154
Forthere, bishop of Sherborne 75
fortification work 46
Fosse Way 8–9, 13, 20–1, 24, 29, 32, 46–7, 68, 103, 113,
	135, 141, 148–9, 154, 163, 170, 187
Foxcote 80
Frances Plantation, nr Priddy 5
free chapels 194, 217–8
Freshford 88, 220
Friesland 26
Frome, 29, 36, 38, 42, 46, 64–5, 102, 137, 152, 154,
	192, 198–9, 205
	monastery 190
funeral monuments 16

Gallic Chronicle 17
Gatcombe 9

Gaul 3, 6, 8, 16, 105, 185
geburs 87
geld 171, 173, 174
	at Bath 164
	geld rating 129
Geraint, king of Dumnonia 33
Gérard of Brogne 203, 208
German Empire 161
Germanic speakers 12
gesiths 83, 87
gesith-born 36
Gilcott 80
Gildas 12, 16, 21, 23, 74
Gillingham, Dorset 65
Giso, bishop of Wells 214–5
glass-ware 17
Glastonbury 29, 140, 148, 192
	abbey 32, 38, 44, 57, 64, 68, 86, 97, 107, 114, 126–7,
		136, 152, 163, 167, 173, 182, 187, 190, 195, 202–4,
	abbey estates 49, 129, 189, 205–7
	island 187–8
	monastery and church rebuilt 205
	Tor 17, 151
		monastic site 185
	wooden church 187
Gloucestershire 8
Godney 187
graves
	'Anglo-Saxon' 23
	grave-goods 22, 23
	orientation 23
Gregorian Reforms 216
Gregory of Tours 16
Gwithian, Cornwall 18

Hædda, bishop of the West Saxons 32, 186, 189
Hæmgils, abbot 32, 43
Hallatrow 200
Ham Hill 140
Hampshire 33
Hamwic 33, 146, 152
Hankerton, Wilts 43
Hardington 42
Harold, earl and king 42, 91, 161, 193
Hatch Beauchamp 69
Hedeby warship 39
Hemington 36, 42
Henley Hill 20, 55
	temple 62, 178
Henley Wood cemetery 24, 51, 54
Henstridge 88

heriots 91
hermits 187
hermitage 180, 190
Hiberno-Norse weight 151
hides and hidage 47, 49, 60, 83–4, 86, 121, 128, 131,
    164, 191
High Ham 68, 168
High Peak, Devon 18
hill-forts 17, 24, 51, 181
    display at 19
    fortifications at 19
    hierarchy 20
    post-Roman reuse 17
    at Worle 4
Hincknoll Slait, South Cadbury 55, 144
hithes and staithes 167–8
Hoar Moor 96
hoards 3–6, 9
    in Wiltshire 5
Holcombe 199
Holton 88
Holway, nr Taunton 5
Holy wells 195
Honorius, emperor 3, 4, 6, 7, 11
Horethorne Hundred 97
Hornblotton 36, 65
horse harness 174–5
Horsecombe 21
Horsington 90
House of Godwin 91
Huish (place-name) 83, 87
Hundreds 92–3
    meeting places 93
    Ordinance 92
    Pence 44
Huntspill 96
Hwicce 8, 34, 142

ieg (place-name element) 114
Ilchester 8, 9, 13, 15, 20, 29, 68, 92, 98, 140–2, 148–9,
    151, 154–5, 163–4, 167, 207, 225
    Ilchester Mead 10
    'Lendiniae' 8
    port 163, 174
Ilminster 42–3, 194, 198, 207, 210, 217
Ilton 210
Imperial administration 3
Ine, king 29, 32, 92
Ine's Laws 27, 33, 36, 74, 84, 101, 105, 112, 128
infield/outfield 120
inland 132

Ireland 39, 150, 165
iron 152, 172
    renders 172
    smelting 8
Isle Abbots 190
Isle of Wight 27
Isle, river 194

jewellery 7

Kent 33, 42
Kewstoke 62, 179, 181, 184
Keynsham 102, 154, 164, 195
Kilmersdon 194
Kilton 64
King Alfred's Will 29, 59, 64
King Ine's church at Glastonbury 187
Kingdom of Wessex 23
    origins 27
Kings
    post-Roman 16
    of Wessex 26
Kingsbury Episcopi 29, 45
Kingsbury Regis 29, 45, 165
Knightcott 82
knives 145

labour services 120, 132, 171
Lamyatt Beacon 55, 184
    post-Romano-British cemetery 51, 54
    temple 65, 178
Langport 45–6, 141, 164–5, 167
Lantocal 32
Lansdown 10
Latin
    language 12, 199
    learning 203
Laverton 132
lay-abbots 198
lead 159
leah 111, 112
leases 91
Leigh (nr Street) 32, 182
Leigh-on-Mendip 88
Leland 180
Leuthere, bishop of the West Saxons 186
Levels 97, 113
Liber Terrarum 182, 205
llan 182
loanland 36, 37
London 161

Long Ashton 9
Long Sutton 68, 101, 211
loot 42, 157
lordship 92
Lotharingia 108, 204
Lottisham 65
Lovington 72
Lufton 133
Lulle, a nun 192
Lullington 42
Lundy, Devon 151
Luxeuil (dep. Haute-Saône, France) 180
Lydford, East and West 71, 123
Lympsham 106
Lyng 45–6

Maes Knoll 21
Magister militum 17
Malmesbury, Wilts 43
manuring 134
Manworthy 90
Marchey 56, 187
    possible early church at 56
Mark 221
markets
    activity, post-Roman 5
    places at minsters 196
    rents and tolls 176
    sites 167
Marksbury 25
marshlands 113, 190
Martock 38
Meare 136, 179, 182
Mediterranean 8
    contacts 20
Mells 136, 207, 212
memorial stones 183
Mendip 32, 13, 34, 46, 113, 135–6, 159, 173
Meon Valley 27
Mercia and Mercians 33, 148, 186
merchants
    Frankish 146
    Frisian 146
    Viking 39, 151–2, 165, 173
metal
    detecting 175
    finds 156
    working 19, 175, 180
Middle Chinnock 122
Midelney 190
Milborne Port 29, 64, 71, 102, 156, 163–5, 196

military obligation and service 34, 48, 50
mills 136–7
minsters 185–186, 192
    at Cheddar 160, 220
    churches 216
    double 186, 192, 208
    enclosures 196
    at Taunton 44, 162–3
    as trade sites 175
    at Wells 213
Minster Lovell Jewel 157
mints and minting 7
    at Bath 47, 163
    at Milborne Port 165
    at Watchet 165, 167
Misterton 194
monasteries
    at Congresbury 181
    monastic communities 100
    reform 202
    revival 93
    in villas 183
    (see also Athelney, Banwell, Bath, Bruton, Carhampton, Muchelney, Glastonbury, Frome)
monks 186
money 8
Moorlinch 168
Mortain, count of 133
Mothecombe, Devon 18
Mons Badonicus (Mount Badon) battle, 21–2
Muchelney Abbey 32, 42, 44, 69, 97, 102, 107, 109, 114, 132, 190–1, 202, 210
    estates 190, 210
    kalendar 180
Mudford 49
Mudgeley 221
multiple estates 63

Nailsea 63, 179
navigation 20
Neroche forest 29, 109, 112, 116
Newton Park 157
Newton St Loe Roman villa 10
North Curry 4, 69, 91, 167
North Petherton 64, 102–3
North Stoke 209
Northmen 1–2, 38
Northover 149, 163
    church 68
Northumbria 37
nuns 186

nuns at Cheddar 219
Nyland (see also Andersey) 187, 220

Odcombe 48
Odo, Abbot of Cluny 203
Offa, King of Mercia 33, 37, 208
Old Cleeve 91
Old English language 26
Old Sarum 13, 15
Old Welsh 2, 11
    language 15
    population 74
    societies 12
open-fields 103
Osric, king of the Hwicce 208
Oswald, king of Northumbria 186
Otterhampton 60, 141
Over Stratton 103
oxen 134–5

Pagans Hill 178
    Temple 68, 151
pagus 15
Panborough 114
pantheistic cults 178
Papal privilege 190
Pardlestone 72
parish system 216
parochiae 197
    of Cheddar 221
    of Taunton 197, 218
Parrett, river 1, 4, 29, 37, 46, 60, 87, 105, 107, 110, 113, 125, 141, 143, 151–3, 167, 170, 190
    battle at the mouth 42
    estuary, fish traps in 96
pastoral communities 96
pasture 134
Patching, Sussex 5
peasants 35
Pedwell 178
Penda, King of the Mercians 25, 186
Penselwood 15
    Battle near 28
Peter's Pence 44
pilgrim saints 178
pilgrimage 181
    to Rome 27
Pilton 13, 82, 112, 191
Pinhoe 48
Pitcombe 66
Pitcot 80

Pitminster 194, 217
Pitney 101
place-names 35, 65
plague 51, 225
planning of
    landscape 126
    settlements 71
    town 165
plough-lands 128–9, 132
ploughs 119–20
    in Domesday 93
plough-teams 128–9, 131
Poldens 13, 122
    estate 71
    ridge 4, 82
Poole, Dorset 15, 141
population
    falling in fifth century 11
    in fourth century 11
    growth 2, 119, 160
Porlock 43, 47–8, 136, 165, 179–80, 184
    wool exports 173
ports and the sea 175
'*portus*' 63
Portbury 20–1, 63, 149
    post-Romano-British cemetery 51
Portishead 20, 55, 63, 136, 148–9, 166
    post-Romano-British cemetery 51, 54
Portland, Dorset 38
post-Roman
    cemeteries 182
    fields 104
    kingdoms 12
    monastic site, Carhampton 19
post-Soviet hoards 5
pottery
    assemblages 19, 56
    African red slip wares 17
    black burnished ware 10
    Byzantine 140
    'E' ware 8, 143
    fifth to seventh centuries 151
    grass-marked 143
    grey-ware 8
    Mediterranean wares 9, 18–20, 185
    medieval, at Wint Hill 54
    at Poundbury, Dorchester 195
    Romano-British industry 8
    sources for late-Anglo-Saxon 171–2
    tenth century 171
Procopius 3, 16

'productive sites' 160
proto-industrial economy 7, 16
provinces of Britannia 15
Puckington 42
Puxton 62, 71, 106

Quantock Hills 29, 32, 60, 105, 113, 141, 172
quarries 172
Queen Camel 137
 sword 29

radio-carbon dating 51
Radstock 13
Rectitudines 82
Reeve 38
Regularis Concordia 208
relics 212
Religious communities 59
 women 184
reproductive success 26
Rexworthy 60
Rhineland 3
Rimpton 72, 83, 88, 123, 128
roads 156, 168–9
Rodney Stoke 80, 220
Roman cantons 13
Roman roads 24
Rome 191
Ryme Intrinseca, Dorset 34

Saltford 154
sea levels 97
seasonal flooding 97
Seaxburh, queen 27
Selwood Forest 13, 20, 21, 65, 109
Selwoodshire 15
Settlement
 abandonment 51
 continuity 55
Severn, river 109
Shapwick 4, 55, 58, 82, 114, 122, 126, 171, 191
 early church 126
 Heath 5, 6
 Turf Moor 5
 Sladwick 55, 57
 timber building 58
Shearston 72
sheep 57, 113, 132, 135, 173, 207
Sheppey, river 65
Shepton Beauchamp 179
Shepton Mallet 13

Shepton Montague 66
Sherborne 67, 104, 184, 192–3
 diocese 29, 33
ships 39
shire court 93
shrine 53
Sigeberht, king 33
silver 146, 159, 163, 171
 from Rammelsburg 161
Skuldelev wrecks 2, 3 and 5 39
slavery and slaves 74–80, 132, 142, 152, 174
 children 75
 emancipation from 76
 as householders 76
 on large estates 77–8
 penal 75–6, 101
 as ploughmen 76
 post-Roman 75
 punishment of 75
soldiers, numbers 50
Somerton 1, 29, 46, 65, 68, 93, 101, 114, 141, 148–9, 165, 174, 190, 195
 Eadred's crown wearing 70
South Cadbury hillfort 15, 17, 19–21, 23–4, 28–9, 55–6, 85–6, 97, 100, 140–1, 148–9, 155, 184
 control of roads 20
 post-Romano-British cemetery 51, 54
South Petherton 29, 45, 64, 102–3, 195
South Saxons 33
South Stoke 44, 209
South Wales 16, 180–2
Sowy 114
Spaxton 60–1
St Æthelwine of Athelncy 210–11
St Aldhelm, abbot and bishop 13, 27, 33, 190, 152, 189, 191–2, 196, 198, 215
St Andrew dedications 220
St Andrew's chapel at Andersey 187
St Andrew's Church, Wells 215
St Andrew's Church, Cheddar 219
St Andrew's Church, Northover 148, 195
St Andrew's Well 194–5
St Bartholomew's Church, Crewkerne 194
St Benedict 202
St Benedict's Rule 203
St Benignus of Meare 179, 182
St-Bertin's monastery, Flanders 164, 203, 208
St Bridget 97, 210
St Cadoc 179–80
St Carantoc 179
 chapel 180

St Columbanus 179–80
    at Cheddar 182
St Cuthbert Without parish, Wells 197
St Cuthbert's Church, Wells 213
    relics 214
St Cyngar 179, 181, 214
St David 212
St Decuman 210
St Decuman's Church 141, 179, 180
    Well 180, 195
St Dubricius (Dyfrig) 179, 180
    Porlock, dedication 166
St Dunstan 127, 202–4
    as Archbishop of Canterbury 205
St Edwold of Cerne 210
St Egwin of Worcester 210
St Erne's Well, Weare 181
St Georges otherwise Puttingthrop 62
St Germanus 16
St Gildas 179, 182
St Hernin 181
St Indracht 212
St John the Baptist Church, Frome 191
St John's Church, Carhampton 63
St Kai 179, 182
St Kew 179, 181
St Leonard's Pitcombe 67
St Martin of Tours 15
St Martin, chapel of 187
St Mary's church, Cannington 59
St Michael's Mount, Cornwall 18
St Nectan 179, 183
St Nicholas's church, Dinnington 197
St Olaf, dedications 165
    relic 164
St-Omer, Flanders 164
St Paternus 179
St Patrick 16, 74, 182, 211
St Peter and St Paul's abbey, Malmesbury 191
St Peter's Abbey, Ghent 203, 205
St Petroc 179, 212
St Swithun's chapel, Claverham 218
Stalbridge, Dorset 71
Stanton Drew 38
Stantonbury hill-fort 21
Steepholm 151, 179, 180
Stigand, Archbishop of Canterbury 194
stoc place-names 62
Stogursey 60
Stoneage Barton 51
Stoney Stoke 66

strǣt 156
Stratford Lane, in Compton Martin 13
Stratton on the Fosse 207
Street 79, 179, 184
    church 182
Stringston 61, 72
Sturminster Newton, Dorset 72
Sussex 33
Swein 48
Swell 69

Talnotrie Hoard 151
Tamar river 33
Tarnock 57
Taunton 29, 32, 34, 38, 46–7, 64, 78, 105, 116, 125, 141,
    162–4, 167, 191–3, 196, 211
    castle 162
    market 174
    minster burial rights 199
    parochia 197, 218
temples 178–9
    at Bath 8
Thames Valley 21–2
thegns 48–50, 87, 90–2, 127, 218
    thegnland 71, 91
    in towns 164
Theodore's Penitential 75
Thorney 190
three common burdens 38
Thurloxton 103
Tickenham 63
Timberscombe 80, 97, 179
tin 20, 22, 139
    trade in 19, 143
Tintagel 18–9, 20, 23, 100, 140–1
Tintinhull 64
tithes 217
Tone, river 4, 32, 46, 125, 163
towns 7, 8, 160, 162, 174
trade 5, 139, 158
    export 3
    with Low Countries 161
transhumance 113
Tregurthy, Cornwall 18
Trent 34
tribute to the Danes 137
tun + personal name 72
tun settlements 61
Twelve Hides of Glastonbury 114
tyrants 3, 16, 225
Tytherington 42

under-kings 27, 33
urban life 8
urban settlements, decay of 9
US dollars 5

vicus 15
Vikings 39, 92
    armies, in Ireland 42
    armies, in Northumbria 42
    attacks on coast 47
    camp at Downend 47
    of Dublin 173
    fleets 40, 42
    in Ireland 152
    raiding 39, 151
    robbers 158
    settlement in Ireland 150
    traders 39, 151, 165
villas 10
    owners 15
    rebuilt 10
villae, Merovingian Gaul 101
villages, nucleated 120
villani 82
virgate 121

Waerstan, bishop of Sherborne 213
Walcot 58
Wales 180
Walton nr Glastonbury 82
Walton-in-Gordano 63
'Waltons' 58
Wansdyke 21, 24–5
    Wiltshire 21
Wareham 15
warrior aristocracy 30, 35
    king 16
warships 39
Watchet 29, 45, 47, 105, 136, 140, 142, 165, 179–80, 184, 196
Waterford 165
weapon burials 22–3
Weare 108, 137, 167, 181, 218, 221
Wearne 10
Wedmore 44, 108, 161, 221
weirs 107
Wellington 215
Wells 29, 46, 148
    cathedral 221
    bishop and bishopric of 29, 114, 193, 203
    estates 194, 214–5
    liturgical life 216
    mausoleum 184

Welsh speakers 28
Welshmen 74
    status 27
Wembdon 20, 55
    post-Roman-British cemetery 51, 54
wergild 27, 33, 75, 150
West Buckland 38
West Camel 210
    cross shaft 173, 216
West Chinnock 122
West Harptree 49, 68
    post-Romano-British cemetery 51, 54, 58
West Huntspill 106
West Monkton 32
West Pennard 112
Western diocese of Wessex 192
Westlands, Yeovil, 9
Weston, nr. Bath 44
Weston-in-Gordano 63
Weston-super-Mare 62
Whatley 141, 207
wics 56
Whitelackington 42, 190
Wigferth, ealdorman 37
William Hosatus 91
William of Malmesbury 187, 190, 203, 211
William Rufus, king 182
Williton 29, 60, 63–4, 105, 141
wills 87
Wiltshire 20, 23, 26, 33
    plough-land 121
Winchester, bishop's seat 27, 186
    monks of 191
    New Minster 207
    Old Minster 44, 88, 162, 202, 206–7, 211
Wine, bishop of the West Saxons 186
Winford 88
Winscombe 62, 87
Winsford Hill 183
Wint Hill in Banwell 55, 62
    post-Romano-British cemetery 51, 54
Winterhead 57
Winterstoke hundred 221
Witham 67
Wiveliscombe 6
wizards, sorcerers, magicians 200
Woden 21
woodland 96, 109–10, 112
    regeneration 96
wood-pasture 112
Wookey 56
wool 173

Woolston, nr. Cannington 61
Woolston, nr. South Cadbury 55
Woolverton 42
Worle 3
Worlebury 17, 178
worth/*wyrth*/worthy 8–4, 60, 87, 105–6, 113
Wraxall 63
Wrington 64, 207
Wulfstan of York 49

Wulfwaru's Will 88
Wyke Champflower 66
Wynflæld's Will 121

'Y' chromosome studies 26
Yarlington 55
Yatton 62–3
Yeo, river 34, 45, 190